METHUEN'S

HANDBOOKS OF ARCHAEOLOGY

Western Asiatic Jewellery
c. 3000–612 B.C.

In this series

ANCIENT EGYPTIAN JEWELLERY
Alix Wilkinson
GREEK AND ROMAN JEWELLERY
R. A. Higgins
GREEK GEOMETRIC POTTERY
J. N. Coldstream
GREEK PAINTED POTTERY
R. M. Cook
GREEK TERRACOTTAS
R. A. Higgins
ENGLISH COINS
G. C. Brooke
ROMAN COINS
Harold Mattingly
GREEK COINS
Charles Seltman
MOSAICS
H. P. L'Orange and P. J. Nordhagen
GREEK AND ROMAN GOLD AND SILVER PLATE
D. E. Strong
THE ARCHAEOLOGY OF ROMAN BRITAIN
R. G. Collingwood and Ian Richmond
THE ARCHAEOLOGY OF CRETE
J. D. S. Pendlebury
WEST AFRICA BEFORE THE EUROPEANS
Oliver Davies

WESTERN ASIATIC JEWELLERY c. 3000-612 B.C.

K. R. MAXWELL-HYSLOP

METHUEN & CO LTD
11 NEW FETTER LANE LONDON EC4

First published 1971
by Methuen & Co. Ltd
11 New Fetter Lane, London EC4

Printed in Great Britain
by W & J Mackay & Co Ltd
Chatham, Kent

SBN 416 15830 7

Distributed in the U.S.A.
by Barnes & Noble Inc.

GILLY

FILIAE DILECTISSIMAE
NOTARIAE PERITISSIMAE
QUAE SUMMA PRAEDITA CUM INDUSTRIA TUM COMITATE
ITA SUADEBAT COGEBAT
UT TANDEM HIC LIBER IN LUCEM PRODIERIT

O quam callida machinae fuisti
claves tundere ; nec dabas quietem
defessis digitis, sed emicantes
huc illuc agilesque paginarum
exemplaria lucida exprimebant.
Segnem me monitu modo incitabas,
lassam blanditiis modo, ut sub auras
tandem prodierit meus libellus.
Magnae nos memores benignitatis
haud parvas tibi gratias habemus.

Contents

List of plates ix
List of colour plates xxx
List of text figures xxxi
Preface xliii
Abbreviations xlvii
Chronological table and map of Western Asia liv
Introduction lxi

1 Mesopotamia: the Early Dynastic period 1
2 Mesopotamia: the Sargonid period *c.* 2370–2200 B.C. 17
3 Anatolia 2500–2000 B.C. 38
4 The Guti-Gudea period, Third Dynasty of Ur to Isin and Larsa dynasties 2250–1894 B.C. 64
5 Babylonia, Mesopotamia and Iran 2017–1750 B.C. 83
6 Anatolia *c.* 1950–1750 B.C.: Kültepe-Kanesh and the Assyrian *Kārum* 97
7 Phoenicia, Syria and Palestine *c.* 2000–1550 B.C. Asiatic-Cypriote relations *c.* 1550–1450 B.C. 102
8 Syria and Palestine *c.* 1550–1300 B.C. 132
9 Iran in the mid-second millennium B.C. 158
10 The Kassite period in Babylonia and the mid-Assyrian period in Assyria 163
11 Assyria and Iran: twelfth to seventh centuries B.C. 180
12 Urartu: ninth to seventh centuries B.C. 198
13 North-west Iran: eighth to seventh centuries B.C. 206
14 Palestine and Syria: twelfth to sixth centuries B.C. 224
15 Assyria and Iran: ninth to seventh centuries B.C. 232

Bibliography 271
Index 275
Plates

LIST OF PLATES

Chapter 1

1–13: Ur Early Dynastic Cemetery

1 Headdresses. British Museum Nos. 120591, 122310. Length of willow leaf 5·8 cm.
Photo: British Museum

2 Jewellery from Ur. British Museum. Length of lapis lazuli and silver pins 15·5 cm.
Photo: British Museum

3 Back view of colour plate A. British Museum No. 122230. Diameter of earring 7·7 cm.
Photo: British Museum

4 Gold earring. British Museum No. 122390. Greatest width 6 cm.
Photo: British Museum

5 (*a*) Hair-ring and (*b*) earring. P.G. 1618. British Museum Nos. 122706, 122707. Diameter of hair-ring 3 cm.
Photo: British Museum

6 (*a*) Necklace; flat diamond-shaped lapis lazuli and gold beads with ring spacers. British Museum No. 122426. Average length 2 cm.
(*b*) Necklace of small double conoid gold, large double conoid lapis lazuli beads and one large lapis lazuli date-shaped bead with gold caps and wire wound spirally in a groove round the length of the bead. P.G. 559. British Museum No. 20583. Length of date-shaped bead 2·7 cm.
(*c*) Beads; five etched carnelian, oval and ball-shaped beads of gold and stone. British Museum No. 122444. Length of etched beads 8 cm.
(*d*) Necklace of fluted spherical gold and lapis lazuli beads with ovoid and flattened double conoid spacers in carnelian. British Museum No. 122314. Average length of large gold bead 1·4 cm.
Photos: British Museum

7 Necklace of large lapis lazuli double conoid and smaller gold ovoid beads. British Museum No. 123330. Length of largest lapis bead 1·3 cm.
Photo: British Museum

8 (*a*) Double conoid gold bead decorated in filigree. P.G. 580. British Museum No. 121427. Length 3·4 cm.
(*b*) Faceted date-shaped bead. British Museum No. 122704. Length 5·8 cm.
Photo: British Museum

9 Necklace with three quadruple spiral pendants. British Museum No. 120587–9. Diameter of pendant 1·8 cm.
Photo: British Museum

10 Necklace with one quadruple spiral pendant, two single gold spirals and two lapis lazuli imitating gold spirals. P.G. 580. British Museum No. 121425. Diameter of quadruple spiral 1·4 cm.
Photo: British Museum

11 (*a*) Ring; twisted wire decoration. P.G. 800. Diameter 2·3 cm.
(*b*) Ring; twisted wire decoration. P.G. 580. Diameter 1·8 cm.
(*c*) Ring with cloisonné inlay. P.G. 800. British Museum No. 121373. Diameter 2·2 cm.
Photo: British Museum

12 Bead and chain fillets, necklace, earrings, hair-ring and plain frontlet. Frontlet British Museum No. 122702, length 26·5 cm.
Photo: British Museum

13 Large lapis lazuli gold capped bead. British Museum No. 120601. Diameter 2·5 cm.
Photo: British Museum

14 Circular silver disc or pendant with filigree decoration and hollow central boss. Uruk. W.21072, 1. Diameter 10·5 cm.
Photo: Courtesy Professor H. Lenzen

Chapter 2

15 (*a*) Necklace of gold coiled wire beads and hair-ring from Vadjalik, Iran, Gilan. St Germain-en-Laye. Diameter of hair-ring 2 cm.
(*b*) Beads, lapis lazuli, and a gold winged disc bead from Djönü, Russia, Azerbaijan (Lenkoran). St Germain-en-Laye. Length 0·75 cm.
(*c*) Silver ring from Agha Evler, Iran, Gilan. Musée de St Germain-en-Laye. Diameter 2·2 cm.
Photos: Musée des Antiquités Nationales

16 Diadem. Ur Early Dynastic Grave P.G. 1054, U.11906. British Museum No. 122241. Length 12·1 cm.
Photo: British Museum

17–23: Ur, Sargonid grave groups

17 (*a*) Necklace; gold flat disc beads and lapis lazuli diamonds. Grave 435. British Museum No. 120586. Average width gold bead 0·75 cm.
(*b*) Earrings; silver lunate earring linked to gold earring. Grave 465. British Museum No. 122234. Width of silver earring 1·5 cm.

(*c*) Earring; gold double lunate. Grave 465. Width 1·1 cm.
Photos: British Museum

18 (*a*) Earrings; pair with hollow lunate ends. Tomb 666. British Museum No. 121568.
(*b*) Earrings; pair, solid thickened ends. Tomb 666. British Museum No. 1928.10.10.285.
(*c*) Finger ring. Tomb 666. British Museum No. 123661. Diameter 2 cm.
Photo: British Museum

19 (*a*) Necklace of carnelian, lapis lazuli, gold fluted and gold flat diamond beads. Grave 703. British Museum No. 121492.
(*b*) Earrings or hair-rings; pair with solid gold lunate ends. Grave 703. British Museum No. 121370. Width 2 cm.
(*c*) Earring (or hair-ring); one of pair with hollow lunate ends. British Museum No. 121371
Photo: British Museum

20 (*a*) and (*b*) Necklace; carnelian, lapis lazuli, gold flanged and gold fluted beads. Grave P.G. 65. British Museum No. 123594. Width of flanged bead 1·8 cm.
Photos: British Museum

21 Four gold ball beads with collars, agate and carnelian barrels and agate cat's eye bead. Grave P.G. 1464. British Museum No. 122720. Length of ball 1 cm.
Photo: British Museum

22 (*a*) String of gold and lapis lazuli beads. P.G. 1284. British Museum No. 122432.
(*b*) Necklace of date-shaped and double conoid lapis lazuli and gold beads with double spiral gold wire pendant. P.G. 1284. British Museum No. 122431. Width of pendant 1·9 cm.
Photo: British Museum

23 Frontlet and necklaces. Grave 1335. Frontlet, British Museum No. 122350, length 11 cm.
Photo: British Museum

24–30: Brak

24 (*a*) Pair of lunate earrings. British Museum No. 125724, 5. Width 1·4 cm.
(*b*) Ribbed earring. British Museum No. 125723. Width 1·4 cm.
(*c*) Double ended lunate earring. British Museum No. 125723. Width 1·4 cm.
(*d*) Pair of penannular flattened end earrings. British Museum No. 125734, 5. Width 1·7 cm.
Photo: British Museum

25 (*a*) Square gold ornament with central boss and two pierced holes. Diameter 1·35 cm. *Iraq*, IX, 1, 1947, pl. 35.
(*b*) Gold button.
Photo: British Museum

26 Earring (or hair-ring); heavy gold, lunate ends. British Museum No. 125736. Width 1·2 cm. *Iraq*, IX, 1, 1947, pl. 36, 10.
Photo: British Museum

27 Pendants with gold strip spacers and tubular gold bead. British Museum No. 125631. Diameter of pendants 1·4 cm. *Iraq*, IX, 1, 1947, pl. 35.

28 Stone mould for circular pendants. British Museum No. 125766. Diameter 4·1 cm.
Photo: British Museum

29 Gold button. British Museum. Diameter 1 cm. *Iraq*, IX, 1, 1947, pl. 35.
Photo: British Museum

30 Necklace of double conoid, tubular, ball, and one central heavy double conoid with sub-spherical ends. British Museum Nos. 125720–1, 125731. Length of central bead 1·8 cm. *Iraq*, IX, 1, 1947, pl. 35.
Photo: British Museum

31 Silver necklace with flat winged disc bead from Byblos. British Museum No. 117798.
Photo: British Museum

Chapter 3

32–36: Alaca

32 Gold pins. Ankara Museum. Length of fluted pin 12·1 cm.
Photo: Olive Kitson

33 Gold clasp and pin *in situ*. Ankara Museum.
Photo: Olive Kitson

34 Quadruple spiral bead from Mari.
Photo: Musée du Louvre

35 Pair of gold bangles. Ankara Museum. Diameter 7·2 cm.
Photo: Olive Kitson

36 Gold double idol. Ankara Museum. Height 4 cm.
Photo: Olive Kitson

37 (*a*) Earring and (*b*) pendant with filigree and granular decoration, from Kültepe. Ankara Museum.
Photo: Courtesy Professor Tahsin Özgüc

38 Disc with filigree decoration, from Ur P.G. 1133. British Museum No. 122208. Diameter 4·2 cm.
Photo: British Museum

39, 40: Troy

39 Basket-shaped earrings made of gold wire decorated with appliqué rosettes; height 1·7 cm, width 2·1 and 2·4 cm. Gold quadruple spiral beads; height 2 cm. Gold bracelet decorated with silver wire bent into looped double spirals and rows of small gold rings; length 15·7 cm, width 2·2 cm. Gold earrings. Gold pin with double spiral top, length 6 cm. Gold pin with vase head with two pairs of double spirals, length 6·6 cm. Gold pin with vase head and double spirals; length 5·5 cm.
Photo: Josephine Powell

40 Gold diadem from Treasure A. Length of ribbon 53·8 cm. Blegen *Troy and the Trojans*, pl. 24.
Photo: Thames & Hudson

41, 42: Poliochni on Lemnos

41 Gold earring with pendants.
Photo: Courtesy Professor Bernabó Brea

42 Gold pin head.
Photo: Courtesy Professor Bernabó Brea

43 Earring with leaf-shaped ends. Ur P.G. 1181. British Museum No. 122223.
Photo: British Museum

44 Earring from Mari. M.640. Musée du Louvre No. AO18240.
Photo: Musée du Louvre

Chapter 4

45 Necklace from Uruk; agate set in gold. Height of central bead 7 cm. Frankfort, *A.A.A.O.*, pl. 676

46 Jewellery from Ur Tomb 1422. Third Dynasty of Ur period.
(*a*) Frontlet. British Museum No. 122242. Length 18·9 cm.
(*b*) Bracelets. British Museum No. 122213, 4. Width 2·3 cm.
(*c*) Hair-ring. British Museum No. 122221. Width 2·3 cm.
(*d*) Earring or hair-ring. British Museum No. 122217 (see fig. 44).
(*e*) Necklace of carnelian and gold ribbed balls, original order. British Museum No. 122433.
Photo: British Museum

47 Frontlets and solid gold bracelets from Ur Tomb 1422. Length of oval frontlet 15 cm. Width of bracelet 8 cm.
Photo: University Museum, Pennsylvania

48 Necklaces from Ur Tomb 1422.
(*a*) Jasper, chalcedony, agate, sard, marble, carnelian, etc. Pennsylvania 30.12.567.
(*b*) Banded sards. Pennsylvania 30.12.568.
(*c*) Banded agate, gold capped, cylinder with central flat gold capped bead (cf. fig. 19a) and gold ball spacers. Pennsylvania 30.12.566.
(*d*) Flat diamonds of gold and carnelian and small gold and carnelian beads. Pennsylvania 30.12.572.
Photo: University Museum, Pennsylvania

49 Beads from Ur.
(*a*) Gold capped agate cat's eye. British Museum No. 120621. Length 4·75 cm.
(*b*) Agate cat's eye. British Museum No. 1919–10–11, 5128. Width 1·8 cm.
Photo: British Museum

50 Necklaces from Ur Tomb 1847.
(*a*) Gold capped bead, gold balls and fluted gold balls. British Museum No. 123135. Length of large bead 2·7 cm.
(*b*) Gold, lapis lazuli and carnelian diamonds. British Museum No. 123137.
Photo: British Museum

51 Gold beads from Trialeti Barrow VIII. Yerevan Museum 595, 598–603.
Photo: Courtesy Professor B. Piotrovski

52–54 Enlargements of beads from pl. 51

55 Jewellery from Tepe Hissar. Necklace with flat disc beads and diadem from Hissar IIIb; necklace with cat's eye and agate, two hair ornaments, from Hissar IIIc Treasure.
Photo: G. Fehevari

56 Gold leaf from Ur. P.G. 783, U.9971. British Museum No. 121367. Width 1 cm.
Photo: British Museum

Chapter 5

57 (*a*) and (*b*) Pair of earrings from Ur. British Museum No. 121416. Height 3·2 cm.
(*c*) Detail showing circle of granules at base of pin and repoussé spiked decoration.
Photos: British Museum

58 (*a*) Silver bangles and fluted earrings from Susa.
(*b*) Detail of left-hand earring showing circular granulation. Musée du Louvre No. SB5890.
Photos: Musée du Louvre

59 Earrings from Susa; (*a*) electrum, (*b*, *c*) gold. Musée du Louvre Nos. (*a*) SB5705, (*b*) SB5704, (*c*) SB5703.
Photo: Musée du Louvre

60 Beads from Khorsabad. Musée du Louvre.
Photo: Musée du Louvre

61–65: Gold jewellery from Dilbat.
Photos: Courtesy Metropolitan Museum of Art, Fletcher Fund, 1947

61 Necklace and associated finds. Metropolitan Museum of Art No. 47.1.

62 (*a*), (*b*) and (*c*) Goddess with raised hands. Height 2·7 cm.

63 (*a*) and (*b*) Part of gold necklace with crescent pendants. Width of crescent 2·5 cm.

64 (*a*) and (*b*) Part of gold necklace; pendants with star and rosette clusters. Diameter 2·5 cm.

65 (*a*) Gold seal caps. 1·1 cm × 1·2 cm.
(*b*) Gold earring. Diameter 2·2 cm.
(*c*) Early Kassite seal impression.
Photo (65*c*): Courtesy Metropolitan Museum of Art, Gift of Georg Hahn, 1947

Chapter 6

66 Toggle pins from the Byblos treasure. Beirut Museum. Length 13 and 12·5 cm, weight 25 and 17 gm.
Photo: Courtesy Emir Maurice Chehab

67 Bronze toggle pin from Ajjul. Middle Bronze I period. Palestine Archaeological Museum No. 13.620.
Photo: Palestine Archaeological Museum

68 Jewellery from Kültepe.
Photo: Courtesy Professor Tahsin Özgüc

Chapter 7

69 Circular pendant from Byblos, Montet Jar. Beirut Museum. Diameter 5·8 cm.
Photo: F. Hadad

70 Gold diadem from Byblos, Montet Jar. Beirut Museum. Diameter 5·7 cm.
Photo: F. Hadad

71 Headband with double spiral clasp from Byblos. Beirut Museum. Length 53 cm, width 3 cm, weight 33 gm.
Photo: Courtesy Emir Maurice Chéhab

72 Rosette made from single piece of gold leaf. Beirut Museum. Diameter 8·6 cm, weight 14 gm.
Photo: Courtesy Emir Maurice Chéhab

73 Gold toggle pin from Ajjul. British Museum No. 130769. Height 5·4 cm.
Photo: Olive Kitson

74 Gold toggle pins with twisted shank. Palestine Archaeological Museum No. 12.667.
Photo: Palestine Archaeological Museum

75 Gold (*a*) strip-twist and (*b*) bar-twist earrings from Ajjul. British Museum Nos. (*a*) 130767, (*b*) 130764.
Photo: Olive Kitson

76 (*a*) Lapis lazuli scaraboid set in gold and (*b*) ribbed earring. 'Cenotaph' deposit, Ajjul. Palestine Archaeological Museum Nos. (*a*) 749, (*b*) 940.
Photo: Palestine Archaeological Museum

77 Gold penannular earrings from Ajjul. British Museum Nos. 130776, 130777, 130778.
Photo: Olive Kitson

78–81: Gold earrings with granular decoration from Ajjul
Photos: Olive Kitson

78 From Hoard 1299. British Museum No. 130762. Width 4·5 cm.

79 From Hoard 1312. Ashmolean Museum No. 1949.314. Width 3·7 cm.

80 From Hoard 1299. British Museum No. 130763. Width 3·6 cm.

81 Unfinished gold earring from Hoard 1299. Ashmolean Museum No. 1949.307. Width 3·2 cm.

82 Winged earring or pendant from Ajjul 1203. British Museum No. 130773.
Photo: Olive Kitson

83 Inlaid earring or pendant from Ajjul. Ashmolean Museum No. 1949.30. Diameter 3·6 cm.
Photo: Olive Kitson

84 Finger rings from Kouklia, Cyprus. Late Cypriote II. Nicosia Museum.
Photo: Nicosia Museum

85 Leech-shaped and bull pendant earrings from Kouklia, Cyprus. Late Cypriote II. Nicosia Museum.
Photo: Nicosia Museum

86 Diadem with rosettes from Ajjul. British Museum No. 130760.
Photo: Olive Kitson

87 Rosettes from Ajjul. British Museum No. 1949.2.12.11.
Photo: Olive Kitson

88 Fragment of diadem with soldered looped double spiral clasp. Ajjul Group 1203. Palestine Archaeological Museum No. 14.569.
Photo: Palestine Archaeological Museum

89 Gold bracelet from Beirut treasure made from thirty-eight longitudinal plaques covered with rows of granules and three pairs of plain hinged strips. Height 4 cm, thickness 0·2 cm.
Photo: Courtesy Emir Maurice Chéhab

90 Solid gold bangle from 'Cenotaph' deposit, Ajjul. Palestine Archaeological Museum No. 32.1308.
Photo: Palestine Archaeological Museum

91 Four gold earrings from Beirut treasure. Diameter 3·9 cm, average weight 9·5 gm.
Photo: Courtesy Emir Maurice Chéhab

92 Silver (?) fibula from Tell Beit Mirsim. Palestine Archaeological Museum No. 732.
Photo: Palestine Archaeological Museum

93 Gold fluted melon-shaped bead with tubular ends from Ajjul Group 1532. Institute of Archaeology, London. Length 1·5 cm.
Photo: Olive Kitson

94 (*a*) Plain, (*b*) fluted and (*c*) barrel-shaped gold beads from Ajjul. British Museum Nos. 130789, 130786. Length 0·9 cm and 3 cm.
Photos: Olive Kitson

95 Gold fly amulet from Ajjul. British Museum No. 130775. Width of wing 1 cm.
Photo: Olive Kitson

96 Gold strip-twist, bar-twist and 'mulberry' earrings and gold toggle pin, from Enkomi Old Tombs 57 and 58. British Museum Nos. 470, 472–6, 544, 358–65.
Photo: British Museum

97 Gold bar-twist earrings from Enkomi Old Tomb 57. Enlargements of bar-twist earrings in pl. 96.
Photo: British Museum

98 Three gold strip-twist (*a–c*), one flange-twist (*d*) earrings from Enkomi Old Tomb 92. British Museum Nos. (*a–c*) 350–3, (*d*) 352.
Photo: British Museum

99 Gold bucranium pendant earrings from Enkomi and Maroni. Top row (left to right) Old Tombs 24, 24, 67; British Museum Nos. 491, 502, 501. Bottom row, Old Tombs 61, 58, Maroni Tomb 2; British Museum Nos. 525, 536, 538.
Photo: British Museum

Chapter 8

100 Jewellery from Alalakh, Atchana.
(1) British Museum No. 125985. Diameter 1·5 cm.
(2) British Museum No. 130093. Diameter 2 cm.
(3) British Museum No. 125987. Length 2·25 cm.
(4) and (5) British Museum No. 125986. Length of (4) 2·3 cm.
(6) British Museum No. 126155.
(7) Bead with cloisons made of gold wire; silver core. British Museum No. 125984. Diameter 1·5 cm.
Photo: British Museum

101 Jewellery from Tomb 4004, Lachish. Ashmolean Museum Nos. 1956.631, 634–6, 647
Photo: Ashmolean Museum

102, 103 Gold Astarte plaques from Ajjul. Ashmolean Museum Nos. 1949. 305–6. Height 8 cm.
Photos: Olive Kitson

Plates 104–107: Gold Astarte plaques from Ugarit
Photos: Courtesy Professor C. F. A. Schaeffer

104 Musée du Louvre Nos. (*a*) AO14719, (*b*) AO14718, (*c*) AO19133.

105 Musée du Louvre No. AO14715.

106 Musée du Louvre No. AO14714.

107 Musée du Louvre Nos. (*a*) AO14716, (*b*) AO14717.

108 Gold eight-pointed star pendant from Ajjul. Palestine Archaeological Museum No. 14.541.
Photo: Palestine Archaeological Museum

109 Gold star pendants with six or four points from Ugarit. Musée du Louvre Nos. (*a*) AO19135, (*b*) AO18551, (*c*) AO17363, (*d*) AO19131.
Photo: Courtesy Professor C. F. A. Schaeffer

110 Gold jewellery from Ugarit. Musée du Louvre Nos. (*a*) AO19143, (*b*) AO19129, (*c*) AO19134.
Photo: Courtesy Professor C. F. A. Schaeffer

111 Gold cut-out eight-pointed star pendant from Ajjul. British Museum No. 130766.
Photo: Olive Kitson

112 Winged female figure on a relief wearing disc pendants on wrist and necklace. British Museum No. 124578.
Photo: British Museum

113 Late Assyrian cylinder seal; worshipper before a goddess; stars behind shrine and above her head. British Museum No. 89846.
Photo: Courtesy Professor D. Wiseman

114 Babylonian cylinder seal; eighth to seventh century B.C.; seated king with divine symbols in sky. British Museum No. 89590.
Photo: Courtesy Professor D. Wiseman

115 Gold jewellery from Sheckem including sun disc pendants. Palestine Archaeological Museum No. 14.577.
Photo: Palestine Archaeological Museum

116 Stele of Ashurnaṣirpal II with divine symbols, from Nimrud.
Photo: British Museum

117 Stele of Ashurnaṣirpal II from Nimrud. Mallowan, *Nimrud*, I, pl. 27, p. 63.
Photo: William Collins & Co. Ltd

118 Cylinder seal; late Kassite; bull before a tree with Kassite cross. British Museum No. 102507.
Photo: Courtesy Professor D. Wiseman

119 Pendant from Ajjul. British Museum No. 130779. Diameter 1·7 cm.
Photo: British Museum

Chapter 9

120 Fluted earring from 'Amlash', Giyan type. Teheran Museum. Diameter 2 cm.
Photo: Bulloz

121 Jewellery from Gök tepe. 1903 excavations. Fitzwilliam Museum, Cambridge, No. E 128–130.
Photo: Reproduced by permission of the Syndics of the Fitzwilliam Museum, Cambridge

122 Jewellery from Gök tepe. Teheran Museum.
Photo: G. Fehevari

123 Jewellery from Daylaman. Museum of Fine Arts, Boston, No. 59.724.733.
Photo: Boston Museum of Fine Arts

124 Beads and pendants from Amlash; modern arrangement.
(*a*) Teheran Museum. Length 26 cm.
(*b*) Teheran Museum. Length 27 cm.
(*c*) Foroughi Collection, Teheran. Length 25·5 cm, diameter of disc 7·4 cm.
Photo: Bulloz

125 Gold disc pendant, (?) Talish area. Museum of Fine Arts, Boston, No. 60.246.
Photo: Boston Museum of Fine Arts

126 Terracotta figurines. Ashmolean Museum, Oxford.
(*a*) With gold earrings and navel. Ashmolean Museum No. 1932.1182. Height 15·3 cm.
(*b*) With copper torque. Ashmolean Museum No. 1914.109. Height 15·5 cm.
Photo: Ashmolean Museum

Chapter 10

127 Gold bracelet with inlay of blue paste from Aqar Qūf. Baghdad Museum.

128 Susa; whetstone; green schist, set in a gold sleeve in the shape of a lion's head decorated with granulation. Musée du Louvre No. SB2769. Length 15·5 cm.
Photo: Musée du Louvre

129 Female mask of glazed frit. Tell Rimah.
Photo: Courtesy Professor D. Oates

130 Gold disc pendant with eight-pointed star. Tell Rimah.
Photo: Courtesy Professor D. Oates

131 Linked earrings with 'mulberry' pendants. Mari. Musée du Louvre Nos. M1424, AO19028, H1266.
Photo: Musée du Louvre

Chapter 11

132 (*a*)–(*d*) Gold rings from Susa, decorated in filigree and granulation. Musée du Louvre. Average diameter 2·2 cm.
Photo: Musée du Louvre

133 (*a*) Gold bead, (*b*) earring and (*c*) unfinished disc from Sialk Cemetery A. Musée du Louvre Nos. (*a*) AO18083, (*b*) AO18085, (*c*) AO18084.
Photo: Musée du Louvre

134 Gold earring from Marlik. Teheran Museum. Width 3 cm.
Photo: Rostamy

135 Pair of earrings from Hasanlu. Teheran Museum.
Photo: G. Fehevari

136 Group of jewellery from Hasanlu. Teheran Museum.
Photo: G. Fehevari

137, 138, 140–148: Marlik
Photos: Courtesy Professor E. Negahban

137 Gold cage pendant with granular decoration. Teheran Museum No. 14689/7689. Weight 28·2 gm.

138 Gold toggle pin with incised shank. Teheran Museum No. 14819/7819. Length 10·9 cm, weight 26·6 gm.

139 Pair of gold pins from 'Amlash'. Height 11·4 cm.
Photo: Messrs. Sotheby & Co.

140 Gold leaf with hooked stem. Teheran Museum No. 14856/7856. Weight 17 gm.

141 Gold serpentine ring made from soldered plain-twisted gold wires. Teheran Museum No. 14725/7725. Diameter 2 cm.

142 Necklace of gold beads and pendant with cloisonné palmette design. Teheran Museum No. 14822/7822. Diameter of pendant 5·8 cm, weight 29·5 gm.

143 Gold bar-twist bracelet. Weight 9·8 gm.

144 Gold earring in the form of a cluster of pomegranates suspended from a loop. Teheran Museum No. 14847/7847. Length 5·2 cm, weight 6·8 gm.

145 Necklace with gold quadruple spiral, date-shaped and spherical beads with pomegranate pendant. Teheran Museum No. 14705/7705.

146 Pair of pins with bronze shafts, decorated with gold; gold lion heads. Teheran Museum No. 14906/77. Length 18 cm and 18·5 cm, weight of pair 50·5 gm.

147 Double pyramid gold earring made of gold balls diminishing in size towards the base. Teheran Museum No. 14738/7738. Weight of pair 8·5 gm.

148 Gold pendant with double eagle head. Teheran Museum No. 14843/7843. Diameter of loop 5·5 cm, weight 11·6 gm.

149 Gold bracelets from 'Amlash'. Teheran Museum.
(*a*) Diameter 8·4 cm, weight 80 gm.
(*b*) Diameter 9 cm, weight 125 gm.
Photo: Bulloz

150 Gold bracelet with two lion heads in lapis lazuli from (?) Hamadan. Cincinnati Art Museum No. 1957.30. Height 12·1 cm.
Photo: Cincinnati Art Museum

151 Gold bracelet with two lion heads. University Museum, Philadelphia. Diameter 11·7 cm.
Photo: Bulloz

152 Gold bracelet, incomplete, from 'Amlash'. Teheran Museum. Diameter 11·5 cm, weight 35 gm.
Photo: Bulloz

Chapter 12

153 Gold pomegranate earring or pendant from Amlash. Teheran, Iran Bastan Museum. Length 4·8 cm, weight 15 gm.
Photo: Bulloz

154 (*a*) Spacer beads. Altintepe. Length 2·2 cm.
(*b*) Enlargement of (*a*).
Photo: Selahattin Oztartan. Courtesy Professor Tahsin Özgüc

155 Gold necklace. Altintepe.
Photo: Selahattin Oztartan. Courtesy Professor Tahsin Özgüc

156 Gold buttons. Altintepe.
Photo: Selahattin Oztartan. Courtesy Professor Tahsin Özgüc

157 Gold disc. North-west Persia. Museum of Fine Arts, Boston, No. 60.959.
Photo: Boston Museum of Fine Arts

158 Jewellery from Karmir Blur; gold earrings, bracelet, part of silver ingot, part of a torque with lion finial (gold over silver), gold stud.
Photo: Courtesy Professor B. Piotrovski

159 Earrings from Ur. U.461, 462. Width 1·5, 1·2 cm.
Photo: Ur Excavations

160 Silver fibula from Kayalidere.
Photo: Courtesy C. A. Burney

161 Gold bracelet with serpent heads from 'Amlash'. Teheran Museum. Diameter 7·5 cm, weight 75 gm.
Photo: Bulloz

162 Agha Evler, Persian Talish. Silver bracelets. Musée de St Germain-en-Laye Nos. 57974–6. Diameter 6·5 cm and 3·9 cm.
Photo: Musée des Antiquités Nationales

Chapter 13

163–166, 168–171: Ziweye

163 Necklace of gold tubular and date-shaped spacer beads. Teheran, Iran Bastan Museum. Length 7 cm, width 2 cm, weight 165 gm.
Photo: Bulloz

164 Necklace of gold beads and pendants with central circular banded agate set in gold with four gold beads suspended by gold chains. Teheran, Iran Bastan Museum. Length 47 cm, weight 21 gm.
Photo: Bulloz

165 Gold necklace, gold capped, fluted spherical and quadruple spiral beads. Cincinnati Art Museum No. 1953.66.
Photo: Cincinnati Art Museum

166 Gold chains threaded through triple spacer beads with gold bells at the ends of the chains which pass through six gold spacers. Teheran, Iran Bastan Museum. Length 109 cm, weight 237 gm.
Photo: Bulloz

167 Gold stag, buttons and gold chain with single tubular beads decorated with lions from Zöldhalompuszta. Nemzeti Museum, Budapest.
Photo: Budapest Museum (1936)

168 Gold earrings. Teheran, Iran Bastan Museum.
(*a*) Boat-shaped, ends bound with gold wire, granular decoration.
(*b*) Boat-shaped, with clusters of granules soldered to body of earring. Average diameter 1·2 cm.
(*c*) Plain boat-shaped, fluted body.
(*d*) Flat boat-shaped, with granular rosettes.
Photo: Bulloz

169 Gold fibula with lion head finials, the pin resting in a human hand. Teheran, Iran Bastan Museum. Length 3 cm, weight 20 gm.
Photo: Bulloz

170 (*a*) Gold fibula; two lions on bow and human hand. Metropolitan Museum of Art No. 54.4.
(*b*) Silver fibula. Metropolitan Museum of Art No. 51.44.1.
Photos: Metropolitan Museum of Art, (*a*) Rogers Fund, 1954, (*b*) Gift of Khalil Rabenou, 1951.

171 (*a*) Bracelet, solid gold with moufflon heads and body incised. Teheran, Iran Bastan Museum. Diameter 9 cm, diameter of moufflon head 2 cm, weight 169 gm.
(*b*) Two gold bracelets, ends in the form of the heads of bull calves. Teheran, Iran Bastan Museum. Diameters 5 cm and 4·7 cm, weight 25 gm.
Photo: Bulloz

172 Bracelet, solid gold with moufflon heads. Provenance unknown. Borowski Collection, Bâle. Diameter 7·7 cm, weight 250 gm.
Photo: Bulloz

173 Gold ajouré bracteates from (?) Hamadan. Teheran, Iran Bastan Museum.
(*a*) Lion head with spreading mane. Diameter 5·7 cm, weight 9 gm.
(*b*) Two pairs of lions with single repoussé head. Diameter 5·5 cm, weight 25 gm.
Photo: Bulloz

174 Gold ajouré bracteate; lion head with speading mane. Museum of Fine Arts, Boston.
Photo: Boston Museum of Fine Arts.

175 Necklace with small granulated beads and ajouré pendants representing two lions, from Hamadan. Teheran, Iran Bastan Museum. Length 41 cm, weight 47 gm.
Photo: Bulloz

176 Limestone Lamaštu plaque from Nimrud. Dimensions 12·5 × 9·6 cm. Mallowan, *Nimrud*, I, pl. 60, p. 117.
Photo: William Collins & Co. Ltd

177 Mythical figure with lion head. British Museum No. 11898.
Photo: British Museum

178 Pair of gold crouching goat appliqués from Ziweye. Teheran, Iran Bastan Museum. Length 1·5 cm, width 2 cm, weight 2 gm.
Photo: Bulloz

179 Examples of appliqués from Ziweye, including Maltese cross, lotus flowers, rosettes and stars. Teheran, Iran Bastan Museum.
Photo: Bulloz

180 Gold jewellery from Ephesus. British Museum 876–7.
Photo: British Museum

181 Gold glove with rings at ends of chains from Ziweye. Teheran, Iran Bastan Museum. Length 19 cm, width 12 cm, weight 139 gm.
Photo: Bulloz

182 Gold mount for a seal, with impression of the stamp, from Ziweye. Teheran, Iran Bastan Museum. Weight 6 gm.
Photo: Bulloz

183 Earring, twisted with lion's head, from Ziweye. Teheran, Iran Bastan Museum.
Photo: Bulloz

184 Gold twisted earring with bull's head or pair of gold twisted earrings, granular decoration and filigree spirals. Provenance unknown. Collection Comte du Puytison, Paris. Weight 8 gm.
Photo: Courtesy Comte du Puytison

185 Pair of gold twisted earrings with ibex heads. Provenance unknown. Ashmolean Museum No. 1965.716a, b. Diameter 2 cm.
Photo: Ashmolean Museum

186 Gold twisted earring with ibex head. Homs region. Collection Comte du Puytison, Paris. Height 2·5 cm, weight 3 gm.
Photo: Courtesy Comte du Puytison

187 Pair of gold ibex-headed bracelets; hoops of multiple twisted wires and separate finials. Pasargadae. Average diameter of upper example 6 cm, weight 41·8 gm. Diameter of lower example 7 cm.
Photo: Olive Kitson

188 Gold pectoral from Ziweye. Teheran Museum.
Photo: Josephine Powell

189 Gold torque of twisted wire; three fragments. Ziweye. Teheran, Iran Bastan Museum. Length 31 cm, weight 30 gm.
Photo: Bulloz

190 Gold pectoral; six fragments with granular decoration. Ziweye. Teheran, Iran Bastan Museum. Length 38 cm, width 2 cm, weight 127 gm.
Photo: Bulloz

191 Gold torque, fluted gold over core; four pieces Ziweye. Length 33 cm, weight 127 gm.
Photo: Bulloz

192 Head of bronze siren figure attached to a cauldron. Vetulonia, Florence Archaeological Museum.
Photo: Florence Archaeological Museum.

193 Bronze winged figure with two heads intended for attachment to a cauldron. Van. Collection of Marquis de Vogué, Paris. Width 37 cm.
Photo: Courtesy Marquis de Vogué.

194 Alabaster figure of a lady. Vulci, Polledrara tomb. British Museum No. D.4. Height 44 cm.
Photo: British Museum

195 Gold pectoral or epaulette. Metropolitan Museum of Art No. L63.6. Height 22·5 cm.
Photo: from the Pomerance Collection

196 Gold roundel from Ghafantlu. Nelson Gallery-Atkins Museum. Diameter 7 cm.
Photo: Nelson Gallery-Atkins Museum, Kansas City, Missouri (Nelson Fund)

Chapter 14

197–207, 209, 210: Tell Fara

197 Earrings from Tombs 204, 222, 240, 506. Institute of Archaeology,

London. (*a*) F.506, height 1·4 cm; (*b*) F.204, height 1·3 cm; (*c*) F.240, height 1·7 cm, (*d*) F.222, height 1·4 cm, gold over bronze; (*e*) F.222, height 1·7 cm, gold over bronze.
Photo: Olive Kitson

198 Gold tassel earrings and drop lunate earrings from Tombs 222 and 518. Institute of Archaeology, London. (*a*) F.222, length 3·3 cm; (*b*) F.222, length 3 cm; (*c*) F.518, length 2·9 cm; (*d*) F.222, length 1·3 cm; (*e*) F.222, length 1·1 cm.
Photo: Olive Kitson

199 Bronze dress pin from Tomb 222. Institute of Archaeology, London. Length 11·7 cm.
Photo: Olive Kitson

200 Gold tassel and mulberry earrings from Tomb 605. Institute of Archaeology, London. Height 1·7 cm and 3 cm.
Photo: Olive Kitson

201 Gold lunate earring with semi-circular gold knob pendant from Tomb 202. Height 1·5 cm.

202 Gold diadem and silver lunate earring from Tomb 202. Length 4·4 cm, height of earring 1·5 cm.
Photo: Olive Kitson

203 Gold diadem from Tomb 201. Ashmolean Museum No. 1937.767. Length 9·5 cm.

204 Bone horse trappings from Tomb 201. Loan from Institute of Archaeology, London. Ashmolean Museum. Blinkers 5·6 × 5.4 cm.
Photo: Ashmolean Museum

205 Gold bull's horn pendant and ring from Tomb 229. Width 1·5 cm and 1·9 cm.
Photo: Olive Kitson

206 Bronze beads imitating gold cylindrical granular beads and melon-shaped beads, from Tomb 837. Length of largest bead 1·3 cm.
Photo: Olive Kitson

207 Necklaces from Tomb 552, with pairs of gold melon-shaped beads on each necklace. Institute of Archaeology, London. Average length of gold beads 5 mm.
Photo: Olive Kitson

208 Solid gold earring and necklace from Tell el Ajjul, Tomb 1074, with one gold melon-shaped fluted bead. Institute of Archaeology, London. Length of gold bead 1 cm.
Photo: Olive Kitson

209 Enlargement of gold melon-shaped fluted bead shown in pl. 208.
Photo: Olive Kitson

210 Silver earring from Tomb 754. Institute of Archaeology, London. Height 4·7 cm.
Photo: Olive Kitson

211 Earrings from Susa. Elamite tombs, eighth to seventh centuries B.C. Musée du Louvre.
(*a*) No. SB5756, height 4·8 cm.
(*b*) No. SB5754, height 5·4 cm.
Photo: Musée du Louvre

212 Pair of gold earrings. Purchased, provenance given as Tello. British Museum No. 90.10.11, 1 and 2.
Photo: British Museum

213 (*a*) and (*b*) Gold boat-shaped earring with granular decoration from Al Mina. Ashmolean Museum No. 1937.769. Height 2·2 cm.
Photo: Ashmolean Museum

214 Pair of gold boat-shaped earrings with granular decoration, from (?) Homs. Collection Comte du Puytison, Paris.
Photo: Courtesy Comte du Puytison

215 Jewellery from Cremation Grave ATG 38/2, Atchana. Ashmolean Museum Nos. 1939. S17, 555–6, 413. Diameter of pendant 3 cm.
Photo: Ashmolean Museum

Chapter 15

216 (*a*) and (*b*) The Nimrud jewel. Diameter of pendant 2·2 × 1·2 cm. Mallowan, *Nimrud* I, p. 114, pl. 58, ND785.
Photo: Willams Collins & Co. Ltd

217 Gold earring from Uruk (Warka). Diameter 3·2 cm.
Photo: Courtesy Professor H. Lenzen

218 Gold granulated earrings. Gutman Collection No. 48. Oberlin College, Allen Art Museum, Oberlin, Ohio.
(*a*) Length 9·8 cm, weight 8·74 gm.
(*b*) Length 9·2 cm, weight 6·24 gm.
Photo: Oberlin College

219 Rock crystal earring with copper loop from Palace of Adad-Nirari III, Nimrud. Height 5 cm. Mallowan, *Nimrud*, I, p. 65, pl. 28, ND3293(B).
Photo: William Collins & Co. Ltd

220 Limestone head of Ashurnaṣirpal II. Fitzwilliam Museum, Cambridge, No. E.3–1942.
Photo: Reproduced by permission of the Syndics of the Fitzwilliam Museum, Cambridge

221 Assyrian cylinder seal; green chalcedony; goddess Ishtar, a worshipper, with earring in sky. British Museum No. 89.769.
Photo: Courtesy Professor D. Wiseman

222 An Assyrian prince; wall panel from the Palace of Sennacherib. Metropolitan Museum of Art No. 32.143.13.
Photo: Metropolitan Museum of Art, Gift of John D. Rockefeller, Jr, 1932.

223 Gold earring from Ur. British Museum No. 116565. U.460B. Width 2 cm.
Photo: British Museum

224 Triple armed electrum earring (one arm missing). From (?) Toprak kale, Van. Museum für Kunst und Gewerbe, Hamburg, No. 1968, 37. Height 5·7 cm.
Photo: Courtesy Dr H. Hoffman

225 Assyrian triple armed gold earrings. Museum für Kunst und Gewerbe, Hamburg.
Photo: Museum für Kunst und Gewerbe, Hamburg

226 Gold earring from Babylon. British Museum No. 124620. Height 3·7 cm.
Photo: British Museum

227 Bronze bracelet, probably Assyrian. Musée du Louvre No. 8255. Diameter 13 cm.
Photo: Musée du Louvre

228 Bronze bracelet originally covered with silver, from Zahleh, Lebanon. Ashmolean Museum No. 1889.5a(3).
Photo: Ashmolean Museum

229 Relief portraying tribute of earrings and armlets from a relief found at Nimrud in the North-west Palace of Ashurnaṣirpal II. Mallowan, *Nimrud*, I, p. 100, pl. 47.
Photo: William Collins & Co. Ltd

230 Bronze bracelet with lion head finials from Luristan. Museum of Fine Arts, Boston, No. 30.616.
Photo: Boston Museum of Fine Arts

231–238: Ivory heads from Nimrud
Photos: William Collins & Co. Ltd

231 Mallowan, *Nimrud*, I, p. 216, pl. 164, ND1145.

232 Mallowan, *Nimrud*, I, p. 212, pl. 151, ND2105.

233 Mallowan, *Nimrud*, I, p. 212, pl. 150, ND2100.

234 Mallowan, *Nimrud*, I, p. 212, pls. (*a*) 148 and (*b*) 149, ND2102.

235 Mallowan, *Nimrud*, I, p. 214, pl. 159, ND2103(B).

236 Mallowan, *Nimrud*, I, p. 212, pl. 152, ND1189.

237 Mallowan, *Nimrud*, I, p. 129, pl. 71, ND2250(B).

238 Mallowan, *Nimrud*, I, p. 133, pl. 73, ND2549.

239 Bronze fibula. Provenance unknown. Ashmolean Museum No. 1913.685. Length of pin 8·3 cm.
Photo: Ashmolean Museum

240 Silver fibula bound with silver wire and hook of chain attached. Ashmolean Museum No. 1937.766. Length of pin 3·5 cm.
Photo: Ashmolean Museum

241 Gold fibula from tomb of Adoni-Nur. Amman Museum No. J1204.
Photo: Amman Museum

242 Terracotta coffin from tomb of Adoni-Nur. Amman Museum No. TJ1231. Height 56 cm, width at square end 66 cm.
Photo: Amman Museum

243 (*a*) and (*b*) Both sides of conical carnelian seal in silver mount from tomb of Adoni-Nur. Amman Museum No. TJ1193. Height *c.* 4 cm.
Photo: Amman Museum

244 Silver earrings from tomb of Adoni-Nur. Amman Museum Nos. TJ1199, TJ1199A.
Photo: Amman Museum

245 Silver finger ring with shank in shape of lotus blossoms forming a setting for a circular bead outlined with a row of globules. Tomb of Adoni-Nur. Amman Museum N. TJ1205.
Photo: Amman Museum

246 Electrum fibula from Gordion, Phrygian city mound. Height 3·4 cm.
Photo: University Museum, Philadelphia.

247 Gold earrings from Gordion, Tumulus A.
Photo: University Museum, Philadelphia

248 Silver earring from Luristan, War Kabud; long pendant decorated with granulations. Length 5·7 cm.
Photo: Professor L. Vanden Berghe

249 Two silver earrings from Luristan, War Kabud; pendant covered with large granulations. Length 2·7 cm and 2·5 cm.
Photo: Professor L. Vanden Berghe

250 Boat-shaped earrings.
(*a*) Silver, diameter 2·5 cm.
(*b*) Gold, diameter 1·5 cm.
Photo: Professor L. Vanden Berghe

251 Silver bracelet from Tepe Sialk Cemetery B. Musée du Louvre No. AO17954.
Photo: Musée du Louvre

252 Four silver double spiral pendants from Tepe Nush-i-Jan; a silver quadruple spiral bead adheres to one of the pendants (*c*). Widths: (*a*) 4 cm, (*b*) 4·3 cm, (*c*) 5 cm, (*d*) 5·1 cm.
Photo: Courtesy David Stronach

253 Silver double spiral from Luristan. Museum of Fine Arts, Boston, No. 15.205.
Photo: Boston Museum of Fine Arts

254 Bronze bracelet with recumbent duck finials. Museum of Fine Arts, Boston, No. 30.613.
Photo: Boston Museum of Fine Arts

255 Gold bracelet with finials in the form of ducks, from Amlash. Teheran, Iran Bastan Museum. Diameter 8 cm, weight 45 gm.
Photo: Bulloz

256 Silver gilt penannular earring from Deve Hüyük. Ashmolean Museum No. 1913.731. Diameter 4·8 cm.
Photo: Ashmolean Museum

257 Pair of gold earrings from Pasargadae; two concentric circles of gold discs and open wire rosettes round the outside, each petal ending in a separate gold granule. Teheran, Iran Bastan Museum. Diameter of each example 4·9 cm, thickness 0·9 cm, weight 19 gm.
Photo: Olive Kitson

258 Pair of gold earrings from Pasargadae with free hanging inlaid pendants, open wire scrolls and oval cloisons inlaid with turquoise coloured paste. Teheran, Iran Bastan Museum. Diameter of each single example 3·6 cm, weight of right hand example 9 gm.
Photo: Olive Kitson

259 Gold earrings with hinged clasp and plain ring pendant. Beirut, private collection. *Paris Cat.* 706 (not 708).
Photo: Bulloz

LIST OF COLOUR PLATES

A Headdress; silver stalks replica, gold flowers original. Ur Early Dynastic Cemetery. British Museum. Height of floral combs 30·5 cm. See Chapter 1.
Photo: British Museum

B Necklace; coiled wire beads, double conoid and twisted double spiral pendants. Ur Early Dynastic Cemetery. P.G. 580. British Museum No. 121426. Diameter of double spiral 1·6 cm. See Chapter 1.
Photo: British Museum

C Necklace with fourteen gold pendants. Alaca. Ankara Museum. Diameter of pendant 2·2 cm. See Chapter 3.
Photo: Olive Kitson

D Gold fenestrated axe head; the wooden shaft decorated with granulated gold foils. Byblos. Beirut Museum. See Chapter 7.
Photo: Woolley, *Mesopotamia and the Middle East*

E Gold falcon earring. Ajjul Hoard 277. See Chapter 7.
Photo: Olive Kitson

F Gold jewellery from Gilan. Mazda Collection, Teheran. See Chapter 12.
Photo: A. Mazda

G Gold bracelet with lion finials and decorated with two pairs of lions. Ziweye. Teheran, Iran Bastan Museum. Length 9·2 cm. See Chapter 13.
Photo: Publications Filmées d'Art et Histoire

H Gold and glass paste earrings from Luristan. Mazda Collection, Teheran. Average length *c.* 4 cm. See Chapter 15.
Photo: A. Mazda

LIST OF TEXT FIGURES

Chapter 1

Figs. 1–5, 7–12: Ur Early Dynastic Cemetery

1 Hair ornament, silver. P.G. 159. Length 22 cm. After *Ur Excavations*, II, pl. 137.

2 Hair ornament, copper. P.G. 1702. Length 5·5 cm. After *Ur Excavations*, II, pl. 219, U.14257.

3 Hair ornament, gold. P.G. 1195. British Museum 122205. Length 7 cm.

4 Earring, gold. Width 8·4 cm. After *Ur Excavations*, II, pl. 219, Type 1.

5 Necklace, 'dog collar'; gold ball beads, lapis lazuli and carnelian ring beads. P.G. 263. Baghdad Museum No. 3933. Scale 1:1. After *Ur Excavations*, II, pl. 220, U.8527.

6 Types of gold and silver beads. Early Dynastic, Sargonid and Third Dynasty of Ur periods. Adapted from *Ur Excavations*, II, pp. 366 ff., figs. 70–8.

7 Necklace; lapis lazuli and gold beads with one lapis lazuli and two gold pendants. Scale 1:1. After *Ur Excavations*, I, pl. 220.

8 Necklace; etched carnelian pendants set in gold. Scale 1:1. After *Ur Excavations*, II, pl. 22, U.8931.

9 Copper pin with gold and lapis lazuli head and silver cylinder seal attached by a copper chain. P.G. 543. After *Ur Excavations*, II, pl. 231, U.9151.

10 (*a*) and (*b*) Copper pins with head and shaft cast in one piece. After *Ur Excavations*, II, pl. 231, U.7080, 8086.

11 Silver pin with head in shape of clenched hand. P.G. 55. Length 19 cm. After *Ur Excavations*, II, p. 231, U.8014.

12 Gold pin with carnelian head. After *Ur Excavations*, II, pl. 231, U.9629.

Chapter 2

Figs. 13–15: Jewellery from Ur

13 Gold frontlets. Lengths: (*a*) 11·5 cm, (*b*) 12·5 cm, (*c*) 19 cm. *Ur Excavations*, II, pl. 219.

14 (*a*) Gold hair-ring. (*b*) Hair ribbon, width 0·64 cm. *Ur Excavations*, II, pl. 219.

15 (*a*)–(*d*) Gold earrings. Average diameter 1·2 cm. *Ur Excavations*, II, pl. 219.

16 Terracottas. (*b*) from Wilayah, height 6 cm; *Sumer*, 16, 1960, fig. 5. (*a*) and (*c*) from Ashur; Andrae, *Archaische Ishtar Tempel*, Taf. 52d and i.

17 Terracotta from Ashur. Andrae, *Archaische Ishtar Tempel*, fig. 53d.

18 Terracottas from Tell Asmar. Heights: (*a*) 9 cm, (*b*) 10 cm. Frankfort *et al.*, *The Gimilsin Temple and the Palace of the Rulers at Tell Asmar*, figs. 109, 110c.

19 Beads from Ur. (*a*) Gold capped V-shaped flattened bead. (*b*) Gold capped banded agate bead, length 4 cm. *Ur Excavations*, II, pl. 132.

Figs. 20–24: Jewellery from Brak

20 Double lunate earring. British Museum No. 125723. Width 1·2 cm. *Iraq*, IX, 1947, pl. XXXVI, 28.

21 (*a*) Silver boss pendant. Width 2·5 cm. After *Iraq*, IX, 1947, pl. XXXIII, 11.
(*b*) Gold or electrum lanceolate pendant. Length 2·7 cm. After *Iraq*, IX, 1947, pl. XXXIII, 10.

22 (*a*) Silver quadruple spiral bead. Width 1 cm. After *Iraq*, IX, 1947, pl. XXXIII, 21.

(*b*) Unfinished silver winged disc bead (?). Width 1·8 cm. After *Iraq*, IX, 1947, pl. XXXIII, 14.
(*c*) Silver ring bead with granulation. After *Iraq*, IX, 1947, pl. XXXIII, part of silver necklace.

23 Silver disc from Brak. Width 3·5 cm. After *Iraq*, IX, 1947, pl. XXXII, 7.

24 (*a*)–(*d*) Copper pins from Brak. Lengths: (*a*) 11·5 cm, (*b*) 10·8 cm, (*c*) 11 cm, (*d*) 8·3 cm. After *Iraq*, IX, pl. XXI, LIII, 3–5. (*e*) Copper pin from Tell Aswad, length 14 cm. After *Iraq*, XIX, pl. XXI, LIII, 30.

Chapter 3

Figs. 25–31: Alaca. 25–28, 30, 31 drawn by Mrs S. Bakker.

25 (*a*) Pin with shank of silver over bronze and gold and carnelian head. Ankara Museum. Length 15·7 cm.
(*b*) Gold and rock crystal pin. Ankara Museum. Length 13 cm.

26 Gold pins. Ankara Museum. Lengths: (*a*) 22·4 cm, (*b*) 11·5 cm.

27 Gold cruciform (*a*), star-shaped (*b*, *c*) and cotton reel (*d*) beads. Ankara Museum. Lengths: (*a*) 6 cm, (*b*) 7 cm.

28 Quadruple disc beads. Ankara Museum.

29 (*a*) Quadruple spiral bead. Length 1·6 cm. After Koşay, *Alaca*, pl. CIX.
(*b*) Quadruple spiral bead from Kültepe. Scale over 2:1. Ankara Museum. After Özgüc, *Horoztepe*, pl. XIX, 8.

30 Gold headband. Ankara Museum. Width of band 1·2 cm, thickness 0·1 cm.

31 (*a*) and (*b*) Gold lock rings. Ankara Museum. Scale 1:1.

Figs. 32–33, 35–41: Troy

32 (*a*) Gold basket earring with rosettes. Width 1·2 cm. After Schmidt, *Sammlung*, 6036.
(*b*) Gold basket earring with granulation. Detail of fig. 35. After Schmidt, *Sammlung*, p. 234, No. 5880.

33 A selection from fifty-six gold earrings, Treasure A. Studs and buttons. Scale 1:1. After Schliemann, *Atlas*, pl. 204.

34 Gold basket earring from Ur. P.G. 1100. Scale 1:1. Adapted from *Ur Excavations*, II, pl. 219, U.11584, and pl. 138.

35 Gold basket earring with idol pendants. Length 8·7 cm. Schmidt, *Sammlung*, Beilage II, 5880.

36 Types of bead adapted from Schmidt, *Sammlung*, No. 5343 and Schliemann, *Ilios*, p. 460, Nos. 715 ff.

37 Beads and buttons. After Schmidt, *Sammlung*, Nos. 5943 ff.

38 Gold beads from Level IIg. Scale 5:1. After Blegen, *Troy*, I, pl. 356.

39 Gold pin from Level IIg. Scale 1:1 After Blegen, *Troy*, I, pl. 356.

40 (*a*) Bronze and (*b*) silver pins. After Schmidt, *Sammlung*, 6401 and 6425. (*c*) Bronze pin from Byblos. Montet, *Byblos*, p. 104, pl. LVIII, 341.

41 Gold pin with cloisonné rosette. After Schmidt, *Sammlung*, 6134.

42 (*a*) Gold pin, (*b*, *c*, *d*) earrings and (*e*) pendant from Tarsus. (*b*) Length 13 cm. After Goldman, *Tarsus*, Vol. II, 434, 1–7.

Chapter 4

43 Silver axe head from Ur. Tomb 1422. Length 18 cm. After *Ur Excavations*, II, pl. 223, 8.

44 Earring (or hair-ring) from Ur. Tomb 1422. Third Dynasty of Ur. British Museum No. 122217. Scale 2:3. After *Ur Excavations*, II, pl. 219.

45 Earring from Ur. Tomb 1850. Third Dynasty of Ur. After *Ur Excavations*, II, pl. 219

46 Jewellery from Ashur. Grave 20. Scale about 1:5. Length of large diadem 28 cm. Third Dynasty of Ur. After Andrae, *Archaische Ishtar Tempel*, Taf. 10a and c.

47 Circular copper ridged pan from Ashur. Grave 20. Length 51 cm. Haller, *Ashur*, Taf. 10h.

48 Clay male figurine from Ashur. Height 11·4 cm. After Andrae, *Archaische Ishtar Tempel*, Abb. 53, p. 77.

49 Gold vase inlaid with sardonyx, amber and colour glass paste from Trialeti. Barrow XVII. Height 8 cm. After Kuftin, *Trialeti*, pl. XCIII.

50 Silver dagger from Trialeti. Barrow XVIII. After Kuftin, *Trialeti*, pl. CV.

51 Copper dagger blade from Ur. Tomb 1422. Length 16 cm. After *Ur Excavations*, II, pl. 228, 2.

52 (*a*) and (*b*) Gold hair ornaments from Lapithos, Cyprus. Heights: (*a*) 4·8 cm, (*b*) 4·5 cm. (*c*) Silver hair ornament from Lapithos, Cyprus. Height 6 cm. (*d*) Bronze hair-rings from Paraskevi, Cyprus.

Chapter 5

53 Fluted earring from Tell Asmar. After Frankfort *et al.*, *Tell Asmar*, fig. 105a.

54 Stone relief from Mari; goddess with necklaces and bangles. Height 13·5 cm. After *Mari*, II, 1959, fig. 21 and pl. XV.

55 Fragment of hairband; steatite. Height 8·2 cm. After *Mari*, II, 1959, fig. 22a.

56 Goddess from Mari; fresco. After *Mari*, II, 1958, pl. XVII.

57 Goddess Lama; bronze; back view showing counterweight. British Museum No. 123040. Height 10 cm.

58 Terracotta from Mari; female head with triple fluted earrings and 'choker' necklaces. Height 15·6 cm. After *Mari*, II, 1959, fig. 27.

59 Male figure wearing necklace and pendants; fresco. After *Mari*, II, 1958, pl. XXIII.

60 Sacrificial scene; two figures, wearing circular pendants, leading a bull, with arm of the king above wearing bracelet; fresco. After *Mari*, II, 1958, pl. VI and fig. 19.

61 (*a*) and (*b*) Male heads wearing circular earrings; fresco. After *Mari*, II, 1958, figs. 70, 83.

62 (*a*) Terracotta with goddess wearing fluted earrings, necklace, bracelet and pelvic beads. After Ruth Opificius, *Old Babylonian Terracottas*, Taf. 2, fig. 114, p. 250.
(*b*) Goddess, terracotta, wearing fringed robe, two rows of fluted earrings and holding rows of necklaces. After Frankfort, *O.I.C.*, 34–35, fig. 67, p. 89.
(*c*) Deity with axes, medallion and moon pendant. After Frankfort, *O.I.C.*, fig. 69, p. 91.
(*d*) Enlargement of pendant shown in (*c*).

63 (*a*) and (*b*) Terracotta goddesses wearing jewellery. After Frankfort, *Tell Asmar*, figs. IIIa and IIIc.

64 Stone relief of Hammurabi from Sipper wearing necklaces and bracelet. British Museum No. 22454. Height from head to elbow 15·3 cm.

65 (*a*) Silver moon pendant. Diameter 2·6 cm.
(*b*) Gold moon pendant. Width 4·5 cm.
(*c*) Gold button with repoussé dot decoration. Diameter 1 cm. After *Mari*, II, fig. 71.

66 Bronze statuette of a worshipper. British Museum No. 91145. Height 30 cm.

67 Head of moon god from Mari; fresco. After *Mari*, II, 1958, pl. XVII and fig. 59.

68 Gold earring from Giyan with centre fluting. After Herzfeld, *I.A.E.*, p. 149, fig. 266, pl. XXX.

69 Necklace on alabaster figure from Susa. After Zervos, *L'art de Mesopotamie*, pl. 241, and Amiet, *Elam*, No. 216.

70 Necklace from a diorite seated statuette of a bearded prince from Susa. After Strommenger, *Mesopotamia*, pl. 150, and Zervos *L'art de Mésopotamie*, pl. 235.

71 (*a*) Necklace and (*b*) bracelet from a statuette. Abu Ḥabbah. British Museum No. 104730.

Chapter 6

Figs. 72–74: Kültepe

72 Gold biconical bead from city mound. Length 10·2 cm. After *Scientific American*, Vol. 208, 2, 1963, p. 96.

73 Gold pin from *kārum* Level Ib. Ankara Museum.

74 Silver toggle pin, upper part of shank covered with gold leaf, from *kārum* Level Ib. Length 10·9 cm. Ankara Museum.

Chapter 7

75 Goldwork from Byblos; decorative gold strips for ornamenting the shaft of a fenestrated axe. Beirut Museum. Lengths: (*a*) 5·5 cm, (*b*) 4·8 cm. Montet, *Byblos*, II, pl. CXXXII.

Figs 76, 77–92: Ajjul

76 Jewellery from Grave 2. Scale 1:2. After Petrie, *A.G.*, I, pl. XV.

77 Diagram of cross-sections of twisted earrings: (*a*) strip-twist, (*b*) bar-twist, (*c*) flange-twist, (*d*) bar-twist with hammered out edges imitating flange-twist. After Hawkes, 'Gold earrings of the Bronze Age', *Folklore*, 72, 1961, p. 451, fig. 3.

78 Penannular earring made from plaited gold wires. Scale 1:1. After Petrie, *A.G.*, IV, pl. XVIII, 127.

79 Jewellery from Grave 1551. Scale 1:3. After Petrie, *A.G.*, IV, pl. XVIII, 101–5 and XXI, 215, 223–5.

80 Jewellery from Group 1532. Scale 1:3. After Petrie, *A.G.*, IV, pl. XXI, 200–5, 214.

81 Gold granulated earring (or pendant), flies, chrysalis pendant and segmented beads from Hoard 1313. Scale 1:1. After Petrie, *A.G.*, IV, pl. XVI.

82 Gold jewellery from child's grave 1740. Scale 1:1. After Petrie, *A.G.*, IV, pl. XVIII.

83 Gold jewellery from Grave 1203; inlaid earrings, spindle-shaped beads, toggle pin and belt. Scale 1:2. After Petrie, *A.G.*, IV, pl. XV and XVI.

84 Gold jewellery from Courtyard Cemetery, Tomb 1416. Scale 1:4. After Petrie, *A.G.*, II, pl. III, 14, 42 and XXII, 7.

85 Gold jewellery from Group 1030. After Petrie, *A.G.*, III, pl. XIV.

86 Gold headband from Grave 309. Scale 1:2. After Petrie, *A.G.*, III, pl. XIV, J.6.

87 Part of gold bracelet or belt from Hoard 1299. Scale 1:1. After Petrie, *A.G.*, IV, pl. XIV, 37.

88 Gold jewellery from Grave 447, a child's burial in a jar. Scale 1:1. After Petrie, *A.G.*, IV, pls. XIX, XX.

89 Bronze weapons and silver dress fastener from Grave 1750. Scale 1:2. After Petrie, *A.G.*, IV, pl. XXII, 237–8.

90 Gold bead, incised decoration. Scale 1:1. After Petrie, *A.G.*, IV, pl. XX, 172.

91 Gold jewellery from Grave 1073. After Petrie, *A.G.*, II, pl. I.

92 Gold spacer bead. After Petrie, *A.G.*, II, pl. 1.

93 White painted Nuzi ware from Alalakh (*a–c*) and Brak (*d–g*). After Woolley, *Alalakh*, pls. CV and CVII, and *Iraq*, IX, pls. LXXVI and LXVII, and *I.L.N.*

94 Terracotta arm-shaped vessel from Atchana Level IV. After Woolley, *Alalakh*, pl. CXXV.

95 Spindle-shaped Syrian flask from Atchana Level IV. After Woolley, *Alalakh*, pl. CXXVI.

Chapter 8

96 (*a*) Star and (*b*) Rosette from frescoes in the Palace at Mari. After *Mari*, II, 1958, figs. 6 and 43.

97 Ornamental coffins from Mari with sun symbols. After *Mari*, II, 1959, figs. 79 and 80.

98 Female figure wearing disc pendants from a relief. Ashurnaṣirpal II, period. British Museum No. 124581.

99 Reconstruction of Middle Assyrian royal seal; (?) Tiglath-Pileser I, *c.* 1100 B.C. From the treaty tablet of Esarhaddon, Nimrud.

100 Cartouche of king Tudhalia IV. Yazilikaya.

101 Necklace from a relief. Ashurnaṣirpal II period. British Museum No. 124562.

Chapter 10

Figs. 102–111: Ashur, jewellery from Tomb 45.

102 Lapis lazuli pendant set in gold; front and back views. Width 1 cm. After Haller, *Ashur*, Taf. 36h.

103 Gold double spiral forehead ornament with lapis lazuli pendants; front and back views. Width 5·7 cm. After Haller, *Ashur*, Taf. 34y and 35p.

104 Gold twisted wire double spiral pendant. Width 7·7 cm. After Haller, *Ashur*, Taf. 34z and 35q.

105 Throat ornament; veined stone in gold granulated setting. Width 3 cm. After Haller, *Ashur*, Taf. 34i and 35b.

106 Cloisonné pectoral; flowers of white shell, lapis lazuli and glass. Width 4·3 cm. After Haller, *Ashur*, Taf. 34x.

107 (*a*) Gold earrings with stone pendants; male skeleton. Width 4·8 cm. After Haller, *Ashur*, Taf. 33a and b. (b) Gold earrings with decoration in gold, lapis lazuli, onyx, jasper and carnelian; female skeleton. Length 5 cm, diameter of gold rings 2 cm, diameter of rosette 2·3 cm. After Haller, *Ashur*, Taf. 36m and mi.

108 Gold ribbed earrings; female skeleton. Height 1·6 cm. After Haller, *Ashur*, Taf. 36i and ki.

109 Plain gold lunate earring; female skeleton. Height 1·2 cm. After Haller *Ashur*, Taf. 36o.

110 Necklace of gold and lapis lazuli plaques; male skeleton. 2·5 cm × 2·3 cm. After Haller, *Ashur*, Taf. 33e.

111 Bull-calf pendants; mottled red stone set in gold. Height 2 cm. After Haller, *Ashur*, Taf. 33di and ii.

Chapter 11

112 Pair of gold earrings; Sialk B type. Private collection, Amsterdam.

113 Gold quadruple spiral bead from Mid-Assyrian grave at Mari. After *Iraq*, XXII, p. 109, fig. 4.

114 Beads from Ur. Yellow faience. British Museum No. 120631. Scale 1:1.

Chapter 12

115 Pomegranate earring from Patnos. Ankara Museum.

116 Earring from painted pot; Patnos. Ankara Museum.

117 Necklace from a relief of Ashurnaṣirpal II. British Museum No. 124584.

118 Jewellery on reliefs of Ashurnaṣirpal II. British Museum No. 124585.

Chapter 13

119 Gold earring from Luristan. Teheran. After Ghirshman, *Iran*, p. 325, No. 400.

120 Gold earring in the form of an ibex head, from Ashdod. Achaemenian period, fifth century B.C. After *I.L.N.*, 7 December 1963, p. 944, fig. 1.

121 Ashurbanipal hunting; from a Kuyunjik relief. British Museum No. 124875. After Madhloom, *Neo-Assyrian Art*, pl. XXXV, 1.

122 Bronze winged sphinx wearing pectoral, armlets and bracelets. British Museum. Madhloom, *Neo-Assyrian Art*, pl. LXXIII, 4.

123 Bronze pectoral from Nor-Aresh Tomb 1. Width between loops 17·2 cm. After *A.S.*, XIII, 1963, fig. 44.

Chapter 15

124 Gold scarab and seal holders and gold earrings from Zincirli. After Von Luschan, *Die Kleinfunde von Sendschirli*, 1934, Taf. 45m, n, i.
(*a*) From treasure in Room J9 of North-west Palace.
(*b*) From Kalamu building. Length 2·3 cm.
(*c*) From Room J9 of Kalamu building. Height 1·7 cm.

125 Chalcedony pendant set in silver mount from Ashur; Late Assyrian Grave 64. Diameter 2 cm. After Haller, *Ashur*, Taf. 38d.

126 Earrings from Assyrian reliefs. Drawn by T. Madhloom. *Type 3*: 1–14 (ninth century B.C.), 15–32 (eighth century B.C.). (1–14 from Nimrud reliefs, Ashurnaṣirpal II).

1 British Museum No. 12568
2 British Museum No. 124570
3 British Museum No. 118802
4 British Museum No. 124581
5 British Museum No. 124565
6–10 Layard, *Monuments of Nineveh*, I, pl. 51
11 British Museum No. 124574
12 British Museum No. 124560
13 British Museum No. 118873
14 British Museum No. 118803
(15–32 from Khorsabad reliefs, Sargon)
15 British Museum No. 118823
16 Botta, II, pl. 41
17 Botta, II, pl. 45
18 A. Moortgat in *A.F.O.*, 4 (1927), Abb. 11
19 Botta, II, pl. 99
20 British Museum No. 118829
21 Botta, II, pl. 27
22 Botta, II, pl. 100
23 Place, *Ninive*, pl. 28
24 Botta, II, pl. 114
25 Botta, II, pl. 113
26 Place, *Ninive*, pl. 28
27 Botta, II, pl. 109
28 Botta, II, pl. 105
29 Botta, II, pl. 113
30, 31 Botta, I, pl. 14
32 British Museum No. 118822

127 Earrings from Assyrian reliefs. Drawn by T. Madhloom. *Type 1*: 1 (ninth century B.C.). *Type 2*: 2–5 (ninth century B.C.). *Type 4*: 6–7 (ninth century B.C.), 8–26 (eighth century B.C.). *Type 5*: 27–31 (seventh century B.C.). (1–7 from Nimrud reliefs, Ashurnaṣirpal II)

1 British Museum No. 118805
2 British Museum No. 124539
3 British Museum No. 124560
4 British Museum No. 124586
5 British Museum No. 124562
6 British Museum No. 124917
7 British Museum No. 124533
8 (from Nimrud relief, Tiglath-Pileser III) British Museum No. 118899 (9–26 from Khorsabad reliefs, Sargon)
9 Botta, I, pl. 76
10 Botta, II, pl. 100
11 Botta, II, pl. 119
12 Botta, I, pl. 19
13 Botta, I, pl. 18
14, 15 Botta, I, pl. 17
16 Botta, II, pl. 110
17 Botta, I, pl. 40
18 Botta, I, pl. 16
19 Botta, II, pl. 89
20 Botta, II pl. 155, fig. 2.
21 Botta, I, pl. 25
22 Botta, I, pl. 40
23, 24 Botta, II, pl. 118
25 Botta, I, pl. 12
26 Botta, I, pl. 74
(27–31 from Kuyunjik reliefs, Ashurbanipal)
27 British Museum No. 124920
28 British Museum No. 124886
29 British Museum No. 124867
30 British Museum No. 124854
31 British Museum No. 124850

128 Relief of Tukulti-Ninurta I from an altar at Ashur. After Madhloom, *Neo-Assyrian Art*, pl. XLI, 5.

129 Gold earrings from Ashur, Late Assyrian Tomb 1. Width 2·1 cm. After Haller, *Ashur*, Taf. 20.

130 Gold earrings from Ashur, Late Assyrian Tomb 51. Width 2.1 cm. After Haller, *Ashur*, Taf. 37d.

131 Heads of attendants from a fresco at Til Barsib. (*a*) After Parrot, *Nineveh*, pl. 102. (*b*) After Madhloom, *Neo-Assyrian Art*, pl. LXIII, 3a.

132 Assyrian soldier leading a captive from a Nimrud relief. British Museum No. 124539. After Madhloom, *Neo-Assyrian Art*, pl. LVII, 1.

133 Gold jewellery from Tell Halaf. After Von Oppenheim, *Tell Halaf* (English edition, undated), pl. III.

134 Tributaries bearing triple earrings on a tray, from an ivory panel of Esarhaddon found at Nimrud. *I.L.N.*, 28 January 1956, fig. 10.

135 Earring from a relief of Sennacherib in the Gomel gorge, Hines region. After Parrot, *Nineveh*, pl. II.

136 Ashurbanipal when crown prince wearing bracelets and earrings, from Zincirli. After Pottier in *Syria*, II, 1921, fig. 111, p. 117.

137 Silver earrings from Ashur, Late Assyrian Graves 864 and 65. Heights: (a) 6·4 cm, (b) 2·7 cm. After Haller, *Ashur*, Taf. 17k, 38c.

138 Deity wearing earrings on a fresco from Khorsabad. After Madhloom, *Neo-Assyrian Art*, pl. LXI, 3.

Figs. 139–145, 148–150, 167: original drawings by T. Madhloom

139 Jewellery from a relief of Ashurnaṣirpal II. British Museum No. 124581.

140 Fly whisk and bracelet from a relief of Ashurnaṣirpal II. British Museum No. 124569.

141 Double bracelet from a relief of Ashurnaṣirpal II. British Museum No. 124575.

142 Bracelets and armlets from a relief of Ashurnaṣirpal II. British Museum No. 124562.

143 Bracelets and armlets from a relief of Ashurnaṣirpal II. British Museum No. 124565.

144 Bracelet with lion head finials from a relief of Ashurbanipal. British Museum No. 124854.

145 Bracelet with rosette from a relief of Ashurnaṣirpal II. British Museum No. 124568.

146 Gold rosette from Ashur, Late Assyrian Grave 807. Diameter 2·9 cm. After Haller, *Ashur*, Taf. 17f.

147 Rosette from Ashur, Late Assyrian Grave 64. Diameter 1·5 cm. After Haller, *Ashur*, Taf. 38d.

148 Bracelets with appliqué rosettes from reliefs of (*a*, *b*) Sargon and (*c*) Ashurbanipal. British Museum Nos. (*a*, *b*) 118822, (*c*) 124920.

149 Bracelets (*a*, *c*) and armlet (*b*) with stylized lion head finials from reliefs of Ashurbanipal. British Museum Nos. (*a*) 124850, (*b*) 124867, (*c*) 124851.

150 Bracelet with floral finials from a relief of Ashurbanipal. British Museum No. 124920.

151 Copper hinged bracelet from Ashur, Late Assyrian Grave 785. After Haller, *Ashur*, Taf. 17e. Height 5·2 cm.

152 Enthroned goddess from a Nimrud relief. Tiglath-Pileser III. After Madhloom, *Neo-Assyrian Art*, pl. LX, 2.

153 King Warpalawas, from the rock relief near Ivriz. After Madhloom, *Neo-Assyrian Art*, pl. LXIV, 1.

154 Diadems decorated with rosettes, from a relief from Khorsabad. After Madhloom, *Neo-Assyrian Art*, pl. LXV, 1.

155 Winged figure from a Nimrud relief wearing diadem. Ashurnaṣirpal II. British Museum No. 124574. After Madhloom, *Neo-Assyrian Art*, pl. LXVI, 3.

156 Relief portraits of (*a*) Ashurnaṣirpal II, (*b*) Tiglath-Pileser III, (*c*) Sargon II, (*d*) Ashurbanipal. British Museum Nos. 118928, 118900, 124867. After Madhloom, *Neo-Assyrian Art*, pl. XL.

157 Wife of king Ashurbanipal, from a Kuyunjik relief. British Museum No. 124920. After Madhloom, *Neo-Assyrian Art*, pl. LXIV.

158 Detail from garment of king Marduk-nadin-aḫḫe. British Museum No. 90841.

159 Assyrian archer from a Nimrud relief. After Madhloom, *Neo-Assyrian Art*, pl. XLV, 5.

160 Divine statue carried by Assyrian soldiers from a Nimrud relief. Tiglath-Pileser III. After Madhloom, *Neo-Assyrian Art*, pl. XLV, 7.

161 Tribute bearer from a Khorsabad relief. After Madhloom, *Neo-Assyrian Art*, pl. XLIII, 5.

162 Sargon II and his *turtan*, from a Khorsabad relief. After Madhloom, *Neo-Assyrian Art*, pl. XXXVIII.

163 Captive wearing fringed garment from a Khorsabad relief. Drawn by T. Madhloom after Botta and Flandin, *Khorsabad*, pl. 82.

164 Ashurbanipal pouring libation after the lion hunt. British Museum No. 124886. After Madhloom, *Neo-Assyrian Art*, pl. XXXIX.

165 Fibula from Tomb 1, Nor-Aresh. Length 11 cm. After *A.S.*, XIII, 1963, fig. 42.

166 Head of a human-headed bull from Nimrud. Tiglath Pileser III. British Museum No. 118879. Height 1·11 m. After Madhloom, *Neo-Assyrian Art*, pl. LXXIII, 1.

167 Earring from colossal winged bull from Khorsabad. Sargon. British Museum.

PREFACE

This book, which is a pioneer attempt to examine synoptically ancient gold and silver jewellery from Western Asia involves recourse to a wide range of specialist branches of learning beyond the purely archaeological. Tentative conclusions have, therefore, to be based on historical, metallurgical, linguistic, technological and archaeological evidence. A work embracing an area stretching from the Hellespont to Susa and covering over three millennia cannot be more than a preliminary to further research on particular aspects and the material in each chapter could easily be expanded into separate detailed studies. Before this can be undertaken a general survey is necessary to present the material against its historical background and to indicate the relationship, if any, between different centres of jewellery production. In many instances, however, the lack of sufficient stratified evidence precludes the formulation of precise conclusions. My purpose, therefore, has been to marshal the evidence now widely scattered and in some cases not easily accessible, so that the material can be considered as a whole and the most profitable lines of future research disclosed. This wide scope necessarily involves much compression and I am conscious of many lacunae; but the rapid advance of the techniques of research, especially in the archaeological field, where new evidence is constantly accruing, demands the publication of the results of the inquiry to date.

The complex question of the translation of Sumerian and Akkadian terms, both for specific objects and for the technical processes, merits a separate study. Here I have only been able to draw attention to these questions and to emphasize that the archaeological, metallurgical and linguistic evidence cannot sensibly be considered separately, although I am fully aware that no single person could presume to bring the necessary expert knowledge to bear on these problems.

The volume forms the predecessor to R. A. Higgins's *Greek and Roman Jewellery*, published in 1961, and is a companion to A. Wilkinson's *Ancient Egyptian Jewellery*, published in 1971. The detailed explanation of the basic technical processes of gold and silver working treated in detail by Higgins have, therefore, not been repeated here.

A work such as this could not have been written without the help of a very large number of friends and colleagues in many different countries.

It is not possible to name them all, but I can, and do, offer them my sincere thanks.

I should, however, like in particular to record my gratitude to the Board of Management of the Gerald Avery Wainwright Fund for Near Eastern Archaeology at Oxford for the generous grants which enabled me to visit museums and excavations in France, Belgium, Cyprus, Turkey, Lebanon, Syria, Jordan, Iraq and Iran. I am glad of the opportunity to thank scholars in these countries, both in museums and in the field, for their unfailing assistance and interest, especially –

M. André Parrot, M. P. Amiet and Mademoiselle Agnes Spycket of the Louvre; Professor C. F. A. Schaeffer of Le Collège de France; M. A. Varagnac, formerly of Musée des Antiquités Nationales, St Germain-en-Laye; Dr D. Homes-Frédéricq of the Musées Royaux d'Art et Histoire, Brussels; Professor L. Vanden Berghe, University of Ghent; Dr V. Karageorghis, Director of Antiquities, Nicosia; Professors Tahsin and Nimet Özgüc, Professor Kemal Balkan and Professor E. Akurgal, all of Ankara University; M. Raci Temizer, Director of the Museum of Archaeology, Ankara; M. Nezih Firath, M. Necati Dolonay, Dr Muazzez Ciğ, of Istanbul, Museum of Archaeology; Emir Maurice Chéhab, Director of Antiquities, Lebanon; Dr Abdul-Hak and M. Bashir Zouhdi, Damascus Museum; the late Dr Awni Dajani, Director of Antiquities, Amman; Dr Yusuf Saad, Palestine Archaeological Museum, Jerusalem; Dr Fawzi Rashid, Curator of the Iraq Museum; Professor H. Lenzen, Baghdad; Professor E. Negahban, Teheran University; Dr R. Ghirshman; Madame Malecki; M. A. Mazda, Teheran; Comte du Puytison, Paris.

I am also deeply indebted to Professor Piotrovski, Director of the Hermitage Museum, Leningrad; Mr Charles Wilkinson and Miss Prudence Harper, Metropolitan Museum, New York; Dr Robert Dyson, Jr, University Museum, Pennsylvania; Professor Rodney Young and Miss E. Kohler, University of Pennsylvania; Professor P. Amandry, University of Strasbourg; Mr W. Culican, University of Melbourne; Dr Machteld J. Mellink; Mr Cyril Stanley Smith; M. H. Seyrig, Institut Français, Beirut; and the Directors and staffs of the British Schools and Institutes of Archaeology in Ankara, Jerusalem, Baghdad and Teheran, for their hospitality and advice.

I have also greatly profited from advice and discussions with Mr Henry Hodges and Mr Peter Parr and colleagues and students at the Institute of Archaeology, London University; as well as Dr Kathleen Kenyon, Miss Nancy Sandars, Professor Oliver Gurney, Dr Roger Moorey, and

Mr Peter Hulin of Oxford University; Mr Kinnier Wilson of Cambridge University and Mr Nichols at the Fitzwilliam Museum; together with Dr Clare Goff, Dr Georgina Hermann, Miss Olga Tufnell, Mrs Leri Davies, Mr Reynold Higgins, British Museum, Greek and Roman Department; and Mrs M. C. Ridley. To Dr Richard Barnett, Dr E. Sollberger and the staff of the British Museum, Western Asiatic Department, I owe far more than I can record here. I am also especially grateful to Sir Max Mallowan of All Souls College, Oxford, Professor Sidney Smith, my first mentor, and Miss Barbara Parker of the Institute of Archaeology, whose counsel and encouragement induced me to undertake and stimulated me to complete what has proved to be an exacting, though rewarding, undertaking.

Jane Cook has been responsible for the map and for most of the drawings and I owe much to her patience and assistance; I must also thank warmly Dr Tariq Madhloom, Director of Excavations, Iraq Department of Antiquities, who specially drew for me details of jewellery on Assyrian reliefs and has generously allowed me to use drawings from his doctoral thesis. A number of photographs were kindly taken for me by Miss Olive Kitson and Mrs Nobbs has given valuable secretarial help. I am especially grateful to Miss Janice Price and Mrs Nicola Kew for their assistance and forbearance, to Miss Sara Wadham for work on the references and to Miss H. Jerrold for the index. Other authors and institutions who have lent photographs are acknowledged in the list of illustrations and I should like to take this opportunity of thanking them.

Finally, I must express my appreciation to my daughter Hilary for her help in arranging illustrations and especially to my daughter Gilly, to whom, in gratitude, the graceful dedications generously composed by Mr R. H. Barrow, C.B.E., pay tribute – and indeed to my husband and all the family who have endured with fortitude continuous exposure to Asiatic jewellery over so many years.

ABBREVIATIONS

A.A.A.	*Annals of Anthropology and Archaeology*, University of Liverpool, 1908–40, Vols 1–26.
A.A.S.O.R.	*Annual of the American School of Oriental Research*, New Haven (in progress).
A.F.O.	*Archiv für Orientforschung*, Berlin (in progress).
A.G., V	E. J. H. Mackay and M. A. Murray, *Ancient Gaza*, V (London, 1952).
A.J.A.	*American Journal of Archaeology*, Princeton, New Jersey (in progress).
A.N.E.T.	Pritchard (ed.), *Ancient Near Eastern Texts relating to the Old Testament* (Princeton, New Jersey, 1950).
Altintepe	T. Özgüc, *Altintepe Architectural Monuments and Wall Paintings* (Ankara, 1966).
Amiet, *Elam*	P. Amiet, *Elam* (Paris, 1966) (references are given to the numbers, not the pages, of the illustrations).
A.R.	D. D. Luckenbill, *Ancient Records of Assyria and Babylonia*, Vols I and II (Chicago, Ill., 1926–7).
A.S.	*Anatolian Studies*, London (in progress).
B.A.S.O.R.	*Bulletin of the American Schools of Oriental Research*, Johns Hopkins University, Baltimore.
Barnett, *Assyrian Reliefs*	R. D. Barnett, *Assyrian Palace Reliefs and their Influence on the Sculptures of Babylonia and Persia* (London, undated).
Barnett, *Tiglath-Pileser III*	R. D. Barnett and M. Falkner, *The Sculptures of Tiglath-Pileser III* (London, 1962).
Belleten	*Türk Tarih Kurumu Belleten* (Ankara – in progress).
Boğazköy	K. Bittel and H. C. Güterbock, *Boğazköy, Neue Untersuchungen in der Hethitischen Hauptstadt* (Berlin, 1935).

Boğazköy, III	K. Bittel *et al. Boğazköy III: Funde aus den Grabungen 1952–5* (Berlin, 1957).
Blegen, *Troy*	C. W. Blegen, J. L. Caskey and J. Sperling, *Troy*, Vols I–IV (Princeton, 1950–8).
B.M.B.	*Bulletin du Musée de Beyrouth* (Beirut – in progress).
B.M.C.J.	F. H. Marshall, *Catalogue of the Jewellery, Greek, Etruscan and Roman, in the British Museum* (London, 1911).
B.M.Q.	*British Museum Quarterly* (London – in progress).
Botta	P. G. Botta and M. E. Flandin, *Monument de Ninive*, Vol. I–V (Paris, 1849–50).
B.P. I	Flinders Petrie, *Beth-Pelet*, I (*Tell Fara*) (London, 1931).
B.P. II	J. L. Starkey and L. Harding, *Beth-Pelet*, II (London, 1932).
Brussels Cat.	*L'Art Iranien Ancien* (Brussels, 1966).
B.S.A.	*Annual of the British School at Athens* (London – in progress).
C.A.H.	*Cambridge Ancient History* (Fascicles; London, 1961 – in progress).
Carchemish, III	C. L. Woolley and R. D. Barnett, *Report on the Excavations at Jerablus on behalf of the British Museum* (London, 1952).
Chronologies	R. W. Ehrich (ed.), *Chronologies in Old World Archaeology* (Chicago, Ill., 1965).
Contenau, *Manuel*	G. Contenau, *Manuel d'Archéologie Oriental*, I–IV (Paris, 1927–47).
D.P.M.	*Délégation en Perse, Mémoires*, I–XXVIII, *Mission Archéologique en Iraq Mémoires*, XXIX (Paris – in progress).
Dacia	*Recherches et découvertes archéologique en Roumanie* (Bucharest – in progress).
Deshayes, *Outils de Bronze*	J. Deshayes, *Les Outils de Bronze de l'Indus au Danube, IVe au IIe millénaire* (Paris, 1960).
Dunand, *Byblos*	M. Dunand, *Fouilles de Byblos*, I, 1926–32 (Paris, 1939); II, 1933–8 (Paris, 1944).
Frankfort, *A.A.A.O.*	H. Frankfort, *The Art and Architecture of the Ancient Orient* (London, 1954).

Frankfort, *O.I.C.*	*Oriental Institute Communications*, No. 17, Iraq excavations of the Oriental Institute, 1932–3 (Chicago, Ill., 1934).
Geneva Cat.	*Trésors de l'Ancien Iran Musée Rath* (Geneva, 1966).
Ghirshman, *Iran*	R. Ghirshman, *Iran from the Earliest Times to the Islamic Conquest* (Harmondsworth, 1954).
Ghirshman, *Persia*	R. Ghirshman, *Persia from the Origins to Alexander the Great* (London, 1964).
Ghirshman, *Sialk*	R. Ghirshman, *Fouilles de Sialk près de Kashan*, II (Paris, 1939).
Gimbutas, *Prehistory of E. Europe*	Marija Gimbutas, *The Prehistory of Eastern Europe, I: Mesolithic, Neolithic and Copper Age Culture in Russia and the Baltic Area*, American School of Prehistoric Research, Peabody Museum, Harvard University, Bulletin No. 20 (Cambridge, Mass., 1956.)
Giyan	G. Contenau and R. Ghirshman, *Fouilles du Tépé Giyan près de Néhavand* (Paris, 1935).
Gjerstad, *S.C.E.*	E. Gjerstad *et al.*, *Swedish Cyprus Expedition*, I–IV (Stockholm, 1934–48).
Godard, *Bronzes*	A. Godard, Les bronzes du Luristan, *Ars Asiatica*, XVII (Paris, 1931).
Godard, *Ziweye*	*Le Trésor de Ziwiye* (*Kurdistan*) (Harlem, 1950).
Goldman, *Tarsus*	Hetty Goldman, *Excavations at Gözlü Kule, Tarsus*, II (Princeton, New Jersey, 1965).
Haller, *Ashur*	A. Haller, *Die Gräber und Grufte von Assur* (Berlin, 1954).
Herzfeld, *I.A.E.*	E. Herzfeld, Iran in the Ancient East (Oxford, 1941).
Higgins, *Jewellery*	R. A. Higgins, *Greek and Roman Jewellery* (London, 1961).
I.E.J.	*Israel Exploration Journal* (Jerusalem – in progress.
I.L.N.	*Illustrated London News* (London – in progress).

Iran	*Iran, Journal of the British Institute of Persian Studies* (London – in progress).
Iraq	*Iraq, Journal of the British School of Archaeology in Iraq* (London – in progress).
J.A.O.S.	*Journal of American Oriental Studies* (Baltimore – in progress).
J.C.S.	*Journal of Cuneiform Studies* (New Haven, Conn. – in progress).
J.D.A.I.	*Jahrbuch des Deutschen Archäologischen Institut* (Berlin – in progress).
J.H.S.	*Journal of Hellenic Studies* (London – in progress).
J.N.E.S.	*Journal of Near Eastern Studies* (Chicago, Ill. – in progress).
Karmir Blur, I–IV	B. B. Piotrovski 'Resul'taty raskopok 1939–49', *Archaeologiceskie raskopki v Armenii*, Nos. 1, 2, 5, 6 (Erevan, 1950, 1952, 1955).
Kenyon, *Amorites*	K. M. Kenyon, *Amorites and Canaanites*, Schweich Lectures, 1963 (London, 1966).
Koşay, *Alaca*	H. Z. Koşay and M. Akok, *Alaca Höyük Kazisi 1940–8* (Ankara, 1966).
Kuftin, *Trialeti*	B. A. Kuftin, *Archaeological Excavations in Trialeti* (Tbilisi, 1941 – Russian with English summary).
Levant	*Journal of the British School of Archaeology in Jerusalem* (London – in progress).
Madhloom, *Neo-Assyrian Art*	T. A. Madhloom, *The Chronological Development of Neo-Assyrian Art* (Athlone Press, University of London, 1970).
Mallowan, *Nimrud*	Sir Max Mallowan, *Nimrud and its Remains*, Vols. I and II (London, 1966) (references are to plate Nos.).
Mari, I	A. Parrot, *Mission Archéologique de Mari, I: Le Temple d'Ishtar* (Paris, 1956).
Mari, II, 1958	A. Parrot, *Mission Archéologique de Mari, II: Le Palais, Peintures Murales* (Paris, 1958).
Mari, II, 1959	*ibid., Le Palais, Documents et Monuments* (Paris, 1959).

Mari, III	A. Parrot, *Les Temples d'Ishtarat et de Ninni-Zaza* (Paris, 1967).
Mari, IV	A. Parrot, *Le 'Trésor d'Ur' Mission Archéologique de Mari, IV* (Paris, 1968).
Marlik, Iran	'A brief report on the excavation of Marlik Tepe', *Iran*, II, 1944, pp. 13–19.
Marlik	E. O. Negahban, *A Preliminary Report on Marlik Excavation, Goher Rud Expedition* (Rudbar, 1961–2; Teheran, 1964).
Megiddo Tombs	P. L. O. Guy and R. M. Engberg, *Megiddo Tombs* (Chicago, 1938, O.I.P. XXXIII).
de Morgan, *La Préhistoire Orientale*	J. de Morgan, *La Préhistoire Orientale, III: l'Asie Antérieure* (Paris, 1927).
Montet, *Byblos*	Pierre Montet, *Byblos et l'Egypte quatre Campagnes de Fouilles à Gebeil, 1921–4* (Paris, 1929).
M.D.O.G.	*Mitteilungen der Deutschen Orient-Gesellshaft* (Berlin – in progress).
Nippur, I	D. E. McCowan and R. Haines, *Nippur, I: Temple of Enlil, Scribal Quarters and Surroundings* (Chicago, 1967).
O.I.C.	Oriental Institute of the University of Chicago communications.
Orfèvrerie Achéménide	P. Amandry 'Orfèvrerie Achéménide', *Antike Kunst*, I (Olten, 1958).
Özgüc, *Horoztepe*	T. Özgüc and M. Akok, *Horoztepe: an Early Bronze Age Settlement and Cemetery* (Ankara, 1958).
Özgüc, *Kültepe* 1948	T. Özgüc, *Kültepe Kazisi Raporu 1948* Ankara, 1950).
Özgüc, *Kültepe* 1949	T. Özgüc and N. Özgüc, *Kültepe Kazisi Raporu 1949* (Ankara, 1953).
Özgüc, *Kültepe-Kanis*	T. Özgüc, *Kültepe-Kanis, New Researches of the Centre of the Assyrian Colonies* (Ankara, 1959).
Paris Cat.	*Sept Mille Ans d'Art en Iran* (Paris, 1961–2).
Parrot, *Nineveh*	A. Parrot, *Nineveh and Babylon* (London, 1961).
Petrie, *Ajjul*	Flinders Petrie, *Tell el Ajjul*, I–IV (London, 1931–4).

Petrie, *A.G.*	Flinders Petrie, *Ancient Gaza*, Vols I–IV (London, 1931–4).
P.E.Q.	*Palestine Exploration Quarterly* (London – in progress).
P.P.S.	*Proceedings of the Prehistoric Society* (in progress).
Piotrovski, *Van*	B. B. Piotrovski, *Il Regno di Van Urartu* (Rome, 1966).
Place, *Ninive*	V. Place, *Ninive et l'Assyrie*, Vols. I–III (Paris, 1869).
Q.D.A.P.	*The Quarterly of the Department of Antiquities in Palestine* (Jerusalem, 1911–53).
R.A.	*Revue d'Assyriologie* (Paris – in progress).
Saggs, *Babylon*	H. W. F. Saggs, *The Greatness that was Babylon* (London, 1962).
Schaeffer, *Cuneiform Texts*	C. F. A. Schaeffer, *The Cuneiform Texts of Ras Shamra-Ugarit*, Schweich Lectures, 1939.
Schaeffer, *Strat. Comp.*	F. A. Schaeffer, *Stratigraphie Comparée et Chronologie de l'Asie Occidentale* (London, 1948).
Schaeffer, *Ugaritica*	C. F. A. Schaeffer, *Ugaritica*, Vols. I–IV Paris, 1939–62).
Schliemann, *Atlas*	H. Schliemann, *Atlas Trojanischer Alterthümer* (Leipzig, 1874).
Schliemann, *Ilios*	H. Schliemann, *Ilios, the City and Country of the Trojans* (London, 1880).
Schmidt, *Sammlung*	H. Schmidt, *Heinrich Schliemanns Sammlung Trojanischer Altertümer* (Berlin, 1902).
Schmidt, *Persepolis*, II	E. F. Schmidt, *Persepolis, II: Contents of the Treasury and other Discoveries* (Chicago, 1953).
Schmidt, *Tepe Hissar*	E. F. Schmidt, *Excavations at Tepe Hissar Damghan* (Philadelphia, 1937).
Smith, *E.H.A.*	Sidney Smith, *Early History of Assyria* (London, 1928).
S.P.A.	Arthur Upham Pope (Ed.), *Survey of Persian Art* (London, 1938).
Starr, *Nuzi*	R. F. Starr, *Report on the Excavations at Yorgan Tepa near Kirkuk, Iraq, 1927–31*, I, II (Cambridge, Mass., 1937, 1939).

Strommenger, *Mesopotamia*	E. Strommenger, *The Art of Mesopotamia* (London, 1964).
Thureau-Dangin, *Til-Barsib*	F. Thureau-Dangin and M. Dunand, *Til Barsib* (Paris, 1936).
Treasure of the Oxus	O. M. Dalton, *The Treasure of the Oxus with other examples of Early Oriental Metalwork* (London, 1963, 3rd edition).
Ur Excavations, II	C. L. Woolley, *Ur Excavations: The Royal Cemetery, II* (Text and plates) (London, 1934).
U.V.B.	*Vorläufige Berichte über die . . . in Uruk-Warka . . . Ausgrabungen* (Abh Berlin, Phil-hist. Klasse – in progress).
Wilkinson, *Egyptian Jewellery*	Alix Wilkinson, *Ancient Egyptian Jewellery* (London, 1971).
Wiseman, *Alalakh Tablets*	D. J. Wiseman, *The Alalakh Tablets* (London, 1963).
Wiseman, *Cylinder Seals*	D. J. Wiseman, *Cylinder Seals of Western Asia* (London, undated).
Woolley, *Alalakh*	Sir Leonard Woolley, *Alalakh: An Account of the Excavations at Tell Atchana in the Hatay, 1937–49* (London, 1955).
Yadin, *Warfare*	Yigael Yadin, *The Art of Warfare in Biblical Lands* (London, 1963).
Z.A.	*Zeitschrift für Assyriologie und Vorderasiatische Archäologie* (Berlin – in progress).
Z.D.P.V.	*Zeitschrift der Deutschen Palästina Vereins* (in progress).

	Mesopotamia *Sumer–Babylonia*	*Assyria*	*Syria*
3000	Early Dynastic [*c.* 3000–2400] I–III		
2500			
	[2375–2230] Akkadian		
	Gudea		
	[2113–2006] 3rd Dynasty of Ur		
2000	[2017–1763] Isin-Larsa		
		Old Assyrian period	
1900		Erishum	
	[1894] 1st Dynasty of Babylon	Sargon I Puzur Ashur II	
1800		Shamshi-Adad I	Zimri Lim
	Hammurabi [1792]	[1813–1781]	of Mari
1700			
1600	[1595] Kassites		Mitanni Alalakh IV [*c.*1550–1
1500			Saushatar
1400			
		[1350] Middle Assyrian Ashur-uballit I [1365–1330]	Tushratta
1300		Tukulti Ninurta I [1244–1208]	
1200			
	[1150] 2nd Dynasty of Isin Nebuchadrezzar I [1124–1103]	Tiglath-Pileser I [1115–1077]	
1100			
		[1000]	

E I *c.* 3000–1000 B.C.

e	*Anatolia*	*Elam*	*Iran*	
				3000
				2500
	Early Bronze III	Akkadian		
ronze – Bronze	Troy II a–g			
		Old Elamite period		
	Karum IV	Destruction of Ur 2006	Hissar IIIb	2000
		Khutran-Temti		
	Karum III		Hissar IIIc	1900
Bronze I	Karum II			
	Karum Ib			1800
Bronze II		Kutir-Nakhunte I		
	Old Hittite Kingdom [*c.*1700–1190]	[*c.* 1730)		1700
onze I			Dinkha Tepe III	1600
			Giyan II	1500
ronze II				1400
		Middle Elamite period		
ge				
				1300
		Untash-GAL	Hasanlu V	
		Kidin-Khutran [*c.* 1230]	Marlik	
				1200
		Shutruk-Nakhunte [*c.* 1170]		
		Shilhak-In-Shushinak [*c.* 1160]		
				1100

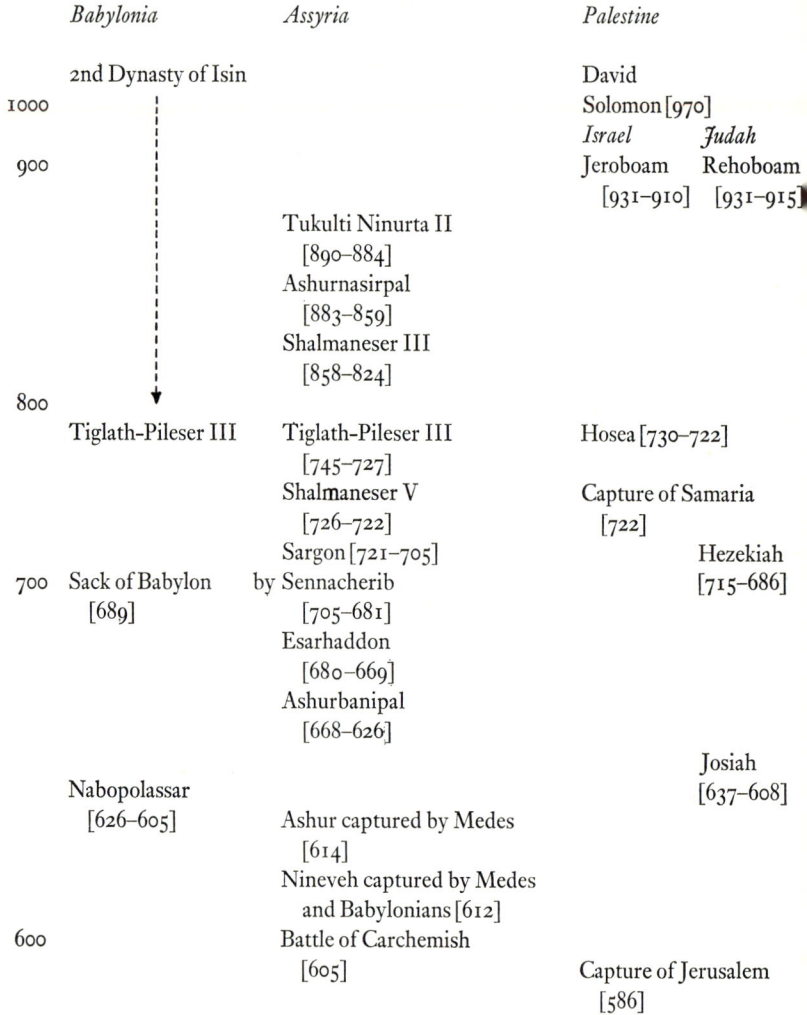

	Babylonia	*Assyria*	*Palestine*	
	2nd Dynasty of Isin		David	
1000			Solomon [970]	
			Israel	*Judah*
900			Jeroboam [931–910]	Rehoboam [931–915]
		Tukulti Ninurta II [890–884]		
		Ashurnasirpal [883–859]		
		Shalmaneser III [858–824]		
800				
	Tiglath-Pileser III	Tiglath-Pileser III [745–727]	Hosea [730–722]	
		Shalmaneser V [726–722]	Capture of Samaria [722]	
		Sargon [721–705]		Hezekiah [715–686]
700	Sack of Babylon [689] by	Sennacherib [705–681]		
		Esarhaddon [680–669]		
		Ashurbanipal [668–626]		
				Josiah [637–608]
	Nabopolassar [626–605]	Ashur captured by Medes [614]		
		Nineveh captured by Medes and Babylonians [612]		
600		Battle of Carchemish [605]		
			Capture of Jerusalem [586]	

II 1000–612 B.C.

	Elam	*Iran*			
		Hasanlu V	Sialk Va	Giyan I	
					1000
		Hasanlu IV	Sialk VIb	↓	
	Neo-Elamite period ↓				900
					800
14]					
		Medes	*Achaemenids*		
I	Shutruk-Nakhunte II [717–699]				
79]		Deioces [*c.* 715]			
	Conflict between Elam and Assyria [700–691]				700
	Elam conquered by Assyria [642–639]				
	Sack of Susa by Ashurbanipal		Cyrus I [*c.* 640–600]		
I		Cyaxares [625–585]			
f Urartu					
errun Urartu			Cambyses I [600–559]		600
		Astyges [585–550]	Cyrus II [559–530]		

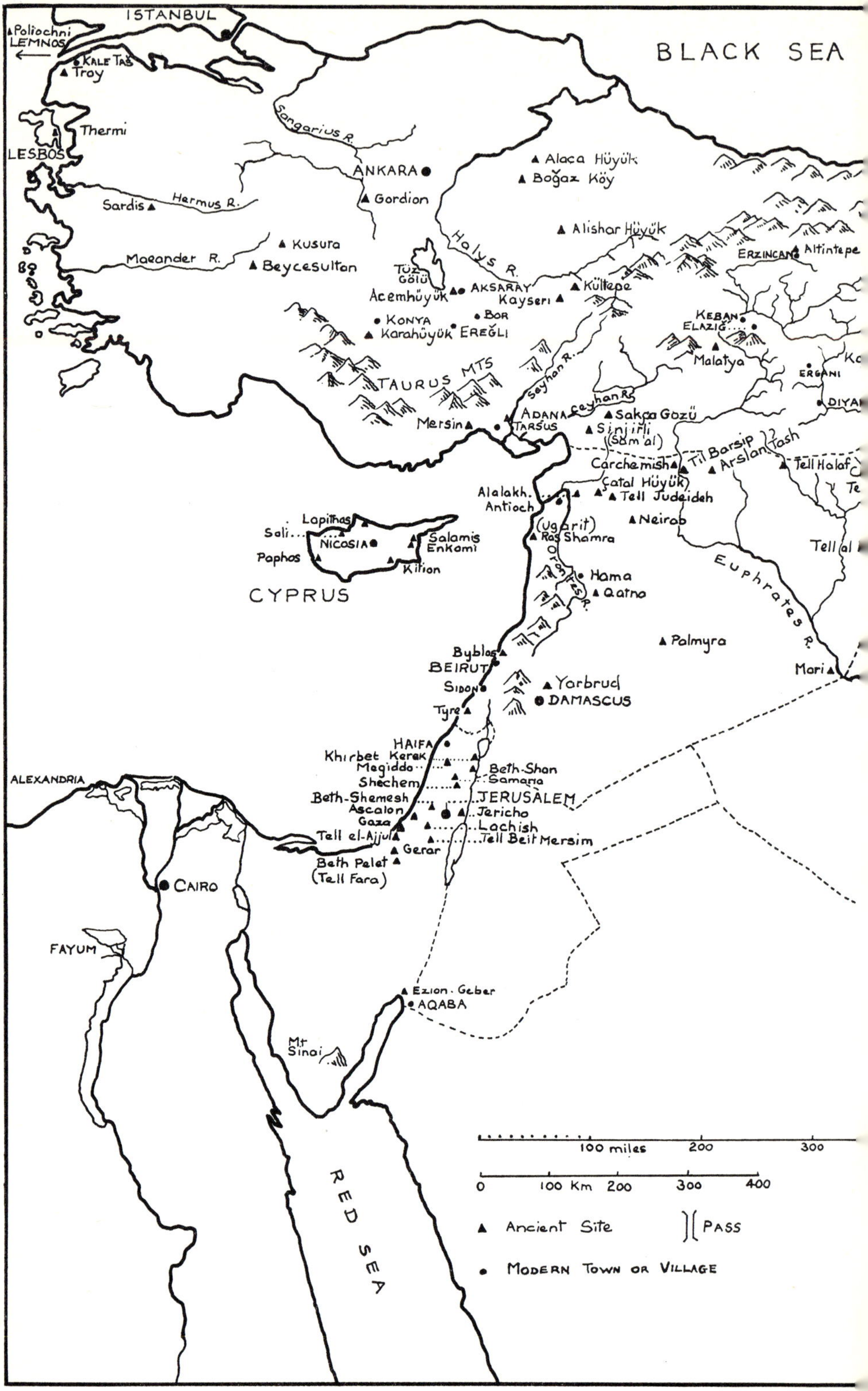
ISTANBUL
Poliochni
LEMNOS
KALE TAŞ
Troy
BLACK SEA
Thermi
LESBOS
Sangarius R.
ANKARA
Alaca Hüyük
Boğaz Köy
Gordion
Sardis
Hermus R.
Alishar Hüyük
Halys R.
Kusura
Maeander R.
Beycesultan
Tüz Gölü
Acemhüyük
AKSARAY
Kültepe
Kayseri
ERZINCAN
Altintepe
KONYA
BOR
Karahüyük
EREĞLI
KEBAN
ELAZIĞ
Malatya
TAURUS MTS
Seyhan R.
Ceyhan R.
ADANA
TARSUS
Mersin
Sakçagözü
Sinjirli
(Sam'al)
ERGANI
DIYA
Carchemish
Til Barsip
Arslan Tash
Tell Halaf
Çatal Hüyük
Alalakh
Antioch
Tell Judeideh
Neirab
Lapithos
Soli
NICOSIA
Salamis
Enkomi
Paphos
Kition
CYPRUS
(Ugarit)
Ras Shamra
Orontes R.
Hama
Qatna
Euphrates R.
Tell
Palmyra
Byblos
BEIRUT
Mari
Sidon
Yabrud
DAMASCUS
Tyre
HAIFA
Khirbet Kerak
Megiddo
Beth-Shan
Samaria
Shechem
ALEXANDRIA
Beth-Shemesh
JERUSALEM
Ascalon
Jericho
Gaza
Lachish
Tell el-Ajjul
Tell Beit Mersim
Gerar
Beth Pelet
(Tell Fara)
CAIRO
FAYUM
Ezion-Geber
AQABA
Mt Sinai
RED SEA
100 miles
200
300
0
100 Km
200
300
400
Ancient Site
PASS
Modern Town or Village

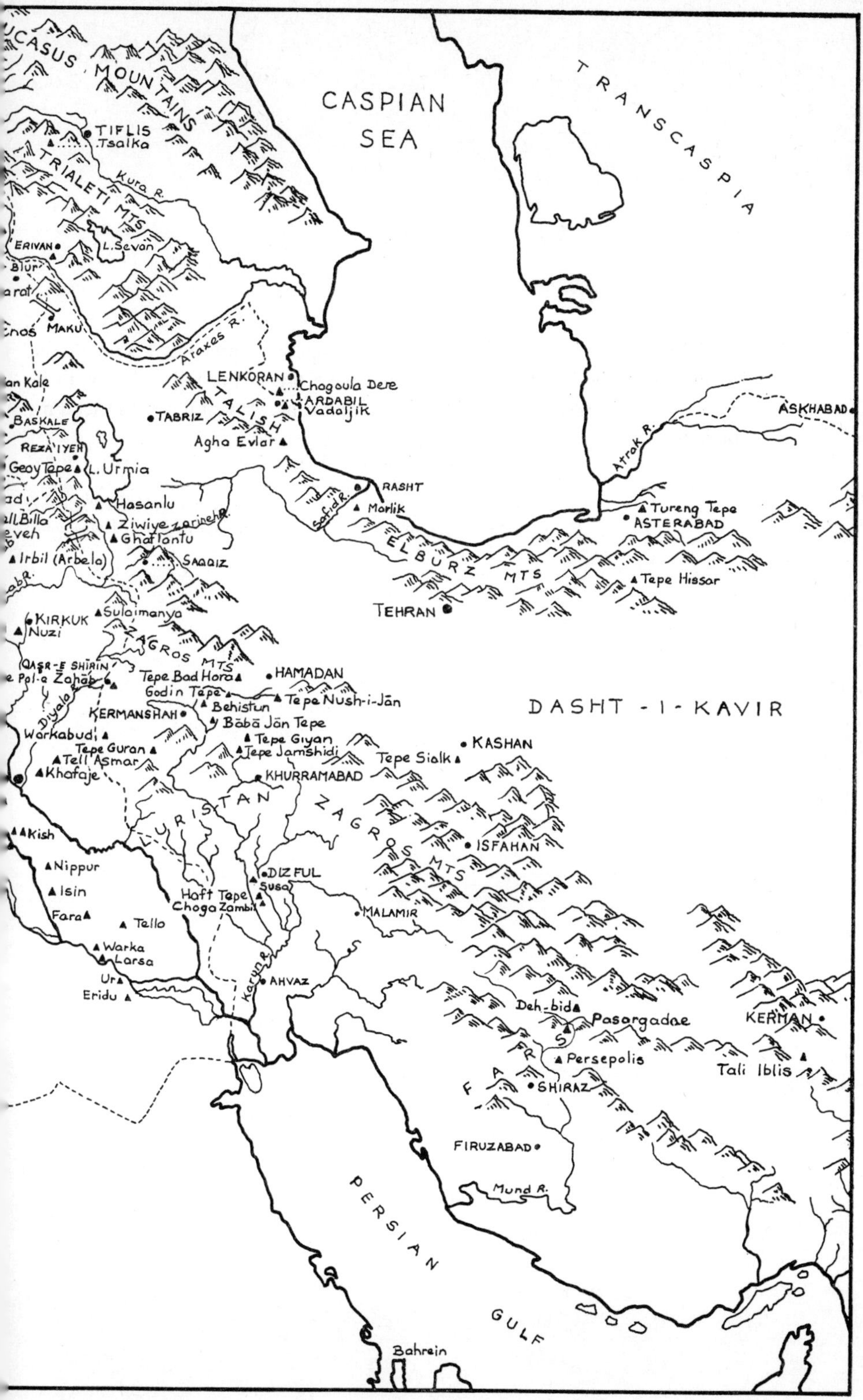
CAUCASUS MOUNTAINS
CASPIAN SEA
TRANSCASPIA
TIFLIS
Tsalka
TRIALETI MTS
Kura R.
ERIVAN
L. Sevan
MAKU
Araxes R.
LENKORAN
Chogoula Dere
ARDABIL
Vadaljik
TALISH
TABRIZ
Agha Evlar
BASKALE
REZA'IYEH
Geoy Tepe
L. Urmia
Hasanlu
Ziwiye
Ghaflantu
Irbil (Arbela)
SAQQIZ
RASHT
Marlik
Safid R.
ASKHABAD
Atrak R.
Tureng Tepe
ASTERABAD
ELBURZ MTS
Tepe Hissar
TEHRAN
KIRKUK
Nuzi
Sulaimanya
ZAGROS MTS
QASR-E SHIRIN
Tepe Bad Hora
HAMADAN
Godin Tepe
Behistun
Tepe Nush-i-Jān
KERMANSHAH
Bābā Jān Tepe
Diyala R.
Warkabud
Tepe Guran
Tell Asmar
Khafaje
Tepe Giyan
Tepe Jamshidi
Tepe Sialk
KASHAN
DASHT-I-KAVIR
KHURRAMABAD
LURISTAN
ZAGROS MTS
ISFAHAN
Kish
Nippur
Isin
Fara
Tello
Warka
Larsa
Ur
Eridu
DIZFUL
Susa
Haft Tepe
Choga Zambil
MALAMIR
Karun R.
AHVAZ
Deh-bid
Pasargadae
KERMAN
FARS
Persepolis
Tali Iblis
SHIRAZ
FIRUZABAD
Mund R.
PERSIAN GULF
Bahrein

. . . I have never before written to you for something precious I wanted. But if you want to be like a father to me, get me a fine string full of beads, to be worn around the head. . . . Establish its price for me, write it down and send me the letter. . . .

Letter from Adad-abum to his father Uzalum, excavated at Tel Abu Harmal by the Iraq Government Department of Antiquities. See A. Goetze, 'Fifty Old Babylonian letters from Harmal', *Sumer*, 1958, p. 71, and A. L. Oppenheim, *Letters from Mesopotamia* p. 87.

In Assyria the general term for jewellery in which gold, silver and semi-precious stones were used as the sole material or combined with ivory, copper or wood was usually *dumāqu*, but this term is generally qualified by a variety of words which denoted different kinds of ornaments. The importance of a collection of fine jewellery for bridal dowries is shown by the references to a widow's *dumāqu* in the Middle Assyrian Law Code, where the woman may keep any jewellery that her husband had settled on her, but only if there were no sons who would then have had prior claim. In the mid-second millennium B.C. the long list of ornaments of precious metal offered to the goddess Ningal at Qatna is prefaced by the word *Šukuttu*, which must have denoted the entire collection of jewellery belonging to the goddess. *Šukuttu* is also used in the fifth tablet of the Creation Epic as a descriptive epithet for the moon when it is ordered by Marduk to shine over the country by night. In secular terms, however, *dumāqu* was generally used, and on a tablet from Nimrud (N.D. 2307), giving the details of the gift given to the daughter of an official of the new palace at Calah on her marriage to a certain Milki-ramu in the mid-seventh century B.C., *dumāqu* is used in a general sense before a detailed list of silver ornaments.[1]

The goldsmith SIMUG GUŠKIN or jeweller KÚ DÌM (Akkadian *kuttimmu*(*m*)) appears in commercial documents not only of the Third Dynasty of Ur, Old Babylonian and Late Assyrian period, but among the lists and accounts from Alalakh-Atchana. Often they are mentioned by name and the exact amount of gold or silver issued to a craftsman is recorded. Although the documents provide us with considerable information about the activities of different classes of craftsmen many problems concerning the organization and status of skilled metalsmiths, such as jewellers, remain to be elucidated.

In the Late Assyrian period we have reference to the *rab nappāḫ ḫurāṣi*, the chief of the goldsmiths, and the craftsmen responsible for each different technical process were highly organized in a guild system whose origin and development has still to be determined. In Sumer we know that goldsmiths and jewellers worked directly for the temple authorities; at Ur in the Third Dynasty officials supervised eight different workshops

[1] B. Parker in *Iraq*, XVI, 1, 1954, pp. 37 f.

whose products included gold vessels, tools, weapons, statues and jewellery, all of which were intended to enrich the temple and to become part of the gods' property. This vast concentration of gold and silver treasure included the jewellery with which the status of the deities were adorned. Different sets of jewellery were made for different rituals and if a temple was sacked jewellery would be the easiest booty to loot. Moreover, it could be carried easily over great distances by merchants travelling along routes where the transport of large and heavy objects must have presented considerable difficulty. Even if donkey caravans, the usual means of overland transport, were raided or failed to arrive, the merchants or their agents, the *tamkāru*, to whom a trading enterprise was entrusted in the old Babylonian period probably carried many pieces on their persons and thus assisted in the diffusion of jewellery over a wide area.

The Assyrians inaugurated a new way of spreading the knowledge of different technical methods; large numbers of skilled craftsmen were removed from conquered cities and transported to the capital where they were required to produce objects for the victors. By the ninth century B.C. it is not easy to determine whether a piece of jewellery was made by local or foreign craftsmen, imported through trade or sent as part of a tribute or dowry. Certain techniques, however, were often associated with defined regions although the place names given in the texts cannot always be identified. Rosettes (*sisṣatu*), eagles (*našru*) and the other ornaments are stated to *ša qati Tu-uk-ri-iš*^{KI}, which can be translated 'made or following the technique of the country of Tukrish'.[1] This, however, does not necessarily mean that the object was actually imported from Tukrish; it could have been made by a craftsman from that area or by a local jeweller copying techniques which were especially associated with the region. It is this attention to detail shown by the scribes recording lists of offerings to deities or booty collected from a successful campaign that was responsible for the fashion of associating certain countries with specific objects, such as Urartu and *Ḫabḫi* with silver vessels and multicoloured garments (possibly made of material with beads sewn on to the actual fabric with gold thread like the fragments of textiles found recently by Professor Nimet Özgüc at Acem Hüyük (see p. 100), or Tabal with incense burners (*niknakke*).

Jewellery can often be related in secular and religious contexts with named individuals and commercial texts provide much instructive information which can be studied alongside the association with deities in

[1] J. Bottero, 'Les inventaires de Qatna', *R.A.*, XLIII, 1949, p. 22.

the ritual and mythological documents. An interesting example of the significance of jewellery occurs in the story of a Sumerian princess, the daughter of Sargon of Agade, Enheduanna, the high-priestess of the Moon god Nanna of Ur, who, at the time of her expulsion from Ur was 'stripped of her tiara appropriate for the high priesthood', an incident which recalls the theft of the jewels and garments of the goddess Inanna by the 'enemy' who clothed his own wife and daughters with them.

Technical methods

Henri Limet's valuable study of the texts of the Third Dynasty of Ur[1] published in 1960 has collected numerous references to the different technical methods used by goldsmiths and silversmiths and the Sumerian verbs used to connote a variety of techniques. Much work, however, still remains to be undertaken on the subject of Akkadian terms concerning specific technical problems in later periods. Some of these can be translated with reasonable certainty: *takāku* (to hammer), *labānu* (to press or flatten, often applied to gold leaf), *šakānu* (to place, when applied to the work of goldsmiths or jewellers), *aḫāzu* (to cover or overlay with gold leaf – *pašallu*), *tamlū* (to incrust or inlay and probably used to signify the technique of cloissoné inlay). The verb *malū* (to attach or set) also occurs in connection with jewellery. Examples of these techniques are discussed and illustrated in this study; the words for other decorative methods such as filigree and granulation have yet to be identified in Akkadian although Limet has proposed that filigree is the technique referred to in a Third Dynasty of Ur text where two silver rings were decorated with forty-seven grains of gold wire.[2]

Sources of gold and silver

In Mesopotamia precious metals were regarded as possessing certain specific properties; gold and silver were associated with the sun and moon; the god Ninurta endowed precious metals and stones with magical powers,[3] while in Sumer Enki, the Lord of Wisdom, was the patron of metallurgists. The prophylactic and apotropaic qualities of gold and silver jewellery were thus based on religious beliefs which were reflected by the myths of their associated temple rituals. For the Sumerians, an

[1] *Le Travail du Métal au Pays de Sumer au Temps de la IIIe Dynastie d'Ur.* [2] Ibid., p. 153.
[3] S. Geller, *Altorientalische texte und Untersuchungen 1, 4 hrsg von B. Meissner* (Leiden, 1917).

important source of gold, GUŠKIN (Akkadian *Ḫurāṣu*), was Ḫaḫḫu from whence Gudea brought *ṣarīru* (gold). *Ṣarīru* denoted a reddish gold which was often used with silver alloys to decorate the jewellery adorning the statues of deities. An identification of Ḫaḫḫu with Cilicia and the Ceyhan and Seyhan rivers as a probable source of alluvial gold was made by Sidney Smith in 1928.[1] Meluḫḫa is also given as a source of gold by Gudea and the identification of Meluḫḫa with the extreme south-east of Iran (to the east of Jāsk on the Persian Gulf and probably extending into Pakistan) suggested by Mallowan in 1965 is supported by convincing evidence.[2] Carnelian, commonly used by Sumerian jewellers, was also imported from Meluḫḫa while lapis lazuli has recently been the subject of an important study by Mrs Herrmann after personal investigation of the mines at Badakshan in Afghanistan (see p. 1).

The importance of Egypt as a source of gold for Babylonia, Assyria and Mitanni in the Amarna letters period (fourteenth and early thirteenth centuries B.C.) is well known, but later references in Assyrian texts do not give detailed information as to whether places mentioned were regular or occasional sources of supply. Tiglath-Pileser III describes *Šikraki*, a town of Media as *ša ḫurāṣi* (of gold), but we do not know if this refers to objects or mines. It is possible that the Pactolus river with its alluvial gold worked by the Lydians in the Persian period was also a source of supply in earlier times, but we have no evidence of this. An investigation of the remains of ancient mining at Kaletas and the area round Canakkale in the Troad should also be useful in solving problems concerning the source of Trojan gold.[3] Assyria, however, must have obtained gold from areas accessible by trade or conquest and Anatolia, north-east Armenia between Lakes Van and Urmia, north Persia and Transcaucasia can all be considered likely sources until definite archaeological evidence is forthcoming.

Gold was often described as red GUŠKIN ḪUŠ-A (gold with copper as the principal impurity), and red *ṣarīru* was regarded as 'the produce of the underworld, the dust of its mountain'. Campbell Thompson suggests that electrum may be denoted by *ebbu*, but references to *zaḫalū* indicate that this means a silver alloy, possibly electrum, used for covering or plating a metal core. Levey considers *ḫurāṣu piṣū* (white gold) as electrum.

More analysis of gold objects is needed before the metallurgical problems concerning words which specify the different qualities of gold

[1] Smith, *E.H.A.*, p. 99. [2] *Iran*, III, 1965, p. 5. [3] W. Leaf, *Strabo on the Troad*, pp. 133 ff.

can be understood. At Ur, the purity of the gold used varied considerably and analysis of a leaf and hair ribbon from the same headdress exemplifies this:

	Leaf	*Hair ribbon*
Gold	67·17%	77·14%
Silver	32·38%	22·06%
Copper	0·45%	0·50%
Approximate carat	16	18

The varying amount of the impurities suggests that native gold was used and it seems unlikely that Sumerian goldsmiths practised refining in the Early Dynastic period. At the time of the Third Dynasty of Ur, however, there is evidence in the texts that smiths and jewellers were able to produce alloys suitable for different kinds of object. Gold is often described as GUŠKIN SÍ-SÁ (refined gold?) and in a text from Ur[1] this quality of gold was mixed with 'red' gold and an alloy, GUŠKIN SÁR-DA, produced. Later in the Qatna inventories gold could be described as *Ḫurāṣu sāmu* (red gold), *ḫurāṣu damqu* (gold of good quality), *ḫurāṣu ellu* (clear or white gold), *ḫurāṣu ṣarpu* (refined gold), *ḫurāṣu arqu* (green gold – gold plus silver?).

Electrum was used at Ur in the Early Dynastic period not only for the famous helmet of Meskalamdug, beaten from sheet metal, but also for handles of silver bowls and on a circular silver plaque with a filigree background of silver wire around a central electrum boss. This juxtaposition of silver and electrum seems to have been preferred to the close association of silver with gold which were usually separated by another material.

Silver, Sumerian KÙ.BABBAR (or KÙ.LUḪ-ḪA), Akkadian *Kaspu*, was brought from the 'mountains' by Gudea, and Elam is also mentioned as a source of silver for Sumerian merchants. Sargon sent expeditions to Anatolia to obtain silver, and his statement that '(Enlil) gave him the upper land, Mari, Yarmuti, Ibla (Byblos) as far as the cedar forest and the silver mountains' is usually taken to signify the Anatolian silver mines at Keban on the Euphrates just south of its junction with the Murat river. Certainly, the rich argentiferous lead ores of Anatolia were the object of much of the commercial trade undertaken by the Assyrian colonist merchants at the beginning of the second millennium B.C. and ores must have continued to supply the needs of Mesopotamia throughout the period of the Assyrian empire.[2]

[1] Limet, op. cit., p. 44. [2] Leaf, op. cit., pp. 212 f.

At Ur the silver was generally of good quality and did not contain a high percentage of copper; traces of gold were common. A silver rein ring was analysed as follows:

Silver	93·5%
Copper	6·10%
Gold	0·08%
Zinc	0·15%

Akkadian epithets for silver include *misū* (washed) and *ṣarpi* (refined), *kima ṣarpi ṣurrupi* ('like refined silver may be bright'). In the Kültepe documents silver is referred to as *kaspum ṣarrupam* and *ṣarpu* is often used as a synonym for *kaspu*. Different qualities of silver are listed and associated with several place names; judging by the price, silver from Kültepe was sometimes regarded as an inferior product. As yet we have no archaeological or textual evidence for the refining of silver in Early Dynastic Sumer and it seems likely that silver must have been imported into southern Mesopotamia in a refined state or as electrum, a natural gold-silver alloy. The analysis shows that Entemena's famous silver vase, now in the Louvre, was made from pure silver and it is described in its inscription as KÙ.LUḪ-ḪA, pure or refined silver. It is probable, however, that in Anatolia the use of the cupellation process for the refining of silver was used as early as the period of Troy II treasures. At Troy the analysis of one of the ingots of silver suggests that an argentiferous lead ore such as galena was used (Silver 95·61 per cent; Copper 3·41 per cent; Gold 1·7 per cent; Iron 0·38 per cent; Lead 0·22 per cent; Nickel traces) and the numerous deposits of galena in Anatolia would naturally attract miners and prospectors from all over the Near East.

As yet we have scanty evidence for the early production of silver in Iran but the current excavations in Media, where silver was far more commonly used in the first millennium than gold, may assist in this problem and analyses are badly needed. There are many important deposits of galena in Iran and remains of ancient mines in the Binalad mountains west of Meshed in the province of Kerman and near Isfahan should be investigated. A survey of the area near the source of the Great Zab river west of Lake Rizayeh, where rich argentiferous lead ores occur, would be useful and essential before many problems concerning the history of silver technology in Assyria can be studied, while more metallurgical evidence is badly needed before work on Elamite jewellery can advance.

CHAPTER I

Mesopotamia: The Early Dynastic Period

INTRODUCTION

The early history of jewellery in Mesopotamia begins in the north at the site of Tepe Gawra, and is closely connected with the early trade in lapis lazuli which was later transferred to the south when supplies from the mines of Badakshan in Afghanistan were diverted to the southern Sumerian cities.[1] At Gawra, in the Jamdat Nasr period (late fourth millennium B.C.), in a rich burial – Tomb 109[2] – which contained gold rosettes (some pierced for attachment) and studs and gold and electrum beads, lapis lazuli was used as inlay and, along with turquoise, was also used for beads. A gold rosette with lapis lazuli centre, the famous electrum wolf's head and a gold and lapis amulet all belong to Gawra level X (Jamdat Nasr period). In Sumer, after this period, it is not until Early Dynastic III that pieces of jewellery have survived and the site of Ur is taken as the starting point of this survey. For the preceding Early Dynastic I and II periods references to gold, silver and precious stones in Sumerian literature are our main sources of evidence for the work of jewellers and silversmiths during the early part of the third millennium B.C.

The epic of King Enmerkar, second king of the First Dynasty of Uruk, who probably reigned in the Early Dynastic II period, is especially relevant for this study.[3] The text records the efforts of the king to obtain gold, silver and semi-precious stones to use for the embellishment of various shrines and temples in Eridu and makes it clear that the people of Aratta, an unlocated state in Iran (which could be located as far from Sumer as the Elburz mountains south or south-east of the Caspian), were themselves skilled craftsmen as well as being capable of transporting gold,

[1] G. Herrmann, 'Lapis lazuli: the early phases of its trade', *Iraq*, XXX, 1, 1968, pp. 21–67.

[2] A. J. Tobler, *Excavations at Tepe Gawra*, II, pl. LVIII, LIX (University Museum, Philadelphia, 1950).

[3] S. N. Kramer, *Enmerkar and the Lord of Aratta, A Sumerian Epic Tale of Iraq and Iran* (University of Pennsylvania, 1952).

silver and lapis lazuli for 'Inanna, the Queen of Eanna'. The text continues, 'In the courtyard they heap them up for the store-house.' In return, Enmerkar sent grain to Aratta on 'crate-carrying donkeys' and 'directed them on the road to Aratta'.

The city of Ur in Sumer (Southern Iraq) was excavated by Sir Leonard Woolley during the years 1926 to 1932 and no other site in western Asia has yielded anything comparable either in quantity or richness to the extraordinary collections of gold and silver jewellery found in the Ur graves. This jewellery is now divided between Baghdad, the British Museum and the University Museum, Philadelphia, and – since the publication of the Royal Cemetery in 1934 – has never been studied in detail as a whole.[1] Recent work, however, on other aspects of the Royal Cemetery has made it easier to re-assess the significance of the gold and silver jewellery and to attempt to date certain classes of objects more precisely than was possible at the time of excavation.

Three studies are of prime importance to this context. The first, 'The date of the so-called Second Dynasty graves of the Royal Cemetery at Ur', was published by Mr Briggs Buchanan in 1954.[2] Working solely from the seals, he suggested that at least 153 graves should be redated. This involved classifying graves which had previously been considered Early Dynastic (called by Woolley pre-Dynastic) as belonging to the full or late Akkadian periods, and others previously included by Woolley in the group called 'Second Dynasty', as belonging to the early part of the Third Dynasty of Ur period. In an unpublished doctoral thesis (University of London) in 1962, Mrs Harriet Crawford reconsidered the stratification of the cemetery, suggesting that six more graves could be added to the Sargonid period.[3] The third and most recent study of the material from the Royal Cemetery with particular reference to the chronological sequence of the graves is H. J. Nissen's detailed study published in 1966,[4] and I am grateful to the author for sending me his section on the beads before publication. This reclassification calls for a reconsideration of jewellery which can demonstrate that, in spite of the great conservatism of the Sumerian jeweller from 2500 B.C. onwards, it is possible to assign the most important types to the period or periods during which they were most in fashion – i.e. Early Dynastic III, Sargonid or Third Dynasty of Ur.

[1] *Ur Excavations*, II, text and plates. [2] *J.A.O.S.*, 74, 1954, p. 147.

[3] *The Archaeology and History of the Early Dynastic Period in Iraq.*

[4] *Zur Datierung des Königsfriedhofes von Ur unter besonderer Berücksichtigung der Stratigraphie der Privatgräber* (Bonn, 1966).

An intelligent study of the jewellery should be based not only on the different types, their variations, technique and purpose, but also on the associated objects in the tomb groups in which they were found. This is not so easy (apart from the publication where the contents of each tomb are listed in detail) as, when the final division of the material was made, tomb groups were split up between the different museums concerned with little thought for the student of the future. Certain grave groups which are important for the dating of certain distinctive types of jewellery will, however, be discussed here and the evidence afforded by associated objects considered alongside that of the jewellery. Certainly the words of Sir Leonard Woolley concerning beads can be applied to most types of jewellery: 'It is more correct to date the fashions in beads by the graves in which they are found than to date the graves by the beads.'

JEWELLERY FROM SELECTED SITES

Ur

The headdress (pls. 1, 2, 3 and colour pl. A)

The headdress of Queen Pu-abi (formerly read Shub-ad) represents the richest and most complicated version of the normal headdress worn by the women in the Ur Cemetery and the various elements can be summarized as follows:

(*a*) Hair ribbon. A narrow gold or silver strip fixed by a short silver pin, the ends coiled into a small loop for the pin.

(*b*) Wreath. This consisted of 'a double string of beads, carnelian rings and short cylinders of lapis lazuli, from which hung pendants whose stems acted as spacers, keeping the ranks of beads in place.'[1] The most common type of pendant was in the form of gold (or sometimes silver) 'beech' leaves followed by gold or silver plain rings, groups of three long willow-shaped leaves or discs of gold with lapis centres.[2] Gold rosettes were sometimes attached to the wreath or fixed as heads to slender silver hairpins. The 'beech' leaf wreath is an invariable part of the headdress;

[1] *Ur Excavations*, II, p. 240.

[2] The leaf is inaccurately identified as beech. There is no evidence of beech growing in Iraq in the third millennium B.C. The leaf is most likely a willow (aspen), *Populus Euphratica*, while the long thin willow leaves used on the headdress can be identified as *Salix Alba*. See W. Walker, *All the Plants of the Bible*, pp. 232, 234 (London, 1958). The young leaves of *Populus Euphratica* are also long and thin and I am grateful to Professor Dimbleby of the Institute of Archaeology, London University, and to the Herbarium of Kew Gardens for identifying a specimen of *Populus Euphratica* which I obtained from the banks of the Tigris in 1970.

the other parts of the headdress are worn with, but not in place of it; as many as four wreaths could be worn at once, one above the other, though this is unusual.

(*c*) Decorative hairpins or combs. These are distinct from and much larger than the silver pins mentioned above and are stuck into the back of the hair. Described by Woolley as 'an upstanding ornament which reminds one of the "Spanish combs" popular in England in the Victorian age, the stem of the pin broadening out to a flat triangular plate from which rise points ending in flower rosettes.'[1] Queen Pu-abi's comb was of

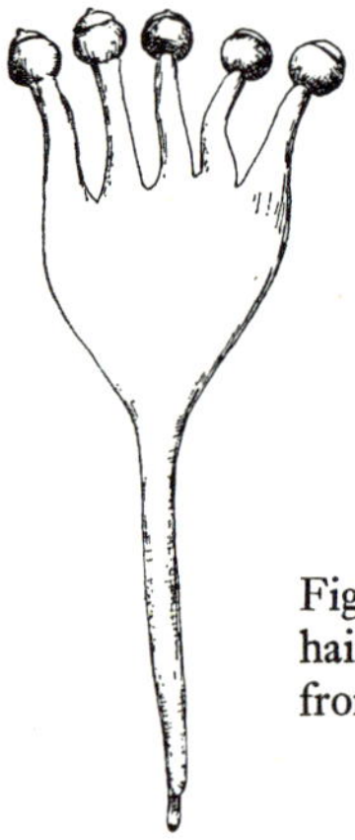

Fig. 1. Silver hair ornament from Ur.

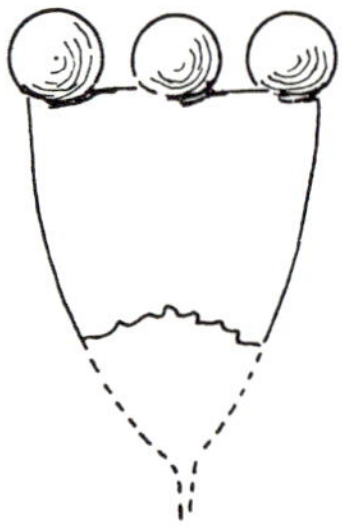

Fig. 2. Copper hair ornament from Ur.

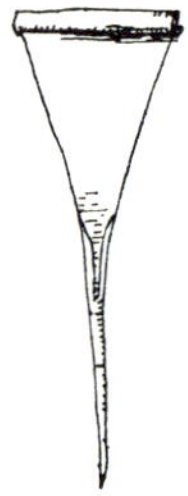

Fig. 3. Gold hair ornament from Ur.

gold and had seven flowers; the ordinary comb (cf. pl. 3 and colour pl. A) was of silver and had three (occasionally five) flowers whose petals were inlaid with gold, shell, lapis lazuli and red limestone; unique among them was a silver comb whose five points ended in round balls of lapis lazuli (fig. 1) and a squat example in which the balls – this time of silver – were soldered directly to the edge of the triangle instead of being at the ends of the branches[2] (cf. fig. 2). Spatulate pins of gold or silver were worn with the 'combs' (see fig. 3). These pins seem designed to be the holders of an ornament which Woolley has suggested might be feathers, though there is no evidence to suggest this was so.

Earrings (pls. 3, 4 and colour pl. A and fig. 4)

Enormous double lunate rings of gold and (less frequently) of silver were invariably worn with the headdress described above. Woolley's description reads: 'The two crescent-shaped lobes, made of thin metal and hollow,

[1] *Ur Excavations*, II, p. 240. [2] Ibid.

were soldered together side by side; from the end of one crescent a curved pin reached across to fit into the tubular end of the second crescent; since the pin is reasonably thin it may have passed through the lobe of the ear, but in view of the weight of the ring (which is in some cases increased by

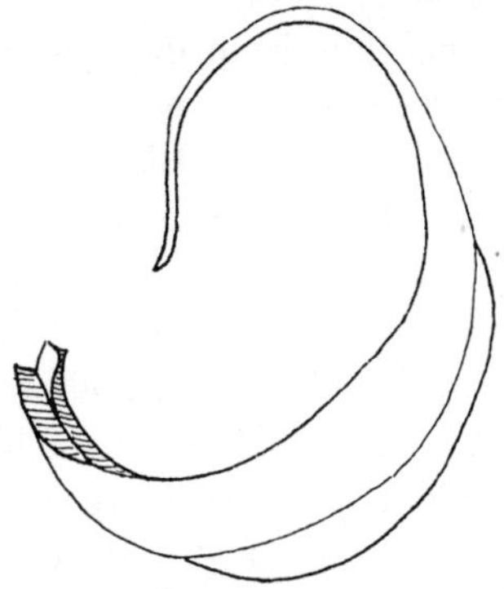

Fig. 4. Gold earring from Ur.

the hollow metal being filled with bitumen) it is likely that it was in part at least supported by a lock of hair passed through it.' It is possible also that the pin of the earring passed over the whole ear as the thickness of some examples suggests that it is unlikely to have pierced the lobe of the ear.

Hair-rings (pl. 5a)

Spirally curled rings of gold wire were called hair-rings by Woolley as they occurred on skulls wearing earrings and examples were found actually inside the enormous hollow earrings described above. That they may also have been used as earrings is suggested by the fact that they occurred where no lunate earrings were found and the spiral rings were sometimes found lying close to the ear. But, as Woolley points out, they have also been found lying in front of the shoulder and could have therefore been threaded over a long lock of hair.

Diadems

An elaborate form of diadem occurred in only four graves, one of which – the most elaborate – was found in the grave of Queen Pu-abi. This was made of gold figures of animals, fruits and flowers against a background of lapis lazuli beads (*Ur Excavations*, II, pl. 140).

Necklaces (pls. 6, 7 and 8)

The materials used are gold, silver combined with lapis lazuli, and carnelian. The magnificent agate beads found with Queen Pu-abi are exceptional for this period and are a distinguishing mark of the succeeding Sargonid period. Gold or silver was never used as the sole material of a necklace and the two metals were not often combined on the same string, although strings of plain lapis often occurred or could be combined with silver. Woolley considered that the use of gold depended on the wealth of the owner, but the quality of the lapis varies considerably and no doubt reflected the conditions prevailing along the trade route to the source of the lapis in distant Badakshan, the sole source of lapis lazuli for the Sumerians.[1] In the same way, the quality of the gold used for beads varies. Usually they are of heavy metal and hollow, although some of the smaller beads (double conoids Type 8, ball-shaped Type 13 and ovoids Type 12) were cast solid. Others are hollow and were made over a core of wood or bitumen which would use less gold.

The main types of bead are shown in fig. 6 (see also pl. 12) and listed on p. 8. To these can be added two elaborate types made of gold wire found in P.G. 580 – the 'dumb-bell' made of twisted wire and the double conoids of coiled wire (colour pl. B). An elaborate large example of a double conoid bead from P.G. 580 (see pl. 8a) was also decorated with applied filigree forming shallow cloisons and a fine example of the jeweller's technical ability is shown where two of these beads are soldered together (U.9657 R.T., pl. 146). Other instances of composite beads of this type are known and P.G. 755 (grave of Meskalamdug) produced double conoids of gold and lapis lazuli. Large spherical lapis lazuli beads could be fluted or capped with gold (pl. 13) and a long biconical lapis lazuli bead was decorated with gold caps and wire spirals which encircled the bead in a groove (pl. 12).

'*Dog collar*' *necklaces* (fig. 5)

This distinctive necklace was the usual form in the Early Dynastic period and could be combined with several larger strings of beads. It was usually made of gold and lapis triangles:

'The lapis beads are cut out of a single piece and pierced with horizontally drilled holes, the gold triangles are made from sheet metal which is folded in half and beaten on to rods placed in a parallel series so as to produce channels for the threads; the two sides were generally soldered together, but sometimes this has been omitted.'[2]

An important variation from the normal type of 'dog collar' described above, which only occurs in a few instances, is where the triangles are

[1] G. Herrmann, *Iraq*, XXX, 1, 1968. [2] *Ur Excavations*, II, p. 369.

composed of small separate ball beads instead of the single solid triangle, and then carnelian could be introduced to vary the colour. In one necklace the balls were soldered or sweated together (fig. 5). This would obviously assist in stringing and is actually a primitive kind of granulation. This

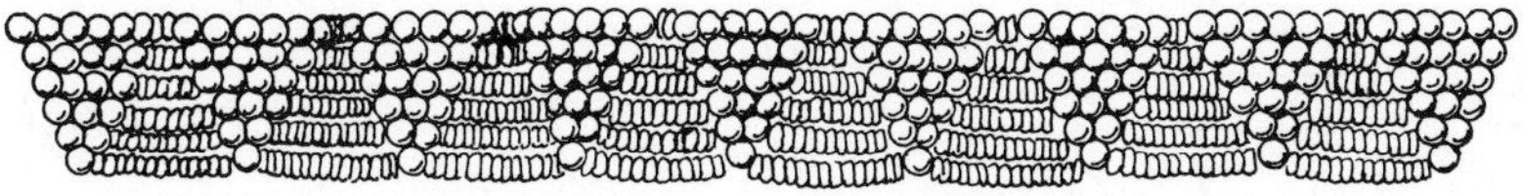

Fig. 5. 'Dog collar' necklace from Ur.

technique is also found on the gold bracelet from Byblos (see p. 123) though here the groups of four granules were soldered to the solid gold background. But the triangular arrangement of minute gold beads invites comparison with the later fine triangular granulation work such as that found on the bracelet from Aqar Qūf (see p. 164) and may well have inspired later smiths to develop the technique of fine granulation using similar triangular patterns. Technically, the Byblos bracelet forms an intermediate stage between the Ur 'dog collar' with minute soldered gold beads and the Aqar Qūf bracelet, where the granules are soldered to a solid gold background and arranged in triangular pattern.

A clear example of a 'dog collar' is shown in paint on a terracotta from Ashur (Smith, *E.H.A.*, fig. 5, p. 66).

Types of gold and silver beads (fig. 6)

Fig. 6 shows the main types of beads which occur in the Ur Cemetery and Woolley's nomenclature has been followed. This agrees with the system adopted by the heads of archaeological missions working in Iraq in 1929. The suggested dating is based on Woolley's comments and descriptions, summarized here with a few additional remarks concerning the dating of certain distinctive types, based on a study of the beads in the British Museum and Baghdad and on Nissen's chronological tables. All Woolley's types are given in fig. 6, including those not actually found in gold, as any change in type number would only cause confusion and most of the types found in stone occur also in gold and, less often, in silver.

Type 1 Square. The thickness is variable. This is one of the types found in carnelian with etched white filled decoration; these distinctive beads are not native to Sumer and were imported from the Indus valley. Early Dynastic III, Sargonid and Third Dynasty of Ur (pl. 6c).

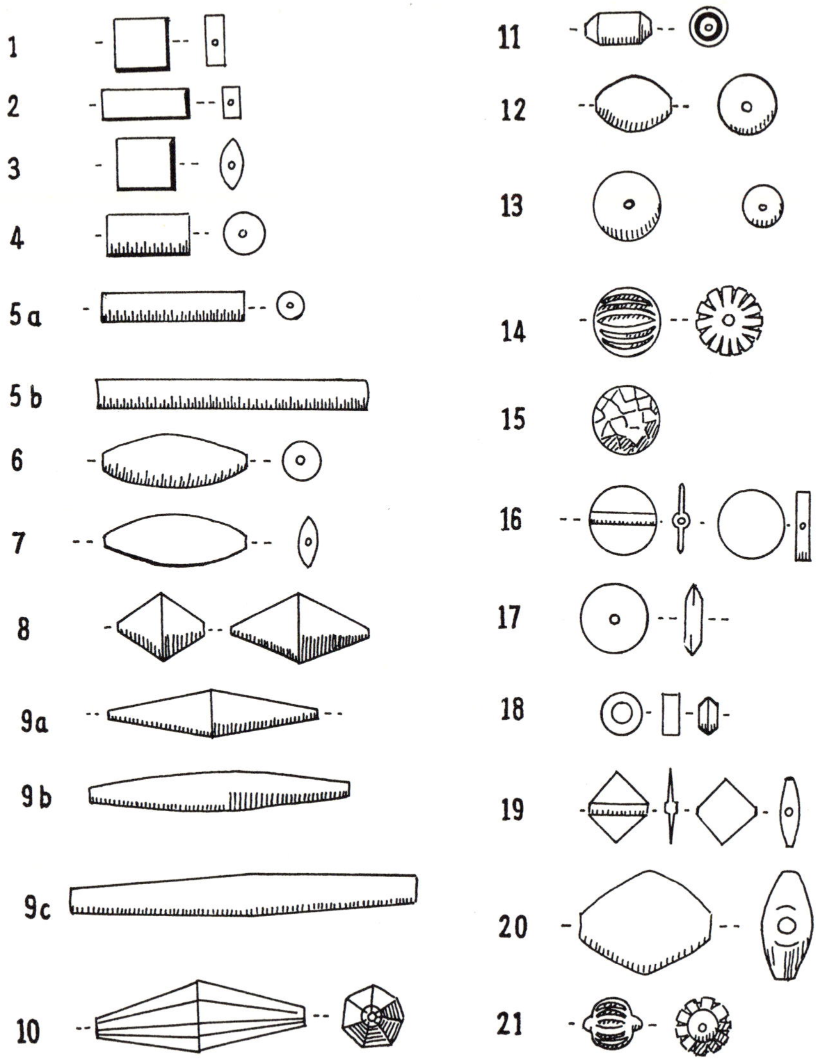

Fig. 6. Types of gold and silver beads from Ur.

Type 2 Rectangular. All examples Early Dynastic III except one Late Akkadian to Third Ur.

Type 3 Biconvex. The section is often lozenge-shaped. Akkadian to Third Ur.

Type 4 Cylindrical. The length is not much more than twice the diameter and generally is less. Common at all periods (pl. 9).

Type 5 Tubular. The length is three or more times the diameter. Common at all periods (pl. 9).

Type 6 Date-shaped. The large faceted date-shaped variety of Type 6 with four to eight facets, combined with Type 10, was used for the men's *brīm* headdress (see below). Woolley states that some were found in the Sargonid graves, but Nissen lists examples for all periods (pls. 8b, 12).

Type 7 Elliptical. The bead is date-shaped in profile, but elliptical instead of circular in section – i.e. a flattened date shape. Nissen lists four examples, all Akkadian period.

Type 8 Double conoid. One of the commonest forms, embracing every degree of proportion. In badly cut beads this type may be scarcely distinguishable from Type 6 (pl. 7).

Type 9 Long double conoid. Length more than three times the diameter. Sometimes the sharp edges tend to disappear and the bead approximates to Type 5 (pls. 6b, 12).

Type 10 Faceted double conoid. Number of facets varies from four to eight. Typical for Early Dynastic III period (pl. 12). None listed by Nissen later than Early Dynastic.

Type 11 Barrel-shaped. A double chamfered cylinder but often very roughly cut and assimilating to Type 12. All periods.

Type 12 Ovoid. Circular in section and elliptical (rather than egg-shaped) in profile. One of the commonest forms, but confined to the Early Dynastic period (pl. 6c).

Type 13 Ball-shaped – i.e. wholly spherical. All periods (pl. 6c).

Type 14 Ribbed ball-shaped. A fluted sphere – i.e. the grooves are concave or V-shaped and the tops of the ridges between them are flat, keeping to the outline of the sphere. In other cases the ribs are convex and the bead might more properly be described as gadrooned. Mostly Early Dynastic, but occurs in Sargonid and Third Ur graves (pls. 6d and 13).

Type 15 Faceted ball-shaped. The surface of the sphere is rubbed down into more or less definite facets.

Type 16 Discoid. Also called flat disc-shaped bead. In its simplest form in stone it is flat and circular in profile and pierced on its diameter. In gold or silver the bead is formed of two discs soldered together, but by hammering these over a wire (or thin rod) a tube is left to take the string, and therefore a convex rib runs across the face of the bead. This important type starts in the Early Dynastic period and becomes increasingly common in the Akkadian and Third Dynasty of Ur periods[1] (see pl. 17a).

Type 17 Lentoid. A disc bead with convex face, giving the lentoid section (pl. 6d).

Type 18 Ring-shaped. The bead may be square, oval or a truncated double-conoid in section, but the sides are mainly flat, so that the beads when strung come close together and produce the effect of an articulated but continuous band rather than of separate elements brought into conjunction (*Ur Excavations*, II, p. 368, fig. 75). All periods (pl. 6a).

Type 19 Diamond-shaped. The gold and silver beads of this type are made in the same way as those of Type 16 and therefore have the same medial rib (pl. 6a). A few Early Dynastic examples; common in Akkadian and Third Dynasty of Ur periods.

Type 20 Rhomboid. Usually large and, although the stone examples are often coarse and of inferior material, the gold examples are well made. Rare form. Woolley states all periods but Nissen lists only one for the Early Dynastic and eight Akkadian to Third Ur inclusive.

Type 21 Hub-shaped. Not found in metal.

Type 22 Pear-shaped pendant.

Pendants (pls. 1 and 3)

Pendants formed either an integral part of the headdress – such as the 'beech' leaves on the wreaths – or were suspended from necklaces, interspersed with gold or stone beads: 'Most of them are made of gold, and even those of carnelian or lapis lazuli are usually attached to gold suspenders. The Sumerians rightly felt that pendants hung from a single rank of beads were likely to prove overweight in effect – something more solid was needed above to put the pendants in proportion, and therefore the pendants are nearly always so made so as to act as spacers for two,

[1] This type of bead is shown on a jeweller's mould of steatite found at Mari (Early Dynastic III level). Parrot, *Mari*, III, figs. 245–6, p. 198.

three or four ranks of beads; the stem is made of a strip of gold cut as a narrow ribbon in the centre and thinned down at one or both ends almost to a wire, it is folded in half and the two sides are alternately looped apart and soldered together so as to make parallel horizontal rings through which the strings of the necklace or wreath may pass, and the pointed ends, in the case of a stone pendant, are put through it and twisted in a knot; in the case of the gold leaves the leaf and stem are in one piece.'[1] This description applies to the long narrow willow or *Populus euphratica* leaf pendants which were always made in sets of three, the pomegranates of Queen Pu-abi's diadem and the plain ring pendants (*Ur Excavations*, II, pl. 142, U.1776).

Pendants of coiled gold wire

(*a*) This is the most elaborate form of pendant. It was made of two pieces of gold wire twisted round each other to form the vertical centre piece of the amulet; the four ends were then coiled into four separate cones; the whole quadruple spiral so formed was then fixed into a circle of gold and attached to the necklace by the gold suspender described above (pls. 9 and 10). A more simple form consisted of a single gold wire cone,

Fig. 7. Necklace from Ur; gold and lapis lazuli.

Fig. 8. Necklace from Ur; carnelian pendants set in gold.

which was also imitated in lapis lazuli (fig. 7 and pl. 10 show the gold and lapis examples on the same necklace from P.G. 580, the 'Gold Dagger' grave).

(*b*) The double spiral pendant shown in colour pl. B is also from Grave 580 and is attached to the necklace by the twisted ends of the wire without the addition of the suspender or enclosing circle. This necklace is especially interesting as it also has two double conoid beads of twisted gold wire, a distinctive type which also occurs at Vadjalik in the Russian Talish (see

[1] *Ur Excavations*, II, p. 374.

p. 20). Etched carnelian beads were also found in this grave; these were sometimes made as pendants with a gold suspender (fig. 8).

(*c*) Fruit pendants in gold, lapis and carnelian were also characteristic of P.G. 580.

Amulets

Amulets are not included here under the heading of jewellery, unless they form part of a necklace or there is evidence that they were actually worn on the person. None of the larger sort have been found suspended from a necklace, although Queen Pu-abi wore two of her amulets (a reclining calf and a bearded bull on a short string with large beads of agate and lapis lazuli). The animals on her diadem certainly had amuletic significance, and the gold bearded bull, U.8269, is considered by Woolley possibly to have come from a diadem. Amulets and beads were probably suspended from the cloak toggle pins; this arrangement is clearly shown on the shell plaques from Mari.[1]

Small amulets were also occasionally strung on to bead necklaces in both the Early Dynastic and Sargonid periods. The frog occurs three times in the Early Dynastic graves and twice in the Sargonid period; the fly occurs in Early Dynastic, Sargonid and Third Ur period graves. Royal Tomb P.G. 789 (King's grave) produced a finely worked hollow gold fly pendant which was bored for suspension down the centre (B.M. 123662). This certain Early Dynastic example is important when considering later examples of fly amulets from Ajjul and Ashur.

Pins

At Ur Woolley distinguished seven types of pin which were made of copper, gold or silver:

Type 1 Plain round shaft with plain or fluted round head of lapis lazuli, carnelian or glazed material, sometimes capped with gold, silver

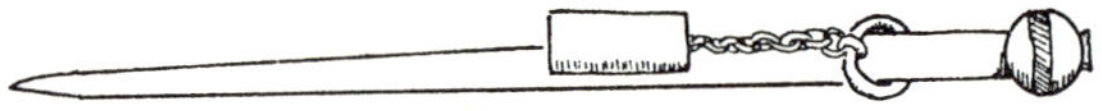

Fig. 9. Pin with attached cylinder seal from Ur.

or copper. Usually pierced to take a metal ring through which a string was threaded for the attachment of either beads or a cylinder seal (fig. 9).

[1] *Ur Excavations*, II, pl. 143; Parrot in *Syria*, XXXIX, 1962, pl. XI.

Type 2 As above, but with rectangular shaft.
Type 3 The shaft and the head are in one piece (fig. 10a and b).
Type 4 The head is made from the coiled-over shaft, in a simple spiral.

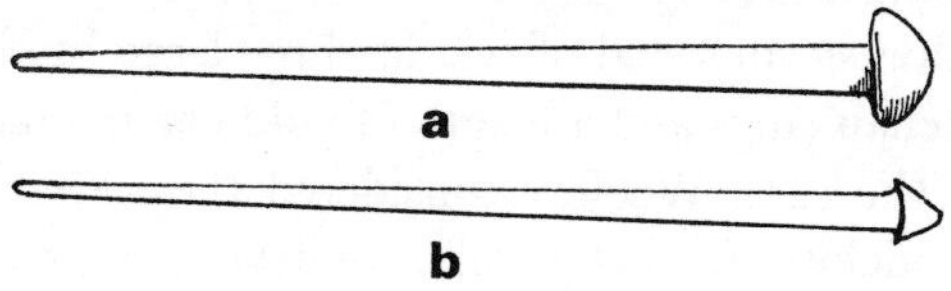

Fig. 10. Copper pins from Ur.

Type 5 The head is expanded to a large triangle with the base curled over into a tube. This type occurred in gold in the grave of Queen Pu-abi, P.G. 800, and in silver in P.G. 337. It is this type which was worn with the 'combs' on the head and which Woolley has suggested was used as a holder for feathers (fig. 3). We have no evidence for this, although the top is bent over in such a way that a thin cord or stalk could have passed through it.
Type 6 With decorated metal head. One example in silver from P.G. 55 has a head in the form of a clenched hand. It occurs at Ashur in a much later context, made of ivory or bone in Grave 45 (see p. 169) and is also common in the 'A' cemetery at Kish (fig. 11).

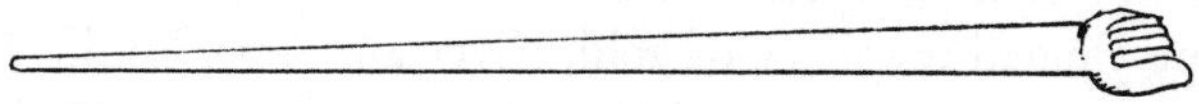

Fig. 11. Silver pin from Ur.

Type 7 This type is typical of the Royal Cemetery: 'The shaft, round at the point, is flattened or brought to a square above and pierced, then thins down again and is curved over at about right angles and ends in a head either made in one piece with the shaft or of some different material.' A fine example came from Royal Tomb P.G. 1054 in gold with a carnelian head (fig. 12).

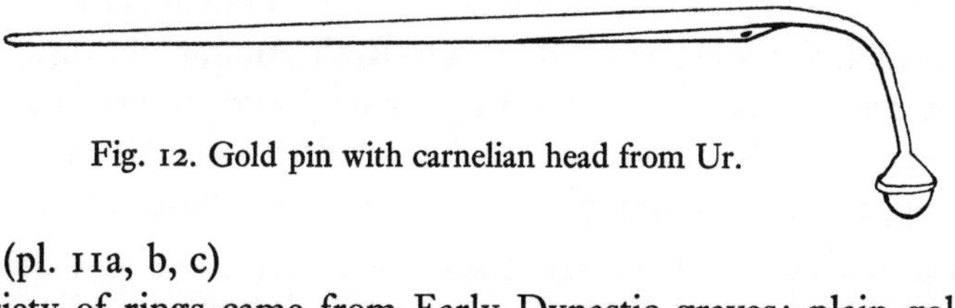

Fig. 12. Gold pin with carnelian head from Ur.

Rings (pl. 11a, b, c)
A variety of rings came from Early Dynastic graves; plain gold strips with curled-over edges could be decorated with twisted filigree wires

(a and b) or cloisons were soldered to the base forming cells for inlay of precious stones (c).[1]

Male Headdress (pl. 12)
The male headdress consisted of two or three large beads of lapis lazuli, gold with carnelian rings and a length of gold chain which passed round the head over the ears. Woolley considered these were intended to be worn over a headcloth. Unfortunately, we have no representations of this headdress.

Mari

The history of the great city of Mari on the Euphrates near the modern Iraqi–Syrian border covers nearly two millennia and the excavations begun by M. Parrot in 1933 are still progressing. Its importance for the history of jewellery in Mesopotamia will be shown from the frequent references to this site (see Chapter 5) and its contribution to Sumerian civilization in the Early Dynastic period is now becoming clear. Two groups of stratified jewellery date from this period.

The first, from Tomb 300[2] (constructed in much the same way as Tomb 1236 at Ur, a vaulted stone tomb), was undisturbed and among a collection of bronze vessels and pottery of Early Dynastic I ('Scarlet ware') type yielded jewellery of gold, silver and lapis lazuli. This tomb, considered by the excavator to belong to one of the rulers of Mari and which provided evidence of human sacrifice, was excavated under the later temple of Ishtar. The collection included part of the gold frontal decorated in eight petalled repoussé rosettes, fragments of silver rosettes, two well-preserved circular plaques (called pectorals in the publication) with seven repoussé cones on the surface, flat winged disc beads in gold and lapis lazuli and gold rings forming the pendants of two necklaces. The circular plaques with the border of punched dots can be compared with the remarkable gold plaque from Kinneret, a cave tomb in Palestine whose Anatolian affinities were studied by Dr Ruth Amiran in 1952.[3] This technique can also be found at Alaca, but its Anatolian origin is by no means proved. A plaque from Ur is decorated in a similar manner (*Ur Excavations*, II, pl. 219, U.8007) with seven repoussé bosses, and another

[1] A fine lapis, carnelian and gold ring from Lagash is now in the Louvre. See G. Herrmann, *Iraq*, XXX, 1, 1968, p. 44; and J. Margueron, 'Mesopotamia', *Archaeologia Mundi*, 1965, pl. 42.
[2] Parrot, *Syria*, XIX, 1938, 1, pl. II, 3.
[3] 'Connections between Anatolia and Palestine in the Early Bronze Age', *I.E.J.*, 2, 1952, pp. 89 ff.

(*Ur Excavations*, II, pl. 219, U.8374) has the bosses made from coiled wire. While the Ur examples belong to Early Dynastic III period, De Vaux places the Kinneret tomb in Phase III of the Early Bronze Age (the pottery suggests a later phase)[1] and the fact that there is evidence of partial cremation at Kinneret – also in certain tombs at Ur and at Mari (Tomb 300) – suggests that the people who wore these plaques may have been foreigners who had come from Anatolia at the time of the introduction to Palestine of the pottery known as Khirbet Kerak ware.

Although, as De Vaux pointed out, there were only limited contacts between Palestine and Mesopotamia during the course of the Early Bronze Age, more evidence for close connections between Mari and Ur has recently appeared in the remarkable treasure jar found by Parrot at Mari which contained a lapis lazuli bead with a dedicatory inscription with the name of Mesannipadda, founder of the First Dynasty of Ur c. 2550 B.C.[2] The treasure included mushroom-headed pins of gold and silver, a bracelet of gold fluted beads, two beads with the flutings developed into semi-circular wings and a remarkable pendant. This was made of gold and consisted of two circles of sheet gold ornamented with twisted gold wires with a central cone of gold and lapis lazuli. It invites comparison with the circular gold pendant from Kültepe (see pl. 68) but the triple ridged 'suspender' is the usual type known at Ur for the suspension of rings and pendants. The cylinders carved in the Tell Fara style can be compared with cylinders of the Ur Royal Cemetery belonging to the earliest period; Parrot dates the treasure and the jewellery to c. 2600 B.C. and considers that it was hidden prior to the destruction of Mari by the Sumerian ruler Lugalzaggisi, king of Umma and Erech, and that it was sent or brought to Mari by Mesannipadda. This remarkable find has recently been discussed by Mallowan,[3] who concludes that the jewellery was probably part of the dowry of a princess of Ur on the occasion of her marriage to a prince of Mari, or a prince of a city subject to Mari.

Uruk

A fine silver disc, with hollow central boss, considered by the excavator to be a breastplate with decoration worked in filigree, belongs to the Early Dynastic period (pl. 14).[4]

[1] De Vaux, *C.A.H.*, No. 46, p. 18. [2] *Mari*, IV.
[3] *Biblioteca Orientalis*, XXVI, 1/2, pp. 86–9.
[4] *U.V.B.*, XXI, 1965, pl. 13, and *Archaeology*, 17, 2, 1964, p. 130.

Kish

A small collection of jewellery from Kish is in the Ashmolean Museum, Oxford, and belongs to the Early Dynastic Period – see especially Burial 344.[1]

[1] Moorey in *Iraq*, XXVIII, 1, 1966, p. 30.

CHAPTER 2

Mesopotamia: The Sargonid Period c. 2370–2200 B.C.

INTRODUCTION

In Mesopotamia the one hundred and seventy years covered by the Dynasty of Agade, founded by Sargon in 2360 B.C., forms a distinct historical and archaeological period whose characteristics – whether architectural, artistic or technological – can be distinguished from the preceding Early Dynastic III period, and should not be regarded as merely the development of earlier Sumerian techniques. I have suggested elsewhere[1] that it is in the Sargonid period that one can discern the gradual secularization of the art of the jeweller, whose activities in earlier times had been primarily religious. The important part played by jewellery in both temple and private rituals seems to have increased considerably in the Sargonid period and was no doubt partly responsible for the tremendous impetus given to the search for raw materials outside Mesopotamia by Sargon and his successors.

The question of trade in the Sargonid period has recently been treated by Professor Mallowan[2] and, as excavations in Anatolia and Persia continue, new information is constantly providing evidence for a re-assessment of the activities of the Sargonid rulers. Until recently there was scanty archaeological evidence to supplement the documentary; now, thanks to Professor Özgüc's work at Kültepe and to recent work in Iran, Pakistan and India, it is becoming possible to link the documentary and archaeological sources of information. In this problem metal objects are important and more analysis to determine the possible sources of the ores would provide valuable data. Mesopotamia had to import all the copper, silver, gold, lead, tin, lapis lazuli and other precious stones she needed for her considerable output of metal objects – whether weapons of war or jewellery for the statues of her deities. A system of open and well-

[1] 'The Ur jewellery', *Iraq*, XXII, 1960, p. 108.
[2] 'The mechanics of ancient trade in western Asia', *Iran*, III, 1965, pp. 1–7.

guarded trade routes was, therefore, essential for the arrival of regular caravans from sources which may have been many hundreds of kilometres distant and necessitated the use of many different forms of transport by sea, land and river.

Unfortunately, we have few commercial texts from the Sargonid period which afford the kind of detailed information given to us by the tablets of the Third Dynasty of Ur or the Isin-Larsa periods. Yet the texts relating to expeditions undertaken by Sargon into Anatolia (although we still do not know the location of the city of 'Purushkhanda' where Sargon sent assistance to merchants, presumably of Akkadian origin, who needed protection) suggest that the search for raw materials in Anatolia began long before the establishment of a regular 'colony' of Mesopotamian merchants which is known from the excavation of the *kārums* at Kültepe and Boğazköy.[1] Single or small groups of prospectors must have been visiting the rich sources of copper at Ergani Maden in the Taurus mountains and other sites in Anatolia during the Early Dynastic period and it may well be that the occurrence of jewellery of Mesopotamian type in Anatolia and Transcaucasia towards the end of the third millennium was due to the activities of early explorers and traders. The subject is beset with difficulties, as we still do not know the exact sources for the copper or the gold used by the metalsmiths of the Sargonid period. If we assume that in the early part of the Sargonid period smiths could smelt copper and tin to make bronze and were not just using ores with a natural tin content, then the search for tin must have led traders to Transcaucasia and Iran and the way would be prepared for the diffusion not only of metal tools and weapons, but also of easily portable objects such as gold jewellery. It is also possible that the spread of Mesopotamian techniques in gold work was due to the widespread search for raw materials into areas previously unvisited by Early Dynastic merchants. Local centres of gold-working in Anatolia and Persia situated near the source of gold would then naturally be stimulated and influenced by the opening up of contact with the urban centres in the Tigris-Euphrates valley.

The site of Troy affords a good illustration of this point. Whether the importance of Troy was due to her position and control of the trade in tin with central European sources in Bohemia or to the shipment of Transcaucasian gold to the Aegean, it cannot be denied that Mesopotamian influence is present in the remarkable gold treasures discovered by

[1] See Güterbock in *J.C.S.*, XVIII, pp. 1–6, 1964, for a reference to Sargon crossing the Euphrates and defeating the troops of Ḫaḫḫum.

Schliemann in 1873 which almost certainly date from the end of Troy IIg (see p. 48). The gold work which was found in a Sargonid context at Tell Brak in north Syria is especially important in this connection. It will be treated in detail on p. 27. Here we may note that the development at Brak of a distinctive form of spiraliform jewellery and the use of the technique of granulation (both known in the Early Dynastic period at Sumer) suggest that it was by the sea routes from the north Syrian coast that the knowledge of these intricate techniques reached the craftsmen at Troy. Similar gold work is found at Poliochni on Lemnos and vessels travelling between the north Syrian coast and the Troad (by keeping close into the coast of Anatolia and using the harbours of Mersin and Antalya and the numerous anchorages of Lycia and Caria) could have covered the distance in perhaps as short a time as four weeks. There is, as yet, no definite evidence for the use of the route through the Cilician gates or up the Calydcadnus valley in Sargonid times as a link between Brak and Troy, but future excavation may well show that these land routes were also used (see p. 63). As far as we know at present it seems that the easiest route for the land trade between Mesopotamia and Anatolia at the end of the Early Dynastic III period and during the Sargonid period was the road which later linked Ashur and Kültepe, although recent finds at Kültepe dating from the end of the third millennium which show close connections with Sargonid work at Brak suggest that other routes were also open. Sargon's Anatolian campaigns were probably undertaken not only to keep open existing routes, but also to find new ways of obtaining the raw materials needed in Mesopotamia.

There are several indications that there was a serious shortage in the supply of both gold and tin at the end of the Sargonid period. The crude hammered copper axes found in the Sargonid graves at Ur, when compared with the well-made bronze weapons with cast sockets of the preceding period, suggest that either the supply of tin had failed at the source or that the routes connecting the mines with the manufacturing centres in Sumer and Akkad had become unsafe for caravans. Naram-Sin's campaigns in the Zagros mountains may well have been due to the need to open up routes for the import of tin from sources in Azerbaijan or Elam. There are also signs of economy in the use of gold in jewellery work. Beads of the Sargonid period at Ur are made of a thin gold covering over a core of copper or paste, the earrings are smaller and beads and pendants of minute size became popular. An increased use of silver suggests that this precious metal was easier to obtain than gold. But, in spite of these difficulties, it must be emphasized that one of the distinguishing marks of the Sargonid period is the spread of Mesopotamian influence into Anatolia, Persia, Transcaucasia and the Caucasus, so that the foundations were laid for the dispersion of Mesopotamian metal types, including tools, weapons and jewellery.

Jewellery from the Persian and Russian Talish region

The material from the site of Vadjalik in the Persian Talish[1] is of importance, both for assessing the evidence for early contact between Mesopotamia and north-western Persia and also for a study of the Talish material in relation to surrounding areas. Tomb 4 at Vadjalik was intact and had not been disturbed in antiquity. It included a lance head, two bracelets of bronze and twenty-five intact pots, of which four have been identified by Professor Schaeffer at the Musée de St Germain-en-Laye.

The excavators mention a small bronze vase 'en form de ciste' which contained a necklace of carnelian, rock crystal, gold and electrum beads (pl. 15a). One lapis lazuli bead also occurs on this necklace, which is preserved in the Musée de St Germain and provides a clue to the foreign relations of the inhabitants of this remote valley of north-west Persia. But it is the electrum and silver beads of coiled wire which are remarkable, as they are of the same type known at Ur in Early Dynastic and Sargonid graves and provide important evidence for some kind of direct contact between smiths in Sumer and north-west Persia during the Sargonid period. Schaeffer has dated the grave to the earliest period he has identified in the Talish region (Talish Moyen 2100–1900 B.C.), but it could be slightly earlier than this. The curious bronze pins, with wide heads, can be compared with the typical Sumerian racquet-headed pin with rolled-over top (Type 5, p. 13), of which examples are known from Ur (Early Dynastic and Sargonid periods) and also from Tell Brak (again in a Sargonid context). The stone mace head could be based on the spiked bronze mace head from Ur, again pointing to Mesopotamia. Two earrings (or spiral hair-rings) of electrum can also be paralleled in Mesopotamia at Ur in the Sargonid and Third Dynasty of Ur period[2] (pl. 15a, fig. 14a).

In the Russian Talish region some beads allegedly from Djönu deserve attention (pl. 15b). This is a string of four beads of which one is of lapis

[1] *D.P.M.*, VIII, pp. 238 ff., and Schaeffer, *Strat. Comp.*, p. 424, pl. LXI.

[2] A necklace with similar electrum and copper beads is shown by J. De Morgan, *La Préhistoire Orientale*, fig. 207, but the only surviving bead is illustrated by Schaeffer in *Strat. Comp.*, pl. LIX.

lazuli and another of gold. The gold bead is the distinctive flat winged disc type (see p. 8) and is the only example of this type I have been able to find among the material from the Russian and Persian Talish areas now in the Musée de St Germain.[1] Its occurrence with lapis lazuli is important and provides evidence for trade connections from north-west Iran to Afghanistan along the route passing through Tepe Hissar in northern Iran.

JEWELLERY FROM SELECTED SITES IN MESOPOTAMIA AND NORTH SYRIA

Ur – Sargonid period graves

The site of Ur is especially important for a study of the jewellery of the Sargonid period, as recent work on the Royal Cemetery has shown that it is possible to subdivide this period into Early, Middle and Late Akkadian. An attempt can also be made to study not only the development of certain distinctive types from the beginning of Early Dynastic III until the end of the Sargonid period, but also to distinguish other types whose use can be confined to Akkadian times. In the original Ur publication, Woolley summarized the changes in dress and costume which can be seen in the Sargonid graves and Dr Nissen's recent exhaustive study of the tombs of the entire cemetery has thrown further light on the problem of the survival of Early Dynastic bead types into the Sargonid period (see p. 2). While it is not yet possible to say whether the new types of jewellery were introduced at the beginning or towards the end of the period, future work on the grave groups should be able to show whether the change in fashion was a gradual process – as seems to have been the case where bronze and copper tools and weapons are concerned – or whether the new types can all be dated to the beginning of the period.

We can, however, be certain that definite changes can be observed and it is, as Woolley has pointed out, in the headdress of both sexes and in the earrings worn by the women that these changes can best be illustrated. In the Sargonid period 'the women's elaborate headdress with its festooned gold ribbons and wreaths of gold pendants set on strings of lapis and carnelian beads which was so common in the earlier time has completely disappeared and so has the *brīm* (bead and chain headdress) usually worn by the men.'[2] In the case of a woman of the upper class, an oval plate of

[1] The catalogue mentions two gold beads, but I could only locate No. 33726.
[2] *Ur Excavations*, II, p. 246.

very thin gold or silver was tied across the forehead by threads passing through holes at the end of the oval (pl. 16). A few examples of a similar decoration have occurred in the Early Dynastic cemetery, so that in this respect we can see the working of a consistent tradition. Frontlets were also worn by the men.

Small lunate earrings (distinct from the large types with exaggerated crescents) are another distinguishing mark of the Sargonid graves and, with the exception of the spiral hair-rings known also in the earlier graves and the thin gold ribbons holding the oval plates in place, the absence of ornament on the head is a specifically Sargonid phenomenon. In contrast to this, the necklaces of the Sargonid period are extremely numerous and can be distinguished from the earlier period by the lavish use of precious stones, including many varieties unknown in the Early Dynastic period. Armlets of beads and metal bangles in gold and silver occur in many female (and some of the male) graves, while the straight pin and not the curved variety survives from the earlier period to fasten the cloak on the shoulder. Flat disc beads of winged and diamond shape (Types 16 and 19 – see fig. 6) are also a distinguishing mark of the Sargonid period (pls. 17, 19).

Frontlets or diadems (pl. 23)

Frontlets of thin gold or silver plates, oval or rectangular, worn across the forehead and attached to the head by 'two pieces of very narrow gold ribbons (fig. 14b) about 15 or 20 cm long . . . wound round two bits of hair which, starting over the ears, were brought one above the other horizontally across the forehead, just above the oval frontlet and so pinned in position.'[1] There are three types (see fig. 13a–c) of frontlet which are pierced at each end.

Sargonid grave groups, with diadems and important bead and pendant types, are as follows:

P.G. 717 contained three oval diadems, one with a rosette chased in the centre (Baghdad No. 7518). The wire was twisted and threaded through the holes in each end (see also pl. 16, B.M. 122241, from Early Dynastic grave P.G. 1054, where the wire is drawn out from each end).

P.G. 1335 (pl. 23) is a typical Sargonid grave group with frontlet and four necklaces.

[1] *Ur Excavations*, II, p. 246.

P.G. 1284 (pl. 22) is noteworthy for the triangular disc beads and necklace with double spiral pendant; a type known in the preceding Early Dynastic period.

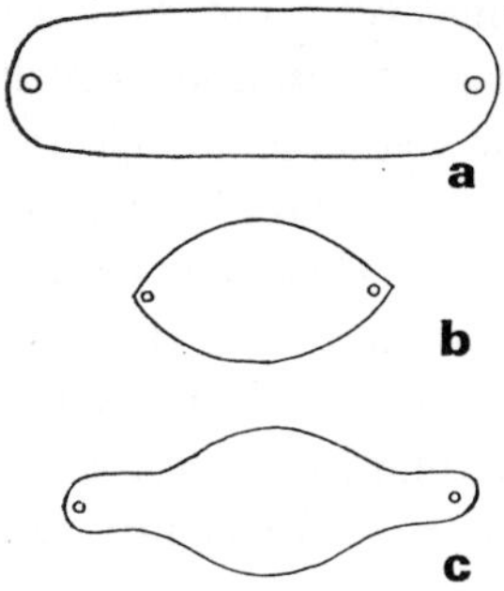

Fig. 13. Gold frontlets from Ur.

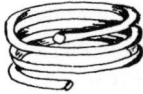

Fig. 14. *a*, gold hair-ring; *b*, hair ribbon; from Ur.

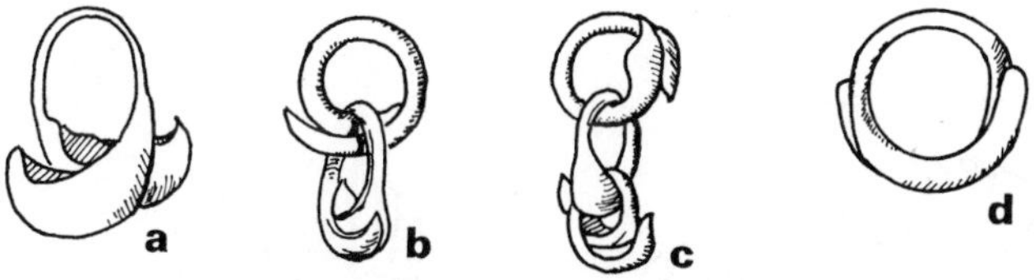

Fig. 15. Gold earrings from Ur.

Hair-rings (fig. 14)

Hair-rings were made of thin spirally coiled wire, usually two or sometimes three coils. Gold or silver (P.G. 666, B.M. 1928.10.10.287 and Tomb 1422 – see p. 65). Hair-rings of this type were found on the heads of men as well as women in Sargonid graves.

Earrings (fig. 15)[1]

Small lunate earrings of gold, silver or copper were often interwoven and worn together. This is typical of Sargonid graves. Fig. 15a, two crescents joined by a thin gold wire, occurs in Sargonid graves (P.G. 465). Figs. 15b and c show two- and three-linked lunate earrings which are also Sargonid. Pl. 17b shows a fine example (B.M. 122234) from P.G. 465 of silver and gold earrings (fig. 15b type) linked together. Fig. 15d, in origin an Early Dynastic type, but smaller, was made with the crescents hollow or made of gold sheet over bitumen core (P.G. 666, U. 9602, B.M. 121568; P.G. 666, U. 9601, B.M. 121568, pl. 18a; P.G. 703, U. 9814, B.M. 121371, pl. 19c,

[1] *Ur Excavations*, II, pl. 219, Types 2–5.

with gold hair-ribbon and frontlet). Solid examples are more rarely found; pls. 18b and 19b are exceptionally heavy.

An interesting series of terracottas comes from Tell el Wilayah, Iraq, and has been published by Tariq Madhloom in *Sumer*, 1960 (fig. 16b). They show that the large hollow crescentic earrings typical of the Early Dynastic period were used as models for earrings on terracotta female figurines, many of which from Wilayah, Ashur (fig. 16a, c; fig. 17), and Tell Asmar (fig. 18a and b) can be dated to the Sargonid period. Most of these are extremely crude with jewellery such as necklaces or a head-dress decorated with a snake-like band, sometimes intertwined (figs. 18a and 16c). None of these terracottas was made in a mould and they can be compared with the later examples dating to the Third Dynasty of Ur, Larsa and Old Babylonian periods when moulds were frequently used (see p. 87).

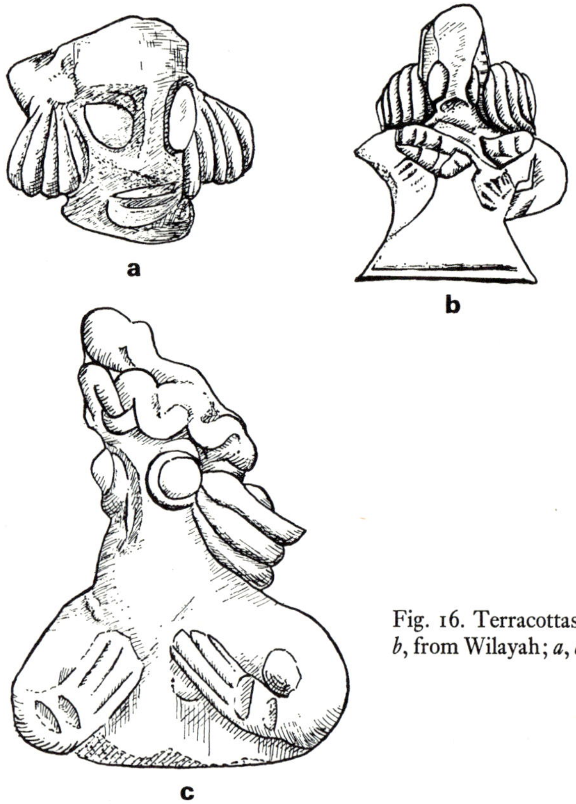

Fig. 16. Terracottas:
b, from Wilayah; *a*, *c*, from Ashur.

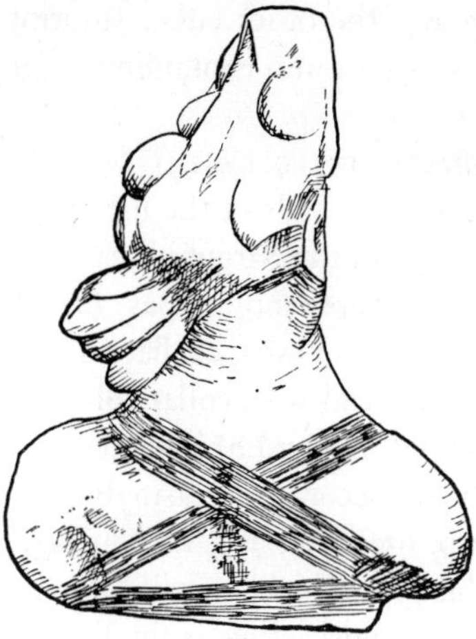

Fig. 17. Terracotta from Ashur.

Fig. 18. Terracottas from Tell Asmar.

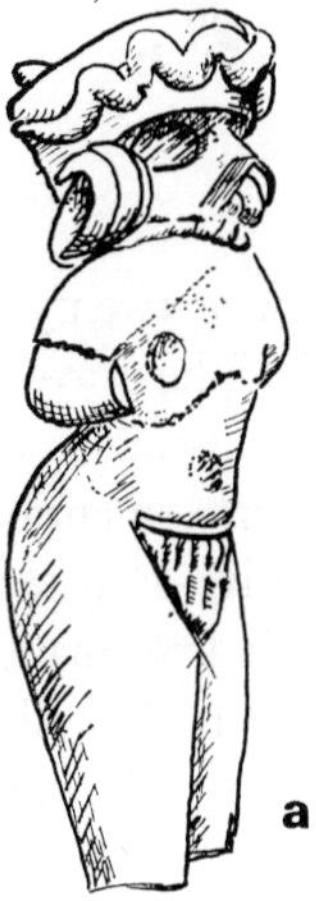

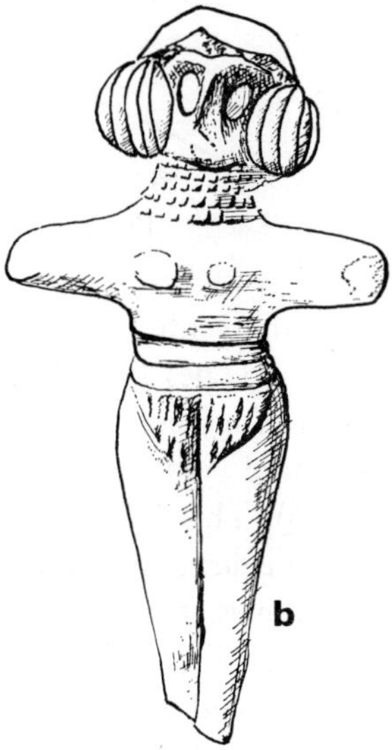

Pins (cf. fig. 24, examples from Tell Brak)

Pins are straight, with plain shafts, or were pierced through the stem through which a string could pass for use as a toggle. A bead or cylinder seal was sometimes attached to the end; this fashion is illustrated by the shell plaques from Mari. In other cases Woolley suggests that the string could have been attached to the edge of the cloak or garment and the pin (a copper pin of Woolley's Type 1 – R.T. pl. 231) could pass through the loop and the other edge. Imprints of strings were found on pins from P.G. 193, a tomb containing a Sargonid seal.

Beads (pls. 17, 19, fig. 19)

Among the beads in the list on p. 9, three distinctive types can be noted as typical of the Sargonid period – Types 16, 19 and 20 – and to these must be added three more types: (*a*) a bead described by Woolley as a lunate (fig. 19a) or V-shaped flattened bead; (*b*) the flanged bead (pl. 20); (*c*) globular bead with collar (pl. 21).

(*a*) (fig. 19a and b) Stone beads usually of agate, fitted with gold caps at each end become increasingly popular in the Third Dynasty of Ur period (see p. 65). P.G. 717, now in Baghdad, contains a fine example of a bead of this type which we will call a gold-capped bead (the term V-shaped, or lunate, is misleading as the P.G. 717 example is in fact flat double-conoid

a b

Fig. 19. Beads from Ur.

in shape). It is the centrepiece for a necklace (U. 9825) of twenty-two gold disc beads of Types 16 and 19 and six crystal beads. The grave also contained a seal of mature Agade style, a pair of small bag earrings (cf. fig. 15a) and three gold diadems, one with chased rosette, mentioned above (cf. pl. 16). This collection of jewellery is instructive as it shows two types: the diadems and disc beads which, although first made in Early Dynastic times, became typical for the Sargonid period; and the gold-capped bead, a distinguishing mark of the Third Dynasty of Ur, here appearing in a Sargonid context.

(*b*) The flanged bead. This is simply a developed form of Type 16, the flat disc bead, with the addition of two further 'wings' or flanges to make four wings each side of the central tube. It is not a common type, but five good examples were found in Grave PJ/G 65a, now in the British Museum (B.M. 123594–see pl. 20). This necklace consists of two nasturtium seed, six carnelian date-shaped and four lapis lazuli date-shaped beads, together with one lapis lazuli cylinder bead. This developed form is important, as it is the prototype for the flanged beads from Alaca (see p. 44). For examples of the same type known on the famous necklace of the priestess Abbabashti of the Third Dynasty of Ur period, see pl. 45.

(*c*) Globular bead with well-marked collar (pl. 21). Sargonid grave P.G. 1464 contained four gold beads unique at Ur.[1] They are globular in shape and fitted with a circular flat gold collar at each end. The surface of the bead is decorated with curvilinear incisions; they were found together with one agate bead of cat's eye type and one carnelian barrel. The material included a frontlet, U. 13508 (Pennsylvania 31.17.80 – cf. fig. 13b), small lunate earrings (U. 13510, Pennsylvania 31.17.78 – cf. fig. 15a), a copper vessel (*Ur Excavations*, II, pl. 233, 15), pottery (*Ur Excavations*, II, pl. 255, 76) and a hammered axe (*Ur Excavations*, II, pl. 226, 19). It is possible that this grave should be dated towards the end of the Akkadian period; this type of hammered axe continues into the Third Dynasty of Ur period and Harriet Crawford has convincingly shown that it was not until the Late Akkadian or post-Akkadian (i.e. Guti-Gudea) periods that cast axes were completely superseded by the hammered type.[2] The cat's eye bead would also point to a date later than middle Akkadian.

Type (*a*) is discussed again on p. 75, for its relations with the Transcaucasian barrow graves in Trialeti. Type (*c*), well known in the second millennium in Babylonia and Syria, here occurs for the first time in Sumer.

Bracelets or Bangles

The term bangle is used here to denote a ring of gold or silver, solid or beaten over a core of bronze, bitumen or other material. This can be distinguished from a bracelet, which could be made of several beads strung together and worn round the wrist. Few examples of metal bangles are known before the Sargonid period; they cannot be found on Early Dynastic statuary or reliefs, but occur in the recently discovered treasure from Mari.

Tell Brak

The site of Brak lies about one and a half kilometres from the west bank of the river Jaghjagha and this enormous mound covering about 120 acres was excavated by Professor Mallowan during three campaigns from 1935 to 1938. The occupation dates from the Jamdat Nasr period, c. 3100 B.C.,

[1] See also *Nippur*, I, pl. 150, for a gold bead of this type in a stratified Akkadian level.
[2] *The Archaeology and History of the Early Dynastic Period in Iraq*. See p. 2 above.

through the Early Dynastic and Sargonid periods, until the site was abandoned around 2000 B.C. There is also evidence of occupation during the Third Dynasty of Ur period and in the first half of the second millennium. The Sargonid levels are the important period for the jewellery and, owing to modern methods of excavation used at this site, we have a vitally important collection of gold and silver jewellery found in stratified contexts and also published in great detail in the excavation report. The main architectural discovery of the Sargonid levels was the great palace or barracks of Naram-Sin identified by the inscribed bricks of its founder and designed as a military fortress of considerable strength. As Mallowan has pointed out, its position was strategically placed about half way between Anatolia, the source of the metal ores needed by the Sargonid monarchs of Mesopotamia, and the areas in Iraq and Persian Kurdistan where Mesopotamian armies were extending the influence of the powerful Akkadian kings. Brak also illustrates the widespread trading contacts between the Tigris valley, the Persian Gulf and the Mediterranean, and the jewellery is especially important as evidence for this contact because – combined with the other metal objects, pottery and seals – it suggests that there must have been a considerable dispersal of craftsmen from Mesopotamian centres spreading new technological achievements into Syria, Anatolia and Persia.

Mallowan has stressed the fact that 'the few gold objects discovered (in the palace) were but small tokens of the considerable wealth which must have once been housed in the palace.'[1] Especially characteristic of the period is the series of clay pots buried beneath the floor of Sargonid houses lying to the east of the palace. Two important groups of jewellery which can be described as treasures were probably buried for reasons of safety before the destruction of the city at the end of the Akkadian period.

Earrings

Fourteen examples of the earrings show slight variations, but most can be compared with types known from Sargonid graves at Ur. They can be divided into simple lunate types (pl. 24a), ribbed lunate (pl. 24b), double-ended lunate (pl. 24c) and penannular with flattened ends (pl. 24d).

Fig. 20, with broad lunate ends, deserves especial attention here. This distinctive form is also known at Ur (see fig. 45, Chapter 4), where the lunate body of the earrings is also split into two separate lobes and the pin

[1] *Iraq*, IX, 1, 1947, p. 67.

is curved and pointed. A comparable earring has recently been found in a grave on the mound at Kültepe by Professor Özgüc (see p. 47 and pl. 37a).

Fig. 20. Double lunate earring from Brak.

A heavy hair-ring from Brak is comparable to Third Dynasty period examples from Ur (pl. 26 and pl. 46d, Chapter 4).

Pendants

(*a*) Circular pendants with suspender strips (pl. 27). A necklace from the treasure found inside a clay pot in Room 12 on the north side of the Sargonid houses on site CH 'belongs by stratification to the last phase of occupation of these levels and may date to the end of that epoch and the turn of the Third Dynasty of Ur'.[1] Eleven circular pendants form an important feature of this necklace which also included gold and silver beads (see below), a glazed steatite cylindrical bead and two serrated discs of lapis lazuli. A mould for circular pendants found at Brak is shown in pl. 28. The gold coil pendants are 'composed of a holder made of strip gold, rolled at the top and fashioned to admit the threading of two strings of beads: the gold rings supported by the suspender strip consist of four concentric coils of gold wire, alternately plain and twisted, held together by tightness of juxtaposition and in places by gold solder. The lower string of beads apparently consisted of little silver disc beads and a few lapis lazuli disc and cylindrical beads. The order was in part given by a section of the necklace which had remained fixed in position owing to corrosion, and this consisted of nine silver disc beads flanked on one side by a lapis lazuli cylindrical bead and on the other by a lapis double conoid.'[2] The centres of these pendants are hollow, but a small gold circular disc was found in the same treasure and fits into the centre of the pendants (see pl. 29). A complete circular pendant of identical type and technique was found at Kültepe with the centre disc (pl. 68); a silver example from Naram-Sin's palace at Brak and another from Tell Asmar belong to the same class.[3] A silver disc decorated with repoussé lines belongs to the Early Dynastic period (fig. 23).

[1] *Iraq*, IX, pl. XXXV and p. 177. [2] Ibid., pp. 177–8.
[3] Ibid., pl. LIII, 26; and Frankfort, *O.I.C.*, 17, fig. 29.

(*b*) Circular pendants with central suspension. A silver boss pendant (fig. 21a), with a flattened rim decorated with a repoussé dot design was found in the hoard discovered in a grey burnished clay cup buried underneath a beaten mud floor of the Sargonid period in Room 6 on Site E.R.[1] This is hemispherical with hollow inside and across the centre there is a loop for suspension, diameter 2·5 cm (Troy II–III has produced related pendants, though of conical shape).[2] In the same house there was a Sargonid-inscribed clay tablet listing cattle, sheep, goats and a pot of wine which suggests that the owner of the hoard was a man of property who may have been an official of the palace or city of Brak. Professor Mallowan has discussed in detail the significance of the discovery of this treasure and the tablets found in the same house, and it is in this treasure that the vitally important minute silver bead with four spiral ends was also found (fig. 22a – see Type 5 below).

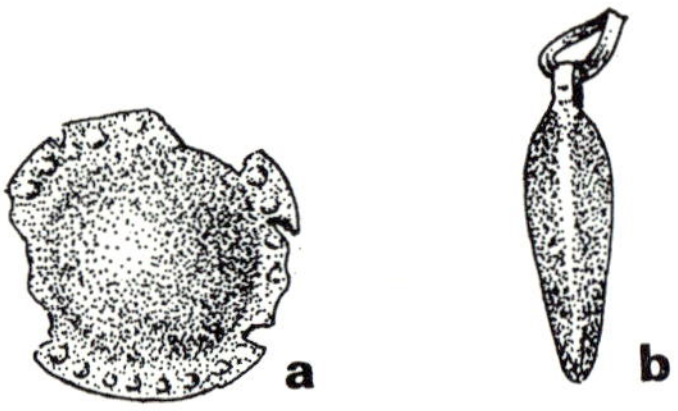

Fig. 21. Pendants from Brak: *a*, silver; *b*, gold or electrum.

(*c*) Lanceolate type (fig. 21b). A gold or electrum lanceolate pendant was found in the same treasure in Room 6. It is made of 'two strips folded over and soldered, leaving at one end a loop to which is attached a gold wire suspender. Length of pendant 2·7 cm, length of loop 0·6 cm'. This unusual type occurs, as Mallowan has pointed out, at Tell Asmar in the hoard from the Agade palace[3] (see p. 33).

Beads (pl. 30)

Six main types can be distinguished among the Brak jewellery:

Type 1 Heavy gold double conoid with sub-spherical ends (pl. 30).
Type 2 Plain double conoids (pl. 30).
Type 3 Flat winged disc – gold and silver (fig. 22b).
Type 4 Barrel and ball beads – gold and silver.
Type 5 Minute quadruple spiral – silver (fig. 22a), width 1 cm.
Type 6 Ring with minute balls soldered on in granulation technique – silver (fig. 22c).

[1] *Iraq*, IX, pl. XXXIII, 11, p. 176. [2] Schmidt, *Sammlung*, p. 236, Nos. 5964–5.
[3] Frankfort, *O.I.C.*, 17, fig. 29, middle pendants in top row.

Of these, Types 1, 2 and 4 are all known from Ur in both Early Dynastic and Sargonid graves, while Type 3 – the disc bead – is important, as at Ur it is confined with two exceptions to Akkadian and Third Ur graves. Type 5 (fig. 22a) – 'a flattened cylindrical tube vertically perforated,

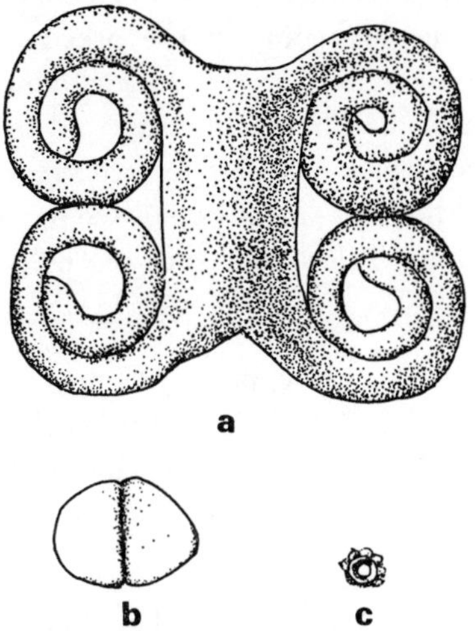

Fig. 22. Beads from Brak: *a*, quadruple spiral, silver; *b*, unfinished winged disc, silver; *c*, ring with granulation, silver.

drawn out at the end to form four spirals or scrolls in continuous pairs on either side of the central tube'[1] – has been discussed in detail by Mallowan (see also p. 34, for discussion of this type and Type 3, the flat disc bead (fig. 22b), which is often associated with it).

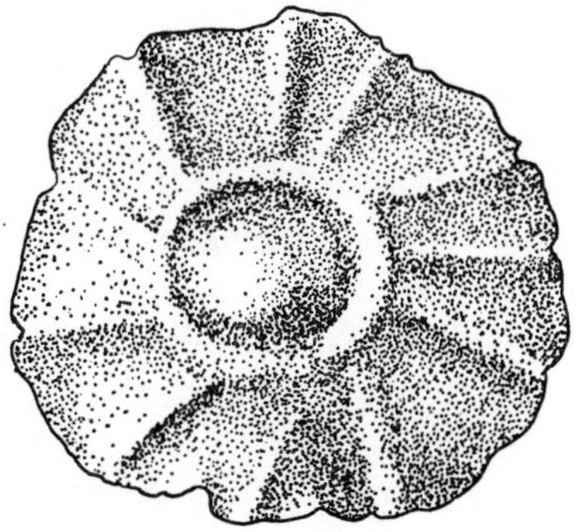

Fig. 23. Silver disc from Brak.

Pins (fig. 24)

The pins found at Brak were all made of copper and are included here as they are important in providing stratified dating evidence for similar

[1] *Iraq*, IX, p. 171.

pins of copper (or bronze), gold and silver which are found in Syria and Palestine. Four types can be distinguished and each has been discussed in detail by Mallowan with a full bibliography of the parallels from other sites. Excavations and publications since the date of the excavation of Brak have also provided more evidence to reinforce Mallowan's conclusions concerning the importance of the Brak pins in the process of diffusion – whereby the products and techniques of Mesopotamian metalsmiths spread across north Syria to the Phoenician coast and then southwards into Palestine and northwards into Anatolia (for occurrences of toggle pins in Syria (Til Barsib) and the coast site of Byblos see p. 105, Chapter 7; and for Megiddo and other Palestinian sites see p. 107, Chapter 7).

Type 1 (see catalogue descriptions, Brak, *Iraq*, IX, p. 166) Copper pin, length 11·5 cm. Conical top, upper part of shank flattened and perforated for use as a toggle. Found in a Sargonid house (fig. 24a).

Type 2 Copper pin, length 10·8 cm. Low conical head, upper part of shank flattened and perforated for suspension. The head is much smaller than Type 1. Found in debris of Naram-Sin's palace (fig. 24b).

Type 3 Copper pin, length 11 cm. Bulbous or low conical head; straight, unperforated shank. Found on the Sargonid floor of Room 14 in Naram-Sin's palace, adjacent to some broken fragments of Sargonid tablets. This type is known in the Early Dynastic period in Sumer, but its use in the Sargonid period is firmly established (fig. 24c).

Type 4 Copper pin, length 8·3 cm. Rolled top, shank unperforated, circular in section. This type was also used in the Early Dynastic II period in Mesopotamia and the Brak example is dated probably to the end of the Early Dynastic II period (fig. 24d).

An example of a 'racquet' pin (fig. 24e) was said to have come from Tell Aswad, but a small example was also found in the Sargonid level at Brak. This has already been mentioned as an important type which seems to have been exported to Vadjalik in the Talish area, but other types from Brak – the toggle pin, Type 1, and the pin with rolled-over head, Type 4 – also reached Transcaucasia and the Talish region (see p. 20).

Tell Asmar

The jewellery from Tell Asmar was found during the 1932–3 season of the Oriental Institute of Chicago excavations[1] and was discovered in the Akkadian palace beneath the floor of the large room (16 E16). A large disc of silver filigree and smaller silver discs used as spacers are similar to those found at Ur in gold dating from Early Dynastic III period, while the carnelian, onyx and lapis lazuli beads can also be paralleled at Ur. The hoard included three fine animal-shaped pendants (one representing the

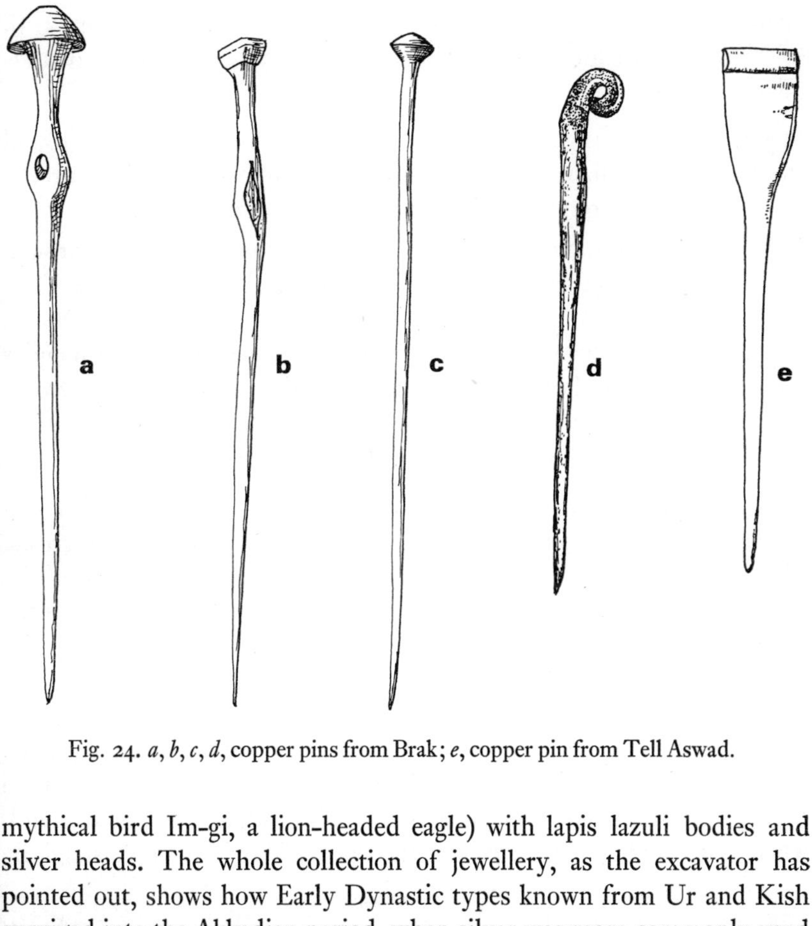

Fig. 24. *a*, *b*, *c*, *d*, copper pins from Brak; *e*, copper pin from Tell Aswad.

mythical bird Im-gi, a lion-headed eagle) with lapis lazuli bodies and silver heads. The whole collection of jewellery, as the excavator has pointed out, shows how Early Dynastic types known from Ur and Kish survived into the Akkadian period, when silver was more commonly used than gold.

[1] Frankfort, *O.I.C.*, 17, fig. 29. See also *O.I.C.*, 16, fig. 31.

QUADRUPLE SPIRAL AND FLAT WINGED DISC BEADS

Quadruple spiral beads (gold and silver) were studied in detail by Professor Mallowan in the Brak publication[1] and little can be added to his remarks about the minute silver example (measuring 1 × 1 cm) which was found in a treasure hoard beneath the floor of the Third Dynasty of Ur period (fig. 22a). Since this date, however, a few more sites can be added to the list; notably the gold example from Kültepe (see p. 44 and fig. 29b, Chapter 3) and an isolated example from Mari (pl. 34, see Chapter 3). At Mari the two main types of quadruple spiral beads can be distinguished:

Type 1 The Brak type. Made from a flat piece of gold sheet bent round to form a flattened tube with the four ends drawn out and wound into four spirals in pairs each side of the central tube.

Type 2 The quadruple spiral is made by twisting the gold wire through and round a central tube (see fig. 113). These are typical of the mid-Assyrian graves at Mari and associated with flat disc beads. Examples belong to the second millennium and include examples from Lchashen, Lake Sevan in Russian Armenia, an example from Lothal and sites in north-west Persia such as Marlik, Ziweye and Amlash (see below).

The association of these beads with flat disc winged beads was noted by the writer in 1963[2] and the jewellery from the Lchashen Sevan barrows, which also contained quadruple spiral and flat disc beads, has been discussed by Culican.[3] Unstratified examples in silver of the flat disc beads from Byblos are in the British Museum (pl. 31). Many problems arise from this evidence.[4]

It has been already pointed out (p. 3) that the use of beads for dating purposes is dangerous and apt to produce extremely misleading results. Jewellery with a particular magical and amuletic significance is apt to become the treasured possession both of individuals and deities and, when a city or temple was attacked, the small gold objects would stand the

[1] *Iraq*, IX, 2, pp. 171 ff. [2] *A.J.*, XLII, 1, 1963, pp. 141 ff.

[3] *Iraq*, XXVI, 1, 1964, p. 38, fig. 1.

[4] See *Iraq*, XXVI, 1, 1964, pp. 36 ff., for references to Transcaucasia and Iran. For Lothal see F. A. Durrani, *Selected Archaeological Material from Harappan sites and their Mesopotamian correlations*, unpublished M.A. thesis (University of London, 1962).

best chance of surviving the depredations of despoilers, as they could be easily buried or carried away by fugitives from the sack. Moreover, hoards of jewellery often contain beads of many different periods and so can only give us a *terminus ante quem* for the find. But, in spite of these difficulties, certain facts emerge from a study of the distribution and dating evidence for these beads. Spiraliform jewellery seems to have been first made in gold from two pieces of twisted coiled wire; examples from Ur, Brak, the Troy treasures, Ashur Grave 20 and Kültepe suggest that this type continued in use in Assyria, Syria and Anatolia during Sargonid times. It became especially fashionable in the period of the Third Dynasty of Ur. The dated examples are often associated with the flat winged disc bead (Ur, Ashur Grave 20, Troy Treasure A, Hissar IIIC) and it seems that spiral jewellery must have had an amuletic significance of such importance that the demand, based on certain fundamental religious concepts, continued throughout many centuries. In Mesopotamia, it is possible to argue that a connection with the goddess Ninhursag implied a fertility significance; its occurrence outside the area of Sumerian and Babylonian religious beliefs might still be due to the efficacy of the magical powers with which it was endowed and its occurrence in Iran at Tepe Hissar in the treasure of IIIC may well attest Babylonian influence.

Although the origin of the quadruple spiral motif may well lie in Iran, it can certainly be found as early as the Jamdat Nasr period in Mesopotamia; a seal impression from Brak portrays a seated figure in front of a gigantic double spiral.[1]

While at Brak we can see the development of the Early Dynastic form, at Troy and Poliochni local smiths elaborated the idea of the double or quadruple spiral designs in a fashion which – although skilled – seems barbarous when compared with Sumerian prototypes. The gold-workers at Alaca were less open to Mesopotamian influence than the Trojan craftsmen, yet the quadruple spiral bead occurs there, together with a local development of the flat disc bead which is given four instead of two wings. Kültepe seems to have been in closer touch with Mesopotamian centres and recently excavated graves have yielded pendants and earrings which can be paralleled at Brak and in the Sargonid graves at Ur (see p. 47). The occurrence of both quadruple spiral beads and flat disc beads at Lothal and Hissar is not surprising; the first reflects the extensive Persian Gulf trade between Mesopotamia and the Indus valley, for which

[1] *Iraq*, IX, 2, 1947, p. 128, pls. XIX, 15, and XXIV, 8, for Jamdat Nasr alabaster seal and Early Dynastic seal impression.

we now have considerable evidence and which seems to have begun in the Early Dynastic period; the latter was probably due to the extensive trade in lapis lazuli between Badakshan and Sumer via the Iranian plateau. Hissar must have been an important entrepôt on the route from Afghanistan to the west.

The question of Transcaucasia and the Talish is not so easy to explain as the dating evidence is uncertain. First, however, we must discard the quadruple spiral bead from Veri in the Russian Talish. This is, as far as one can judge from the published drawing, a different type from those discussed above. It is more related to the Mycenean relief beads and probably belongs to the latter part of the second millennium B.C. The flat disc bead from Djönu of Type 1, however, has to be considered along with the instances of Mesopotamian earrings and pins in Transcaucasia and the Caucasus, to which attention was first drawn by Frankfort as early as 1931.[1] Since then the Russian excavations in Trialeti and the chariot burials at Lchashen[2] have provided us with important evidence for the early and mid-second millennium B.C. and can assist in any attempt to consider the extent of Sumerian influence on Transcaucasian metallurgy and reciprocal Transcaucasian-Mesopotamian contacts. In this problem the question of granulation is of prime importance.

THE TECHNIQUE OF GRANULATION

The earliest datable instance of this intricate and highly skilled technique is in the Ur Cemetery from Pu-abi's grave, P.G. 800, where 'a fine example of minute craftsmanship in the latter (i.e. granulation) technique is afforded by a gold ring measuring only 0·2 cm in diameter and composed of six gold balls sweated together'.[3] Unfortunately, I have been unable to identify this piece in the collections in London, Baghdad or Pennsylvania. A crude form of granular decoration was also used on the sheath of the gold dagger from P.G. 580, yet – while the technique was certainly known in the Sargonid period – the available evidence suggests that it is possible to trace a continuous history for the development of this technique in

[1] Frankfort, *Archaeology and the Sumerian problem* (Chicago, 1932). This question should now be studied in the light of published and unpublished Russian excavations.

[2] For a recent assessment of the dating evidence from Lchashen, see Piggott in *P.P.S.*, XXXIV, 1968, pp. 285 ff.

[3] H. J. Plenderleith in *Ur Excavations*, II, p. 297. See also E. A. Smith, 'Solders used by the goldsmiths of Ur', *Discovery*, January, 1930.

Mesopotamia which was probably spread by Sumerian goldsmiths to the Mediterranean coast at Byblos (see p. 102).

Examples of this technique from Susa and Giyan suggest that knowledge of the skill reached Trialeti in Transcaucasia via Persia. The dating of the Trialeti barrows is discussed in Chapter 4 and the Lake Sevan jewellery must be considered in this context. The jewellery contained examples of both quadruple spiral (Type 2) and flat disc beads. Lchashen has also produced the only known occurrence of the quadruple spiral beads with granulated decoration and also large round beads finely decorated with granulation. Similar large spherical granulated beads found in the barrow graves of Trialeti (see p. 75) may date as early as the Third Dynasty of Ur period or the early centuries of the second millennium.[1] That the Lake Sevan jewellery cannot be far removed in date from the Trialeti barrow containing gold work and jewellery is evident; it is possible that the knowledge of the technique of granulation spread to Transcaucasia during, or soon after, the expansion of Assyrian commercial interests at the time of the Third Ur period and continued throughout the period of the First Dynasty of Babylon.

Contacts between Anatolia and Transcaucasia may have been responsible for the sudden flowering of the goldsmiths' work in Trialeti and other areas of Transcaucasia; if it could be proved that local Transcaucasian mines were being worked as early as the second millennium B.C., this would explain the production of so many fine pieces of gold and silver work in this area, which was relatively far removed from the centres of civilization. It must also be remembered that Russian Armenia, although a mountainous and difficult region, is linked by the valley of the river Khram and a route which, in ancient times, may have followed the course of the modern Tiflis to Leninakan-Kars road, whence the route to Kültepe or Assyria is fairly straightforward.

[1] The same technique occurs on comparable beads in the National Museum at Athens, from Tiryns, Chamber Tomb 28.

CHAPTER 3

Anatolia
2500-2000 B.C.

INTRODUCTION

The question of Mesopotamian influence on the goldsmiths of Anatolia during the Sargonid period has been discussed in general terms in the preceding chapter; here we shall attempt to consider the question of the relationship of gold jewellery from Troy and other rich finds,[1] such as Alaca (see p. 46), with Transcaucasian material from the Trialeti area discussed in Chapter 4. In 1954 Frankfort related Anatolian gold work and jewellery to Mesopotamia in the following terms: 'Everywhere (in Anatolia) the products of the smiths and jewellers betray a greater or less dependence on the brilliant achievements of the Third Early Dynastic period in Sumer, and the influence of southern prototypes is noticeable, although they were not slavishly copied.'[2]

New evidence calls for a slight amendment to this statement and we can add that this influence continued into the early part of the second millennium B.C. Sites such as Alaca illustrate Frankfort's point easily, but it is also possible to demonstrate the homogeneity of the western and central Anatolian schools of jewellery working and the strength of the local traditions. The close connections between western centres such as Troy and Poliochni are easily discernible; there are only a few pieces of jewellery from central Anatolian sites apart from Alaca, yet other metal artifacts from Horoztepe (Tokat vilayet) and Mahmatlar (twenty-five kilometres south-east of Amasya) enable us to relate the Alaca gold work to the products of sites in the Pontic region.

2500–2250 B.C.

The period discussed in this chapter covers the Anatolian Early Bronze period, beginning c. 2500 B.C. or later and ending c. 2000 B.C. – i.e. at a

[1] The Dorak treasure is not considered here, as no photographs are available.
[2] Frankfort, *A.A.A.O.*, p. 113.

time shortly before the end of the Third Dynasty of Ur period in Mesopotamia. The chronology of the period in Anatolia has been discussed in the *Cambridge Ancient History* (Fasc. 8) by Mellaart[1] and an examination of his arguments from a Mesopotamian historical point of view is useful. The historical framework provided by the Mesopotamian evidence is especially relevant here and can help in many ways for understanding the complex problems arising from the study of Anatolian metal work and jewellery dating from the end of the Early Bronze II period.

If we take the accession of Sargon as 2371 B.C. and the reign of Naram-Sin as 2291–2255 B.C., it is evident that the date of 2300 B.C. proposed for the destruction of Troy II would have taken place a short time before the reign of Naram-Sin during the time of Rimush or Manishtusu – while the later date of 2200 B.C., also proposed, would fall during the time of the Guti invasions of Babylonia and about the time of the beginning of the Second Dynasty of Lagash and, therefore, probably before the reign of Gudea (c. 2150 B.C.). Arguments for the earlier date can be based on later texts which present a confused picture of revolts occurring at the beginning of Naram-Sin's reign, where the rebels are said to have come from regions extending from Anatolia to the shores of the Persian Gulf (in one list the rebels include Anatolian 'kings'). But, as Gadd has so clearly shown, Naram-Sin must have campaigned for many years in Syria and the north-west and the mention of the town of Talkhatum (known from later business documents of Assyrian merchants engaged in Cappodocian trade) does suggest that unsettled conditions in Anatolia required Naram-Sin's armies to put down revolts and keep open the trade routes. Gadd summarizes the position: 'It will hardly be too much, therefore, to believe that Naram-Sin exercised some authority, however incomplete, over districts in the south-east of Asia Minor, where his grandfather before him had accomplished the same phenomenal march which Naram-Sin or his flatterers heralded as a pioneer effort.'[2]

Now Mellaart has suggested that the activities of the invaders who destroyed the city of Troy IIg can be detected in the destruction levels of Poliochni, Beycesultan (Level XIIIa), Kusura B, Ahlatlibel, Polatli, Tarsus and over one hundred other sites; he has also pointed out that the Cilician plain is one of the areas where there was a great decline in the number of settlements at this time. It is certainly conceivable that an invasion on the scale envisaged by Mellaart, starting from the north-west and continuing as far to the south-east as the Cilician plain, would have

[1] *C.A.H.*, No. 20, pp. 43 ff. [2] *C.A.H.*, No. 17, pp. 28–9.

important secondary effects; Naram-Sin's campaign in Syria and possibly Anatolia may well have been related to this event.[1]

It is, however, possible to argue that the date of 2300 B.C. for the end of Troy II allows very little time for the spread of the influence of Sargonid goldsmiths in Troy and that one should allow for 'a lag of a century for the diffusion of Mesopotamian metal objects', as Mallowan suggested in his account of the excavations at Tell Brak. The establishment of the great palace by Naram-Sin at Brak, with bricks bearing his name, in order to collect and store the tribute collected from surrounding regions may well have coincided with the spread of Mesopotamian influence in Anatolia and the activities of Sargonid traders at Troy. A period of one hundred or perhaps fifty years was not too long in which to learn the advanced Mesopotamian technical methods and to adapt them to their own needs. The palace at Brak was destroyed at the end of the Sargonid period (probably not before the end of Shar-kali-sharri's reign, c. 2230 B.C.) and this destruction, in Mallowan's opinion, may well be attributed to the Gutian invaders of the Sargonid empire.

More evidence is badly needed to tell us whether the 'Troy IIg invaders' were ultimately responsible for creating the conditions resulting in the descent of the Guti into Mesopotamia and the incursions of the 'Amorite in Bashar' which necessitated Shar-kali-sharri's campaigns in north Syria – probably between the Khabur and Balikh rivers. The mention in a text chronicle relating to Naram-Sin of the foreign enemy, the 'Umman Manda', which seems to denote a hoard of foreign barbarians, and the mention of the town of Purushkhanda, are also suggestive. Gadd has pointed out how the descent of the 'Umman Manda' apparently started from somewhere in the north-west, for the 'course of its devastation is a great sweep from the city of Purushkhanda, seemingly the town in Asia Minor where Sargon made his epic march, and continuing south-eastwards until it swept over Gutium itself, over Elam, and did not end before it had overrun also the lands beyond the Persian Gulf, Telmun, Magan and Melluhha.'[2]

It is also important to remember that there is evidence of Hurrian penetration, presumably from the mountains of east Anatolia, into Mesopotamia as early as the Sargonid period, as we know that there were Hurrian workers at Nippur and that they were already settled in north Mesopotamia: a settlement which may have also been prompted by the 'Umman Manda' invasions from the north-west. However, if we take the

[1] See Mellink in *Anatolia*, VII, 1963, pp. 101–15. [2] *C.A.H.*, No. 17, p. 40.

beginning of the Gutian period at 2250 B.C. in the reign of Shar-kali-sharri and allow for the possibility that their raids may have started in the reign of Naram-Sin, a date for the destruction of Troy IIg at about 2250–2100 B.C. is possible (arguments for dating the end of Troy IIg to a period corresponding with the first part of the Isin-Larsa period in Mesopotamia – c. 2023–1830 B.C. – are discussed on p. 17).

2250–2000 B.C.

After Troy, the key sites in Anatolia for any study of jewellery are Alaca and Kültepe, as it is from these sites that we have numerous examples of the products of goldsmiths from graves and tombs which have escaped looting in antiquity, while the important sites of Beycesultan in the west and Tarsus in the Cilician plain afford invaluable stratified evidence for the dating of certain distinctive types. Any conclusions based on this material must of necessity be tentative, because the site of Kültepe is still in the course of excavation by Professors Tahsin and Nimet Özgüc – the earliest levels here are yielding evidence which will be of great importance for the vexed problem of the date of the 'Royal Tombs' at Alaca. We shall, therefore, not discuss in detail the various views expressed by scholars on Alaca, but note that the results from Kültepe suggest that Özgüc's opinion (first published in 1957[1]) that the Alaca graves must have covered a period of more than one generation and scarcely more than two – i.e. about one hundred years – is reinforced by recent evidence and that his date of 2200 or 2150–2050 B.C. is more reasonable, in the author's opinion, than earlier dates proposed by other scholars.

Özgüc's excavations at Horoztepe provide important evidence for the chronology of this period and there is no serious objection to his statement in the final Horoztepe publication: 'that the tomb at Horoztepe is contemporary with or a little more advanced than the latest tombs at Alaca höyük. If we take the level Ib at *kārum* Kanesh as c. 1840 the highest date we should like to propose for the tomb at Horoztepe is 2100 B.C. This figure in our opinion may have to be lowered slightly but hardly raised.'[2] The discovery of a tablet of the Assyrian king, Puzur-Ashur II, at the *kārum* level II is vital evidence for the dating of this level at not much later than 1850 B.C. and reinforces Özgüc's suggestion of c. 2100 B.C. for the date of the tomb at Horoztepe.

Mellaart has suggested[3] that the movement of peoples responsible for

[1] 'Objects from Horoztepe', *Belleten*, XXI, No. 82, 1957. [2] Özgüc, *Horoztepe*, p. 58.
[3] *C.A.H.*, No. 20, p. 33.

the destruction of Troy IIg, Beycesultan XIIIa and the sites of this period in south-west Anatolia, the Konya plain and Cilicia did not affect central and Pontic Anatolia and, therefore, the dynasty buried in the Royal Tombs at Alaca could have been brought to an end by the users of the earliest painted Cappadocian pottery. This pottery is known in all its phases at Kültepe and future work there will no doubt elucidate many problems concerning the identity of the makers of this pottery. For Alaca it is important to remember that the jewellery, while showing some links with western Anatolian work, is remarkable for its local character and its lack of Mesopotamian influence. This is not surprising if, as seems probable, Mesopotamian influence in Anatolia temporarily ceased during the unsettled conditions of the period of the Guti invasions c. 2200 B.C. Circumstances would not have been conducive to trading expeditions or the movement of smiths or craftsmen. Even if trade did continue and the routes leading to Kültepe were being used, Alaca could have been left in a comparative backwater, its links being – as Özgüc has suggested – with the Pontic sites, rich in metal objects. Kültepe, as we shall see in Chapter 6, p. 101, later shows connections with north Syrian centres, which also seem to have by-passed Alaca.

JEWELLERY FROM SELECTED SITES

Alaca

Pins and clasps

Six main types of pins can be distinguished:

(*a*) Fluted, six wings – gold (pl. 32a).

(*b*) Date-shaped, fluted spiral – gold (pl. 32b). Tomb K.

(*c*) Globular and studs (figs. 25a and b). Tomb K.

(*d*) Plain globular – silver (fig. 26a).

(*e*) Double spiral – gold and silver (fig. 26b). Tomb K.

(*f*) Hammer head – silver. Tomb H. Two examples, length 13·3 cm and 10·9 cm.

All the above types were of solid gold cast in two parts, with the exception of types (*e*) and (*f*). One example of (*c*) has a silver shank and a gold head decorated with jade knobs capped with gold. The body of the head is deeply incised round the base of the knobs. A second (fig. 25b) has a head of rock crystal and is decorated with four gold studs in the form of a cross; a third (fig. 25a) has a bronze shank covered with silver

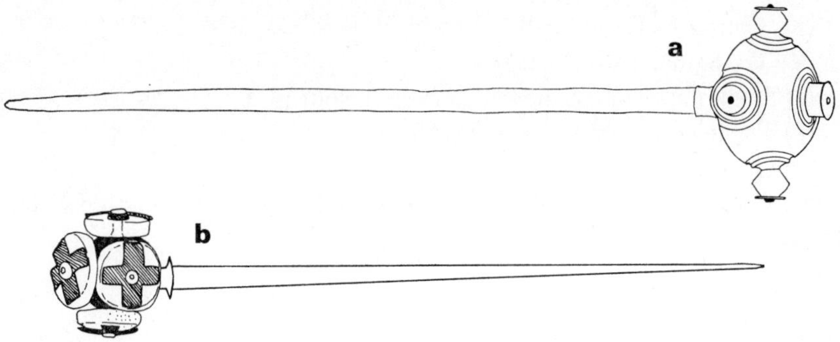

Fig. 25. Pins from Alaca: *a*, silver over bronze, gold and carnelian head; *b*, gold and rock crystal.

and a gold and carnelian head. The techniques used on the pins combining gold, silver and precious stones are notable in that the jewellers were apparently unaware of the more intricate techniques of cloisonné inlay and granulation. Both of these decorative methods were used with great skill by the jewellers responsible for comparable beads and pins from Trialeti (see p. 75, Chapter 4) and future work in Transcaucasia may provide a link between the Alaca and Trialeti jewellery.

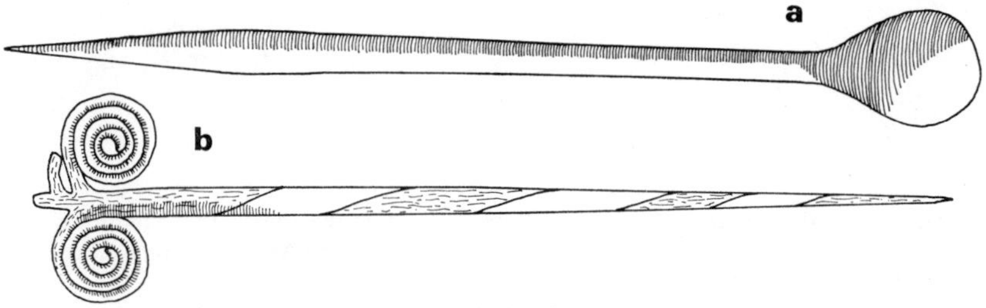

Fig. 26. Gold pins from Alaca.

The clasps were often found with the pin *in situ*, placed through two holes. The centre and circular wings of the clasp were usually decorated with seven repoussé circles enclosing a central dot, each circle within a pattern of small repoussé dots (pl. 33).

Necklaces, beads and pendants

The main types of bead can be summarized as follows:

(*a*) Cruciform (fig. 27a).

(*b*) Star-shaped. This is composed of diamond-shaped segments (fig. 27b and c).

(*c*) 'Cotton reel' (fig. 27d).
(*d*) Triangular with flat base.
(*e*) Small flat pendant pierced at base (colour pl. C).
(*f*) Triple cotton reel (colour pl. C).
(*g*) Quadruple disc beads (fig. 28).
(*h*) Quadruple spiral bead. Twelve examples. Average length 1·6 cm (fig. 29a – see also pl. 34 from Mari and p. 34).

Fig. 27. Gold beads from Alaca: *a*, cruciform; *b*, *c*, star-shaped; *d*, cotton reel.

Necklaces were often composed of examples of one of these types only or, as in colour pl. C, two different types were combined with large flat round pendants decorated with repoussé dots and the base pierced for suspension. The quadruple disc bead (fig. 28) and quadruple spiral

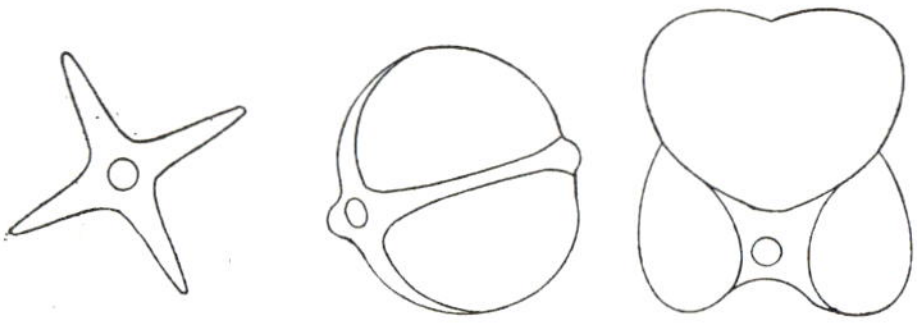

Fig. 28. Quadruple disc beads from Alaca.

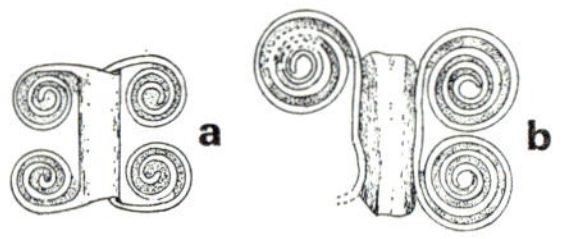

Fig. 29. Quadruple spiral beads: *a*, from Alaca; *b*, from Kültepe.

bead (fig. 29) are both related to Mesopotamian Early Dynastic types which became common in the Third Dynasty of Ur period. The quadruple spiral bead was made in one piece from a flat oblong piece of gold sheet bent round to form a flattened tube with the four ends drawn out and wound into four spirals in pairs on each side of the central tube. The minute quadruple spiral bead from Kültepe has been published and studied by Özgüc[1] and is especially important for the method of manufacture which is extremely crude technically. Fig. 29b shows how the wires were soldered to the edge of the central tube. Horoztepe has produced one example of a flat round pendant similar to the Alaca example.

[1] Özgüc, *Horoztepe*, pl. XIX, 8, p. 58.

Headbands or 'diadems'

These were worn by men and women and five main types can be distinguished:

(*a*) Plain gold band.

(*b*) Plain band with repoussé 'blobs' round edge. Joined by two rivets behind.

(*c*) The diadem is composed of four rows of open work forming a pattern of diagonal crosses. Width 1·4 cm. From Tomb H.

(*d*) Narrow band composed of one row of open work diagonal crosses with each end twisted and then cut into two long separate strips.

(*e*) Plain band with ends tied as in Type (*d*) ending in four strips (fig. 30). Width of band 1·2 cm. Thickness of gold diadem 0·1 cm.

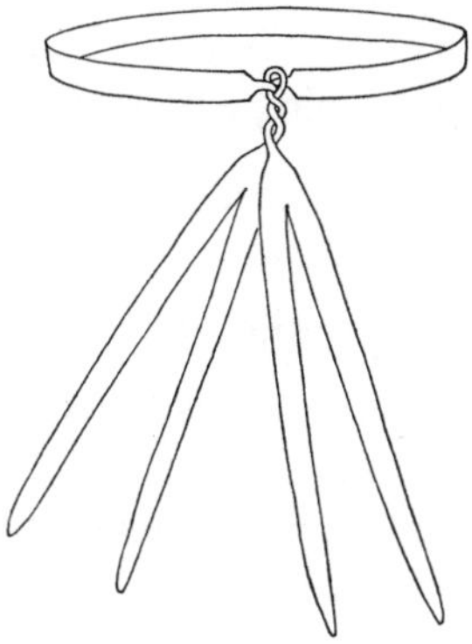

Fig. 30. Gold headband from Alaca.

Bangles

These are not common at Alaca but one pair is cast solid and is decorated with deep incisions (pl. 35).

'Lock rings'

Small curved rings, usually blunt at one end, have been called lock rings and this rather unsatisfactory term will be used here until definite evidence as to their use is forthcoming. At Alaca they were found near the heads of the skeletons and it has been assumed that strands of hair were threaded through the rings and the open ends were designed to facilitate the threading. One would expect these ornaments to be light in weight, so that they would keep easily in place but, although the standard type (fig. 31a) is made of plain thin gold wire, another type (fig. 31b) is made of solid gold with deeply incised decoration on the surface.

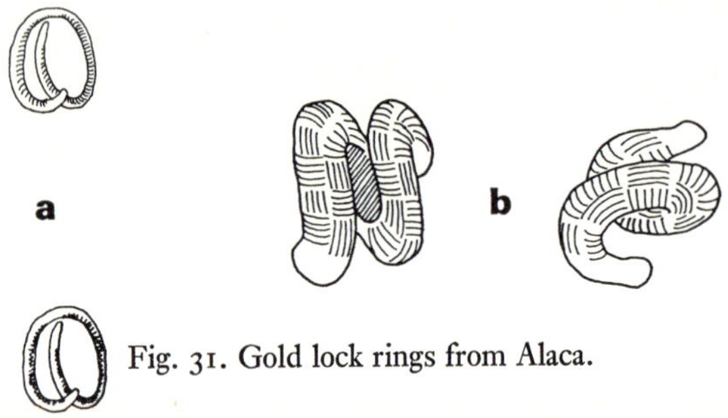

Fig. 31. Gold lock rings from Alaca.

Double violin-shaped female idols (pl. 36)
Made from a single sheet of gold, the eyes, breasts and navel indicated by repoussé bosses, with two circular holes probably intended to facilitate attachment to a garment or as holders for nails. They can be compared with the series of marble idols known from Kültepe and other sites in Anatolia.

Alaca and Pontic sites – Maikop and Tsarskaia

The question of possible trade connections between Alaca and the north Caucasian sites has often been discussed; Özgüc has written, 'there are undeniable similarities in jewellery, in weapons and in some of the bull and deer figurines.'[1] He has also established the importance of the Samsun–Ordu–Tokat–Amasya area of northern Anatolia as the centre of the production for the metal objects found in the Alaca tombs. There is strong evidence that this view is correct and it then becomes possible to envisage trade contacts across the Black Sea between the Caucasian sites of Maikop and Tsarskaia, which can be dated to c. 2200–2100 B.C.[2]

Among the jewellery from these sites, the long narrow gold diadem decorated with gold rosettes and the plain gold earrings may well have been imported across the Black Sea, as there is not yet evidence of local gold-working in this area at the end of the third millennium B.C. Gimbutas has, however, shown that there is evidence of working of copper from local ores at this period and the Alaca hammer pin – a rare type at Alaca – may have been copied from the Caucasian copper prototypes. A distinctive thick gold earring (or hair-ring) from Tsarskaia (Gimbutas, *Prehistory*

[1] Özgüc, *Horoztepe*, p. 59.
[2] Gimbutas, *Prehistory of E. Europe*, pp. 58, 91; and in *Chronologies*, p. 492. Piggott, *Ancient Europe*, p. 82.

of E. Europe, fig. 30, 8) could also have a local copper prototype from Kislovolsk (ibid., fig. 38, 10), where several examples were found. This type with narrow slit occurs in Palestine at Ajjul (Petrie, *A.G.*, IV, pl. XV) where it is described as a hair-ring–the slit being only wide enough for hair to pass through.[1] It is interesting that Tsarskaia shows connections not only with Hissar and north-west Iran, but also with Ras Shamra in north Syria; if Tsarskaia – as Gimbutas suggests – is later than Maikop, a possible connection with the Ajjul gold work is not impossible. The rosettes on the gold diadem are comparable with those of the Ajjul diadem and, together with the hair-rings, may indicate a possible connection with Palestine and Egypt.

Kültepe

The recently published finds from Kültepe near Kayseri in central Anatolia are of the greatest importance as evidence of contact between Sargonid Mesopotamia and Anatolia long before the establishment of the first Assyrian merchants at the *kārum* of Kültepe. Graves on the city mound, dating from the lowest level C of Özgüc's Early Bronze period, contained 'objects utterly foreign to central Anatolia.'[2] Two pieces of gold jewellery, an earring of Mesopotamian type (pl. 37a; see also fig. 45, Chapter 4) and a gold circular disc (pl. 37b), also comparable with examples from Brak, Ur (pl. 38) and Uruk, could either have been imported or have been made by goldsmiths from Mesopotamia who had travelled to Anatolia and settled at Kültepe where the raw material may have been easier to obtain than in their original home. The discovery of a large building of megaron type – probably a palace (or possibly a temple) – shows that the rulers of Kültepe at this period were sufficiently prosperous to attract foreign craftsmen. Other imported goods, such as pottery of Syrian type, show them able to organize the trade routes so that caravans could travel between central Anatolia, Cilicia, north Syria and Mesopotamia in reasonable safety, without interruption by invading bands of marauders.

Kültepe provides evidence for catastrophes such as burning, but these were of a scale which does not seem to have interfered seriously with the development of civilization at the site. It seems that the transition from

[1] Exactly similar rings are known in Ireland, where they are regarded as a form of currency. Several examples are in the National Museum, Dublin. See A. Hartmann, *Prähistorische Goldfunden aus Europa* (Berlin, 1970), Taf. 14.

[2] 'Early Anatolian archaeology in the light of recent research', *Anatolia*, VII, 1963, p. 13.

the Early Bronze Age to the Middle Bronze Age, starting about 1900 B.C., shows a continuous and gradual development and the choice of this site by the Assyrian merchants as a suitable place to found a trading colony, or *kārum*, must have been due to the importance of the site as an administrative and metallurgical centre. The excavations, still in progress, conducted by Professors Tahsin and Nimet Özgüc on the mound at Kültepe and in the neighbouring *kārum* have enlarged our knowledge not only of the early and later Hittite periods, but also of the important earlier Bronze Age period.

Troy

The jewellery from the treasures found by Schliemann at Troy is remarkably homogeneous and many of the types found in the Great Treasure A can be found in the smaller hoards. Any detailed description of this jewellery is unfortunately hampered by the fact that very little Trojan jewellery survives today (there is a small collection in the National Museum at Athens, the gift of Madame Schliemann, and part of the three treasures stolen at the time of excavation in 1873 is now in the Museum at Istanbul, together with pieces found in the excavations conducted by the University of Cincinnati by Professor Blegen between 1932 and 1938). Blegen's opinion that the treasures should be assigned to Troy IIg is followed here. The entire collection in Berlin, displayed in the Kaiser Friedrich Museum prior to 1939, disappeared in 1945. The following descriptions are, therefore, entirely based on the few pieces in Athens and Istanbul, Schliemann's detailed descriptions, my visit to Berlin in 1931 and the catalogue of the Schliemann collection published by H. Schmidt in 1902. This latter publication includes many additional drawings, photographs and descriptions and needs to be studied with the accounts of the actual excavation of the treasures given by Schliemann, in order that an attempt can be made to study this extraordinary collection of gold work as a whole.

Earrings

(*a*) Basket earrings (figs. 32 and 35) decorated with applied rosettes or rows of granules mounted on a narrow strip, to which small flat circular pendants or leaf-shaped pendants are attached. There are many different varieties of this basic form, which can be seen with pendants missing in pl. 39; the developed type has five or six long chains or wires threaded with small gold leaves supporting triangular-shaped stylized idols decorated with punched dots and shows considerable variety in both shape and decoration. Four magnificent and complete examples of the developed form were found in the large Treasure A and are illustrated by photographs in the catalogue (Schmidt, *Sammlung*, p. 234, Beilage II). The granulation work is extremely fine and the rosettes often contain a small circle of granules.

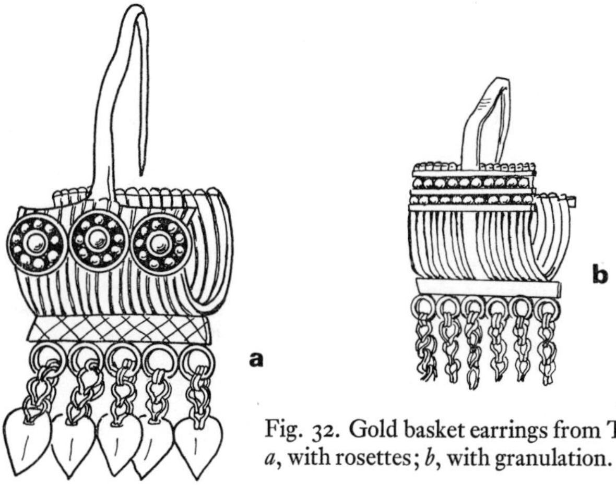

Fig. 32. Gold basket earrings from Troy: *a*, with rosettes; *b*, with granulation.

(*b*) Lunate earrings (fig. 33). Fifty-six gold earrings were found in Treasure A and are of great importance for any attempt to date the jewellery in the treasures found by Schliemann at Troy. All the jewellery was found together in a large silver tankard. With the exception of three examples in Athens (Athens Museum 4331–4333), the gift of Madame Schliemann, these can only be studied from Schliemann's drawings, the photographs in Schmidt's catalogue and the original photographs in the Schliemann *Atlas*. Drawings from these photographs are shown in fig. 33, where the main types are illustrated. Some of the simple types are similar to earrings from the site of Poliochni on Lemnos, but the more elaborate examples, including the three in Athens, are decorated with granulation work of a kind unknown in the Early Dynastic period in Mesopotamia and of which we only possess one small bead from Brak from a Sargonid context. Comparable minute granulation work can only be found on earrings dating from the Third Dynasty of Ur period at Ashur and Susa (see Chapters 4 and 5, fig. 46g and pls. 57 and 58). Three main types can be distinguished:

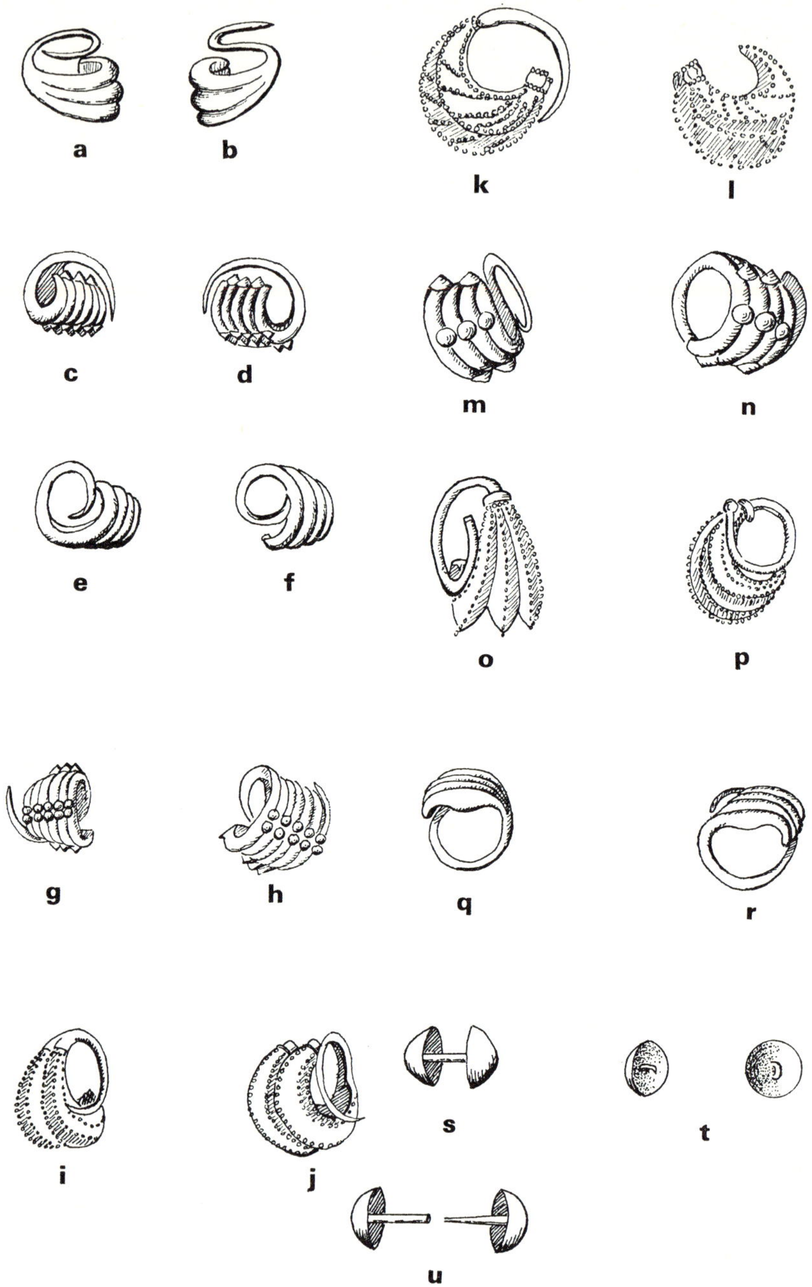

Fig. 33. Gold earrings, studs and buttons from Troy Treasure A.

Type 1 Earring or lock ring. Made from one piece of gold, three lobes ending in a single point (fig. 33a, b, q and r).

Type 2 Solid gold wires, five or more soldered together and one end beaten out and pointed to form a ring. Small pointed blobs of gold in single or double rows were then applied as decoration (fig. 33c, d, g, h, m and n).

Type 3 Lunate-shaped earring with flat-sided lobes decorated with fine granulation. There is a well-marked rib where the pin joins the main body of the earring (fig. 33i and j). There are many variations of this form. Minute granules were applied to the surface of the lobes and along the edges and often there are granules between the lobes. The ring of gold wire was soldered on to the separate gold base of the two or three bossed-out plates, which form the lobes of the earring (fig. 33, o and p).

A unique type of earring from Ur, Tomb 1100, is comparable in technique with the Troy basket earrings. Woolley's catalogue entry is as follows: 'Gold earring, one only; from a spiral ring with lunate ends hangs a second ring decorated with appliqué spirals and striated lines and a pendant fringe with bar and dot ornament.' (*Ur Excavations*, II, pls. 138, 219, U. 11584; Baghdad 8256, 9607; see also fig. 34). The dating evidence for this grave with its gabled wooden coffin does not preclude a date later than Early Dynastic III and the earring may possibly have been the prototype from which the later elaborate Trojan forms were developed. Alternatively, it may be an import to Ur.

Fig. 34. Gold basket earring from Ur.

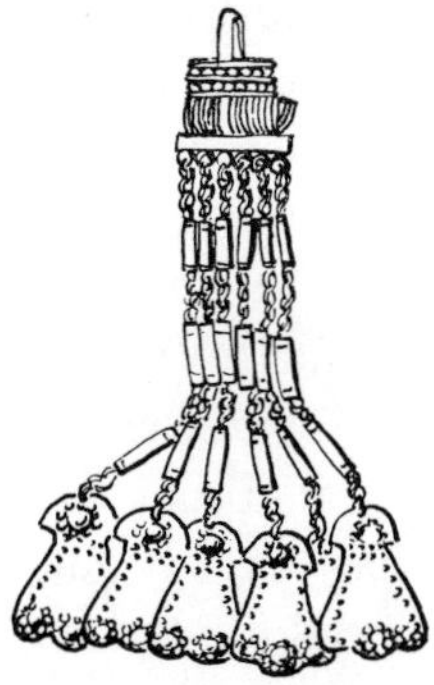

Fig. 35. Gold basket earring with idol pendants from Troy.

Diadems

The two magnificent diadems from the Great Treasure A were made from plain gold sheets; one had elaborate stylized idols as pendants (pl. 40), which are comparable with the pendants on some of the basket earrings (fig. 35); the technique of the diadems and the pendant basket earrings is also similar. One diadem (Schliemann, *Ilios*, 685, p. 455) is 56 cm long with sixty-four gold chains attached to the edge of the diadem strip; lozenge-shaped flat disc winged beads with central tube are threaded on to the chains like gold beads and the stylized idols attached to the end of the chains. The diadem is pierced at each end. The larger diadem (Schmidt, *Sammlung*, 5875 and Schliemann, *Ilios*, 687, p. 457) was distinguished from the smaller by the lancet-shaped leaves fastened to the chains composed of rings of double gold wire (Schmidt, *Sammlung*, Beilage I).

Bracelets

Six gold bracelets, or torques, from the Great Treasure A were found entangled together but were reasonably well preserved (Schliemann, *Ilios*, 689, p. 458). Two pairs were of plain gold – one 0·6 cm and the other 0·2 cm in thickness – with knobbed ends. If worn as bracelets they would easily pass twice round the wrist. Schmidt No. 5942 is made of a piece of quadrangular wire twisted and ending in two hooks. Schliemann describes, but does not illustrate, a sixth made from two pieces of gold wire, twisted in opposite directions, 'then a gold wire was soldered to the twist on each as is evident from the many places in which the soldering was deficient.'[1]

Beads

The figure of 8,700 gold beads was given as the total of the beads from the Great Treasure A and comprised types shown in fig. 36. They show that the Trojan jewellers were capable of fine granular work, in many cases finer than that used on the earrings. It is important to note that the different types catalogued by Schmidt (Nos. 5943–5966) and illustrated here (figs. 36 and 37) were all found in the silver two-handled tankard (Schmidt 5873) with the bracelets or torques, diadems and the fifty-six earrings (fig. 33). Beads found by Blegen in the IIg level (fig. 38) all belong to types already found by Schliemann in the Great Treasure. Several types call for comment:

(*a*) Circular bead with one or two rows of granules (fig. 38c and d).

[1] Schliemann, *Ilios*, p. 458.

(*b*) Flat disc winged bead with central tube, well known among the jewellery from Ur (fig. 38i).

(*c*) Quadruple spiral bead (see p. 35, fig. 37b and pl. 39). These quadruple beads also occurred in two of the smaller treasures (Schmidt D. 5988 and J. 6042).

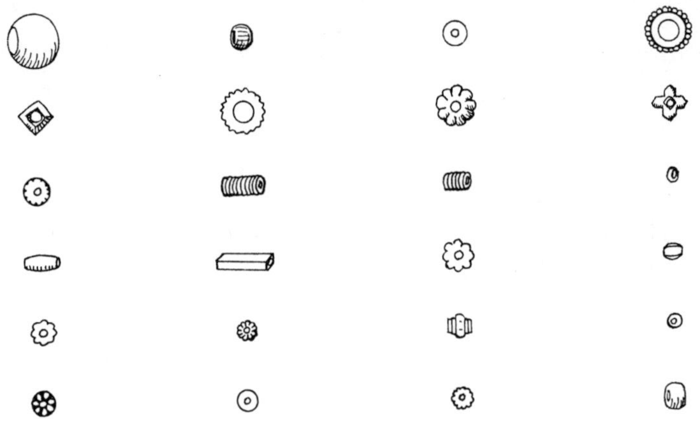

Fig. 36. Types of bead from Troy.

(*d*) Small conical 'beads', better described as buttons, with loop behind for suspension (fig. 37d and e; for a comparable example from Brak, see pl. 25b, Chapter 2).

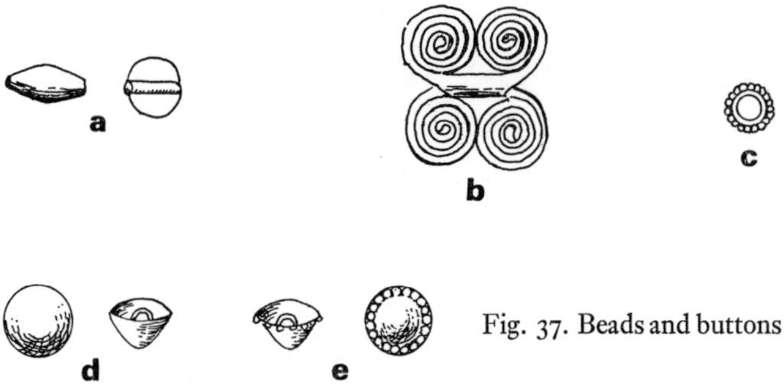

Fig. 37. Beads and buttons from Troy.

Curious studs with conical heads like the buttons described above, but with a hollow tube soldered into one cap and a pin into the other which could be inserted into the tube, also belong to Treasure A. These have been described as earrings; their purpose is not clear (fig. 33s and u).

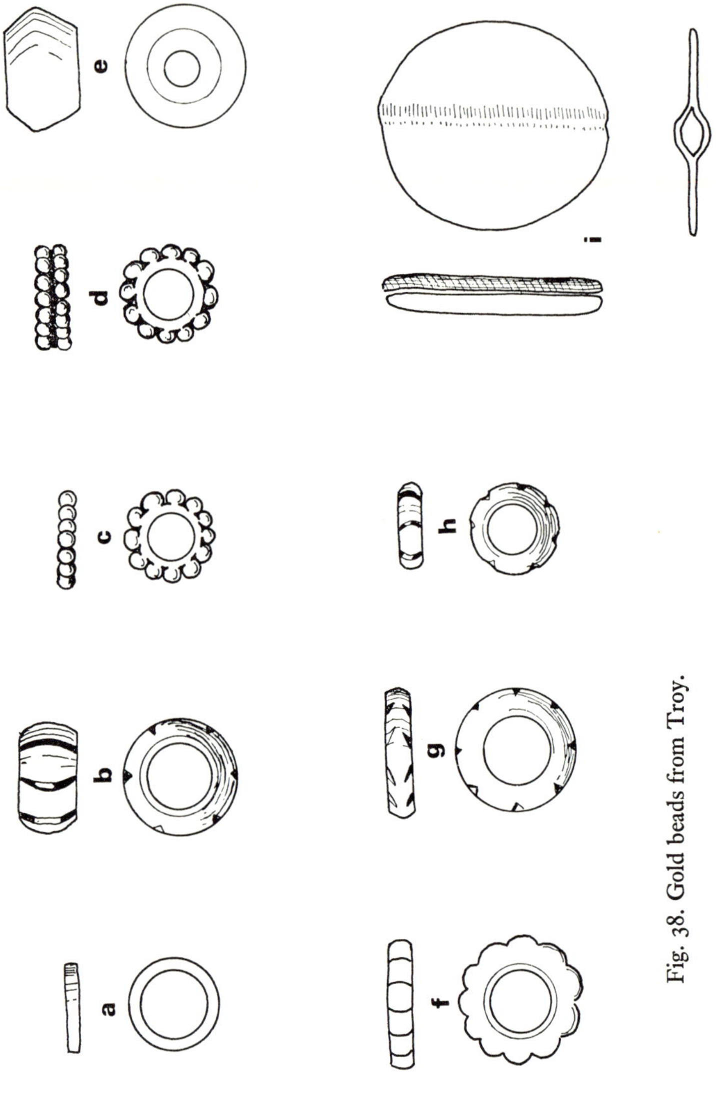

Fig. 38. Gold beads from Troy.

Jewellery from Treasure F

Treasure F contained the two remarkable gold bracelets (Schmidt 6003, Schliemann 873, 874, p. 495) and also included a *depas* (two-handled pottery vessel), basket earrings with lines of fine granulation (Schmidt 6004, 6005), gold lock rings and a bronze (or copper) dagger or lance head with curved tang. From the *depas* protruded sixteen bars of gold, each being 11 cm long, which after analysis turned out to be electrum. Below the gold bars were two basket earrings (Schliemann 842, 843) with rosette decoration, like that on one of the bracelets, soldered to the body of the earring and a unique earring (Schliemann 837) with an appliqué running spiral decoration in gold wire.

The bracelets (Schmidt 6003) were made of thick gold plate decorated in one case with gold, in the other with silver wire, with a design formed by looped double spirals and lines of rosettes (pl. 39). With these bracelets were found large lumps of melted gold and a lump of gold which seemed to have been cut from a bar.

Pins (figs. 39 and 40a and b)

A gold pin with the head in the shape of a squat pot between double spirals made from coiled wire was found by Blegen in room 252 of a

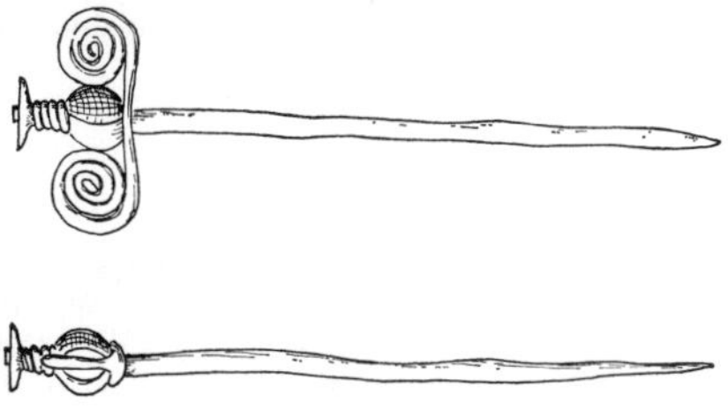

Fig. 39. Silver pin from Troy.

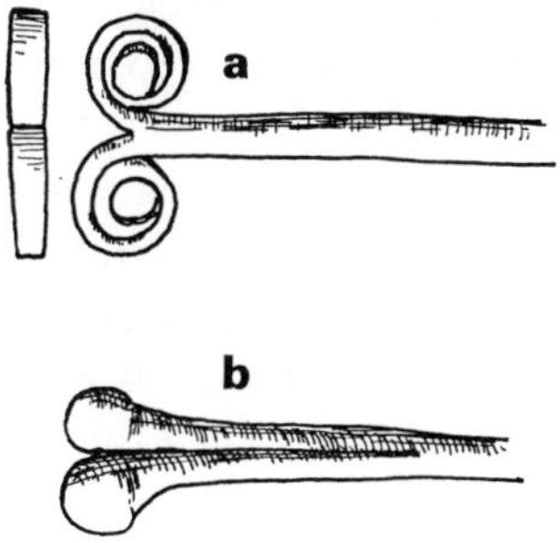

Fig. 40. *a*, bronze, *b*, silver, pins from Troy; *c*, bronze pin from Byblos.

building of the IIg period (see pl. 39 and fig. 39). This belongs to a type of which Schliemann found a comparable gold example, not in a treasure but in a context he considered to be Troy III, i.e. Troy IIg (pl. 39, with four spirals). This was not catalogued by Schmidt (Schliemann,

Ilios, 849) but it is in the Trojan collection in Istanbul along with another double spiral pin found by Schliemann (pl. 39).

Schliemann states (p. 488) that the gold pin with four spirals was found together with another remarkable pin (Schliemann 834, Schmidt 6133). Here, the double spirals form the basis of a rectangular gold mount, decorated with four rows of looped double spirals and supporting six small two-handled pots.

A third pin of gold was illustrated by Schliemann (No. 835; Schmidt, *Sammlung*, 6134). Schmidt says that Schliemann does not describe it but in fact the description, as a 'dress pin', is given on p. 498 (fig. 41). This pin is unique for Troy, the head being formed of a rosette of eleven petals forming cloisons for inlay, with central repoussé boss inside a circular gold setting, flanked by four gold spirals, one pair circling upwards and the other downwards. The skill of the jeweller in making the cloisons suggests that this piece may perhaps be later than the jewellery described hitherto. Schliemann's description is as follows:

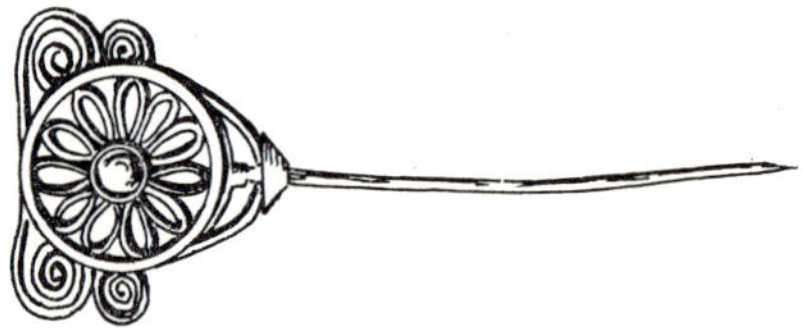

Fig. 41. Gold pin with cloisonné rosette from Troy.

'A small semi-globular gold plate was soldered in the centre, and around it a border of gold wire; then the leaves were formed on gold wire and soldered on symmetrically. When the two discs had thus been decorated, they were joined by a broad flat gold band, which projects slightly over both of them. Then this double disc was soldered on the long pin, the upper part of which is decorated with incisions. The pin was then stuck through a flat gold band, which was soldered on both sides of the double gold disc and coiled at both ends into a spiral with three turns. The pin was further pierced through a small gold disc, which we see soldered below the gold band. Lastly, a gold band was soldered on the top of the disc, and turned on either side into spirals of five turns.'

The importance of this piece is due to the fact that Schliemann states that it formed part of a cache of two earrings, one of which was a crescentic example decorated with granules (see fig. 33, o and p, for the type), and hundreds of flat gold winged disc beads (fig. 37a). From Schliemann's meagre description of the find, little can be deduced except that it is conceivable that it may belong to a period as late as Troy VI.[1]

The simple form of Trojan double spiral pin is shown in fig. 40a in bronze. A silver double club-headed pin, Troy II–V (fig. 40b), can be compared with a bronze example from Byblos (fig. 40c) found in a deposit in Building II, which can be dated post 2000 B.C. – probably mid-nineteenth century B.C.

Foreign relations and the date of the Trojan jewellery

The brief account of some of the more important pieces of the extraordinary amount of gold and, to a much less extent, silver jewellery found at Troy demands an assessment of parallels with other sites. Poliochni on Lemnos is discussed below. The connection between the two sites is undoubtedly close, in both jewellery and the architectural and other material remains. The hoard of jewellery is obviously Trojan in character and although the work there is rougher and some pieces may have been crude imitations of Trojan work, the distinctive earrings with pendants in the form of the calyx of a flower with separate stamens occur at least once at Troy (Schliemann 844, p. 489).

The beads with single and double lines of granular decoration (fig. 38c and d) recall the silver example from a Sargonid level at Tell Brak (fig. 22c, p. 31) and a few interesting comparisons can be made with jewellery from Byblos. Among the bronze pins from Byblos can be found an example with the head in the shape of a pot,[2] comparable with the Troy pin (fig. 39), while a peculiar bronze pin with a double head of two knobs was found at Byblos (fig. 40c) in one of the deposits probably contemporary with the Montet jar, and at Troy in silver (fig. 40b). Another possible Byblos connection is the decoration of rosettes on the magnificent pair of gold bracelets (see pl. 39) found by Schliemann in Treasure F.

The whole question of the relations between Troy and Kültepe needs to be studied from every angle, not solely from the jewellery; here we would like to draw attention to the remarkable silver dagger found in 1878 by Schliemann in the large level IIg megaron or royal palace. This is the same form as the bronze daggers found in the large Treasure A (Schmidt, *Sammlung*, 5842, etc.), and exactly the same type as the dagger found at Kültepe engraved with the name of the Hittite king, Anittas, which can

[1] Schliemann, *Ilios*, pp. 498 and No. 841, p. 489.
[2] Dunand, *Byblos*, II, pl. CLXXIX, 19361, 1930.

be dated to c. 1850 B.C. A lead figurine from Troy (Schmidt 6446) is comparable with the numerous Kültepe examples; the Trojan metal vessels with curled handles which occur in the treasures, together with other examples from the Troad – studied in detail by Bittel[1] – could be regarded as imitations of the more developed examples now known from Kaypinar and Alaca and other examples from the Black Sea area.

The contents of Tomb 20 at Ashur (figs. 46–7) are especially important. This is a well-dated Third Dynasty of Ur group which included, as well as the necklace with quadruple spiral beads, the curious object shaped like a frying pan with ridges round the central boss – a type also studied by Bittel who pointed out that many examples are known from the Troad.[2] The object catalogued by Schmidt as an axe has been identified as the handle of one of these 'frying pans' which Schliemann found in his Treasure A and thought was a shield. The Ashur example (see fig. 47, Chapter IV) is the only instance where the type has appeared outside the Troad; a possible terracotta prototype may perhaps be found at Til Barsib[3] in the large tomb excavated by Dunand, but this can have little chronological significance as this tomb was certainly used over a long period. The Ashur tomb, however, is securely dated and, in view of the history of the early trade relations between Ashur and Kültepe, it is difficult to regard the Troadic 'frying pan' as an heirloom over 200 years old, as it would have to be if a date of 2300 B.C. is taken for the end of Troy IIg.

The Mesopotamian connection discernible in the earrings from the large Treasure A is also relevant when considering the date of the Trojan jewellery and is one of the many different reasons for postulating a lowering of the date of the end of period Troy IIg. From a purely technical point of view, the pairs of earrings shown in fig. 33j, k and l are the most developed, with fine granular decoration; fig. 33k and l shows the distinctive small circle or border of granules at the end of the body of the earring where the pin would be fixed. This feature can be found in Mesopotamia, but not before the Third Dynasty of Ur period. Ashur Tomb 20 (fig. 46) provides good examples and the type becomes common in the Larsa period in Babylonia and Assyria and at Susa. The popularity of the type is also shown by the evidence of the terracotta female figurines of the Larsa period. It seems unlikely that this particular type of lunate-shaped

[1] Bittel, 'Beitrag zur kenntis Anatolischer Metallgefässe der Zweifen hälfte des Dritten Jahrtausends v. Chr.', *J.D.A.I.*, 74, 1959, pp. 1–34.

[2] Ibid. See also K. R. Maxwell-Hyslop in *Antiquity*, September 1970, pp. 227 ff.

[3] Thureau-Dangin, *Til Barsib*, pl. XXVI, 7.

earring with granulation is Anatolian in origin and, if they are to be regarded as imports, then the earliest date for their deposition in the Trojan Treasure A must be after the beginning of the Third Dynasty of Ur period in Mesopotamia – i.e. 2113 B.C.

Moreover, the great increase in the use of silver in the Third Dynasty of Ur period in Babylonia and the occurrence of many silver ingots at Troy suggest that Assyrian-Trojan contacts may have been one of the reasons for the decision of the Assyrian merchants to establish their colony at Kültepe and to trade their lead and other goods for Anatolian copper, with which they could buy silver. Silver was the common currency used in Babylonia and Assyria and it is possible that Troy was one of the main suppliers of the metal to the Anatolian traders and Assyrian merchants settled at Kültepe.

If a date of 2000 B.C. (or even later) for the end of Troy IIg proves correct, then we have to consider a period corresponding with the first part of the Isin-Larsa period in Mesopotamia – 2017–1830 B.C. The arguments depend on a study of both Asiatic and Aegean evidence and also the comparative stratigraphy of Troy and Kültepe-Kanesh. This is outside the scope of this study but, in addition to the connections mentioned above, two further points must be stressed. One is that the use of the fast wheel occurs in the lowest Early Bronze Age levels dug on the city mound at Kültepe; secondly, many techniques and artifacts previously considered Trojan or western Anatolian in origin, could in fact have originated in central Anatolia – probably at Kültepe itself. The fast wheel, hooked tang daggers and spear heads – even the *depas*, or two-handled cup – could all have reached Troy from central Anatolia. If the jewellery is regarded more as dependent on Mesopotamian techniques and craftsmanship of the Third Dynasty of Ur rather than the Sargonid period (see p. 70), then the use of fine granulation and the latest objects in Treasure A (the earrings, fig. 33k, l) can be reasonably dated in relation to the technical standards of production of the great centres of Asiatic craftsmanship, such as Ur, Ashur or Byblos. Finally, the publication of the Karahöyük (near Konya) seals and seal impressions by Professor Sedat Alp[1] has shown that the impression with a distinctive kind of interlacing design found on a sherd of Troy IIb by Blegen must be central Anatolian in origin. Blegen describes the sherd as 'imported'[2] and it must now be regarded as a central Anatolian rather than an Aegean import to Troy. At

[1] *Zylinder und Stempelsiegel aus Karahöyük bei Konya*, figs. 183 ff. (Ankara, 1968).
[2] Blegen, *Troy*, I, pl. 408b.

Karahöyük this seal impression belongs to a stratified level equated with Kültepe *kārum* II. This would suggest that Hood's proposed date of c. 2100 for the beginning of Troy II is correct;[1] the jewellery could then be as late as the mid-Larsa period, c. 1900–1850 B.C.

Poliochni on Lemnos (pls. 41 and 42)

The remarkable collection of gold jewellery found at Poliochni by Professor Bernabó Brea belongs to a level contemporary with Troy IIg; the bracelets, basket-shaped earrings with pendants of stylized idols (pl. 41) and 'shell' earrings can all be paralleled at Troy.

Flat disc-shaped beads and a quadruple spiral bead also occur, together with other types known at Troy, but one group of earrings calls for comment. These are different from Trojan types, and are made in the form of the calyx of a flower with the stamens attached to a hollow central holder below the plain circular hoop of the ring. The technique of the pins, compared with the fine filigree and granular work on the earrings and beads, is remarkably crude. Two bird-like figures in roughly cut gold sheet with the details made from thin gold wire are attached by rough lines of gold balls to a transverse bar of gold ending in upward curling double spirals (pl. 42). The bar is fixed to the shaft of the double spiral pin by twisted gold wire. Compared with the Trojan vase pins, this work seems extremely crude.

The 'shell' earrings are made of gold or electrum, six being found linked together. They vary according to the number of lobes of the parallel wirings and are sometimes decorated with appliqué bosses.

Hoard of jewellery alleged to have come from the Troad, recently purchased by the University Museum, Pennsylvania[2]

If all or part of this hoard is genuine, it deserves mention here on account of the 'shell' or lobed earrings made of cast, solid, ribbed pieces in imitation of separate wires soldered together, and then curled into 'shell'

[1] See also *Annuario di R. Scuola Archaeologica di Atene*, N.S. XIX–XX, 1957–8, p. 95, fig. 217, for a comparable Cretan sealing, probably central Anatolian in origin. I owe this reference to Mr Sinclair Hood. See also Newberry, *Scarabs* (London, 1906), fig. 100, with inscription of Sesostris III.

[2] See *Expedition*, 8, 14, 1966 (cover illustration). It is possible that this is a made-up collection, part genuine and part modern copies, with some pieces of a mixture of antique and modern. I have not yet been able to make a personal study of this collection.

shapes which are remarkably similar to the Poliochni earrings mentioned above, and also to many of the Trojan examples illustrated in fig. 33.

A type with a single appliqué boss is comparable with Poliochni examples, while other 'shell' or lobed earrings are decorated with rows of granulation like many of the Trojan basket earrings (cf. fig. 35).

A particularly interesting 'shell' earring is decorated with filigree spirals each side of an appliqué conical boss, which should be compared with the unique earring from Ur from P.G. 1100 (fig. 34), mentioned above on p. 51. An even more remarkable piece in this collection is an earring made of five wires, each formed of curled sheet metal and soldered together in the same way as the 'shell' earrings. 'From the five wires protrude five tiny rods, each scored with fine lines, which spread apart slightly just before ending in touching nailhead-like ends. Hanging from rings attached to these ends are loop-in-loop chains ending in leaves of sheet metal decorated with repoussé dots (one of the chains is broken and its leaf missing).'[1] The Ur earring from P.G. 1100 (fig. 34), now in the Baghdad Museum, also has similar scored rods protruding from the wires and an appliqué boss. One must seriously consider the possibility that these rare earrings may be products of a source known to Trojan and Sumerian jewellers and unknown today.

An important study of three steatite moulds by J. V. Canby[2] makes the suggestion that these moulds were especially designed for use by itinerant smiths who travelled over the trade routes linking the Troad and Mesopotamia via Cilicia and central Anatolia; there is ample evidence to support this conclusion. A negative mould for an earring of this type is actually shown on one of these moulds.

Tarsus

The important Cilician site of Tarsus excavated by Professor Hetty Goldman between 1935 and 1939 has produced jewellery which is comparable with material from Brak dating from the Sargonid period, with Mesopotamian jewellery of the Third Dynasty of Ur and Larsa periods and with the jewellery from the Trojan treasures. These pieces are interesting not only as examples of Mesopotamian influence in Cilicia – which is not in any way confined to gold work – but also for the Trojan connections, suggesting that Tarsus may have played an important part as an entrepôt on the overland route between Sumer, north Syria and the Troad which

[1] Ibid., p. 38. [2] 'Early Bronze Age "trinket" moulds', *Iraq*, XXVII, 1, 1965, pl. IX, b.

may well have been in use either at the same time or later than the link by sea.

The problem of the absolute chronology of Tarsus is too complex to be discussed here. It should, however, be noted that the parallels between Troy and Tarsus quoted by the excavator for the gold pin (fig. 42a) are not relevant; it is more likely to be related to the simple Brak type (fig. 24c, p. 33) in copper and to date from the Third Dynasty of Ur period. A date of c. 2000 B.C. for the end of the Early Bronze period at Tarsus can hardly be too high and may well have to be lowered if a general lowering of the dates of the end of Troy II proves to be correct.

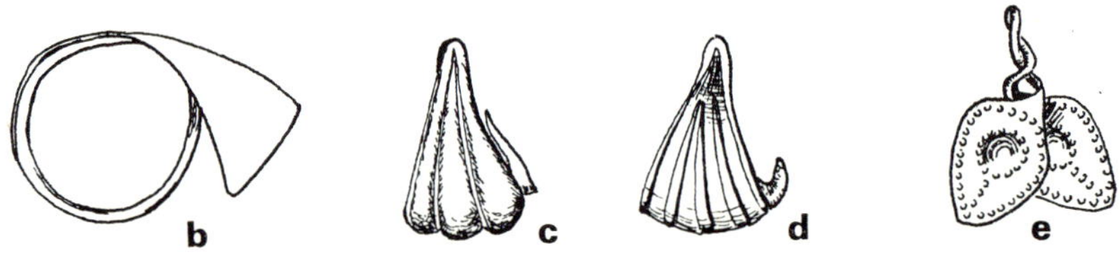

Fig. 42. *a*, gold pin; *b*, *c*, *d*, earrings; *e*, pendant; from Tarsus.

The earliest example of an earring at Tarsus comes from the Early Bronze Age II level and is of simple type (fig. 42b): a single loop of gold is flattened to a thin triangular plaque and pulled out to a slightly flat end after being bent over to form the loop. This is comparable with an unusual example from Ur (B.M. 122223) from the Royal Cemetery tomb 1181. Woolley classes this piece as his Type 6, which is a rare type at Ur and may be Anatolian in origin (pl. 43). Another comparable example comes from Byblos.[1]

The Early Bronze III level yielded two pairs of more developed earrings. One pair (fig. 42c) from Room 55 was made of heavy gold wire with one end tapering to a point, the other splayed into three lobes comparable with a fluted lunate earring from the large Trojan Treasure A, discussed above on p. 50 (fig. 33a and b). The other similar pair (fig. 42d) has four incised flutings and the excavator quotes a good central Anatolian

[1] 'Byblos', *Dacia*, N.S. III, 1959. E. Zaharia, 'Die Lockenringe von Sărata-Monteoru und ihre typologischen und chronologischen Beziehung', *Dacia*, III, 1959, pp. 103–34.

parallel from Alaca found in the Hittite level,[1] while other examples come from Mari (pl. 44) and Brak (pl. 24b).

The gold pin with rounded nail head (fig. 42a) shows skilful workmanship and is decorated with incised bands on the shaft.

An interesting pendant (or possibly part of an earring – fig. 42e) comes from the second millennium, Late Bronze II level. Here, two gold leaves were joined together with twisted wire and decorated with punched decoration round the leaves; each leaf has a repoussé boss in the centre.

A bracelet of bronze covered with thin gold plate, with the centre thickened and pierced and the surface decorated with parallel grooves, completes the inventory of jewellery from this period (*Tarsus*, II, figs. 454–8).

Karataş-Semayük, Lycia

Excavations in progress at Karatas-Semayük, directed by Professor Machteld Mellink,[2] have produced gold and silver jewellery from pithos burials in the extra-mural cemetery. The beads – gold and unusually large silver winged disc beads from Tomb 357 – are important evidence for providing a link between Ur and Troy. Bracelets and pins of silver, gold ear studs of central Anatolian type and a unique 'claw' bead attest that Lycia was in touch with the main centres of jewellery working at the end of the third millennium B.C.

[1] Kosay, *Alaca*, 1937–9, pl. LXXXVIII, fig. 4. [2] *A.J.A.*, 73, 1969, figs. 15–17.

CHAPTER 4

The Guti-Gudea Period, Third Dynasty of Ur to Isin and Larsa Dynasties 2250-1894 B.C.

INTRODUCTION

The period of the Third Dynasty of Ur kings in Mesopotamia is characterized by a paucity of archaeological material where jewellery is concerned; yet there is a wealth of documentary evidence to prove that, while a mass of gold work was produced, its absence is due to the fact that few tombs dating from this period have been dug. Texts from Ur constantly mention goldsmiths and jewellers and afford detailed information about the activities of the temple workshops, where carpenters, coppersmiths and stone workers, as well as goldsmiths and jewellers, were kept constantly employed. Their output can be calculated from the lists and receipts of finished goods; the complex and efficient organization of the temple authorities facilitated production, which was supported by the widespread trading activities of the merchants of Ur. These trading activities have been discussed by many scholars and the work of Oppenheim and Limet is especially important for our subject.[1]

Among the commodities traded via Telmun (identified with the island of Bahrein), gold is often mentioned and, although the texts date mainly from the First Dynasty of Babylon period, they are of vital importance for the earlier period when merchants from Ur were importing much of their raw materials via the Persian Gulf and sea traffic with the east was flourishing. It was during the Third Dynasty of Ur period that Telmun was becoming a centre which attained its greatest importance in the succeeding Larsa period. Other raw materials imported from Telmun included copper, lapis lazuli and various precious stones and ivory.

[1] A. L. Oppenheim, 'The seafaring merchants of Ur', *J.A.O.S.*, 74, 1954, pp. 6 ff.

THE JEWELLERY

Uruk (Warka)

The magnificent necklace of large onyx beads set in gold, belonging to the priestess Abbabashti (pl. 45), is one of the few surviving pieces of jewellery which can be certainly dated to the Third Dynasty of Ur. It was found in the temple of Eanna at Uruk (Warka) and is now in the Baghdad Museum. The use of cloisonné inlay is especially important and must be remembered in any assessment of the influence of the Sumerian jewellers of this period on contemporary centres of gold-working. The beads are large biconical banded agate, set in gold, and the smallest bead is inscribed with the name of the priestess. The stones are capped by heavy gold rims ornamented with filigree work and along the top and lower ridges are gold borders ornamented with small circular cloisons. Some of the larger beads have another pattern of double twisted wire at the base of the gold caps and the remains of silver wire suggest that the thread was of silver.

Between each large agate bead are small fluted disc beads, with six distinct wings, forming a spacer between the caps of the larger beads. There is no granulation on this necklace but the jeweller was such an obvious master of his craft that there is little doubt that he could have included this technique if he had thought it necessary. The height of the central bead is 7 cm (3 inches) and the necklace is more comparable with a present-day mayoral chain of office than anything yet found in western Asia. This unique necklace, with the few pieces of jewellery mentioned in this chapter, comprise the meagre archaeological evidence which can be related to the contemporary texts dating from the Third Dynasty of Ur period.

Nippur

Nippur has produced a few pieces of jewellery from graves of the Third Dynasty of Ur period; fluted and melon-shaped beads and six carnelian beads with gold caps decorated with filigree work come from graves of this period.[1]

Ur – Grave P.G. 1422 (Pls. 46–48)

This rich grave contained one of the few groups of jewellery which can be assigned to the early part of the Third Dynasty of Ur period and it

[1] *Nippur*, I, pl. 150, 6, 11, 12.

deserves to be studied as a whole. It is unfortunately divided between the British Museum and Pennsylvania and I am indebted to Dr Robert Dyson for the photographs (pls. 47 and 48) of the Pennsylvania group.

The grave contained one skeleton in a wooden coffin with a gabled lid. The silver pin of Type 1 (U. 12480), with a silver ring round it, was found on the right shoulder, as though it was a toggle fastening for a garment. In addition to the jewellery discussed below, there was a plain penannular gold bangle of solid gold on the right arm, and three bangles on the left arm of which one was made of gold and two made by hammering a thick gold plate over a core which was then withdrawn. Woolley suggests the core could have been wire (B.M. 1222213–4). A pair of silver penannular bangles (Pl. 46b), solid and heavy, are also mentioned (U. 12473). A large cylinder seal of lapis lazuli with gold caps (U. 12470, B.M. 122216) has the inscription apparently intentionally defaced (for another lapis lazuli seal with gold caps see U.12471). By the hands of the skeleton were a silver bowl and a decayed silver vase. A copper dagger with gold mounts and studs lay by the wrist and the other weapons included a silver axe of rare type (fig. 43).

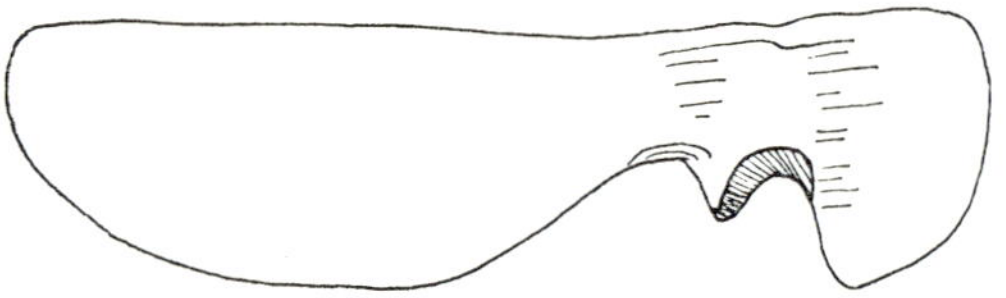

Fig. 43. Silver axe head from Ur.

The pottery consisted of three pots with haematite slip and lightly burnished surface and two copper vessels (*Ur Excavations*, II, pls. 254, Type 60; 233, Type 20; and 232, Type 10).

Between the coffin and wall of the shaft were a number of offerings: four examples of pottery jar (*Ur Excavations*, II, pl. 264, Type 200), a remarkable number of copper vessels and vases corroded on to a ribbed tray, and a curious open pan ribbed horizontally like the tray but having a long handle. A large cauldron was at the foot of the coffin with attached handles (*Ur Excavations*, II, pls. 234, 31; 235, 49; and 184a). Three copper spear heads with the typical Sumerian 'poker butt' retained the tube of thin copper which acted as a binding at the head of the wooden shaft and also the copper disc from the butt end of the shaft. A copper box (U. 12482) with a flat knob on its lid and a cylinder seal (U. 12471) with the usual Third Dynasty of Ur introduction scene complete the inventory of the offerings.

Frontlets (pls. 46a, 47)
Six gold frontlets of thin sheet metal (U. 12463, B.M. 122242) were all on the head. Average size 17 cm × 5 cm. They are the oval type narrowing into a strip of gold ribbon (U. 12465).

Hair-ring (pl. 46c)
A hair-ring (U. 12466, B.M. 122221), made of three hoops of spirally coiled gold wire, fairly thick, diameter 2·3 cm. Found not on the head but by the hands, near the silver vase between two earrings (U. 12467) as if the three of them had been tied together.

Pair of gold earrings or hair-rings (pl. 46d, fig. 44)
Thin metal over a core probably of bitumen. The ring consists of a thick spiral coil with lunate ends but, whereas one end is of the normal sort, the other splits into two lobes, each lunate (U. 12467, B.M. 122217).

Gold earrings
Normal small type with solid lunate ends (Pennsylvania 30. 12. 623, 626).

Gold goat amulet
(U. 12469, B.M. 122202).

Four necklaces
Catalogue descriptions as follows:

U. 12474 Beads, a very long chain of large and small jasper, chalcedony, agate, sard, marble, carnelian, etc., cut as cylinders, date-shaped, barrels, flattened square-ended date-shaped, alternating with gold balls, some plain, some ribbed, and one with relief pattern. These seemed to have one chain which passed two or three times round the neck; the beads lay very thickly under the head. Re-strung as two necklaces, but not strictly in original order (pl. 48a and c; Pennsylvania 30.12.566–7).

U. 12475 Beads, banded sard, square with bevelled faces. Pennsylvania 30.12.568 (cf. pl. 48a–b).

U. 12476 A necklace of carnelian balls and gold ribbed beads strung alternately except in front (B.M. 122433). See pl. 46e.

U. 12477 Beads, flat winged diamonds of gold and carnelian, small gold carnelian balls. Re-strung mostly in original order (Pennsylvania 30.12.572). See pl. 48d.

The beads composing these necklaces merit especially attention. In the centre of U. 12474 (pl. 48c) is a fine agate bead, flat rhomboid in shape, with gold caps fitted to each end. Long, thin, date-shaped beads with gold caps are on the same necklace and the fashion of attaching caps of gold to beads or seals is a distinguishing mark of this period which continued in Babylonia through the First Dynasty of Babylon and into the Kassite period (for a comparable agate bead with gold caps from Barrow VIII in Trialeti, see pl. 52). Agate beads of cat's eyes also occur on this necklace (see pl. 49b, for example, not from 1422 but similar; and pl. 49a, a gold capped bead – B.M. 120621).

Ur – Graves P.G. 671, 871, 1847, 1850

Two graves at Ur – P.G. 671 and 871 – both rich in jewellery, have yielded comparable material and, if they cannot be dated quite as late as the Third Dynasty of Ur period, certainly belong to the Guti-Gudea times.

P.G. 871 included a large copper cauldron, a cylinder seal with gold caps (U. 10757, *Ur Excavations*, II), plain hoop bangles, silver pin with plain ball head, diadem and ribbon and three necklaces (U. 10753, Pennsylvania 16920). The earrings were two gold lunate-ended rings of different sizes linked together (Type 3, U. 10758) (fig. 15a, Chapter 2).

Noteworthy among the jewellery in grave P.G. 671 are the earrings or hair-rings (U. 9637, Baghdad 8041, see fig. 44) with large coils of hollow metal with lunate ends and a third lobe added so that at one end of the coil there are two crescents. This type is similar to U. 12467 in Tomb 1422 (pl. 46d).

The large shaft graves numbered P.G. 1845–1850 by Woolley produced a collection of gold and silver jewellery which, when considered with the finds of P.G. 1422, can be regarded as typical products of the Ur temple workshops at the time of the Third Dynasty. In all these graves the jewellery is remarkably homogeneous. Some of the pieces are shown in pl. 50.

P.G. 1847, the largest, contained no less than sixteen burials, most of which contained jewellery *in situ*. This grave produced no less than three gold fillets, oval in shape, pierced at each end for the attachment of a length of narrow gold ribbon which had been twisted round a lock of hair. The two coiled hair-rings were found on the chest of the skeleton, about level with the elbow, which suggests that in this case the description of 'hair-rings' rather than 'earrings' is likely to be correct. Woolley considered that they may have been attached to the end of long tresses of hair, though the possibility that they could have rolled to that position after the deposition of the body must not be entirely disregarded. The blunt ends of these objects, when compared with the usual type of earring which was often found in position at the ears, points to the correctness of Woolley's interpretation. Two strings of beads were composed of very small gold and carnelian balls with large gold balls, agate, carnelian, marble and lapis beads, with the addition of a long, thin, date-shaped agate bead with gold caps (pl. 50). Of the four bracelets, one was gold (thin gold plate over a copper core), the second silver and two were of copper. The axe was of hammered copper, a technique used for most of the axes in these Third Dynasty of Ur shaft graves, and hammered copper cauldrons and bowls are also typical of the grave offerings.

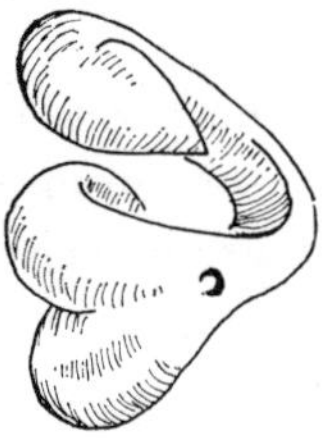

Fig. 44. Earring (or hair-ring) from Ur.

Fig. 45. Earring from Ur.

P.G. 1850, with multiple burials, is noteworthy for the fine lapis lazuli seal and a cast bronze axe of late Early Dynastic type. The pair of earrings of Burial 8 (U. 17913 – fig. 45) is unique and the catalogue description is: 'Gold earrings, a pair, a single loop widening to a lunate form below but split into two flat plates which are soldered together along the inner curve of the crescent but are bent apart below' (see p. 47 for mention of an earring of this type in discussion of jewellery from Kültepe). A rich collection of jewellery, oval gold frontlets with elongated ends with narrow fillets for attachment round the forehead, small hollow gold lunate earrings (which can be distinguished from the hair-rings discussed above), silver bracelets, a finger ring of spirally coiled gold wire, a silver pin and two necklaces of small gold, agate, carnelian and lapis lazuli beads with a shell cylinder seal complete the inventory of the ornaments of this grave.

Ashur

The Assyrian site of Ashur affords valuable information for the continuation of Sumerian techniques during the period of the Third Dynasty of Ur and the succeeding Isin-Larsa periods, and one of the graves excavated by the German expedition is especially important in this respect.

Ashur Tomb 20 (fig. 46)

Among the graves classified as Old Assyrian by Andrae, Tomb 20 is of particular interest as it contained a fine collection of jewellery. This included oval diadems of normal Sargonid type (fig. 46a), though longer than the Ur examples, earrings of triple-lobed type (fig. 46b and g), a necklace including many examples of quadruple spiral beads (fig. 46c) and a cylinder seal of lapis lazuli with the usual introduction scene characteristic of seals of the Third Dynasty of Ur. A curious bronze or copper object, shaped like a round 'frying pan' with upstanding circular ridges on the inside, is discussed below (fig. 47). A socketed spear and pins with conical fluted heads (fig. 46h and i) were also in this grave. It is to be regretted that this material is not now in Berlin and available for study, so that conclusions are based only on a study of the photographs under a microscope.

The earrings are decorated with triangles of fine granulation; round the juncture of the pin and the body of the earring and where the pin meets the body are two well-marked circles of gold filigree surrounded by a circle of granulated dots (fig. 46g). These pieces are of prime importance in the history of Sumerian jewellery, as there is little reason to doubt a date in the Third Dynasty of Ur period for this grave. This is, therefore, one of the few extant examples of the technique of granulation which can be dated just before 2000 B.C.

The same feature (circle surrounded by granulated dots) occurs on a comparable pair of earrings from Susa, now in the Louvre, which also probably belongs to this period – and also on the fine pair of earrings of Larsa period date from Ur (see p. 83 and pl. 57). In a much cruder technique it also can be found on Trojan earrings from the Troy treasures (fig. 33k, l) and at Poliochni. It is possible (though unlikely, in my view) that these earrings represent an imitation of Trojan technique by the more highly skilled Mesopotamian craftsmen and thus a reflection of the Sargonid-Trojan contact discussed in Chapter 3. A later, post 2000 B.C. date for the Trojan treasures is put forward in Chapter 4 and the earrings and the 'frying pan' discussed below could then be regarded as evidence

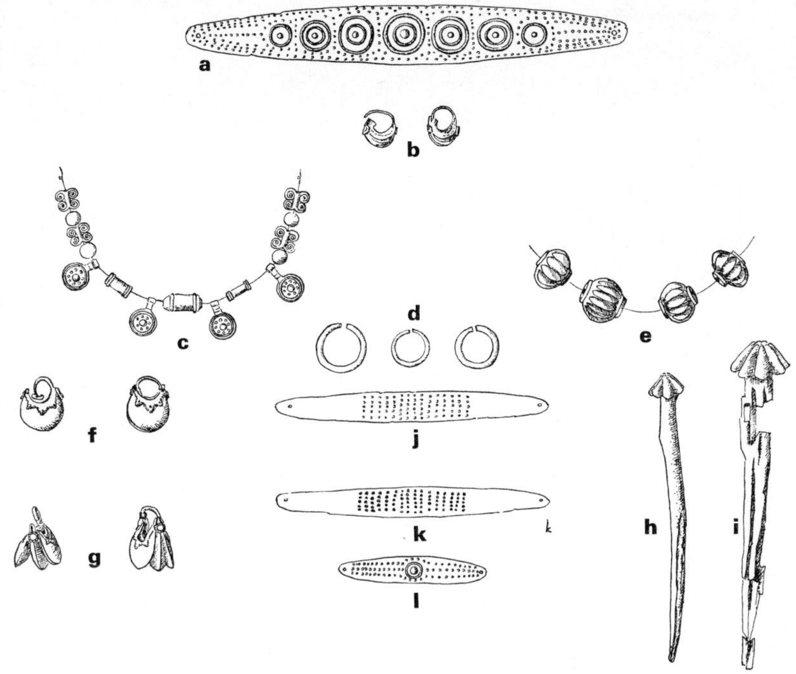

Fig. 46. Jewellery from Ashur Grave 20.

of Assyrian contact with Anatolia before the establishment of the trading centre at Kültepe-Kanesh.[1] Comparable earrings from Tarsus (in the Early Bronze Age III level) would also suggest Trojan-Assyrian contact between goldsmiths – in this case via Cilicia rather than Kültepe.

The curious 'frying pan' (fig. 47) is a type well known in the Troad and discussed in detail by Bittel, but he omitted to mention the Ashur example. One occurred in Troy Treasure A (see p. 58) and was thought by Schliemann to be a shield, while the handle which was found separately was catalogued by Schmidt as an axe. Its purpose remains obscure, unless it was intended actually for use as a frying pan for cooking meat – in which case its presence in the grave seems odd. There is no evidence for thinking that it is a crucible used in metal working (the excavator calls it a *tiegel*), although it could have been used effectively for panning gold (see p. 58, footnote 2). It can be compared with not unsimilar ribbed pans in Grave 1422 at Ur (*Ur Excavations*, II, pl. 184a), also of Third Dynasty of Ur date, and must be later than the Trojan ones.

[1] Lewy in *C.A.H.*, No. 40, pp. 7 f., suggests that Kanesh and parts of the surrounding country might have been under the domination of Ibbi-Sin of Ur.

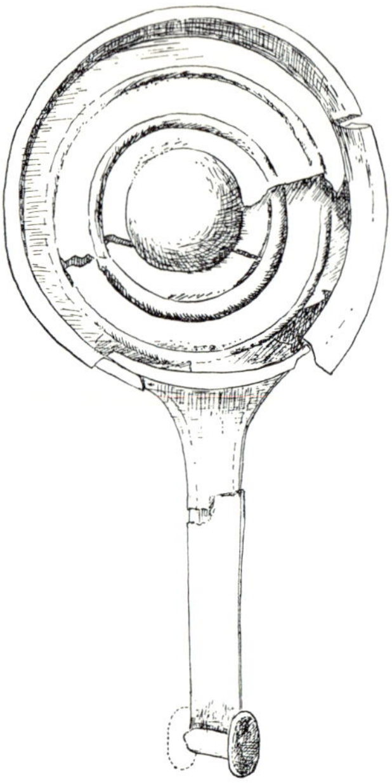

Fig. 47. Circular copper ridged pan from Ashur.

Ashur Grave 18

Grave 18 also provides evidence of Assyrian-Anatolian connections during this period. It contained a male terracotta (fig. 48) wearing copper earrings, a lead figure of a gazelle and toggle pin of Trojan type. A cast, socketed axe from the same grave belongs to an interesting class,[1] of which a fine

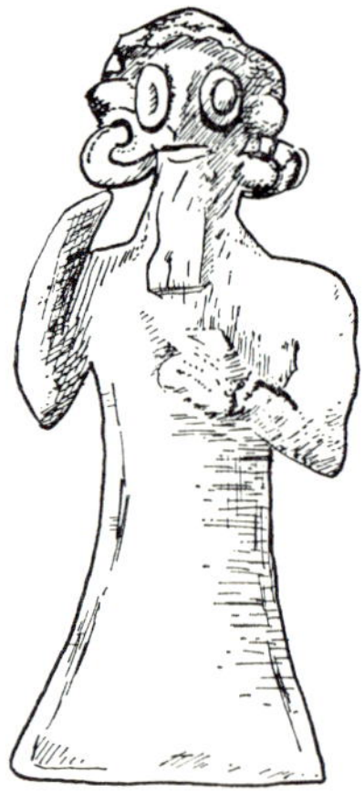

Fig. 48. Terracotta male figurine from Ashur.

[1] See K. R. Maxwell-Hyslop, 'Western Asiatic shafthole axes', *Iraq*, XI, 1, 1949 – Type 12a, p. 102; and J. Deshayes, *Outils de Bronze*, p. 305.

example of mould and castings has recently turned up in the grave of a warrior at Shemshāra near Kirkuk.[1] The axes and mould at Shemshāra can be closely dated by the tablets in Level 5 to a period contemporary or slightly older than the time of the Assyrian king Shamshi-Adad I (1813–1781 B.C.), so there is good reason for regarding it as a native Assyrian or possibly Hurrian type. Its appearance at Kültepe is not, therefore, surprising at the time of the colony of merchants (see p. 101).

Relations between Trialeti and Mesopotamia in the Guti-Gudea[2] and Third Dynasty of Ur periods

The problem of the occurrence of Mesopotamian types in both Transcaucasia and at sites north of the main Caucasus range was discussed by Frankfort as early as 1932. With his usual acumen, he published a table showing how many objects found at Ur and Kish were already known from Russian sources. His conclusion, that 'a close connection between the metal industry of the early Dynastic period and the Caucasus must be admitted', is still valid – although his view that 'the geographical distribution of the various types excludes Sumer as the centre of dispersion'[3] must now be amended in view of more recent evidence, especially that concerned with the chronology of recently excavated Russian sites. It is not possible to estimate how much interruption to the trade which distributed these types as far afield from Sumer as the north Caucasus was caused by the Guti invasions which began c. 2250 B.C., but possibly the disorganization caused in Sumer and Akkad could have been avoided by traders and craftsmen using routes via Susa and the Iranian plateau. Transcaucasia and the Caucasus could then be reached via Gilan and the valleys of the Kura and Araxes rivers afforded access to the Russian centres. There must have been three main routes to Transcaucasia and the Caucasus from Mesopotamia presumably used by prospectors in search of gold. Danger and disturbance among hostile tribes in one area would not necessarily stop intercourse between the two areas. From Sumer their routes were:

1 The Iran route starting from Susa (see above).

2 Up the Tigris until Ashur and then via Rowanduz, the Kelishin pass

[1] J. Laessøe, *People of Ancient Assyria*, pl. 12b (London, 1963).

[2] See Gadd in *C.A.H.*, No. 17. The last four kings of the Akkadian Dynasty, after the fall of Shar-kali-sharri, were contemporary with the early Gutian kings.

[3] Frankfort, *Archaeology and the Sumerian problem*, pp. 52–3.

to Tabriz, the Araxes valley and Erivan. From here, the Kura valley could easily be reached.

3 From Assyria to Lake Van and then via Bayazid and Kars to Tiflis and the Trialeti area.

Evidence for contact between Mesopotamia and Transcaucasia during the period of about 115 years between the end of the Sargonid period and the beginning of the Third Dynasty of Ur, which includes the period of Guti invasions and reign of Gudea at Lagash, is becoming gradually clearer. In this context, P.G. 1422 discussed on p. 66 is particularly interesting. The diadem (pl. 46a) is typical of the preceding Sargonid period, but the earrings and the dagger are unique types at Ur. The type of triple coiled earring is known in Transcaucasia and occurs in Barrow XXIX at Trialeti, while the dagger may well be a Transcaucasian type traded or copied by Mesopotamian smiths, as it occurs in several Transcausian burials. The axe types are also non-Mesopotamian in origin and reflect Persian influence coming probably via the Persian routes to the Caucasus region.

The barrow graves in Trialeti, Georgia

The region of Trialeti is part of Georgia lying about sixty-four kilometres west of Tbilisi and comprises the valley of the Khram river, a western tributary of the Kura. Forty-two barrow graves were dug by the Russians between 1936 and 1940 and the results have been published by Kuftin in 1941.[1] Minns, in his summary,[2] points out some of the difficulties in using this important archaeological material when we have incomplete information for many of the graves and no full description of any. However, while attempts have been made by many scholars to date these important finds and more published information is badly needed, there are certain points worth noting where the jewellery is concerned which can contribute to any final assessment of the chronology of the barrows. Three barrows which are especially important are numbers VIII, V and XVII.

Barrow VIII (pls. 51–54) contained a remarkable bead which can be related to the Uruk necklace of the priestess Abbabashti (see pl. 45) and associated in the same grave were spherical granulated beads and pins with silver shanks and round heads with granulated decoration. These

[1] Kuftin, *Trialeti*. [2] *Antiquity*, XVII, 1943, pp. 129–35.

beads are illustrated by Kuftin in colour in *Trialeti*, pl. XCIV. The first is made of a thin agate plate which is bored for suspension and capped with gold at each end; the curved shape of this remarkable bead is known from Ur (fig. 19a, Chapter 2) and the filigree work and inlay is technically similar to the Uruk bead. Granulation and filigree is typical of the Trialeti gold work and is combined with inlay on the spherical beads (pls. 52–54). The large hemispherical beads, decorated with filigree and inlay set in small round cloisons which are surrounded with fine granulation work, were also found in Barrow VIII (pls. 53 and 54). A round-headed pin decorated in similar technique has a silver shank.[1]

The relationship of these pieces to the Alaca pin has been noted on p. 43; here we must consider the evidence of the pottery which was discussed by Burney in 1958.[2] Burney pointed out that this barrow contained a sherd of eastern Anatolian Early Bronze II ware, probably a survival, but important evidence for placing this barrow as the earliest of the series, probably c. 2100 B.C. It is difficult to believe that the Uruk necklace and the gold agate bead from Barrow VIII were made at widely separated periods[3] and a date around 2000 B.C. seems reasonable.

Barrow V is assigned by Burney to not later than 1900 B.C. on the pottery evidence; here there is no jewellery to corroborate this suggestion and parallels for the remarkable silver cup with the procession of figures with pointed boots and wolves' tails are not easy to find. One would hesitate in assigning this cup to so early a period (a date towards the end of the second millennium or the beginning of the first can be argued), yet it is possible to detect a connection between the silver cup of Barrow V and the silver bucket of Barrow XVII where the pottery with swastikas and Maltese crosses also recalls Alaca and Alishar.

Barrow XVII is also assigned by Burney to a date 'probably not much later than 1900 B.C.' The silver bucket of Barrow XVII with twisted gold handle and animal decoration, shows a tree in similar style to that of the cup in Barrow V, but is also comparable with the tree on the silver bowl from Maikop.[4] This again suggests a date not long after 2000 B.C. and the other objects in this rich Barrow XVII are not inconsistent with a date soon after 2000 B.C. Among the jewellery, which includes granulated spherical beads and pins similar to those in Barrow VIII, the most remarkable piece

[1] Kuftin, *Trialeti*, pl. XCVII.
[2] C. A. Burney, 'Early Anatolia in the Chalcolithic and Early Bronze Age', *A.S.*, VIII, 1958, pp. 175 ff.
[3] Kuftin, *Trialeti*, pl. XCIV.
[4] See Piggott, *Ancient Europe*, fig. 37, p. 82.

is a circular disc with three rows of granules round the edge and a central row enclosing nine circles with the centre and four surrounding ones enclosed in a ring of fine granules. A remarkable gold cup (fig. 49) with a looped spiral design enclosing cloisons inlaid with turquoise and carnelian,[1] each cloison being surrounded with granules, has a floral inlaid decoration on the base which is comparable with the gold circular medallion from Byblos (see p. 102 and pl. 69).

49

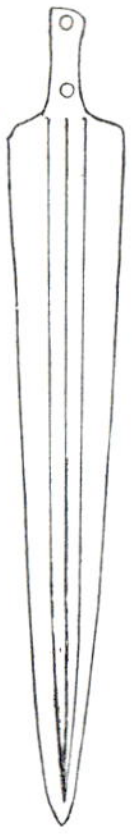

50

51

Fig. 49. Gold vase from Trialeti; sardonyx, amber and glass paste inlay.
Fig. 50. Silver dagger from Trialeti.
Fig. 51. Copper dagger blade from Ur.

Finally, a silver dagger (fig. 50) with the blade finely incised, suggesting Mesopotamian contact, also comes from Barrow XVII. The type is known at Ur in a Third Dynasty of Ur context, in Grave P.G. 1422 (see p. 65 and fig. 51), where it occurred in association with the distinctive gold triple earring or hair-ring (pl. 46d). This association of daggers with incised or reeded mid-ribs and triple earrings can also be found at Trialeti in Barrow XXIX; this barrow, on the evidence of the jewellery, could be dated roughly contemporaneous with Barrow XVII, but for the pottery which belongs to a later phase of the Kura-Araxes tradition and was therefore dated by Piggott to a period not later than 2200 B.C.[2]

[1] The inlay includes sardonyx, coloured paste and amber.
[2] See Piggott, *P.P.S.*, XXXIV, 1968, pp. 266–318, for a detailed study of the Transcaucasian barrow burials.

IRAN AT THE PERIOD OF THE THIRD DYNASTY OF UR

New light was shed on the vexed question of the date of the two periods at Tepe Hissar, near Damghan in north Iran, by Professor Mallowan[1] who drew attention to the similarities between the plan of the 'burnt building' at Hissar (Level IIIb) and the temple at Ashur, dedicated to the goddess Ishtar, Temple E. He suggested that the building at Hissar, which may well have contained a shrine, reflects the influence of Mesopotamia at a time when the two regions were in increasingly close contact with each other before the fall of the Third Ur Dynasty and the capture of its king, Ibi-Sin, by the Elamites. The richness of Tepe Hissar during the periods IIIb and IIIc was certainly due to its key position on the route which led to the west from the great lapis lazuli mines at Badakshan in the Hindu Kush mountains in Afghanistan;[2] the trade in lapis which reached urban centres in Mesopotamia, Syria and Anatolia would explain some of the peculiar non-Iranian features of the civilization of Tepe Hissar. A date around 2000 B.C. would fit in well for the occurrence of long spouted stone and silver vessels of Anatolian shape (known from the *kārum* at Kültepe), while the use of lead for vessels also suggests contact with Assyria and Cappadocia. The spears with stop ridge belong to a type widely distributed over western Asia and Iran in the late third and early second millennium B.C., while many other objects can be cited to show the extraordinary wealth accumulated at Hissar owing to the trade in Trans-Caspian lapis lazuli.

It is against this background that the jewellery must be considered and, while some of the gold ornaments are obviously local in design and technique, it is easy to discern the influence of Sumerian smiths in the use of agate and carnelian stones for beads of types well known in the Sargonid and Third Dynasty of Ur graves at Ur.

The use of silver rather than gold as the normal material for jewellery at this period in Iran is again indicative of a date in the period of the Third Dynasty of Ur for much of the unstratified jewellery said to have come from Giyan and published by Herzfeld.[3] Triple earrings (or hair-rings)

[1] *The Dawn of Civilisation*, p. 95 (London, 1961).

[2] G. Herrmann, *Iraq*, XXX, 1, 1968, p. 21. See also unpublished D.Phil. thesis, *The source, distribution, history and use of lapis lazuli in western Asia from the earliest times to the end of the Seleucid era*, presented by G. Herrmann at Oxford, 1966.

[3] *I.A.E.*, fig. 266, pl. XXX.

of silver are made in the same way as the gold examples discussed above (p. 67 and pl. 46d) from Grave 1422 from Ur, a well-dated Third Dynasty of Ur group, while the plain crescent-shaped earring with one large drop at the base[1] can also be related to Babylonian examples belonging to the period of the First Dynasty of Babylon from Mari and other unstratified Mesopotamian examples. Here again, the Iranian examples are of silver and the Babylonian of gold. From Gilan, however, there are many gold earrings with several drops at the base (colour pl. F, see Chapter 12) now in the Mazda Collection which belong to the more developed type known from stratified mid-Assyrian contexts at Mari and may well prove to be imports from Babylonia.

Tepe Hissar

The jewellery from Tepe Hissar can be divided into material from the periods designated by the excavators as Hissar IIa and IIb, IIIb and IIIc. Until more study has been made of the entire archaeological record from Hissar and its relations with sites such as Giyan and Sialk and other sites in the south and south-east where excavations have recently been started, the question of absolute chronology must be regarded as uncertain and the suggestions advanced by R. H. Dyson[2] will be used here as the best that can be adduced from the available evidence, combined with the radiocarbon date of c. 2100 B.C. for Hissar IIIb material obtained by Mr Stronach at Yanik Tepe. The excavations in progress directed by Professor Jean Deshayes at Tureng Tepe will no doubt provide evidence for a reassessment of the Hissar sequence and its chronological problems – one of the most important being the length and actual end of the period Hissar IIIc, which is particularly relevant to any study of the jewellery.[3] Hissar IIa and IIb can be tentatively dated to the Early Dynastic period I–III in Mesopotamia and the jewellery can give little assistance to the pottery evidence in determining the absolute dates, with the exception that – unlike the pottery – it is possible to detect foreign links in some of the silver objects from graves allocated to IIa; if it proves correct to regard the silver looped double spiral pendants made in rough and primitive technique as distant imitations of Sumerian gold originals, then a slight lowering of these dates becomes possible. The occurrence of gold date-

[1] Herzfeld, *I.A.E.*, figs. 267–8.
[2] 'Problems in the relative chronology of Iran 6000–2000', pp. 215–56 in *Chronologies.*
[3] J. Deshayes in *Iranica Antiqua*, VI, p. 1, 1966; and in *Ugaritica*, VI, pp. 139–63.

B. Necklace from Ur. See p. 11

A. Headdress from Ur. See p. 4

C. Necklace from Alaca. See p. 44

D. Axe head from Byblos. See p. 103

shaped beads of the usual Early Dynastic III type at Ur would also point in this direction.

On the other hand, the two silver double spiral pendants, one with a loop (H. 2982, Schmidt, *Tepe Hissar*, pl. XXX), are comparable in shape with the pendant (H. 2659, Schmidt, *Tepe Hissar*, pl. XXX) and could have been the prototype for the similar gold example at Ur (colour pl. B), also from an Early Dynastic III context. Both these pendants at Hissar could then be regarded as reflecting the contacts which must have existed between Sumer and the Iranian plateau at a time when the trade in lapis lazuli between Badakshan in Afghanistan and southern Mesopotamia was beginning to resume its former importance after its surprising eclipse in the Early Dynastic I period. The relatively large amount of silver jewellery, of non-Sumerian type, combined with the frequent use of lapis in period II at Hissar, also suggests that the site may have been an important centre of silver-working whose products were considered worth imitating by Sumerian smiths. Furthermore, alongside the import of lapis lazuli to Sumer, jewellery would be one of the easiest of commodities to export or use as barter.

To Hissar IIIb can be allocated the jewellery from Grave CF55 X 1 and the gold beads and diadem from the period IIIb 'burnt building'. This group of jewellery from the 'burnt building', now in the Teheran Museum (pl. 55), is remarkable for the crudity of workmanship and rough finish; the beads are the flat disc shape known from Sumerian examples, but show a surprising lack of technical skill; some attempt at repoussé decoration has been made, but the whole group, with the simple oblong diadem pierced at each end with two holes like the Sumerian series, contrasts with the fine copper dagger with silver grip and developed hooked tang and the gold cup and silver vessels which are far more skilfully made. The jewellery from Grave CF55 X 1[1] suggests that the Hissar craftsmen were technically more skilled when working in silver, rather than in gold. A curious silver double spiral pendant with open looped top (H. 2389) can only be paralleled by the much later example from Tepe Nush-i-Jan. This seems to be a primitive type whose development can be seen on the examples from a grave of Hissar IIIc date (H. 3609) where the neck is perforated laterally. The size of the earlier IIIb example – height 4·8 cm, breadth 6·6 cm – and two large crescent-shaped silver pendants from IIIb graves H. 4039 and H. 2809[2] invites comparison with the pendant shown on the rock relief of Tar-Lunni, sculptured on a rock near Sar-i-pol

[1] Schmidt, *Tepe Hissar*, p. 244 and pl. LV. [2] Ibid., pls. LV, LXIX.

on the road from Qasr-i-Shin to Kermanshah, where the figure of a local chieftain, probably of the Lullubi tribe, is wearing a large crescent-shaped pendant at the centre of his necklace (see also p. 215 for discussion of these rock reliefs).

Hissar IIIc has produced an important collection of jewellery not only from the treasure hoard, but also from graves of this period. In the same grave as the double spiral silver pendant mentioned above came a unique silver button (H. 3609) with pierced loop for attachment and several plain silver bracelets. The period is noted for its use of new materials – such as amber, ivory, lead, frit and etched carnelian. Banded chalcedony is used for a bead of typically Sumerian Third Dynasty of Ur shape (H. 2856), while turquoise had already been used in the preceding IIIb period (CF55 X 1).

The treasure hoard now in the Teheran Museum (pl. 55) shows considerable skill in using gold for jewellery – in contrast to the preceding period – and the necklaces of gold tubular beads combined with cat's eye carnelian, banded agate beads of typical Sumerian Third Dynasty of Ur type, and the triple gold spacers, suggest a date not far removed from the beginning of the second millennium B.C. Four pieces, however, can probably be considered as local in inspiration. These are the hair ornaments in the shape of elongated leaves made out of sheet gold with the ends twisted over in a loop of gold wire. It is possible that these ornaments were intended as earrings; for similar ornaments we have to look to Cyprus (see p. 82), but these are not the same shape and are probably earlier in date. An isolated gold leaf from Ur from P.G. 783 (pl. 56), though here recognizable as a willow leaf like the type of long willow leaf used on the Early Dynastic headdresses (see pl. 1), may possibly provide a prototype. If this is correct, then the Hissar examples are rather crude imitations. The popularity of this form in Iran in a much later period is attested by the occurrence of large gold leaves at Marlik (see p. 191, pl. 140, Chapter 11), but here they were found on the skeleton in one instance and were not connected in any way with hair ornaments.

The gold beads in the treasure hoard (Hissar IIIc) consist of plain long tubular beads and the distinctive gold triple spacer faceted beads, combined with small oval and hollow cones (pl. 55). The triple spacers are more often found in paste or blue glass and are commonly known in mid-second millennium contexts (see p. 126) in western Asia; they may well prove to be the prototypes of the Iranian examples from Gök tepe, Dinkha tepe and other Iranian sites. A glass paste example from Giyan

Tomb 92, which also yielded painted tripod pots and a silver ring, must belong to Giyan period III, which can be equated with the First Dynasty of Babylon before 1600 B.C. (see p. 91).

CYPRUS IN THE EARLY CYPRIOTE III PERIOD (c. 2100–2000 B.C.)

The jewellery found in the island of Cyprus was first known from the systematic looting of tombs carried out by General Cesnola in the latter part of the nineteenth century; organized excavation dates only from A. S. Murray's work at Enkomi for the British Museum.[1] These tomb groups are in the British Museum and the Cesnola collection was admirably catalogued by Myres in 1914.[2] Since 1927, however, systematic excavation of numerous sites dating from the Early Bronze to the Roman period by the Swedish-Cyprus expedition and, more recently, by the Cyprus Department of Antiquities has provided a mass of jewellery (mainly from tombs) which can be reasonably dated by the associated pottery. Today there is no lack of material from the Later Cypriote period onwards and here we shall only attempt to survey the history and development of jewellery working in the island and to indicate the relationship of those pieces which show distinct Asiatic, as opposed to Mycenaean and Greek, characteristics. Whenever possible, dated pieces will be referred to and the Swedish chronology (with slight amendments noted) for different archaeological periods will be followed.

The earliest gold in Cyprus dates from the Early Cypriote III period (c. 2100–2000 B.C.) and occurs at a period when there is evidence from the pottery of connections with the Syrian coast and when quantities of gold were presumably being imported into the island. Lapithos, on the north coast, is the source of the two important early pieces of jewellery found by the Pennsylvanian Museum expedition of 1931 and J. L. Myres and Markides in 1913. Both objects are forms of hair ornament and were found near the skull of a woman. They consist of two pieces of sheet gold decorated in repoussé and presumably intended for clipping round locks of hair (fig. 52a and b). They have recently been discussed along with similar Cypriote examples in gold, silver and bronze (fig. 52c) by Dr

[1] Murray *et. al.*, *Excavations in Cyprus* (London, 1900).
[2] J. N. L. Myres, *Handbook of the Cesnola Collection of Antiquities from Cyprus* (New York, 1914).

Karageorghis.[1] As there are no close parallels[2] for these remarkable ornaments outside Cyprus, it is not possible to say whether the gold pair was imported and then copied in silver and bronze or whether they were made in Cyprus with imported gold. Simple bronze examples from Ayia Paraskevi (fig. 52d) can be dated earlier in the Early Cypriote period and provide evidence for Dr Karageorghis's view that these ornaments are Cypriote in origin.

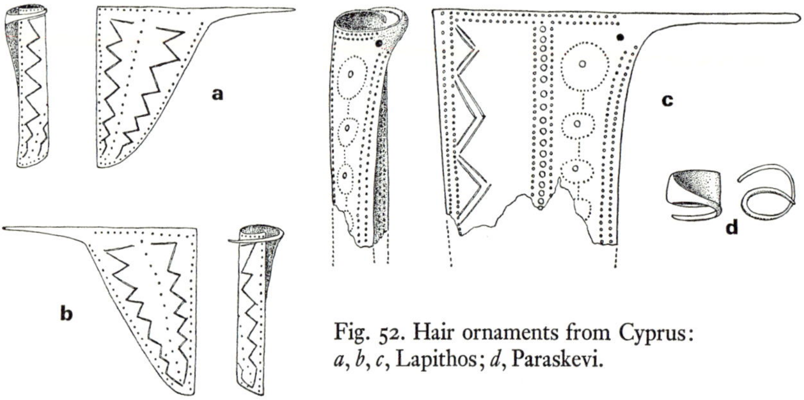

Fig. 52. Hair ornaments from Cyprus: *a*, *b*, *c*, Lapithos; *d*, Paraskevi.

The second pair of objects consists of simple spiral hair ornaments in gold, found in an Early Cypriote III tomb[3] and of the type known in Mesopotamia in the Third Dynasty of Ur period (Ur Grave 1422) and in Syria.

Apart from these gold hair ornaments, we have no other objects of gold jewellery which can be dated to the end of the third and beginning of the second millennia and the Middle Cypriote period (c. 2000–1600 B.C.) is equally barren – due, no doubt certainly in part, to the absence of gold in the island and difficulties of obtaining supplies from abroad. Yet contact with Syria is shown not only from pottery, which shows Syrian influence, but by the presence of a few seals of north Syrian origin. The seals, however, were probably not imported until the succeeding Late Cypriote period; an inscribed haematite cylinder with gold mounts found on a necklace from Ajios Jakovos belongs to this period.[4]

[1] V. Karageorghis, 'Sur quelques ornaments de chevelure du bronze ancien de Chypre', *Syria*, XLII, 1–2, 1965.

[2] The gold hair ornaments from the Hissar IIIc treasure (see p. 80) may possibly be related (see Schmidt, *Tepe Hissar*, pl. XXXV, H. 3218).

[3] Gjerstad, *S.C.E.*, I, pl. XXXV, 2, 31, 33, and pl. CXLV, L.322A, 29.

[4] Ibid., pl. CXLVII, 9, p. 357, 12.

CHAPTER 5

Babylonia, Mesopotamia and Iran 2017–1750 B.C.

INTRODUCTION

The first three hundred years of the second millennium in Mesopotamia are characterized by an extraordinary lack of material where fine jewellery is concerned. The reasons for this lacuna are partly historical and partly due to the fact that few cemeteries of this period have been excavated. At a site such as Ur the destruction wrought by the Elamites and the chaotic condition in Sumer prior to the establishment of the Isin Dynasty by Ishbi-Erra of Mari would not have been particularly conducive to the production of gold and silver work by the skilled craftsmen we know flourished in the temple workshops during the preceding period of the Third Dynasty of Ur. But one important result of the break up of the empire of the Third Ur kings and the advance of the Amurru (Amorites) from the desert into the settled lands of Mesopotamia must certainly have begun even before the disastrous sack of the city of Ur by the Elamites. This was the dispersion or capture of skilled temple jewellers and goldsmiths who may well have been taken off to Elam by the captors of Ibi-Sin, the last king of the Third Dynasty of Ur. The loot taken by the invaders would certainly have included easily portable objects such as jewellery; certain gold pieces from Susa[1] and Tello (Lagash) now in the Louvre afford evidence that the techniques developed by Sumerian smiths were not entirely lost in the succeeding Isin-Larsa period.

A pair of earrings from Ur now in the British Museum (pl. 57a, b, c) is important as it illustrates that the fine art of granulation continued to be used by the craftsmen at Ur during the Larsa period; this pair may well date from the time of Gugunum of Larsa (c. 1932–1906 B.C.), when the city seems to have recovered some of the prosperity known in the preceding century. Documents relating to private business and the increasing

[1] Many of the finest pieces of jewellery from Susa have been published in Amiet, *Elam*, with excellent photographs and detailed references to the original Susa publications.

practice of the dedication of votive gifts in the temples both attest to a certain stability favourable to the production of objects in precious metals.

We know there was only one short conflict between Larsa and Isin during the period of the Isin-Larsa domination at Ur and excavations have shown that considerable restoration work on the zigurrat terrace was undertaken by the successors of Gugunum. Here, a shrine with five chambers was surrounded by a long range of storehouses and the inscriptions refer to the temple of E-nun-maḫ as 'the house of silver and gold'. The statues and other gifts dedicated to the goddess Ninmah by the Larsa kings could thus be safely housed. Elsewhere in southern Babylonia, at Larsa and Eridu, restoration of temples was undertaken by the later kings of the Larsa Dynasty; and at Ur the seventy years of rule under Kudur-magug (who was of Elamite origin) and his sons, Warad-Sin and Rim-Sin, constituted a period of relative prosperity.

It is against a background of considerable architectural, literary and commercial activity that we have to consider the few examples of gold work which survive. A pair of earrings found in a tomb at Susa, now in the Louvre (pl. 59c), is worked in the same technique as the British Museum pair from Ur – both having a small circular cloison for inlay surrounded by minute granulation at the base of the pin. Earrings from Tell Asmar (fig. 53) and Tello, Larsa period, belong to the same type, with the body of the earring made of fluted gold, usually three or more flutings, and round cloison to hold the inlay (for both of these, cf. Ashur, fig. 46). Similar earrings from Susa (pl. 58b) in the Louvre, dating from about this period, are of silver and show the skill of the jeweller in working in granulation both in gold and silver. Other pieces of jewellery from Susa–earrings (pl. 59a, b), bracelets and beads – are evidence for the spread of Sumerian techniques into Elam during the first two centuries of the second millennium; and a few other pieces from Tello show that there was no break in the development of jewellery working during the Isin-Larsa period.

After this period there is a gap in our knowledge of Babylonian jewellery work until the end of the First Dynasty of Babylon, but a certain amount of information can be gained from a study of the frescoes at the site of Mari on the Euphrates, where jewellery is portrayed. We have few extant dated examples from this period, but there is no reason to suppose that jewellery was not being made. The statue of the goddess with the flowing vase, now in the Aleppo Museum, and the intercessory goddesses on the relief and frescoes from the huge palace of Zimri-Lim at Mari, dating from the earlier part of the eighteenth century (Parrot, *Sumer*, Nos. 339,

340), are all shown wearing many necklaces of beads, which entirely cover the neck like a 'choker' (figs. 54, 56 and 58) and which must have been kept in place by a large counterweight attached to a long tassel worn below the neck on the shoulders.[1] A bronze statue of the goddess Lama (fig. 57), now in the British Museum,[2] shows the counterweight in position. Triple bracelets and armlets (fig. 56) are also portrayed in the frescoes. The absence of earrings on the frescoes is probably due to the fact that the painter was not concerned with small details of dress; the terracotta plaque from Mari (fig. 58) shows a female head with triple fluted earrings and 'choker' necklaces, while the priests and other male figures wear small circular earrings (fig. 61a and b). Necklaces with enormous beads and large circular pendants are characteristic of the priests in the sacrificial scenes (figs. 59 and 60). The goddess with the flowing vase has a complicated arrangement of multiple earrings composed of several crescentic earrings fixed into a circular ring, of a type quite possibly similar to the granulated penannular earrings with hollow centre from Ajjul (see p. 116). Alternatively, she is wearing a large earring of the type known from Susa (pl. 58a, b) with multiple fluted body, probably dating from the Larsa period, which is also shown on the Mari terracotta plaque (fig. 58).

This plaque is useful for determining whether the female figures or goddesses on the numerous terracottas and terracotta plaques dating from the Larsa and Old Babylonian periods are wearing double or triple rows of multiple fluted earrings, or whether the opinion of some scholars is correct and these loops each side of the face should be interpreted as locks of hair. On the plaque from Mari (fig. 58) there is no doubt that a pair of triple fluted earrings and long loops of hair resting on the shoulders are both portrayed. In our opinion, a plaque showing the goddess Ishtar from the Kititum temple at Ischali (fig. 62b) also shows two rows of multiple fluted earrings with four large loops of hair below; the goddess wears a 'choker' necklace similar to that worn by the female figure in fig. 58, together with an elaborate series of five necklaces with large central rhomboid and curved beads of types well known in earlier periods in Babylonia and Sumer. A similar plaque in the Ashmolean Museum shows the goddess with 'choker' and five necklaces, but here the identification of the three loops each side of the face is more problematical. Two figures from Tell Asmar are shown with a double row of possibly triple fluted

[1] See A. Spycket, 'La Déesse Lama', *R.A.*, LIV, 1960, pp. 73–84. Strommenger, *Mesopotamia*, pls. 162–3.
[2] Wiseman, 'The Goddess Lama at Ur', *Iraq*, XXII, 1960, pp. 166–71, pl. XXIII.

earrings (fig. 63a and b), but fig. 63a shows extra flat extensions which are pierced by five and three holes on each side of the face, obviously for the insertion of metal earrings (see also fig. 62a, where the goddess wears fluted earrings, necklace, bracelet and pelvic beads).

54

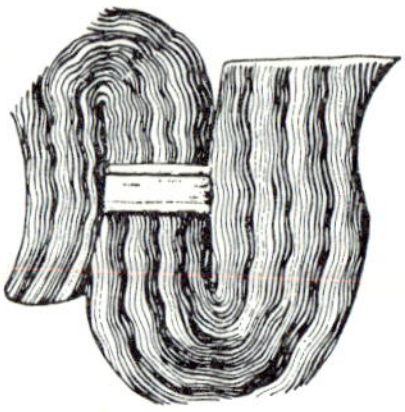

55

53

56

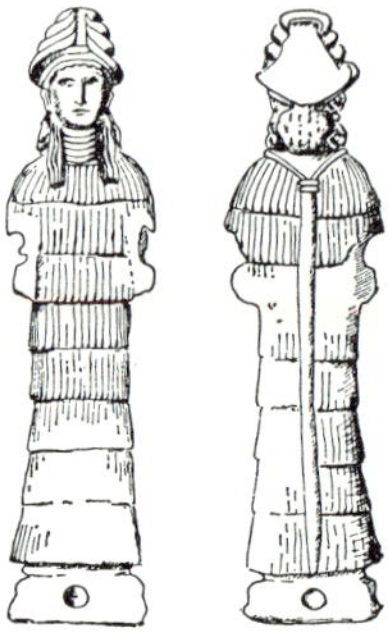

57

58

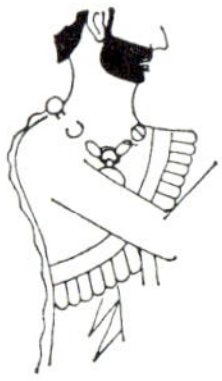

59

60

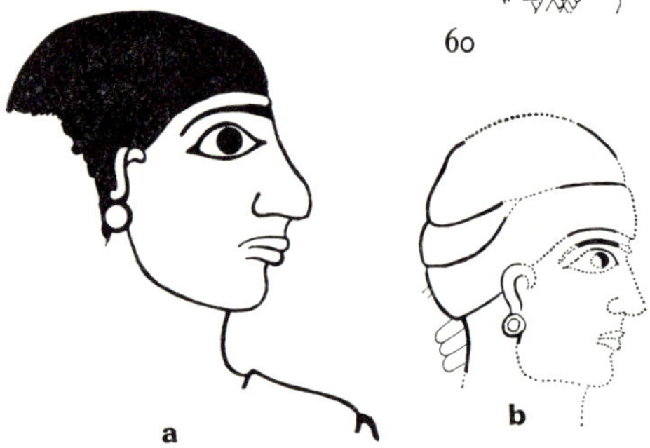

a b

61

Fig. 53. Fluted earrings from Tell Asmar.

Fig. 54. Goddess with necklaces and bangles from a Mari relief.

Fig. 55. Fragment of hairband from Mari.

Fig. 56. Goddess from a Mari fresco.

Fig. 57. Bronze goddess from Mari, showing counterweight.

Fig. 58. Terracotta from Mari, showing triple fluted earrings and 'choker' necklaces.

Fig. 59. Male figure with necklace and pendants from a Mari fresco.

Fig. 60. Sacrificial scene from a Mari fresco.

Fig. 61. Male heads with circular earrings from a Mari fresco.

Jewellery was not confined to goddesses or females on terracottas; a bearded warrior god with bull's ears and carrying two axes is shown on a fine plaque (fig. 62c and d) wearing an elaborate circular disc pendant with six petals round a central knob, probably denoting cloisonné work. Below is a thin crescent pendant.

62

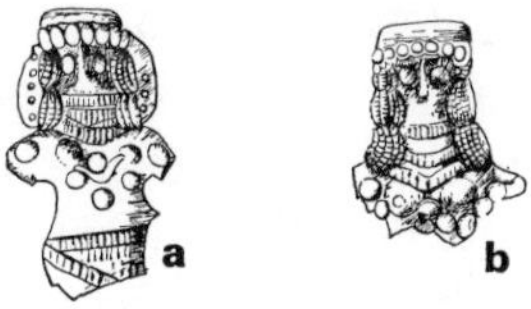

63

64

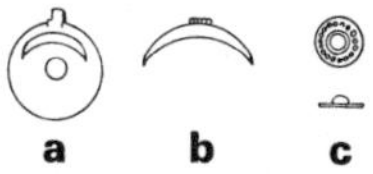

65

66

Fig. 62. *a*, goddess with fluted earrings, necklace, bracelet and pelvic beads; *b*, goddess with fringed robe, two rows of fluted earrings and holding necklaces; *c*, deity with axes, medallion and moon pendant; *d*, enlargement of moon pendant shown in *c*; from Old Babylonian terracottas.

Fig. 63. Terracotta goddesses with jewellery from Tell Asmar.

Fig. 64. Hammurabi with necklaces and bracelet from a Sippar relief.

Fig. 65. *a*, silver moon pendant; *b*, gold moon pendant; *c*, gold button with repoussé decoration; from Mari.

Fig. 66. Bronze statuette of a worshipper from Mari.

The importance of Mari as an artistic and commercial centre during the reign of Hammurabi of Babylon (1792–1750 B.C.) cannot be overstressed, especially when one considers the high quality of the metal work belonging to this period as illustrated by the bronzes, not only from Mari, but also from Larsa and Ischali in central Babylonia, where the use of gold for decorating bronze is also found. One can, therefore, reasonably infer that the jewellers' workshops at Mari must have produced many varied products which would have been used to decorate the statues in the temples or as votive offerings to the deities. The use of jewellery in everyday life is also attested by the fact that, on many terracotta plaques, musicians and even boxers are wearing necklaces, while Hammurabi is shown on a relief now in the British Museum (fig. 64) with a necklace of large beads round his neck of a size comparable with those worn by the priests on the Mari frescoes (fig. 59).

Unfortunately, the palace at Mari has produced few examples of jewellery, but the pieces which survived the sack of the palace by the soldiers of Hammurabi are particularly informative. A circular pendant, with the usual rolled-over attachment for suspension, is decorated with a crescent above a central circle (fig. 65a), while a gold pendant with rolled-over attachment in the form of a crescent (fig. 65b) invites comparison with similar pendants from Ajjul and the elaborate granulated example from Dilbat (pl. 61). Repoussé work is shown on the small circular disc with central boss from Mari (fig. 65c). Two beads call for especial attention: these are of gold, melon-shaped and fluted (cf. pl. 60 for the type) and are of the same type as those discussed on p. 125 from both Ajjul and Dilbat.

A bronze figure of a lady in the British Museum shows a pendant of the type found at Mari (fig. 66) worn suspended from a necklace or neckband which is twisted behind the head and hangs down the back. A minute circular button (fig. 65c) with repoussé dots round a central boss may be the cap of a paste bead similar to an unstratified example from Khorsabad (pl. 60).[1]

THE DILBAT NECKLACE (Pls. 61–64)

A remarkable necklace, now in the Metropolitan Museum of Art, New York, must now be considered against the background of the foregoing remarks. The information concerning its history is – as is so often the

[1] This unusual type occurs at Troy in Treasure L, but nowhere else to my knowledge (see Schmidt, *Sammlung*, Nos. 6108, 6109).

case with collections of gold jewellery – very uninformative, but can be briefly summarized. The original account states that the beads, pendants, two gold caps for cylinder seals, four early Kassite seals (see below) and an earring (pl. 65b) were found in a jar at Dilbat. The seals do not belong to the gold caps (pl. 65a), so that the original collection may have included five seals in all.

From a double row of fluted melon-shaped beads are suspended seven pendants: a lunar crescent (pl. 63a, b), the forked lightning symbol and two circular rosettes (pl. 64a, b), all decorated in the finest granulation work, a central circular pendant of the 'disc with rays' type which is worked in repoussé and incision (pl. 61), and a pair of gold figures of a goddess (pls. 62a, b, c) with horned headdress and long kaunakes and raised hands who can be identified as the goddess Lama. One of the seals shows a goddess – probably also Lama – with a bull with the lightning symbol on his back behind her (pl. 65c).

Reference should be made to an article published by Professor Wiseman in 1960,[1] where various representations of the goddess Lama are discussed and mention is made of a Kassite stele from Uruk, where an inscribed figure of the goddess informs us that she is wearing a *gadmāḫu* garment. As Professor Wiseman points out, this is a ritual dress which was not worn by ordinary humans at this period, and the *gadmāḫu* of the texts was worn by goddesses down to the end of the First Babylonian Dynasty. A detailed description of the sanctuary where the Ur goddess Lama was found is given. This sanctuary dates from the Larsa period and, if the seals and all the gold objects of the Dilbat find were actually found together in the jar (and we have no evidence to disprove the statement), then the deposit in the jar cannot be later than the Early Kassite period, with a *terminus ante quem* of about 1600 B.C.

The importance of this collection of jewellery cannot be overstressed, as we have hardly any other gold jewellery from Mesopotamia which can be assigned to this period, owing to the lack of excavation of First Dynasty levels in Babylonia. The extremely fine granulation work can only be compared with that of Aqar Qūf (see p. 163) or the gold work from Ajjul in Palestine (see Chapter 7), but there is no reason to doubt that the workmanship is Babylonian, especially when the symbolic form of the pendants and the presence of the pair of Lama figures is considered. If a date of c. 1600 B.C. for the find is correct, then it is possible to deduce two vitally important points in the history of jewellery work in the first part of the

[1] *Iraq*, XXII, 1960, pp. 166–71.

second millennium B.C. It would seem likely that the Kassites, when they finally consolidated their position in Babylonia to the point where they began to rule the country, not only took over the religious ideas and iconography of the Babylonians, but must also have learnt the art of fine goldworking from the Sumerian and Babylonian craftsmen who had developed the intricate techniques, such as the art of granulation, to a standard which invites comparison with the finest Greek or Etruscan examples. If this is correct, then the sudden appearance of the art of granulation at Aqar Qūf in the reign of Kurigalzu is not surprising and its use by Assyrian craftsmen at Ashur in the thirteenth century B.C. is also understandable. It is quite possible that Babylon was the centre from which Asiatic jewellers learnt their trade and that it was from Babylon that new techniques spread over to the Syrian coast and down into Palestine. The subsequent history of the art of granulation will be discussed in Chapters 7 and 10 and any suggestions concerning the possible part played by the Hurri in this development must not be obscured by the important influence of Babylonia on the artistic productions of the surrounding countries.

Fig. 67. Head of moon god from a Mari fresco.

Of the four seals, one is definitely Kassite, because its inscription is a short prayer to the god Nabu, and on two of the others the names of the fathers of the donors are well known in Kassite texts. The fourth seal is stylistically Kassite. There is no necessity, however, to date the jewellery as late as the seals. It is more probable – in view of the pendants, the lunar crescent, the forked lightning (both of which are symbols used extensively in the First Dynasty of Babylon period) and the gold goddess Lama (who is not likely to date later than the earlier part of the First Dynasty period) – that the necklace belongs to the eighteenth or seventeenth century B.C.

There are several features which connect this necklace with the palace period at Mari. First, the lunar crescent, worked in extremely fine granulation and portrayed on the headdress of the seated moon god on the palace frescoes (fig. 67); secondly, the rosette (pl. 64a) with nine granulated circles between the rays of an eight-rayed star; and lastly the gold goddess (pl. 62) whose dress with necklace and counterweight is similar to that of the Mari statue of the goddess with streams. Fluted melon beads are also found at Mari and at Ajjul and are discussed below.

IRAN IN THE END OF THE THIRD AND BEGINNING OF THE SECOND MILLENNIUM B.C. (GIYAN PERIOD IV)

Tepe Giyan

The site of Tepe Giyan, excavated in 1931–2 by Contenau and Ghirshman, was one of the first sites excavated on the Iranian plateau and recently the material from the tombs has been discussed by R. H. Dyson, T. Cuyler Young and C. Goff.[1] A chronological framework can be constructed, based on the ceramic evidence from the graves, but this may need considerable amendment when Young's excavations at Godin Tepe are completed and when Clare Goff has completed her excavation at Baba Jan, Luristan. Several tombs, however, which contained jewellery can be related to the Dinkha tepe-Gök tepe tombs discussed below. Dates of c. 2100–1800 B.C. for Giyan IV, c. 1800–1650 B.C. (corresponding with the period of the First Dynasty of Babylon) for Giyan III, and c. 1650–1250 B.C. for Giyan II are used here until further evidence from Godin tepe or Giyan itself suggests amendment.

Several examples of the type of earring with fluted body known from Susa also occur among unstratified examples from Tepe Giyan. An earring of this type was found in Giyan Tomb 108 and another in the collection of the late Professor E. Herzfeld (fig. 68). The silver examples from Susa (pl. 58) now in the Louvre show variations in detail; there can be as many as nine flutings on the body of the earring or three well-marked lobes similar to the Ashur examples (fig. 46b and g, Chapter 4), but the general resemblance is remarkable and provides evidence for the view that goldsmiths in centres separated by many hundreds of kilometres

[1] Dyson in *Chronologies*, pp. 232f. C. Goff, *New Evidence of Cultural Development in Luristan in the late 2nd and early 1st Millennia*, unpublished Ph.D. thesis (University of London, 1966).

must either have been working in close contact with each other or have been trained in the same school of jewellery working. It is becoming increasingly certain, as more evidence accumulates, that the Sumerian-Elamite tradition with its long history of technical skill must have continued to influence goldsmiths all over western Asia, long after the end of

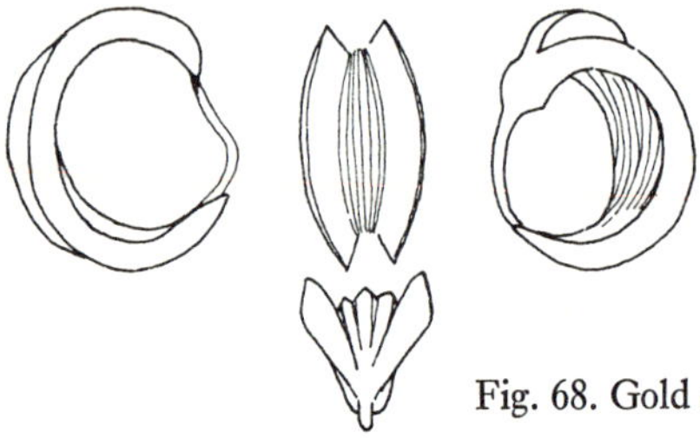

Fig. 68. Gold earring with centre fluting from Giyan.

the Third Dynasty of Ur. In Assyria, the continuity of tradition is to be expected, as it is also in Elam. It is, therefore, not surprising to find examples as far away from Susa as Giyan. Dyson has noted that Tomb 108, Giyan IV, shows western connections; the stemmed goblet with loop handle is a type distributed over Palestine, Syria and the Phoenician coast where it does not appear before 2000 B.C.[1] A fine silver pair of earrings in the Teheran Museum has over eleven flutings and each circle at the base of the pin is surrounded with granules.

Four tombs from Tepe Djamshidi, a site dug by Professor R. Ghirshman[2] which yielded material comparable to the Giyan sequence, contained silver jewellery. Here the silver work suggests a late Sargonid – Third Dynasty of Ur date which does not contradict Dyson's suggested date for the earlier part of Giyan IVb. Tombs 16, 18 and 19 produced plain looped silver earrings, a hair-ring and a rough silver disc decorated in repoussé, while a silver torque with an agate pendant came from Tomb 13. The geographical situation of Tepe Djamshidi is important as it is situated fifteen kilometres (as the crow flies) from Tepe Giyan the other side of the pass through the Kuh-i-Garri mountain range in a wide upland valley, inside the area which can be correctly called Luristan, while Giyan lies to the east of the range and far more open to communication from the Median plateau.

[1] Dyson in *Chronologies*, p. 233. See also *C.A.H.*, No. 66, 'The archaeological evidence of the second millennium B.C. on the Persian plateau', where Giyan IV–III are treated as a single regional culture.

[2] *Giyan*, pls. 79–81.

The distribution of the earrings discussed above is further complicated by the enormous mass of gold and silver jewellery in the Mazda Collection in Teheran, the origin of which is said to be Gilan, the province of Iran lying along the south-east coast of the Caspian which includes both the fertile coastal plain and the mountainous region behind. Many examples of the Susa fluted type of earring from this area (including the fine pair in the Teheran Museum mentioned above) are unstratified and without any associated pottery or objects. Pl. 120 (see Chapter 9) shows a gold fluted example from 'Amlash' now in the Teheran Museum and, although this type has not, as yet, occurred in Luristan, the distribution suggests that the production of Elamite goldsmiths at the beginning of the second millennium may have been on a scale much larger than the relatively small amount of stratified material suggests. Alternatively, the Gilan examples may reflect the activities of a group or groups of travelling skilled goldsmiths and jewellers who were attracted to centres where gold and silver were easily available and where the social organization provided a ready market for objects made with skilled techniques and a long tradition of craftsmanship. But until a site in Gilan giving a stratified series of pottery and gold work dating from the beginning of the second to the beginning of the first millennium is excavated, there is little that can be said about this problem.[1] There can be little doubt, however, that among the quite astonishing amount of jewellery which exists mainly in private collections and whose provenance is given as Gilan, there is a surprising amount which one would be inclined to date to the second millennium B.C.

The results of Dr Cuyler Young's excavations at Godin tepe near Kangavar in Luristan, where pottery of Giyan periods II, III and IV occurs, are awaited with great interest and should shed light on the vexed problem of the chronology of the Giyan sequence. This will be of great importance for any further attempt to date the jewellery from the earlier excavation at Giyan. Already, Giyan-Hasanlu relationships are becoming evident and it may well be that the information which can be gleaned from the relatively small amount of stratified jewellery from Susa and Giyan, when considered alongside the Gilan material, will corroborate the view based on the pottery that there was a 'spread of basic forms and style northward from Elam to the southern shore of Lake Rizayeh'[2] along the route from Susa to north-west Iran.

[1] The work of Dr Hakemi may give us the necessary evidence.
[2] Dyson in *Chronologies*, p. 233. See also Goff in *Iran*, 1970, pp. 141–56.

IRAN AT THE FIRST HALF OF THE SECOND MILLENNIUM B.C.

Susa

The earrings from the first part of this period at Susa have been discussed in the preceding section; to these must be added the information which can be found on reliefs, statues and terracottas and the surprising amount of pieces of gold and silver jewellery which has survived the depredation of pillage and loot at Susa. Many of these pieces are in the Louvre and will be the subject of a special study by P. Amiet who has also illustrated some of the finest in his book, *Elam*. The richness of this period, as shown in the jewellery, presents a sharp contrast to the preceding period at Susa when Susiana had been subject to Ur. During the time of Shulgi, Susa had to provide mercenaries to help the Sumerians defend both the frontier province of Lagash and the Elamite frontier against the mountain tribes to the north-west. In spite of Shulgi's building activity at Ur and the dedication of offerings in the temple of Susa, little jewellery has survived; this may be fortuitous, but the texts giving accounts of the marriage between the daughter of Shu-Sin of Ur and a governor of Anshan tell us that her dowry consisted entirely of food and drink – oil, butter, cream, milk and beer – but no jewellery. It may be that the flow of precious metals from the Zagros mountains was diverted from Ur and Nippur at this period. Shu-Sin's campaigns against the so-called 'Su' people and the country of Zabshali (located by Hinz in the mountains of Luristan west of Khurrumābād[1]) were undertaken not only to quell the turbulent mountain people, but also to obtain lead, copper, bronze and, presumably, gold, as after one of these forays Shu-Sin had a statute of himself cast in gold.

While we have no jewellery which can be dated with certainty to the time of the Elamite Dynasty of Simash (probably the area round Khurrumabad) during the time of the suzerainty of the kings of the Third Dynasty of Ur, one of the later kings of the Simash Dynasty is known to have married a Babylonian princess, Me-kubi (daughter of Bilalama, the governor of Eshnunna) who brought a rich dowry with her and founded a special temple to Inanna at Susa. This may have provided the impetus for the organization of temple workshops and the production of fine jewellery, such as the material which has been found in tombs and deposits dating from the first two centuries of the second millennium B.C.

[1] *C.A.H.*, No. 19, p. 16.

E. Falcon earring from Ajjul. See p. 118

F. Gold jewellery from Gilan. See p. 205

G. Bracelet from Ziweye. See p. 209

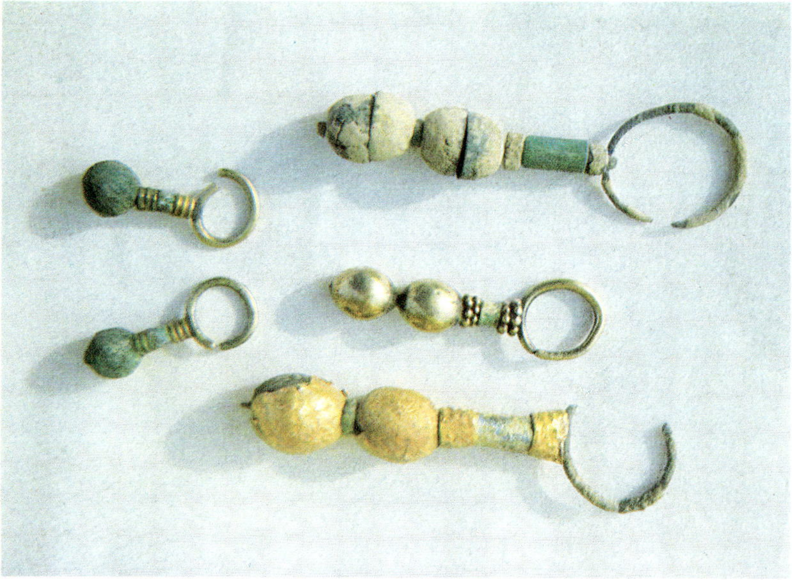

H. Earrings from Luristan. See p. 265

The distinctive types can be divided into the following groups:

Earrings (pls. 58 and 59, p. 84)
To the fluted type discussed above can be added a fine pair of plain silver earrings in the form of an open penannular ring (Amiet, *Elam*, No. 194).

Beads
Fluted melon-shaped beads are common, and occur on a bracelet or necklace of agate and hollow gold beads with a distinctive long tubular-shaped bead with curved body decorated with incisions (Amiet, *Elam*, 195). This type can also be found on an alabaster figure of a prince or local official from Susa (fig. 69) and on the stele from Susa with a seated god in

69

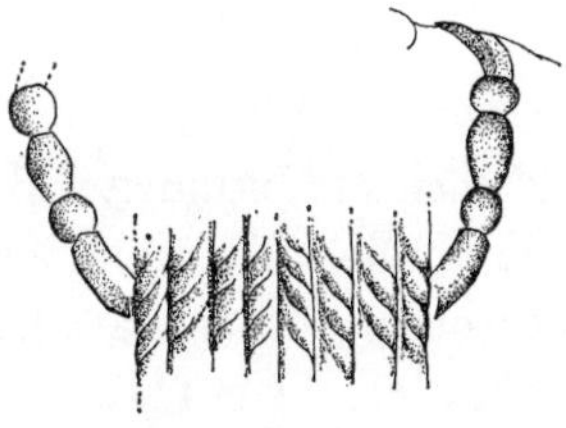

70

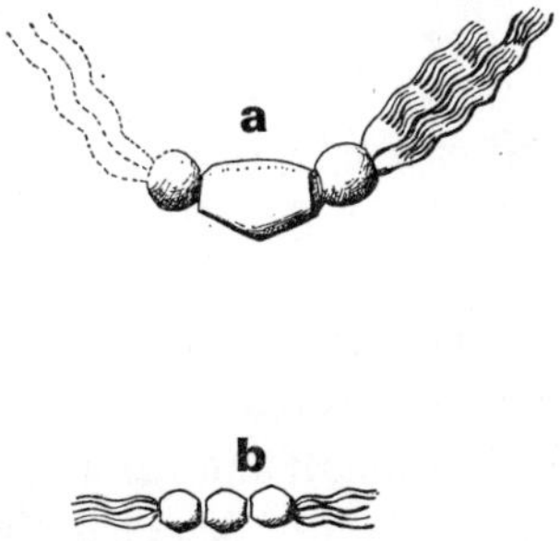

71

Fig. 69. Necklace on an alabaster figure from Susa.
Fig. 70. Necklace from a Susa statuette.
Fig. 71. Necklace and bracelet from a statuette from Sippar.

front of the palm tree in a tall pot.[1] Necklaces of large beads were part of the usual dress of governors or princes of Susa, as shown by the male statues found at Susa (some of them booty from Eshnunna), now in the Louvre (fig. 70; cf. fig. 71, British Museum), while an ivory female statuette shows no less than seven rows of necklaces. This ivory statuette (Amiet, *Elam*, No. 217) is instructive for the study of jewellery. The necklaces must have been held in place by a long counterweight (see p. 86) which was shown on the statuette by an inlay of presumably precious metal, gold or silver, which was probably looted in antiquity; the slot for the inlay remains down the back of the statuette, while large heavy bangles must have been worn above the elbows where a deep incision is

[1] *Encyclopédie Photographique de l'Art*, I, pl. 247 (Musée du Louvre, 1935).

also made in the ivory to receive the gold or silver inlay to represent the bangles.

Bracelets

The ivory female statuette (above) wears at least three bracelets on the wrist and these may be of a type found at Susa which consists of two solid gold flat strips soldered together longitudinally with incised ends. Other bracelets of this period are made of gold over a bronze or copper core (Louvre No. 5711). Heavy bracelets were also worn by the men; the alabaster statue mentioned above (fig. 69) and the diorite statues[1] (cf. fig. 70) found at Susa, but in fact booty from Eshnunna, show double and single bracelets certainly decorated, but the detail is not possible to identify owing to the fragmentary condition of the original. A plain bracelet of three beads threaded on several strands of some kind of thread is combined with a necklace of large beads on a female statuette from Abu Ḥabbah (Sippar) (fig. 71a, b).

Pins

Various kinds of pins occur, often made of shell and bitumen with bronze or copper heads covered with gold; a fine example with bronze shank was covered with gold leaf and has a head of carnelian; others have thin rings of schist and chalk threaded on to the shank, while the heads are of bronze or copper covered with gold (Amiet, *Elam*, Nos. 190, 191, p. 261).

A pair of plain gold toggle pins, pierced for the threading of a cord to attach to the material of a garment, belongs to the mid-second millennium, seventeenth to sixteenth centuries B.C. (Amiet, *Elam*, No. 246, p. 327); the way they were used is shown on two female terracottas (Amiet, *Elam*, No. 245A, B, p. 326) now in the Teheran Museum, where the back of the cloak is brought forward over the shoulders and secured on each side with a pin.

[1] Strommenger, *Mesopotamia*, pls. 148, 150.

CHAPTER 6

Anatolia c. 1950–1750 B.C. Kültepe-Kanesh and the Assyrian *Kārum*

INTRODUCTION

The main source for the economic history of this period came from Kültepe-Kanesh where outside the old walled city the new settlement was built and occupied by Assyrian merchant colonists. This Assyrian *kārum* or trading colony became one of the most important centres of the metal trade in Anatolia – gold, silver, copper, precious stones and iron being exported to Ashur on the Tigris in exchange for textiles, wool, tin and various other commodities.[1]

The excavations on the city mound at Kültepe and the neighbouring Assyrian *kārum* have yielded some remarkable pieces of gold jewellery, found in stratified contexts, as well as silver, bronze and copper artifacts. The large level II palace on the city mound is famous for the bronze spear head of Trojan type, inscribed with the name of the Hittite king, Anittas (c. 1850 B.C.). A fine gold cup and a large gold biconical ornamental bead about 10·2 cm long (fig. 72) which may have formed the centre piece of

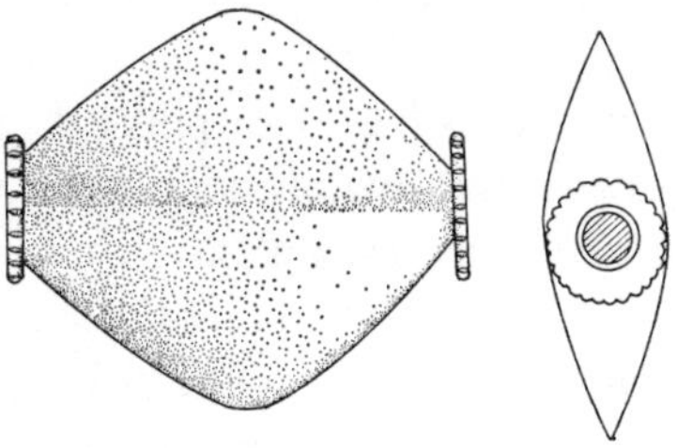

Fig. 72. Gold biconical bead from Kültepe.

a necklace belong to the period on the mound at Kültepe contemporary with the first colony period (*kārum* level II), which can be dated between 1952 and 1852 B.C. The existence of metal working shops shows that the

[1] For a detailed study of the documentary evidence, see P. Garelli, *Les Assyriens en Cappadoce* (Paris, 1963) with references to original sources. See p. 77 for discussion of the chronology proposed on p. 79.

jewellery, such as the large biconical bead (fig. 72), could represent local work, possibly skilfully executed by a jeweller familiar with Assyrian and Babylonian jewellery. The bead invites comparison with the large biconical gold-capped beads of banded agate from Uruk (see pl. 45) which, although earlier in date, could have formed the prototype for the gold Anatolian example.

The jewellery from level II in the *kārum* came mainly from graves, where in two instances the skeleton was wearing a conical gold or silver cap of a type known from seal impressions where it is worn by deities. A child's grave in the *kārum* level II produced a minute gold quadruple spiral bead made in a different way from the Mesopotamian examples of this type, where the spirals are formed from the drawn-out ends of the central tube. At Kültepe the four spirals of gold wire are attached to a central cylindrical tube (fig. 29b), suggesting that the jewellery was imitating the more intricate Mesopotamian technique (see pl. 34 and fig. 46c, Chapters 3 and 4, and fig. 22a, Chapter 2).

Pins from kārum *level II*

Three main types can be distinguished; bronze examples are included here, as gold and silver pins belong to these types and the bronze is often gold-plated.

(*a*) With oval-shaped fluted head, plain and ribbed shank (*Belleten*, XIX, 73, 1955, figs. 75, 77).

(*b*) Flat mushroom-shaped fluted head, incised or ribbed shank (*Belleten*, XIX, 73, 1955, figs. 76, 91).

(*c*) Rounded or angular conical head (*Belleten*, XIX, 73, 1955, figs. 78, 80).

Types (*a*) and (*c*) can be technically related to the Alaca pins (pl. 32 and figs. 25 and 26a) and can be regarded as native Anatolian types. Type (*b*) is unknown at Alaca. The technique used on the examples which were not made in one piece was to pierce the head of the pin so that the shank could pass through the head, thus securing a firm fit. The more elaborate pins found in succeeding level Ib of the *kārum*, when the site was re-occupied about fifty years after a disastrous fire destroyed the earlier level II, can all be related to these basic types.

Pins from kārum *level Ib* (figs. 73 and 74)

These pins are technically more advanced than those in level II and the toggle pin (pin with the shank pierced, through which a cord could be threaded) appears here, being apparently unknown at Kültepe in earlier levels. Several examples occur of pins with bronze cores plated with gold or fluted bronze heads combining gold and lapis lazuli. A white stone was used for the head of one pin, also fluted, while a silver pin had a head in

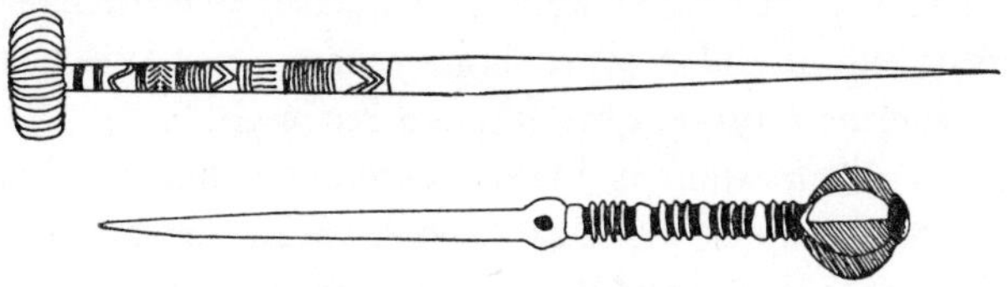

Fig. 73. Gold pin from Kültepe *kārum*.
Fig. 74. Toggle pin from Kültepe *kārum*.

the shape of a perched bird.[1] A fine gold pin (fig. 73) with flat mushroom-shaped fluted head has an elaborately decorated shank which was made in the same way as those of Type (*b*) in the earlier level II period with the shank passing through the head.

Jewellery from kārum *level Ib*

The material from the graves of the *kārum* level Ib (c. 1812–1730 B.C.) shows close connections with north Syria, especially the Ḫabur area, and also a knowledge of Mesopotamian burial fashion. A gold diadem pierced at each end and two simple gold earrings, as well as gold strips for placing on the mouth and eyes of the dead, came from *kārum* level Ib, while Grave 14 contained nine gold rings, fluted melon-shaped beads of Meso-potamian-north Syrian type and a pin with gold shaft and bronze tip and head. In the same grave were two silver dress or toggle pins with fluted heads, the shanks between the hole and the head being heavily ribbed and covered with gold leaf (fig. 74). Bronze fluted toggle pins are well known from Hittite sites in Anatolia, north Syria and Palestine, with rare examples in the Ḫabur valley at Chagar Bazar, but several from Byblos and examples in gold from the so-called Byblos treasure, whose exact origin is unknown, are shown in pl. 66 for comparison. In these examples the ring is *in situ*, threaded through the hole of the pin and it may be that the gold rings in Grave 14 were intended as rings for the fluted pins, rather than for earrings. An example in bronze from Ajjul belonging to the early second millennium (Middle Bronze I period) and similar to the Kül-tepe examples is shown in pl. 67. Others from Yabrud in Syria associated

[1] Özgüc in *Belleten*, XIX, 73, 1955, figs. 35, 36, 68–73, 79–89. See also pins with flat mushroom-shaped and fluted heads from Alaca in Kosay, *Alaca*, pls. 121–4.

with a fenestrated axe and seal of the First Dynasty of Babylon must belong to the early part of the second millennium B.C.[1] and are among the earliest examples of fluted pins in Syria – probably reflecting Anatolian influence on Syrian metallurgy.

Grave 11 contained silver jewellery; a circular pendant, a small silver seated female figure and a silver lunate-shaped pendant could, as the excavator suggests, represent the sun and moon goddess.[2]

The 'lunula' is important as it is also used as a pendant at Mari (see fig. 65b and p. 88, Chapter 5); it can also be seen on the necklace from Dilbat (pl. 61, Chapter 5) and worn by the bronze figure of a lady in the British Museum (fig. 66, Chapter 5). It occurs in Hittite levels (fourteenth-thirteenth century B.C. at Boğazköy[3] and in gold at Ras Shamra (No. 23. 476, Damascus Museum).

Pl. 68 shows a group of jewellery from the *kārum* Ib period. It is especially interesting for the circular plaques decorated in repoussé punched dots, one of them pierced with four holes to facilitate attachment to material, probably a garment. Recently, at Acem Hüyük near Aksaray, Professor Nimet Özgüc has found remains of woven material to which small gold beads had been attached.[4] This could have belonged to a statue and have been an early Anatolian example of the 'golden garments of the gods' (see p. 259). The pendant (pl. 68) with central boss surrounded by twisted gold wires and rolled-over top for suspension is a Sumerian-north Syrian type closely comparable in technique with the recently published pair from the Sumerian treasure from Mari; many examples in this circular form are known from Chagar Bazar, Ras Shamara and Mari. The Chagar Bazar examples are well dated, in graves from level I, which in its first and second phases is contemporary with the colony period at Kültepe. Here Grave G. 141 contained an electrum pendant, a gold earring and a gold fillet placed round the forehead of the skeleton.[5] All the jewellery from Chagar Bazar level I, especially the gold, silver or electrum pendants with central boss, is closely related to the Kültepe jewellery; Boğazköy has produced a similar pendant, but in bronze, from a grave of the Hittite period.[6]

[1] *Annales Archaeologiques Arabes Syriennes*, XVII, 1967, 1–2.

[2] Özgüc, *Kültepe*, 1949, pl. LVII, Nos. 319–21.

[3] *M.D.O.G.*, 76, 1938, p. 21, Abb. 10.

[4] *Anatolia*, X, 1968. For recent discoveries of jewellery from Acem Hüyük, see summary by Mellink in *A.J.A.*, April 1969.

[5] *Iraq*, IV, 1942, figs. 12, 12 and 13, pl. XIIIA.

[6] *Boğazköy*, 1935, Taf 11, 22.

The earrings from Kültepe (pl. 68) are plain with narrow opening; two thicker rings of gold (over bronze) with narrow opening may have been designed as hair-rings. The long silver chain may have been a bracelet.

Bronzes from kārum *level Ib*

Certain objects from the *kārum* level Ib are certainly imported, such as the bronze shaft-hole axe with ribbed socket,[1] a type known from Chagar Bazar in north Syria and foreign to Anatolia. But, although north Syrian influence at the time of the Ib *kārum* (probably transmitted via Mari and Chagar Bazar) is especially strong, the occurrence of a mould for casting the typical Sumerian fenestrated type of axe and the discovery of metalsmiths' shops and a mould for the production of simple types of earring show that local production of metal objects, including jewellery, flourished.

[1] *Belleten*, XIX, 73, 1955, fig. 40a.

CHAPTER 7

Phoenicia, Syria and Palestine c. 2000-1550 B.C. Asiatic-Cypriote relations

INTRODUCTION

The remarkable finds from the site of Byblos, twenty-four kilometres north of Beirut, lie for the most part outside the scope of this book as the jewellery is mainly related to Egypt.[1] There are, however, a considerable number of objects whose Mesopotamian relationship must be considered and an attempt should be made to solve some of the outstanding and puzzling problems.

One remarkable piece of jewellery, the circular medallion found in the Montet jar, has recently been republished by Miss Olga Tufnell, who has studied the jar itself and its contents of nearly one thousand objects.[2] Her conclusions for the date of the deposit place it around 2000 B.C. and the latest objects in the jar appear to be the two cylinder seals of 'Syrian style', assigned by Porada to the twentieth to nineteenth centuries B.C. The circular medallion is unique and an isolated example of the techniques of granulation for this period (pl. 69). The inlay invites comparison with inlay work on the magnificent necklace of the priestess Abbabashti of Shu-Sin (see pl. 45) from Uruk and the use of this technique, combined with the non-Egyptian appearance of the medallion, suggests that it may have been the product of a local craftsman who had learned the technique of granulation from Mesopotamia and was copying Mesopotamian work. There is a crudeness of execution which is not typical of Mesopotamian work, either of the Third Dynasty of Ur or Isin-Larsa periods, and yet there is nothing to suggest that it was an import from Anatolia, where cloisonné inlay was not known until the first millennium B.C.

[1] Wilkinson, *Egyptian Jewellery*.

[2] O. Tufnell and W. A. Ward, 'Relations between Byblos, Egypt and Mesopotamia at the end of the third millennium B.C.: a study of the Montet Jar', *Syria*, XLIII, 3–4, 1966, pp. 166–241. E. Porada in *Syria*, XLIII, 34, 1966, pp. 243–258.

There is evidence that Byblos might have formed part of the empire of the Third Dynasty of Ur and, if this is so, the movement of craftsmen from Mesopotamia to the Phoenician coast should not have presented many difficulties. A dispersion of Sumerian craftsmen after the sack of Ur by the Elamites in 2003 B.C. might explain the extraordinary abundance of the technique of granulation, as found on the shafts of the gold fenestrated axes (colour pl. D and fig. 75) deposited as votive offerings in the temple

a

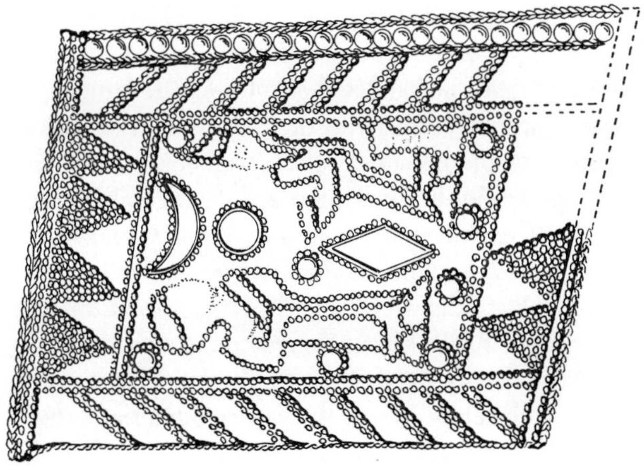

b

Fig. 75. Goldwork from Byblos.

of the obelisks at Byblos. It is on one of the gold strips decorating the shafts of these axes and on three gold axe foils that we find further evidence for Mesopotamian influence.[1] One of these pieces (see fig. 75a) has a pair of bull-men crudely designed but executed in fine granulation work; each bears a similar crescent in cloisonné border (though here the inlay is missing) to that found on the circular medallion from the Montet jar. The rectangular plaque (fig. 75b) is decorated with a border of fine triangular granulation and shows the same circular and crescent-shaped cloisons as the circular pendant (pl. 69). Two figures, one standing with folded hands before a seated figure, are portrayed. This scene is again a crude imitation of Mesopotamian work. The standing figure is dressed in long robes with one shoulder bare, typical of the period of Gudea of Lagash in south Babylonia, and the stance is comparable with that of worshippers on many seals of the Third Dynasty of Ur period. The details of the seated figure are more difficult to distinguish but the long robe and beard are both crudely executed in fine granules. Fig. 75b shows wire and granule cloisons which formerly held a paste inlay and appliqué wire twisted into a guilloche design round the edge.

These axes are, in their simpler bronze form, especially interesting, as they are one of the distinctive metal types which, with other artifacts, have been used by Dr Kenyon[2] as evidence for an Amorite penetration of Palestine at the end of the second and beginning of the first millennium B.C. (Intermediate Early Bronze – Middle Bronze period). Professor Yadin[3] has pointed out that the famous Beni Hasan tomb painting, with the caravan of Semites en route for Egypt, shows a 'duck bill' variety of the fenestrated axe in the hands of one of the male figures. The last group shows a procession of smiths with the bellows on the back of the donkey and is a pointer to the possibility that metalsmiths were included among the Amorite groups infiltrating into north Syria and Mesopotamia at the beginning of the second millennium B.C. We have, however, no evidence that the Amorites were skilled craftsmen themselves and the extreme skill shown by the goldsmiths who made the Byblos fenestrated axes suggests that they learnt their skill from Mesopotamian smiths and applied the art of granulation to the socketed fenestrated axes. This was a typical Syrian form which was developed from the earlier Sumerian tanged fenestrated blade.

[1] Culican, 'Essay on a Phoenician Earring', *P.E.Q.*, July–Dec. 1958, pp. 90–103, pl. 9.
[2] Kenyon, *Amorites and Canaanites*, Schweich Lectures 1963, pp. 6 ff. (London, 1966).
[3] Yadin, *Warfare*, p. 167.

But in trying to present evidence to identify specific metal types with the Amorites, it should be remembered that, even if it can be established that a certain well-defined ethnic group could use a particular kind of weapon or wear a distinctive type of ornament or jewellery, it does not necessarily follow that they actually made these objects. There are many instances of nomadic groups borrowing ideas from the skilled craftsmen of the settled populations and obtaining by trade the products of goldsmiths and bronze workers. There are, however, certain facts which cannot be disregarded concerning Palestine and to which Dr Kenyon has recently drawn attention in her Schweich lectures. Briefly, there is ample archaeological evidence to show that intrusive groups of people, using well-defined metal types and distinctive types of pottery, appeared in Palestine towards the end of the third millennium B.C. These people buried their dead in tombs which, at sites such as Jericho, are typical of the period between the end of the Early Bronze period and the beginning of the Middle Bronze (Dr Kenyon's Intermediate Early Bronze – Middle Bronze period=Albright's Middle Bronze I).

The metal types associated with this phenomenon are toggle pins (types with mushroom heads and the swollen or club heads), pins with a curled head, thin spear heads of the 'poker butt' variety, crescentic axe heads and long daggers with several rivets in the base. All these types, with the exception of the daggers, can be found in Sargonid contexts in Mesopotamia; and the site of Brak (see p. 27) provides stratified examples of the pins and spearheads mentioned above. Mrs Crawford has discussed the whole question of the diffusion of Mesopotamian metal types in Syria and Palestine[1] and her study certainly reinforces Dr Kenyon's proposal that these intrusive groups came to Palestine from Syria. But the metal types they used were known in Mesopotamia and north Syria in the Sargonid period and their origin can be traced back into the Early Dynastic period; if they are to be associated with the Amorites, they cannot have been invented by Amorite smiths. The subsequent development of types such as the toggle pins and the fenestrated axe in Syria and Palestine may well have been due to Amorite penetration; the stable conditions at the time of the great Amorite kingdoms of Aleppo, Mari and Babylon would also favour a development of metallurgical knowledge, together with the spread of new techniques. The equipment of the armies of these kingdoms alone implies an organized production of weapons from workshops enjoying a steady supply of raw materials.

[1] *The Archaeology and History of the Early Dynastic period in Iraq.* See p. 2 above.

PALESTINE AT THE TIME OF THE FIRST DYNASTY OF BABYLON

In Palestine, the period corresponding to the First Dynasty of Babylon, 1830–1595 B.C. (Sidney Smith's dating), consists of the middle and later phases of the Middle Bronze II periods (Kenyon) or Albright's Middle Bronze IIa, IIb and the earlier part of IIc. It is not until the seventeenth century B.C. at the earliest that there is any gold jewellery extant. This lack of material, however, is not – as is probable in Babylonia at this time – due to lack of excavation, but to the absence during the late nineteenth and early eighteenth centuries of craftsmen sufficiently skilled in the methods necessary to produce gold jewellery. It seems that the Amorite penetration of Palestine and the debt owed to Byblos for many of the cultural features, as shown in the pottery, did not include skilled craftsmen in fine gold work. Nor is there any instance in Palestine of fenestrated axes made of gold and decorated in advanced techniques of granulation, such as found at Byblos in the votive deposits from the temple of the obelisks. As we have stressed in the preceding section, there is little reason to credit the Amorites with a knowledge of advanced gold technology, although there is evidence for the use of well-made metal weapons among groups who can be designated as Amorite. In Palestine, however, gold work, including granulation, appears suddenly at the site of Tell el Ajjul,[1] ancient Gaza, presenting us with a number of problems – none of which can be satisfactorily solved until more jewellery is excavated in carefully stratified contexts.

At Ajjul the jewellery is found in a few graves or in hoards, with some pieces in the city or unstratified levels. It is generally agreed that the graves are earlier than the hoards, but some of the objects in the hoards could be considerably earlier than the date of deposit and, if so, would be contemporary with objects from the graves, whose occupants were buried before a well-marked destruction level.

It seems likely, as far as one can judge from the published evidence, that a considerable amount of the gold work is contemporary with the first 'palace' which was erected on the site in the seventeenth century B.C. However, some of the gold jewellery must have been in use during the period of the second 'palace', which was built shortly after the destruction of the first. Albright dates this destruction to c. 1550 B.C. and suggests

[1] Petrie, *Ajjul*, I–IV.

that it was the result of the Palestinian campaign undertaken by the Egyptians in the reign of Amosis I (the founder of the Eighteenth Dynasty). Ajjul I was surrounded by a large fortification of a type well known elsewhere in Palestine – at Jericho (where it can be dated in phase II of the Middle Bronze Age II period), Hazor and Lachish, as well as at sites in Syria such as Carchemish, Ras Shamra and Qadesh and at Tell el Yahudiyeh in Egypt. This type of fortification, probably erected as a defence against battering rams,[1] is often connected with the Asiatic Hyksos invaders of Egypt.

While there is no reason to connect the Ajjul gold work with the Hyksos in so far as they can be identified after their arrival in Egypt, it is a distinct possibility that the later phase at Ajjul, contemporary with the second 'palace', is represented by the distinctive Bichrome pottery.[2] This is important when considering the gold work as, although there are no certain associations between Bichrome pottery and jewellery at Ajjul, the evidence points to the fact that some of the gold work must be contemporary with the period of Bichrome pottery, a period when we know that trade with Cyprus was flourishing – Cypriote imports being found in increasing quantities at Ajjul. This distinctive painted pottery is found in great quantities in Cyprus, where it was not only imported, but also imitated locally. The connections of Cyprus with Ajjul in the Late Cypriote I period are discussed on p. 127, and it is important to remember the influence of Ajjul jewellery workers on Cypriote craftsmen when considering the extent of the spread of technical knowledge in later years of the sixteenth century B.C. Here, however, we have to consider the question of the origin of this remarkable industry, which shows few signs of Egyptian influence and no sign of earlier development, either at Ajjul or anywhere else in Palestine.

A few observations can, however, be made before the question of origin is discussed. First, it is not difficult to find analogies for some of the pieces of Ajjul jewellery from the few other sites in Palestine where gold jewellery has been found in any quantity. Megiddo, Shechem and Beth-Shan have produced comparable jewellery (see p. 151 below), but it seems unlikely that these finds can be dated earlier than the Ajjul examples – many of the types of earrings, rosettes, circular pendants or 'Astarte' plaques belong to the fifteenth, fourteenth and thirteen centuries B.C. The origin has thus

[1] Yadin, 'Hyksos fortifications and the battering ram', *B.A.S.O.R.*, 137, 1955, pp. 23–32. Peter Parr, 'The origin of the rampart fortifications of Middle Bronze Age Palestine and Syria', *Z.D.P.V.*, Bd. 84, 1968, pp. 18–45.

[2] See Clare Epstein, *Palestinian Bichrome Ware* (Leiden, 1966).

to be sought outside Palestine and it is when we are looking for the antecedents of the developed granulation work at Ajjul that the site of Byblos, already mentioned in this chapter, provides some clues. Recently, in her Schweich lectures, Dr Kenyon has suggested that the origin of the Middle Bronze I culture must be sought at Byblos; she has shown that prototypes for Middle Bronze pottery types can be found in the temple deposits and royal tombs of Byblos and has designated this culture as Canaanite – as opposed to the preceding 'Amorite' Early Bronze – Middle Bronze period. The Middle Bronze I period is represented at Ajjul by the courtyard cemetery;[1] here there is no gold work (except in one tomb, see fig. 84) but the pottery, made on a fast wheel, shows connections with coastal Syria and Byblos in particular.[2] In fact, it is at a coastal site like Ajjul where one would expect to find the links with Phoenicia not only well represented at their inception around 1900 B.C., but also continuing into the succeeding period – the Middle Bronze II period, which seems to have developed without any apparent break directly from the preceding Middle Bronze I period. It is within this period, probably in the beginning of the seventeenth century B.C., that the earliest pieces of jewellery at Ajjul should be dated. The evidence from Byblos which points to Ajjul connections can be briefly summarized.[3]

(1) A long tradition of gold work and the manufacture of jewellery goes back certainly to the mid-third millennium B.C. The skill of the goldsmiths working for the kings of Byblos has already been mentioned (p. 102). All the techniques practised by the maker of the Ajjul jewellery can be found at Byblos – granulation, filigree and cloisonné work – and moulds for pendants in the form of a bull's or ram's head have been found at Byblos among quantities of other moulds for jewellery. A gold pendant in the form of a pair of outstretched wings may well have inspired the maker of the remarkable Ajjul pendants (or earrings) in which the centre piece is designed in the form of wings, then inlaid with paste in cloisons decorated with granules round the edge and a stylized bull's head in strip gold being added below the wings (see p. 118 and pl. 82).

(2) The technique of fastening diadems, bracelets or belts by means of a pin passing through alternate sockets (see p. 123) occurs at Byblos (pl. 71) and Ajjul (fig. 87). The diadem with double looped spiral clasp can be

[1] O. Tufnell, 'The courtyard cemetery of Tell el Ajjul, Palestine', *Institute of Archaeology Bulletin*, III, 1962, pp. 1–37 (London University).

[2] For drawings and descriptions of the pottery from the first three Royal Tombs, dated by objects bearing the name of Ammenemes III and IV, see O. Tufnell in *Berytus*, 1970.

[3] See Dunand, *Byblos*, II, especially pls. CXXII, CXXXII–IV.

paralleled by a diadem with similar clasp from Byblos (pl. 70, fig. 83).

(3) A rosette in thin gold leaf (pl. 72) from the Beirut treasure published by Emir Maurice Chéhab[1] may come from further south than Byblos, but is comparable with rosettes from Ajjul.

(4) There are many parallels for the amethyst and gold beads from Ajjul among the jewellery from Byblos, the distinctive fluted beads with prolonged tubes or spindle beads occurring at both sites. These, however, must be compared with the fluted beads on the Dilbat necklace (see pl. 61) and are almost certainly developed from Babylonian prototypes.

(5) The granular decoration of small circles on the earrings or 'nose rings' from Ajjul may well be inspired by the similar motifs on gold work from Byblos where the inside of the circles are plain but surrounded by a circle of granules (pl. 79, fig. 75).

On the present evidence, therefore, we can suggest that the knowledge of the intricate technique of granulation was brought to Ajjul from Byblos, possibly by metal workers who came south by sea and whose ancestors at Byblos had probably learnt this technique from Mesopotamian goldsmiths at least as early as the Isin-Larsa period and the period of Hammurabi of Babylon.

The part played by Mari in the dissemination of this knowledge is easy to envisage when the documentary evidence for the trading activities of Mari is considered. It was not only lapis lazuli from the mines at Badakshan or copper from Cyprus that passed through Mari, but also raw materials for many of the luxury goods supplied to the temples and palaces of rulers rich enough to employ quantities of skilled craftsmen to fulfil their needs. It is interesting that both Mari and Byblos had west Semitic rulers who at Mari (as in Babylonia) had taken over almost entirely Babylonian material and religious culture, while at Byblos Egyptian influence is seen at its strongest in the rich tombs of the king Abi-shemu and his successors. Yet the jewellers at Byblos were using the techniques of granulation and filigree, which are not known in Egypt before the Twelfth Dynasty and which, as they appear then without any previous history in Egypt, are assumed to have come to Egypt from Asia.

Is it possible that the spread of the knowledge of gold jewellery working in its most developed stage, from Mesopotamia to Syria and then to Palestine, can be linked with the Hurrian advance from northern Syria, which Kupper[2] has shown began as early as c. 1800 B.C.? Certainly the

[1] *B.M.B.*, I, pp. 2–21.

[2] See J. R. Kupper, 'Northern Mesopotamia and Syria', *C.A.H.*, No. 14.

Ḫurri, after crossing the Euphrates in the eighteenth century B.C., established principalities in Upper Mesopotamia, and we know that by the time of Alalakh level VII Hurrians were holding high religious and civil offices in that city. The existence of Hurrian kingdoms in north Syria had begun at the time of the Mari documents. Speiser[1] has stressed the debt owed by the Hurrians to Mesopotamia where law, administration, religion and literature are concerned – the Hurrian seals of Kirkuk type attest their versatility in the artistic field and it is unlikely, from the evidence given by the texts for their activities in the economic sphere, that they did not include skilled craftsmen among the groups who spread far away from their original homeland. Speiser has recently discussed the part played by the Hurrians in Palestine and it may well be that the Hurrian penetration of Palestine was on a far greater scale than has hitherto been envisaged. This could mean that, by the time of the Patriarchs or in the seventeenth century (c. 1600 B.C.), there was a considerable population of Hurrians in Palestine and if, as Speiser suggests, places such as Shechem were in fact Hurrian centres, then many problems – both archaeological and relating to the Old Testament – could be more easily solved.

Certain archaeological facts and documentary information can, however, be noted in this discussion. First, it is clear from the Hurrian gods and goddesses, as portrayed in the rock sanctuary at Yazilikaya near the Hittite capital of Boğazköy, that earrings were an essential part of the equipment of Hurrian deities.[2] Secondly, the important Akkadian text found at Boğazköy in 1957[3] throws much light on the problems of gold work and the Hurrians. Here, the Hittite king, Khattushilis I (1650–1620 B.C.), says that he destroyed Alalakh and that 'on my way back I destroyed the land of Ursa and filled my house with treasure.' He also mentions that, while campaigning in Arzawa, he was attacked in the rear by the Hurrians who, however, were unable to prevent the town of Hassu (wa) also being plundered by the Hittites. The list of booty from the temple of the goddess Mezulla is instructive: 'Two silver bulls, three statues of gold and silver, a door of gold and two gold statues.' This list, from the chief cities of the two principalities which were occupied by the Hurrians about 150 years earlier, attests to the richness of Hurrian temples and implies that

[1] E. A. Speiser, 'The Hurrian participation in the civilisations of Mesopotamia, Syria and Palestine', *Cahiers Histoire Mondiale*, I, 2, 1953, pp. 311–27.

[2] E. Akurgal, *The Art of the Hittites*, pl. 82–6.

[3] Otten, 'Vorlafiger Bericht über die Ausgrabungen in Boğazköy in Jahre 1957', *M.D.O.G.*, 91, 1950, pp. 73–84.

there must have been skilled craftsmen and jewellers who could produce the necessary amount of jewellery for the adornment of the statues and for votive offerings, such as are described in such detail in the Qatna inventories. Thirdly, there is considerable documentary evidence to show that jewellery was regarded as an essential part of the dowry of a Mitannian princess in the Amarna period (cf. p. 133), while the inventories of the gifts dedicated to the temple of Ningal, the Sumerian moon goddess, at Qatna show the important part played by jewellery in religious practice.[1]

Fourthly, in nearly all cases of levels which can be designated as Hurrian (on the grounds that the inhabitants included people speaking the Hurrian language and bearing Hurrian names – and which are also distinguished by the use of pottery of Hurrian or Nuzi type, such as at Nuzi or Alalakh) we find jewellery of a high technical standard using all the most advanced techniques of granulation, filigree and cloisonné inlay. The excavations at Tell Brak in the Khabur valley in north Syria have shown that the use of the distinctive painted Hurrian ware began c. 1600 B.C. and continued throughout the fifteenth and fourteenth centuries B.C.; the jewellery from this period in Syria and Palestine is discussed in Chapter 8 and comes mainly from the sites of Ras Shamra, Alalakh, Megiddo, Beth-Shan and Ajjul. The Palestinian variant of this ware is the Bichrome pottery mentioned above, which has recently been the subject of a study by Dr Clare Epstein. Her conclusions, however, have been questioned by R. de Vaux[2] who cannot agree that there is a connection between the Palestinian Bichrome pottery and Hurrian-speaking peoples. It is the chronologically later Nuzi ware which has more claim to be identified as Hurrian and it is this distinctive north Syrian pottery whose patterns can be compared with some of the designs on contemporary jewellery (see fig. 93).

Other objects, such as the face urn from Jericho (possibly closely related to the well-known vase from Brak) made in the form of a double-human face surmounted with what appears to be a feathered crown,[3] and the appearance of a distinctive type of socketed axe head[4] developed from a north Syrian type (which, from its archaeological associations, can now be described as Hurrian) are only a few of the pointers to suggest that the

[1] J. Bottero, *R.A.*, XLIII, 1949, pp. 1 ff.

[2] 'Les Hurrites de l'histoire et les Hurrites de la Bible', *Revue Biblique*, LXXIV, 1967, p. 37.

[3] Mallowan, *Twenty-five Years of Mesopotamian Discovery, 1932–56*, p. 37, fig. 15 (London, 1956).

[4] K. R. Maxwell-Hyslop, *Iraq*, XI, 1, 1949, pls. XXI–XXII. Types 12 and 13. Deshayes, *Outils de Bronze*, pp. 102–3.

Hurrian penetration of Palestine began at least as early as c. 1600 B.C. This continued in increasing numbers until we know that in the fourteenth century B.C. a number of rulers bore Hurrian names.

If this view proves correct, and the decisive evidence of the mention of Hurrian individuals who are jewellers and goldsmiths in the texts is still missing (we have Hurrian dancers, singers, magicians and weavers but as yet no mention of craftsmen), then it must be recognized that probably there is a second influence – i.e. Hurrian – to be taken into account where the Ajjul gold work is concerned, especially in the material that belongs to the fifteenth, fourteenth and thirteenth centuries B.C. It is in this period that the links with Ras Shamra, Megiddo and Shechem are most apparent.

The jewellery from Tell el Ajjul

The gold and silver jewellery from Ajjul is now displayed in the Palestine Archaeological Museum (pre-1967), the British Museum and the Ashmolean Museum, Oxford. Since the appearance of the five-volume account of the excavations, no published study has been made of this important material. Two unpublished studies have been made. One consists of the extensive notes made by J. R. Stewart for seminars at the University of Sydney, but this was done before the publication of *Ajjul*, Vol. V. Olga Tufnell has also made a study of some of the more distinctive types of toggle pin and earring and has produced lists which are invaluable for collating the published material with each individual object now in the three different museums. Any conclusions set forth here owe much to these two studies and we have attempted to isolate those more important pieces which have definite associations and which can be used for an attempt to arrange the jewellery in some sort of chronological order, in so far as this is possible from the published evidence of the actual excavations. Pieces which have definite foreign connections in Syria and Mesopotamia are also noted (see also note in Bibliography, p. 272).

It is possible to distinguish grave groups which can, by their contents and position in the excavation, be dated to within the Middle Bronze II Age (1700–1550 B.C.) and also to the Late Bronze Age (1550–1350 B.C.), but the hoards – many of which were rich in jewellery – can only provide limited information for dating purposes. Even in the graves we can only infer a date for the actual interment, when the objects were in use, and not the date of manufacture for each individual piece of jewellery – some of which could, of course, be older than others in the same tomb or hoard.

In certain cases, however, it is possible to determine the period when a distinctive type of earring or pendant, etc., is in common use and the time when it ceased to be fashionable.

Information concerning the different types can be briefly summarized.

Toggle Pins

The toggle pins at Ajjul number over one hundred examples and were mostly found in graves, where a large number were of gold, though they were also made in copper, silver and electrum. Tufnell has divided them into three main types and has shown that examples can be found at Ajjul of the nine types identified by Mme Henschel-Simon.[1] Here we will refer to Tufnell's classification and summarize her conclusions.

Type 1 Nail with flat head (pl. 73). This is the earliest and rarest type at Ajjul – an example comes from Grave 1416 in the Middle Bronze I courtyard cemetery[2] (fig. 84).

Type 2 Pin with plain head and no thickening to the shaft. This is the usual form at Ajjul. An important variation of Type 2 has a bar-twisted shaft (Henschel-Simon's Type 7), frequently made in gold or silver (pl. 74). It is comparable, from the point of view of technique, with the bar-twisted earring (see below) and seems to be contemporary with it. Two plain pins of Type 2 (each measuring 10 cm in length) were found with a scarab of Sheshi, a Hyksos ruler of the Fifteenth Dynasty, c. 1674 B.C. (*A.G.*, IV, pl. XXXIII, 478a).

Type 3 Knob-headed pin with head of gold or agate, amethyst, etc. These tend to be late in the series. A gold pin of this type was found in a single grave with a group of scarabs including one of Auserre-Apophis whose reign began in c. 1634 B.C. (Petrie, *A.G.*, II, pl. III, 13). The decorative principle of the use of coloured beads to form the top of the shaft of the pin is comparable with the rings of cylinder seal type with stone or gold beads threaded on the pin. The gold heads are sometimes elaborately worked with milling on the sides and can be compared with the gold 'washer beads' on these rings (*A.G.*, IV, pl. XVIII).

[1] E. Henschel-Simon, 'Toggle pins in the Palestine Archaeological Museum', *Q.D.A.P.*, 6, 1938, pp. 169–209.

[2] See O. Tufnell, *London University Institute of Archaeology Bulletin*, III, 1962, p. 20.

Earrings

(*a*) *Earrings of penannular shape*

These are common at Ajjul and can be divided into seven distinctive types, apart from the plain form which occurs in all periods.

Fig. 76. Jewellery from Ajjul Grave II.

(i) Plain with incisions on the surface (pl. 76b). These incisions can make deep raised ribs round the body of the ring. An example comes from Grave 2 (fig. 76) from the 'Cenotaph' deposit (Petrie, *A.G.*, II, pl. I, with gold toggle pin) and Grave H.771 (Petrie, *A.G.*, IV, Pl. XXII, 250), as well as other isolated finds. The ribbing is comparable with the ribbing on a gold torque from Byblos, Tomb II of the early eighteenth century B.C., and may be derived from the earrings or rings strung with beads (Petrie, *A.G.*, I, p. 8, pl. XV, 6), as Professor Hawkes has suggested.[1]

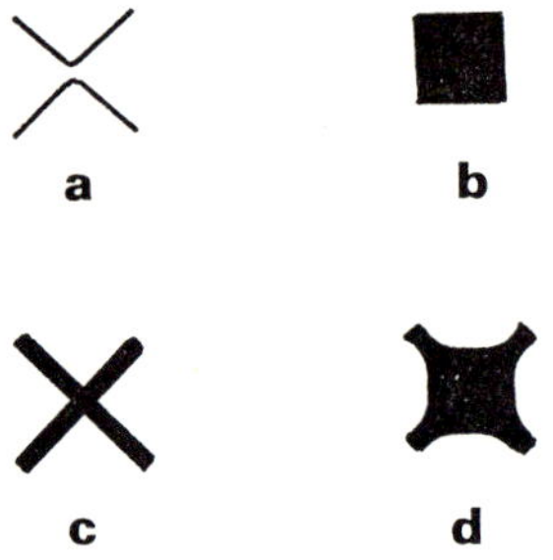

Fig. 77. Cross-sections of twisted earrings: *a*, strip-twist; *b*, bar-twist; *c*, flange-twist; *d*, bar-twist with hammered-out edges.

Fig. 78. Plaited gold wire earring from Ajjul.

(ii) 'Bar-twist' type (pl. 75b and fig. 77b). This type occurs in lead and was made by twisting a thin bar or rod of gold or lead with square section round on itself, so that the surface of the earring is ribbed by means of the upstanding edge of the metal. The lead examples are probably the proto-

[1] C. F. C. Hawkes, 'Gold earrings of the Bronze Age, East and West', *Folklore*, 2, September 1961, p. 446.

types for the gold, as lead would lend itself to this treatment easily. This type seems to have begun earlier than the next type (iii) and at Ajjul has not been found in association with it.

(iii) 'Strip-twist' type (pl. 75a and fig. 77a). Technique: 'Two gold strips were taken and bent lengthways down the middle to give them an angle 'V' or 'U' cross section; they were set beside each other, with the angles opposed and touching; twisted together in that position, the twist of course forcing the angles into firm conjunction along the centre line of what was now an 'X' cross section . . . the ends, left untwisted, were then hammered together into tapering points; and lastly the whole was

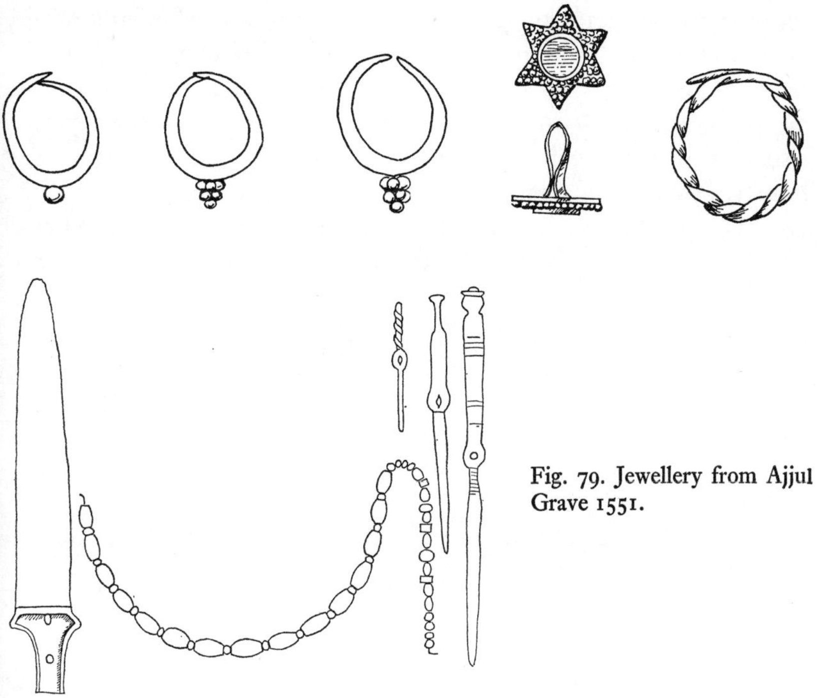

Fig. 79. Jewellery from Ajjul Grave 1551.

bent into the required penannular shape.'[1] It occurs in a grave group from Ras Shamra of eighteenth or seventeenth century B.C. date and is now in the Damascus Museum (Schaeffer, *Ugaritica*, IV, p. 308, fig. 6).

(iv) Penannular earrings made of plaited gold wires (fig. 78). Only one example of this type occurred at Ajjul. Similar wire binding can be found

[1] Ibid., p. 451.

on a bracelet from Megiddo,[1] and also on scarab mounts from the same site. A large earring from Ajios Jakovos is also comparable (see p. 128).

(v) Penannular with single drop at base of the ring (pl. 77d and e). The addition of a single large granule of gold to the simple penannular earring was a simple decorative device and a silver solder was used to attach the ball to the body of the ring. At Ajjul the type belongs to the Middle Bronze IIc period, or c. 1625–1500 B.C., and a similar example from Megiddo (Tomb 251) can also be dated to this period.[2]

(vi) Penannular with several granules at base of ring (pl. 77a and b). This type is referred to in archaeological publications as the 'mulberry', 'clustered' or 'grape cluster' type. The granules are sometimes attached with a silver solder and the gold of the granules is often of inferior quality to that of the ring. The type can be dated towards the end of the sixteenth century and belongs particularly to the fifteenth, continuing in use into the fourteenth century B.C. In Grave 1551 (fig. 79) at Ajjul this type was associated with an earring of Type (v) above, toggle pins of Types 1 and 2, a strip-twist earring and a flanged horned dagger. In Group 1532 the associated jewellery included a strip-twist earring, a spindle-shaped bead (fig. 80), fluted melon beads (pl. 93) and a Type 2 toggle pin. 'Mulberry'

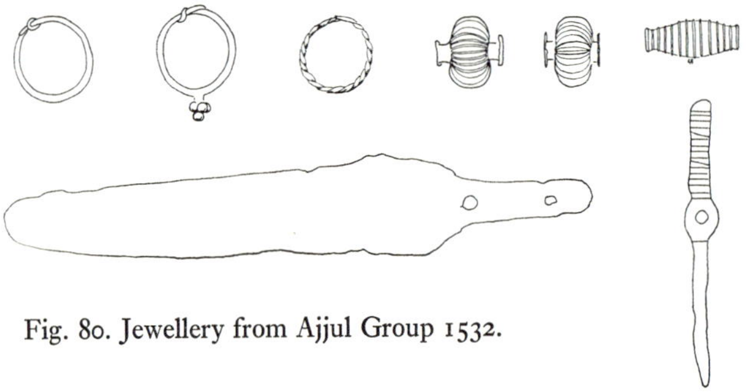

Fig. 80. Jewellery from Ajjul Group 1532.

earrings are also found at Enkomi Tomb 8 and at many Syrian and Palestinian sites, such as Megiddo Tomb 251 and Atchana, where the examples date from the fifteenth to twelfth centuries B.C. It is a common type in the mid-Assyrian period at Mari (see pl. 131).

(vii) Earrings with granular decoration (pls. 78–81 and colour pl. E). This class is distinguished by the decoration worked in either coarse or

[1] *Megiddo Tombs*, p. 178, figs. 179, 1, and 176, 16–17.

[2] Petrie, *A.G.*, IV, pl. XIV, 28–9, Hoard 1299; pl. XVI, 67, Hoard 1313. *Megiddo Tombs*, pl. 115, 10.

fine granular triangles or clusters and all examples come from hoards or isolated finds. None can be definitely associated with burials. Miss Tufnell considers that the hoards were deposited at the time of the destruction of the first 'palace', which can be assigned to Middle Bronze Age II. The method of manufacture for two examples from Hoards 1299–1313 has been described by Petrie as follows: 'The plate of each side was swaged into a raised ridge, and the grains piled in position on the slopes. The junctions were all sweated together, and no trace of free solder could be found, all fine interstices were unjoined except by surface contacts. The loops for suspension were not soldered.'[1] The joint of two sheets of gold was then concealed by a wire with granular clusters.

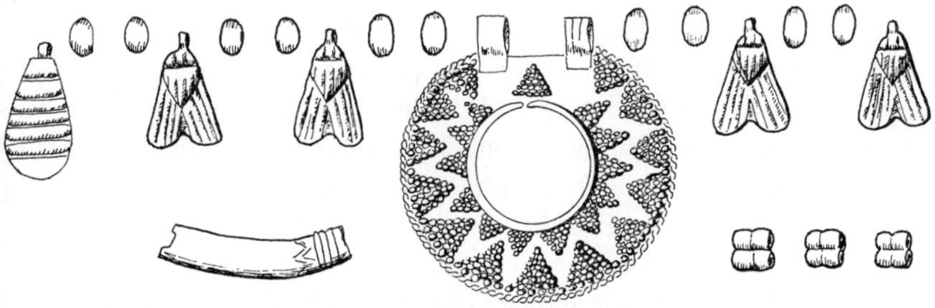

Fig. 81. Jewellery from Ajjul Hoard 1313.

The example from Hoard 1313 (fig. 81) was 'worked with two bossed up plates attached to the edges' which were 'covered by two counter-twisted square wires joined by sweating; inner edges coerced with a V-shaped strip, sweated on at the ends. After this, the grains were attached by piling and sweating, no solder and the hoops sweated on.'[2]

An example of this type in the Ashmolean Museum (pl. 81) is interesting as it shows a rough attempt to produce the same fine workmanship that is found on all the twelve other examples found at Ajjul. Here the surface is flat, not curved, there are no granules round the edge or wire round the centre and the granulation is uneven and coarse. The granular decoration on these earrings must be related to that found in the Dilbat pendant (see p. 89) where the blobs are covered with granules. Among a group of jewellery from (?) Ajjul now in the Museum at Leiden is a round pendant with rosette and falcon granular decoration which was noted by

[1] Petrie, *A.G.*, IV, p. 6. [2] Ibid., p. 7

Miss Tufnell. The technique is so close to the Dilbat pendant (see p. 89) that it could have come from the same workshop as the Babylonian piece.[1]

(*b*) *Falcon earrings* (colour pl. E)

Only three examples of this remarkable type were found at Ajjul and no comparable earring has been found as yet in either western Asia or Egypt. The earring is made of one sheet of gold, the back plain and undecorated, while the front is made in the form of a bird with outstretched wings, the outlines made of fine gold wire filled with an inner row of globules; the wings are decorated with granulation in both clusters and triangles each formed of five × five granules (*Falco biarmicus* is a possible identification).

It has been suggested that the inspiration for these remarkable pieces is Egyptian, but the motif is also comparable with the eagle-headed bird on a standard carried by one of the priests on the stele of Gudea. Here the head is turned to one side and the treatment of the quadrangular tail is also comparable with the Ajjul bird. This bird, although distinct from the lion-headed bird Inannak, symbol of Ningirsu, was also associated with Ningirsu-Ninurta, god of the thunderstorm.[2] It is possible that the the rare Ajjul bird earring may be the prototype for the commoner penannular-shaped earring or pendant; the final stage of development would then be the example shown in fig. 81, where the top of the earring is no longer open but solid.[3]

(*c*) *Inlaid 'earrings' or pendants* (pls. 82 and 83)

Four earrings (or pendants) combine cloisonné inlay with granulation on a gold base. They are made in the form of a winged disc surrounded by an oval with a small disc placed in the angles of the wings and the central disc; below the wings there is a pointed stylized animal's head with long horns rendered in strip gold without inlay. A large hook is fixed to the back of the jewel and, unless this was intended to be worn right over the ear (it is possible to fix the piece in position in this way), it would seem likely that it was intended to be worn flat hooked over a neck band or belt of the same width as the hook. A comparable inlaid pendant from Megiddo is the only other example of this type known in western Asia. This comes from level IX, datable to the sixteenth century B.C.[4]

[1] *Monuments Egyptiens du Musée d'Antiquités des Pays-Bas à Leide* (1893–1905), pls. XLVI, XLII, 37.

[2] G. Cros *et al.*, *Nouvelles fouilles de Tello*, pl. X, 2, and fig. 6, p. 290, (Paris, 1910–14).

[3] I owe this suggestion to Mr Michael Roaf.

[4] G. Loud, *Megiddo*, II, seasons of 1935–9, pl. 225, 12, 13 (Chicago, 1945). See also Kenyon in *Levant*, I, 1969, p. 59.

The association of the winged disc and the animal horns has not been explained; the amuletic properties of different pieces of jewellery and the fact that in Mesopotamia symbols of the gods were often made in the form of pendants suggest that a deity associated with the bull is represented by the stylized animal head and that the combination with solar disc may denote the Canaanite god El, rather than Baal. A stele from Ras Shamra[1] showing a seated deity with bull's horns on his conical headdress may represent El and here a winged sun disc is shown above him – possibly denoting the solar aspect. The god Reshef is also depicted with horns, but these are gazelle's rather than bull's horns. On two stelae, his symbol is a gazelle and in an omen text he appears as an astral deity – the 'porter of the sun goddess'[2] – and so it is possible that these pieces may be symbols of Reshef rather than El. The discovery of the bronze-horned god at Enkomi who has been identified with Reshef and the popularity of earrings in the form of a stylized bull's head in Cyprus (see pl. 99) also suggest that these pieces were originally intended as symbols of Canaanite deities and were regarded as having prophylactic as well as ornamental functions. It is relevant in this connection to remember that Reshef was regarded as the god of good fortune; therefore, his symbol (if this interpretation of these pieces of jewellery is correct) would have an attractive amuletic value.

Another possibility is that the inlaid earrings or pendants are symbols of the goddess Anat, the sister and wife of Aliyan, son of Baal, who is represented on the ivory plaque from Ras Shamra, winged, with the curls and horns of the Egyptian cow goddess Hathor, surrounded with an astral disc.[3] In this case, the earrings would have been used as fertility amulets and also especially in childbirth, in the same way as the more common Astarte plaques, of which many terracotta examples come from sites all over Syria and Palestine.

One of these earrings comes from a tomb group, Tomb 1740 (fig. 82), a child's burial, which also contained a headband, necklace with triangular pendants of sheet gold and a circular disc decorated with granules, possibly part of a large inlaid pendant of the type with hook described above.

Group 1203 (fig. 83) is important for the association of these earrings with the fluted spindle-shaped beads (see below) and the diadem with

1 Schaeffer, *Cuneiform Texts*, pl. XXXI.

2 J. Gray, *The Canaanites*, pl. 19, 20 (London, 1964).

3 Schaeffer, *Syria*, XXXI, 1954, pl. VII, pl. 48. Gray, op. cit., pl. 9. Petrie's identification of the animals as rams may, however, be correct.

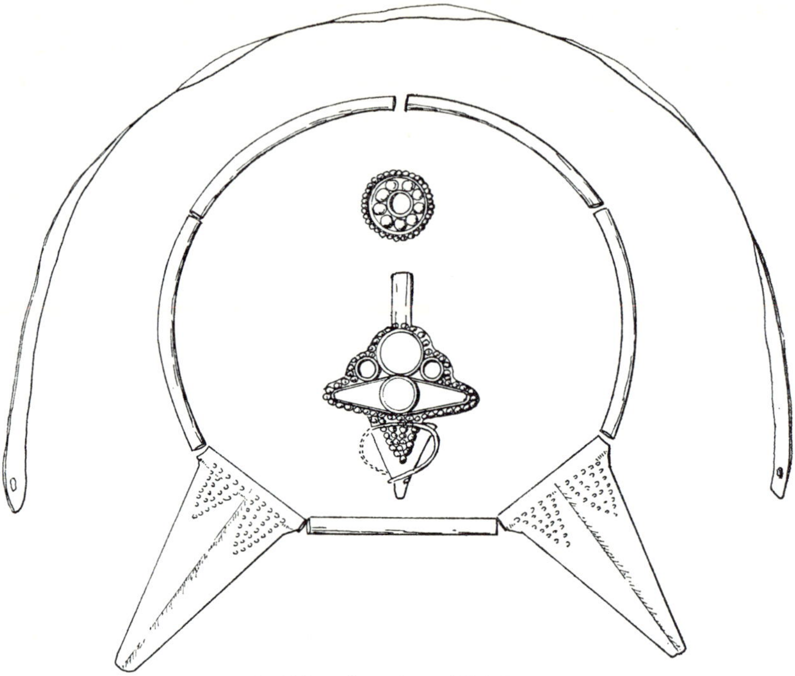

Fig. 82. Gold jewellery from Ajjul Grave 1740.

double loop spiral clasp and hinge comparable with Byblos jewellery. In this tomb, plain circular gold earrings were found in position near each ear.

The technique of glass paste inlay combined with granulation may be compared with the finger rings of Late Cypriote II date from a hoard from Kouklia in Cyprus which can be described as true enamel.[1] The finger rings shown in pl. 84, dated to the thirteenth century B.C., are also important for the comparison which can be made between the curvilinear cloisonné design on the face and the gold pendants from Ashur.[2]

The leech-shaped earrings[3] (pl. 85), described by Higgins as 'neo-Mycenaean', may be Asiatic imports. Similar examples are in private collections allegedly from Gilan in north-west Persia.

Diadems

At Ajjul a simple type of gold headband with rounded ends, each pierced for a string to fix round the forehead, occurs in the early sixteenth century

[1] Higgins, *Jewellery*, p. 25. [2] K. R. Maxwell-Hyslop, *Iraq*, XXII, fig. 6, p. 112.
[3] Ibid., pl. 12 H.

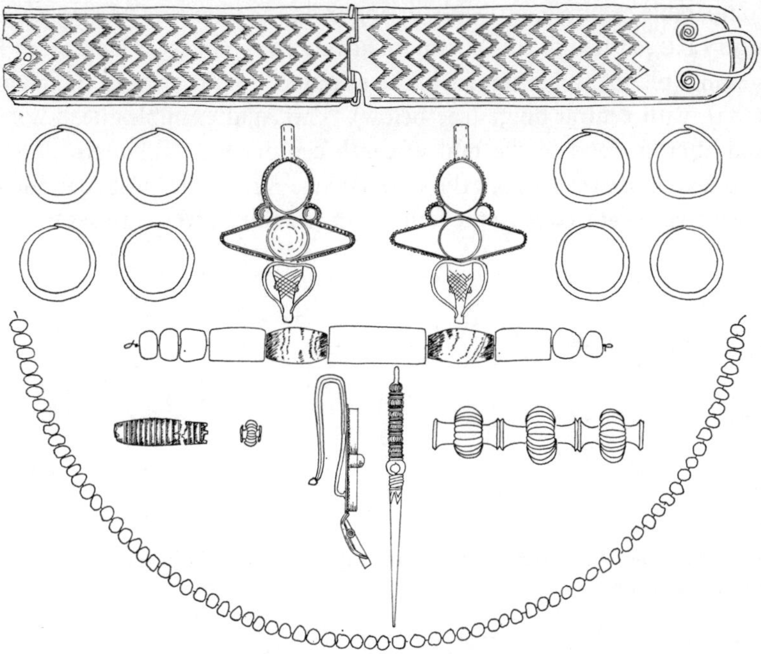

Fig. 83. Gold jewellery from Ajjul Grave 1203.

B.C. (Grave 1416, courtyard cemetery) in association with a gold toggle pin of Type 1 (see fig. 84). Grave I in the city (probably late seventeenth to sixteenth century B.C., Middle Bronze IIc) produced a silver example; a similar plain example comes from Grave 1740 (fig. 82) associated with an inlaid and granulated earring pendant (see p. 118) The headband (fig. 84) was made of two gold strips pressed together (PAM 919).

These headbands could be decorated with punched dots along the borders and this variety occurs in two instances with earrings of the drop-cluster or 'mulberry' type (Tomb 860: Petrie, *A.G.*, IV, pl. XVIII, 113, 125, 126; see also fig. 85 of this chapter) and level 731 AF (Petrie, *A.G.*, III, pl. XIV, 6, PAM 1218) produced a more elaborate example with a design in repoussé chevrons, combined with punched dots (fig. 86). An important example comes from Hoard 1209 (Petrie, *A.G.*, IV, pl. XIV, 7, PAM 145). Here the band is made of a simple solid strip of electrum and there are tubular cloisons soldered to the band for the insertion of inlay of coloured stones or for the attachment of gold rosettes. On the diadem from Hoard 277 (pl. 86) petalled rosettes of gold foil are inserted into narrow collars soldered on to the band (see also pl. 87). The treasure from Byblos contains a comparable example, probably dating from the nineteenth or eighteenth century B.C., although this is a more advanced type with a loop catch for fastening (pl. 70) and is similar to the example, unique at Ajjul (pl. 88 and fig. 83), with central hinge (see below). The Ajjul examples need not be dated after the end of the mid-fifteenth century B.C., although the type continued in use throughout the Late Bronze Age and is most common on the western Asiatic coast in the fourteenth and thirteenth centuries B.C.

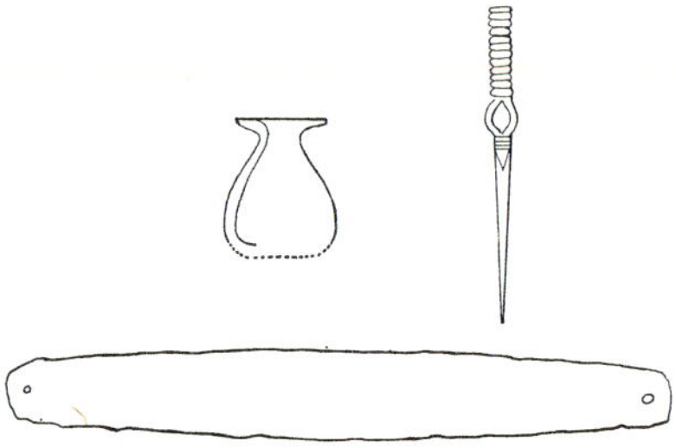

Fig. 84. Gold jewellery from Ajjul burial, 1416, Courtyard cemetery.

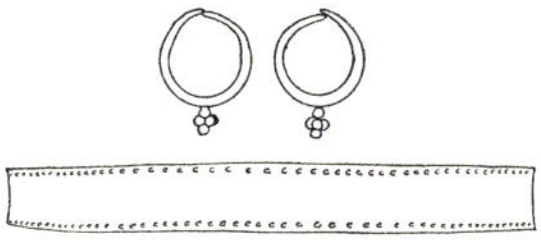

Fig. 85. Gold jewellery from Ajjul Group 1030.

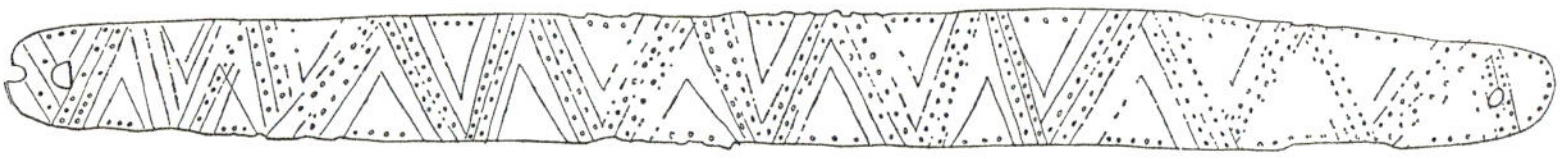

Fig. 86. Gold headband from Ajjul Grave 309.

Diadems of a more elaborate kind are common in Cyprus in the Late Cypriote period 1400–1200 B.C. (Enkomi Tombs 11 and 18) and have been discussed by Higgins.[1] There seem to be no dated Late Cypriote I examples.

Belts or 'headbands'

Objects described by Petrie as 'belts' and 'headbands' were found in a fragmentary condition in Hoards 1299 and Grave 1203 (fig. 83). They are more likely to be bracelets or possibly belts, rather than headbands. They were made of laminated plates, joined by a pin passing through sockets, arranged alternatively on each unit to interlock with the sockets in its neighbour. They were decorated with repoussé and the one from Hoard 1299 (PAM 1161) has an attachment for a pendant (fig. 87). A wire loop with double spiral ends is soldered to one end of No. 42 from Grave 1203 (fig. 83 and pl. 88, PAM 1179) and gold pins were used to fix the separate

[1] Higgins, *Jewellery*, p. 87 and pl. IID.

plates together. The hinge was made by bending the end of the flat strip over a piece of wire which was bent back on itself to keep the wire in place. There is fine geometric repoussé decoration on the surface.

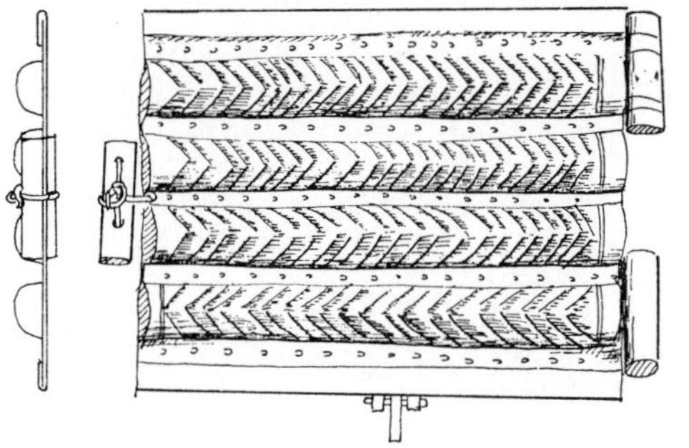

Fig. 87. Part of gold bracelet or belt from Ajjul Hoard 1299.

Although similar methods of fastening with a pin passing through sockets in the individual plates can be found in Egyptian jewellery of the time of Thotmes III and Hatshepsut, the inspiration for these pieces is more likely to be Phoenician. A bracelet of narrow gold strips decorated with globules (pl. 89) was found in the Byblos treasure, along with the gold headband with a similar double spiral wire loop (pls. 71 and 88). A silver bracelet from Megiddo Tomb 1100B (*Megiddo Tombs*, pl. 145, 22, p. 178, fig. 179, 1) should be noted.

Bracelets or armlets

Ten gold armlets were found in the deposit in the 'Cenotaph' (see pl. 90). 'These are in two sets of five each, and each individual band in each set is marked I to IIIII by incisions near one end. Engraved linear decoration encircles the ends of each. The three middle armlets in each set are flattened on both sides so that they can lie close together, while the end pieces are flattened on the side in contact with the next one but rounded on the outside faces. . . . The end of a similar object cut up for melting was found in Hoard 1200.' (Petrie, *A.G.*, IV, pl. XX, 155–8, PAM 1140).

Grave 447 (fig. 88) produced four examples in gold with incised linear decoration at the ends and silver examples come from Hoard 1299 (Petrie, *A.G.*, IV, pl. XII, PAM 1134 and PAM 1141). An unfinished silver example also occurs (PAM 1139).

Stewart has suggested that the armlets, although possibly buried in the fifteenth century B.C. (if that date is correct for the 'Cenotaph' deposit), were in use during the late seventeenth to sixteenth century B.C.

(Middle Bronze IIc period) and possibly earlier. They can be related to the four gold earrings from the treasure from Beirut (pl. 91). On these examples the section is slightly flattened like the 'Cenotaph' deposit examples and there is a decoration of grooves at each end. They are made

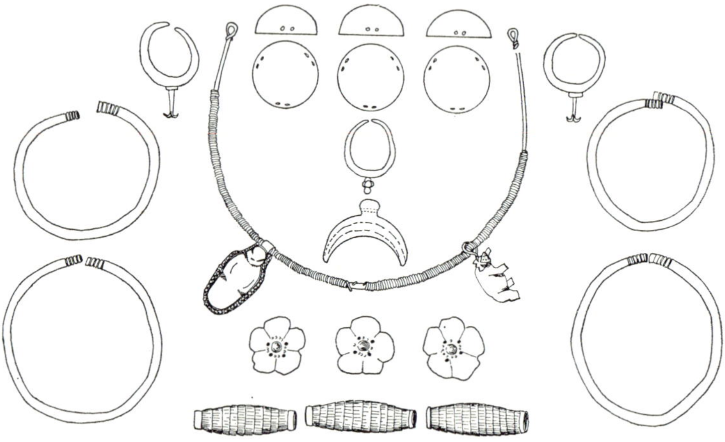

Fig. 88. Gold jewellery from Ajjul Grave 447.

from a sheet of gold rolled over to form a tube. A date in the nineteenth or eighteenth century B.C. is probable for this treasure; it is possible that the earliest Ajjul examples may not be far removed in date and that they should be dated to the earlier part of the seventeenth century B.C.

Dress fasteners

While the toggle pin seems to have passed out of use in Palestine by the end of the fifteenth century B.C. (although a few later survivals can be found), it must have existed alongside a more developed form of dress fastener which occurs in bronze and also in silver at Ajjul in Middle Bronze II contexts. This is a solid, heavy, penannular 'fibula' with either circular or oval discs at each end of the bow. Grave 1750 (fig. 89) produced two examples in bronze with heart-shaped ends. This 'warrior' grave is important because it also contained a fine 'veined' dagger blade and a socketed axe, both types being common in the Middle Bronze II period in Palestine.[1]

At Tell Beit Mirsim a fine example in silver, now in the Palestine Museum (PAM 732 – see pl. 92), comes from Level D (seventeenth–

[1] P. R. S. Moorey in *Levant*, I, pp. 97 f.

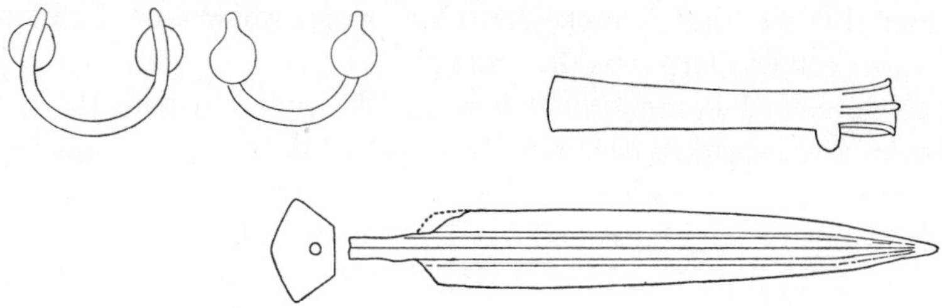

Fig. 89. Bronze weapons and silver dress fastener from Ajjul Grave 1750.

sixteenth centuries B.C.) and a movable pin may have passed across the bow from loop to loop. At Ajjul examples were found with the pin *in situ* and it seems that these primitive brooches or dress fasteners must have been the predecessors of the fibula where the pin is attached by a spring or hinge to the bow. Fig. 161, p. 256, however, shows an object fastening two long braids of material which resembles the dress fastener under discussion and seems to be directly attached to the braid at each end.

Beads

The most important forms can be briefly summarized.

(*a*) Fluted beads with elongated or plain collars. Fluted melon-shaped beads with elongated collars are common in both graves and hoards. In Group 1532 (fig. 80) two gold fluted spindle-shaped beads occurred with an electrum barrel-shaped bead (see below), a clustered 'mulberry' earring and a strip-twist earring. On some examples there is no attempt made to form a rolled edge to the collar and the bead is roughly made from one piece. A variety is incised instead of fluted and shows more care in execution (fig. 90). Fluted spindle beads are also found at Tell Beit Mirsim level D (*A.A.S.O.R.*, 17, pl. 32, 1–3), late seventeenth or early sixteenth century, and the form occurs in faience at the same site in level E (*A.A.S.O.R.*, 17, pl. 39, 34), so that the history of these beads in Palestine may well date from as early as the late eighteenth century B.C. At Ajjul a single fluted example occurs on a necklace of carnelian beads found in Tomb 1074 (pls. 208 and 209, see Chapter 14) and isolated examples also occur at Tell Fara. In Cyprus, Tomb 8 at Enkomi produced a gold example which can be dated to the Late Cypriote Ia period, 1550–1450 B.C. This dating evidence is important when considering the ultimate origin of the type, as fine examples with slightly less accentuated collars occur on the necklace from Dilbat (see p. 89) which are not likely to date much later than the eighteenth or seventeenth centuries B.C. It cannot be doubted that the Ajjul examples are related and it would seem likely that the Mesopotamian form was the prototype.

The developed form, without long spindle ends but with the same fluting and well-marked edge round the collar (pl. 93) is less common at Ajjul but a few well-made examples occur which can be compared with similar beads of the Dilbat necklace and also with later Mesopotamian examples from Aqar Qūf (*Iraq*, VIII, pl. XXI; see also p. 131 below). Ajjul also produced a plain example with collars but no fluting and also fluted types (pl. 94a, b).

(*b*) Barrel-shaped beads (pl. 94c). These are decorated with vertical ribbing and were found in three graves – 1203 (pl. 94c), 447 (fig. 88) and, in electrum, 1532 (fig. 80). A smaller, plain variety is common (Petrie, *A.G.*, IV, pl. XX, 167).

(*c*) Segmented beads (fig. 81). These are divided into four sections and were found in Hoard 1313. They can be compared with the more elaborate example on the Dilbat necklace.

(*d*) Globular beads (fig. 81). These occur in both gold and silver (Petrie, *A.G.*, IV, pl. XVI, 62).

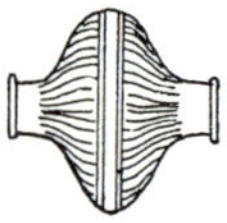

90

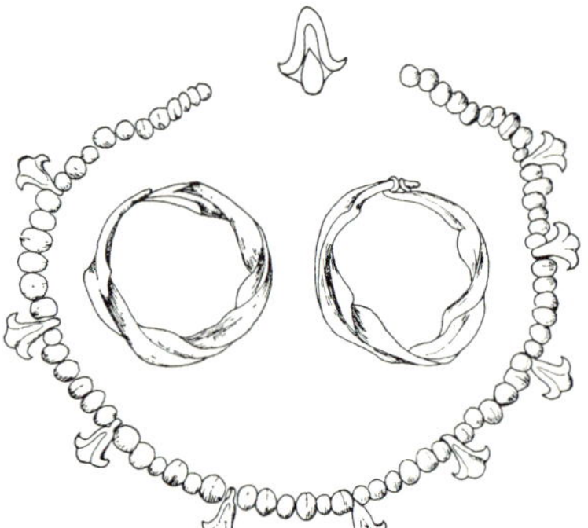

91

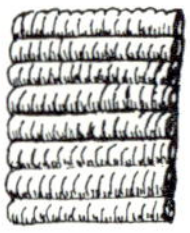

92

Fig. 90. Gold bead from Ajjul.
Fig. 91. Gold jewellery from Ajjul Grave 1073.
Fig. 92. Gold spacer bead from Ajjul.

(*e*) Biconical beads. An example from Grave 1089, datable to the fifteenth–fourteenth centuries B.C. (Petrie, *A.G.*, II, pl. XXV, 93) can be noted.

(*f*) Gold lily or lotus beads (fig. 91). These were found in Grave 1073, datable to the fifteenth century.

(*g*) Spacer beads (fig. 92). A spacer bead for dividing a necklace of eight strings occurred in the 'Cenotaph' deposit.

(*h*) Amulets. The 'fly' amulet (pl. 95) is known at Ajjul in gold and was made with rolled-over hooks for suspension. Four examples from Hoard 1313 (fig. 81) were intended to be part of a necklace and an oval-shaped pendant from the same group has been identified as a chrysalis.

The association of flies with Baal-zebub does not preclude an ultimate Babylonian origin. Fly amulets in lapis lazuli are mentioned in the Old Babylonian Atra-ḫasīs myth when the mother goddess Anu announced she would wear them round her neck as a reminder of the disaster of the flood. The fly amulets would have been worn by divine statues and an aetiological explanation for the insertion of this detail by the author of the myth is reasonable.[1]

RELATIONS BETWEEN SYRIA, PALESTINE AND CYPRUS IN THE LATE CYPRIOTE Ia PERIOD (1550–1450 B.C.)

The fact that many of the motifs found on the Hurrian pottery in Syria and the Bichrome pottery in Palestine and Cyprus can also be found in the contemporary gold work is important when considering Palestinian, Syrian and Cypriote relations at the beginning of the Late Bronze Age. Tress patterns, worked in twisted wire or granulation, twisted spirals with a dot in the centre of the loop, triangles in fine granulation, rosettes and star patterns were common to both painter and jeweller, suggesting that the two crafts were not working in isolation (fig. 93).

The twisted spiral with dot motif is also found in twisted gold wire on an ivory tusk vessel whose thin neck terminates in a woman's head topped by an oval cup. This object, found at Megiddo, is one of a class of vessel recently studied by Dr Amiran[2] who concludes that they are probably the prototype of the long arm-shaped vessels where the cup is held in the palm of a right hand (fig. 94, from Atchana). These pottery arm-shaped vessels are of interest here and have been listed and studied by Bittel,[3] who concludes that their origin is probably north Syria and that, although many examples are known from Hittite levels in Anatolia, they are more likely to be connected with Hurrian rather than Hittite religious practice. There can be little doubt of their ritual significance and there are several

[1] See Peake's *Commentary of the Bible*, 1962, p. 347, 300b. W. Lambert and Millard, *Atra-ḫasīs, the Babylonian Story of the Flood*, pp. 99 f. (Oxford, 1969).
[2] *J.N.E.S.*, XXI, 3, pp. 161–74, fig. 2. [3] *Boğazköy*, III, pp. 37 ff.

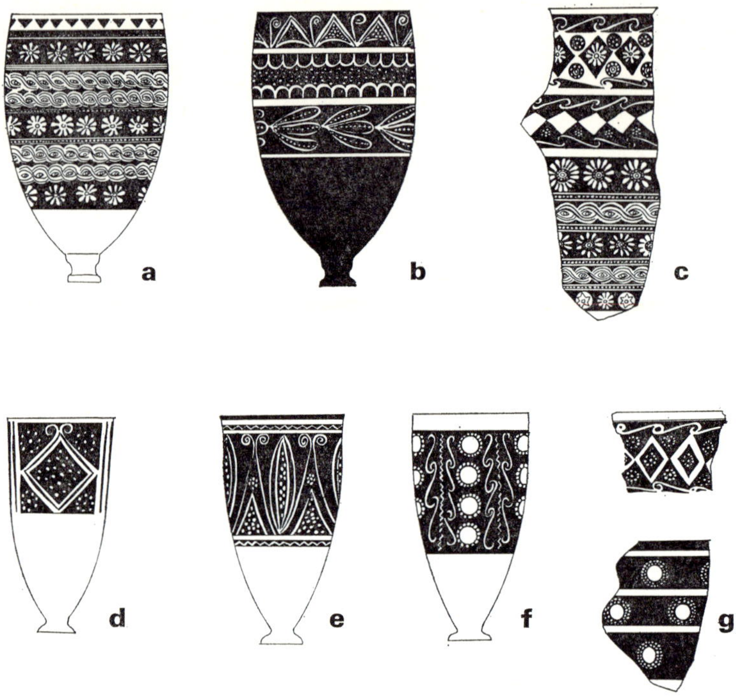

Fig. 93. White painted Nuzi ware: *a*, *b*, *c*, from Alalakh; *d*, *e*, *f*, *g*, from Brak.

examples from Cyprus where they are sometimes associated with another distinctive flask of Syrian origin – the so-called spindle-shaped flask (fig. 95). This type is relevant to the study of the jewellery of the Late Cypriote period in Cyprus as it occurs in Tomb 18 (Enkomi); the arm-shaped vessel and the Syrian flask are also found together in the Late Bronze Age sanctuary of Ajios Jakovos and in Tomb 2 from Enkomi.

These last two instances belong to the Late Cypriote II or fourteenth century B.C. and have been noted by Amiran. They are mentioned here as evidence for the suggestion that it may well have been Hurrian ritual practices and religious ideas which provided the impetus for the Asiatic influence visible in both the pottery and the gold work in the Late Cypriote period. Ras Shamra and Ajjul, whose trade with Cyprus at this period is well known, must have been important centres for the dissemination of this influence. And it may well prove to be more than just influence – as the large amounts of Palestinian Bichrome pottery found in Cyprus in the Late Cypriote I period might represent an actual colonization of groups from the Asiatic mainland. There is little doubt, however, that some of this

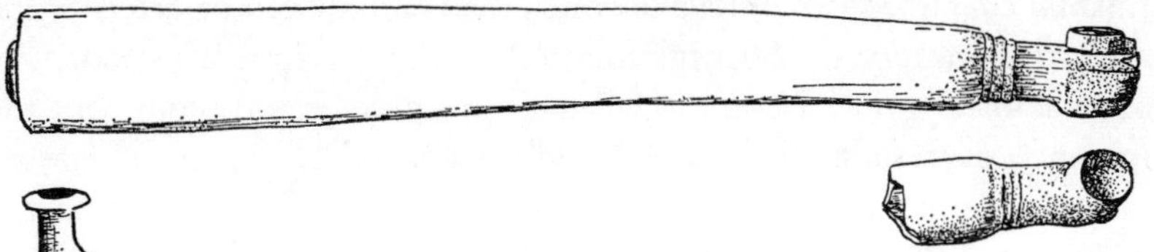

94

95

Fig. 94. Terracotta vessel from Atchana Level IV.

Fig. 95. Syrian flask from Atchana Level IV.

pottery was actually made in Cyprus and these incoming groups would naturally bring their religious ideas with them. The bronze god, probably Reshef, found at Enkomi and dating from the twelfth century B.C., is an instance of this transfer of religious ideas at a later period.[1]

CYPRIOTE JEWELLERY IN THE LATE CYPRIOTE Ia PERIOD

The Late Cypriote I period, divided into periods Ia (1550–1450 B.C.) and Ib (1450–1400 B.C.), is important both for the history of Cypriote jewellery and for its relationship with Syrian and Palestinian gold work. While there are few tomb groups of the earlier Ia period which contain jewellery of any significance, one of the tombs excavated by the Swedish Cyprus expedition does provide vital evidence for the origin of some of the techniques used in Cyprus in this period. Cypriote jewellery which is either Mycenaean in origin or can be related to Mycenaean work has already been considered by Higgins;[2] here we are concerned only with such pieces as can be shown to be Asiatic rather than Mycenaean in origin. Tomb 8 at

[1] H. W. Catling, *Cypriote Bronzework in the Mycenean World*, pp. 255 f. and pl. 46 (Oxford, 1964). I am grateful to Mr Catling for generous assistance concerning Enkomi.

[2] Higgins, *Jewellery*, pp. 87 f., pl. 12.

Enkomi contained two burials of which the jewellery can be dated by the associated pottery to the beginning of the Late Cypriote period. The absence of Cypriote Levanto-Helladic ware may be fortuitous, but the presence of certain distinctive Middle Cypriote III types of pottery justifies the opinion of the excavators that the burial took place in the early part of the Late Cypriote period (i.e. 1550–1500 B.C.). The jewellery is especially interesting as it includes not only plain strips or 'mouth-pieces' and toggle pins, but distinctive types of earrings (pl. 96) and beads which can be related to similar jewellery from Ajjul and Megiddo in Palestine (see p. 125).

Earrings

The earrings fall into three main types:

Type 1 Gold strip-twist and bar-twist earrings (pls. 96, 97 and 98 a–c).

Type 2 Oval earrings with 'mulberry' pendants (pl. 96).

Type 3 Penannular earrings with pendants in the form of stylized bull's heads decorated with granulation (pl. 99).

The method of manufacture of the gold strip earrings has been described above (p. 114); one isolated flange-twisted example comes from Enkomi Old Tomb 92 (pl. 98d). Here the gold bar was 'not left solid but cut into, lengthwise down its (normally) four faces, to allow the ribs thus left projecting, along the corners between the cuts, to be hammered out each into a flange (fig. 77c). The bar so flanged, with its terminal portions alone left plain and now most often tapered to a point . . . was then twisted, like a strip-twist earring.'[1] This technique is difficult to distinguish from the strip-twist type except with the aid of a microscope. It is, as Professor Hawkes has pointed out, a cruder method. Exactly similar examples to the Cypriote form are known from Ajjul and an example from Tomb 1073 (fig. 91) belongs to the Late Cypriote period when connections between Cyprus and Ajjul were particularly close. One can reasonably infer that it was not only potters but also jewellers who profited from these conditions of easy access between Cyprus and the Asiatic mainland.

The development of the strip-twisted type from the Palestinian bar-twisted types has been postulated by Hawkes and the evidence all points to the fact that the Cypriote examples of the strip-twist variety must have been 'devised within the sixteenth century, by goldsmiths serving the

[1] Hawkes, op. cit., p. 452.

consortium of interest established between Cyprus and the mainland, which is represented so conspicuously at Gaza.'[1]

The granulated earrings in Tomb 8 at Enkomi with a bucranium pendant in wire and granulation in the form of an ox's head are important as they are the earliest example of the technique of granulation known from Cyprus. They can be related to the remarkable inlaid pendants from Ajjul (pls. 82 and 83) which are also decorated with granulation and *bucrania* and which may well be the prototypes for the Cypriote examples. Higgins has described Cypriote examples of this type (where the tapered hoop has an elongated granulated pendant) as Cypriote imitations of a Minoan type, quoting examples from Enkomi Old Tombs 19 and 58 (pl. 99) of the thirteenth and twelfth centuries B.C. respectively.[2] However, the Enkomi Tomb 8 evidence suggests that in fact the Minoan examples may not be earlier than the Cypriote.

Enkomi Old Tomb 57 contained two bar-twist earrings associated with four or more small oval earrings with 'mulberry' pendants composed of granules soldered together and joined to the base of the ring (pl. 96). These can also be related to Syrian and Palestinian types and may be regarded as a development from the simplest form with one single drop pendant which is common at Ajjul in the Middle Bronze IIc period. Megiddo Tomb 251 (*Megiddo Tombs*, pl. 115, 10) is another well-dated example. A gold toggle pin of Palestinian type also comes from Enkomi Old Tomb 57.

Beads

(*a*) Fluted spindle beads with tubular collars occur in Tomb 8 and many examples of this distinctive type are known from Ajjul. Their Mesopotamian origin and subsequent development in Syria has been noted on p. 126.

(*b*) A flat square bead composed of four tubes with one side covered with granulation (Gjerstad, *S.C.E.*, I, pl. CXLVII) comes from Tomb 8 and belongs to the second burial dated not earlier than 1550 B.C. The example is unique for Cyprus and the granular decoration in panels of triangles is comparable with granular decoration at Ajjul.

[1] Hawkes, op. cit., p. 450. [2] Higgins, *Jewellery*, p. 72.

CHAPTER 8

Syria: and Palestine c. 1550–1300 B.C.

INTRODUCTION

The jewellery which can be dated to this period cannot be adequately studied without reference to the textual evidence, where many objects are described in detail and valuable information for different technical processes is given. Certain objects can be translated from the Akkadian with a reasonable degree of certainty: *šamšatu hurāṣu* as golden sun-discs, *anṣabtu* as earring, *kišadu* and *hīšu* as necklaces, *guḫaṣṣu* as braided wire or torque for suspending jewellery. But the terms used for different varieties of beads or rings need to be related to extant examples of both in gold and precious stones, and there are many problems which need detailed study before adequate translations can be made. The *tudittu* is discussed below. In the absence of a full linguistic archaeological and technical study of the evidence, reference can be made to the Chicago Assyrian Dictionary and to two of the main sources of evidence – the Qatna inventories and the Amarna letters[1] – together with an Old Babylonian text enumerating the clothes and jewellery worn by a statue of the goddess Ishtar.

The Qatna inventories consist of long lists of jewellery given by various donors to the goddess Ningal at Qatna (Misrifé, Syria), intended not only for the adornment of her statue in the temple, but also as gifts to the rich temple treasury. This enormous collection, which was probably started early in the second millennium B.C. when the cult of Ningal (of Sumerian origin) arose in Syria, must have covered several centuries, but the actual tablets can be dated to the fifteenth century B.C. and therefore antedate the Amarna letters. It is not surprising that nothing as yet has been found at Qatna of these offerings, jewellery being the easiest material to loot when a sanctuary was sacked, but future excavation may possibly yield some pieces. Reference should be made to the texts, translations and commentary by J. Bottéro[2] and it is relevant to note here that

[1] J. A. Knudtzon, *Die El-Armana Tafeln* (Leipzig, 1915).
S. A. Mercer, *The Tell el-Armarna Tablets* (Toronto, 1939).
W. F. Leemans, *Ishtar of Lagaba and her Dress* (Leiden, 1952).
[2] *R.A.*, XLIII, 1949, pp. 1–40, 137–218.

Bottéro has clearly shown that many Hurrian words and Hurrian proper names occur in the Qatna inventories; he considers it possible that some of the scribes may have been as familiar with Hurrian as with Akkadian. One unidentified piece of jewellery is described as an object of *Tukriš*, and a necklace could be described as inlaid in the manner of *Tukriš*. The land of *Tukriš*, often mentioned in cuneiform literature, must lie north of Elam and east of the Tigris and Bottéro suggests it may have formed part of Luristan.

The Armana letters also provide textual evidence for the identification of different types of jewellery in the fourteenth century B.C. Here again we find many Hurrian terms. The writer of many of the letters was king Tushratta of Mitanni, who sent urgent requests to Egypt for the despatch of gold and lists the appropriate gifts which were sent in exchange. The quantities mentioned imply a large output by the goldsmiths supplying Mitanni: 400 silver anklets (*šimirē šēpi*), pendants, earrings, bracelets (*šimir qāti*) and other jewellery are mentioned,[1] while the technique of cloisonné inlay with lapis lazuli and different precious stones was common practice.

The tablet listing the clothes and ornaments worn by the goddess Ishtar, dating from the Old Babylonian period and published by W. F. Leemans,[2] gives valuable information about the terms used by the scribes when describing types of jewellery. One can infer, from the quantities given, that the statue of the goddess would have different clothes and jewellery for different ritual occasions (two *tudinatu* were of gold, six of ivory) and we know that these ornaments were not only used by goddesses, but formed part of the normal collection of jewellery worn by women of high rank. Eleven pairs made of gold and precious stones and a hundred pairs of silver formed part of the dowry of Tushratta's daughter and were sent to Egypt on the occasion of her marriage with Amenophis IV.

JEWELLERY FROM SELECTED SITES, SYRIA AND PALESTINE

Alalakh (Atchana)

The site of Alalakh was strategically placed on the direct route from the cities of Mesopotamia and north Syria to Antioch and the Mediterranean coast, close to the Orontes river and sixty-four kilometres west of Aleppo.

[1] Knudtzon, op. cit., 25, col. 3, line 64 f. [2] W. F. Leemans, op. cit.

As a commercial centre on the west side of the 'Amuq plain, it has been described by Sir Leonard Woolley as a 'meeting place of the Great Powers' and routes from Egypt, Palestine and Syria to the south, Marash and the Hittite empire to the north, and Mitanni and eastern Anatolia to the north-east, all converged on Alalakh, which was also conveniently placed for the control of the timber trade from the Amanus mountains. This is exactly the kind of centre from which one would hope to find evidence of jewellery working, both in actual objects and from tablets, and we are fortunate that a considerable amount of gold and, to a lesser extent, silver jewellery has survived which must be considered in relation to the textual evidence which has been studied and catalogued by Professor Wiseman.[1]

The great palace of the ruler Niqmepa (the vassal of Saushatar of Mitanni) belonged to Level IV and the jewellers' moulds found in the palace along with many of the finest pieces of gold jewellery attest that Alalakh was an important centre of production in the fifteenth century B.C. This activity seems to have had a long history at this site; a bronze crucible (diameter 2 cm, depth 3 cm) found at Level V was considered by the excavator to have been used for precious metals, while a steatite jeweller's mould was found in an early temple of Level XIV which can be dated to the Jamdat Nasr period in Mesopotamia.[2]

Actual examples of gold or silver jewellery before the period of Niqmepa are not common; apart from gold ribbed or fluted ball beads made of thin gold leaf over a core, two pieces call for comment. An example of simple granular technique occurs in Level VI, where a small ring bead of solid gold was made by soldering small gold pellets together in a circle. This same technique was used in silver at Tell Brak (see p. 30), but at a much earlier period than the Alalakh bead, which dates from a period ending between 1750 and 1600 B.C., when Aleppo fell to the Hittites. A fine gold ornament with a circular disc and two long narrow tubular extensions covered with fine granules was found in a rubbish pit in the temple area of Level V and, therefore, belongs to the sixteenth century B.C. The close resemblance of the central disc with the pendant from the Kültepe *kārum* period Ib (pl. 68) suggests that Alalakh may well have played an important part in the trade between central Anatolia and north Syria (of which there is increasing evidence from Kültepe) and that the free movement of goldsmiths between the two centres was prevalent in the eighteenth and seventeenth centuries B.C.

[1] Wiseman, *Alalakh Tablets.* [2] Woolley, *Alalakh*, p. 273 (AT/39/143, AT/49/11).

By the fifteenth century B.C., however, it is clear (as Woolley has stated) that 'the Alalakh goldsmith was reasonably expert and was familiar with the techniques of cloisonné, filigree, granulation, casting and repoussé work and with the making of very thin gold foil for application to a base of another material.'[1] From the texts we learn that the majority of fifteenth-century B.C. personal names were Hurrian; many of these were craftsmen, but only one goldsmith is mentioned by name – Abban, the goldsmith who apparently received a sheep 'to dedicate in a ritual to the goddess Ishtar'. The seal of the great ruler Idri-mi, whose statue with its important historical inscription is now in the British Museum, mentions three houses of the jewellers (3 *bītāti amēli* (*meš*) *ša-aš-ši-nu*). A steady supply of gold (perhaps from local mines – see p. 230) is inferred from the monthly payment to the king of sixty sheep and fifty shekels of gold. This requirement is found on the seal impression of Idri-mi.[2]

Among a list of objects named in Hurrian, a pair of silver earrings (*išten*(*en*)*-nu-tum* (*a*)*n-ṣa-ab-tum*: KÙ.BABBAR) is included; the *tu-di-it-tum* (see p. 154) is also mentioned with the jewellery given as presents when the daughter of the governor of Alalakh was married.[3]

Pl. 100 (1–7) shows jewellery and gold work from Level IV, now in the British Museum:

(1) Gold pendant. Tang rolled for suspension; repoussé design of dots and linear design (imitating filigree work) perhaps of a lily (B.M. 125985).

(2) 'Ishtar' circular pendants, with six rays, one central boss and six bosses between each ray in repoussé, each surrounded with punched dots imitating granulation; curled-over tang made in one piece with the circle (B.M. 130093).

(3) Lozenge-shaped pendant with curled-over suspension, hook broken; central boss and border of dots. From 1937 house site. Unstratified. Level III–IV (B.M. 125987).

(4) and (5) One complete and one fragmentary piece of tubular sheet gold with gold wire round the edges and triangular pattern of double lines of granules; electrum. Level IV, courtyard of Niqmepa's palace. Probably plating for a staff (B.M. 125984, 125986).

(6) Described in Woolley's catalogue as a (?) tassel, this gold cone, broken at the top, may be the pendant of an earring; triangular granular decoration and overlapping scales of gold, possibly imitating the petals

[1] Woolley, *Alalakh*, p. 272. [2] Wiseman, *Alalakh Tablets*, Nos. 100, 227, 348.
[3] Ibid., Nos. 440, 441

of a closed bud – or, as Woolley suggests, the whole piece is shaped as a fir cone. Level IV, Niqmepa palace.

(7) Spherical bead with silver core pierced for threading and covered with gold wire forming cloisons for lapis lazuli and green and yellow stones. Level IV, Niqmepa palace (cf. the earlier example of this technique on a ring from Ur – pl. 11c).

Among the rest of the rich collection of gold jewellery from the level IV palace published by Woolley, the earrings should be noted (Woolley, *Alalakh*, pl. LXIX, g). They include the open penannular earring with cone-shaped granulated pendants (see pl. 131, Chapter 10, for type), sometimes two linked together. Another of the same type is from a grave not later than Level IV; this has fine granulation round the base of the hoop. An example of the variety with small granules at the base of the hoop instead of a pendant is important as it was cast in a mould. The catalogue entry is as follows: 'AT/39/95, pl. LXIX, J. Gold earring, a hoop, open at the top and decorated with three minute balls at the base. This type of earring was much favoured, but since real granulated work required time and skill a cheaper version having more or less the same effect was produced by direct casting. The mould AT/47/147 (misprint for 139) makes an earring of precisely the same sort as this; other examples in gold were found, and some in silver and in bronze. From grave ATG/39/45 attributed to Level IV.'[1] Similar moulds from Ugarit (Ras Shamra) are in the Damascus Museum.

This type is extremely common in Palestine and Syria and the distribution extends to Cyprus (Enkomi). The close connection between Alalakh, Ajjul and Cyprus is evident when the different varieties of the open penannular earring with pendants are considered, the fifteenth century to the end of the twelfth century B.C. being the main period of production. The actual use of these earrings could, of course, extend for much longer, but the existence of many different kinds of mould for jewellery making from Ugarit and Byblos, as well as Alalakh, is evidence for regarding the Phoenician coastal cities as extremely important centres of production of gold and silver jewellery as well as other types of fine metal work. Earrings from Levels I and O, just before and after the destruction of the city by the 'Sea Peoples' (c. 1200 B.C.) are noted in the section on Al Mina (Chapter 14).

Among the many female terracottas from Alalakh, two made from moulds (Woolley, *Alalakh*, pl. LVI, b and d, AT/48/4 and AT/37/77e)

[1] Woolley, *Alalakh*, p. 273.

clearly show the jewellery they are wearing. This type of moulded figurine belonged to the period of Yarim-Lim, Level VII, where a large brazier and pot stand from the level VII temple had five terracotta 'naked votaresses' or goddesses fixed to its side (Woolley, *Alalakh*, pl. LVIII, a). AT/48/4 holds her breasts in the usual fashion but wears an open torque round her neck, while AT/37/77e wears a wide necklace with circular 'Ishtar' pendant, large triple earrings and multiple bracelets. The earrings are the usual First Dynasty of Babylon type known from Mari and Larsa, etc. (see p. 87), while the crude hand-made female figures of typically Syrian type usually wear an incised clay necklace and have their ears pierced with several holes for the insertion of earrings. Two examples of this type are illustrated in pl. 107 wearing gold earrings and a bronze torque or necklace.

Ugarit (Ras Shamra)

In the mythological texts from Ugarit many references can be found to gold, silver and precious stones, which reflect the fact that the city was, especially in the fifteenth and fourteenth centuries B.C., an international centre for the production of fine metal work and jewellery.[1] The activities of the craftsman god Hayin, the divine craftsmen, Kathair and Khasis, and the account of the building and furnishing of the house of the god Baal, all testify to the accessibility of the raw materials and the richness of the objects associated with the Canaanite pantheon. Although the exact translations for words denoting different objects are often uncertain, the references to processes such as the smelting and (?) refining of silver and objects overlaid with gold link up with the discovery of magnificent treasures such as the famous gold cup and patera, both decorated in elaborate repoussé work, or the bronze falcon inlaid with gold found at Minet-el-Beida, the port of Ugarit.[2]

That the craftsmen at Ugarit were skilled in the most intricate metallurgical techniques is also clear from a study of both the texts and the actual objects discovered during the excavations undertaken by Professor Schaeffer, now on show in the Damascus Museum and the Louvre. The jewellery is of a uniformly high standard; it can be related to contemporary work from Atchana to the north and also to Ajjul in the south.

[1] See G. R. Driver, *Canaanite Myths and Legends*, pp. 91 ff. (Edinburgh, 1956) and *A.N.E.T.*, p. 133.

[2] Schaeffer, *Ugaritica*, II, pl. I–V; *Ugaritica*, I, fig. 24.

The surviving pieces must form an extremely small part of the production of jewellers working at Ugarit during the Late Bronze Age.

The Astarte plaques and circular disc pendants are noted below (p. 139). Moulds for 'mulberry' earrings, a bird pendant, and a double set of long narrow triple beads are in the Damascus Museum (Nos. 16.20, 16.69, 16.01). Among the gold beads, a melon-shaped fluted bead with collars (Damascus Museum 21.190) belongs to the type well known in Babylonia and Ajjul (see pls. 61 and 209), while single and quadruple oval-shaped beads (Damascus Museum Nos. 15.285, 21.160) and a flat circular bead pierced at each side with minute granular decoration in circles are typical for Ugarit.

Earrings combine the use of gold and precious stone, often lapis lazuli, and are often decorated in fine granular work. A particularly elaborate pair in Damascus Museum (Nos. 20.57, 20.26) are hollow, lunate-shaped, with attached gold and lapis lazuli pendant. A small circular earring (Damascus Museum) has a stylized bull's head pendant attached to the hoop and belongs to the same type previously noted from Atchana and Cyprus.

Lachish

The site of Lachish, Tell-ed-Duweir, has yielded a group of jewellery, now in the Ashmolean Museum, from Cave 4004 (pl. 101). This belongs to the Late Bronze III period, c. 1225–1175 B.C. The end of a diadem has a looped spiral attachment (cf. Ajjul, pl. 88 and fig. 83), while the 'mulberry' earring belongs to the usual Syro-Palestinian type discussed above (pl. 77). A circular mount for a scarab is decorated in granular triangles.[1] As at least two periods are represented in Cave 4004, an earlier date for the jewellery is not precluded.

DISTINCTIVE TYPES OF JEWELLERY FROM SYRIA AND PALESTINE

Nude goddess pendants and plaques

Ajjul has produced several examples of the well-known 'Astarte' pendants which can be divided into three main classes.

(*a*) Representational. Made from sheet gold, piriform in shape, with a

[1] O. Tufnell, *Lachish IV: The Bronze Age*, pl. 40, 393 (Oxford, 1957).

curled-over ribbon loop, worked with ribs and banded edges and cut as a continuation in a ribbon from the top of the piriform sheet. The design treats the whole field as if it was a human body, detailing in relief the head, breasts and pubic region. Of the four examples from Ajjul of this type, two are from Hoard 1299 (Petrie, *A.G.*, IV, pl. XIII – see also pls. 102 and 103). These examples, if Hoard 1299 was buried before the end of Ajjul II, should not be dated much later than c. 1500 and could belong to the late sixteenth century B.C.

Ras Shamra (Ugarit) has also produced Astarte pendants of representational type (pl. 104b). These are dated to the fifteenth to fourteenth century B.C. and, while they may well have begun in the late sixteenth, they continue to the fourteenth century B.C. Usually the head is stylized with a minimum of detail, but one example from Ras Shamra (pl. 105) is remarkable for the realism of the head, which is worked in repoussé.

(*b*) Pictorial – probably the prototype for Type (*a*). The plaque shows a picture of the nude goddess worked in repoussé or incised on the surface of the pendant, sometimes with Hathor curls and holding a plant (probably a lily) or an animal in each hand (pls. 106 and 107a). This variation has not been found at Ajjul, but is known from Ras Shamra (Minet-el-Beida) where a particularly fine example is now in the Aleppo Museum.[1] Here the goddess is shown front face standing on a lion, accompanied by two serpents and holding an animal in each hand. Her necklace, bracelets and armlets are clearly shown, while on another Ras Shamra example she wears four bracelets, holds the serpents and appears between two lilies and two gazelles (pl. 107b).

An example of Type (*b*) from Beth-Shan[2] comes from the level designated by the excavators 'Thotmes III', but its date has now been amended to the fourteenth century B.C. This is an oval-shaped pendant showing Ashtoreth holding the war sceptre.

A variation of the pictorial type from Ras Shamra shows a seated goddess holding a flower. Indications of a robe are shown and the goddess is portrayed side face, seated on a high-backed chair. Dated fourteenth to thirteenth century B.C.[3]

(*c*) Cut from sheet gold in the form of a stylized human outline (pl. 104c). Details of the face and breasts are in relief and necklaces, navel and pubic region are indicated by punched dots. Three published

[1] Schaeffer, *Ugaritica*, II, fig. 10, p. 36.

[2] A. Rowe, *The Four Canaanite Temples of Beth-Shan*, pl. LXVIIIA, 5 (Philadelphia, 1940). A new study of this site will shortly be published by E. Oren.

[3] Schaeffer, *Ugaritica*, I, figs. 114, p. 130; 120, p. 138.

examples from Ajjul (Petrie, *A.G.*, IV, pl. XX, 134) come from hoards: two from Hoard 1299, both with conical hats, while the third from Hoard 1312 has indications of a garment. The type is found at Ugarit (Ras Shamra) dated to the fifteenth to fourteenth century B.C.

The origin of these distinctive fertility pendants has ultimately to be found in Mesopotamia, where clay plaques and figurines of the nude goddess known from the Jamdat Nasr period onwards developed into terracotta plaques, which became extremely popular from the time of the Third Dynasty of Ur. The type was probably borrowed by the Egyptians at the time of the Eighteenth Dynasty; Mesopotamian and Egyptian influence can be seen on the Syrian and Palestinian versions, which are common in pottery on almost all sites in the Late Bronze period. The pottery plaques are usually oval in shape and, as they were made from a mould, could be produced in large numbers for use in childbirth and for prophylactic purposes at other times. The gold plaques are naturally far fewer in number and are probably the prototypes for the clay examples which occur as early as the Middle Bronze period IIb (eighteenth to seventeenth centuries B.C.) at Tell Beit Mirsim.[1] Type (*c*) can be compared with the clay figurines also common on sites in Syria and Palestine in the fifteenth to fourteenth centuries B.C. and also with Syrian bronze figurines of the type known from Ras Shamra in the seventeenth to sixteenth centuries B.C.[2] and at Byblos among the foundation deposits of the Temple of the Lady of Byblos.

It is clear that two goddesses are represented on both the gold and the clay plaques. The first has the Egyptian Hathor curls well emphasized and large cow's ears, while the second wears a tall feathered crown, sometimes pointed. Both types hold lilies in each hand while the feature of the hands supporting the breasts seems to be found on the Hathor type only. It is possible that the second type may represent a Hurrian goddess and – if this is so – then the goddess Shaushga, the Hurrian form of Ishtar (see p. 143), would be a likely candidate; the eight-pointed star, discussed below, could be regarded in Palestine (as in Anatolia) as her particular symbol.

Star pendants

Eight-pointed star, with variations for number of points.

(*a*) Circular pendant in sheet gold. A round pendant from Ajjul with

[1] W. F. Albright, 'Tell Beit Mirsim, II', *A.A.S.O.R.*, XVII, 1936–7, pl. 26–8.
[2] Schaeffer, *Ugaritica*, I, pl. XXVII–XXXII.

an eight-pointed star worked in repoussé with central boss and smaller bosses between each ray of the star has a milled edge and curled-over loop at the top for suspension (pl. 108). Similar pendants are known from Ugarit (Ras Shamra) with eight points (Damascus Museum No. 21.192 – *Syria*, XIII, pl. XVI, 2) and with six points (Damascus Museum No. 20.28). One group from Ras Shamra is important, as it included round star pendants (pl. 109d) with six and four points, a moon-shaped crescent pendant (pl. 110c) and a nude goddess pendant.

The six-pointed star pendant has been identified as a solar emblem, owing to its similarity with the six-pointed star forming the centre of the winged disc on the stele of El from Ras Shamra. This find of pendants was discovered near the El stele and Schaeffer[1] refers to the texts where gold pendants are mentioned by the names of 'Astarte' and 'Shapash'. It is, therefore, probable that either the six- or the four-pointed star pendants (or probably both) should be regarded as sun pendants and symbols of and the Ugaritic sun goddess, Shapash.

Nuzi has produced a bone star pendant from Level I which can be dated to c. 1475 B.C., owing to the letter of Saushatar of Mitanni found in this level (Starr, *Nuzi*, pl. 127, B1).

(*b*) Star pendants cut from sheet gold (pl. 111). Pendants cut from sheet gold in the shape of an eight-pointed star with a rolled-over loop at the top for suspension are a simpler form of the circular disc star pendant. In both forms the points spring from a central repoussé boss. The star motif on Bichrome pottery found at Ajjul (Petrie, *A.G.*, I, pl. XXX, 22) should be compared with these gold examples, which may well have been inspired by the use of the star symbol on pottery.[2] Unfinished star pendants cut from sheet gold where the rays are not pointed but rectangular in shape occur at Ugarit (Ras Shamra) (Damascus Museum No. 23.343) and Ajjul (PAM 1162, 1168). These have rolled-over loops for suspension and were clearly intended as pendants, not rosettes (see p. 151).

The origin for both these types of star pendant, which can be found in many varying forms all over western Asia, must lie in Mesopotamia where they were known as early as the Sargonid period. The stele of Naram-Sin shows the symbols of Ishtar and Shamash and the association between the eight-pointed star of Ishtar, the crescent of Sin, the moon god,

[1] Schaeffer, *Cuneiform Texts*, p. 62 and pl. XXXII.

[2] *A.G.*, V, coloured frontispiece, pl. A & pl. B, and pl. VI shows three examples which were included in a large hoard of gold jewellery (Group 277).

and the sun disc of Shamash can be found throughout the Babylonian and Assyrian periods. In Babylonia, Ishtar as goddess of love and war was manifested in the form of the morning and evening star and her dual aspect had an astral character linked to the planet Venus. Often the eight-pointed star was inscribed on a disc and there was very little difference between conventionalized rendering of the star and the rosette, which was also used from the earliest times as a symbol of the goddess Inanna-Ishtar (see fig. 96a and b).

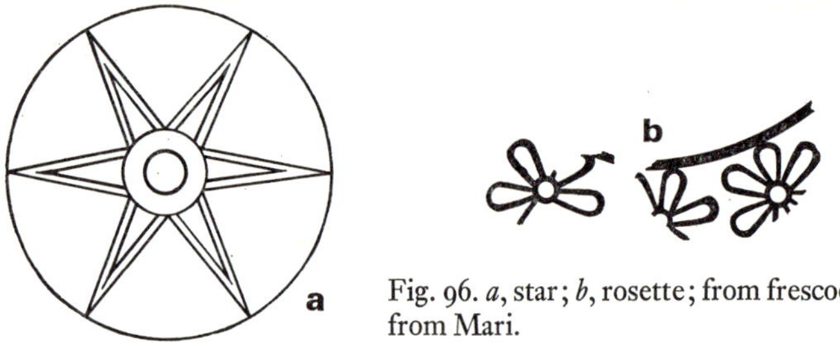

Fig. 96. *a*, star; *b*, rosette; from frescoes from Mari.

Documentary references in the texts to the use of the divine symbols in Babylonia are useful when considering the purpose of the gold examples which concern us here. Cult scenes show that the symbols were set up and used for ritual purposes – as Gudea says: *aš-me šu-nir Ninni-kam sag-bi-a mu-gub* ('the (star) disc, symbol of Innina, he set up').[1] Terracotta reliefs also show the symbol either beside the goddess Ishtar standing on her lion or associated with the sun disc and crescent in cult scenes dating from the Larsa or Early Babylonian period.

The amulets of these symbols were in fact simply small editions of the large cult symbols and their apotropaic powers ensured that they were an essential part of the equipment, both of the actual statues of the goddess in the temple and also of the king himself. Many examples in Mesopotamia illustrate this; a goddess described as *ṣalman Ishtar* is portrayed wearing an eight-pointed star inscribed on a disc on her wrist on the stele of Shamash-resh-uṣur, a governor of Mari, in the eighth century B.C.[2] – while the pendants in the shape of divine symbols, including the star of Ishtar, can be seen worn by Ashurnaṣirpal II and other Assyrian emperors of the ninth and eighth centuries B.C. (cf. figs. 118b, 98).

A female figure with four wings and horned headdress wearing a neck-

[1] E. D. van Buren, *Symbols of the Gods in Mesopotamian Art*, pp. 84 f. (Rome, 1945).
[2] Ibid., pp. 85 f.

lace of charms including the star and carrying a chaplet of beads may possibly represent Ishtar herself (pl. 112) and a clear representation of the goddess with the eight-pointed star placed actually on the top of her headdress can be seen on a relief from Nimrud (fig. 152) and on the famous rock reliefs of the Assyrian divinities at Maltai, 120 kilometres north of Mosul, in a valley through which runs the route to Armenia and Lake Van. In the procession of gods and goddesses they are shown standing or sitting on their animal attributes and Ishtar on her lion is the seventh and last divinity portrayed.

The widespread popularity of the pendant or circular amulet in the form of a star, all over western Asia in the second and early first millennium B.C., can partly be explained by the important part played by the goddess Ishtar in the Hurrian pantheon and the assimilation of the goddess not only in the Babylonian form, but also in the guise of such goddesses as the Hurrian Shaushga and the Canaanite Anat-Astarte, whose characters were closely allied to that of Ishtar – although the warlike character emphasized in the Ras Shamra mythological texts was less in evidence in Syrian and Phoenician iconography. The fame of Ishtar of Nineveh at the time of the *floruit* of the kingdom of Mitanni in the fifteenth century B.C. extended all over the civilized Asiatic mainland and the Amarna letters tell us how Tushratta of Mitanni sent a letter to Amenophis III announcing that the goddess Ishtar of Nineveh desired to make another visit to the Egyptian court; the first visit apparently took place in the reign of Tushratta's grandfather, Artatama, which enabled the Mitannian king to increase his prestige at the Egyptian court. The extensive devotion to the Semitic Ishtar among the Hurrians is further shown by the fact that Ishtar plays an important part in Hurrian myths of the serpent Hedammu. On the Syrian coast at Atchana there was a temple dedicated to the goddess and the site of Al Mina, the port of Atchana, has yielded a cylinder seal on which she is shown with other divinities who emerge from their symbols: an immense star, a winged disc and a crescent.[1]

In Anatolia the eight-pointed star appears in connection with the goddess Shaushga, the Hurrian form of Ishtar, who has been studied in detail by Mlle Damanville.[2] The goddess Shaushga is represented on several occasions and yet on only one of these instances can the symbol of the star be found. This is on the seal of the prince Taki-Sharruma, where the goddess Shaushga is shown with axe, wings and horned headdress, carrying the triangular-shaped object with which she is usually portrayed.

[1] R. D. Barnett, *Iraq*, VI, pl. 1, p. 2. [2] In *R.A.*, LVI, 1, 3 and 4, 1962.

Behind the goddess is a star. Carchemish also provides another instance of a goddess and the eight-pointed star symbol shown in the exact form known in Assyria and on the *kudurru*, or boundary stones. This is the goddess with horned headdress striding forward with one leg bare in the manner of the Hurrian Shaushga mentioned above, but here she has no wings or axe. Instead she carries a bucket in her left hand in the manner of Assyrian winged figures who are engaged in the ritual of the sacred tree; the right hand is raised, but unfortunately a break in the relief has damaged the hand; on the head is a large eight-pointed star and another is worn on the breast.[1] Here we may have an Assyrianized version of the Hurrian Ishtar-Shaushga, which can be closely related to many representations of Ishtar on Late Assyrian seals of the ninth and eighth centuries B.C. where the goddess Ishtar is shown in her guise as a war goddess with weapons and star above her head. A comparable seal (pl. 113) shows the goddess holding a short curved weapon facing a worshipper. She stands in front of her shrine which is embellished by stars and her usual eight-pointed star is above her head.

Sun disc with 'rays' (*Akkadian* šamšatu)

A group of jewellery, found on the refuse heap of a Late Bronze Age house at Shechem included circular pendants with varying numbers of points, together with a fine example of the four-pointed star combined with four curved rays (pl. 115). This distinctive type does not occur at Ajjul, but is found on the ivory panel from Ras Shamra surmounting the headdress of the winged fertility goddess whom we have suggested might be identified with Anat, the sister and wife of Baal. It is also found at Atchana and was often represented on ornamental coffins at Mari (figs. 97a and b).

In Mesopotamia the sun disc was the symbol of the sun god Shamash (the Sumerian Utu) who, like Ishtar, was regarded as the child of the moon god Sin. Many representations of his symbol of the sun with four points and four rays between are preserved. In the British Museum can be seen the stone tablet of Nabu-apal-iddina decorated in relief with a scene in which the king is conducted by a priest into the presence of the sun god enthroned in his temple at Sippar.[2] A huge solar disc is shown in front of the god resting on a base; two divinities above hold cords to keep the disc upright. On a Babylonian seal of the eighth–seventh century B.C. (pl. 114)

[1] *Carchemish*, III, pl. B.36, b.

[2] R. D. Barnett, *Fifty Masterpieces of Ancient Near Eastern Art*, p. 40 (London, 1960).

the god emerges from the sun disc clearly shown with its four points and curved rays amid other divine symbols – including Ishtar's eight-pointed star and the moon crescent of Sin. Shamash as the god of justice is shown on the stele of Hammurabi where the god is portrayed as handing over the law to the king.[1] The rod and ring, symbols of justice and right, are also often shown in the hands of Shamash and there is reference in the texts to the *šurennu* (symbol or emblem) of Shamash, before which an oath would be taken or a judgement given.

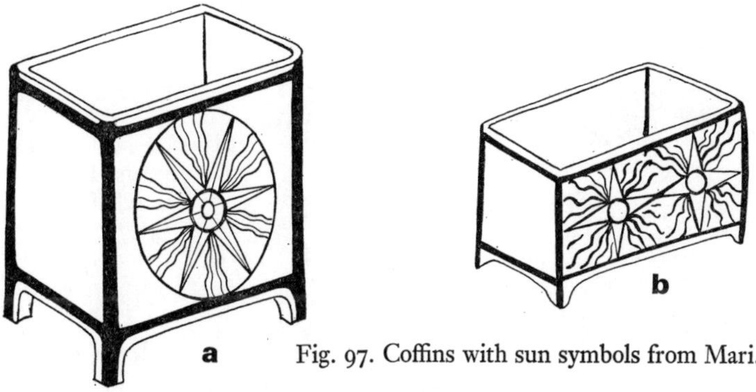

Fig. 97. Coffins with sun symbols from Mari.

Representations of the sun disc symbol include instances where it is shown on a support or post. Stone moulds for casting sun discs for use as amulets have been found at various sites in Iraq. The extant gold necklace from Dilbat (see pl. 61) shows amulets and symbols similar to those known from Assyrian reliefs where they are worn by the king or winged figures (fig. 98); among the divine symbols is a pendant in the shape of the sun disc. In Assyria the symbol of Shamash was the winged disc, later used as the symbol of Ashur, but the question of the origin and history of this important symbol has been treated in detail by many scholars and need not be repeated here.

The symbol of the sun disc on a post is, however, relevant. This is the symbol which in Early Assyrian and Cappadocian texts is denoted as *nipḫu paššūru*, which implies that it was made of metal. In a letter to Sargon II of Assyria the writer mentions palaces which 'are brilliant as the sun disc of Shamash'. The term *šurennu* was also used for the divine symbol set up on a post at the entrance to the temple and instances are given where 'a ceremony performed to attest the veracity of a witness who, after giving his testimony, was obliged to "pull up" or "take away" the

[1] Frankfort, *A.A.A.O.*, pl. 65.

šurennu of Shamash from its base, with the implication that it would be impossible for him to uproot it from its socket if he has committed perjury.' In Anatolia the same custom occurred where witnesses had to pull out the *šugariaum* of Ashur after they had sworn by it.[1]

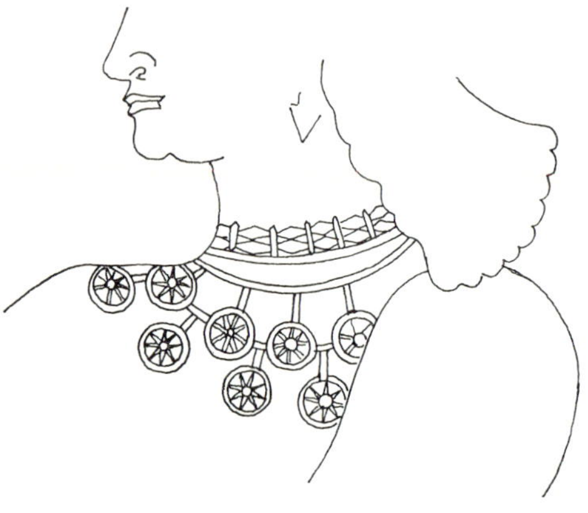

Fig. 98. Female figure with disc pendants from an Assyrian relief.

Cylinder seals of the Mitannian period can provide plenty of representations of the winged disc on a post. A good example can be found on the seal of Saushatar of Mitanni, which is the earliest example of the motif on the Asiatic mainland. But this device, which, as Frankfort suggests, was used to symbolize the Indo-European conception of a pillar supporting the sky surmounted by a disc[2] in fact differs little from the sun disc of the Mesopotamian sun standard or *šurennu.*

In view of the fact that we now know that Hittite religion was strongly influenced by Hurrian cults and that the gods and goddesses of the rock reliefs at Yazilikaya belong to the Hurrian pantheon, it is not surprising that the sun disc should be used in Hittite monuments usually supported by two pillars above outstretched wings. Documents from Boğazköy mention the sun disc as *šittar(i)*: AŠ.ME, and in these texts the *šittar* was always made of metal; in one instance it was apparently strung on a necklace as a pendant. There are references to six gold sun discs on the breast of the cult statue and during rituals and festivals the *šittar* was placed near the window of the temple. At Yazilikaya the king holds up the royal symbol consisting of the winged sun disc and his royal monogram. However, it is important to distinguish between the sun disc and

[1] E. D. van Buren, op. cit., pp. 90 ff. Oppenheim in *A.F.O.*, XII, p. 344.
[2] Frankfort, *Cylinder Seals* (London, 1939), p. 277.

the so-called Cappadocian royal symbol, known in Anatolia as early as the early part of the second millennium B.C. and studied in detail by G. R. Wainright.[1] Three important examples of the sun disc with rays or thunderbolts must be noted in this connection, as they are made of gold with rolled-over tops designed for suspension and come from Alalakh and Shechem (see p. 144 and pl. 115).

It is difficult to identify some of these disc pendants with the symbol of any particular divinity with certainty, as although they can easily be related to the symbol of Shamash, it is arguable that the curved 'rays' shown between the four-pointed star might represent thunderbolts. Alternatively, they might represent the double lightning of the Mesopotamian god Adad, who, after the period of the First Dynasty of Babylon, was represented with double rather than the triple lightning which was the usual symbol in Mesopotamia prior to the First Dynasty. It is worth noting in this connection that the god shown on many of the cylinder seals and seal impressions from Kültepe, standing on a bull or dragon, holds the double lightning or thunderbolt.[2] It may be that in Syria the double lightning (also the symbol of the Hurrian storm god Teshub) replaced the rays of the original Shamash symbol, but was combined with the four-pointed Shamash star.

In Assyria the double lightning, the symbol of Adad, is portrayed in the twelfth century B.C. on a Middle Assyrian seal used on the treaty tablet of Esarhaddon, where the god Adad, standing on his winged bull, holds the double lightning (fig. 99). This seal, which had been taken to Babylon and found there in 689 B.C. by Sennacherib when he sacked the city, was then used by his son Esarhaddon on treaty tablets recording the terms imposed on his Median and other vassals whom he summoned to Nineveh in 672 B.C. to acknowledge his son Ashurbanipal as crown prince and successor to the throne. On one of the *kudurru*, or boundary stones, this symbol is labelled 'Adad' in the inscription; on the stele of Ashurnaṣirpal II found at the entrance to a temple of the god Ninurta at Nimrud (pl. 116) the king is shown standing below five divine emblems which can clearly be identified with the crown of the sky god Anu, the winged disc, the crescent of the god Sin, the double fork of Adad and the eight-pointed star of the goddess Ishtar. Identical symbols can be seen on the stele of Shamshi-Adad V found in the Nabu temple at Nimrud (B.M. No.

[1] *A.S.*, VI, 1956, pp. 137–43.

[2] Özgüc, *The Anatolian Group of Cylinder Seal Impressions from Kültepe*, pl. 1: 2 (Ankara, 1965).

Fig. 99. Reconstruction of Middle Assyrian royal seal from Nimrud.

118892). The gold necklace from Dilbat (see p. 88 and pl. 61) includes a pendant in the shape of double lightning.

The recently discovered stele of Ashurnaṣirpal II from Nimrud (pl. 117) also shows the symbol of the god Adad – in this case triple lightning; it is interesting in this connection, as it clearly shows the emblems of Sin, Ashur, Ishtar, Enlil, Adad and the *sibitti* or Seven Stars. Here the Maltese cross, which is combined with rays from the carefully executed eight-pointed star symbol of Ishtar, can be clearly distinguished in the sun disc. It is probable that in Assyria the Maltese cross represented Ashur and this symbol was combined with the rays of Shamash. The Maltese cross occurs separately as a pendant; both Ashurnaṣirpal II (pl. 116), Shamshi-Adad V and Tiglath-Pileser III[1] are shown wearing a necklace to which is attached a Maltese cross pendant. A Late Kassite seal in the British Museum (Wiseman, *Cylinder Seals*, No. 56 – see pl. 118) also shows the Maltese or 'Kassite' cross with rays.

In Anatolia the question of the identification of divine symbols needs to be studied in relation to the texts and the seals and more information is needed before many problems can be solved. First, we find that the winged sun disc is shown at Yazilikaya and on certain of the royal seals, not only with six rays (cf. the stelae of Ashurnaṣirpal II from Nimrud), but also with another eight-pointed star in a disc placed immediately above it. The fact that the king is shown on the seal protected by a large

[1] Barnett, *Tiglath-Pileser III*, pl. XIX.

divine figure, the weather god, and standing opposite a goddess suggests that the second eight-pointed disc may represent the symbol of a goddess. She can be certainly distinguished from the Hurrian goddess Hepat who, wearing a *polos* headdress, faces the Hurrian storm god Teshub at Yazilikaya. Laroche, when discussing this seal,[1] has suggested that this goddess with her conical headdress of Anatolian type could represent the Hittite sun goddess of Arinna whose importance in the Hittite pantheon was such that she was known as 'queen of the land of Hatti, queen of heaven and earth, mistress of the kings and queens of the land of Hatti, directing the government of the king and queen of Hatti.' The conception of a sun goddess, which is entirely alien to Babylonian religion, was natural to the Hittites of the empire period. A comparable seal, mentioned above (pl. 113) shows the goddess facing a worshipper and holding a short weapon. She stands in front of her shrine which is embellished by stars and her usual eight-pointed star is above her head.

Gurney has discussed the relationship of the Hittite sun goddess to the sun god and pointed out that there is evidence that in official theology the husband of the sun goddess was the weather god of Hatti – and not the sun god, whose position in the pantheon, although important, is more difficult to define.[2] But on the seal of Tudhalia IV found at Ugarit and on the cartouche of the same king at Yazilikaya (fig. 100) the symbol of a six-rayed sun disc flanked by a pair of wings is clearly portrayed above the deity; immediately above this is another disc with rays. It seems likely that these are examples of the symbols of the Hittite sun god and sun goddess placed together to symbolize their dual character as supreme protectors of the king. The disc with rays can, therefore, be distinguished from the eight-pointed star which we have noted above in connection with the Hurrian goddess Shaushga (see p. 143). In view of the importance of both the sun symbol and the star symbol in Semitic, Hurrian and Hittite religion, the circular disc pendants can, therefore, be regarded as amulets which were small versions of the divine symbols and which – as in the case of the sun disc with rays from Atchana and Shechem – may have combined the apotropaic qualities of two deities.

Crescent or horn-shaped pendants

Many sites in Syria and Palestine have produced examples of pendants made in the form of a crescent with rolled-over hollow loop for attach-

[1] Schaeffer, *Ugaritica*, III, p. 114, fig. 24 and p. 17.
[2] O. R. Gurney, *The Hittites*, p. 140 (Harmondsworth, 1961).

ment: Ajjul (pl. 119), Megiddo, Beth-Shan, Shechem (pl. 115) and Ras Shamra (pl. 110c). Two types can be distinguished – a thin crescent moon comparable with the Ajjul example and the moon pendant on the Dilbat necklace (see p. 88 and pl. 63) and the flatter type from Megiddo and Shechem which is more like a pair of animal horns. In Palestine, Reshef and Baal are probably represented by the horn symbols. At Hazor in the

Fig. 100. Cartouche of Tudhalia IV from Yazilikaya.

Late Bronze Age temple the crescent is not only depicted on a stele with two elongated hands, but is also shown round the neck of an adjacent basalt figure of a seated god – probably the moon god Yerah. Some of these crescent-shaped pendants are probably also the symbol of the Moon god's consort, Nikkal (Sumerian Ningal), whose temple at Qatna was renowned for the richness of its offerings in gold, silver and precious stones (see p. 132 for a discussion of the jewellery included in these gifts).

In Babylonia it is possible that both forms of this pendant represent the Moon. In the Creation Epic, when Marduk orders the Moon, the 'jewel (*šukuttu*) of the night', to determine the counting of the days within a month, first the Moon is 'drawn in (the form) of a dim circle . . . to shine over the country' and then the horns of the Moon are mentioned with the phrase, 'Make your horns (increasingly) brilliant to indicate the first six days.'[1]

[1] See A. L. Oppenheim, *Orientalia*, N.S., 16, 1947, p. 231.

The Ajjul examples are mostly silver of the moon-shaped type, although the 'horn' type also occurs. The loops are plain, incised or ribbed. Megiddo, Beth-Shan, Gezer and Ras Shamra[1] have all produced similar pendants of both types, while a fine example in onyx from Ajjul with a pierced knob replacing the loop is without parallel elsewhere (fig. 88, Chapter 7). Nuzi has produced an example in composition paste.[2] The evidence suggests that the type was introduced in the sixteenth century B.C., but the most popular period for the use of these pendants seems to have been the fifteenth and fourteenth centuries (for a discussion of Anatolian examples from Kültepe, Karahöyük and Boğazköy, see p. 100). At Beth-Shan[3] three gold examples come from the level designated Amenophis III (now amended to thirteenth century B.C.); they were found in the different rooms of the temple and are the flat horn-like type.

Rosettes – Akkadian ajaru (fig. 88, Chapter 7)

Each petal is carefully cut from sheet gold and the centre of the rosette often pierced by four holes. The edges are decorated with repoussé dots. The type is found at Ajjul, Beth-Shan and many other sites. These were intended to be sewn on to garments and some examples realistically portray the natural original. Sometimes the rosette was made in the form of a circular disc with the petal worked in repoussé and the disc was pierced by four holes to facilitate attachment to the garment.

Symbols and jewellery of Inanna-Ishtar

The history of the rosette in Mesopotamian art begins with the earliest representations on cylinder seals of the Jamdat Nasr period at the end of the fourth millennium B.C. at the Sumerian site of Uruk in southern Iraq. The motif often resembles a flower, but the petals are so slender and pointed that it could represent a star and it is clear that the motif cannot be regarded as purely decorative. It symbolized the great Sumerian goddess Inanna (later the Akkadian Ishtar) and therefore 'the motif, whether typifying star or flower, was equally appropriate to her.'[4] Like so many other Mesopotamian symbolic motifs it could have been used for ornamental purposes, but the magical function of the symbol was the main reason for its widespread use in early Sumerian art.

[1] On the Ugarit (Ras Shamra) example No. 23.476 in the Damascus Museum a small ring for suspension is fixed to the base of the crescent instead of the usual rolled-over top.

[2] Starr, *Nuzi*, II, pl. 120, TT, UU, VV.

[3] A. Rowe, op. cit., pl. XXX, 53, and XXXIV, 12, 13.

[4] E. D. van Buren, *Z.A.*, II (45), 1939, 2–3, pp. 99–107.

On the Uruk seals it is often shown at the end of branches with eight petals and it is important to note that, although sheep and other animals play an important part in these early agricultural scenes, the figures of gods or goddesses are rarely represented. Instead, it is the symbols which are portrayed and these seals are an apt illustration of the view recently put forward by Jacobsen that 'the earliest expressions of the nature of the gods, their names and their external forms are like those of the phenomena in which they were seen to reveal themselves.'[1] Thus, the power of the god or goddess was regarded to be in the actual natural phenomena with which they were associated: Nanna was the power in the moon, Utu was the heat of the sun disc, while an important aspect of the goddess Inanna, the sister of Utu, was the power of growth and fertility. Jacobsen has also stressed the fact that in Sumer the idea of representing the gods in human form occurs relatively late; we can trace its beginning on the seals of the Early Dynastic period, but it was not until the Sargonid period that anthropomorphic forms developed and different deities can be identified with any degree of certainty. The divine emblems, however, survived the changes in name and importance undergone by different Sumerian deities when worshipped by the Semitic Akkadians, the Amorite Babylonians, the Indo-European Kassites or the Assyrians of the first millennium B.C. The emblems were carried into battle to show that the gods were accompanying the Babylonian and Assyrian rulers on their campaigns over Syria and Palestine, into Anatolia to the north and Persia to the east. It is not surprising, therefore, that the symbols should have been translated into amulet form by the craftsmen and jewellers and used in decoration of temples, as foundation deposits and simply as amulets in private ritual practices.

At the end of the second millennium B.C. in Mesopotamia and Syria we can find many examples of the rosette and the eight-pointed star of Ishtar. The existence of these two symbols can perhaps be explained by the fact that the Akkadian Ishtar under her Semitic form as a sky deity was embodying the dual nature of the Sumerian Inanna, goddess of fertility, who was 'queen of Erech', 'goddess of the sheepfold', 'goddess of war' and 'queen of Heaven'. It was especially suitable that the symbols of Inanna should be made by gold-workers in the form of amulets which could be worn on the wrist as a bracelet or as a pendant forming part of a necklace – as in the myth describing the transfer of the arts of civilization

[1] G. E. Wright (ed.), *The Bible and the Ancient Near East: Essays in Honour of William Foxwell Albright*, p. 268 (Cambridge, Mass., 1960).

from Eridu to Erech where Enki actually presents the arts of 'woodworking, metalworking, writing, toolmaking, leather working . . . building, basket weaving' and 'pure Inanna took them.'[1] The subsequent adventures of Inanna who, after being presented with over a hundred divine decrees – including 'lordship, godship, the exalted and enduring crown, the throne of kingship, the exalted sceptre, the exalted shrine, shepherdship, kingship, wisdom and understanding, judgement and decision'[2] – placed her gifts into the boat of heaven and departed for Erech need not be described here. It may be noted, however, as Kramer has pointed out, that the whole basis of Sumerian culture is found in the list of these divine decrees.

The myth of the descent of Inanna to the Underworld, the prototype of the Akkadian Ishtar's descent, is again relevant in any study of the jewellery.[3] Exactly why Inanna decided to visit the Underworld is still not clear, but the myth tells how the goddess first had to collect the seven ordinances, translated by Kramer as follows:

(1) The *šurgurra*, the crown of the plain, she put on her head.
(2) The measuring rod (and) line of lapis lazuli.
(3) A necklace of lapis lazuli.
(4) Twin *nunuz* stones (sparkling stones) on her breasts.
(5) A gold ring in her hand.
(6) The *tudittu* which she tightened on her breast.
(7) The *pala*-garment on her body.

Then, after instructing her messenger, Ninshubur, that if she does not return within three days, he is to set up a hue and cry for her in heaven at the assembly of the gods, she descends to the nether world and approaches the temple of her elder sister and enemy, Ereshkigal. The gate keeper leads her through the seven gates and myth describes how at each gate Inanna has to allow the removal of one of the seven ordinances. It is instructive at this point to consider the Akkadian version of the myth, where Ishtar is adorned with seven objects:

(1) The great crown on her head.
(2) The pendants on her ears – i.e. earrings.
(3) The *erimmati* – necklaces.
(4) The *tudittu* ornaments on her breast.
(5) Girdle of birthstones on her hips.

[1] S. N. Kramer, *Sumerian Mythology*, p. 64 (Philadelphia, 1944). [2] Ibid, p. 66.
[3] See S. N. Kramer in *A.N.E.T.*, p. 52, and Speiser, ibid., p. 106. See also Kramer in *Proceedings of the American Philosophical Society*, 1963, pp. 491 ff.

(6) The clasps round her hands and feet – i.e. anklets and bracelets.

(7) The clasps round her body.

The differences in the Sumerian and Akkadian versions of the myth raise many problems where the jewellery is concerned, but an attempt may be made to identify some of the objects which are shed by Inanna-Ishtar as she passes through the seven gates. There can be little doubt about the first object, the *šurgurra* crown worn on her head, which in both versions is removed at the first gate. Recently, Mr G. F. Dales[1] has made suggestions towards the identification of the objects named in the two accounts. He points out that, while there is a divergence between the two versions not only in the objects, but in the order in which they were removed, it is possible to equate the objects in certain instances and to amend certain translations. In the Semitic account the *erimmati* was removed at the third gate and Speiser's 'chains' could be more accurately translated as 'a necklace made of egg-shaped beads', owing to the correspondence which is now established between Akkadian *erimmatu* and Sumerian *nunuz*. In the Sumerian version the twin *nunuz* stones on her breasts were removed at the fourth gate.

Another object mentioned in both versions, but removed at different gates, is the *tudittu* – at the fourth gate for Ishtar and the sixth gate for Inanna. Dales has collected a mass of evidence from clay figurines to query Kramer's translation of *tudittu* as breast-plate, which implies a large heavy object, and considers that the *tudittu* was an ornament or pendant probably suspended from a necklace. Textual references to the weight of the *tudittu* suggest that it was light and that it possessed powerful apotropaic powers. If this suggestion is correct, then the *tudittu* may be shown on an Old Babylonian terracotta,[2] where the figure wears a large pendant suspended on a special necklace falling between the breasts in addition to the triple row of short necklaces. On the other hand, the passage 'her (evil demon Lamaštu) *tudittu* is broken, her breast exposed' would not make sense if the *tudittu* is a single pendant worn between the breasts without any functional purpose. The other passages quoted by Dales – 'The curse for rending a (woman's) cloak, breaking her *tudittu* and snipping off her *didu* garment' and 'If the ghost is that of a woman, you clothe her (a figurine) in a black garment (you put on her) *d/tudittu*' – also suggest that the *tudittu* had some connection with a cloak or garment and that either the garment or the *tudittu* itself actually concealed the whole or part of the breasts.

[1] *R.A.*, LVII, 1, 1963, p. 21. [2] Ibid., fig. 19.

A letter written by Tushratta of Mitanni to the king of Egypt in the fourteenth century B.C. from the Amarna collection provides a clue that the *tudittu* was composed of several parts as the phrase *ištenutum tudinatum ḫurāṣu* ('one set of *tudinatum* (plural) of gold') is used along with one pair of *anṣabatum ḫurāṣu* ('a pair of gold earrings') as a 'gift for my sister.'[1] Textual references to the *tudittu* from Alalakh and Mari also show that among the jewellery given to a bride for her dowry the *tudittu* was always included. It was often decorated with precious stones and lapis lazuli is constantly mentioned. It included a part called either the *rešu* or *qaqqādu* (the head) and the *tudittu* could be made of bronze or ivory as well as gold. A *tudittu* with the head of a bison is given as one of the presents offered to the underworld god Ningišzida on the occasion of the death of Ur-Nammu.[2] At Alalakh it was included among the jewellery given to the king's daughter.

With this rather incomplete evidence one further suggestion can be made. Sumerian statues of goddesses usually wear multiple rows of beads or rings which entirely cover the neck up to the chin and cover the bare area of the breast below the neck. The goddess with the vase from Mari and the goddess Lama from Ur (see p. 89) are two good examples of the use of this type of ornament and Mlle Agnes Spycket has shown how the row of beads or rings did not encircle the neck at the back but was secured by a knot or clasp, behind which a counterweight kept the ornament in place.[3] A long fringe was fixed to the weight at the back and this falls to below the knees behind. If we are correct in associating the *tudittu* with the 'collier à contrepoids', then the fact that Ishtar 'tightened the *tudittu* on her breast' would appear intelligible and it is important to remember that the word *irtu* (breast) is expressly used in this context.

The 'collier à contrepoids' first appears during the time of Shu-Sin (the penultimate king of the Third Dynasty of Ur) and became popular at the time of the First Dynasty of Babylon. It can be found on Kassite seals, is more frequent on seals from Nuzi and its history can be traced back to the Early Dynastic III period. But it is the spread of the use of this distinctive type of ornament, its portrayal in the artistic repertoire of Syria and its continued use into the Late Assyrian period which are important facts where any study of individual pieces of jewellery is concerned. An interesting example from the time of Ashurnaṣirpal II can

[1] J. A. Knudtzon, *Die El-Amarna-Tafeln* (1915), No. 17, line 42 f.
[2] S. N. Kramer, 'Death of Ur-Nammu', *J.C.S.*, 21, 1967, line 120.
[3] *R.A.*, LIV, 1960, pp. 73–84.

be seen in the British Museum (fig. 98) where a goddess wears not only a double row of necklaces, but another double row of beads from which are suspended four circular rosette pendants above a second row of four rosettes. There seems to be a connection between the breast ornaments and the double necklaces round the neck and, while the hair of the goddess conceals the place where one would expect to find the counter-weight, the fringed tassels are clearly shown on another contemporary relief – though in this period considerably shortened to just below the shoulders (fig. 101). These two reliefs suggest that the necklace and double rows of rosette pendants formed one single ornament which may have been designated by the term *tudittu* and would explain the use of the phrase *ištenutum tudinatum.*

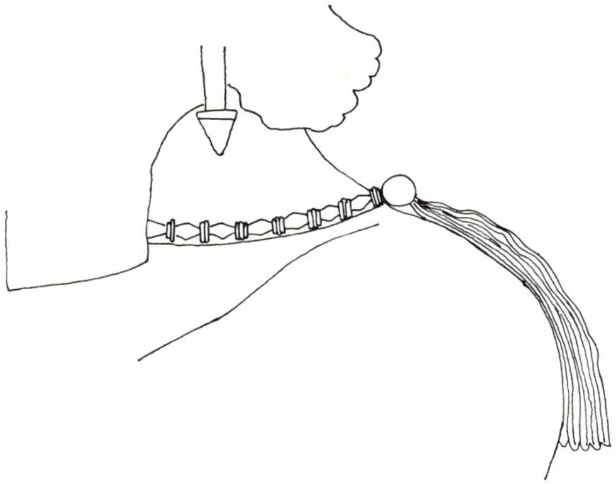

Fig. 101. Necklace from a relief, Ashurnaṣirpal II period.

It is, therefore, possible to regard the circular rosette pendants, the 'Ishtar' and the 'Shamash' types of circular disc pendant, as part of the *tudittu* ornaments which were an essential part of the wedding jewellery of the daughters of rulers in the second half of the second millennium B.C. It is probable that the *tudittu*, in simplified form, was also used by ordinary women. The undoubted apotropaic power of the *tudittu* would ensure that the bride would not consider herself properly equipped for both the marriage ceremony and the future hazards of married life without her *tudittu*. The association of the rosette with the goddess Inanna mentioned earlier in this section would also mean that fertility was ensured and the pendants, therefore, were particularly appropriate to a bride's dowry.

The concept of Ishtar as the goddess who embodied the ideas of fertility and procreation was one of the bases of Babylonian religion and the development of the Sumerian Inanna, whose fertility cult had been practised in Erech from as early a period as the Jamdat Nasr (c. 3400 B.C.), can be traced through succeeding periods in Sumer, Babylonia and Assyria. Sumerian religious ideas certainly began to influence Syria as early as the Third Dynasty of Ur period (c. 2113–2006 B.C.), so that it is not surprising to find archaeological evidence of this fact alongside a mass of textual evidence which affords ample proof for the strength of Mesopotamian religious ideas.

The translation of *tudittu* as pectoral in the Chicago Assyrian Dictionary has still to be proved correct; pectoral is used by Bottero to translate Akkadian *ṭuppu ḫurāṣu libba* in the Qatna inventories.[1]

[1] *R.A.*, XLIII, 1949, p. 11, notes 2 and 4, and 'cache seins' to denote the *tudittu*.

CHAPTER 9

Iran in the Mid-Second Millennium B.C.

INTRODUCTION

There is little stratified jewellery which can be assigned to this period, but the recent excavation by the Pennsylvania Museum expedition, directed by Dr R. H. Dyson, of tombs at Dinkha tepe containing pottery, bronzes and gold work provides important evidence which can be used as a basis for dating similar jewellery found without associations but with the place of origin sometimes known. In addition to this find, the grave groups from Gök tepe, excavated by Professor Earp in 1903 and recently discovered in the Fitzwilliam Museum, Cambridge, provide confirmatory evidence for regarding this period as an important period of jewellery production in Kurdistan and the western part of the Iranian plateau east of Luristan. The site of Giyan (see p. 91 above) is well known as a source of unstratified jewellery, especially fluted earrings (fig. 68, Chapter 5), which also come from 'Amlash' (pl. 120); some of this material can now be related to the Dinkha tepe and Gök tepe finds. It is unlikely that it can be far removed from the central mid-second millennium B.C. date established for similar material from Azerbaijan.

Among the large quantity of gold jewellery (much of which is now in private collections) shown at the various exhibitions of Iranian art and archaeology, two groups are especially important, as they can, although unstratified, be related to Middle Assyrian dated groups, so providing evidence for any attempt to date this varied material. Until scientific excavation takes place, it is impossible to make any useful or accurate study of this jewellery. Only one conclusion can be made with any certainty. It is evident that, even if only half the pieces which have been given findspots such as Daylaman, 'Amlash' or Ardebil actually come from these areas, a vast amount of gold jewellery has, without any doubt, turned up in the region which includes the valleys of the Elburz mountains round Ardebil (especially in the upper valleys of the Sefid Rud and its tributaries.

JEWELLERY FROM SELECTED SITES

Dinkha tepe[1]

The jewellery from this site (in course of excavation by Dr R. H. Dyson Jnr) is remarkable for its western connections, in particular those with the sites of Ajjul and Alalakh (see pp. 140 and 135). A tomb group included an eight-rayed star pendant of 'Ishtar' type, a crescent-shaped pendant, a single gold lunate earring and a pair of twisted penannular earrings of strip-twist type. A silver pendant, made of two crescents joined at each end, and agate and carnelian beads complete the inventory of the jewellery. Grave B.28 contained a long gold tubular bead comparable with the Gök tepe example (see below) and Grave B.26 a pair of gold earrings with large gold blobs below the pin which can be related to earrings of this type from Marlik (pl. 134, see p. 188). The radio-carbon date of 1550 ± 52 B.C. for the level in which these tombs were dug suggests that the jewellery should be assigned to the sixteenth century B.C.

Gök tepe

Tomb 1 (pl. 121) contained a pair of double hollow lunate decorated earrings with lapis lazuli set in cloisonné inlay and surrounded with a border of triangular granulation; the filigree border is made of twisted and plaited wire. The standard of workmanship is of fair quality, although this is difficult to judge because the granulation is very worn in places. A necklace of agate and carnelian beads (comparable with the Dinkha tepe examples) also included triple blue glazed spacer beads of normal faceted type (three long tubes joined longitudinally together) and a distinctive long gold tubular bead. This tubular type also occurs in Tomb 4 and a curved variety of the same type in Tomb 3. It is interesting that fragments of earrings similar to the gold examples but made of undecorated sheet bronze filled with paste and fragments of long bronze cylindrical beads, both straight and curved, were found in these tombs – suggesting that gold was not in ample supply in this area.

Another group of jewellery from Gök tepe is in the Teheran Museum (pl. 122). A pair of gold earrings is similar in type to the pair from Tomb 1,

[1] I am grateful to Dr Dyson for information concerning the jewellery. See Dyson, *C.A.H.*, No. 66, pp. 21 ff., and in *Iran*, 5, 1967, pp. 136 ff.

but without decoration. A third (single) earring is slightly larger. A necklace of dark stone and fluted gold melon-shaped beads also belongs to this series, but details of discovery and the associations of this find are not known.

Giyan

Tombs 80, 79 and 74, related by Dyson[1] to Hasanlu period VI on the basis of the pottery (late Ḫabur ware type), contained silver rings and simple coil earrings of silver, a bronze circular 'Ishtar' pendant and triple tubular spacer beads of paste. All three tombs belong to Giyan II period – probably towards the beginning of the period, as similar paste spacer beads and a silver ring occurred in an earlier period III grave, Tomb 92. A date of around fifteenth to fourteenth century B.C. should not be far wrong for Tombs 74 and 79.

A fine gold 'Ishtar' pendant was published by Herzfeld[2] with Giyan as its provenance. This example is decorated with fine granulation work on the pierced suspension knob, round the centre circle and outlining the rays of the star and the rosettes between the rays, as well as forming the border. The fine workmanship of this pendant suggests that it may well be closer to the Dilbat necklace (dated to c. 1650 B.C. or the end of the First Dynasty of Babylon period – see pl. 61) than to a not unsimilar but less elaborate example from the In-Shushinak deposit at Susa (Amiet, *Elam*, fig. 314a).

Daylaman

The Japanese excavations at Daylaman have not produced a great deal of jewellery and what was found belongs mostly to the later centuries of the first millennium B.C. or early centuries of the first millennium A.D. However, a group acquired by the Boston Museum of Fine Arts,[3] said to be from Daylaman, is noted here and provides a pointer for thinking that a considerable amount of the unstratified material from this region may belong to the second millennium and even as early as the period of the Third Dynasty of Ur in Assyria.

[1] R. H. Dyson, 'Problems of protohistoric Iran as seen from Hasanlu', *J.N.E.S.*, XXIV, 3, 1965, p. 195.
[2] *I.A.E.*, pl. XXX.
[3] E. B. Terrace, 'Some recent finds from N.W. Persia', *Syria*, 39, 1962, pp. 212–24. See also W. Culican, 'Spiral end beads in western Asia', *Iraq*, XXVI, 1, 1964, pp. 36 ff.

Pl. 123 shows this group, which was allegedly found together, although the centre piece in the top row is considered by Terrace to be possibly a later or even modern addition.

(1) Diadem. Oval-shaped with vertical rows of concentric circles separated by bands of repoussé dots (often described as the 'punched dot' style) surrounding bosses in their centre; length 3·5 cm, greatest width 6·4 cm. This can be compared with a dated diadem from Ashur (fig. 46, p. 71) from a grave of the Third Dynasty of Ur period.

(2) Two cone-shaped buttons 'with flanged bases', pierced for attachment (pl. 123). Top row, cone-shaped buttons; second row, outer examples 'decorated with raised bosses surrounded by pointillage, these being divided into six and eight vertical sections respectively by repoussé dividing lines'.

The right hand example has four punched dot dividing lines and a double row of punched dots on the flange; the left hand example has simple raised divisions, each with a boss and oblique repoussé lines on the flange.

All these buttons are pierced for attachment to leather or material, presumably garments.

Dimensions: average diameter of discs and cones 3 cm; average height of discs and cones 3 cm.

'Amlash'

Three necklaces from 'Amlash' (pl. 124) were exhibited at Paris in 1962–3 and, as there is no evidence to prove or disprove that the individual beads were found together, they must be regarded as a collection strung together in modern times. The round disc pendants, the flat disc beads and the pomegranate beads, however, suggest that a date in the second millennium B.C. is possible for this group and that, while the disc pendants could be dated to the middle or end of the second millennium, the flat disc winged beads (a well-known Third Dynasty of Ur type – see p. 68) could have been made as early as the beginning of the second millennium B.C.

Right hand necklace: length 25·5 cm, diameter of disc 7·4 cm. The large disc pendant is decorated with repoussé triangles, concentric circles in two registers, with an agate in the centre. The necklace is composed of barrel-shaped agate beads and divided by small flat gold circular disc beads.

Centre necklace (Iran Bastan Museum, Teheran): gold animal beads (ducks' heads and rams' heads), pomegranates, flat disc date-shaped beads with six circular disc pendants ornamented in punched dot technique with repoussé centre; length 27 cm.

Left hand necklace (Iran Bastan Museum, Teheran): flat disc, melon-shaped with collar and plain beads, four disc pendants with six-pointed star and centre repoussé boss and large circular disc pendant decorated with punched dots and centre (?) animal design; length 26 cm.

A gold disc pendant with six-pointed star and repoussé bosses between the rays is also in the Boston Museum of Fine Arts, No. 60.246 (pl. 125). It is said to have come from the Talish region and can be compared with similar pieces from Ras Shamra and Palestine (see pls. 108–9) and also with a fine example from Susa (Amiet, *Elam.* fig. 314A). It could be dated fifteenth to fourteenth century B.C., or as late as the end of the second millennium B.C.

Terracotta figurines from 'Amlash'[1] are often decorated with concentric circles which probably denote gold or bronze discs either worn as pendants or sewn on to clothing; a terracotta from Kazvin[2] is represented with bracelets, necklace, pendant-pectoral and possibly some kind of breast-plate. The ears on this type of female figurine are often pierced and, while the style of the Iranian examples is different from that of the Mesopotamian or Syrian female figurines of this class, the crude indications of jewellery are often comparable.

Of two Syrian figurines now in the Ashmolean Museum (pl. 126), one wears gold earrings, the navel marked by a gold bead (pl. 126a), while the other (pl. 126b) wears a bronze necklace as well as the usual incised necklace or pectoral often worn by these terracottas, whether Syrian or Iranian in origin.

[1] *Geneva Cat.*, No. 478, pl. 12. [2] Ibid., No. 593, pl. 45.

CHAPTER 10

The Kassite Period in Babylonia and the Mid-Assyrian Period in Assyria c. 1350–1000 B.C.

INTRODUCTION

The capital of the Early Assyrian empire founded by Shamshi-Adad I about 1814 B.C. at Ashur has yielded several graves of the Middle Assyrian period which contain jewellery of the greatest importance for dating purposes. In Babylonia, the site of Dur Kurigalzu[1] (Aqar Qūf, near Baghdad, capital of the Kassite kings), excavated by the Iraq Department of Antiquities and Professor Seton Lloyd, has also yielded a collection of stratified gold work. These two sites provide a reasonably firm basis for any attempt to date unstratified material in both Babylonia and Iran. This is the only large collection of Kassite jewellery extant and, while Kassite art in Babylonia is known to us from cylinder seals and other archaeological material, including the boundary stones, we still know practically nothing about the Kassites prior to their arrival in Babylonia around 1600 B.C. It is probable that they came from the Zagros mountains, possibly from the area round Sar-i-pol, and we know that in the reign of Samsuiluna (1749–1712 B.C.) Kassite soldiers raided Babylonia and managed to conquer Ur and Erech. Kassites were also in Elam and there is evidence of gradual Kassite infiltration into Babylonia for the next 150 years, when they appear in business documents as labourers and harvesters.

It has been suggested that movements of tribes of Indo-European speaking peoples in the Caucasus and Transcaucasian area were responsible for the migration of the Kassites southwards and that pressure from the north resulted in their invasion of Babylonia. Of their original homeland we know nothing and, although there is evidence that some of the Kassite gods are of Indo-European origin and that their language was a

[1] *Iraq* Supplements, 1944, VIII, 1945.

Caucasian language, there is no definite archaeological evidence to suggest that their ultimate origin might lie in the Caucasus or Transcaucasia. Until further excavation provides more evidence for this problem, two possible clues can be noted here. These are the chariot burials on Lake Sevan and the rich barrow graves in the Trialeti region of Transcaucasia (where chariots were also buried in the graves) which have yielded an astonishing amount of gold jewellery decorated with granulation – a technique used with great effect by Kassite smiths at Aqar Qūf. Certain features on the silver cup from Trialeti, which shows a procession of figures with wolves' tails approaching an altar, can be found in Iran and also on a much later boundary stone of the period of the Kassite Melishipak, king of Babylonia in the early twelfth century B.C.[1]

The question of the use of an extremely developed kind of granulation by goldsmiths in this period raises many problems. Did they bring the knowledge of this intricate technique with them? Or did they acquire the knowledge from Assyrian, Babylonian or Elamite smiths? At the time of Kurigalzu II (c. 1345–1324 B.C.), contemporary of Khurpatila, king of Elam, war broke out and the Kassite king made various dedicatory gifts to the gods Sataran and Enlil in Susa after his victory and left an inscribed statuette of himself recording the defeat of Elam on the acropolis at Susa. He also brought back to Nippur an agate tablet, which Shulgi of the Third Dynasty of Ur had presented to the goddess Inanna in Susa, and – although Elam did not remain long under Kassite overlordship – contact between the Kassites and Elam remained close. We know that the Elamite Shutruk-Nakhunte exacted tribute from Dur Kurigalzu which attests to the wealth of the city around 1170 B.C. Elamite metallurgy, which had attained its climax in the reign of Untash-GAL (1265–1245 B.C.) when the great life-size bronze statue of Queen Napir-Asu was cast, continued to produce objects of a high technical standard. It is unfortunate that we have no examples of jewellery from the Susa excavations dated to the period immediately prior to the thirteenth century to compare with the jewellery from Aqar Qūf (for twelfth-century B.C. Elamite work see below, p. 186).

Egyptian influence, however, has been shown by Edith Porada[2] to have been easily discernible on both seals and mosaic work. The gold bracelet from Aqar Qūf, now in the Iraq Museum (pl. 127), finely decorated with

[1] L. W. King, *Babylonian Boundary Stones*, pl. XXIX. Cf. Kuftin, *Trialeti*, pl. XCII.
[2] 'On the problem of Kassite art', *Archaeologica Orientalia in Memoriam Ernst Herzfeld*, pp. 179 ff. (New York, 1952). Porada follows Van der Meer, Kurigalzu III (1333–1309 B.C.).

granulation and a blue paste inlay, may well be the result of Egyptian influence on Kassite jewellers. Granulation in Egypt at this period was practised with extreme skill – as shown by the examples from Dahshur and Lahun.[1] Diplomatic contact with Egypt and Mitanni is attested by the correspondence of the Kassite Burnaburiash II with Amenophis IV – while Mitannian, or perhaps more correctly Hurrian, influence cannot be discounted in the jewellery; it is certainly evident on the products of the later Kassite seal cutters. It is also possible that the knowledge of the technique of granulation was derived from Egypt via the Hurrian workshops on the Syrian coast at sites such as Atchana or Ugarit, where fine examples dating from the fifteenth and fourteenth centuries B.C. can be found (see p. 133).

But it is perhaps more likely that the knowledge of this technique was learnt from Babylonian craftsmen who had not forgotten how to use it during the preceding period of the First Dynasty of Babylon. Unfortunately, we have practically no jewellery which can be dated to this period (see Chapter 5), but this is probably due to the fact that there are hardly any tombs of the First Dynasty excavated. At Ashur, Tomb 35 contained a seal of this period and a minute bead with granular decoration, while the famous cylinder seal found at Platanos in Crete belonging to the First Dynasty of Babylon style has gold caps decorated in granulation work.[2] Granular decoration in triangles on the gold caps of seals is characteristic of Kassite seals and may well represent the continuation of a tradition which had not died out in Babylonia since the Sargonid period.[3]

In Assyria the site of Ashur has given us an astonishingly rich collection of gold and silver jewellery found in graves and tombs dating from the period of the Third Dynasty of Ur onwards, through the Mid-Assyrian period starting c. 1350 B.C., and into the Late Assyrian period of the ninth, eighth and seventh centuries B.C. I have elsewhere suggested[4] that the purpose of the activities of Mesopotamian jewellers from the earliest historical periods in Sumer onwards was primarily religious and that Tomb 45 at Ashur (dated to the thirteenth century B.C.), where the design and technique of many of the objects of jewellery show striking similarities to material from the Royal tombs at Ur, has provided us with instructive

[1] Wilkinson, *Egyptian Jewellery*.
[2] Smith, *E.H.A.*, p. 203, fig. 16; Alalakh and Chronology, p. 16.
[3] T. Beran, 'Assyrische Glyptik des 14 Jahrhunderts', *A.F.O.*, 18, 1957–8, p. 266. For earlier examples from the Dynasty of Babylon period see B. Buchanan, 'On the seal impressions of some Old Babylonian Tablets', *J.C.S.*, XI, 1957, pp. 45 ff.
[4] *Iraq*, XXII, 1960, pp. 105–15.

material to illustrate this point. Andrae's suggestion that this tomb, with both its male and female inmates adorned with such an extraordinary wealth of gold, silver and precious stones, could be regarded as an example of the *ἱερος γαμος*, in which a priest and priestess acted the parts of Tammuz and Ishtar, is certainly reasonable. This collection of jewellery is also an apt illustration of the underlying conservatism of the Assyrian jewellers when their products were needed for ritual and magical purposes. The importance of performing a ritual correctly with all the necessary accompaniments was a basic necessity in Babylonian and Assyrian religious practice; further work on the texts may soon make it possible to relate the head ornaments, earrings, necklaces, pendants and other jewels found on the body of the lady to the description of the ornaments worn by the goddess Ishtar in the myth of her descent to the Underworld (see p. 153).

The ritual significance of the jewellery found at Ashur would not have been lessened by the fact that certain forms of spiraliform jewellery, such as the double spiral (known earlier at Brak and Ur, p. 11), are developed with great skill into elaborate patterns for double spiral forehead ornaments with a loop between the two spirals. If these looped double spirals represent, as Frankfort has suggested, fertility symbols and can be related to the ancient symbol of the goddess Ninhursag, they reflect the strength of the belief in amulets of this form, which would explain their widespread distribution.[1] In Tomb 45 at Ashur the forehead ornaments which show the looped double spiral in an elaborate form, made from gold wire and sometimes decorated in granulation, were all found on or near the female skeleton. These pendants can be regarded as purely Mesopotamian in inspiration, but it is possible to discern Egyptian influence among the magnificent collection of jewellery found in Tomb 45. However, the extent of this is not easy to assess and the problem has to be considered in relation to the question of Egyptian influence in Babylonian jewellery of the Kassite period.

A study of the cylinder seal impressions is essential to understand the significance of the Ashur jewellery. Edith Porada has convincingly shown that the distinctive representational style of cylinders of Kassite origin dating from the reign of Kurigalzu II can be summarized as 'motifs which can be shown to have been of Kassite origin . . . combined with Mitannian designs and with some Egyptian elements' and has established that this new phase in the glyptic art of Mesopotamia can be ascribed to southern

[1] Ibid., p. 108, footnote 7.

seal cutters in the Late Kassite period.[1] She has also stressed the important fact that the reign of Kurigalzu II, as shown by the excavations at Aqar Qūf, was a prosperous period in which relations with Egypt may have been intensified, resulting in the influence evident at Dur Kurigalzu not only on the seals and the mosaic decoration, but also on the jewellery.

At Ashur, however, if Egyptian influence exists, it is later than the reign of Kurigalzu II in Babylonia, both seals and jewellery providing evidence for this. Moortgat's study of the Ashur seal impressions[2] showed that this group must be dated to the thirteenth century B.C. and Edith Porada has remarked that the earliest dated Assyrian impressions which show a representational style similar to that of Kurigalzu II are dated at least one generation later. Andrae's date for Tomb 45 at Ashur (i.e. Tukulti-Ninurta I, 1244–1208 B.C.) is important because, if Egyptian influence in the north did not become apparent until the thirteenth century B.C., the question has to be asked whether this influence was the result of direct contact between Egyptian and Assyrian craftsmen or of indirect contact via the Phoenician coast and north Syria.

Any attempt to answer this question also has to consider the seal impressions with the representational Kassite style mentioned above. Three of the best examples of this style studied by Miss Porada are dated – two to the reign of Kurigalzu II and one to the reign of his successor, Nazimaruttash (1308–1283 B.C.). The interesting point about the latter sealing and one of the Kurigalzu II examples is that the borders show the imprint of the intricate triangular patterns of the granular decoration of the gold caps which formed the setting of the cylinder. The fact that many Kassite cylinders are mounted in gold settings showing fine granulation work is extremely important in this context: if we could establish the source of the knowledge of this highly intricate technique at this period, we would have evidence of great value for assessing the extent of Egyptian influence at Ashur and also the part played by Syria in transmitting Egyptian techniques and motifs to Assyria and Babylonia.

Another technique which occurs at Ashur is cloisonné inlay, which may well represent the influence of Egyptian techniques. Cloisonné inlay occurs in Babylonia at the time of the Third Dynasty of Ur (see p. 165) but the necklace made of gold and lapis lazuli and decorated by cloisonné inlay, worn by the man in Tomb 45, can be compared with that of Tutankhamun on the gold-plated throne, suggesting strong Egyptian influence.[3]

[1] 'On the problem of Kassite art', *Archaeologia Orientalia in Memoriam Ernst Herzfeld*, p. 186.
[2] *Z.A.*, 47, 1942, pp. 50 ff. [3] Wilkinson, *Egyptian Jewellery*.

The round pectoral with inlay of precious stones also has Egyptian parallels and has no known Babylonian or Assyrian prototype. A pair of earrings, with attached circular rosette of lapis and gold (fig. 107b) can be compared with the ear ornaments of Tutankhamun which, although of a far more intricate design and workmanship, suggest that they or similar less complicated Egyptian examples may easily have served as the model for the Ashur jewellery. The circular pendants on this type of earring which form the setting for a precious stone (usually malachite) with the attachment for suspension formed of an onyx drilled longitudinally (fig. 107b) suggest that the jeweller might be imitating the central part of an Egyptian earring such as the pair of Tutankhamun, already mentioned. The edging of these pendants, however, with the distinctive 'cup spiral' pattern is not Egyptian. The pattern can be found on an Assyrian seal published by Moortgat[1] and dated by him to the time of Tukulti-Ninurta I, thus being contemporary with the jewellery from Tomb 45. Here, the 'cup spirals' form a palmette cross which is simply an elaborate form of the Kassite cross known on earlier Kassite seals.

The possible influence of Kassite jewellery on Elamite work of the twelfth century B.C. must now be considered. The technique of granulation is known among the jewellery found at Susa and a fine example is the whetstone with a gold lion's head (pl. 128) discovered in the deposit of the In-Shushinak temple at Susa, which was restored and reconstructed with rich decoration by Shilhak-in-Shushinak c. 1125 B.C. The votive deposits may well have included objects from an earlier period, but a *terminus ante quem* is provided by Shilhak-in-Shushinak. It may well be that this example of Elamite granulation can be explained by the fact that not only gold work as booty, but also smiths as prisoners were brought back to Elam from the campaigns in Babylonia of Shutruk-Nakhunte. We know that the Elamites sacked Babylon and that Kutir-Nakhunte, Shutruk-Nakhunte's successor, captured the Kassite Enlil-nadin-aḫḫe, whom he exiled to Elam.

Labat[2] has suggested that the difficult art of moulding panels of brick in decorative forms, which have been found in the temple of In-Shushinak dating from this period, may have been introduced into Elam by Babylonian prisoners familiar with the technique used at the temple of Inanna at Uruk which was built by the Kassite king, Karaindash, in the fifteenth century B.C. It is also probable that the intricate technique of granulation in jewellery owed its origin in Elam to captured craftsmen. An alternative

[1] *Z.A.*, 47, 1942, Abb. 52, p. 76. [2] *C.A.H.*, No, 23, p. 8.

explanation is that the whetstone with lion's head may be plunder from Aqar Qūf which is not likely to have escaped the depredations of the Elamites when Babylon was captured. Shutruk-Nakhunte dedicated a vast booty to his god In-Shushinak and the whetstone could have been originally included in this deposit and then been re-dedicated about fifty years later by Shilhak-in-Shushinak. The importance of this object in the history of granulation cannot be overstressed as, although comparable examples with granulation have been found in Persia, there is no other stratified example.

Jewellery from Ashur – Middle Assyrian period c. 1500–1100 B.C.

Tomb 45[1] was a well-preserved vaulted brick tomb whose stratigraphical position can be dated to the period of Tukulti-Ninurta I (1244–1208 B.C.). The male and female skeletons were each placed flat on their backs with legs outstretched and were found with jewellery *in situ* as it was placed on the bodies and the clothes. In the absence of an anthropological study of the skeletons, the sex was determined from the evidence of size, weight of the bones and the nature of the offerings: ivory pyxis, ivory and bone hair-pins and an extremely rich collection of jewellery accompanied the skeleton identified as female. Fewer and heavier pieces of jewellery were found on the skeleton identified as male, but the absence of weapons is puzzling if this identification is correct.

The male skeleton was adorned with earrings and a unique gold and lapis lazuli necklace. The earrings differed only from those of the female in size, while smaller examples of the same types were also found with the male. The bulk of the jewellery, however, belonged to the female skeleton. The excavation suggests that this represented the entire stock of jewellery owned by the woman.

Necklaces

(*a*) Five gold and six lapis lazuli plaques. Found on the male skeleton, round the neck (see p. 176, fig. 110).

(*b*) Diadem in the form of a necklace. Eighteen pendants suspended from a cord now perished. Found on the female skeleton, on or near the skull (Haller, *Ashur*, Abb. 166).

[1] For detailed descriptions, see Haller, *Ashur*. I am indebted to Mrs M. C. Ridley for detailed translations of the German technical descriptions.

Details of pendants from necklace (b) above

(*a*) Pair of pomegranate-shaped pendants; the globular fruit has five angular sepal spikes on the crown. A gold tube passes through a vertical boring which is fixed to a small curved gold clasp with upturned rim (Haller, *Ashur*, Abb. 167a). At the top is attached a conical gold stopper. The tube is drawn out into a broad gold loop, with triple ribbing below the curved clasp.

(*b*) Two small vases imitating the alabaster vases found among the grave goods. Hexagonal beads in red carnelian, one with ribbed edges, the other plain. Gold sheet mountings at the head and foot connected by a gold tube passing through a vertical boring splayed out over a flat perforated mount with hammered rims (Haller, *Ashur*, Abb. 167c, Taf. 34c, d).

(*c*) Pair of disc pendants (Haller, *Ashur*, Abb. 166).

(i) With ram's head of lapis lazuli set in gold mount and surrounded with fifteen semi-circular 'cup spiral' attachments decorated in granulation. An onyx with gold caps is pierced to hold the thread or cord (Haller, *Ashur*, Taf. 34s). The gold setting is made with a ring of cylindrical wire surrounded by a larger ring of twisted quadrangular wire. Gold granules lie in the groove between the two and the whole is joined to a base of gold sheet. The fifteen 'cup spirals' which decorate the periphery are outlined in twisted quadrangular wire, inside which seven gold granules form a rosette. A tubular lug, in the form of a 1·5 cm long black and white onyx bead, is soldered by two gold bands to the upper rim, where the cup spirals are lacking.

(ii) The centre is of malachite, drilled vertically and the edge of the gold backing decorated with looped spirals with granulation (Haller, *Ashur*, Taf. 34w). The gold sheet base is slightly oval in shape and measures 3·4 × 3·6 cm. The stone inlay is enriched by double cylindrical wire, a ring of large granules and twisted quadrangular wire. The rim of the disc is formed by 'cup spirals' of cylindrical wire. A cylinder bead of highly coloured stone attached by two gold bands soldered to the rim provides the means of suspension.

(*d*) A pair of gold-mounted, double onyx cat's eye spacers with granulated gold mount (Haller, *Ashur*, Abb. 166, Taf. 34h, k).

(*e*) Onyx pendant of triangular shape, mounted in gold with gold backing; twenty-seven gold 'petals' round the edge strengthened and outlined by plain gold wire; the setting is of cylindrical gold wire and granulation, bent so that the stone lies in a shallow saucer. The suspension ring consists of three gold bands soldered to the underside of the base (Haller, *Ashur*, Abb. 166, Taf. 34u).

(*f*) Pair of rock crystal pendants, set in gold. The crystal, transparent as glass, is shaped like a large drop with oval section. It is 2·8 cm long, including a short angular projection at the top, perforated for suspension. The periphery is overlaid with gold; a regularly denticulated thin strip of gold runs round the crystal from one side of the perforation to the other. It is held in position by two cylindrical wires, which are soldered to it; at the top these are hammered into a band, forming the upper projection and closing the circle. The gold band is perforated on both sides for threading the string of the necklace (Haller, *Ashur*, Abb. 166, Taf. 34a, f).

(*g*) Triple cat's eye in gold mount of cylindrical wire linked at back by double gold bands between each disc, which are provided with five eyelets to keep the piece vertical when suspended. Length 4·8 cm, width 1·7 cm (Haller, *Ashur*, Abb. 166, Taf. 34o, Taf. 35f).

(*h*) Melon-shaped pendants of dark red carnelian set in gold mount and pierced longitudinally. Triple ribbed gold bands at either end crowned by gold caps with double ribbed profile. Round the central perforation the edges of the caps are hammered up to support the three ribbed suspension rings. This has been drawn out of a gold tube which passes through the boring from end to end. At the lower end it is covered by a small gold cap into which the two wires of the palmette volutes have been inserted and firmly soldered, as well as the massive gold palmette itself. This consists of hammered gold sheet, the leaves and volutes bordered with gold wire (Haller, *Ashur*, Abb. 166, Taf. 34m, q).

(*i*) Pair of lapis lazuli pendants of four cylinders joined and set in gold with palmette decoration at base similar to (*h*) above. Two gold rings, ribbed for suspension, are joined to the quadripartite cappings by two invisible gold tubes (Haller, *Ashur*, Abb. 166, Taf. 34n, p, Taf. 35e, g).

(*j*) Pair of carnelian vase-shaped pendants in gold settings (Haller, *Ashur*, Abb. 166, Taf. 34b, e).

(*k*) Pair of disc pendants. The borders of both examples are 'cup spirals' with granulation similar to (*c*) above:

(i) With lentoid lapis lazuli centre and pierced cylindrical onyx with gold caps for suspension (Haller, *Ashur*, Abb. 166, Taf. 34t).

(ii) With lentoid light green jasper centre and pierced cylindrical lapis lazuli with gold caps for suspension (Haller, *Ashur*, Taf. 34v).

(*l*) A pair of gold-mounted lapis lazuli drop-shaped pendants (fig. 102), each with a single eyelet and decorated round the edge with granulation, were found near the right knee of the female skeleton. Their original position is not clear.

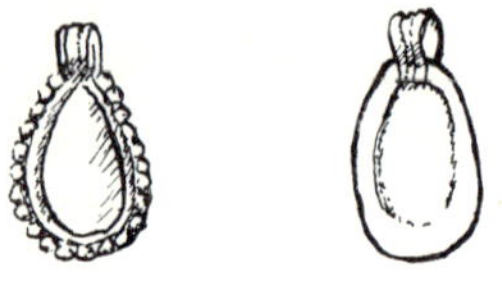

102

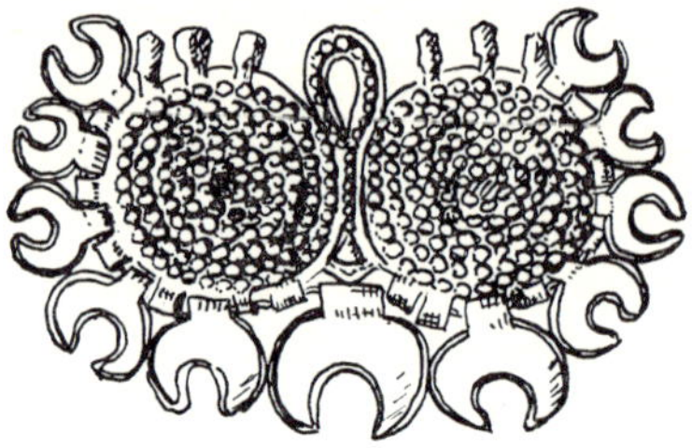

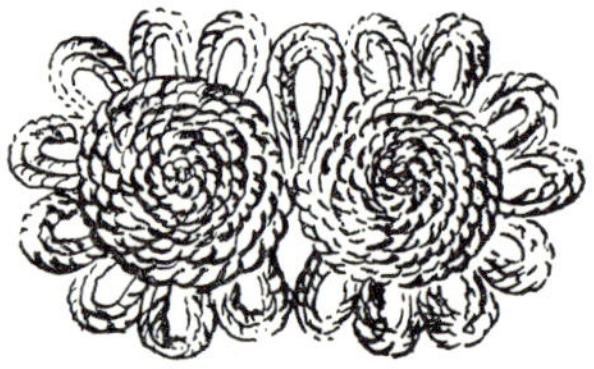

104

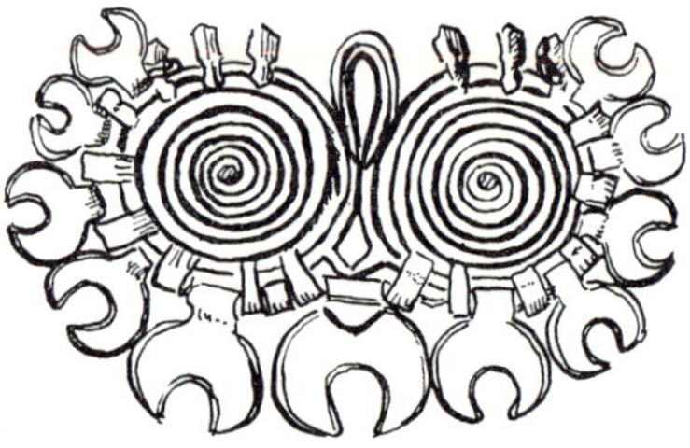

103

Fig. 102. Gold and lapis lazuli pendant from Ashur.
Fig. 103. Gold double spiral forehead ornament with lapis lazuli pendants from Ashur.
Fig. 104. Gold twisted wire double spiral pendant from Ashur.

Forehead ornament

In addition to the diadem of gold pendants listed above, a remarkable forehead ornament (fig. 103) was found *in situ* on the forehead which, as Andrae suggests, must have either been separately fastened to the hair, or been connected to the diadem of pendants discussed above. It is formed of plain gold wire, about 0·1 cm thick, tapered at both ends. From these ends, it is wound up in two flat spirals of eight coils, while the remaining central length of wire is drawn upwards in a slightly projecting loop and strengthened on the inner side by wire backing. The coils and the loop are decorated by granules placed on the grooves between the coils with great exactitude. Nine loops were soldered, pincer fashion, on to the periphery of each spiral or threaded on the wire and soldered to the back plate. The two uppermost remained free to serve for suspension (the central loop of wire was presumably not intended for this purpose). Eleven lapis lazuli crescents in gold settings were flexibly attached by means of finely drawn gold wire to the outside of each of the spirals. These crescents, which have suspension eyelets, are graded in size decreasing from the bottom centre upwards. The largest measure 1·2 × 1·3 cm high, the smallest 0·7 × 0·7 cm. The overall measurement is 4 × 2 cm.

Breast ornament

Two double spirals (fig. 104) were found on the left breast of the woman and are much lighter and simpler than the forehead ornament. They consist of very thin gold wire coiled in eight spirals, beginning from the end, with a central loop projecting upwards, stiffened by a small wire noose, as in the forehead ornament. The spirals are fastened together by two small bands joined on to their backs. Andrae suggests that, although it is scarcely perceptible, the coils of the spirals must be soldered together. None of the seventeen loops bordering the spirals is distinguished in any way for use as suspension and one can infer that the ornaments were intended to be sewn on to the dress, with the thread passing through sixteen peripheral eyes; if it was worn as a clasp, the central loops would have been tied together by a cord, to close the two edges of a garment.

Throat ornament (fig. 105)

Veined stone disc in a gold setting. Lentoid in form, with suspension eyelets, cut into the stone. The gold setting is denticulated, on both obverse and reverse, and hammered over the sharp rim of the lentoid. Three rows of granulation are carefully joined to the outer border. This exceptionally fine piece hung from the necklace over the throat not far above the pectoral (see below).

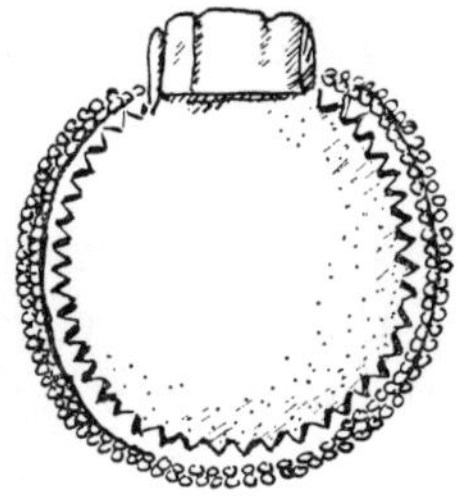

105

Fig. 105. Throat ornament, veined stone in gold setting, from Ashur.

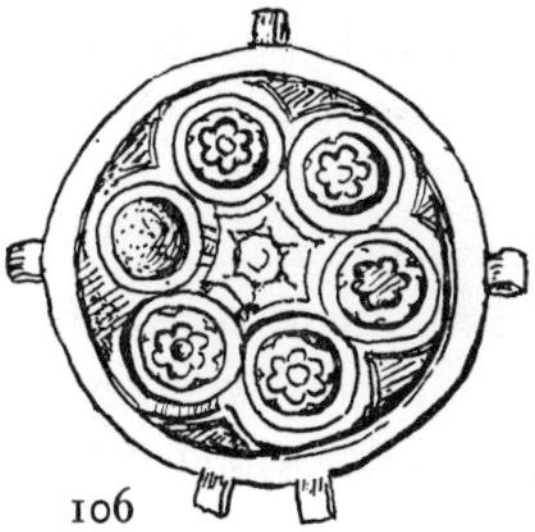

106

Fig. 106. Cloisonné pectoral from Ashur.

The cloisonné pectoral (fig. 106)

This magnificent piece was inlaid on both sides with stone and other materials and only partly preserved. It was found *in situ* on the middle of the chest. It must have been intended to form the climax of the elaborate system of necklaces. Three strings of beads could be attached to the three single eyelets on the rim, fixing the pectoral in position; many of the loose beads recovered from the tomb must have formed several strings of necklaces which may have been attached to this pectoral. When intact the necklaces and pectoral may have been the ornament denoted by the term *tudittu* (see p. 154).[1] Over 1,100 beads were found, the material being mainly semi-precious stones: carnelian, onyx, rock crystal, jasper, lapis lazuli, shell, serpentine, frit, glass paste, limestone and marble, with gold used chiefly as a setting. Animal beads were common and an attractive white carnelian mouse has a gold head. A frog's head is made of hollow gold. The lower pair of eyelets served perhaps for the suspension of two tassel pendants.

The method of manufacture was as follows. Two round plates of identical size were placed together with the edges turned over, closed on the inner side by a gold band, creating a double hollow ring, quadrangular in section; to this the five suspension eyelets are attached. Then the double-sided gold circular plate was fitted with designs in fine strips of gold, laid out symmetrically as regards the eyelets. These strips stand vertically on the gold base to which they are welded, forming separate cloisons to hold the inlay. The design produced symmetrical sixfold patterns consisting first of six broad gold sheet rings, each enclosing a white six-petalled flower; the central space is filled by a printed star motif surrounded by strips of lapis lazuli. The inlaid flowers in the cloisons are worked in different colours by strips of lapis lazuli and the space outside the design was filled with a black substance (bitumen?) into which tiny fragments of glass and stones were impressed. Unfortunately, many of these have worked loose and disappeared. The material employed included gold, lapis lazuli and white shell.

Earrings

Three main types of earring occur in Tomb 45, of which the largest example of Type 1 was found on the skeleton of the man, while the other examples belonged to the female skeleton (four pairs of single and one pair of triple variety).

Type 1 Large gold earrings, with single or triple hoops and single or triple tassel pendants of precious stones; the loops decorated with circular setting for a stone inlay. On the triple pair worn by the female the rosette is shallow and saucer-shaped, decorated with petals edged with twisted gold wire (fig. 107a and b).

Type 2 Lunate-shaped with body fluted (fig. 108).

[1] A comparable pectoral with attached strings of beads is shown on a figurine of a goddess in the Louvre. *Encyclopédie Photographique de l'Art*, I, p. 263B.

Type 3 Lunate, plain, with moulding round base opposite end of pin (fig. 109).

The method of manufacture for both the single and triple varieties of Type 1 was as follows. The basis of the earring is a penannular hollow ring, tapering from the centre upwards to the open ends which are reverted and bound by a gold band. On the single earrings, one end is rolled together,

107

108

109

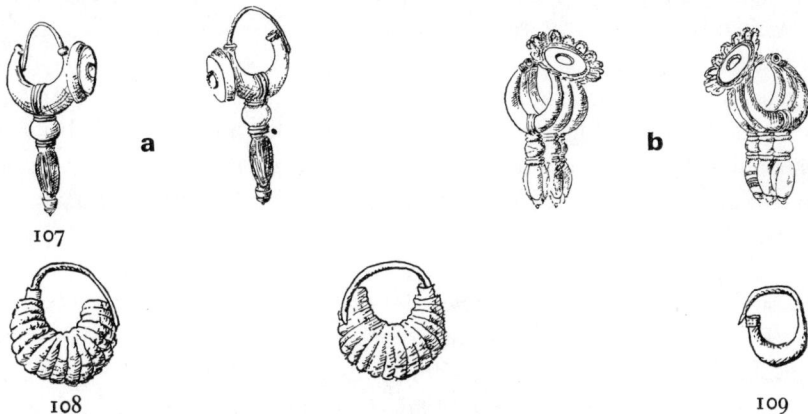

Fig. 107. Gold earrings from Ashur.
Fig. 108. Gold ribbed earrings from Ashur.
Fig. 109. Gold lunate earring from Ashur.

hammered into wire and sharpened to form the crooked pin. This, after passing through the ear, could be inserted into the socket formed by the other end. On the triple earrings no pin was present. The three penannular rings were joined together at the top. Tripartite loops united together to form a little tube were connected by three little ribbed rings welded to the free ends of the penannular rings. The penannular rings are made of fine gold sheet with an internal seam and hang free except at the top where they are joined together. Each is clasped by a tripartite suspension ring passing round the bottom centre, to which is joined a fine hollow gold tube. On this is threaded (from top to bottom):

(1) A double ribbed gold ring.

(2) A round bead of onyx, jasper or carnelian. Each single earring had a different stone and on the triple variety all three kinds of stone were used.

(3) A gold ring like (1).

(4) A pendant lotus bud, half-open, of variegated lapis lazuli, jasper or carnelian.

(5) A plain gold ring with a lapis lazuli bead.

(6) On the man's earring, a disc or plaque. On all other examples a gold cap perforated at the base and held in place by the out-turned lower rim of the tube.

The ornament is completed by a cockade-like setting for a stone inlay, usually two-coloured and resembling an eye, welded on to the narrow side of the pair of tubular rings. In the case of the woman's large pair of earrings of this type (fig. 107b), this is enlarged to form a rosette. The rosette is attached by claws to the central arc of the three hollow rings. It is tilted obliquely upwards, as if opening to the sun. The small gold petalled saucer bears a lapis lazuli ring as corolla, the underside flat, the upper domed. In the middle a small circular recess, set apart by a gold fillet, surrounded a gem, now missing. The fifteen petals are edged with twisted quadrangular gold wire. Pierced ears were not essential for the wearing of these earrings. If the lobe was pushed between the tubes at the upper end of the hollow rings, the ornament was firmly attached, although likely to become uncomfortable in time.

The ear ornaments of the woman were completed by four pairs of small tubular crescent-shaped earrings, finely ribbed with thin wire crooks. This is a developed form and related to Babylonian earrings of the Larsa period.

Jewellery found on the male skeleton

Necklace found near the cervical vertebrae (fig. 110). This consisted of five gold and six lapis lazuli plaques, probably strung alternately. Both have double borings, so they were presumably threaded on two strings. The plaques were made of sheet gold squares with edges hammered over at right angles on all four sides. The edges in contact with the preceding and following links were stiffened by three transverse struts of plain gold wire. Four half-cylinders of open-work gold sheet were then joined on to the bottom plate and the edges, parallel to the struts (which remain visible). The half-cylinders each bear three rows of perforations, a central row on top of five circular holes; two on either side of six oval holes. The small round holes have plain edges, those of the oval holes are reverted and outlined by granulated borders. The lapis lazuli links are also almost square, with flat under surfaces, the upper sides being longitudinally segmented in four half-cylinders, as if four strings of long tubular beads surrounded the neck.

A single hemispherical stone bead, capped with gold at either end, was recorded as belonging to the male skeleton (Haller, *Ashur*, Taf. 33g).

The earrings which were assigned by the excavators to the male skeleton were two large pendant earrings (cf. fig. 107a) but larger and heavier than those found on the female skeleton.

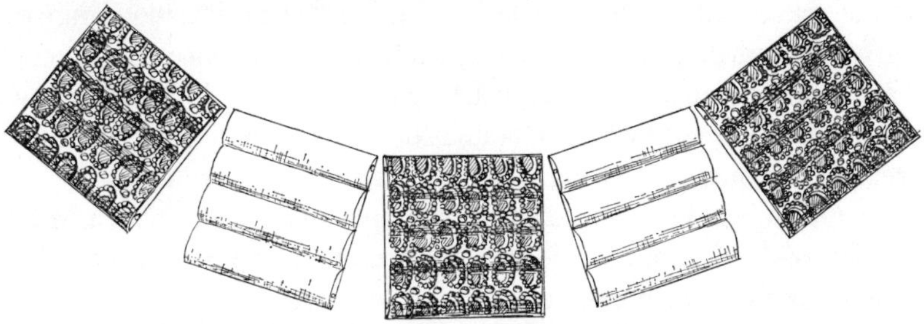

Fig. 110. Gold and lapis lazuli plaques on necklace from Ashur.

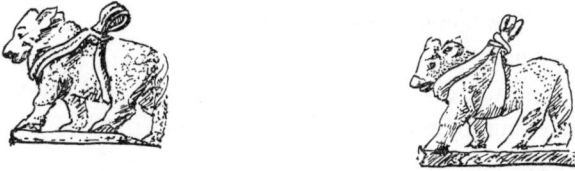

Fig. 111. Bull-calf pendants from Ashur.

Two pendants (fig. 111) in the form of bull-calves of mottled red-brown stone, with gold loops round the body, probably belonged to the necklace of gold and lapis lazuli plaques described above (fig. 110).

Jewellery from Tell al-Rimah and Mari (Mid-Assyrian graves)

Excavations at Tell al-Rimah, situated in northern Iraq about seventy-five kilometres west of Mosul in the Sinjar plain, were started by the British School of Archaeology in Iraq and are still in progress (1968). This important site has yielded valuable evidence for the accurate dating of some important pieces of jewellery and other objects of frit and glass. The fortified mound of Tell al-Rimah was situated on the trade route from Ashur to the important centres of north Syria and central and eastern Anatolia. The stratification at this site, when considered alongside that of Tell Brak, Chagar Bazar in the Ḫabur valley to the north-west and Mari on the Euphrates, provides a firm basis for any attempt to date gold and silver jewellery of the mid-second millennium B.C., both in Syria and Iran.

A remarkable series of female masks made of frit have their ears pierced with three or four holes for the insertion of earrings; a magnificent example found in 1965 had the eyes and eyeballs of glazed frit set in bitumen (pl. 129). 'Tresses of hair ending in ringlets are represented by spiral rods of frit inlaid in pairs on either side of the neck and terminating in groups of small glass discs. Black, white and yellow discs are also used to indicate a jewelled necklace, collar and diadem . . .'[1] This mask was associated with a gold disc perforated for suspension and decorated with a repoussé pattern of an eight-pointed star with linear rays (pl. 130). These pieces belong to Phase I of the temple which represents a Middle Assyrian re-occupation, considered by Oates to have begun some time in the fourteenth century B.C. and certainly to have come to an end in the second half of the thirteenth century B.C. A tablet of Shalmaneser I (1274–1245 B.C.) belongs to Phase I.

Mid-Assyrian graves at Mari[2] also produced comparable frit masks and Tomb 236 also contained earrings and necklaces. Of the six earrings in this tomb, five have 'mulberry' pendants composed of a pyramid of gold balls attached to the circular gold ring; this type could be embellished also with three minute granules attached to each ball. Five plain rings are shown linked together above the 'mulberry' earring (Tomb 149k pl. 131). Tomb 236 also contained a necklace of carnelian beads made in the shape of stylized pomegranates.

Tomb 125 is especially important, as it produced a fine necklace of gold quadruple spiral beads (fig. 113) alternating with flat winged disc beads of lapis lazuli, carnelian and blue paste. The quadruple spirals on this necklace have been discussed above (p. 34) and it was noted by Mallowan in the Brak report that the Mari series, unlike the Brak and Anatolian examples, show that the 'four coils or spirals, instead of being drawn out of the central tube, appear to be twisted or bound around the ends of it'.[3] This is the same technique used for the quadruple spiral beads from Marlik, Hasanlu and many unstratified specimens allegedly from 'Amlash' (see p. 158 and pls. 145 and 136). A fourteenth to thirteenth century B.C. date, even if the Mari examples are to be dated around 1300 B.C., can be given to the use of this particular type of quadruple spiral bead and it is probable that their period of use continued well into the early first millennium B.C. One example from Mari[4] (pl. 34, see Chapter 3), however, is made in

[1] D. Oates, 'The excavations at Tell al-Rimah 1965', *Iraq*, XXVIII, 2, 1966, pls. XXXIV XXXV, p. 125.

[2] A. Parrot, 'Les fouilles de Mari 1935–36', *Syria*, XVIII, 1937, pl. XV.

[3] *Iraq*, IX, 2, 1947, p. 174. [4] *Syria*, XVIII, 1937, pl. XV, 2.

the same technique as the Brak, Troy and Alaca type, where two strips of gold are twisted round each other (with the join down the centre still visible) forming a single tube with the ends pulled out into wire to form four spirals. This single early example at Mari may have been the model for the later series.

The associated objects in Tomb 125 – frit masks, faience vases, etc. – cannot only be paralleled at Tell al-Rimah, but also, as Mallowan has pointed out, at Ashur and at Ur at the time of the Kassite king Kurigalzu II (c. 1330 B.C.). A boat-shaped earring made of gold leaf over a core of bitumen belongs to Tomb 125 and is now in the Louvre with two smaller examples from the same tomb.

The lapis lazuli beads supply certain evidence for trade between Iran and Assyria at this time; and it may well be that the transport of lapis lazuli from Badakshan in Afghanistan across Iran facilitated contacts between craftsmen in north-west Iran and Assyria working in many different materials. The remarkable glass mosaic vessel found at Rimah is closely comparable with an example from Marlik; this remarkable mosaic beaker[1] cannot be far removed in date from the Rimah pieces dating from the second half of the thirteenth century B.C. (Level Ib) or, as Mr Oates suggests, possibly earlier.

Tomb 135 at Mari was noteworthy for a remarkable series of twelve gold discs with central repoussé boss surrounded by two circles of smaller bosses and an eleven-petalled rosette with the petals outlined by twisted gold wire. These discs are not pierced and probably formed part of a headdress, as there is a loop on the back through which a cord could pass.

[1] *Marlik*, pl. XVII. *Iraq*, XXVIII, 1966, pl. XXXVc.

CHAPTER 11

Assyria and Iran: Twelfth to Seventh Centuries B.C.

INTRODUCTION

Among the list of booty and tribute obtained by the Assyrians in their campaigns in the mountains north, east and south-east of Assyria, gold is often mentioned, but unfortunately the texts do not usually give specific details of gold objects. Tiglath-Pileser I (1115–1077 B.C.) records that he carried off 'one hundred and eighty vessels of bronze, five bowls of copper, together with their gods, gold and silver, the choicest of their possessions', in addition to the wives and sons of Kili-Teshub, king of the Papkhi, who had come to help the people of Kummukh, west of the upper Tigris. After marching further to the east to the fortress of another local king, Shadi-Teshub of Urraṭinash, he was offered 'sixty vessels of bronze, bowls of copper, great cauldrons of copper', as well as slaves and animals, but there is no mention of gold.[1] The jewellery would certainly have been included in the tribute when deities were mentioned, as the statues would carry the best products of the local metalsmiths and would have been placed in the temple at Ashur, alongside the vessels of bronze and the copper cauldrons which the scribe tells us were offered by Tiglath-Pileser to the gods Ashur and Adad.

The identification of the geographical areas and the people mentioned in the Assyrian records as inhabiting the different kingdoms situated in the difficult mountainous country east of Assyria has recently attracted the attention of many scholars[2] and certain points relevant to the study of gold jewellery may be briefly noted. It must be remembered, however, that the rulers of small territories on the eastern borders of Assyria were constantly expanding or contracting the areas over which they exercised control and, until the Assyrians managed to introduce a small measure of stability into the region by organizing these essentially tribal areas into

[1] See *A.R.I.*, pp. 75, 76.
[2] Wiseman, *C.A.H.*, No. 41, pp. 17 ff. Kinnier Wilson in *Iraq*, XXIV, 2, 1962, pp. 90–115.

acknowledging the Assyrian overlordship, revolt and internecine warfare was the usual order. But even when an area had been invaded and conquered and tribute was secured, countries beyond the borders of those already conquered had to be visited and some recognition of suzerainty obtained. The preliminary organization of these eastern areas before they were finally absorbed into the empire necessitated constant invasion and the collection of tribute and this was regarded as the best means of securing the more turbulent areas within Assyria from plunder and raids from the mountains.

It is not surprising that the scribes and compilers of the historical texts should give accounts which show considerable variation at different periods concerning the geographical location of neighbouring tribes or areas. The areas covered by certain kingdoms changed or were split up and tribes could migrate from one region to another; but it is possible to deduce that certain regions seem to have been a rich source of metal goods in the tribute lists, while others were recorded as contributing sheep, horses or other animals. In this connection it is interesting to note that the Papkhi, mentioned above in the reign of Tiglath-Pileser I, seem to have had some kind of association with the land of Ḫabḫi (previously read Kirḫi), a land which is constantly occurring in the records as a source of metal goods of all kinds. If Kirruri is correctly located east of Arbela and south-east of Raniyah, then it is conceivable that the pass of the land of Kirruri could be across the mountain range along the Iraqi-Persian frontier and the land of Ḫabḫi could be located in the Saqqiz area. The three mountains, Usu, Amra and Arardi of Ashurnaṣirpal II's records, could then be peaks in the Kandil Dağ range. A location for Ḫabḫi west or south-west of Lake Van is arguable, however, if earlier Assyrian references are considered; in Ashurnaṣirpal II's reign Ḫabḫi may simply mean the land where the Ḫabḫi people dwelt and imply a settlement of Ḫabḫi from their original homeland.[1] Mirjo Salvini[2] identifies Ḫabḫi as a kingdom in the upper reaches of the Great Zab river which, by the time of Ashurnaṣirpal II, had expanded as far as the Euphrates in the west.

Gilzanu, which may be located in Persian Kurdistan, perhaps between the Upper Zab valley and the river Zarineh, also sent silver, gold, lead and copper vessels to Shalmaneser III (858–824 B.C.) and its king, Sua, is shown on Shalmaneser's black obelisk now in the British Museum.

[1] See W. Lambert, *A.S.*, XI, 1961, pl. XIX, p. 156. Burney, *A.S.*, XVI, 1966, pp. 58 ff. For routes see also C. J. Edmonds, 'Some ancient monuments on the Iraqi-Persian boundary', *Iraq*, XXVIII, 2, 1966, Map pl. XLVIII.

[2] *Nairi e Ur(u)aṭri*, pp. 92 ff., (Rome, 1967).

Shalmaneser III's campaign in the sixteenth year of his reign is worth noting, as, after campaigning in Zamua (the hill country to the east and north of Sulimaniya), he records that he sacked the city of Ianzi in Allabria and carried away the 'beautiful gold door-leaves of his palace, (the treasures) of his palace in large number.'[1] Allabria probably lies in the region between the Upper Zab and the modern town of Saqqiz which is an area today renowned for its metal working.

Further to the east or south-east lies Gizilbunda and from the city of Urash, Shamshi-Adad V (823–811 B.C.) carried away 'Pirishati, their king, together with 1,200 of his fighters . . . flocks . . . horses, vessels of silver, splendid gold, and copper in countless numbers'. A possible clue to the location of Gizilbunda is the fact that, on his march from the Nairi regions where he had received the tribute of Dadi of Hubushkia and of the lands of Manai and Parsua, he crossed the ŠIM.BI.ZI.DA (Musi) stone mountain. Kinnier Wilson has suggested that Hubushkia should be sought to the south or south-west of Lake Rizayeh (Urmia); Hulin places it in the upper reaches of the Little Zab[2] and it is generally accepted that Manai is located to the south or south-east of the lake. Parsua has been identified by Minorski with the mound of Paswē which lies on a small tributary of the Gadir river and, whether or not this proves to be correct (as only excavation can show), we can assume that the starting place of Shamshi-Adad's march across the ŠIM.BI.ZI.DA stone mountain lay somewhere south of Lake Urmia. If ŠIM.BI.ZI.DA denotes arsenic, it is probable that the mountain could be Takht-i-Sulaiman mountain beyond the Zarineh river.[3] Today arsenic is mined at Zara Shuran near Sain Qaleh in Azerbaijan. This pure arsenic ore, orpiment, was a sulphur compound of a bright yellow colour and in classical times was used as a pigment; its poisonous property was also known.

The campaign undertaken by Tiglath-Pileser III in 734 B.C. contains some interesting references to gold. We are told how Merodach-baladan came before Tiglath-Pileser in the city of Sapia, in the marsh country on the lower Euphrates and presented 'gold, the dust of his mountains, in great quantity, articles of gold, golden necklaces (?), precious stones' among a mass of other gifts including wood, plants and woven garments.[4] The tablet on which this account is inscribed is in the British Museum (Nimrud K. 3751) and continues with a long list of the countries brought

[1] *A.R.*, I, p. 235.
[2] Kinnier Wilson, *Iraq*, XXIV, 2, 1962, pp. 90–115. P. Hulin, *Iraq*, XXV, 1963, 1, p. 59.
[3] See R. Campbell Thompson, *A Dictionary of Assyrian Chemistry and Geology*, pp. 50 f.
[4] *A.R.*, I, pp. 285 f.

under Assyrian rule, including a reference to 'the land of Rū(a), as far as the alkali desert, the lands of Ushkakkāna, Shikraki, (the land) of gold, provinces of the mighty Medes'. But it is interesting to note that, in all the references to the tribute presented by the Medes to the Assyrian emperors, there is no other reference to gold. In every case, horses, mules, cattle and other animals are the accepted tribute. Sargon II (721–705 B.C.) records that he imposed a yearly tribute of horses.

The text which affords more information than anything considered here so far is the celebrated letter to the god Ashur sent by Sargon II, in which he described the events in the Urartian campaign of 714 B.C. against Urzana of Urartu, which led up to the sack of the city-state of Musasir, an important religious centre with its great temple of the god Haldi.[1] The sack of this temple, which is represented on a relief found at Khorsabad,[2] produced an astonishing amount of treasure of all kinds. We are given a mass of detailed descriptions of different objects, some of which cannot as yet be translated but which give a vivid picture of the extraordinary skill of the goldsmiths, silversmiths, jewellery and bronze workers in this remote kingdom. The booty from the palace treasure house, 'overflowing, the heaped up stores', is listed and the scribe records that it contained large stores of raw minerals, thirty-four talents, eighteen minas of gold, 167 talents, two and a half minas of silver, white bronze, lead, carnelian, lapis lazuli, banded agate, *aban* UD.AŠ., *aban sāmti*, a red stone often mentioned alongside *uknu* (lapis lazuli). The pommels of staves of ivory, maple and boxwood were inlaid with gold and silver, vases were decorated with gold and silver inlay, while the hilts were also encrusted with gold. Fifty-four cups are listed as being covered with silver and rings (*šemirē*) were also made of silver – these were probably not finger rings but intended for use in the cult ceremonies of the god Haldi.

In the list of the treasure pillaged from the temple of the god are many entries which merit consideration here. After detailed description of the votive shields, spears and other weapons of silver and gold, again inlaid with gold, special mention is made of 393 cups of silver, the work of the countries of Ashur, Urartu and Ḫabḫi, and of the seal which was used for confirming the oracular instructions of the goddess. This was completely covered with precious stones. An interesting entry (Line 386) mentioned

[1] F. Thureau-Dangin, *Une Relation de la Huitième Campagne de Sargon* (Paris, 1912), lines 350–409.
[2] Unfortunately lost in the Tigris river but recorded by a drawing in Botta, pl. 141.

nine garments of the goddess, whose borders were presumably decorated with rosettes (*ajaru*) and discs (*nipḫu*) of gold. The list of the divine furniture from the shrine included mention of the *šukani* or jewels of the goddess and also those of her husband Haldi, which is followed by a long list of bronze statues including a bull and a cow, together with its calf, cast in the temple foundry. This would imply that Musasir was an important centre, where craftsmen skilled in working metals of all kinds were producing vast quantities of objects for the embellishment of the temple. It is also especially stated (Lines 406–7) that the lists of this enormous treasure did not include the objects of gold, silver, lead, copper, iron and different kinds of wood which the Urartians had pillaged from towns, palaces and temples dedicated to Ashur and Marduk and had brought back to add to the palace and temple treasuries. Sargon states that his soldiers were ordered to take this enormous booty back to Ashur and that men of the Urartian province of Musasir were forced to accompany them. Without doubt, a large number of goldsmiths, silversmiths and jewellers were taken back to Assyria and the text is a good illustration of the difficulty which confronts us when attempting to distinguish the origin of gold objects and jewellery when found in Assyria itself. A brooch or necklace may have been made by an Assyrian craftsman, been the result of an Assyrian campaign where booty was taken or been made by a foreign smith captive in Assyria who might be making types similar to those of the country he has left or copying Assyrian types using the same techniques which he had been using in his homeland.

Sargon's historical records also afford interesting sidelights on the use of jewellery in the Assyrian task of subjugating the rulers of the mountainous country which was eventually incorporated into the eastern provinces. In Prism B, now in the British Museum, we read how the king of Izirtu, described as the 'Royal City of Mannaeans', 'rushed forth in great haste and in the land of Laruete of the land of Allabria he came before me and his heavy tribute – horses, cattle and sheep I received, and he kissed my feet. (With) a girdle dagger and brightly coloured (woollen) and linen garments I clothed him. With inlaid rings, —— I bound (his fingers?) with a joyful countenance he returned to his land.'[1]

The sixth campaign of Sennacherib (704–681 B.C.) against the king of Elam who had come to help the Babylonians in their revolt against Assyria also contains some interesting reference to goldwork. We read how the men of Parsuash, Anzan, Pashiru and Ellipi were among the

[1] *A.R.*, II, pp. 108 f.

forces of the king of Babylon and, after their defeat in the plain of Halule (which can be located on the left bank of the Diyala river), their leaders were described as standing on 'silver chariots . . . bedecked with golden daggers, their fingers covered with golden rings'.[1] In a later campaign the Babylonians had apparently attempted to bribe the Elamites to come again to their aid by opening the treasury of Esagila in Babylon and 'gold, silver and precious stones to the king of Elam they sent'.[2] Later, many objects in the Susa treasury must have been taken off to Assyria, as the sack of Susa by Ashurbanipal (668–626 B.C.) was conducted with characteristic Assyrian efficiency.

IRAN AT THE END OF THE SECOND MILLENNIUM c. 1350–1000 B.C.

The stratified material for this period comes mainly from Susa, Sialk (Cemetery A) and sites in the north-west of Iran, of which the site of Hasanlu provides the clearest stratigraphical sequence. The archaeological background of the period can best be studied by relating, as far as possible, the material from Sialk, Giyan, Marlik and Khurvin, as well as part of the mass of unstratified finds, to the Hasanlu sequence.

Two important factors must be stressed before any assessment of the evidence provided by the jewellery can be made. First, the meagre amount of jewellery which has survived in stratified contexts must bear no relation to the amount of gold work actually used by the inhabitants of Persia at this period. This supposition is based on the enormous amount, which increases year by year, of gold jewellery which has appeared in the hands of dealers with no known provenance, or sometimes with the name of a region such as Amlash or Daylaman attached to it. Some of this material has found its way to museums where it can be studied and every effort made to ascertain all available details as to its original provenance. Often it has proved impossible to obtain even generalized information, especially when objects have passed through several hands, with no record made of any associated objects which might have afforded some clue as to date and/or origin. It is understandable, in view of the intrinsic value of gold jewellery, that illicit excavators should ignore pottery or metal objects if they are found in a bad state of preservation, but which could have provided valuable evidence for dating the jewellery.

[1] Ibid, p. 156. [2] Ibid, p. 157.

The second factor which must be borne in mind is the danger of attributing dates to jewellery of unknown provenance which are based on stylistic considerations when our knowledge of the stratified jewellery of the pre-Achaemenian periods in Persia is so limited. The origin of Achaemenian jewellery work must be sought in the early centuries of the last millennium not only in Persia itself, but also in eastern Anatolia and Transcaucasia; it may well be that many pieces of jewellery at present confidently labelled Achaemenian in museums and private collections should in fact be attributed to the eighth century B.C. or even earlier. All that can be done at the present state of our knowledge is to consider the unstratified material in certain defined groups, note any parallels with stratified finds and, at the same time, remember that any suggestions put forward from this study may have to be drastically altered when more excavation has taken place.

Susa: The In-Shushinak deposits

An important collection of gold jewellery was found in deposits near the great temple of In-Shushinak on the Acropolis of Susa, which may have been funerary offerings or intended as foundation deposits. The objects belong to the period when Elam, under its ruler Shilhak-in-Shushinak (c. 1130 B.C.) attained a position at the centre of a considerable empire whose power was reflected in the magnificent buildings and the material output of many different kinds of craftsmen. The conquests of Shilhak-in-Shushinak (the son of Shutruk-Nahhunte who had captured Babylon in 1160 B.C. and brought a large booty back to Susa) and his brother Kutir-Nahhunte, who had made Babylonia the vassal of Elam, extended into the Zagros mountains beyond Anzan and Susiana and to the eastern shores of the Persian Gulf. It is possible that the remarkable jewellery in the In-Shushinak deposits may have been made in Babylonia or have been the work of Babylonian goldsmiths who were probably among the large numbers of Babylonians deported to Susa after the last Kassite ruler Enlil-nadin-aḫḫe was captured and exiled to Elam by Kutir-Nahhunte; but more evidence is needed before this theory can be advanced with any certainty. The fine granulation and the obvious technical skill of the jewellers invite comparison with Kassite jewellery working from Aqar Qūf, yet the long tradition of craftsmanship in Elam and the known skill of the bronze smiths at this period make it perhaps more likely that this jewellery should be regarded as native Elamite work.

Three gold rings (pl. 132) were decorated with fine granulation and one shows a combination of filigree and granular work. The technical skill of the work contrasts with the cruder granular decoration noted above (p. 159) from Gök tepe and is of the same standard as that shown on the gold lion-headed whetstone from Susa (see p. 165 and pl. 128) and some of the gold capped Elamite and Kassite cylinder seals. On pl. 132d the twisted filigree pattern is embellished with a single granule in the centre of each twist and invites comparison with the same patterns which can be found on painted pottery of the so-called Nuzi or Hurrian type belonging to a slightly earlier period (fig. 93 – see Chapter 7).

Two circular pendants of the 'Ishtar' variety (see p. 141) belonged to another deposit (Amiet, *Elam*, 314A, B). Both are decorated in repoussé and show an eight-pointed star with repoussé circles and dots between the points of the star. They can be compared with examples from Ugarit (Ras Shamra) and many other examples from Syria, Palestine and Iran (see pls. 108, 109).

Sialk Cemetery A (pl. 133)

The jewellery from Cemetery A at Sialk includes a long tubular gold bead and a pair of plain lunate-shaped earrings decorated in rough granular triangles (pl. 133b). A similar pair allegedly from 'Amlash' was recently on exhibition in Holland[1] (fig. 112). Compared with the jewellery from

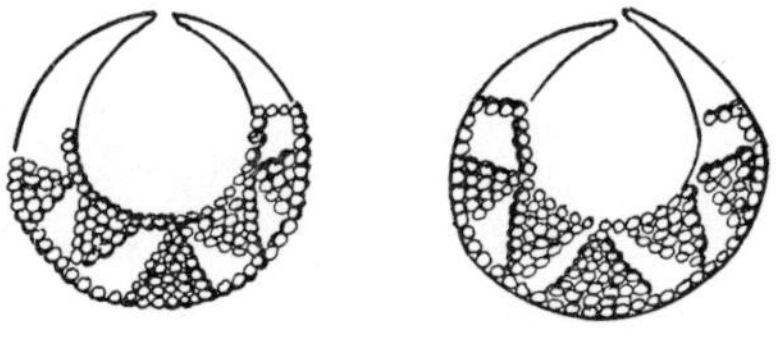

Fig. 112. Gold earrings, Sialk B type.

the In-Shushinak deposits at Susa, the crudeness of the technique is remarkable, and the rough circular gold piece from Cemetery A (pl. 133c) is either unfinished or represents the attempt of a smith who was unfamiliar in working in gold or who was beginning to learn his job (pl. 133b). The decoration is found on each side of the flat crescent and a plain example of this can be found *in situ* on one of the terracotta bulls from Marlik (see p. 193).

[1] *Vroeg aadewerk brons en sieraden uit Noord-Iran* (Amsterdam, 1966–7).

Giyan tombs of Period I

Two tombs belonging to Period I at Giyan produced jewellery. Tomb 38, dated to Giyan I, Phase 4, by T. Cuyler Young,[1] contained a silver earring of the same type as the gold Sialk Cemetery A example mentioned above and a silver 'Ishtar' pendant with six points. A bronze toggle pin with ring and plain button base was also found. Pottery fixes this tomb in the Sialk A – Hasanlu V period starting around 1350 B.C.

Tomb 53 can also be dated to this period. This contained two gold boat-shaped earrings with large balls below the pin (cf. pl. 134 from Marlik) and a silver crescent-shaped pendant and a bronze bracelet. A bracelet with sliding twisted ends also comes from Giyan[2] and can be compared with a similar example from Susa now in the Louvre (Louvre No. 9137).

Khurvin

The cemetery of Khurvin[3] has produced a mass of unstratified gold jewellery and a distinctive type of boat-shaped earring closely related to the earring from Marlik (pl. 134), where the surface of the earring is decorated with round repoussé blobs surrounded with a circle of granules. Two large knobs are fixed at the base of the pin. This feature can be found on the fine Middle Assyrian examples from Ashur (fig. 107, Chapter 10) and may represent Assyrian influence on the products of Gilan and north-west Persia.

Hasanlu

The stratigraphical system established by the excavations of the University Museum of Pennsylvania University, directed by R. H. Dyson, forms an indispensable framework for Azerbaijan material and can afford considerable assistance in any attempt to relate the jewellery of the periods c. 1200–800 B.C. to the historical background. It is also important for north-west Persian sites such as Marlik (see p. 189). The radio-carbon dates for Periods V and IV of c. 1200–1000 B.C. and c. 1000–800 B.C. correspond reasonably well with the archaeological evidence.[4] Some fine

[1] *Iran*, III, 1965, p. 66. [2] Herzfeld, *I.A.E.*, fig. 264, p. 148.
[3] L. Vanden Berghe, *La Necropole de Khurvin*, pl. L (Istanbul, 1964).
[4] The published date of c. 1200 should probably now be revised to c. 1350 B.C. (information from Dr Dyson, 1969).

pieces of gold jewellery from Hasanlu (now in the Teheran Museum), found before the American excavations began, probably belong to the end of Period V or the beginning of Period IV and are particularly important for their relationship with Marlik.

(1) A plain solid gold bracelet.

(2) A pair of large gold earring pendants made of large and smaller gold balls (sheet gold over a core) soldered together in triangular shape, attached to a gold ring through which the hoop of the earring must have passed (pl. 135). These earrings are known from Assyrian reliefs (see Chapter 15).

(3) A pair of earrings, similar in type to (2) above, but the balls are smaller.

(4) Necklaces (pl. 136). One with quadruple spiral beads with the wire wound round the top and bottom of a central tube. In this type two pieces of wire are used in the same way as the quadruple spiral beads found at Mari (fig. 113) and they can be contrasted with the earlier type of quadruple spiral bead discussed above from Ur, Brak or Troy (p. 34). A small double circular pendant belonged to this necklace and is decorated in fine granular decoration. It is comparable with the earlier Sumerian example (pl. 22b).

Fig. 113. Gold quadruple spiral bead from Mari.

The second necklace included rectangular gold beads, soldered together in three or more rows, combined with carnelian and paste beads.

(5) A small gold mouthpiece, or central part of a diadem, with repoussé and punched decoration, completes this group.

Marlik (First Period)

The site of Marlik is situated in the valley of the Gohar Rūd, a tributary of the Sefid Rud, and lies on the southern slopes of the Elburz mountains, 500 metres above sea level. The results of the excavations directed by Professor E. O. Negahban are renowned for the extraordinary richness of the material from the tombs and have been published in a preliminary report in 1964. Two magnificent exhibitions in Teheran have shown scholars these remarkable finds, of which only the jewellery can be discussed here. But the associated objects are especially relevant for any attempt to date the gold jewellery with any hope of precision; the different classes of jewellery will be as far as possible related to the other datable objects in the tomb and to jewellery from other sites.

Dr Negahban concludes that the tombs at Marlik must have covered a period of two to three centuries and he places this period at the end of the second and the beginning of the first millennium B.C. This would allow for Middle Assyrian connections discernible for certain of the gold vessels, the cylinder seal with a broken Assyrian inscription and also various distinctive features among the bronze work which suggests contact with Sialk Cemetery B. Here, we will divide the jewellery into two groups – an earlier group which, until more work is done on this material, might be dated c. 1350–1150 B.C., and a later period from the eleventh to the end of the tenth century B.C., and possibly a little later.

Tomb XVIIB included the splendid gold vase with two rampant winged bulls, the heads in high relief each side of a sacred tree. The style suggests comparisons with mid-Assyrian art of the thirteenth and twelfth centuries B.C. and the fine bronze sword (*Marlik*, fig. 51) with blunt end also points to a date in this period. This type of sword is uncommon at Marlik and its Transcaucasian connections also belong to this period.

The jewellery consisted of:

(1) Gold button with an intricate design of dots and circles executed in repoussé round a central cone (*Marlik*, fig. 83).

(2) Gold disc pendant decorated with granular triangles (*Marlik*, fig. 68).

(3) A fine gold cage pendant composed of a hollow gold ball soldered to a cone-shaped base, to which is attached a 'cage' formed of twisted gold wires and pendant granular triangles with granular circles for inlay on the base of the 'cage'. A filigree loop which passes through the top of the gold ball forms the holder for a large ring of solid gold (pl. 137).

These three pieces from Tomb XVIIB show that the development of the most intricate techniques of jewellery working can be found at Marlik: the rather crude repoussé technique executed by punches and shown on the gold button, the comparatively crude granular work on the disc pendant and the extremely fine work on the 'cage' pendant. The pieces may well have been executed in the same workshop and show either varying degrees of skill or the gradual development of techniques over a relatively short period. Another disc pendant, from Tomb XVD (*Marlik*, fig. 71), also shows the early stages of granular decoration, here combined with repoussé on a rather rough gold disc pendant with central boss and six-pointed star worked with a tracer.

Tomb XXIH–XXIIH is another rich tomb which included among the grave goods the remarkable mosaic vase (*Marlik*, pl. XVII) of blue and white stone (possibly glass) with small pedestal foot and comparable with the fine example recently found by David Oates at Tell al-Rimah in Assyria. The site of Rimah lies west of Mosul in northern Iraq (see p. 177) and this type of beaker with small foot is known from the painted Nuzi ware of Assyria and Syria and is datable to the fifteenth to fourteenth centuries B.C. The magnificent 'Unicorn' gold vase (*Marlik*, pl. XVI) from Tomb XXIH–XXIIH also suggests an early date for the tomb, whose richness is similar to Tomb XVIIB. The silver cup,[1] the unique bronze dagger with marble hilt and blade inlaid with lapis lazuli (*Marlik*, fig. 48) and a bronze mace head with attached human heads (*Marlik*, pl. XIIIA and fig. 57) were also found along with the largest gold button found at Marlik (*Marlik*, pl. VIA). This button (diameter 10·5 cm) had the usual central cone and the decoration is entirely carried out by means of punches, with dotted bosses and triangles arranged alternately round the edge, with an inner circle round the boss. There is no granular work and this button provides a prototype for the granular decoration on other pieces where the same patterns can be found, but worked in a far more difficult technique.

Tomb XXIK–L contained a silver teapot (*Marlik*, pl. II) with a gold design of animals, a human figure and a fantastic winged creature with two lion's heads holding a sphinx in each hand. Similar monsters can be found on mid-Assyrian seals and we would, therefore, tentatively ascribe this tomb to the thirteenth- to twelfth-century group. The jewellery consisted of the following:

(1) A gold toggle pin with mushroom-shaped head and incised design on the shank (pl. 138). A smaller, but similar pair of toggle pins (pl. 139) with slightly flatter top were sold at Sotheby's in 1965.[2] The decoration is the same 'bead and reel' incised patterns as seen on the Marlik example and many other dress pins allegedly from Amlash probably belong to this thirteenth- to twelfth-century B.C. period.

(2) A large gold leaf (weight 17 g) with a hooked stem for fastening (pl. 140). From the position in the tomb the excavator suggests that this and similar pieces were used for fastening a cloak or garment or possibly denoted a mark of rank.

[1] *I.L.N.*, 28 April 1962, p. 664, fig. 11; and *Iran*, II, 1964, p. 13, pl. IIIC.
[2] *Catalogue*, 28 June 1965, No. 76.

(3) A pair of serpentine rings (pl. 141) made of three narrow twisted gold wires and five plain wires soldered together side by side. Weight of the pair: 13·4 g.

Tomb XVIIIF is included in this group, as it contained a bronze dirk with flanged and ribbed hilt of early type and the cloisonné design on the pendants recall mid-Assyrian motifs. The jewellery consists of the following:

(1) A necklace of seven spherical hollow and eight barrel-shaped gold beads with a fine gold pendant, whose flat circular surface is decorated in sacred tree patterns in applied cloisons for an inlay of paste or precious stones which is now lost. The edge is bound with twisted gold wire (pl. 142). Weight 29·5 g, diameter of pendant 5·8 cm.

(2) Gold pendant practically identical to (1) above (*Marlik*, fig. 67).

(3) Gold bracelet made of one piece of twisted bar gold (pl. 143). Weight 9·8 g.

(4) Gold earring in the form of clustered pomegranates suspended from a circular loop of gold (pl. 144). The pomegranates are decorated with twisted gold wires (cf. Hasanlu, pl. 135, where the same ribbed loop occurs on the clusters of gold balls).

Tomb XVIIE contained a fine gold necklace with ten hollow, spherical gold beads, six quadruple spiral beads and six date-shaped beads, with a pomegranate pendant attached by a loop (pl. 145). The quadruple spiral beads are common among collections of jewellery from Iran with 'Amlash' given as the provenance and many have been exhibited in the exhibitions of Persian art in Iran, Europe and America. This is the first time that these beads have been recovered from a scientifically excavated site. Two of these beads were shown on a necklace from a private collection in Brussels in 1965.[1] A large quantity of similar quadruple spiral beads are in the collection of Mr A. Mazda in Teheran and are said to come from the Ardebil area.

A fine necklace of fourteen carnelian beads, long double conoids with gold caps, belongs to this tomb (*Marlik*, fig. 64). Three of these beads are considerably longer than the others and recall much earlier beads of this type from Ur (Grave 1422, pl. 48) though here without the gold caps. The smaller beads of this type on the Marlik necklace also recall Sumerian gold-capped beads of the Third Dynasty of Ur period (see pl. 49) and it is possible that the necklace may be considerably older than the other objects in the tomb.

[1] *Brussels Cat.*, No. 414.

A fine pair of decorative pins with gold lion's heads, bronze shanks covered with gold sheet, decorated with a granular pattern of outlined triangles, completes the inventory of the jewellery from Tomb XVIIE (pl. 146). In their original state these pins must have been extremely fine examples of the skill of the Marlik craftsmen. Between the head and the bronze and gold body of the pin the shank must have been covered with some kind of organic material, possibly ivory or lapis lazuli, now lost.

The six gold date-shaped beads on the necklace from Tomb XVIIE (pl. 145) recall Sumerian lapis lazuli beads of the Early Dynastic period (pl. 6b) which are also date-shaped and bound with gold wire; the circular incisions on the Marlik examples could well be imitating the gold wire binding on the Sumerian examples. It is possible that this necklace is considerably older than other objects in the tomb. Tomb XIIIB contained a hollow gold date-shaped bead (*Marlik*, fig. 128) decorated with longitudinal incised lines and punched dots. A similar gold bead, although slightly longer and thinner, was found in Sialk Cemetery A (see pl. 133a).

Tomb XIVD is included among the early group as it contained the striking red pottery humped bull fitted with a pair of small gold earrings through each ear (*Marlik*, pl. I, and *I.L.N.* 26 December 1964, fig. 6). These earrings are lunate-shaped and plain, but are important as they may well be the prototype for the similar lunate earrings already noted above from Sialk Cemetery A, though these are decorated with a triangular granular pattern (pl. 133b). Small solid lunate-shaped earrings are also worn by terracotta human figures.

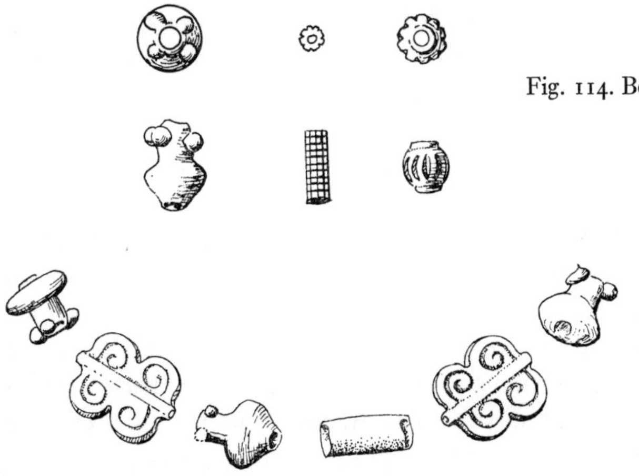

Fig. 114. Beads from Ur.

Tomb IIII is noteworthy for the necklace of oblong frit beads with gold caps. This technique of capping stone or paste beads with gold was known much earlier in Babylonia and Assyria, but here the beads are usually wider and flatter in shape (*Marlik*, pl. III). A small frit winged bead on the same necklace may imitate the gold quadruple spiral beads noted above. To the necklace is attached a pomegranate pendant of the same type as those mentioned above. The frit beads are strikingly similar to the beads found at Ur in 1927 by Woolley (shown in fig. 114) and now in the British Museum.[1]

Marlik (later tombs c. tenth to ninth centuries B.C.)

The tentative ascription of this group of four tombs at Marlik to the two centuries after c. 1000 B.C. is based on the relationship which can be detected between jewellery in these tombs and dated Urartian jewellery in eastern Anatolia and Transcaucasia belonging to the ninth, eighth and seventh centuries B.C. In Anatolia and Transcaucasia the earlier stages of the developed Urartian techniques have not been found; there are no Urartian architectural or archaeological remains of the tenth century yet excavated and it is probable that the origins of Urartian jewellery work may in fact lie in north-west Iran and – if not at Marlik – somewhere not far from this site. Far more evidence is needed before this problem can begin to be solved; at present, all we can do is to record the jewellery from tombs at Marlik and related pieces from Urartu and sites in Azerbaijan, such as Ziweye, until more stratified examples can be considered.

Tomb XIIIC contained a gold bead formed of two cylinders, fastened by a band of gold at each end. Each bead is pierced through its length. This may have been the centrepiece or part of a double cord necklace. Length 3·5 cm, weight 4·2 g (*Marlik*, fig. 130).

The gold bead can be compared with the later Urartian beads from Altin tepe (see p. 200 and pl. 154) made from four narrow cylinders joined together with gold wire at the centre and each end and decorated in fine granular triangles. It is possible that the plain Marlik bead with only two cylinders may represent the first attempts of the jewellers to make a bead of this type. Similar beads, also decorated in fine granulation technique, are known from Ziweye and are now in the Teheran Museum. These are more elaborate than the Altin tepe examples and have seven narrow cylinders joined together longitudinally. The granular patterns are also more

[1] See Mallowan in *Iraq*, IX, p. 173. No details of findspot are known.

intricate and combine triangles with rosettes and extremely minute granules (see p. 207 and pl. 163).

Earlier examples of this type of spacer bead are known in stone in the Talish region, several examples being in the Museum at St Germain-en-Laye, from Hassan Zamini (No. 57787 Dolmen No. 20, which also contained two seals[1]), Chagula Derre, Agha Evler and Tchila Khane.

A gold diadem made from a narrow strip of gold decorated with repoussé and punched decoration of circles and running spirals was also found in Tomb XIIIC (*Marlik*, fig. 86). Length 53·5 cm, weight 10·2 g.

Tomb XVIID is important for the fact that it contained a pair of fine gold earrings built up from graduated gold balls in a double pyramid design (pl. 147). A large double circular gold loop is soldered to the top of the earring. This earring should be compared with the double pyramid earrings from Patnos (see p. 198) now in the Ankara Museum and probably dating from the ninth century B.C.

The bronze model of a plough drawn by a yoked pair of humped bulls was also found in this tomb.[2]

Tomb XVE contained a pendant threaded on to a gold chain, similar to the double pyramid earrings from Tomb XVIIB, and the gold bowl (*Marlik*, fig. 107) with a humped mountain goat in front of a tree and a bird. The excavator has noted that the designs bordering the rim and the base of crudely executed punched design and a rosette on the base are different from those on the other gold bowls.

A double-headed eagle pendant, suspended by a small loop which joins a bar fitted round the centre of the pendant to a larger twisted gold ring, was also found in this tomb (pl. 148). Diameter of loop 5·5 cm, weight 11·6 g. A silver bracelet completes the inventory of jewellery. It is made of a hollow curved tube in two pieces with one piece inserted into the other. Weight 20 g (*Marlik*, fig. 74).

Among the rest of the material, a bronze spouted cup (*Marlik*, fig. 29) may be noted as a type often found in pottery, both at Marlik and Sialk Cemetery B.

Tomb XVIIIC was one of the richest tombs at Marlik and is mentioned here with the possibly later group as it contained the famous gold cup with the striding winged bulls and griffins and the distinctive motif of a tree in a small spherical pot in the plain background. We cannot discuss here the style and reasons for considering this cup to be one of the latest of the gold cups and vases of Marlik, but the attribution of a date in the

[1] Schaeffer, *Strat. Comp.*, fig. 301, p. 410. [2] *I.L.N.*, 8 May 1965, fig. 2.

tenth to ninth centuries B.C. to the cup does not, of course, preclude the attribution of some of the other objects, such as the famous gold figure of a goddess (see below), to an earlier period. Edith Porada considers that the curious bronze female figures from this tomb (*Marlik*, fig. 99) should be dated in the twelfth to eleventh centuries[1] and, therefore, the jewellery in the tomb may belong to a period earlier than the tenth to ninth centuries B.C. The jewellery can be briefly listed with quotations from published catalogue entries:

(1) 'Broad gold ring incised with a design of birds, animals and humans. The ring which tapers underneath is bordered with a raised band edge.' Diameter 2·8 cm, weight 23·4 g. The use of the drill on the design on this ring suggests comparison with ninth-century Assyrian work, but the style is local and may well be earlier (*Marlik*, fig. 81).

(2) 'A compound chain of fine silver loops with loops at the end for fastening.' Length 44 cm, weight 48 g. The chain is made of several plaited silver wires bound together at each end by wire to which the fastening hook is attached. Probably intended as a bracelet (*Marlik*, fig. 127).

(3) 'Gold bracelet formed of two curved hollow tubes, one inserted into the other. The finials are lions' heads with a chain band of decoration at the point at which the lion's head is joined to the body of the bracelet.' Diameter 7·3 cm (*Marlik*, fig. 77). This is the earliest known gold bracelet of this type to have come from a scientific excavation and – with the exception of the bracelets with animal finials from Pasagadae, Susa and Karmir Blur – all the other examples now in museums and private collections and called Achaemenian have no known provenance beyond in many cases a general label indicating a possible region, such as 'Amlash'. It is, therefore, possible that some of these examples may in fact be earlier than the Achaemenian period. The bracelets shown in pl. 149 may well belong to the eighth to seventh centuries B.C. The work is technically more advanced than that of the Marlik examples; the bracelet in pl. 149a, now in the Teheran Museum, is made like the Marlik example, in two pieces, but joined together by a hook at the point where one half is inserted into the other.

The binding of gold wire on the magnificent fluted example from (?) Hamadan, where the lions' heads are of lapis lazuli (pl. 150) is comparable with the binding on the Marlik bracelet, though here – as on the Philadelphia Museum piece – the bracelet is made on one piece of hollow

[1] *Ancient Iran*, p. 102, fig. 65.

gold tubing. The Philadelphia bracelet (pl. 151) is typologically the latest in this series. On this example, the inside of the bracelet is made of a piece of plain gold sheet soldered to the outer fluting, and the binding where the lions' heads join the body of the bracelet is shown by incisions. An incomplete bracelet, also from 'Amlash', in the Teheran Museum is also plain like the Marlik piece, and made in two halves, but the finials are missing (pl. 152).

(4) The gold bust of the goddess or king is described in the catalogue as follows: 'Gold bust of a king in ceremonial dress. His crown is a separate twisted loop of gold wire. His ears are pierced and in one a single loop earring still remains. His dress or chain armour is indicated by wavy lines. Two large decorative buttons can be seen on his chest above his crossed hands.' Height 11·7 cm, weight 43·5 g. Professor Negahban considers this gold figure to be male and to denote a young prince. The hands crossed supporting the breasts, the necklace and round pendants, the lower acting as a fronted counterweight, suspended in the same way as those worn by Babylonian goddesses with a counterweight behind the neck and the triple 'chokers' or torques round the neck, all suggest this was the tutelary goddess of a male, probably a prince or ruler buried in Tomb XVIIIC.

There are many points of interest in this figure. First the headband and the base are decorated with a twisted guilloche pattern of double gold wire which is comparable with that on one of the gold rings found at Susa in the In-Shushinak deposit, but, although the Elamite work is combined with fine granulation, the similarity of technique is remarkable (cf. pl. 132a; see also p. 187 above). Many of the Susa terracottas and statuettes wear pendants, necklaces and bracelets, but these are always female figures and the male figures are bearded. This magnificent hollow gold figure, with twisted guilloche headdress, single earring and smiling expression, could have been inspired by stone or terracotta Elamite, Babylonian or Assyrian models and is unique in western Asia.

CHAPTER 12

Urartu: Ninth to Seventh Centuries B.C.

INTRODUCTION

The earliest gold jewellery from Urartian sites in Anatolia and Transcaucasia comes from Patnos (Girik tepe), excavated by Professor Kemal Balkan and now in the Ankara Museum. The detailed publication of this rich material is awaited with great interest; meanwhile I am grateful to Professor Balkan and the Director of the Ankara Museum, Dr Raci Temizer, for giving me facilities to study the jewellery. The Urartian palace at Girik tepe was destroyed towards the end of the eighth century B.C., either by the Assyrians or the Cimmerians; this event can probably be dated around 714 B.C.

The techniques used by the goldsmiths are advanced and may well have developed from the earlier jewellery from Marlik. Certain pieces show similar technical methods and it is instructive to compare some of the earrings with those portrayed on the Assyrian reliefs which may represent Urartian work, either looted by the Assyrians during their campaigns against Urartu, or the products of Urartian jewellers captured by the Assyrians and deported home to work for the victors. A wheel-shaped pendant or earring with extremely fine triangular granulation work is comparable with the gold pendant from Marlik in the form of a cage (pl. 137, see Chapter 11), but the work is even finer than the Marlik example.

A pair of silver gilt double pyramid earrings made of graduated balls with a collar of minute granules round the base is also comparable with the Marlik double pyramid earrings (pl. 147). A pomegranate-shaped earring or pendant decorated in very fine granular patterns (fig. 115) could have been inspired by the Marlik pendant composed of a group of undecorated stylized pomegranates, and is of the same type as a pendant in the Teheran Museum said to have come from the Amlash region (pl. 153). The earring of the lady on the painted pot (fig. 116) from Patnos may also represent an earring of this circular type. This may be the kind of pendant often portrayed on Assyrian reliefs at the end of a necklace and the examples shown here (figs. 117 and 118a) date from the reign of Ashurnaṣirpal II.

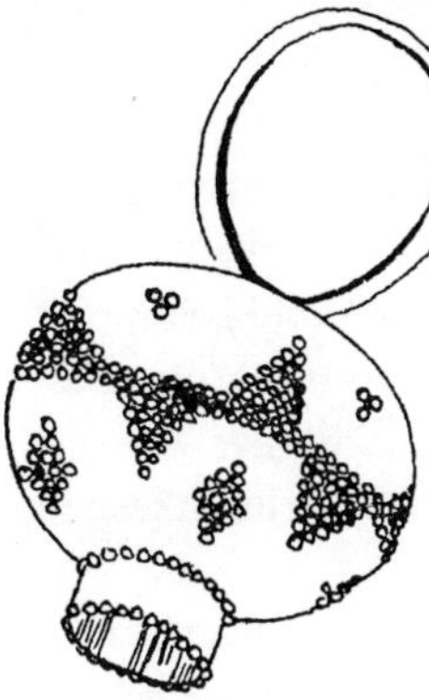

Fig. 115. Pomegranate earring from Patnos.

Fig. 116. Earring from painted pot from Patnos.

Other links with Assyria include a silver earring made of two separate rings of silver wire, gilded, with a short stalk ending in a triangle of coarse granules, and possibly of the type represented on an Assyrian relief of the time of Ashurnaṣirpal II (figs. 117b, 126, 166, Chapter 15). A plain gold circular looped earring with curled ends suspending a long stone pendant may also be of the type shown on reliefs of Sargon from Khorsabad (fig. 126: 25, 26, Chapter 15). Cloisonné work was combined with granulation on

Fig. 117. Necklace from a relief of Ashurnaṣirpal II.

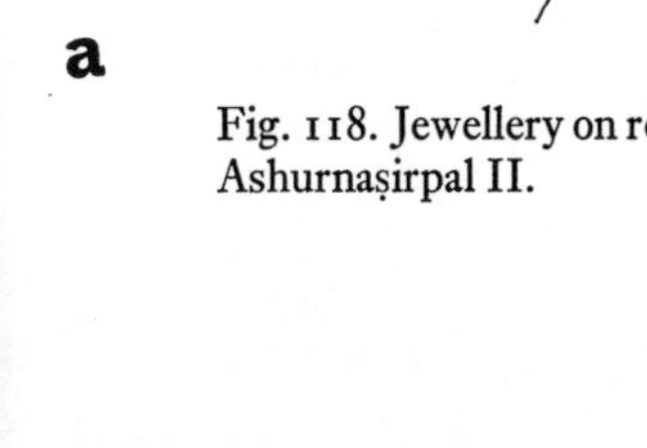

a

b

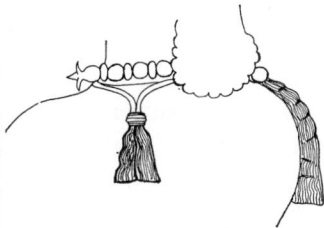

Fig. 118. Jewellery on reliefs of Ashurnaṣirpal II.

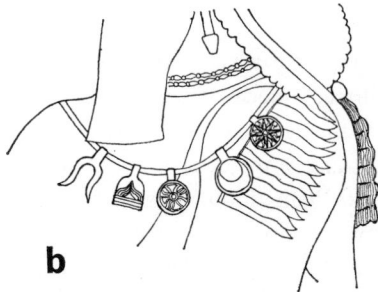

a fine ring of twisted silver wire, the cloison at the side of the ring forming a setting for a red stone, possibly carnelian, each row being made from one piece of sheet gold bent over and joined longitudinally.

Altintepe

The site of Altintepe (the hill of gold) lying in the plains of Erzincan on the road to Erzerum was excavated by Professor Tahsin Özgüc in 1959 and successive years; it has produced some remarkable gold jewellery which is especially important as it comes from a stratified context in a scientifically conducted excavation.[1] The beads and circular buttons, all decorated in extremely fine granulation, are now in the Museum at Ankara.

The jewellery was found in a large stone-built tomb, excavated in 1959, with three rectangular rooms, one of which contained two stone sarcophagi in which a male and a female had been deposited with the appropriate funeral gifts. The remains of a chariot, bronze cauldrons, furniture, iron weapons and other objects have been described by the excavator and the jewellery was found *in situ* on the female skeleton and also outside the male coffin.

Beads

At least four necklaces had been placed in the woman's tomb. The beads included the following:

(*a*) Three gold spacer beads (pl. 154a, b) composed of eight hollow tube-like beads soldered together in two rows of four beads. The openings are bound with gold wire and the surfaces, decorated in triangles, rosettes and lines of minute granules, show the developed technical skill of the jewellers who produced this work. The total length of these beads is only just over 2 cm. The joins are only visible through a strong magnifying glass.

(*b*) Seven date-shaped beads (pl. 155) made from a single piece of coiled gold wire, finished off at each end by a circular collar formed by a separate piece of wire. The traces of paste at the end of one of these beads suggest that the wire was originally wound round a core of some perishable material. Length 1 cm.

(*c*) Plain globular beads with collar (pl. 155). Length 0·4 cm, width 0·35 cm. Two examples, each made in two pieces.

[1] *Altintepe*, I, II.

(*d*) Two melon-shaped beads (pl. 155). Length 0·35 cm. Made from five separate curved pieces soldered together.

(*e*) Double cone-shaped beads (pl. 155). Length 0·35 cm, width 0·15 cm. Made in two pieces with two pieces of wire round the centre join. Each curved surface is decorated with granular triangles with a border of grains round the centre and upper and lower collars. Three examples.

(*f*) Circular fluted beads, silver.

(*g*) Spacer bead comparable with the quadruple spacers described above but constructed differently. A single piece of gold sheet (width under 1 cm) encases three tubes, the openings (as on the quadruple spacers) bound with wire and decorated with granules, but the surface of the bead is flat and decorated with a border and triangles of granules (pl. 154a).

Rings and buttons

Gold ring. Width 1·8 cm. The surface decorated in gold balls between a border of minute granular triangles.

Gold buttons were found outside the male coffin and also sewn on to the dress of the woman. These are circular; of two of them (pl. 156), the larger one (diameter 1·75 cm) with curved surface decorated with a central rosette with six petals surrounded with six repoussé circles and triangles – each element of the decoration being surrounded with granular borders and the outer circular gold wire border set between two continuous rows of grains. On the back are two small loops soldered on to the body of the button to use for attaching it to the material. The smaller of the two buttons illustrated here (under 1 cm diameter) is simpler, with a design of seven petals outlined in granules. Six smaller buttons of silver were also found at Altintepe.

A rectangular gold plaque with a human-headed winged bull in Assyrian style executed in repoussé (height 7·8 cm) was also found at Altin tepe.

The jewellery from the tomb can be dated by the Altintepe inscriptions to the period of Argistis II (713–679 B.C.) and the presence of an imported Assyrian faience vase raises the question whether the jewellery was also imported to this important Urartian provincial centre, or whether it was the product of Urartian workshops. Some of the jewellery portrayed on Assyrian reliefs could well be Urartian and the Assyrian lists of booty taken from Urartian cities suggest that this may be correct. In the time of the greatest strength of Assyria in the ninth to eighth centuries B.C. the possibility of large quantities of gold jewellery being obtained as loot from Assyrian centres of production by invaders from the northern and eastern mountains seems unlikely, although this explanation could reasonably account for much of the jewellery found in these regions after the fall of Nineveh in 612 B.C. However, the reference in the account of Sargon's eighth campaign (see p. 184) to objects at Musasir pillaged from the temples of the gods Ashur and Marduk suggests that many gold and silver objects had been looted from Assyria by 714 B.C. and transported to Musasir. Jewellery was easily transportable through the normal methods of trade and often formed part of the dowries of princesses whose marriages were used as links between Assyria and surrounding nations.

The standardization of technical methods from the ninth to eighth centuries B.C. onwards makes this problem difficult to solve until more stratified material is available for study. We have already compared the necklaces on the Assyrian reliefs (figs. 118a and b) with the pomegranate earrings or pendants. It is also possible that the globular part of the earring (fig. 115) from Patnos may have been intended to be placed as a kind of holder for a tassel at the back of necklaces such as those portrayed in fig. 118a and b, which would act as a kind of counterweight. The gold wire beads may also be represented on the necklaces shown in fig. 118. Gold buttons have also been noted at Marlik and the pendants worn by the figure in fig. 118b can be compared with the Marlik pendants and another circular gold pendant now in the Boston Museum of Fine Art (pl. 157), whose provenance is simply given as north-west Persia–it could possibly have come from an Urartian site in Persian Azerbaijan.

Karmir Blur

The Urartian site of Karmir Blur[1] lies in the valley of the Zangu river, a tributary of the Araxes, close to Erivan. It was excavated by Professor Piotrovski and has produced some fine pieces of gold jewellery, forming a valuable collection which can be dated to the seventh to sixth centuries B.C., when Karmir Blur succeeded the site of Argishti as the most important Urartian centre in Transcaucasia. Karmir Blur or Tesheba survived until shortly after Tushpa fell to the Medes in 590 B.C.; the destruction was the work of the Scyths and, in spite of the fire which devastated the citadel, excavators showed that tribute and loot from the Urartian empire was stored here in vast quantities and that far-reaching commercial contacts were enjoyed by the inhabitants. We know from the annals of the

[1] *Karmir Blur*, I–IV.

Urartian kings that large quantities of metal were received as tribute from conquered and dependent territories; the king of Diauehi (an Urartian principality whose control seems to have included Altin tepe) sent forty-one minas of gold, thirty-seven minas of silver and more than ten minas of copper to Argistis I; the king of Kummuḫ sent Sarduras forty minas of gold and 800 minas of silver. These imports presumably would have been used for the local manufacture of gold and silver jewellery, but finished objects were also imported or sent as tribute or gifts; the fine pair of earrings of Phoenician type found at Karmir Blur was undoubtedly an import (pl. 158).

The jewellery is listed as follows:

(1) A pair of gold boat-shaped earrings, the ends bound with gold wire and the body decorated with lines and triangles of granulation (pl. 158). This type is common in Syria and Phoenicia in the seventh to sixth centuries B.C.[1] A pair of earrings from Ur (pl. 159) belongs to the same class (see p. 208). An example in the Teheran Museum (pl. 168b, see Chapter 13), said to have come from Ziweye, is of exactly the same type as the Karmir Blur example. Another earring from Karmir Blur (pl. 158) belongs to the same class as the pair described above but is crude work with a circular cloison on the base as the setting for inlay and two large triangles of twisted wire soldered to the body of the earring. This could be a local imitation of the Phoenician import.

(2) Part of a silver torque ending in the figure of a crouching lion, covered with gold leaf (pl. 158). From the north-west part of the citadel.

(3) Gold bracelet; the two ends which form part of the body of the bracelet and are not separately attached are in the form of lions' heads with the details of head and neck incised. This is the earliest stratified example of this type of bracelet with animal heads and was found in one of the magazines in the palace (No. 47) (pl. 158).

(4) Plain biconical gold bead with attached collars of gold.

(5) Stud or button of gold, mushroom-shaped and decorated in fine granulation (pl. 158).

(6) A fragment of a gold ingot came from Deposit 36, weight 14·85 g. (pl. 158).

(7) Gold pin with flat head (pl. 158).

(8) Medallions – two silver examples:

[1] cf. a pair from Amrit, illustrated by E. Coche de la Ferté in *Les Bijoux Antiques*, pl. 11, 3, and an example from a private collection (pl. VI). For parallels from Tharros see *B.M.C.J.*, pl. XXIII, 1495; and R. D. Barnett in *Iraq*, XIV, 2, p. 142, footnote 1, with references for Cretan and Ionic types.

(*a*) A female figure holding an animal, probably a goat, by the horns confronts a seated deity. This is rough work, but it can be compared with the gold medallion from Tushpa (Van).

(*b*) Standing deity with raised hands confronting a figure conducting an animal, imitating an Assyrian ritual scene.[1]

Van

A silver armband from Toprak Kale in the Berlin Antiquarium was published by G. Pudelko in 1934.[2] The ends are in the form of two bull calves and the style of carving can be compared with the bronze bracelet now in the Louvre (see pl. 227). A date in the seventh century B.C. is likely.

Kayalidere

The site of Kayalidere lies north-west of Lake Van, at the junction of two natural routes: from the Murat river north to Erzerum, and along the Murat valley to the plain of Bulanik and Malazgirt, which was an important part of the Urartian homeland from the early formation of the kingdom. The excavation of this important site was begun in 1965 by Professor Seton Lloyd and C. A. Burney. A group of jewellery was found in a rock-cut tomb (Tomb A) which, although plundered, is important for the association of the silver jewellery with glazed pottery, fragments of bronze furniture and iron objects.[3]

The fibula (pl. 160) is described on p. 263. The variety of personal ornaments combined with the small size of the rock-cut sarcophagus suggests that these objects were buried with a woman. Among the small silver rings and bronze bracelets a silver earring calls for comment. This is crescent-shaped with each end pointed and six small grains in a cluster soldered to the base.[4]

BRACELETS WITH SERPENTS' HEADS

Bracelets with serpent head finials often occur among the unstratified 'Amlash' jewellery, but a few examples whose provenance is known sug-

[1] Piotrovski, *Van*, Tav. XLVII b & c.

[2] G. Pudelko, 'Altpersische Armbänder', *A.F.O.*, 1933–4, Taf. IV, 4 & 5, p. 86.

[3] C. A. Burney, 'A first season of excavation at the Urartian citadel of Kayalidere', *A.S.*, XVI, 1966, pp. 55–111, fig. 23, Nos. 7, 11.

[4] Silver earrings of this type are known from the Kassite period in Mesopotamia. See *Ur Excavations*, VIII, pl. 36, U.18166.

gest that this distinctive type belongs to the ninth to eighth centuries B.C. and that they should probably be designated as Urartian. There are no bracelets with serpents' heads from Assyria and the few examples with known findspots come from the area included in the Urartian empire. An example (pl. 161) from 'Amlash' in the Iran Bastan Museum, Teheran, has a square section; the head and neck of the serpent, which is bent back along the body of the bracelet, are ornamented with incisions.

The same type, but in bronze, comes from Transcaucasia (Mkart in Georgia) from the Urartian cemetery at Idgyr on the southern slopes of Mount Ararat and from tombs at Chagula Derre in the Persian Talish, associated with weapons of bronze and iron.[1] Another in solid gold from 'Amlash' was exhibited in Brussels in 1966 (*Brussels Cat.* 464), but the stylized finials, although catalogued as serpents' heads, more closely resemble bull calves. A group of silver bracelets from Agha Evler is now in the Museum at St Germain-en-Laye (pl. 162). The larger of the three (diameter 6·5 cm) has snake's head finials, while the ends of the two smaller pairs, decorated with incisions, are in the shape of stylized bull calves' heads (diameter 3·9 cm). This group was associated with iron and the silver serpent head bracelet was found in a tomb along with an iron spear and a curious circular bronze ornament with pin – a type often allegedly found in Luristan. Colour pl. F shows an example in gold from the Mazda Collection, which is said to have come from Pir Kuh, Gilan. A silver example with rams' heads is in the Helen Stathatos collection.[2]

An important group from the Iron Age dolmens at Agha Evler, excavated by De Morgan, was identified by Schaeffer as coming from Dolmen 8.[3] This included a silver ring with an animal design (pl. 15c), a sword with bronze blade and silver or electrum head. Schaeffer had dated the Agha Evler and Chagula Derre Iron Age graves to c. 1200–1000 B.C. and certainly the use of bronze weapons alongside the combination of bronze and iron, as well as weapons made solely from iron, suggests that these groups belong to a period when iron was beginning to be used but had not yet ousted bronze for armament.

[1] Schaeffer, *Strat. Comp.*, fig. 271. Barnett, 'The Urartian Cemetery at Igdyr', *A.S.*, XIII, 1963, fig. 32, No. 10. *D.P.M.*, VIII, fig. 477, p. 284.

[2] Cf. Ghirshman, *Iranica Antiqua*, 4, 1964, pp. 90–107, fig. 1. Amandry, *Collection Hélène Stathatos*, pl. XXXII, 146.

[3] Schaeffer, *Strat. Comp.*, p. 441, fig. 237.

CHAPTER 13

North-West Iran: Eighth to Seventh Centuries B.C.

Ziweye

The site of Ziweye lies forty kilometres east of Saqqiz and has been identified with the Zibie of Assyrian records.[1] A short three-week season by the University of Pennsylvania directed by R. H. Dyson on the fortifications which still crown the mound established that the main period of occupation can be confined to the seventh century B.C. and that the site was abandoned early in the sixth century B.C. The famous treasure which was discovered in 1947 apparently came from the site, but its subsequent dispersal into private collections and museums all over the world makes the study of the jewellery particularly difficult. It is also probable that many pieces whose provenance is given as Ziweye may not in fact belong to the original treasure. With this caveat, the jewellery will be discussed under the general heading of Ziweye.

The treasure was found in a large bronze coffin (or bath tub), which has been discussed in detail by both Barnett and Wilkinson.[2] They conclude that the date of the burial of the objects in the 'coffin' cannot be later than the seventh century B.C., but it is generally agreed that many of the objects should be dated to the eighth century B.C. It is thus possible for the earliest and latest objects to be separated by as much as two hundred years, so the jewellery cannot be used as a dating criterion for related pieces; all we know is that the collection existed at the time of burial some time during the seventh century B.C. The treasure is not homogeneous in style; Scythian, Median, Assyrian and Urartian elements have been identified among the bronzes and ivories and some of these influences can also be found in the jewellery. Some of the pieces could have been imported, via trade, to the Saqqiz area in antiquity, or have been looted

[1] Godard, *Ziweye*, p. 7.

[2] In *Iraq*, XVIII, 2, 1956, p. 111 and XXII, 1960, p. 213. Wilkinson calls the 'coffin' an Assyrian bath tub; Barnett assigns it to the Neo-Babylonian period.

from Assyria or Urartu; some may be modern imports from dealers in Beirut or Europe and added to the collection in recent times. There seems to be little evidence of unskilled local work; if some of the jewellery can be attributed to Mannean or Median craftsmen, then they were as skilled as jewellers working in Assyrian and Phoenician centres and their technique is of a uniformly high standard. The skill of Mannean gold-workers is known from Hasanlu but this site has not produced comparable gold or silver jewellery.

A summary is given below of the types of gold and silver jewellery alleged to have come from Ziweye, which can be related to other distinctive pieces from surrounding areas whose provenance can be determined with certainty.

Necklaces

(*a*) Necklace of spacer beads composed of six tubes soldered together, decorated in fine granulation, and also five or seven date-shaped coiled wire beads, soldered together at the centre (pl. 163 – cf. similar beads from Altintepe, pl. 154).

(*b*) Necklace of gold globular beads, date-shaped wire beads and pointed lantern-shaped pendants (pl. 164). The inverted conoid base of the pendant is decorated with triangles of minute granules and the upper part is composed of loops of gold wire topped by a cap and ring for suspension, In the centre is a round agate (?) in a gold circular setting with the outer band covered with fine granulation. Similar pendants, with a double row of wire loops above the point, were found in the Achaemenid Treasury at Persepolis.[1] If the Ziweye necklace is correctly assigned to this site, then one would suspect that the Persepolis pendants were antiquities when they were deposited in the treasury. Comparable pointed pendants can be found on earrings of the Sargonid period in Assyria (fig. 126:19, 22). A necklace from Ziweye now in the Cincinnati Art Museum (pl. 165)[2] is composed of gold-capped stone beads, three quadruple spiral beads and fluted melon-shaped beads with collars. The arrangement may not be original and the oval-shaped gold capped beads and fluted beads recall Third Dynasty of Ur types from Ashur (Tomb 20) and Ur (Grave 1422). The quadruple spiral, however, is comparable with the Mari quadruple spiral beads where the gold wire forming the spiral is twisted round the top of the tube. A date in the early part of the second

[1] Schmidt, *Persepolis*, II, pl. 43, 6.
[2] *Iraq*, XXVI, 1, 1964, pl. VIII; and *Cincinnati Art Museum Bulletin*, V, 2, 1957, fig. 4, p. 14.

millennium B.C. for this group is possible, with the quadruple spirals added later (see pl. 48 and figs. 46, 113).

(*c*) Gold chain (pl. 166) made from three lengths of twisted gold wire which pass through six spacer beads composed of three tubes and decorated with granular triangles. To the ends are attached small gold bells by rings. The three chains pass through a larger spacer composed of six gold tubes soldered together in two rows of three each.

A gold chain which passed through five gold tubes, three of which are decorated with lions, in Budapest,[1] found in a grave at Zöldhalompuszta with the famous gold stag, may represent a Scythian imitation of the much finer Ziweye necklace (pl. 167). Alternatively, it could have been, along with the gold buttons, brought to Hungary in the course of the Scythian movement to Europe.

Earrings (pl. 168 a-c)

(*a*) Boat-shaped, decorated with triangles of granules, the ends bound with gold wire. This is the same type as found at Karmir Blur (see p. 203, pl. 158) and considered by Piotrovski to be a Phoenician import (see also pl. 213 from Al Mina, Chapter 14).

(*b*) Boat-shaped with the body fluted and decorated in lines of granules. Small balls of gold with attached granules are soldered to the body of the earrings. This type is comparable with a pair found at Ur (pl. 223, see Chapter 15, U.460 A and B), but here the attachments are much larger. Type (*a*) was also found at Ur in a stratified Neo-Babylonian level (pl. 159).

(*c*) Plain boat-shaped earrings, with bound ends and fluted body. This pair is crudely made, with thick pins and may well be local work imitating Type (*b*) above.

(*d*) Flat boat-shaped with bound ends, decorated with granular rosettes and applied granular triangles.

(*e*) Basket-shaped earrings with applied rosettes and granular border; ends bound as on Types (*a*) to (*d*) (not illustrated).

Fibulae

Two typical features of the fibulae from Ziweye are the hook for the pin formed in the shape of a human hand and the use of the lion motif either applied or as an integral part of the body of the fibula. These two features can be found on a single fibula of gold shown here (pl. 169) and also on a

[1] *Guide à travers la collection des Trouvailles de l'Époque de la migration des peuples exposée au Musée Historique de Hongrie*, p. 5 (Budapest, 1935).

fibula in the Metropolitan Museum of Art, New York (pl. 170a), where two lions are placed head to tail on the bow of the fibula. The triangular-shaped bow with the mark of a join across the centre, visible on the Ziweye gold fibula (pl. 169), is also found on a stratified bronze fibula from Hasanlu[1] from Period IIIb, seventh century B.C. A silver brooch from Ziweye, also in the Metropolitan Museum, has the human hand forming the hook for the pin (pl. 170b). An elaborate version of the Ziweye fibula with each end of the bow ending in a lion's head comes from Ephesus[2] and, when more stratified examples of this class of fibula are available, it will be possible to work out the development of the typology from the early eighth-century to the seventh- and sixth-century B.C. examples.

Bracelets

(*a*) A magnificent gold bracelet now in the Teheran Museum (colour pl. G) is decorated with confronted pairs of crouching lions and two stylized lions' heads (both detachable) at each end of the gold bar which forms the body of the bracelet. Urartian workmanship for this piece is suggested by the treatment of the four lions' heads, where the 'gable' above the forehead is typically Urartian, and by the stylization of the two confronted lions. A comparable gold bracelet with three pairs of confronted lions' heads, now in the Louvre, is said to have come from Luristan.[3]

(*b*) Open bracelet in solid gold (pl. 171a). The ring is deeply cut into flat segments which are incised and each end is carved in the shape of a moufflon head. Decoration of the heads is by incision. A thick plain bracelet worn by Ashurnaṣirpal II (fig. 142, Chapter 15) on a relief in the British Museum ends in comparable moufflon heads. The bronze bracelet in the Louvre (pl. 227) belongs to the same class of animal-headed bracelet; the ends have been identified as lions' heads and compared with the bracelets worn by the colossal figure of Gilgamesh from Khorsabad, also in the Louvre, but the heads are perhaps better identified as those of bull calves. Amandry considers this bracelet to belong to the Persian period; the Ziweye evidence suggests that the original dating to the eighth century may well be correct.

(*c*) A pair of gold bracelets with the ends in the form of bull calves' heads. Diameters 5 and 4·7 cm. Three incised lines around the neck of each animal (pl. 171b).

[1] *I.L.N.*, 12 September 1964, fig. 5, pp. 372–3.
[2] P. Jacobstahl, 'The date of the Ephesian foundation deposit', *J.H.S.*, LXXI, pl. XXXI.
[3] Ghirshman, *Persia*, p. 343, fig. 435.

(*d*) Gold bracelet with ends in the form of bull calves' heads, now in the University Museum, Pennsylvania. Diameter 4·2 and 4·7 cm. Details finely incised. This type can be found on Assyrian reliefs of the time of Ashurnaṣirpal II (figs. 142, 143).

The silver bracelet published by G. Pudelko in 1933[1] from a private collection in Lausanne can probably be related to the Ziweye class of armbands. The goat head finials are carved with incised detail and the bracelet should probably be dated to the seventh century B.C. Another gold bracelet with moufflon heads exhibited at Paris in 1961–2 as Achaemenian can be included here; it is made of solid gold (pl. 172).

The development of this class of Persian animal-headed bracelet in the sixth century and throughout Achaemenid times has been studied in detail by Amandry and further discussion is outside the scope of this book.[2] For another gold bracelet with moufflon heads and granular decoration, see p. 223, reputedly from Amlash and probably eighth to seventh century B.C.

Appliqués

(*a*) *Ajouré lion head roundels and bracteates.* Two remarkable roundels in the Iran Bastan Museum, Teheran, whose provenance is given as Hamadan, are shown in pl. 173b and noted here as they are clearly related to gold work from Ziweye and could possibly have come from this site. The design is in the shape of two rampant lions, back to back, with hindquarters touching and the necks joined by a single head. The feet rest on the incised circular gold strip forming the border. Diameter 5·5 cm.

The motif of the lion head with two bodies can be found on a gold plaque from Ziweye, now in the Metropolitan Museum, New York,[3] where two rampant winged lions are joined with one head below a sacred tree, and also on a gold cup exhibited at the Paris exhibition of Persian art in 1961–2 (*Paris Cat.*, No. 159, pl. LI). This and another cup (*Paris Cat.*, No. 674, pl. LII) in the Cincinnati Art Museum with handles in the form of double-headed ibexes decorated with a frieze of striding winged lions have been described as specifically Median in style – an attribution which cannot be proved until a Median site is completely excavated.

Certain other gold plaques, the famous Kelermes scabbard and a gold and silver rhyton from Marash in south-east Turkey, now in the British

[1] *A.F.O.*, IX, 1933, 4, Taf. IV, 1 and 2, p. 86. [2] *Orfèvrerie achéménide.*
[3] *Metropolitan Museum of Art Bulletin*, March 1955, p. 216.

Museum,[1] have also been attributed to the Medes and no doubt when current excavations in Media develop we shall be able to identify Median jewellery. The two roundels in pl. 173b could be regarded as the product of a Median goldsmith. The lion's head and circular mane are closely comparable in style with the head of the lion on the gold cup (*Paris Cat.*, No. 159, pl. LI) and the bodies have features known from Assyrian and north Syrian art, such as the flame-like pattern on the hindquarters and the well-defined muscles above the forelegs; these features, although more stylized, are also found on the gold cup whose applied gold handles, also in the form of lions, are made in the same style. It is also possible that some of the ajouré lion head bracteates allegedly from Hamadan, which have been discussed in detail by Helene Kantor,[2] may originate further north in the Ziweye area and belong to the end of the seventh century or the beginning of the sixth century B.C. Two examples are shown here from Ziweye (pls. 173a and 174), with the magnificent necklace (pl. 175) which could also be regarded as an early Achaemenian development from the Median style, possibly also to be dated in the early part of the sixth century B.C.

The purpose of these lion head bracteates was undoubtedly apotropaic and they were presumably sewn on to clothing worn either by the statues of deities or by human beings. A distinctive feature which occurs on all of these pieces is the series of single circles with repoussé centres which are placed between each strand of the mane of the lion. On a roundel with two rampant lions from Hamadan, now in the Seattle Art Museum,[3] the treatment of the heads is comparable in style, although here the end of each strand of the mane ends in a round blob. It is possible that the inspiration for the treatment of the mane and the prophylactic purpose of the Iranian lion bracteate was provided by the Babylonian and Assyrian demon Lamaštu, well known from the stone and bronze plaques where both this demon and the ritual for exorcising her evil influence from a sick man are vividly portrayed. A fine limestone plaque of this class was found by Mallowan at Nimrud (pl. 176) where the mane of the lion-headed Lamaštu demon is carved as a series of rough circular blobs. The Iranian bracteates could also be related to the Assyrian demon Pazuzu, who also appears on the same magical exorcism plaques and whose head was often made in bronze for use as an amulet. A fine bronze example from Nimrud

[1] R. D. Barnett, 'Median art', *Iranica Antiqua*, II, 1, 1962, pp. 77–95. W. Culican, *Medes and Persians*, 1965, pl. 32.

[2] *J.N.E.S.*, XVI, 1957, pp. 1–23.

[3] Culican, *Medes and Persians*, pl. 69.

has a loop for suspension.[1] The fighting half-human lion-headed demons on Assyrian reliefs of the seventh century B.C. are also comparable in style with the Hamadan bracteates (pl. 177).

(*b*) *Crouching goats* (pl. 178). One pair is now in the Iran Bastan Museum, Teheran. To this pair can be added four more exhibited at Geneva in 1966 and now in a private collection in Geneva (*Geneva Cat.*, No. 602, p. 7). All are said to have come from Ziweye. Certain technical and stylistic features, such as the muscles emphasized by double incisions and the circular eye surrounded by an incised border, link these goats with the lions on the ajouré roundel discussed above (pl. 173b) and the bracelet with moufflon heads (pl. 171a). The cutting and incision is finely and accurately done.

(*c*) *Lotus flowers* (pl. 179). Four examples from Ziweye, one in the Iran Bastan Museum, Teheran, and three in Geneva.

(*d*) *Maltese cross* (pl. 179). Five examples (*Paris Cat.*, No. 548). These are not pendants, but intended to be fixed or sewn on to material. The Maltese cross, typical of Kassite times in Babylonia, is shown as a pendant worn by the Assyrian king Shamshi-Adad V on a stele from Nimrud, now in the British Museum (see also pl. 116). A Ziweye variant of the cross motif has four points and cup spirals between. Three examples in the Iran Bastan Museum, Teheran (pl. 179). This design is also found among the jewellery at the Ephesus Artemision (pl. 180).

(*e*) *Rosettes and stars* (pl. 179). These were intended to be sewn on to garments or decorate gold strip diadems, such as that shown in fig. 154, Chapter 15.

(i) With eight petals. Nine examples in the Iran Bastan Museum, Teheran, from Ziweye (pl. 179; *Paris Cat.*, No. 548). The Achaemenid development of this type can be seen among the jewellery dating from the sixth century B.C. from Gordion and the slightly earlier example with granular decoration from Altintepe (pl. 156).

(ii) With repoussé circles and fine granular decoration outlining each circle and the centre (cf. Altintepe, pl. 156). Three examples, all in Teheran.

(iii) With many petals and milled edge. Three examples, all in Teheran (pl. 179).

[1] Mallowan, *Nimrud*, I, p. 119; *I.L.N.*, 29 July 1960, fig. 6. A bronze plaque belonging to this class from Luristan is now in the museum at Geneva: A. Alfoldi, 'Der Iranische Weltriese auf archäeologischen Denkmälern', *40 Jahrbuch der Schweizerischen Gesellschaft für Urgeschichte*, 1949–50, p. 17, Abb. 1, 2. Another bronze plaque portraying the lion-headed Lamaštu demon from Carchemish is in the British Museum: Saggs, *Babylon*, pl. 55.

(iv) With the edge surrounded with fine granules. One example in Teheran Museum. This type is known from Ashur in a Late Assyrian grave, No. 807 (fig. 146).

(v) Eight-pointed stars. Five examples in Teheran Museum.

Rings (pl. 181)

A gold 'glove' made of chains of twisted gold wire with six ends with gold rings attached. The other four rings are missing. The rings are made from a gold strip with punched dots round the centre and twisted filigree wire round each edge. Rough work with the join clearly visible. The clasp is a modern addition.

Gold mount for a seal (pl. 182)

The two gold caps have been joined by modern plaster; the lower cap (which could be used as a stamp seal) has a tree design in Urartian style, three branches ending in pomegranates, with two falling fruits attached to the outer pair. This design can be compared with the fragments of the large gold appliqué from Ziweye discussed in detail by Helene Kantor,[1] but the nearest analogy is the 'tree' at the end of the bronze belt from Ani-pemza in Russian Armenia, now in the Museum at Erivan, where the falling fruit can be found, though here attached to the stem of the tree.[2] The fine granulation round the top of the mount and the triangular designs related this gold mount to the fine work known on Urartian jewellery and it is a development of the Babylonian gold caps of cylinder seals of the Kassite period (see p. 165).

Bar-twist earring with lion's head (pl. 183)

Among the Ziweye jewellery now in the Iran Bastan Museum in Teheran is a remarkable earring made from a solid gold bar deeply incised to give the impression that the bar is bound with twisted gold wire. This technique and its variations have been discussed on p. 130 and until a similar earring was excavated in a stratified context at Gordion (cf. pl. 247, see Chapter 15), one would have assumed that this piece was an example of Hellenistic workmanship and did not come from Ziweye. There is evidence, however, that the origin of these earrings is to be sought in Persia; recently many examples of earrings with one end made in the shape of an animal have been coming from the region of Ardebil in the north-west Caspian area. No stratified examples are yet known, but a

[1] *J.N.E.S.*, XIX, 1, fig. 2. [2] Piotrovski, *Van*, fig. 86, p. 360.

crude example was published by Ghirshman, said to have come from Luristan (fig. 119); this gold earring, now in the Fouroughi Collection in Teheran, with one end in the shape of a gazelle's head, is typical of these Iranian animal earrings, which must be the prototype of the more sophisticated Greek and Hellenistic examples. In these early types the pin is placed directly into the mouth of the animal; the Gordion lion earring has the loop below the mouth for the insertion of the pin, a feature found on a stratified Achaemenian earring from Ashdod in the form of an ibex head (fig. 120), and also on a fine example from Sidon in the Istanbul Archaeological Museum (No. 825) decorated with triangular designs in minute granulation and an inlay of blue enamel (?) or lapis lazuli.[1]

Fig. 119. Gold earring from Luristan.

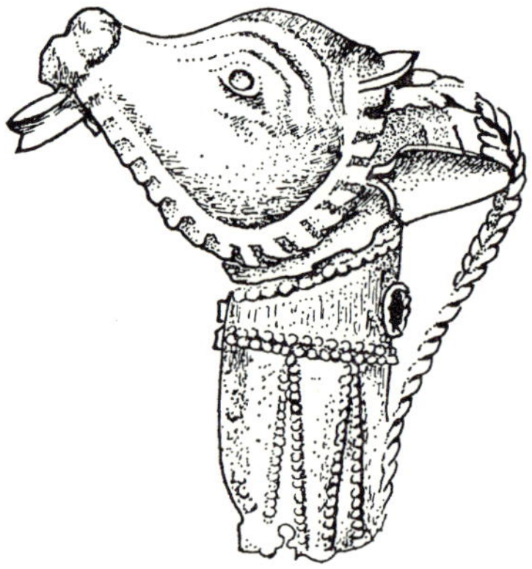

Fig. 120. Gold earring from Ashdod.

The Achaemenian and Greek forms of this type of earring fall outside the scope of this book; they merit a detailed study when more stratified examples are available. For comparison, some of these are shown in pls. 184–186, none of them from known sites, but useful for comparison with the ibex heads on the bracelets from Pasargadae, two of the few pieces of stratified Achaemenian jewellery[2] (pl. 187).

Diadem[3]

Arrangement of a gold strip diadem decorated with six rosettes, the petals forming cloisons for inlay (length 0·59 cm, width 0·012 cm). This is remarkable for the fragments of enamel of yellow and greenish colour

[1] *Art Treasures of Turkey*, No. 124 (Smithsonian Institute, 1966).

[2] For a detailed discussion of this bracelet see Stronach in *Iran*, 3, 1965, pp. 33 f.

[3] Godard, *Ziweye*, fig. 90; Ghirshman, *Persia*, fig. 531.

which remain *in situ*. This is an example of true enamel (powdered glass fused *in situ*) and the one surviving fastener is a gold wire double looped spiral (cf. the Ajjul diadem, fig. 86, p. 122).

Torques

Fragments of three gold torques from Ziweye are now in the Iran Bastan Museum, Teheran.

(*a*) Thick gold wire, twisted (pl. 189). This may have been large enough to put over the head without fasteners.

(*b*) Four fragments of a heavy gold torque, solid, with deep lateral incisions (pl. 191).

(*c*) Fragments of a solid gold torque, decorated with unbroken line of moufflon heads.[1] These heads are carved in great detail; the style is the same as that of the moufflon heads on the gold bracelet described above (pl. 171a) and the eyes are round with the same circular rib encircling the sockets. Fragments of a necklace composed of eight moufflon heads of steatite (length of each bead 2·7 cm) are said to have come from Ghafantlu near Ziweye (see p. 222).

On the reliefs it is not easy to distinguish between necklaces made of large beads and torques, but it is worth noting that torques have a long history in Iran and were worn by local chieftains on the rock reliefs at Sar-i-Pol who caused themselves to be portrayed in a manner obviously inspired by earlier rock reliefs of the Akkadian king Naram-Sin. Of the five reliefs in the Sar-i-Pol area[2] two of them have inscriptions which mention the names of the chieftains Anubanini and Tar-Lunni. Anubanini wears a large torque (or necklace) and confronts a goddess wearing several strings of beads, which, if fixed to a solid backing, could provide the origin for the solid pectoral discussed below. Tar-Lunni has a large circular pendant attached to his torque (or necklace). This relief may be slightly earlier than the carving portraying Anubanini, which should be dated to the period of Gudea or the Third Dynasty of Ur.

Another interesting example of a torque can be found on the stele from Susa,[3] on which the seated deity wears a torque comparable with the Ziweye types. Various dates have been given to this relief, which is considered by Parrot to be Elamite work of the period of the First Dynasty of Babylon and by Amiet as loot from Babylon carried off to

[1] Ghirshman, *Persia*, fig. 148, p. 113.
[2] For drawings of these reliefs see Ghirshman, *Iran*, figs. 21, 22; Contenau, *Manuel*, II, fig. 541, p. 764.
[3] Amiet, *Elam*, 310 p. 410 with refs.

Susa by Shutruk-Nakhunte around 1160 B.C., with the figure of the worshipper carved at this period. Another scholar would date the figure of the worshipper to the Neo-Elamite period, eighth to seventh centuries B.C., but whatever the actual date of the seated god, it was quite likely visible to craftsmen of this later period at the time when the Ziweye gold work was produced.

The Ziweye pectoral (pl. 188)

The gold pectoral from Ziweye belongs to a class of ornament worn in Urartu which will be included here under the heading of jewellery, while the oblong or trapezoidal plaques (which were probably sewn on to leather or other material) can be considered as part of body armour or breastplates and are thus outside the scope of this study. Gold shoulder pieces or epaulettes from Ziweye have also been classified as armour and Mr Wilkinson has made the suggestion that all these gold plaques may have been intended to have been fastened to the shroud containing the dead person.[1]

The Ziweye pectoral has two registers and is decorated with two sacred trees flanked by ibexes and winged bulls who are followed by a procession of sphinxes, human-headed bulls, lions, griffins, bullmen and rams (all winged), with two bears and two hares at each end (length 34 cm). The bears and hares are undoubtedly Scythian in style, but the winged bulls imitating the Assyrian *lamassu* figures (see fig. 166) and the sphinxes, griffins and rams with their Syrian or Phoenician skirts suggest that the goldsmith responsible for this pectoral was familiar with Urartian, Assyrian, Phoenician and local Mannaean styles; the result has been identified by one scholar as an example of Median work.[2] It may be that the Scythians owed much to the Medes in the formation of their own peculiar style which is known to us mainly from south Russia; the suggestion that the Ziweye treasure belongs to the burial of a Scythian chieftain has still to be proved; the Scythians are not known to have been in this region before the reign of Ashurbanipal and many of the objects in the Ziweye treasure can be dated earlier than the period 675–625 B.C., when the Scythians were a powerful force in Transcaucasia and north-west Iran. It is perhaps more likely that the pectoral was made for an Assyrian governor by local goldsmiths at the same time as the ivories which have been convincingly dated to the reign of Tiglath-Pileser III (745–727

[1] C. Wilkinson, *Metropolitan Museum of Art Bulletin*, March 1955, p. 218.

[2] Faulkner, *A.F.O.*, XVI, pp. 129–132.

B.C.) or that the treasure in the bronze coffin (or bath tub) belonged to a Median chief who lived around the middle of the seventh century B.C.

Ghirshman[1] has drawn attention to a series of comparable gold pectorals from Bulgaria (Dalboki and Trebenishte) and the famous example from Cerveteri in Etruria (the Regolini-Galassi tomb) which must be related to the Ziweye example – although the exact nature of this relationship is still to be defined. Hencken has recently re-published the fragments of a fine gold pectoral which has been cleaned and restored by the Museo Nazional, Tarquinia,[2] and relates its ornamentation closely to that of the Regolini-Galassi pectoral. The Tarquinia pectoral is, however, rectangular in shape and could be better described as a breastplate or plaque like the Ziweye plaques mentioned above. The oriental influence discernible on the decoration and ultimate Persian inspiration of these pieces is indubitable. The tomb of the gold pectoral at Tarquinia is dated by Hencken to the Villanovan III period, starting 700 B.C., but – while it seems unlikely that these pieces were imported to Etruria – the similarity of style suggests that they were made in Italy by goldsmiths familiar with oriental models.

Pectorals on Urartian bronzes are important as evidence for connection between the Urartian-Median area and the West, and they can also be found on the Nimrud ivories, especially those carved in an Egyptianizing-Phoenician style.[3] Six fragments of narrow curved gold pectoral from Ziweye (pl. 190) now in the Teheran Iran Bastan Museum, decorated in filigree, can be compared with a pectoral worn by an unusual Nimrud ivory of a bearded male sphinx which Mallowan has described as a 'rare example of the blending of Syrian-Phoenician and Assyrian styles.'[4]

The bronze 'siren' figures, of which fine examples are known from Vetulonia and Gordion, also wear this type of curved pectoral; one of the Gordion figures and another from the Barbarini tomb at Cerveteri (pl. 192) both wear curved pectorals of the type shown in pl. 188 from Ziweye. These figures are usually considered products of Urartian–north Syrian workshops.[5] An unusual double-headed siren figure in the collection of the Marquis de Vogué shows a different type (pl. 193). Below each head a trapezoidal slot is gouged out of the metal with holes in the flat

[1] Ghirshman, *Persia*, p. 310, figs. 373–5.
[2] H. Hencken, *Tarquinia, Villanovans and Early Etruscans*, I, figs. 389, 390, pp. 402 f.
[3] Mallowan, *Nimrud*, I, p. 279, pl. 260, II, pl. 504, and many other examples.
[4] Ibid., II, pl. 538.
[5] K. R. Maxwell-Hyslop, 'Urartian bronzes in Etruscan tombs', *Iraq*, XVIII, 2, 1956, pp. 150–67. Ghirshman, *Persia*, p. 295.

surface to hold an inlay for a pectoral of gold, bone or other precious material. In this case, unlike the appliqués mentioned above from Ziweye, the width is greater than the height and the design would therefore run across the pectoral in the same way as the design shown on the pectoral worn by Ashurbanipal when he is shown on horseback hunting lions (fig. 121). Ashurbanipal's example, with two large rosettes and a square central

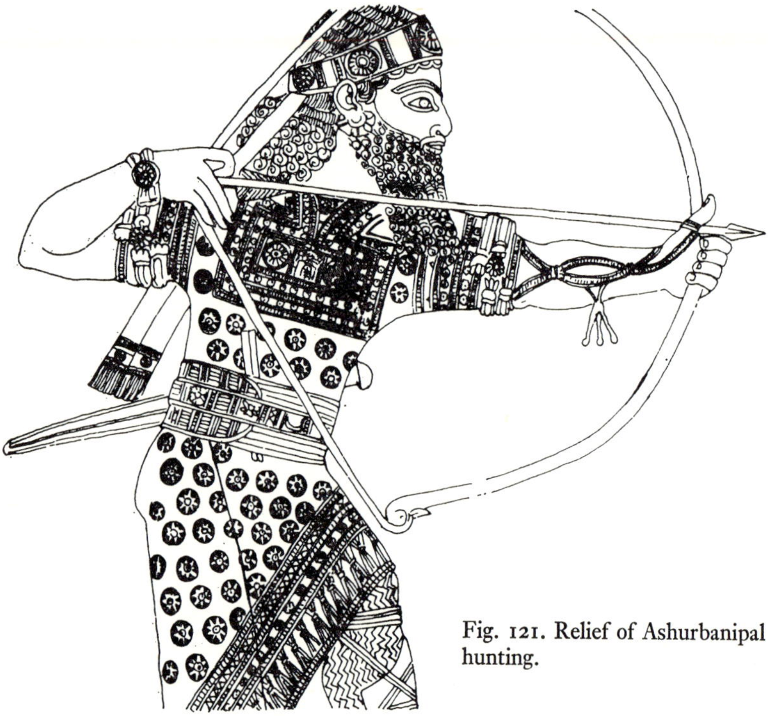

Fig. 121. Relief of Ashurbanipal hunting.

plaque of two standing figures, the sacred tree and sun disc, probably represents a pectoral whose base was leather covered with ornaments of gold, each piece placed so close together that the effect would have been the same as if the whole pectoral had been made of metal. The king's garment is covered with rosettes and these were probably metal, like the rosettes we have noted from Ziweye and elsewhere in Persia and Urartu. The king's wide diadem is also adorned with rosettes. The earrings and bracelets will be discussed on pp. 243, 248.

The bronze siren figures have been listed and studied by many scholars.[1] The examples from Gordion excavated by Professor Rodney Young have provided more important evidence for the Asiatic influence on the metallurgy of Greece and Italy, and recent excavations at Salamis[2] have contributed much to help define the exact nature of this influence. Trade, settlement of craftsmen whose livelihood was threatened by Assyrian occupation and the copying of oriental motifs and techniques by western smiths, familiar with oriental models, all contributed to the increasing close contact between Italy, Greece, Crete, Cyprus and Asia. This began in the eighth century B.C. and during the seventh century the foundations were laid for the widespread commercial contact between Asia and Europe at the time of the Achaemenian empire. In this context, there are certain objects related to the bronze siren figures which are relevant to the study of pectorals, and which reflect the influence of oriental religious conceptions on the west.

The winged siren lady can also be found above the sun disc on the Nimrud ivories,[3] holding a lily in each hand, and on the engraved *tridachna* shells from Ashur where she also wears a pectoral; this ornament can also be found on a winged sphinx engraved on a white limestone oliphant from Nimrud.[4] The lady is often associated with a lion; one of the Ashur shells shows her with a lion's body and at Gordion an alabastron of a lady (now in the Istanbul Museum) wearing elaborate necklaces in the shape of a pectoral holds a lion upside down between her hands. The same lady can be found in Italy, from the Polledrara tomb at Vulci where she holds the winged disc. This piece is now in the British Museum (pl. 194). On the *tridachna* shells and on many of the alabastra, which have been studied in detail by Riis,[5] the lady holds a flower. It is possible to link these representations of a lady, who must be a goddess, with the Babylonian Ishtar, whose attribute was the lion, the Hurrian Shaushga (also associated with the lion) and the Phoenician Astarte who, as we have seen on the gold plaques from Ras Shamra and other sites, holds the Plant of Life (pl. 106, see Chapter 8).

In the Ugaritic texts we can find mention of the goddess Shapash, a sun goddess who can also be linked with the lady in the sun disc on the Nimrud ivories. Another lady on the Nimrud ivories, portrayed seated

[1] See H. V. Herrmann, *Olympische forshungen*, VI, 1966, 'Die Kessel der Orientalisierenden Zeit'; and R. F. Young, 'A bronze bowl in Philadelphia', *J.N.E.S.*, 26, 3, 1967, pp. 145–54.

[2] V. Karageorghis, *Excavations in the Necropolis of Salamis*, I & II (Nicosia, 1967).

[3] Mallowan, *Nimrud*, II, pls. 392–4.

[4] Andrae, 'Gravierte Tridacna Muscheln aus Assur', *Z.A.*, 11(45), 1939, p. 88. *Nimrud*, I, p. 295.

[5] P. Riis, 'Sculptural Alabastra', *Acta Archaeologica*, XXVII, 1956, p. 28, fig. 4.

below a winged sun disc (Mallowan, *Nimrud*, II, 401, 402), wears a pectoral, holds a ring with beaded coil (similar to the centre of the sun disc with the lady above) in her right hand and the lotus tree in her left. On another panel the same lady is shown seated at a table holding an elaborate plant which is unique on the Nimrud panels. Mallowan quotes an inscription of Adad-Nirari III 'as agreeable to the people of Assyria as (is the smell of) the Plant of Life',[1] and he suggests that the enthroned ladies with banquet tables (of which the legs actually rest in the branches of a lily tree) may be protective spirits or goddesses. There is considerable evidence from north Syria and Asia Minor to reinforce this view and he cites a number of parallels from these areas. If the ladies are protective spirits, the female equivalent to the Assyrian *šēdu* or winged human-headed bulls, then texts from Boğazköy about the beneficent spirit, the Hittite *annariš*, should be noted.[2]

The pectorals may, therefore, be closely linked with the spread of the oriental idea of a goddess of love and fertility, although by the time that goldsmiths in Bulgaria and Yugoslavia were copying the oriental models in the sixth and fifth centuries B.C., this connection was probably entirely forgotten. The Regolini-Galassi and Tarquinia examples, however, may well have reflected a strand in the oriental religious influence which can be found in Etruscan religious practice.

Two triangular-shaped pieces from Ziweye (pl. 195) have been identified as possible shoulder guards or epaulettes, but they are ornamented in the same style as the trapezoidal pieces and it is possible that these should be classified as pectorals. Wilkinson has drawn attention to a seal from Babylon where a deity wears a similarly shaped pointed pectoral; another seal of Neo-Babylonian date in the British Museum shows two winged figures wearing similar ornaments.[3] Perhaps the best representation can be found on the rock reliefs near Ivriz in Cilicia where king Warpalawas wears a pointed pectoral as he stands worshipping the vegetation god Tarchon (fig. 153, Chapter 15). It is the head of this figure which has been compared with the fantastic winged figure on the base of the Barbarini cauldron and it is possible that this pointed form of pectoral was the model for the unusually long curved Regolini-Galassi example.[4]

1 *A.N.E.T.*, p. 281. *Nimrud*, II, p. 502, pl. 403.
2 M. H. Otten, 'Hittite *tarpiš* and Hebrew *terāphîm*', *J.N.E.S.*, XXVII, 1968.
3 C. Wilkinson, *Metropolitan Museum of Art Bulletin*, April 1963, p. 280; E. Unger, *Babylon, die Heilige stadt nach der Beschreibung der Babylonier*, p. 212, Abb. 43 (Berlin, Leipzig, 1931); Wiseman, *Cylinder Seals*, 71.
4 R. D. Barnett, 'Early Greek and oriental ivories', *J.H.S.*, LXVIII, 1948, p. 9.

Wilkinson has described the Ziweye pointed pectoral or epaulette (pl. 195) which is now lent to the Metropolitan Museum of Art, New York, as follows: 'The same sort of mythical beings that adorn the plaques decorate the border of this piece, with a similar guilloche running around the outer edge, but in the centre is a scene that occurs on no other gold fragment from Ziweye. Dominant is a large flying bird, somewhat resembling an eagle but with a curious long rope-like crest. In the grasp of its talons are two odd little creatures, perhaps infant griffins or the young of *Mischwesen*. One has the head of a young bird with an open beak, and the other the head of a young bullock, though with exposed, triangular teeth; both have animal bodies and the tails of antelopes or goats. Underneath the bird's beak and in much larger scale than the lion is a bearded human head, and the scene is completed by a small roaring lion that confronts the bird.'[1]

The curved crest on the bird's head is certainly the same as the crest on the striding winged griffins on the border of the pectoral and the association of lion and griffin recalls the use of these two animals on the bronze cauldron from the Barbarini tomb at Cerveteri in Italy (see p. 217) where the bronze protomes form the handles of the vessel. Winged sphinxes are often portrayed wearing pectorals (cf. the Philadelphia bowl, see p. 219, note 1) and the two naked ladies on the curious chariot attachment recently studied by Barnett also wear the same ornament.[2]

Finally, we can draw attention to the best analogies for the curved Ziweye pectoral. On the bronze figure of a man (now in the Berlin Museum) from Toprak Kale, a curved pectoral with five holes, presumably for inlay of gold or precious stones, is shown suspended round the neck of the figure; the sphinx from the same site (now in the British Museum) wears a similar curved pectoral decorated with rosettes (fig. 122). The sphinx from Toprak Kale now in the Hermitage[3] wears a plain curved pectoral, a rosette on each shoulder and a crown with centre rosette.

There are few extant pectorals of this type, apart from the Ziweye example. A bronze pectoral from Nor Aresh near Erivan[4] is decorated with repoussé circles and dots and has incised borders with the hooks for attachment to a cord which would pass round the neck still in place

[1] C. Wilkinson, op. cit., pp. 278 ff.
[2] R. D. Barnett, 'North Syrian and related harness decoration', *Vorderasiatische Archäeologie: Festschrift Anton Moortgat*, pp. 21 ff. (Berlin, 1964).
[3] Piotrovski, *Van*, fig. 34, p. 252. Akurgal, *Die kunst Anatoliens* (Berlin, 1961), p. 30.
[4] *A.S.*, XIII, 1963, p. 196, fig. 44.

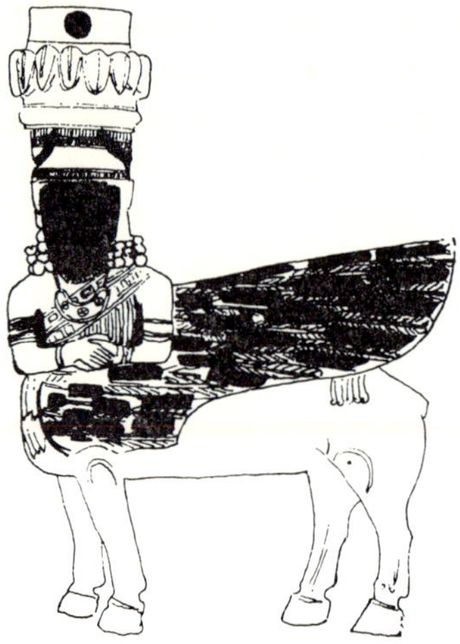

Fig. 122. Bronze sphinx with pectoral, armlets and bracelets.

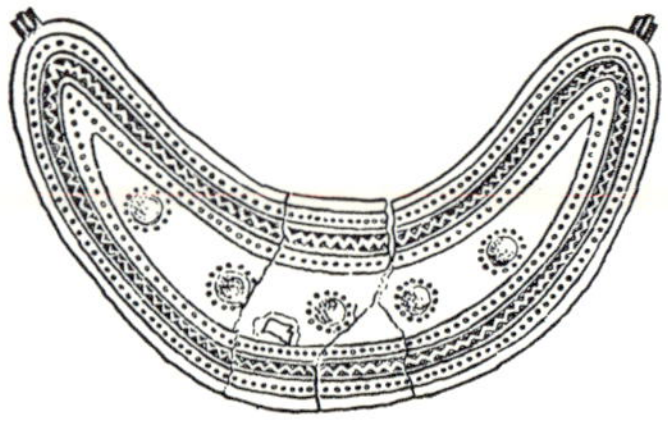

Fig. 123. Bronze pectoral from Nor-Aresh.

(fig. 123). Bronze pectorals with curved ends are also alleged to come from Luristan.[1]

Ghafantlu

Five kilometres from Ziweye, the village of Ghafantlu (or Khafantlu), possibly the Assyrian Izirtu and capital of the land of Mannai, known from the records of Sargon (722–705 B.C.), is given as the source of several gold roundels, one of which is now in the Nelson Galley, Atkins Museum, Kansas City, Missouri (pl. 196), and was recently published by Culican.[2] This piece is larger than the Ziweye examples, depicting a bearded figure holding two lions by the legs in a style which, while obviously Assyrian in inspiration, reflects local Iranian characteristics. The technique is skilled, with the design worked in repoussé and surrounded by applied filigree wires and granular triangles. There is a pair of holes on each side for attachment to material. Probably seventh century B.C.

The exaggerated left hand paw of each lion, which is depicted in a manner quite out of proportion to the body of the animal, is a distinctive feature which can also be found on the lion confronting the figure armed with shield and sword on one of the finest of the ivories from Ziweye[3] and also on the relief from Malatya now in the Ankara Museum.[4] It also

[1] Ghirshman, *Persia*, p. 314, 380(b). [2] Culican, *Medes and Persians*, pl. 18.
[3] Godard, *Ziweye*, fig. 81, p. 93. [4] E. Akurgal, *Art of the Hittites*, pl. 105.

occurs on the scabbards of Assyrian swords on reliefs, where two confronted lions turned their heads towards their tails,[1] and on the lions on Ashurbanipal's hunting reliefs.

Amlash

A gold moufflon head from Amlash, although not classified as jewellery, should be mentioned here, as the style and technique are comparable with a gold bracelet[2] with terminals in the shape of rams' heads also reputedly from Amlash and made in two halves with a band of gold decorated with granular triangles. Two similar bands encircle the bracelet below the head of each animal.

These pieces belong to the same class of object as the Ziweye bracelet (pl. 171a) and probably belong to the eighth to seventh centuries B.C. The moufflon head is bound with gold wire and decorated with granular triangles and may have been intended as the end of a fly whisk such as is portrayed on Assyrian reliefs of the ninth to eighth centuries B.C. (see fig. 140, Chapter 15). Whether or not these pieces and others executed in a similar style which have appeared on the market and in exhibitions of Iranian art, often from private collections, can be regarded as the products of Median goldsmiths is impossible to say until several Median sites have been scientifically excavated.

[1] J. C. Reade, 'Two slabs from Sennacherib's palace', *Iraq*, XXIX, 1, 1967, pl. XIII.
[2] *I.L.N.*, 2 April 1960, figs. 4 and 7.

CHAPTER 14

Palestine and Syria: Twelfth to Sixth Centuries B.C.

INTRODUCTION

The period covered in this chapter in Palestine deserves a full-scale study based on a detailed index of all the stratified gold and silver jewellery and the numerous pieces found in tombs. Studies of the associations of the jewellery and the distribution of the different types, together with detailed technical studies, all need to be undertaken. Here we can only draw attention to some of the problems which await solution and discuss some of the more important types based on those pieces of jewellery from selected sites which were easily accessible for study.

JEWELLERY FROM SELECTED SITES

Tell Fara (Beth-Pelet)

The introduction of painted Philistine pottery and the increasing use of iron for weapons, tools and small ornaments during the course of the twelfth century B.C. seem to coincide with the appearance of distinctive types of earrings in gold and silver, although the evidence from tombs containing Iron Age painted pottery does not suggest that gold or silver jewellery was used in any great quantities by the Philistines. The types now to be described could reasonably be regarded as the products of local Canaanite smiths, while during the later tenth and eighth centuries B.C., however, until the capture of Samaria by Sargon in 722 B.C., Urartian and Assyrian influence is discernible in the jewellery, continuing throughout the seventh century B.C. until the Babylonian king Nebuchadnezzar annexed Judah and sacked Jerusalem in 587 B.C.

The site of Tell Fara (Beth-Pelet) excavated by Sir Flinders Petrie in 1928–9 lies twenty-nine kilometres south of Ajjul (Gaza). A considerable amount of material is now in the Institute of Archaeology at London University. Apart from simple penannular earrings of bronze and occasionally of gold, there are two types illustrated here which come from published tomb groups and can be dated by the associated pottery and scarabs with reasonable accuracy.

Earrings

Tomb 552 is one of the few examples where gold and silver jewellery can be found associated with examples of painted Philistine pottery. A solid gold earring of drop-lunate type (cf. pl. 197) probably came from the same workshop as one from the neighbouring site of Gerar, where a similar piece has the same arrow-shaped mark on the base (*B.P.*, I, pl. XXII, 197). Tomb 552 was one of a distinctive group of five large chamber tombs which contained both Philistine pottery and a characteristic anthropoid coffin lid; it can be dated early in the twelfth century B.C. The occurrence of a dagger with bronze hilt cast on to an iron blade in the contemporary Tomb 542 shows that iron was beginning to be used. The drop-lunate type of solid gold earring is shown in pl. 197, with examples from Tomb 222 belonging to a cemetery which can be dated by the associated pottery to the Solomonic period – i.e. the tenth century B.C.

Tomb 222 is especially important for the dated earrings. Here, as well as the drop-lunate types (pl. 198d and e, for gold, silver, bronze and electrum examples) is a unique variety of the so-called tassel earrings, of which many examples were found at Tell Fara; here, however, the pendant, in the form of the calyx of a flower bud, is composed of gold strips and rows of coarse granules (pl. 198a, b and c). This granulated tassel earring comes late in the series. There is no evidence to connect them with Philistine pottery and the material prosperity which we can discern in tombs of the Solomonic period is reflected by the considerable amount of gold and silver work found in dated tenth-century tombs. Pl. 198a and c (from Tombs 222 and 518) shows different varieties of the tassel earrings, sometimes with a binding of gold wire between the tassel or calyx and the lunate body of the earring. A bronze dress pin, with the round head decorated with incised lines and pierced shank also comes from Tomb 222 (pl. 199).

In Tomb 605 a crude tassel earring with the gold binding simply shown by incised lines was associated with 'mulberry' earrings – i.e. earrings with lunate body and attached pendant of five large gold balls (pl. 200). This type also occurs in silver at Tell Fara and, on present evidence, a dating of eleventh to tenth century B.C. for the tassels and 'mulberry' earrings seems reasonable. A detailed typological study of these types with distribution maps would be useful. At present, the tassel earrings seem to be confined to the Gaza area. One example in Tomb 368 was associated with a scarab of Ramesses XI (1113–1085 B.C.), but this does not, of course, preclude a later date for the earring.

Assyrian influence at Tell Fara is evident among the jewellery from Tombs 201 and 202, both stone-built tombs with covering slabs in the same manner as those in cemeteries designated by Petrie as 100 and 200 and dated to the Solomonic period. The pottery and jewellery from Tomb 202, now in the Institute of Archaeology, London University, can be dated to the tenth century B.C. (possibly extending into the early ninth century B.C.), and the jewellery is clearly modelled on Assyrian originals. The gold earring with single large knob (pl. 201) is comparable with the gold earring with single knob found at Tell Halaf under the statue of the great goddess (see fig. 133 and p. 240). The Tell Halaf earrings are well-known types from the reliefs of Ashurnaṣirpal II (884–859 B.C.) and the variety with one knob is the simplest of the series. From the technical point of view, the Tell Halaf gold work is far more sophisticated and finely made.

Pl. 202 shows a wide gold strip with perforations in each corner, which may have formed part of a diadem, while a plain silver earring was made of silver plating over a bitumen core.

Tomb 201, of which the material is divided between the Institute of Archaeology, London University, and the Ashmolean Museum, covered a long period of use; the disordered contents included 120 bodies, fragments of bone horse trappings (blinkers and a frontlet – pl. 204), iron weapons, bracelets of bronze and iron and two gold strips perforated to form part of a diadem (pl. 203). The pottery here can be dated to the tenth to ninth centuries B.C. and to this period also belongs the pottery from Tomb 229. This included many small black-on-red juglets and a remarkable pottery chalice (*B.P.*, I, pl. XXXIX, 17) with a painted lotus flower and bud design well known from Assyria and Iran, especially on the Nimrud ivories and Ziweye silver work (Godard, *Ziweye*, fig. 102), where it is normally regarded as Phoenician in origin.

The jewellery from this large Tomb 229 (pl. 205) is noteworthy only for the 'pendant in the shape of a bull's horn'; this is clearly different from the crescent pendants discussed in Chapter 7, p. 149, and is roughly made from solid gold. A date around 900 B.C. is likely. The pendant can also be distinguished from the chariot yoke pendants with knobs discussed by Barnett in 1964.[1]

Beads

Associated with the 'tassel' and drop-lunate earrings in tombs of the Solomonic period at Tell Fara were silver melon-shaped beads of the type common in Syria and Mesopotamia in the mid and late second millennium B.C. and small cylindrical beads composed of a series of small gold balls soldered together. Ring beads made in the same technique also occurred (*B.P.*, I, pl. XXXVII). Tomb 204 produced fifteen gold beads of these latter two types and a gold earring. The small cylinder gold beads were also imitated in bronze (see pl. 206) in Tomb 837. The gold granulated cylinder beads are associated with the painted Philistine pottery in Tomb 552 (see above) and, while in Assyria the technique of granulation was certainly being practised in the twelfth century B.C., it was probably also used in Palestine.

Another twelfth-century B.C. instance of the occurrence of gold beads (fluted melon-shaped) is important, as the type was found at Tell Fara in Tomb 552 (see above) with Philistine painted pottery (pl. 207). An example from Ajjul (Tomb 1074, Institute of Archaeology – pls. 208 and 209) can be dated from the associated pottery to the tenth century B.C., or possibly to the eleventh or tenth centuries B.C. The Tomb 552 bead, however, is the earliest example at Tell Fara of a type which is especially common in Palestine in the tenth century B.C.

Silver earrings, eighth to sixth centuries B.C.

The problem of Urartian influence among the rich furnishing of Tomb 650 at Tell Fara, with the silver ladle with handle in the shape of a swimming lady and the bronze bed fittings, has been discussed by Barnett,[2] but no jewellery was found in this tomb. Assyrian influence is also apparent among the silver and bronze bowls found in other tombs and a study of these would be especially valuable now that the Nimrud material is published and comparisons can be made with Assyrian examples from the reliefs.

A pair of silver earrings, however, have survived from later tombs at Tell Fara (Tomb 754, see pl. 210) and these are made of hollow silver

[1] R. D. Barnett, *Comte Rendu de l'onzième rencontre Assyriologique Internationale*, p. 69 (Leiden, 1962).

[2] *Iranica Antiqua*, II, 1, p. 90. J. H. Iliffe, *Q.D.A.P.*, IV, pl. LXXXIX and XCI

balls soldered to a large hoop, with the base of the pendant composed of a triangle of small granules.[1] The particular technique and method of construction of the body of the earrings from large balls is more comparable with Iranian and Elamite work of this class; two fine examples from Susa (pl. 211), now in the Louvre, are important in this connection, as they come from dated eighth- to seventh-century B.C. neo-Elamite graves. Another example of this type (pl. 212), provenance unknown, is in the British Museum; here the pendant of gold balls with granular tips is fixed to a circular base supporting a loop through which passes an earring with wide pointed base. Hasanlu and Marlik also have produced simpler forms of the same basic type, while a fine gold example from Lachish[2] with the loop bound with wire was dated by Starkey to the sixth century B.C. (c. 597 B.C. – date of the destruction of Level III). A crude example of the type also occurs at Deve Hüyük[3] near Carchemish, where it may be as late as the fifth century B.C.

Petrie dates the Tell Fara example to c. 600 B.C., but Assyrian and Elamite examples suggest that its use must have spanned at least most of the seventh century B.C., as well as extending into the sixth century B.C.

Megiddo

Gold jewellery from the site of Megiddo was (pre-1967) in the Palestine Archaeological Museum and a few pieces dating from the Iron Age (1200–1000 B.C.) must be noted. References are to the 1961 Museum Gallery book. A pin (PAM 117 from Megiddo) is the only gold example among the many bronze examples from Palestinian sites which can be dated to the twelfth to tenth centuries B.C. It belongs to the same type as the bronze pin from Tell Fara noted above (pl. 199). The Iron Age dress pins are clumsier in design than the bronze and gold examples belonging to the Bronze Age (see pl. 74 and p. 113) and, by the end of the tenth century B.C., these pins began to be replaced in general use by the fibula (or safety pin) for dress fastening.

Gold mouthpieces which were placed on the mouths of the dead (several have been found *in situ*) were pierced at each end for attachment round the head in the same way as a diadem. PAM 120, from Beth-Shan, was found inside an anthropoid clay sarcophagus of a type well known

[1] See Fara Tomb 725 (Institute of Archaeology) for another silver example; Petrie *B.P.*, I, pl. XLVIII. This is closely comparable with the gold Lachish example.

[2] O. Tufnell, *Lachish, III: The Iron Age*, p. 160, fig. 15 (Oxford, 1957).

[3] *A.A.A.*, VII, pl. XXIII.

from Beth-Shan and Tell Fara (Tombs 552 and 562 – *B.P.*, I, pl. XXIV).

Gold melon-shaped plain and fluted beads, with and without collars, were plentiful in the Iron Age levels at Megiddo; the same fluted varieties with collars, of varying sizes, are known from Beth-Shemesh.

Beth-Shemesh

Ain-Shems (Beth-Shemesh or House of the Sun God) lies on the road between Jerusalem and Gaza at a natural junction of routes. This site produced a considerable amount of gold jewellery which was displayed (pre-1967) in the Palestine Museum. Many beads (asymmetrical barrel-shaped, large and small varieties, fluted melon-shaped beads with collars and minute plain spherical beads) are types known on Palestinian sites of this period – while the gold and silver drop-lunate earrings and a crescent-shaped pendant can be paralleled at Tell Fara.

A gold pendant, probably for attachment to an earring, also comes from Beth-Shemesh; this is in the form of the bud of a flower, probably a pomegranate, and the petals are clearly marked. It can be closely related to Assyrian examples (fig. 127: 28) and may date from the time of the Assyrian invasion of Palestine under Sennacherib in 701 B.C., or may have been imported during the earlier centuries of the first millennium B.C.

Al Mina

The site of Al Mina, at the mouth of the river Orontes in the Sanjak of Alexandretta, was excavated by Sir Leonard Woolley in 1936 and 1937. After the destruction of Alalakh, the harbour town of Al Mina was rebuilt and has provided important evidence for Asiatic-Greek trade from c. 825 B.C. (the beginning of the lowest level X) and continuing into the fourth century B.C. Remains of large warehouses were excavated and the site yielded Syrian, Cypriote and Greek pottery.[1] A fine gold and electrum necklace (Greek work of the fifth century B.C.) is outside the scope of this study. A jeweller's workshop also belonged to this period, but the lower levels produced a mould for making jewellery (Level VIII), some gold casings for beads with attached circular gold pendants (Ashmolean Museum 1938 293A) and a fine earring (pl. 213) now in the Ashmolean Museum (1937. 769).

[1] *J.H.S.*, LVIII, pp. 1–30, 133–70; *Iraq*, XXI, 1, 1959, pp. 62–92; *B.S.A.*, 52, 1957, pp. 5 ff., *J.H.S.*, LX, pp. 2 ff.

Gold is known to occur near Al Mina in the Melas valley and the occurrence of considerable quantities of liquid mercury both at Seleucia and Al Mina (probably, as Woolley suggests, imported from the Almaden mines of Spain), used for the extraction of gold, suggests that the tradition of jewellery working at Al Mina may date from the earliest period of the occupation of the site. This source of gold may also have been used by the jewellers at Alalakh.

The magnificent earring (pl. 213) was unstratified but can be dated to the seventh to sixth centuries B.C. It is the normal boat-shaped Phoenician type and a closely comparable example from Cyprus could have originated in the same workshop.[1] Two similar pairs of earrings of this type, from Amrit in Syria, in the collection of the Comte de Putyison (pl. 214) in Paris, also show the distinctive filigree looped spiral pattern on each end of the body of the earring, combined with an arrangement of triangles executed in minute granules, which is identical on all three pairs. The ends of the earrings, which act as the sockets for the pin, are also identical on all three pairs; two circles of gold wire enclose a ring of gold balls.

Alalakh – Levels 1 and 0

The cremation graves at Alalakh[2] represent an intrusive element in the population; the fashion of cremation began as early as the fifteenth century B.C. at Alalakh, but it was not until after the invasions of the 'Sea Peoples' in the early twelfth century B.C. that the practice became common for a large proportion of the inhabitants of Syria and Palestine. At Alalakh, five intact cremation burials were excavated, of which two (ATG 38/2 (pl. 215) and ATG 37/2) deserve special mention for the jewellery included among the grave contents.

ATG 38/2, the burial of a child (Woolley, *Alalakh*, fig. 70), now in the Ashmolean Museum, contained a remarkable gold circular plaque with two clasps on the back to facilitate fastening to a strip of material or leather – probably a headband or narrow belt. The edges are bound with a double twisted gold wire and two circles of running spirals finely executed in filigree encircle a setting for a central inlay of paste and probably a central precious stone, now missing. Ashmolean Museum 1939 413 – diameter 1·3 cm. Four circular gold buttons, a pair of fragmentary penannular earrings of gold and silver and a gold crescent (also damaged) are included in the inventory of the jewellery.

[1] Gjerstad, *S.C.E.*, IV, 2, fig. 34, 2, Nicosia Museum.

[2] Woolley, *Alalakh*, pp. 203 ff.

ATG 37/2, with a scarab with a cartouche of Ramesses VI, can be definitely assigned to the post-destruction period and not earlier than the middle of the twelfth century B.C. (Level 0). A gold pendant with impressed cruciform design, gold, amber, frit and glass beads, and a penannular gold earring with a globular pendant of blue glass comprise the inventory of the jewellery. The earring is a simpler type of a well preserved example found in an inhumation grave belonging to Level 1, where three blue beads were strung on a gold rod pendant.

Plain penannular earrings from Level 1 were usually made of silver, but the elaborate example described above was of gold.

CHAPTER 15

Assyria and Iran: Ninth to Seventh Centuries B.C.

INTRODUCTION

The expansion of Assyria under Ashurnaṣirpal II (884–859 B.C.) is the start of a period during which, in contrast to the preceding three centuries, we have a wealth of archaeological evidence for the activities of jewellers and goldsmiths. This is mainly based on the detailed portrayal of jewellery on the reliefs; extant examples are few, due to the fact that jewellery is the easiest kind of valuable loot to carry away and therefore it is not surprising that little has been recovered from either tombs or buildings dating from this period. The systematic sacking of Nineveh by the Medes, Scythians and Babylonians in 612 B.C. ensured that few gold objects should be left for modern excavators; the main Assyrian sites of this period, Ashur, Nimrud, Khorsabad and Nineveh, have yielded only isolated examples of jewellery.

However, the reliefs provide a mass of important dated material and the few extant examples of Assyrian jewellery which exist can usually be dated by reference to the representations. It must also be remembered that the wealth of gold jewellery which has recently been discovered in Persia and which has found its way into private collections or to dealers, with often no or extremely inadequate information as to its source, may in fact have been pillaged from Nineveh and carried to Iran as loot. It might then have been buried in the tomb of a local ruler and later looted by peasants in present-day Iran. Ghirshman has discussed this question when considering the inscribed 'Luristan' bronzes and the part played by the Cimmerians in the seventh century B.C., employed as mercenaries by the Assyrians and possibly used by Sennacherib who destroyed many Elamite cities in his campaign of 693 B.C.[1] While there is little evidence for the activities of specific groups of looters, the part played by the Medes in this kind of activity all over the vast area they controlled in the

[1] In *Iraq*, XXII, 1960, pp. 210–12.

west in the seventh century B.C. needs little imagination to assess; the fact that jewellery was not only used as votive offerings but formed an essential part of the clothing and adornment of both gods and goddesses in the temple would ensure that it was unlikely to be missed either by an invading army or by the marauders in their train. The chronological value of the evidence given by the reliefs is, therefore, obvious in comparison with that afforded by extant examples of this period, especially when found in areas outside the confines of the Assyrian empire; we have discussed the question of jewellery as imports, tribute or presents in Chapter 11. Here, we would stress the importance of a detailed study of the Assyrian reliefs before any attempt is made to date or determine the origin of the mass of unstratified material which is being discovered in Persia today.

The few outstanding pieces of stratified Assyrian jewellery give some indication of the richness of the material which was dispersed in 612 B.C. The site of Zincirli has yielded many examples of seventh century B.C. craftsmanship, whose designs can be traced to Assyrian, Phoenician or Urartian origins, but the techniques used were common to all western Asiatic centres of jewellery working at this time. Nimrud has produced one superb example of the jeweller's art, but modern excavators were preceded by ancient looters at other Assyrian sites.

EXTANT ASSYRIAN JEWELLERY

The Nimrud jewel

The most remarkable piece of extant Assyrian jewellery is the Nimrud jewel, found in the grave of a princess in a room of the north-west palace at Nimrud (pl. 216). The jewel was attached to a bronze fibula by a gold chain composed of thick double links. It consisted of an oval pendant of pale mauve chalcedony (2·2 × 1·2 cm) engraved with 'two figures playing the pipes on either side of the sacred tree . . . The gold chain is attached to a link on a swivel; the pear-shaped drops on either side of the ogival holder are soldered to the heavy wire binding'.[1] As Professor Mallowan has stated, this jewel is a triumph of the goldsmith's art and suggests a date of 681–669 B.C.

A badly corroded silver seal holder, which can be dated to a period contemporary with the Nimrud grave containing the jewel, comes from

[1] Mallowan, *Nimrud*, I, pp. 114 f.

the Amman cave-tomb with the seal of Adoni-Nur (see p. 261). Other parallels for the Nimrud jewel come from Khorsabad and Zincirli.

The Zincirli Treasure

A group of gold objects from the site of Zincirli in south-east Turkey belongs to the early first millennium B.C. However, some of these, as Mallowan has shown, can be dated to the last quarter of the ninth century B.C., as a gold tube (probably the covering of a staff or sceptre) is inscribed with the name of Kalamu, a local ruler contemporary with Shalmaneser III.[1]

A gold scarab holder and a gold seal pendant (fig. 124a and b) are comparable in technique with the Nimrud jewel and are probably contemporary with it. The mount of the seal pendant has ram's head terminals which encase a dark stone engraved with a bull. This superb example of seventh-century craftsmanship was found at the entrance to the Kalamu building whose destruction is fixed by a tablet to 676 B.C.

Other finds from Zincirli[2] include an oval gold pendant with a figure of the nude goddess, round silver pendants decorated in gold leaf with rolled-over top portraying the goddess Ishtar on her lion, a square electrum pendant with a seated figure before a table, a circular electrum pendant and silver earrings of ninth-century type (see fig. 127:4). A silver fibula with flat bow and angular beadings below the pin may be the prototype for the Gordion fibula (pl. 246). A gold earring (fig. 124c) is decorated with triangular granules and a bordering of gold wire at the base of the pin; three hollow gold circles attached to the base suggest that an inlay of stones is missing and the type may be a simple variety of Ashurbanipal's earring (fig. 127:31).

Pendant from Ashur

A chalcedony pendant set in a silver mount comes from the Late Assyrian Grave 64 (fig. 125).

Electrum triple-armed earrings from (?) Toprak Kale, Van

A fine pair of triple-armed earrings has recently been discovered in the Museum für Kunst und Gewerbe, Hamburg, and I am indebted to Dr H. Hoffman for the photograph and for permission to publish it here (pl.

[1] Mallowan, *Nimrud*, I, p. 328, note 21; W. Andrae, *Ausgrabungen in Sendschirli*, V, Taf. 47 f, g.
[2] Ibid., Taf. 46i, 46a–h, 44q, 45g, 43w.

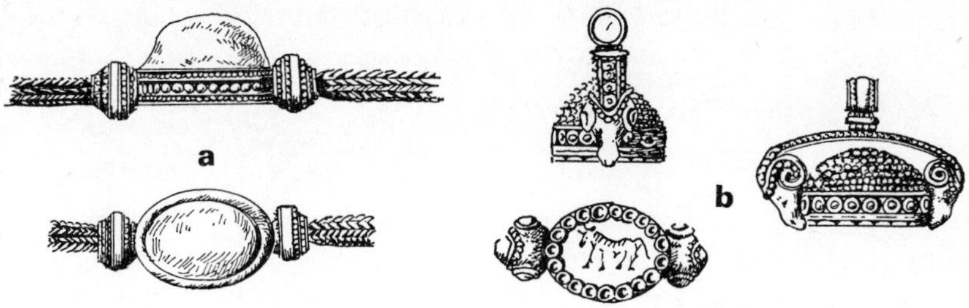

Fig. 124. Gold scarab and seal holders and gold earrings from Zincirli.

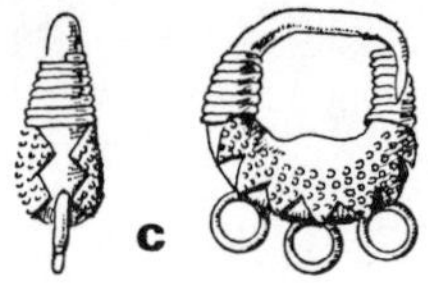

Fig. 125. Chalcedony pendant set in silver from Ashur.

225).[1] This is undoubtedly the type portrayed on Assyrian reliefs (fig. 127:6–8) from the time of Ashurnaṣirpal II, including the reign of Tiglath-Pileser III. Hoffman considers it probable that this pair of earrings may have been brought to Hamburg by Lehmann-Haupt with the famous Urartian candelabrum. It is clear that these earrings must have been produced on a large scale, but it is not known whether the centre of production was Urartu or Assyria, or both areas.

JEWELLERY PORTRAYED ON ASSYRIAN RELIEFS

Earrings

A comprehensive catalogue of Assyrian earrings portrayed on Assyrian reliefs, with a discussion of the few extant examples, has been made by Dr Tariq Madhloom.[2] I am grateful to Dr Madhloom for the drawings of sixty-three different earrings especially made for this work, shown here in figs. 126 and 127, which (with some additions and omissions) correspond to the two figures of earrings reproduced in his book. Type 1 (fig.

[1] H. Hoffman in *Archaeologisher Anzeiger*, 1969, 3, p. 369, Abb. 55a–d. [2] *Neo-Assyrian Art*.

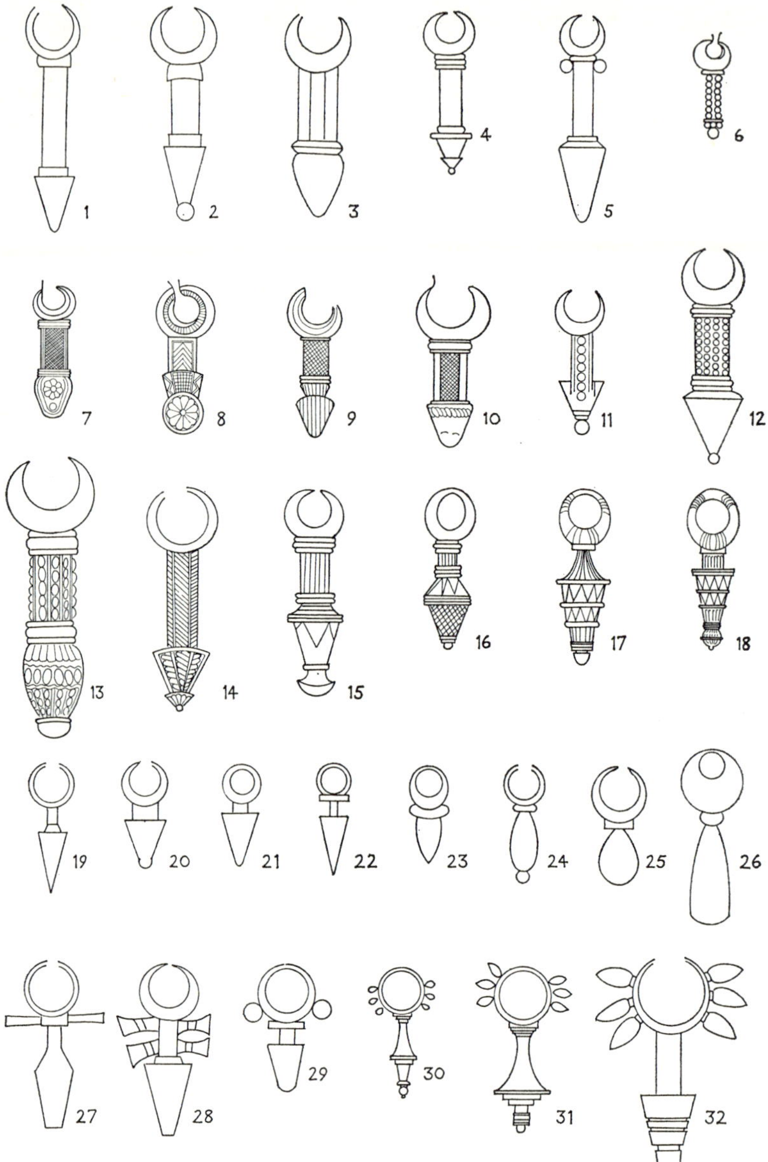

Fig. 126. Earrings from Assyrian reliefs. Type 3.

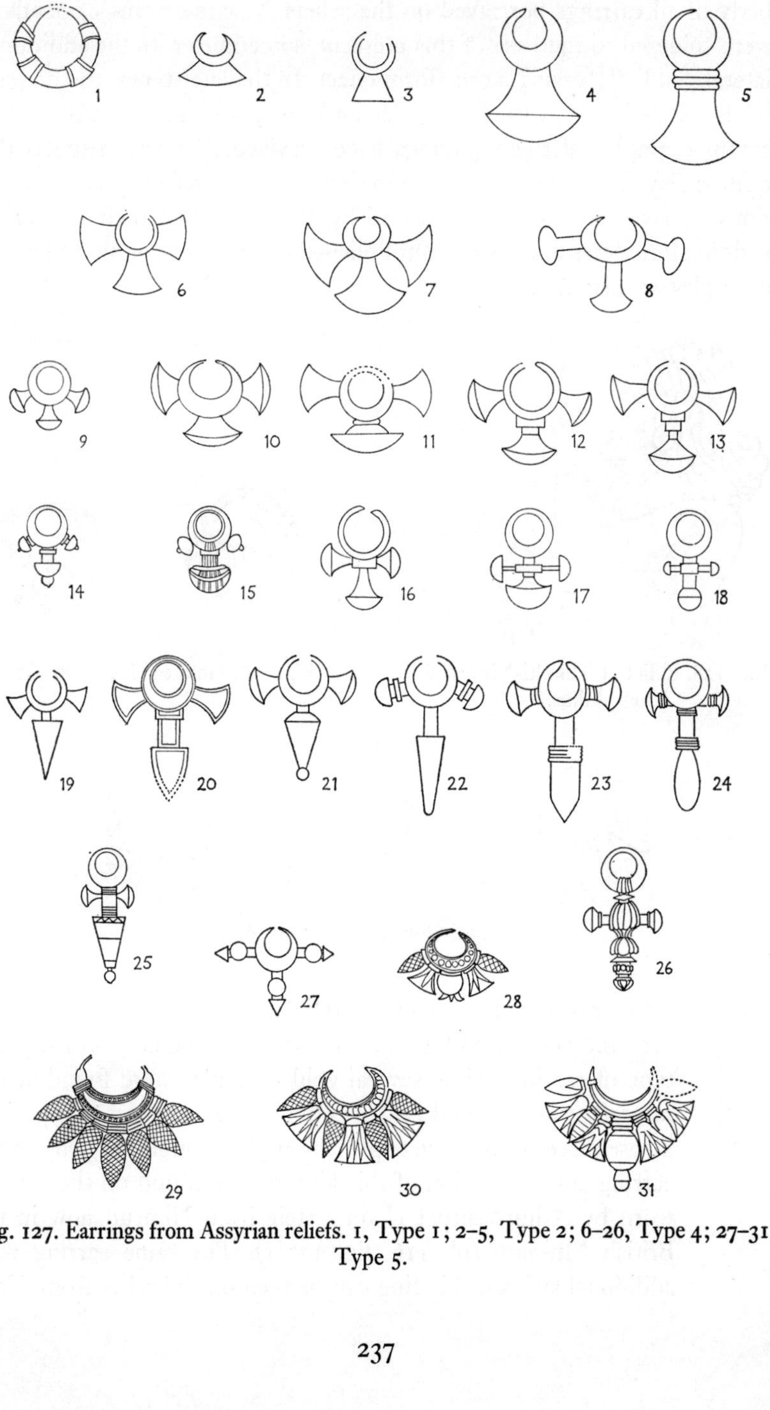

Fig. 127. Earrings from Assyrian reliefs. 1, Type 1; 2–5, Type 2; 6–26, Type 4; 27–31, Type 5.

127:1) is the simplest form in the shape of a crescent which is used as the body of all earrings portrayed on the reliefs. Varying forms of pendants were soldered to the base of this crescent, sometimes with the addition of lateral pendants, giving a cruciform effect. In the later types, the crescent is also embellished with lotus buds and flowers or pomegranates. Few extant examples of these earrings have survived, but one suspects that quite a few Assyrian earrings are in fact unrecognized in private collections or have been used and restored by dealers, so that their true origin is difficult to determine. Some unpublished and recently published extant examples are also noted.

Fig. 128. Relief of Tukulti-Ninurta I from Ashur.

Fig. 129. Gold earrings from Ashur.

Fig. 130. Gold earrings from Ashur.

Type 1 Crescent-shaped earrings. A relief of Tukulti-Ninurta (1244–1208 B.C.) (fig. 128) found at Ashur shows the king wearing this type of earring, while several gold examples were found at the same site (figs. 129 and 130) in graves of the Late Assyrian period. These pieces have three triple ribs applied round the body of the earring and decoration of this kind can be found on the earring worn by Ashurnaṣirpal II on a stele from Nimrud now in the British Museum (pl. 116, fig. 127:1). The same earring with additional strips of binding can be seen on the relief from Alaca now in the Museum of Archaeology, Istanbul, worn by the 'sword eater' and the two small figures, one of whom climbs a ladder.[1] A similar example was found at Ephesus.[2] The earring worn by one of the soldiers on the frescoes from Til Barsib[3] with triangular decoration, probably indicating granulation (fig. 131a) is a development from this type, while the plain crescent shape is also found on the Til Barsib frescoes (fig. 131b). This type has been described as 'Lydian'[4] and an example in gold from north-

131 (a)

131 (b)

132

Fig. 131. Heads of attendants from a Til Barsib fresco.

Fig. 132. Relief from Nimrud showing Assyrian soldier and captive.

west Persia (fig. 112) where the body of the earring is divided into segments by triangles of granules must represent the final development of this type, which seems to have been borrowed by the Lydians, as it is typical of the jewellery from Sardis. It also occurs in Cyprus.[5] The Neo-Babylonian variety is shown in pl. 217 in a group of jewellery from Uruk with the thin gold wire hoop decorated with small gold balls.

[1] M Vieyra, *Hittite Art 2300–750 B.C.*, pl. 30 (London, 1955).
[2] D. G. Hogarth, *Excavations at Ephesus*, pl. XII, 16 (London, 1908); *B.M.C.J.*, pl. X, No. 1065.
[3] Thureau-Dangin, *Til Barsib*, pl. LXIV, 4. [4] R. D. Barnett, *C.A.H.*, No. 56, p. 13.
[5] Gjerstad, *S.C.E.*, IV, 2, fig. 34, 3.

The so-called boat- or leech-shaped earring is uncommon on ninth-century Assyrian reliefs, as it is basically a Mid-Assyrian type known from extant examples from Ashur (see fig. 108). A captive chieftain of the time of Ashurnaṣirpal II, however, is shown wearing a small boat-shaped earring (fig. 132), while a gold example was found at Tell Halaf in a pot under the great goddess with other earrings of Assyrian type which are noted on p. 241 (fig. 133; see also pl. 250 from War Kabud, Luristan).

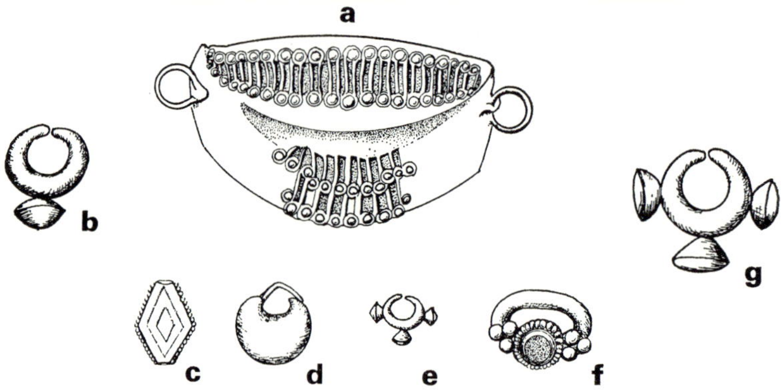

Fig. 133. Gold jewellery from Tell Halaf.

Type 2 Crescent-shaped earring with single mushroom-shaped pendant (fig. 127:2–5). All the examples, in various forms, come from the reliefs of Ashurnaṣirpal II, with the exception of one unusual type (of which we now only have a drawing) on a relief of Tiglath-Pileser III where the pendant is exceptionally long.[1] This may be the origin of the next type listed here (Type 3). A fine gold example with mushroom-shaped single pendant comes from the collection of jewellery found in the pot under the great goddess at Tell Halaf (fig. 133b).

Type 3 Earring with single pendant and conical tip (fig. 126:1–5, 7–18). This is the commonest form of Assyrian earring and was worn from the ninth century B.C. onwards. There are many variations of the basic type and different kinds of decoration are shown on the reliefs. The period covered includes the reigns of Ashurnaṣirpal II, Shalmaneser III Shamshi-Adad V, Tiglath-Pileser III,

[1] Barnett, *Tiglath-Pileser III*, pls. XCV, XCVI.

and Sargon, where both granulation and filigree work are portrayed. Two examples now in the Allen Art Museum, Oberlin, Ohio, are shown in pl. 218a and b, and can be compared with fig. 126:12. One of the rare pieces of extant Assyrian jewellery was found in the palace of Adad-Nirari III at Nimrud. This was an earring of a copper ring with cylindrical socket, into which was fitted a rock crystal pendant (pl. 219). A fine example with gold ring and paste (glass?) pendant is in the Mazda Collection, Teheran (colour pl. H); this piece is said to have come from Luristan, but is obviously Assyrian.

This type of pendant earring is sometimes embellished with small round projections on the body of the earring and fig. 126:5 shows an example from the reign of Ashurnaṣirpal II. Other examples date from the reign of Sargon and there may be as many as six round or cone-shaped additions (fig. 126:29–32). Earrings of this type have been found on bronze statuettes from Luristan and also in bronze, imitating the Assyrian type in Luristan. Crude examples in silver were found in Cemetery B at Sialk (see p. 265).

Type 4 Triple-armed earring (fig. 127:6–27). There are many variations of this type, which can be dated from the ninth century B.C. onwards; the evolution from the simple solid type with three projections, one on each side and one at the base of the crescent-shaped body of the earring, to the elaborate forms dating from the reign of Sargon can be followed from the numerous examples portrayed on the reliefs. This earring is sometimes shown on the trays of jewellery carried by tribute-bearers, both on stone reliefs and ivories (fig. 134) dating from Ashurnaṣirpal II and Shalmaneser III. It is worn by Ashurnaṣirpal himself on a limestone head in the Fitzwilliam Museum, Cambridge (pl. 220). It is interesting that the triple-armed earring seems to have been brought as tribute to the Assyrians by tributaries from the west – Aramaens, Phoenicians and the land of Qalparunda[1] – and also from Iranian chieftains, possibly Medes, as well as Babylonians. A fine gold earring of this type is in the Museum für Kunst und Gewerbe in Hamburg (pl. 225). One magnificent example in gold was found at Tell Halaf with jewellery under the great goddess (fig. 133g).

[1] See P. Hulin in *Iraq*, XXV, pp. 48–69; Mallowan, *Nimrud*, II, pp. 446 ff.

Another interesting example can be seen on one of the reliefs from Carchemish from the Citadel Staircase[1] (c. 820 B.C.), now in the British Museum (B.M. No. 125010). In the reign of Tiglath-Pileser III the arms of the earring are longer and thinner than on the ninth-century examples (fig. 127:8). This form can be seen in the field on a cylinder seal in the British Museum, which can be dated to the reign of Tiglath-Pileser III or Sargon (pl. 221).

Fig. 134. Ivory panel from Nimrud showing triple earrings as tribute.

During the Sargonid period a combination of the triple-armed and the pendant type of earring was common (fig. 127:19–25); there were many different varieties of this form, which was also worn by Sennacherib and by the Assyrian provincial governor of Gozan (Tell Halaf) in 727 B.C.[2]

The final development of the triple-armed earring can be found in the reign of Sargon, when the arms were given the addition of small balls or granules of gold (fig. 127:14) and this variation continued into the reign of Esarhaddon and Ashurbanipal. It can also be found on a Greek vase of the sixth century B.C., where it may represent one of the types either imported or copied by Greek jewellers in the seventh century B.C.[3]

Type 5 The earliest form of this type can be found on the rock reliefs of Sennacherib and the gods at Hines, where it is worn by the god

[1] *Carchemish*, III, p. 161, pl. B35d. [2] A. Moortgat, *A.F.O.*, 4, 1927, pl. VII, 5, p. 197.
[3] C. Kardara, *A.J.A.*, 1961, pp. 62–4, pl. 36, fig. 8.

Ashur and by the king himself (fig. 135). Rows of pomegranate-shaped pendants are attached to the crescent-shaped body of the earring; the same use of pomegranates (the symbol of fertility) can be found on an earring on the side of the relief of Esarhaddon (681–669 B.C.) worn by a figure identified by Thureau-Dangin as the crown prince of Assyria, the future king Ashurbanipal (fig. 136). Recently, J. M. Reade has suggested that two reliefs from the palace of Sennacherib, one in Berlin and the other in the Metropolitan Museum, New York (pl. 222), should be identified not with the vizier or *turtan*, but with a crown prince who was the heir to the throne designated by Sennacherib. The legitimate heir to the throne nominated by Sennacherib was his son Esarhaddon; the evidence of this earring, however, suggests that the relief may portray Ashurbanipal, the grandson of Sennacherib.

Fig. 135. Earring from a rock relief of Sennacherib.

Fig. 136. Ashurbanipal wearing bracelets and earrings, from a Zincirli relief.

The earring is clearly the same elaborate type known from the reliefs of the time of Ashurbanipal (see fig. 127:28–31), where it is worn by the king; this type with buds and flowers is unknown in Assyria before the seventh century B.C. The earrings worn by Ashurbanipal and his queen[1] show clearly that the crescent-shaped body of the earring was usually decorated with fine granulation, often the ends were bound with gold wire (fig. 127:29) and the series of lotus buds and flowers could be

[1] Barnett, *Assyrian Reliefs*, pl. 105.

combined with a central pomegranate or stylized pomegranate pendant.

These earrings certainly mark the apogee of technical skill of the Assyrian jewellers, and, while we have very little in the way of extant examples to compare with the fine pieces shown on the reliefs, two sites (Ashur and Ur) have produced earrings which can be compared with this elaborate type. At Ur a remarkable hoard of jewellery and other objects was found in the temple of E-nun-maḫ under the Persian pavement and above a floor of the period of Nebuchadnezzar.[1] These objects, however, as Woolley has pointed out, are of widely differing dates – as one would expect in any collection of precious objects stored in a temple treasury; the earrings (pl. 223), U.460 A and B, can be more closely related to the earrings on Ashurbanipal's reliefs than to any jewellery definitely dated to the Persian period. The catalogue entry reads: 'A pair of gold earrings, crescent shaped, width 2 cm. The sides are decorated with bands of granulated work and were inlaid with lapis lazuli, the ends are formed of coils of fine wire with knobs above, one of which takes the spring of the pin and the other is hollow and acts as the pin's socket. From the base project silver wires which probably held stone beads.' These beads would have probably been made in the shape of the lotus buds and flowers attached to Ashurbanipal's earrings (fig. 127:30, 31). An electrum earring from (?) Van (pl. 224) is possibly related to the earrings on Ashurbanipal's hunting reliefs.[2]

At Ashur two silver earrings, one from Grave 864 (fig. 137a) and the other in the Berlin Museum,[3] have the central pendant in the same shape as that in fig. 127:31, possibly a stylized pomegranate; the side blobs could have been (before corrosion) parts of the lotus flowers.

A type not usually shown on the reliefs is known from many extant gold and silver examples, of which several come from Ashur in dated tombs. Four examples from Babylon in the British Museum are of gold. Pl. 226 (B.M. 124620) shows the pendant in the shape of a lotus bud with three petals fixed with

[1] *Ur Excavations*, IX, pp. 29 ff. [2] Hoffman, op. cit., Abb. 56.

[3] Liane Jacob Rost, 'Zum Orhschmuck der Assyrer in Staatliche Museum zu Berlin', *Forchungen und Berichte*, 5, pp. 37 ff., Abb. 15.

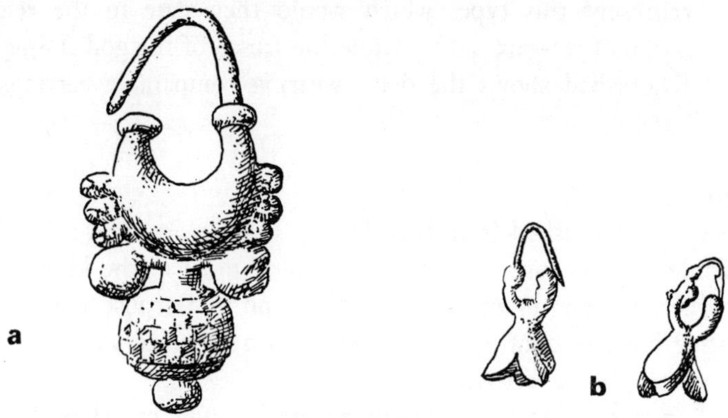

Fig. 137. Silver earrings from Ashur.

Fig. 138. Deity with earrings from a Khorsabad fresco.

circular bands decorated in granulation to a plain crescent-shaped pin.

Two examples from Ashur, Late Assyrian Tomb 64 (fig. 137b), are in silver, with no granular decoration, and the lotus flower is fixed directly to the crescent-shaped body of the earring. Another example from Ashur in silver is now in the Berlin Museum;[1] the bud and three petals are attached to the crescent-shaped body of the earring, whose ends are bound with gold wire. It is possible that the earrings shown on the reliefs from Khorsabad, worn by the soldiers (fig. 126:23, 24, 25), may

[1] Ibid., Abb. 14.

represent this type, which would then date to the reign of Sargon (722–705 B.C.) – while the fresco of the god Ashur from Khorsabad shows the deity wearing comparable earrings (fig. 138).

Armlets

These are distinguished from bracelets by being worn above the elbow. The armlet was an essential part of the adornment of the king and the priest when engaged in ritual ceremonies, and its purpose was not only decorative but also apotropaic. It is also worn by officers and courtiers. There are two main varieties.

(*a*) Plain (fig. 139). The open-ended armlets and bracelets (figs. 140 and 141) of the same type were often worn by officials and differ only in size. The two ends are shown overlapping and many of the examples portrayed may well have been of bronze. More frequently, the plain open-ended armlet was worn with a rosette bracelet (fig. 139); this occurs frequently on representations of winged deities.

(*b*) With animal heads at each end (figs. 142 and 143). The ends could be in the form of a lion, moufflon or bull calf and the accuracy of the sculptor makes it possible usually to distinguish the different animals' heads (figs. 142, 143 and 144). The *Apkallu* figure from Khorsabad, usually referred to as 'Gilgamesh and the Lion',[1] wears elaborate armlets with bull's head finials and lion-headed bracelets. Another bronze example of this type (pl. 227) is in the Louvre with bull-calf heads (see p. 204). A bronze bracelet, originally covered with silver plating and terminals of moufflon heads is in the Ashmolean Museum (pl. 228) and has Zahleh, Lebanon, as provenance. It can probably be identified as Assyrian. The same type is shown as tribute on a dish with a pair of triple earrings carried by a foreign tributary (pl. 229). These reliefs come from Nimrud and belong to Ashurnaṣirpal's time. One was found by Layard and two more fragments by Mallowan in 1952. It is not possible to say whether they are intended as armlets or bracelets.

Bracelets

In the ninth century B.C. single or double armlets, either plain or with animal head finials, were combined with thick bracelets to which a rosette was attached (fig. 145). These rosettes were probably gold or covered with gold leaf (figs. 146 and 147) and the body of the bracelet when worn

[1] H. H. Rowley (ed.), *Atlas of Mesopotamia*, pl. 216 (London, 1962).

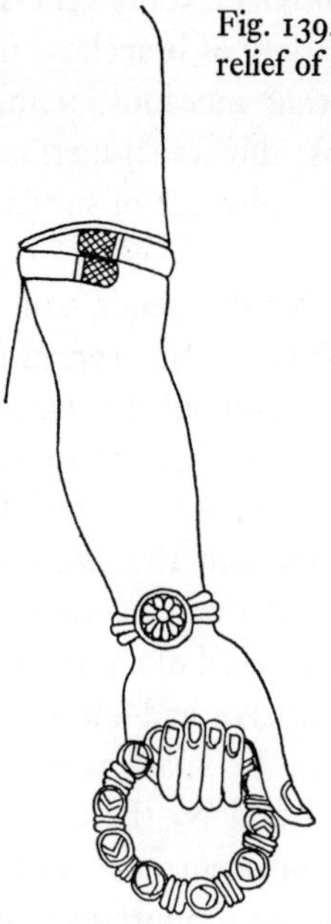

Fig. 139. Jewellery from a relief of Ashurnaṣirpal II.

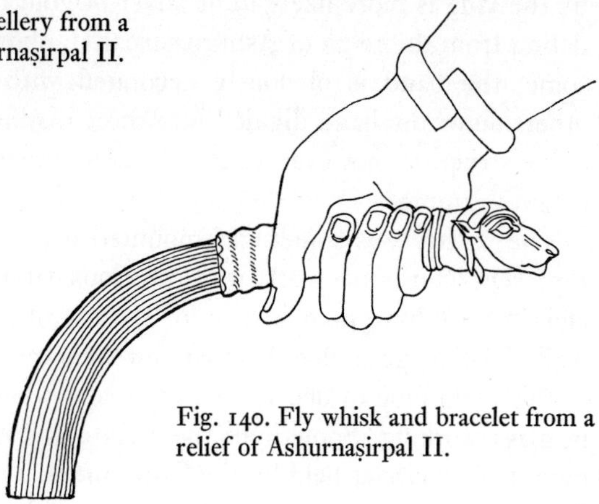

Fig. 140. Fly whisk and bracelet from a relief of Ashurnaṣirpal II.

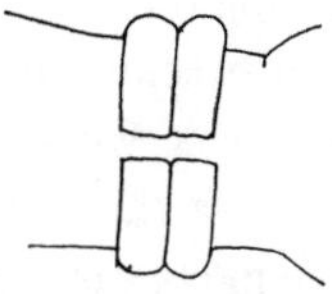

Fig. 141. Double bracelet from a relief of Ashurnaṣirpal II.

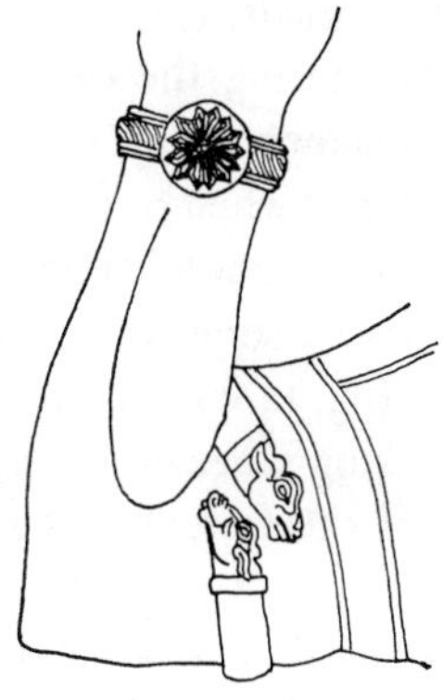

Fig. 142. Bracelets and armlets from a relief of Ashurnaṣirpal II.

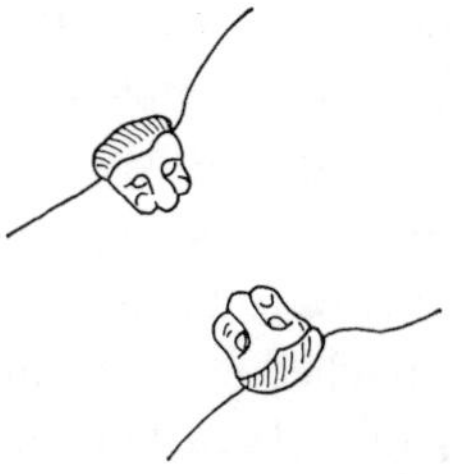

Fig. 144. Bracelet with lion head finials from a relief of Ashurbanipal.

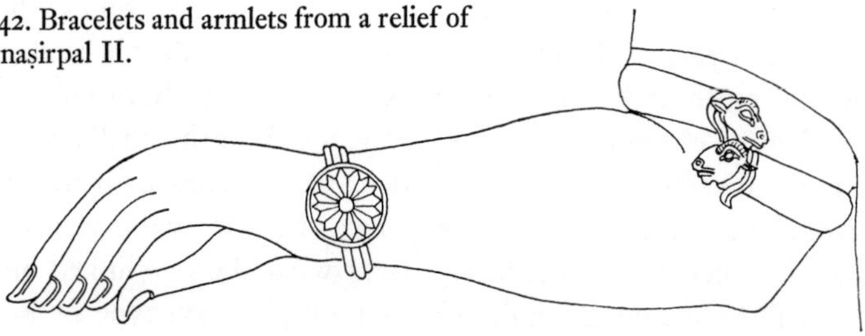

Fig. 143. Bracelets and armlets from a relief of Ashurnaṣirpal II.

by the king is more likely to be silver or gold than bronze. Many reliefs, dating from the reign of Ashurnaṣirpal II, show a variety of bracelets; in some, the band is obviously decorated with slanting incisions, while others show the band divided into three distinct ribs; the actual method of construction, however, cannot be determined in the absence of similar extant examples.

The rosette was sometimes mounted inside a circle; the petals could represent cloisonné work with precious stones inlaid in the separate cloisons; we have no evidence for the use of enamel, although its use at Tell Halaf suggests that Assyrian jewellers can hardly have been unaware of this technique of decoration, especially when one considers their skill in glass working. Sometimes the rosette is cut out without the circular mount. The circlet held by the figure in fig. 139, one of a pair of winged female figures facing the sacred tree, was probably composed of a mixture of gold beads and precious stones, all of which would have had amuletic significance. Bracelets with rosettes were also worn by male winged apotropaic figures on the reliefs of Ashurnaṣirpal II and by the eagle-headed winged demons carrying cone and bucket; their occurrence on so many reliefs depicting ritual ceremonies attests to the importance of jewellery in the attire of the priests taking part in the rituals.

The bracelet with single rosette continued in use during the eighth century; a fine example from the reign of Sargon is shown in fig. 148b, a relief in the British Museum; Tiglath-Pileser III wears it when receiving homage from an enemy,[1] but by the reign of Ashurbanipal more complicated forms were being made. The bracelet could have a series of small rosettes attached to a flat gold strip with thick borders (fig. 148c) or double bracelets of stylized lions' heads were worn by the king when hunting, the large central rosette presumably forming part of the fastening (fig. 149a; see also figs. 144, 149c and 150).

Armlets also combined the use of stylized lions' heads and a single rosette (fig. 149b); these can also be seen on the lion hunt reliefs of Ashurbanipal's reign, when the bracelets ending in bull calf heads, common in the ninth and eighth centuries B.C., seem to have gone out of fashion. A good example can be seen worn by Ashurbanipal's charioteer on the lion hunt reliefs in the British Museum. An elaborate plain bracelet made from four rings, was worn by the queen on her left wrist on an eighth-century B.C. relief from Zincirli. Her right wrist shows a linked bracelet (see below). An extant example of this multiple plain type of bracelet

[1] Barnett, *Tiglath-Pileser III*, pls. XVIII, XIX.

Fig. 145. Bracelet with rosette from a relief of Ashurnaṣirpal II.

Fig. 146. Gold rosette from Ashur.

Fig. 147. Rosette from Ashur.

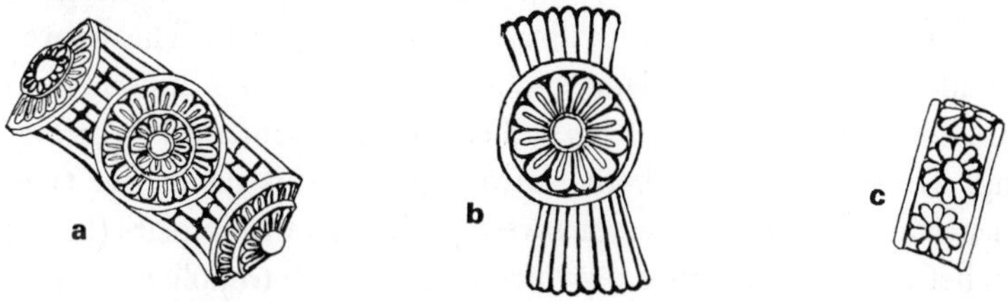

Fig. 148. Bracelets with appliqué rosettes from reliefs of: *a*, *b*, Sargon; *c*, Ashurbanipal.

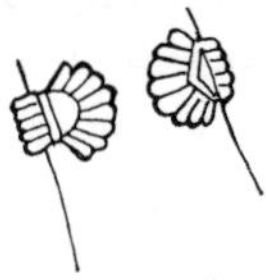

Fig. 150. Bracelet with floral finials from a relief of Ashurbanipal.

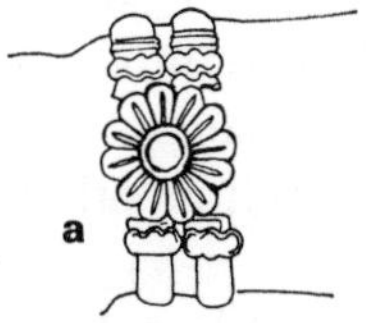

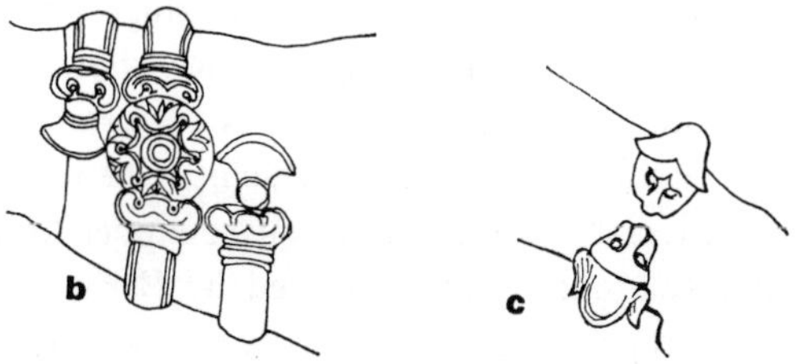

Fig. 149. Bracelets (*a*, *c*) and armlet (*b*) with stylized lion head finials from reliefs of Ashurbanipal.

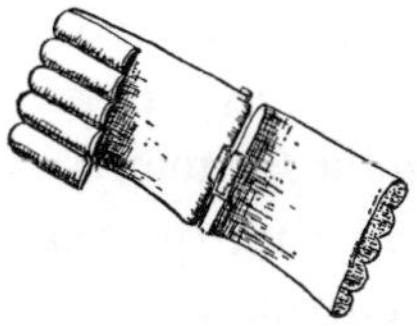

Fig. 151. Copper hinged bracelet from Ashur.

could be the copper hinged bracelet (or anklet) from a late Assyrian grave at Ashur (fig. 151); here five ribs are soldered to a copper backing.

In Assyria the distinctive type of linked bracelet can be dated to the late eighth to seventh centuries B.C. It can be found on reliefs of the time of Sennacherib and Esarhaddon and was often worn at the same time as the earrings discussed above (fig. 135). This bracelet was made of four linked discs and the prototype is probably the example worn by a courtier on one of the frescoes from Til Barsib, usually dated to the late eighth century B.C.[1] Three circular discs are shown on a relief of Sargon in the British Museum; one can assume there was a fourth at the back of the bracelet out of sight of the sculptor (fig. 148a). The discs are clearly shown on the rock relief of Sennacherib in the Gomel gorge in the region of Hines[2] and also on the stele of Esarhaddon at Zincirli. The figures of Esarhaddon's two sons – Shamash-shum-ukin, who was appointed king of Babylon in the lifetime of his father, and Ashurbanipal (wearing an earring, see p. 243) – are both shown wearing this distinctive type of bracelet, one on each hand, so they were probably worn in pairs (fig. 136). The relief of the Assyrian crown prince in the Metropolitan Museum, New York, wearing the earring typical of Ashurbanipal's time, also wears a linked disc bracelet (pl. 222).

An important unpublished example comes from Marlik and here the three surviving discs are decorated with inlaid stones set in eight oval-shaped cloisons round a central oval-shaped stone. On the second fragment the hinges are visible and are two hollow gold tubes through which a pin could pass to join one disc to the next. These important fragments must have either been imported or come from Assyria; no other extant example of this type exists to my knowledge.

The bracelets or armlets carried as tribute on the Nimrud frieze are depicted as extremely thick and heavy and the distinctive fringe round the lower part of the jaw of the calf's head (which is also clearly shown on the Louvre bronze bracelet mentioned above – pl. 227) is important to note. This feature occurs on the double calves' heads which can be found on the Certomlyk sword hilt, an Urartian mirror and a silver dipper from Tell Fara (p. 224). The latter two objects are regarded by Barnett as Urartian, while the sword may represent Median art with the calves' heads worked in Urartian style.[3] A silver bracelet with calf's head and

[1] Thureau-Dangin, *Til Barsib*, pl. LI. Examples can also be found on Sargonid reliefs from Khorsabad; Botta, II, pl. 161.

[2] Parrot, *Nineveh*, p. 73. [3] *Iranica Antiqua*, II, pp. 77–95.

lower jaw fringe (in a private collection in Basle) belongs to this series and could well be Urartian work.[1]

R. Moorey, in his unpublished thesis on Luristan bronzes,[2] has pointed out that the feature of the calves' heads with lower jaw fringe does not appear among the bronze bracelets allegedly from Luristan, but the feature can be found on many later Achaemenian pieces. Many bronze bracelets from Luristan have lion-head terminals – single, double or triple – and these are closely comparable with the few examples of lion bracelets on the Assyrian reliefs (cf. fig. 144). The bracelet shown in pl. 230, now in the Boston Museum of Fine Arts, is a fine extant example.

Jewellery on headdresses and garments

Jewellery was used in many different ways by the Assyrians to ornament the tiaras or fillets worn by the king, the *turtan* or commander-in-chief, and also the diadems of half-human apotropaic figures who appear in many ritual scenes on the Assyrian reliefs of the ninth century B.C. The king's headdress or *polos*, which became progressively higher and more elaborate during the seventh century B.C., was also richly ornamented and the caps and feather headdresses of various deities and winged bulls were often covered with rosettes or could be ornamented with a circular disc with rays on the top. The garments of royal personages, officials, gods and goddesses were also ornamented with appliqué rosettes and squares, some of which may well have been of gold or silver; we know that the statues of the gods and goddesses were adorned with gold and silver and wore elaborate jewellery. A divine statue carried by Assyrian soldiers of the enthroned goddess (fig. 152) shows decorated garments; these reliefs date from the time of Tiglath-Pileser III when the fashion was widespread. It can be seen on the relief of king Warpalawas at Ivriz in south-east Anatolia, which shows the influence of this method of decoration on the appearance of provincial rulers at the time of Tiglath-Pileser III (fig. 153).

The simple form of diadem decorated with rosettes can be seen in fig. 154. The rosettes vary in design and were presumably sewn or fixed to the diadem which must have been made of material or leather. It is possible that in some instances (fig. 155) the diadem itself may have been made of metal, to which the rosettes could have been attached, but we have no evidence to prove this.

[1] *Orfèvrerie achéménide*, pl. 13, 35.
[2] Unpublished doctoral thesis, presented at Oxford, 1967.

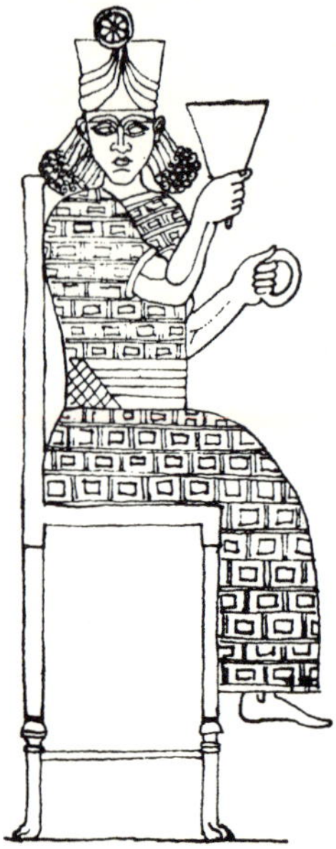

Fig. 152. Enthroned goddess from a Nimrud relief.

Fig. 153. King Warpalawas from relief near Ivriz.

Fig. 154. Diadems with rosettes from a relief from Khorsabad.

The fillet was a plain headdress, widening at the front where a large rosette could be fixed and, in the case of royalty, was often combined with the high *polos*. Fig. 156 shows the development of the high *polos* with the richly ornamented form worn in the seventh century B.C. by Ashurbanipal, who is also portrayed wearing the fillet alone when hunting lions. The eighth-century type, worn by Tiglath-Pileser III (fig. 156b) with three fillets, is not so richly decorated; Esarhaddon's *polos* is similar to that of Ashurbanipal, while Shamshi-Adad V on his stele in the British Museum wears a *polos* of eighth-century type similar in design to that of Ashurnaṣirpal II.

Fig. 155. Winged figure with diadem from a Nimrud relief.

Fig. 156. Relief portraits: *a*, Ashurnaṣirpal II; *b*, Tiglath-Pileser III; *c*, Sargon II; *c*, Ashurbanipal.

The Nimrud ivories provide detailed evidence for the ornamentation of the headdresses worn by women in the eighth and seventh centuries B.C. A remarkable series of ivory heads from the Burnt Palace of Ashurnaṣirpal II is considered by Professor Mallowan to portray the 'many and varied types of female beauty gathered together for the king's pleasure from distant parts of the Assyrian empire.'[1] Many different types of headdresses, which can be described sometimes as crowns or as fillets, are worn by these ladies. In this collection, only one head is male and he wears a narrow plain fillet (pl. 231). The crowns can be distinguished from the fillets by being worn on the top of the head; they are usually wide and sit on the hair, while the fillet can be described as a narrow band worn low down on the forehead, and sometimes knotted behind the head. The crowns could be decorated with gold discs or lotus buds (pl. 232), bands of gold granules (pl. 233), rosettes and rectangular plaques with tassels of pomegranates below in the centre (pl. 234a and b). The fillets could be plain or decorated with lotus buds and gold discs, which were inlaid with precious stones or some kind of perishable material (pl. 235). Sometimes the headdress was made of cloth, to which was sewn the plaque (presumably gold), rectangular in shape, and finely decorated with a row of pomegranates below (pl. 236). The 'Mona Lisa' of Nimrud, found at the bottom of a well and dated c. 715 B.C. by Professor Mallowan (pl. 237) wears a plain double crown, to which ivory studs had been affixed, while one of the finest of the ivory heads, the 'Ugly Lady', shown without a headdress, wears four necklaces with a row of gold pendants (these were carved in the ivory and still carried the remains of gold inlay – pl. 238).

A dated example of a seventh-century B.C. headdress can be found on the relief in the British Museum of Ashurbanipal reclining at a banquet in a garden with his wife, who is seated on a throne and wears a wide crown made in the shape of the battlements of a city (fig. 157). She also wears earrings of the same type as the king (fig. 127:29–31).

Appliqué ornaments of precious metal

Small gold and silver appliqué ornaments shown on the reliefs decorating the garments of gods or goddesses were made of gold, silver or woven thread and then attached by thread or cord to the surface of the material. Similar decoration can be found on the garments of kings and the fashion became widely used at the time of Tiglath-Pileser III. An early instance is shown on the boundary stone of Marduk-nadin-aḫḫe, king of Babylonia

[1] *I.L.N.*, 16 August 1952, p. 255.

Fig. 157. Relief from Kuyunjik showing the wife of Ashurbanipal.

(1096–1068 B.C.), now in the British Museum (fig. 158), where rosettes, semi-circles and hexagonal-shaped ornaments cover the sleeves of the garment. In the ninth century B.C., however, decoration of garments by appliqué plaques, presumably of metal, is shown more often on military costume (an Assyrian archer at the time of Ashurnaṣirpal II wears a skirt covered with rosettes and square plaques – fig. 159) than on royal costume, while the statues of gods and goddesses were richly adorned in this manner (fig. 160). King Warpalawas at Ivriz (fig. 153; see p. 260), a contemporary of Tiglath-Pileser III, however, had an elaborately decorated garment comparable with that worn by Assyrian deities (while Tiglath-Pileser III is shown wearing a fringed garment with a decoration of concentric squares confined to a narrow band along the borders, his officials wear long robes covered with square appliqué ornaments[1]); even

[1] Barnett, *Tiglath-Pileser III*, pl. LIX.

Fig. 158. Detail from garment of Marduk-nadin-aḫḫe.

Fig. 159. Assyrian archer from a Nimrud relief.

Fig. 160. Divine statue carried by Assyrian soldiers from a Nimrud relief.

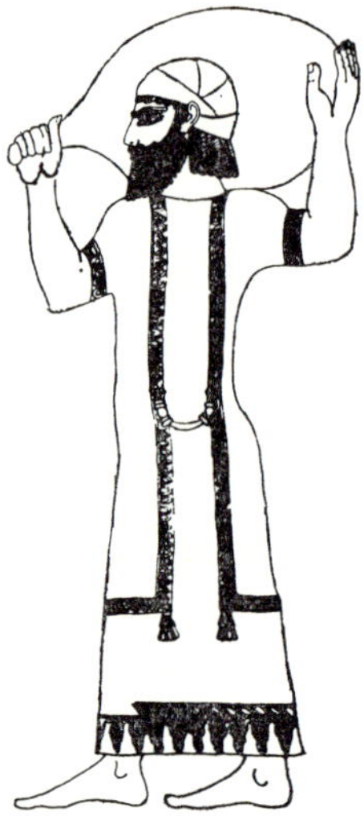

Fig. 161. Tribute bearers from a Khorsabad relief.

if these patterns represent woven appliqué ornaments, they were probably imitating the Assyrian 'golden garments of the gods' and were perhaps the source of the classical idea that the Phrygians were the 'inventors of embroidery'. A Phrygian tributary on a relief from Sargon's palace (fig. 161) at Khorsabad wears a garment with richly decorated fringes and borders and the magnificent robe worn by Sargon himself (fig. 162) probably represents a mixture of 'Phrygian' embroidery and golden appliqué ornaments, already used in Assyria for the decoration of the statutes in the temple. A prisoner from Iran on a Sargonid relief (fig. 163)

Fig. 162. Sargon II and his *turtan* from a Khorsabad relief.

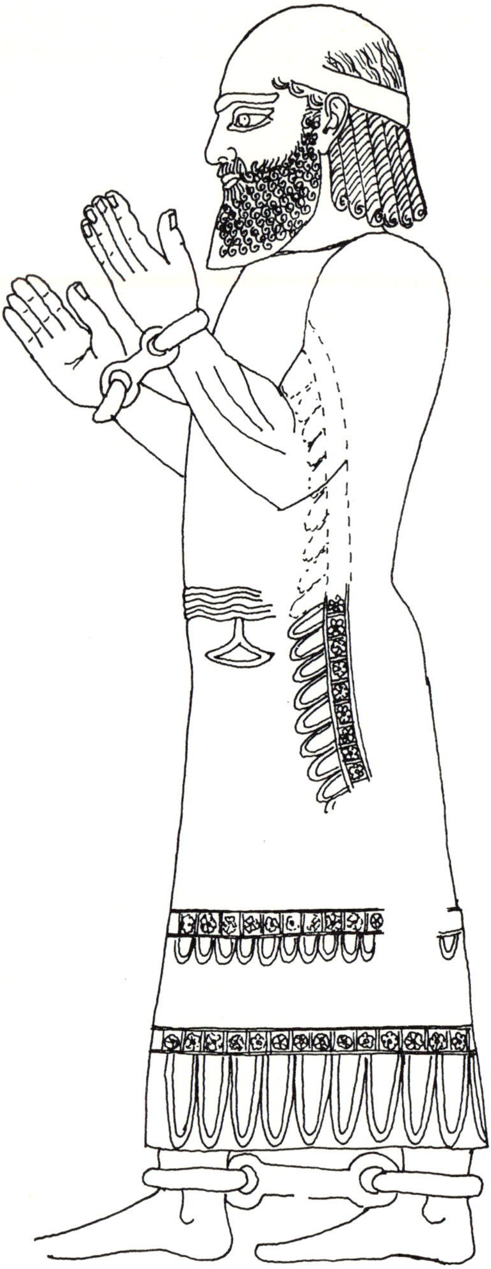

Fig. 163. Captive with fringed garment from a Khorsabad relief.

also wears a robe with the fringed borders decorated with squares containing rosettes.

After the reign of Sargon the fashion continued and can be seen on the royal costumes of Sennacherib and Ashurbanipal (fig. 164).

The textual references to this subject have been studied in detail by Oppenheim.[1] Especially relevant are references to goldsmiths responsible for the attachment of gold ornaments such as the rosettes (*ajaru*) or discs (*nipḫu*).

Fig. 164. Libation scene of Ashurbanipal.

The 703 golden stars and 688 golden ornaments from the *kusītu* garment of the Lady of Uruk are mentioned and sixty-one damaged golden stars from the *kusītu* garment were sent to named goldsmiths for repair. Rosettes are listed as being made in different sizes with especially large ones to be worn on the forehead, 'the front rosette of the Lady of Uruk'. Other references contain Akkadian words which obviously denote some kind of jewellery, but which cannot yet be translated with certainty. The *tenšu* ornaments (usually of gold) and the *ḫašu* ornaments, both of which are associated with the *kusītu* garment of a goddess, frequently occur in the texts; on one occasion they are mentioned as being at the

[1] 'The golden garments of the gods', *J.N.E.S.*, 8, 1949, pp. 172–93.

disposal of a certain named goldsmith for cleaning. Oppenheim would translate *tenšu* or *tenšia* as the small squares or rectangles sewn on to garments, and *šibṭu* as a border decorated with gold ornaments.

In Babylonia in the twelfth century B.C. a representation of Marduk wearing a feathered crown decorated with small rosettes also shows that his robe was covered with large circular plaques and a huge circular pendant suspended from his shoulders to below the belt. The sleeves of the god's garment are also covered with rosettes, while another Babylonian representation of the storm god Adad shows similar decoration on the robe, though here the rosettes enclose stars with four, six and eight points.[1] These figures were found on cylinder seals from Babylon during the German excavations undertaken between 1899 and 1914.

Fibulae

Fibulae do not seem to have been worn by Assyrian kings or officials and do not appear on the reliefs as part of the dress of deities or mythical figures. The fibula was a Mediterranean invention and, while many bronze examples have been found in excavations all over western Asia, there are few examples in gold and silver. Stronach[2] has studied the development and distribution of the types which can specifically be called Near Eastern; here we will relate the few stratified gold and silver examples to this typology.

A few instances of fibulae as portrayed on reliefs should be noted, as their material is not known. First, the fibula worn by king Warpalawas on the rock relief at Ivriz (fig. 153) is closely dated, as we know that this local ruler paid tribute to Tiglath-Pileser III in 738 B.C. The type, with round bow and round-headed studs, is the normal Phrygian form known from Gordion, where 175 bronze examples were found in the royal tomb excavated by Dr Rodney Young in 1937. Warpalawas' earring is also a western Anatolian type, as noted by Barnett, who compares it with an example from Ephesus.[3]

At Zincirli, however, Bar-rekub's queen wears a fibula (Stronach Type I.5, semi-circular with continuously ribbed bow) which is a Near Eastern type unknown on the Anatolian plateau. The bronze examples show that this was a type particularly popular in north Syria and a fragmentary relief at Carchemish, probably to be dated to the seventh century B.C.,

[1] H. H. Rowley, op. cit., p. 139. Oppenheim, op. cit., fig. 8.
[2] Stronach, 'The development of the fibula in the Near East', *Iraq*, XXI, 2, 1959, p. 181.
[3] R. D. Barnett, 'Early Greek and oriental ivories', *J.H.S.*, LXVIII, 1948, p. 9.

shows two identical fibulae of this form attached to the hem of a garment.[1] A Mid-Assyrian bronze example from Mari (Tomb 287) belongs to this type, which seems to have had a long history in northern Mesopotamia. Similar examples from Luristan could therefore be as early as the twelfth century B.C.[2]

Stronach's Type III.7[3] (triangular fibula with ribbed and beaded mouldings) is important here, not only because it is the most common variety of the triangular Near Eastern class, but also because among the thirteen bronze examples from Nimrud, one of them can be closely dated as it was found in a grave which belongs to a period not earlier than the reign of Sargon (722–705 B.C.). To this fibula was attached a magnificent stamp seal with gold chain and clasp – the famous Nimrud jewel (see p. 233 and pl. 216). A comparable silver example in the Ashmolean Museum (pl. 240) has the hook of the chain still attached. Bronze examples of this type should be noted here from the comprehensive list published by Stronach, as they have the catch developed into the form of a hand (see also pl. 170b, from Ziweye in silver, and an example in the Ashmolean Museum, pl. 239).

A variant of Stronach's third main class of Near Eastern fibulae (Type III.6, the triangular fibula) has the same ribbed mouldings as Type III.7, but no intermediate beads. A fine gold example comes from Amman (pl. 241) in a tomb that can be closely dated, as it contained a carnelian seal inscribed with the name of Adoni-Nur, who is known to have fought against Ashurbanipal in 650 B.C.[4] The fibula was found in a large terracotta coffin (or bath tub) (pl. 242) of the same shape as the large bronze coffins known from Ur, Ziweye and Zincirli and was associated with pottery, silver jewellery and seals. A simpler bronze fibula of the same basic type, also in the Museum at Amman, is from Shahab and datable to the eighth century B.C. This is the same kind of fibula often depicted on the Lamaštu plaques, of which a good example can be seen on the seventh-century Lamaštu plaque from Nimrud (pl. 176), where it is shown in the field as one of the objects used in the ritual to ward off the evil Lamaštu demon from attacking a sick man.

The Lamaštu evil spirit is also shown on one side of one of the Amman seals (pl. 243a), which has a silver mount and hook and had an obviously

[1] Von Luschan, *Ausgrabungen in Sendschirli*, IV, p. 325, Abb. 236.
[2] Parrot, *Syria*, XIX, 1938, p. 20, fig. 12.
[3] Godard, *Bronzes*, pl. XXIX, 103, and many other examples.
[4] G. Lankester Harding, 'Four tomb groups from Jordan', *Palestine Exploration Fund Annual*, VI, 1963.

prophylactic purpose. The other side shows the goddess Gula and her dog (pl. 243b). A pair of silver earrings, boat-shaped and badly corroded, also belongs to this group (pl. 244); this pair seems to be made all in one piece without the pin being attached separately. A similar silver pair of earrings from Madaba is also in the Museum at Amman. A comparable silver earring comes from Luristan, War Kabud, in a stratified eighth- to seventh-century context (pl. 250).

The silver ring from the tomb of Adoni-Nur (pl. 245), although badly corroded, is made in the shape of a lotus flower whose petals support the circular setting for the missing stone which is decorated with a circle of attached bosses. The setting is soldered on to the lotus-shaped ring. It is comparable with the silver example from Tell Halaf (see pl. 245 and fig. 133f) and shows that this Assyrian form of ring continued in use from the ninth to the seventh century B.C. A silver bracelet is made of a hollow silver ring with two flat knob heads added afterwards and then bound round with silver wire and engraved. This is one of the few dated silver bracelets of the seventh century B.C. A lunate-shaped silver earring has the base of the pin bound with silver wire and belongs to a common eighth- to seventh-century type with a widespread distribution, including western Iran. A badly corroded bronze fibula in this tomb finally deserves notice, as it belongs to Stronach's Type I.3 (semi-circular fibula with single or multiple ribs at the base of each arm). Stronach remarks that this type is almost as popular in Babylonia as in Palestine and that stratified examples appear to be seventh century or later in date.

A fine electrum fibula from Gordion, found in the Phrygian city level (the terrace building excavated in 1959), belongs to this type (pl. 246), along with a group of gold and silver objects which show that Phrygian jewellers were capable of producing as fine work in precious metals as their colleagues could in bronze. The small gold and silver fibulae also found in this group are common Phrygian types, known at Gordion in bronze, while the electrum example is exactly the same as the bronze examples found in one of the Gordion tumuli. Although the ivory horse trappings found in the same room as the jewellery were certainly imports to Gordion, these fibulae are more likely to have been made at Gordion or at some other accessible Phrygian centre farther east. Most of the Mesopotamian and Syrian examples of the type are later in date than the Gordion group, which must belong to the period before the burning of the building at the time of the Cimmerian destruction of the city early in the sixth century B.C.

A silver fibula from Zincirli (seventh century B.C.) belongs to a type whose Near Eastern distribution has been studied by J. M. Birmingham[1] and is closely related to the Gordion electrum fibula (pl. 246) and to a variant which is known in bronze in Tumulus III at Gordion (eighth century B.C.). Zincirli seems to have produced the sole eastern example of the type which is found either on the Anatolian plateau or on the western seaboard and islands; here there are many examples noted by Mrs Birmingham, including Ephesus, Samos and Delos.

Later sixth-century B.C. jewellery from Gordion lies outside the scope of this book, although the cremation graves excavated in 1950 are important for their east Greek and Lydian connections. A gold bracelet with lion's head and the gold earrings with granulated knobs on the boat-shaped body should, however, be related to Asiatic work and an Iranian origin could be postulated for these pieces (pl. 247). Another fine pair of gold boat-shaped earrings has round sockets of gold for stone inlay, now missing, and is Asiatic in origin; this pair can be closely related to Ashurbanipal's earrings (fig. 127:31) and its maker must have been inspired by Asiatic models.[2]

A small silver fibula was found in Tomb A at Kayalidere (pl. 160) with the group of Urartian jewellery described on p. 204. It is an unusual type which has two angular collared beads on the arched bow and an exaggerated wide catch plate. These features would place it in Stronach's Type II.4, but the nearest analogy is the fibula from Nor-Aresh (fig. 165),

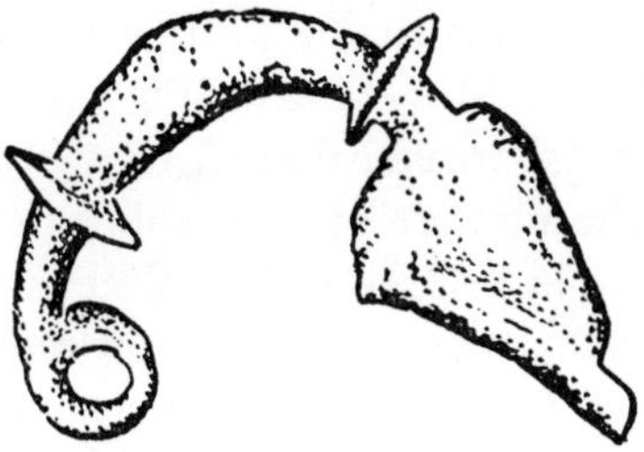

Fig. 165. Fibula from Nor-Aresh.

a site on the outskirts of Erivan, where three Urartian cremation burials were found. This fibula had the wide flat catch plate, well known from Greek examples from the Cerameicus Cemetery at Athens (Tomb 41) and reference should be made to Higgins's discussion of the question of oriental influence on Greek art and craftsmanship during the course of

1 As noted by J. M. Birmingham, 'The oriental route across Anatolia', *A.S.*, XI, 1961, p. 187, fig. 2. This type occurs in bronze in Phrygian levels at Boğazköy and at Ankara – *Boğazköy*, Taf. 11, 10 and 14; E. Akurgal, *Phrygische Kunst*, Taf. 60b (Ankara, 1935).

2 *Bulletin of the University Museum, Philadelphia*, 1953, fig. 25.

the eighth and seventh centuries B.C. and the possibility that Phoenician craftsmen actually established centres of jewellery working in some of the principal Greek cities.[1] It seems likely that Urartian craftsmen reached the shores of Greece and provided new models for Greek craftsmen to copy and improve upon, but this requires definite evidence; the gold Greek examples from the Elgin collection are unstratified and are obviously the products of extremely skilled workmen; the examples from Tomb 41 at the Cerameicus cemetery are bronze and the date of the tomb (875–825 B.C.) could imply that the Urartian examples are local copies of Greek originals. Barnett considers the Nor-Aresh cemetery to belong to the seventh century B.C., but it is possible that the fibulae are earlier and more dated Urartian examples are needed before this question can be discussed further. Fibulae with swollen bows, like those shown on the Kayalidere and Nor-Aresh examples, have a wide distribution in Syria, Palestine and Cilicia and, as Stronach has pointed out, examples with this feature are known in the Near East as early as the ninth century B.C.

JEWELLERY FROM LURISTAN AND MEDIA

Stratified jewellery from Luristan has recently been excavated from the cemetery at War Kabud by Professor Vanden Berghe and was exhibited in Brussels in 1966.[2] The site is dated to the end of the eighth and beginning of the seventh century B.C. A silver earring with long pendant showing traces of silver granulation (pl. 248) is the same type as in fig. 126:1, the usual type for the reign of Ashurnaṣirpal II. A close analogy can be seen on a marble relief from Nimrud worn by a winged figure now in the Musées Royaux d'Art et Histoire in Brussels.[3] Two silver earrings from the same cemetery with crude granulation on the pendant could be as early as Ashurnaṣirpal II (pl. 249–cf. fig. 126:13). A gold boat-shaped earring (pl. 250b) belongs to the type discussed on p. 239 (fig. 132). A crescent-shaped silver example (pl. 250a) with silver wire bound round the base of the pin and silver granules forming a border along the body of the earring, can be compared with later seventh-century B.C. Assyrian earrings (cf. fig. 127:28–30).

[1] Higgins, *Jewellery*, pp. 95 ff.
[2] L. Vanden Berghe, 'Het archeologisch onderzoek naar de bronscultuur van Luristan', *Opgravingen in Pusht-i Kuh*, I; *Kalwali en War Kabud* (Brussels, 1968).
[3] G. Goosens, *Art de la Mesopotamie*, fig. 16 (Musées Royaux d'Art et Histoire, Brussels).

Other pieces of gold jewellery from Luristan are in private collections with no definite information concerning their provenance. Certain pieces with the attribution Luristan may well come from other parts of Persia. A boat-shaped earring, gold over a core of bitumen, was published by Godard and came from a tomb in Luristan[1] but its associations are not known. A similar example is in the Mazda Collection in Teheran. These pieces and the War Kabud earring could well have been imported from Assyria; the five fine Assyrian earrings (colour pl. H) in the same collection must undoubtedly be imports to Luristan or taken there as booty from Assyria. The bottom pair in colour pl. H have simple gold rings, to which a round pendant of bronze is attached; the neck of the pendant is bound with gold and the pendant itself would probably have been covered with gold leaf. The earring is comparable with the Nimrud earring (pl. 219) found in the palace of Adad-Nirari III (see p. 241). The two outside examples (top row, colour pl. H) have the rings of bronze and the left hand piece has a tubular pendant with acorn-shaped attachments of a kind that can be found on the relief of the head of a human-headed bull (fig. 166) wearing a feathered headdress, whose earrings are comparable with this extant example. This relief dates from the reign of Tiglath-Pileser III (see also fig. 167, from the colossal winged bull in the British Museum). On the right hand outer example the acorns of bronze are covered with gold and the tubular pendant has gold bands top and bottom. On the centre earring, top row, the bands of gold leaf are replaced by two rows of granules and this example may belong to the Sargonid period.

Tepe Sialk Cemetery B

Cemetery B at Sialk was remarkable in that the numerous ornaments and jewellery worn by the men, women and children were of silver, bronze, iron or occasionally lead, but never of gold. The jewellery is crude and barbarous in appearance.

A circular silver ornament with attached blobs of silver[2] is comparable with a broken bracelet from Ashur found in a Kassite grave of the mid second millennium (Haller, *Ashur*, Taf. 16d), which may be the prototype for the later Sialk examples. A bracelet now in the Louvre (pl. 251) is decorated with rough incised patterns. Silver button pendants with the glass paste core covered in silver and the hook of bronze, combined with

[1] Godard, *Bronzes*, pl. XXIX, 102.
[2] Ghirshman, *Sialk*, II, pl. L, S 545b; see also pls. XXVII–XXIX, XCIII.

triangular silver plaques, seem to have formed parts of a headdress, while a variety of silver hair ornaments were combined with narrow silver ribbons to decorate the hair. The earrings were either of bronze or silver balls soldered together; a pendant of small silver balls may have formed the pendant of an earring; torques were of bronze, silver and, in one case,

Fig. 166. Head of a human-headed bull from Nimrud.

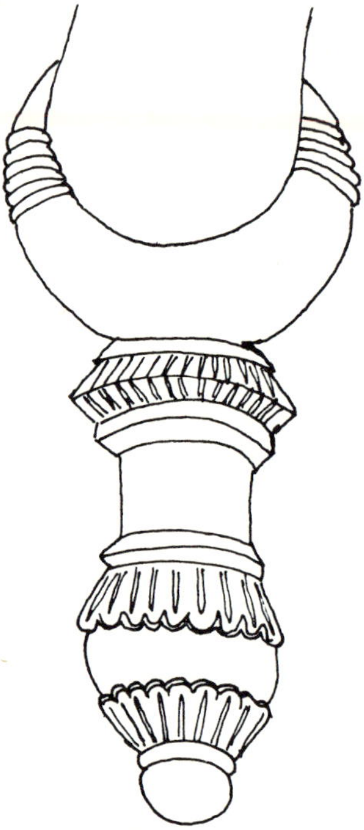

Fig. 167. Earring from winged bull from Khorsabad.

iron. One silver example was made of twisted silver wire with a ring at each end. Rings were of thin silver or bronze, open and widening towards the centre. Pins were usually of bronze, but two remarkable specimens have iron shanks and silver heads. The bad state of preservation of this jewellery precludes detailed discussion.

Sialk Cemetery B has sometimes been identified as Median; there is nothing definite to prove this attribution, which may well have to await the excavation of Hamadan, as well as future work at Nūsh-i-Jān, before Median jewellery can be studied in any detail.

Tepe Nūsh-i-Jān

In 1967 a remarkable hoard of silver jewellery was found in a stratified context in the Median fort excavated by Mr David Stronach at Tepe Nūsh-i-Jān, fifty kilometres south of Hamadan. This is the first collection of Iranian jewellery which can undoubtedly be identified as Median;[1] its importance cannot be overstressed.

Found inside a bronze bowl and including six silver bars, numerous scraps of silver ingots and half-finished objects, the hoard was probably part of a silversmith's stock and was buried at the time when the fort had been abandoned in the first half of the sixth century B.C. The pottery from Nūsh-i-Jān is, however, mostly dated to the seventh century B.C. and the jewellery could have been contemporary; when more stratified Median jewellery and pottery is forthcoming, a more definite chronology can be put forward.

The hoard included three quadruple spiral silver beads (greatest width 2·6 cm) made in the same technique as the much earlier western Asiatic examples from Mesopotamia and Anatolia (fig. 22a) in contrast to the Syrian and Iranian types from Mari and Marlik (fig. 113). Some large double spiral pendants (pl. 252) are of a type which recalls spirals from Tepe Hissar of much earlier date (see p. 79). A silver earring (length 2·2 cm) decorated with crude granulation work, badly worn, belongs to the same type as the Elamite earring (pl. 211, see Chapter 14) where hollow silver balls decorated with granules form a pendant below a circular ring (cf. also War Kabud, pl. 249).

A curious double spiral ornament of silver, now in the Boston Museum of Fine Arts (pl. 253) from Luristan can be compared with the silver double spirals from Nūsh-i-Jān.

Bracelets with duck's head finials

Luristan has been given as the source for several bronze bracelets with the finials in the shape of a duck with head bent back over the body. A good example (pl. 254), now in the Boston Museum of Fine Arts, with twisted hoop made in the same way as many of the bronze torques, also allegedly from Luristan, cannot be paralleled on any Assyrian relief, but the motif was well known in Babylonia and Assyria where it was often used for weights. A good example from 'Amlash' (pl. 255) could be earlier than Achaemenian, the period to which it was dated in the Paris exhibi-

[1] *Iran*, VII, 1969, pls. VIIIa–Xa.

tion, and could be related to part of the material from Marlik (tenth to ninth century B.C.); another example with similar finials from the Oxus treasure, in the British Museum, may be pre-Achaemenian.[1]

Several other gold bracelets in private collections with Luristan given as the source may also be pre-Achaemenian; a fine example with triple animal terminals could, on analogy with Ashurbanipal triple armlets, be dated to the seventh century B.C.[2] Stratified examples of all these types of armlets and bracelets are badly needed before any certain chronological development can be postulated. A magnificent gold example from Ziweye with a thick twisted hoop and terminals in sheet gold in the form of ducks with heads bent back may be the prototype for this series.[3]

Gold and silver pennanular earrings

The magnificent Neo-Babylonian earring from Uruk composed of a double row of gold balls soldered to a central wire (pl. 217) is probably the origin for the form of the silver circular earrings with solid body, to which a series of silver balls is attached. This is a common type in north Syria. There are many variations of the basic type shown in pl. 256 (Ashmolean Museum No. 1913.731) from the later cemetery excavated at Deve Hüyük near Carchemish; these are usually dated to the end of the sixth century B.C., but, while some of the contents of these graves (such as the sword chapes and iron swords) could date from the period of Median domination of north Syria in the early part of the sixth century B.C., the silver jewellery may well belong to the period when the whole of Palestine and Syria had fallen into the hands of Nebuchadnezzar after the battle of Carchemish in 605 B.C.

Five more examples similar to the Ashmolean earring from Deve Hüyük are in the Archaeological Museum at Istanbul; they are marked Carchemish and probably came from Deve Hüyük. Tombs at Neirab near Aleppo have produced several silver examples which can also be dated to the Neo-Babylonian period.[4] The Lydian examples from Sardis and the fine examples shown on the ivory head from Sardis[5] suggest that it was via the Medes (who controlled the trade routes across Asia Minor to the Aegean coast after the treaty between Cyaxares the Mede and Croesus of Lydia) that the type became so popular in Lydia. These earrings were

[1] *Treasure of the Oxus*, pl. XIX, 142.
[2] *Orfèvrerie achéménide*, pl. 14, Nos. 44, 45; see also No. 46, p. 19.
[3] Ghirshman, *Iran*, pl. 11b.
[4] *Syria*, VIII, 1927, p. 211, pl. LIV. Ibid., IX, p. 194, fig. 2, pl. LVI.
[5] E. Coche de la Ferté, *Les Bijoux Antiques*, p. 45, fig. 6.

almost certainly worn by Medes, Babylonians and Lydians; it is worth remembering that the treaty defining the boundary between the Medes and Lydians was negotiated by the Babylonian Nabonidus, who was then an officer. The craftsmen who actually made them have often been local and there is a distinct relationship to the much earlier solid gold earring from Ajjul (pl. 77) which has been noted by Coche de la Ferté.[1] Two unstratified gold examples of the Ajjul type with a falcon outlined in minute granules on the solid body of the earring (one in Leiden, the second in the Louvre) are closely related to the Ajjul examples and may well have come from this site.[2]

Much work needs to be done on the earrings of the seventh to sixth centuries in Syria; Lydian and Achaemenian jewellery falls outside the scope of this book, but the early Iranian development is beginning to become clear. The magnificent early Achaemenian earrings from Pasargadae have been published and studied in detail by Stronach;[3] they are shown here in pls. 257 and 258 and form a suitable end to this survey of western Asiatic jewellery. Their relationship to the silver type discussed above, to the Assyrian examples from the reliefs of Ashurbanipal (fig. 127:28–31) and to Phoenician examples of the same type from Aliseda is obvious and a fitting example of the internationalism prevalent among jewellers in Asia in the late seventh and early sixth centuries B.C. A cruder unstratified pair of gold earrings from Iran (provenance unknown and exhibited in Paris in 1961) is representative of the mass of unstratified examples from Iran of this type (pl. 259).

[1] Ibid., p. 45.
[2] *Monuments Egyptiens du Musée d'Antiquités des Pays-Bas at Leide*, pl. XLVII, 1272 (Leiden, 1839–1905) – I owe this reference to Miss O. Tufnell. Coche de la Ferté, op. cit., pl. V.
[3] *Iran*, III, pp. 9–40, pls. X–XIV.

BIBLIOGRAPHY

There is no general work devoted to the gold and silver jewellery of the whole of Western Asia; the principal sources are reports of excavations (many in progress), the collections of jewellery in museums (and to a lesser extent private collections) and the Sumerian, Old Babylonian and Assyrian texts relating to goldwork and jewellery. Reference has also been made to texts of the Neo-Babylonian period, although Neo-Babylonian jewellery falls outside the scope of this survey.

For a brief introduction see E. Coche de la Ferté, *Les Bijoux Antiques*, Chapter 1 (Paris, 1956), and C. V. Sutherland, *Gold*, Chapter III (London, 1959). For general background see *Bibliographie Analytique de l'Assyriologie et de l'Archaéologie du Proche-Orient*, *Philologie*, *1954–6*, *Archaéologie*, *1960* (Leiden, 1957, 1960).

The following lists are given as a guide to further reading; they do not pretend to be exhaustive. The titles of excavation reports and articles in periodicals are given in the footnotes to each chapter. See also abbreviations, p. xlvii.

Introduction

Archives Royales de Mari: VII, J. Bottero, *Textes Economiques et Administratifs* (Paris, 1957); IX, M. Birot, *Textes Administratifs* (Paris, 1960).

The Assyrian Dictionary of the Oriental Institute of Chicago (1964 – in progress).

R. Campbell-Thompson, *A Dictionary of Assyrian Chemistry and Geology* (Oxford, 1936).

G. R. Driver and J. C. Miles, *The Assyrian Laws* (Oxford, 1935), see Nos. 26, 38.

G. Essen and J. Levy, *Die Altassyrischen Rechturkunden vom Kültepe* (Mitteilungun der Vorderasiatische Aegyptischen Geschellschaft, 33, Leipzig, 1930).

R. J. Forbes, *Studies in Ancient Technology*, VIII (Leiden, 1964).

P. Garelli, *Les Assyriens en Cappadoce* (Paris, 1963).

A. Guillaume, 'Metallurgy in the Old Testament', *P.E.Q.*, 1962, pp. 129–32.

H. Hodges, *Artifacts* (London, 1963).

M. Y. Larsen, *Old Assyrian Caravan Procedures* (Istanbul, 1967).

W. Leaf, *Strabo on the Troad* (Cambridge, 1923).

W. F. Leemans, *Foreign Trade in the Old Babylonian Period* (Leiden, 1960).

E. Legrain, *Ur Excavations, III: Business Documents of the Third Dynasty of Ur* (London, 1947).

M. Levey, *Chemistry and Chemical Technology in Ancient Mesopotamia* (Elsevier Publishing Co., London and New York, 1959).

H. Limet, *Le Travail du Métal au Pays de Sumer au temps de la IIIe Dynastie d'Ur* (Paris, 1960).
H. Maryon, 'Metal working in the ancient world', *A.J.A.*, 53, 2, 1949.
C. Singer *et al.* (eds.), *History of Technology*, Chapters 21–23.
Strabo XII, 549; XIII, 591; XIII, 603.
W. Von Soden, *Akkadische Handwörterbuch* (Wiesbaden, 1959 – in progress).
D. Wiseman, *The Alalakh Tablets* (London, 1953).
For a discussion of the techniques used by modern forgers, see H. Hoffmann '"Greek gold" reconsidered', *A.J.A.*, 73, 4, 1969.

Chapters 1, 2, 4 and 5

Cambridge Ancient History, Fascicles 62, 9, 17, 28, 35 (listed below in chronological order), with detailed bibliographies.
A. Moortgat, *Tell Chuēra in Nordost Syrien. Bericht über die vierte Grabungskampagne 1963* (Köln, 1965).
XVe Rencontre Assyriologique Internationale, *La Civilisation de Mari* (Liège, 1967).
A. Spycket, *Les Statue de Culte dans les textes Mesopotamiens des origines à la Ière Dynastie de Babylone* (Paris, 1968).

Chapters 3 and 6

E. Akurgal, *Art of the Hittites* (London, 1962).
Cambridge Ancient History, Fascicles 8, 1, 20, 40.
Catalogue of the Exhibition of Hittite Art and the Antiquities of Anatolia (London, 1964).
A. Goetze, *Kleinasien* (Handbuch der Atlertumswissenschaft (Munich, 1957).
Seton Lloyd, *Early Anatolia* (Harmondsworth, 1956).
Treasures of Turkey, Catalogue (Washington, 1966).

Chapters 7 and 8

K. Kenyon, *Archaeology in the Holy Land*, Site lists and Bibliography (London, 1970).
Cambridge Ancient History, Fascicles 55, 46, 48, 29, 14, 37, 63, 51.
V. Karageorghis, *The Ancient Civilisation of Cyprus* (London, 1970).
O. Negbi's *The Hoards of Goldwork from Tell el Ajjul* (Gotëborg, 1970) appeared during the printing of this volume.

Chapter 9

Cambridge Ancient History, Fascicles 19, 66, 21, 16.

Chapter 10

Cambridge Ancient History, Fascicles 49, 42.

Chapter 11

See Bibliographies in:
P. Amiet, *Elam* (Archée Editeur, Auvais-sur-Dise, 1966).
Cambridge Ancient History, Fascicles 16, 23, 41.
P. Ghirshmann, *Persia from the Origins to Alexander the Great* (London, 1964).
E. Porada, *Iran* (London, 1965).
L. Vanden Berghe, *Archaeologie de l'Iran Ancien* (Leiden, 1959).

Chapter 12

See Bibliographies in:
A. Akurgal, *Urartäische und Altiranische Kunstzentren* (Ankara, 1968).
M. Van Loon, *Urartian Art* (Istanbul, 1966).

Chapter 13

Catalogues:
Sept Mille Ans d'Art en Iran (Paris, 1961).
Trésor de l'Ancien Iran, Musée Rath (Geneva, 1966).
Art Iranien Ancien (Brussels, 1966).

Chapter 14

Cambridge Ancient History, Fascicles 31, 67, 51, 32.

Chapter 15

V. Karageorghis, *Salamis in Cyprus* (London, 1970).
T. A. Madhloom, *The Chronological Development of Neo-Assyrian Art* (London, 1970).
Sir Max Mallowan, *Nimrud and its Remains*, I–II, Bibliography and Notes (London, 1966).
A. Parrot, *Nineveh and Babylon*, Bibliography (London, 1961).
E. Strommenger, *The Art of Mesopotamia*, Bibliography and Excavation Reports, Section V (London, 1964).
The few pieces of extant Hittite jewellery merit a separate study and are not included here. See R. D. Barnett 'Ancient oriental goldwork', *B.M.Q.*, XXII, 1, 2, 1960, pl. VIII, pp. 29ff.; C. L. Woolley and R. D. Barnett, *Carchemish*, III, 1952, pl. 64, pp. 252-6; M. Riemschneider, *Die Welt der Hethiter*, pls. 107, 108 (Paris, 1955). In addition, a magnificent gold ring is in the Ashmolean Museum, Oxford, No. 1896–1908.0.6. See D. G. Hogarth, *Hittite Seals* Oxford, 1920), p. 22.

Index of Sites

(Main references are indicated in bold type)

Abu Ḥabbah, 96
Acem Hüyük, lxii, 100
Agha Evler, 195, 205
Ain-Shems (Beth-Shemesh), 229
Ajios Jakovos, 82, 116, 128
Ajjul (Gaza), 12, 47, 85, 88–9, 91, 99, **106–9**, 111, **112–27**, 128, 130–1, 137–41, 150–1, 159, 224, 227, 269
Alaca, 14, 26, 35, 38, 41, **42–7**, 58, 63, 75, 98, 99 n., 238–9
Alalakh (Atchana), lxi, 110–11, 116, 128, **133–7**, 143–4, 147, 155, 159, 165, 229 **230–1**
Aliseda, 269
Alishar, 75
Al Mina, 136, 143, 229–30
Altintepe, 194, **200–2**, 203, 212
Amlash, 34, 93, 158, **161–2**, 178, 185, 191–2, 196–7, 198, 204–5, 210, **223**, 267
Amman, 234, 261–2
Amrit, 230
Ani-pemza, Armenia, 213
Aqar Qūf (Dur Kurigalzu), 7, 89–90, 126, 163–4, 167, 169, 186
Ardebil, 158, 192, 213
Argishti, 202
Arzawa, 110
Ashdod, 214
Ashur, 7, 12–13, 19, 24, 35, 49, 59, 70, 72–3, 77, 90, 97, 120, 161, 163, 165–8, 178, 183–4, 188, 207, 213, 219, 232, 234, 238, 240, 244–5, 249–50, 265; Tomb 20, 58, **70–1**; Tomb 45, 165–7, **169–77**
Asmar, Tell, 24, 29–30, **33**, 84–6
Aswad, 32
Atchana, *see* Alalakh
Athens, Cerameicus cemetery, 263–4
Ayia Paraskevi, 82

Baba Jan, 91
Babylon, 90, 105, 168–9, 185–6, 215, 244
Beirut, 109, 124
Beit Mirsim, 124–5, 140
Beni Hasan tomb painting, 104
Beth-Pelet, *see* Fara, Tell
Beth-Shan, 107, 111, 139, 150–1, 228–9
Beth-Shemesh (Ain-Shems), 229
Beycesultan, 39, 41–2
Boğazköy, 18, 100, 110, 146, 151, 220
Brak, 19–20, **27–32**, 34–5, 40, 47, 49, 53, 57, 61, 63, 105, 111, 128, 134, 166, 177–9
Byblos, lxv, 7, 32, 37, 57, 59, 62, 76, 99, **102–4**, 106, 114, 121–3, 140; connections with Ajjul, **108–9**

Carchemish, 107, 144, 228, 242, 260, 268
Certomlyk, 250
Cerveteri, 217, 221
Chagar Bazar, 99, 100–1, 177
Chagula Derre, 195, 205
Cyprus (*see also* Enkomi), 80, **81–2**, 107, 119–20, 122, **127–31**, 136, 219, 229–30, 239

Dahshur, 165
Dalboki, Bulgaria, 217
Daylaman, 158, **160–1**, 185
Delos, 263
Deve Hüyük, 228, 268
Dilbat, 88; necklace, **88–91**, 100, 117–18, 125–6, 145, 147, 160
Dinkha tepe, 80, 91, 158, **159**
Djamshidi, Tepe, 92
Djönu, 20, 36
Dur Kurigalzu, *see* Aqar Qūf

Enkomi, Cyprus, 81, 116, 119, 125, 128–9, **130–1**
Erech, *see* Uruk
Eridu, 1, 84, 153

Fara, Tell (Beth-Pelet), 125, **224–8**, 229, 250

Gawra, 1
Gaza, *see* Ajjul
Gerar, 225
Gezer, 151
Ghafantlu, 215, 222–3
Gilan, 73, 78, **93**, 120, 188, 205
Girik tepe, 198
Giyan, 37, 77–8, 80–1, **91–3**, 158, **160**, 185, **188**
Godin Tepe, 91, 93
Gök tepe, 80, 91, 158, **159–60**, 187
Gomel gorge, 250
Gordion, 212–14, 217, 219, 260, **262–3**
Gozan, *see* Halaf, Tell

Ḫabur valley, 99, 177

Halaf, Tell, 226, 240–2, 248, 262
Hamadan, 196, 210–11, 266–7
Hasanlu, 93, 178, 185, **188–9**, 207, 209, 228
Hassan Zamini, 195
Hassu, 110
Hazor, 107, 150
Hines rock reliefs, 242, 250
Hissar, 21, 35–6, 47, 77, **78–81**, 267
Horoztepe, 38, 41, 44

Idgyr, 205
Ischali, 85, 88
Ivriz rock relief, 220, 251, 255, 260

Jericho, 105, 107, 111

Karahöyük, 59–60, 151
Karatas-Semayük, 63
Karmir Blur, 196, **202–4**, 208
Kasvin, 162
Kayalidere, **204**, 263–4
Kaypinar, 58
Kelermes, 210
Khorsabad, 88, 232, 234; rock reliefs, 245–6, 256–8
Khurvin, 185, 188
Kinneret, 14–15
Kish, 13, 16, 33, 73
Kislovolsk, 47
Kouklia, 120
Kültepe, lxvi, 15, 17–19, 29, 34–5, 41–2, 44, **47–8**, 57–9, 73, 77, **97–101**, 134, 147, 151
Kültepe-Kanesh, 71, 97–101
Kuyunjik, 255

Lachish, 106, **138**, 228
Lagash (Tello), 14 n., 83–4
Lahun, 165
Lapithos, 81
Larsa, 84, 88
Lchashen, 34, 36–7
Lothal, 34–5
Luristan, 91–2, 133, 158, 205, 209, 214, 222, 240–1, 261–2, **264–9**; bronzes, 232, 251

Madaba, 262
Mahmatlar, 38
Maikop, 46–7, 75
Malatya, 222
Maltai rock reliefs, 143
Marash, 210
Mari, 10 n., 12, **14–15**, 25, 27, 34, 63, 78, 88, 91, 100, 105, 109, 116, 144, 155, **177–9**, 189, 207, 261, 267; frescoes, 84–5, 91, 142
Marlik, 34, 80, 159, 178–9, 185, 187–8, **189–97**, 198, 202, 228, 250, 267–8

Media, 266–9
Megiddo, 32, 107, 111–12, 116, 118, 127, 130–1, 150–1, **228–9**
Minet-el-Beida, 137, 139
Mkart, 205
Musasir, 202

Neirab, Aleppo, 268
Nimrud, lxi, 211, 232–3, 241, 261, 265; ivories, 217, 219–20, 226, 242, **254**; jewel, **233–4**, 261; reliefs, 143, 147, 212, 238, 246, 250, 252, 256
Nineveh, 143, 147, 232
Nippur, 65, 164
Nor Aresh, 221, 263–4
Nūsh-i-Jān, Tepe, 78, 266, **267**
Nuzi, 111, 141, 151, 155; pottery, 111, 128, 187, 191

Paraskevi, 82
Pasargadae, 196, 214, 269
Paswē, 182
Patnos, 195, 198, 202
Persepolis, 207
Pir Kuh, 205
Platanos, 165
Poliochni, Lemnos, 19, 35, 38–9, 49, 57, **60**, 61, 70

Qadesh, 107
Qatna, 132, 150; inventories, lxi, lxv, 110–11, 132–3, 157

Ras Shamra (Ugarit), 47, 100, 106, 111–12, 114, 119, 128, 136, **137–8**, 139–41, 143–4, 149–51, 162, 165, 187, 219
Rimah, Tell al-, 177–9, 191

Salamis, 219
Samos, 263
Saqqiz area, 181–2, 206
Sardis, 239, 268
Sar-i-pol rock reliefs, 79, 163, 215
Sevan, Lake, 34, 37, 164
Shahab, 261
Shechem, 107, 110, 112, 144, 147, 150
Shemshāra, 73
Sialk, 78; Cemetery A, 185, **187**, 193; Cemetery B, 190, 195, 241, **265–6**
Sidon, 214
Sippar, 95–6, 144
Susa, 37, 49, 58, 70, 73, 83–4, 91, 93, **94–6**, 160, 162, 164, 185, 196, 228; In-Shushinak deposit, 160, 168–9, **186–7**, 197; stele, 215–16

Tabal, lxii
Talish region, 11, **20–1**, 32, 36, 162, 195, 205
Tar-Lunni rock relief, 79–80
Tarquinia, 217, 220
Tarsus, 39, 41, **61–3**, 71
Tchila Khane, 195
Tell-el-Duweir, *see* Lachish
Tello, *see* Lagash
Tepe Hissar, *see* Hissar
Tesheba, 202
Til Barsib, 32, 58; frescoes, 239, 250
Toprak Kale, 204, 221
Trebenishte, Bulgaria, 217
Trialeti region, 27, 36–7, 38, 43, 68, **74–6**, 164; relations with Mesopotamia, 73–4
Troy, lxiv, lxvi, 18–19, 35, 38, **48–60**, 70–1; date of destruction, **39–42**; Great Treasure A, **48–53**, 57–8, 62, 88 n.; Treasure F, 55–7
Tsarskaia, 46–7
Tureng Tepe, 78
Tushpa, *see* Van

Ugarit, *see* Ras Shamra
Ur, lxv, lxvi, **2–14**, 15, 19–20, **21–7**, 33, 35–6, 46, 51, 59, 61–3, 64, **65–9**, 73, 75, 77–80, 83–4, 94, 103, 155, 165–6, 179, 192, 194, 203, 207–8, **244**
Urartu, lxii, 183, 194, **198–205**, 209, 216–18, 227, 235, 250–1, 263–4
Uruk (Erech, Warka), 1, 15, 46, 65, **74–5**, 98, 151–3, 157, 163, 168, 239, 259, 268; stele, 89

Vadjalik, 11, 20, 32
Van, 204, 244; Lake, area of, lxiv, 74, 181, 204
Veri, 36
Vetulonia, 217
Vulci, 219

Warka, *see* Uruk
War Kabud, 240, 262, **264–5**
Wilayah, 24

Yabrud, 99–100
Yahudiyeh, 107
Yanik Tepe, 78
Yazilikaya rock reliefs, 110, 146, 148–9

Zahleh, 246
Zincirli, 233, **234**, 243, 248, 250, 260, 263
Ziweye, 34, 194, 203, **206–22**, 226, 261, 268
Zöldhalompuszta, Hungary, 208

General Index

Abbabashti, necklace of, 27, 65, 74, 102
Achaemenian jewellery, 186–97, 207, 210, 214, 219, 251, 267, 269
Adad, storm god, 147–8, 180, 260
Afghanistan, lapis lazuli from, 21, 36, 77, 179
agate, 5–6, 12, 26–7, 65, 68, 75, 77, 80, 159
Akkadian: terms, lxi, lxiii, lxvi, 132–3, 259–60; periods, 9–10, 21, 27, 31, 33, 73 n.; kings, 28, 73 n., 215; text on Hurrian booty, 110–11, 133; deities, 151–2
alabastron, 219
Albright, W. F., 106
Allabria, 182, 184
Alp, Sedat, 59
Amandry, P., 209–10
Amarna letters, lxiv, 111, 132–3, 155
amber, 80
Amiet, P., 94 215
Amiran, Ruth, 14, 127–8
Amorites (Amurru), 83, 104–6
amulets, 1, 119, 152; animal, 12, 67, 127; fertility, 119, 140, 166; spiral jewellery as, 35; sun, moon and star symbols as, 142–3, 145, 149
Anat, Anat-Astarte, goddess, 119, 143–4
Anatolia: ores of, lxiv-lxvi, 18, 28; contacts with Palestine, 14–15; excavations in, 17; influence of Mesopotamia on, 18–20, 28, 35, 38, 40, 47, 71; contacts with Transcaucasia, 37, 38, 77; Early Bronze period in, 38–63, 75; rebellion and unrest in, 39–40; contacts with Caucasia, 46–7; contacts with Assyria, 70–3; *kārum* periods in, 97–101; Hittite sites in, 98; contacts with Syria, 100, 134; inlay work in, 102; deities of, 143, 146, 148–9; mid second millennium B.C. in, 177; early first millennium B.C. in, 234
Andrae, W., 166–7, 172–3
animal heads: on amulets, 204, 246–8; on bracelets, 204–5, 209–10, 212, 246–51; on roundels and bracteates, 210–12; stylized, on earrings or pendants, 218–19
Anu, sky god, 147
appliqués, 151, 210–13, 219, 251, 253–5, 259–60
Ararat, Mount, 205
Araxes river, 73–4, 202
Arinna, sun goddess, 149
Armenia, lxiv, 37, 213
armlets, 22, 85, 123–4, 204, 246–8
armlets, periods: Sargonid, 22; Larsa, 85; Middle Bronze Age, 123–4; Late Assyrian, 246–8; Urartian, seventh century B.C., 204
arm-shaped vessels, 127–8
arsenic ore (orpiment), 182
Ashtoreth, goddess, 139
Ashur, god, 146, 148, 180, 183–4, 202, 243, 246
Ashurbanipal, 147, 185, 218, 242–4, 248, 250, 252–4, 259, 261, 263, 269; wife of, 254
Ashurnaṣirpal II, jewellery on reliefs of, 142, 148, 209–10, 226, 234, 238, 240–1, 246–9, 252–5; stele of, 147–8; period of, 155–6, 181, 199, 232, 235, 255
Assyria, sources of gold, lxiv; trading colony at Kültepe, 47–8, 59, 71, 97–101; contacts with Anatolia and Troy, 70–3; contacts with Hissar, 77; metal-work tradition in, 92; deities of, 142–5, 147, 152; Egyptian influence on, 166–7; booty taken in campaigns of, 180–5; influence on Iran, 188; associations with Urartian sites, 199–200; gold looted from, 202; reliefs of, 209–10, 212, 232–3, 235–6; lions of, 222–3; influence on Palestine, 226–9
Assyrian periods: Old, 70; Middle, lxi, 147, 158, 163–79, 180–1, 188, 190–2; Late, lxi, 155, 180–5, 232–64
Astarte, goddess, 219; plaques and pendants, 107, 138–9
Atra-hasīs myth, Old Babylonian, 127
axe heads, 19, 27, 66, 69, 72–4, 100, 103–6, 111, 124
Azerbaijan, 19, 158, 188, 194, 202

Baal, god, 137, 150
Baal-zebub, god, 127
Babylonia, Third Dynasty of Ur in, lxi–lxiii, lxv, 2, 26–9, 31, 33–5, 37, 44, 58–9; Old Babylonian period in, lxi, 132–3, 154; source of gold in, lxiv; use of divine symbols in, 35, 141, 144–5, 150, 152, 260; First Dynasty of, 37, 64, 68, 78, 81, 84–5, 90–1, 100, 106, 137, 147, 155, 160, 165, 215; Guti invasion of, 39; Larsa period in, 58–60, 83–91, 142; Kassite period in, 90, 163–79, 212–13; influence of, on Kassite jewellery, 165; revolts against Assyria, 184–5, 232; conquered by Elam, 186; captures Jeru-

salem, 224; tribute to Assyria from, 241; negotiates between Media and Lydia, 269
Badakshan, Afghanistan, lxiv, 1, 6, 36, 77, 179
Balkan, K., 198
bangles, 22, 27, 45, 66, 68, 95–6
Barbarini cauldron, 220–1
Barnett, R. D., 206, 221, 227, 250, 260, 264
barrow graves, Trialeti, 74–6
beads, attached to woven material, 100; used as head or threaded on shank of pin, 113
beads, periods: Jamdat Nasr, 1; Early Dynastic, 3, 5–10, 15, 20–1; Sargonid, 7, 9, 19–21, 26–7, 33, 77; Third Dynasty of Ur, 7, 9, 10, 65, 67–70, 77, 80, 192; Akkadian, 9, 10; Early Bronze, Anatolian, 43–4; Troy IIg, 52–4; First Dynasty of Babylon, 68; Kassite, 68; Hissar III, 80; Larsa, 85–6; Simash Dynasty, 95; *kārum* level II, 97–8; Middle Bronze II, Palestine, 125–7; Late Cypriote Ia, 125, 130–1; mid second millennium B.C., Iran, 134, 159–62; Mid-Assyrian, 173–4, 178–9; late second millennium B.C., Iran, 189, 192; early first millennium B.C., Iran, 194–6; Urartian, 200–3; Solomonic, 227; Iron Age, Palestine, 227, 229, 231
beads, principal forms: animal, 161, 174, 215; ball-shaped (spherical, globular), 6, 9, 27, 30, 37, 67–9, 74, 126, 136, 192, 207, 229, (collared) 26, 75, 200, (faceted) 9, (fluted or ribbed) 9, 67, 134; barrel-shaped, 9, 27, 30, 67, 125–6, 161, 192, 229; biconvex, 9; circular, 138, 201; claw, 63; coiled wire, 20, 200, 202, 207; conoid, double (biconical), 6, 9, 11, 29–30, 97–8, 126, 201, 203, (faceted) 9, (long) 9, 192; 'cotton reel', 44, (triple) 44; cruciform, 43; cylindrical, 9, 29, 67, 170, (cylinders joined longitudinally) 194–5, (of soldered balls) 227; date-shaped, 9, 26, 67–9, 78–9, 161, 192–3, 200, 207; diamond-shaped, 10, 22, 26, (flat-winged) 68; discoid (flat disc-shaped), 10, 26, 29, 35, 37, 60, 79, 161–2; 'dumb bell', 6; elliptical, 9; flanged, 26; fluted with long collars, 109, 125, 131; frit, 194, 231; gold-capped, 6, 26–7, 65, 68–9, 75, 176, 192, 194, 207; granulated, 37, 74, 131; hemispherical, 75, 176; hexagonal, 170; hub-shaped, 10; lentoid, 10; lily or lotus, 126; lunate, 26; melon-shaped, 201, 227, 229, (collared) 162, (fluted) 65, 88–9, 91, 95, 99, 116, 125, 138, 160, 207; oval, single or multiple, 138; ovoid, 6, 9; pomegranate, 161, 178, 202; quadruple disc, 44; quadruple spiral, 30–1, 34–7, 44, 53, 58, 60, 70, 98, 178–9, 189, 192, 207–8, 267; rectangular, 9, 189, 194; rhomboid, 10, 26, 68; ring-shaped, 10, 120, (granulated) 30, 52, 57, (of soldered balls) 134, 227; spacer, 80, 126, 159–60, 194–5, 200–1, 207–8; spindle-shaped, 109, 116, 119, 125, 131; square, 7, 67, (segmented) 126, 131; star-shaped, 43; triangular, 23, 44; tubular, 9, 80, 159, 187, (curved) 95, 159; winged disc, flat, 14, 21–2, 30–1, 34–6, 52–3, 56, 63, 65, 161, 178, 194
bells, gold, 208
belts (or headbands), 122–3
Birmingham, J. M., 263
Bittel, K., 58, 71, 127
Black Sea, 46, 58
Blegen, C. W., 48, 52, 55, 59
Bottéro, J., 132–3, 157
boundary stones, 147, 163–4
bracelet, of Adoni-Nur, 262
bracelets, periods: Early Dynastic, 15; Troy IIg, 52, 55, 60; Third Dynasty of Ur, 69; Larsa, 85; Kassite, 164–5; second millennium B.C., Iran, 187–9, 192; first millennium B.C., Iran, 194–7, 209–10, 223, 267–8; Urartian, 203–5, Late Assyrian, 246–51
bracelets, principal types: animal-headed, 196–7, 203, 209–10, 223, 248, 250–1, 263, 268; bead, 96; bronze, 20, 63, (and iron) 263, (gold plated) 63; duck-headed, 267–8; granulated, 7, 164–5; hinged, 250; inlaid, 250; linked, 248, 250; laminated plates, 122–3; multiple, 85, 248–50, 268; plaited wire, 116; serpent-headed, 204–5; silver, plain, 80; solid gold, plain, 180; tubular, 124, (one tube within another) 195–6; twisted bar, 192; with rosette or rosettes, 57, 152, 246–50; with sliding ends, 188
bracteates, lion-head, 211–12
Brea, Bernabó, 60
breast ornament, 173
breastplate, 15, 216
bronze and bronzes, 18–19, 88, 101
Buchanan, Briggs, 2
bucranium pendant, 131, 226
Bulgaria, pectorals from, 217
bull: bearded, on amulet, 12; calf finials, 204–5, 209–10, 246, 248, 250–1; humped, drawing plough, 195; stylized, on inlaid earrings, 119; terracotta, 187, 193; winged, 147, 195, 251, (human-headed) 201, 216, 220, 265
Burney, C. A., 75, 204
bust, gold, of goddess or king, 197
buttons, 80, 202, 230; conical, 53, 161; granulated, 190, 200, 203; punched dot, 191; repoussé, 88, 190

calf amulet (*see also* bull calf), 12
Canaanite culture, 108, 224; deities, 119, 137, 143
Canby, J. V., 61
cap, gold or silver conical, 98
Cappadocia, 42, 77, 145, 147
carnelian, lxiv, 3, 5, 7, 10, 12, 26–7, 33, 65, 77, 80, 125, 159, 170–1, 178, 192
cat's eye: beads, 27, 68, 80; pendants, 170–1
Caucasus, Mesopotamian influence in, 20, 73–4; connection between Alaca and sites in, 46–7; Kassites and, 163–4
Cesnola, General, 81
chain, silver, 101, 196; gold, 208
chalcedony, 80, 233
chariot burials, 36, 164
Chehab, Emir Maurice, 109
chrysalis amulet, 127
Cilicia, lxiv, 39, 41–2, 61, 264; Mesopotamian influence in, 61, 71
Cimmerians, 198, 232, 262
clasps, 43, 108
cloisons and cloisonné work, 14, 56, 65, 75–6, 102, 118, 133, 136, 167, 173–4, 192, 199–200
Coche de la Ferté, E., 269
'collier à contrepoids', 155
combs, Sumerian, 4
Contenau, G., 91
copper, sources of, 18, 46–7, 64; axes, 19; pans and weapons, 66; hammered, 69; earrings on terracotta figure, 72
counterweight for necklace, 85, 95, 155; fronted, 197; tassel as, 202
Crawford, Harriet, 2, 27, 105
cremation graves, 230
crescent (lunula) (*see also* earrings, lunate; pendants, crescent-shaped) 100; and horn-shaped pendants, 149–51
Crete, 165, 219
crowns, Assyrian, 254
Culican, W., 34, 222
'cup spirals', 168
cylinder: beads, 9, 29, 67, 170; gold-mounted haematite, 82; seals, *see* seals, cylinder
Cypriote periods: Early, 81–2; Middle, 82, 130; Late I, 82, 107, 127–31; Late II, 128

daggers, 57, 66, 74, 76, 79, 105, 116, 124, 191–2, 225
Dales, G. F., 154
Damanville, Mlle, 143
De Morgan, J., 205
De Vaux, R., 15, 111
Deshayes, Jean, 78
diadems, periods: Early Dynastic, 5, 11; Sargonid, 22, 26, 74; Early Bronze, Anatolian, 45; Pontic, 46–7; Troy IIg, 52; Guti-Gudea, 68, 79; Third Dynasty of Ur, 70; *kārum* level Ib, 99; First Dynasty of Babylon, 108–9, 119–22; Late Assyrian, 251; first millennium B.C., Iran, 214–15
diadems, principal types: centrally hinged, 122; necklace, with pendants, 169–71; pierced at each end or corner, 99, 120, 226; repoussé, 189, 195; with beaded chains and pendants, 52; with looped spiral clasp, 108–9, 119–20, 122–3, 138; with rosettes, 121, 218, 251, (and enamel) 214–15
discs, 29, 33, 47, 76, 88, 179; winged, 118–19, 145
dress fasteners (*see also* fibulae), 124–5
Dunand, M., 58
Dyson, R. H., 78, 91–2, 158, 159, 160, 188, 206

eagle-headed demons, 248
Earp, Professor, 158
earrings, of Hurrian deities, 110; on Assyrian reliefs, 235–46
earrings, periods: Early Dynastic, 3–4, 24; Sargonid, 19, 22–4, 28–9, 35, 47, 207; Talish Moyen, 20; Troy IIg, 48–51, 55–6, 58, 60; Troy VI, 56–7; Third Dynasty of Ur, 58–9; Early Bronze II and III, Anatolia, 62–3; Larsa, 70, 83–4; Guti-Gudea, 74; First Dynasty of Babylon, 78; Giyan IV, 92–3; Shimash Dynasty, 91, 95; *kārum* level Ib, 99–101; Middle Bronze II, Palestine, 106, 112, 114–20, 125; Late Cypriote Ia, 130–1; second millennium B.C., Iran, 159–60, 162, 187–9, 192–3; Mid-Assyrian, 168–9, 174–9; early first millennium B.C., Iran, 195, 208, 213–14; Urartian, 198–9, 203; Solomonic, 224–6; Iron Age, Palestine, 227–8; Late Assyrian, 234–46, 261–5
earrings, principal types: animal-head, 119, 130–1, 138, 213; bag, 26; bar-twisted, 113–15, 130–1, 213; basket-shaped, 48–9, 51–2, 60–1, (with rosette) 208; boat-shaped, 179, 188, 203, 208, 230, 240, 262–5; circular (hoop), 85, (with balls) 239, (with balls and granules) 227–8, 267, (with pendant) 199, 266, (with triangle of balls) 189; coiled, 74, 160, (or hair-rings) 45–7; double pyramid, 195, (ring) 199; drop-lunate, 78, 225, 229; falcon, 118; flange-twisted, 130; flower calyx, 57, 60, 224–5; fluted, 84–5, 91–3, 95, 158; granulated, 70, 84, 109, 116–17, 225, 130–1, 138, 230, 234, 264, (and inlaid) 118–21, 131; leaf-shaped, 80; leech-shaped, 120, 240; lunate (crescent-shaped),

22–3, 27–8, 49, 69, 159, 175, 193, 238–40, 243, 262, 264, (double) 4–5, 24, 159, (double-ended) 28, 67, (fluted) 28, 62, 174, 176, (triple) 67, 76–8, (with bud and flower pendant) 243–4, (with granulation) 49, 51, 56, 58, 187–8, 193, 204, (with knob) 226, (with pendant) 138, 174, 234, 240; mulberry, 116, 121, 125, 138, 178, 225–6, (oval) 130–1; penannular, 28, 85, 95, 101, 114–18, 130–1, 136, 159, 175, 225, 230–1, 268–9, (bar-twisted) 114–15, (granulated) 116–18, (incised) 114, (plaited wire) 115–16, (strip-twisted) 115, (with drop or clustered granules) 116; pomegranate, 198, 202, 243–4, (clustered) 192, 198, 243; 'shell', 51, 60–1; soldered balls, 266; strip-twisted, 115–16, 125, 130, 159; tassel, 225–6; triangular plaque, 62; triple-armed, 234–5, 241–2; triple-lobed, 70, 137; with pendant and conical tip, 240–1, 264–5, (and rosette), 168, 174–7
Egypt, source of gold, lxiv; Tsarskaia relations of, 47; Hyksos invaders of, 107; relations of, with Mitanni, 133, 143, 155, 165; influence on Kassite and Assyrian jewellers, 164–8
El, Canaanite god, 119, 141
Elam, source of silver and tin, lxv, 19; invasions of, 40; conquers Ur, 77, 83–4, 103; metal-work in, 92–3, 164, 168, 228, 267; Simash Dynasty of, 94; Kassites in, 163–4; sacks Babylon, 168–9; helps Babylon against Assyria, 184–5
Elburz mountains, 158, 189
electrum, lxiv–lxvi, 20, 55
enamel, 214–15, 248
Enki, god, 153
Enlil, god, 148, 164
Enmerkar, king of Uruk, 1–2
Entemena vase, lxvi
Epstein, Clare, 111
Esarhaddon, 147, 242–3, 252; reliefs of period, 250
Eshnunna, booty from, 94–6
Etruria, Asiatic influence on, 217, 220

face-urn, 111
falcon, in granular decoration, 117, 269; earring in form of, 118; bronze, 137
fertility: goddess, 35, 152, 156–7, 220; amulets, 119, 140, 166; symbols, 243
fibulae, 204, 208–9, 233–4; predecessors of, 125; Stronach's classification of Assyrian, 260–4
figurines, terracotta, 24, 58, 72, 85–6, 136–7, 162, 193, 197; lead, 58; bronze, 140, 196
filigree work, 65, 70, 75, 230; with granules, 187, 230
fillets, 69, 100, 251, 254; with rosettes, 252
fly: amulet, 12, 127; whisk, 223
forehead ornaments, double spiral, 166
Frankfort, H., 36, 38, 73, 146, 166
frescoes, Mari, 84–5; Til Barsib, 239
frit, 80; beads, 174, 194; masks, 178–9
frog amulet, 12
frontal (frontlet), 22, 27, 67, 69
'frying pan', 58, 66, 70–1

galena, lxvi
gazelle, lead, 72
Georgia, 204
Ghirshman, R., 91–2, 214, 217, 232
Gilgamesh, 209, 246
Gilzanu, 181
Gimbutas, Marija, 46–7
Giyan Period IV, 91–3
Gizilbunda, 182
glass: spacers, 80; paste, 80, 120, 174; mosaic, 179
goat: amulet, 67; crouching, from Ziweye, 212
Godard, A., 265
Goff, Clare, 91
gold, sources of, lxiii–lv, 18–19, 133, 230; shortage of, 19; lacking in Cyprus, 82
Goldman, Hetty, 61
granulation, 7, 19, 36–7, 117
Great Zab river, lxvi, 181–2
Greece, animal earrings from, 214; Asiatic influence on, 219, 263–4; connections with Al Mina, 229
griffins, 221
Gudea, king, lxiv, lxv, 39, 74, 118, 142; period of, *see* Guti-Gudea
Gula, goddess, 262
Gurney, O. R., 149
Guti, invasions of, 39–40, 42, 73–4
Guti-Gudea period, 27, 41, 64–81, 215
Gutium, 40

Ḫabḫi, land of, 181, 183
Ḫaḫḫu, Cilicia, lxiv
hair ornaments, periods: Early Dynastic, 3; Sargonid, 22–3, Hissar, 80; Early Cypriote III, 81; Late Assyrian, 266
hair ornaments, principal types: leaf-shaped, 3, 80; pins, 4; ribbon, gold and silver, 3, 22, 69, 266; sheet gold, 81–2; spiral, 82
hair-rings (lock rings), 5, 20, 22–3, 29, 45–7, 67, 69, 76, 101
Haldi, god, 183–4

Hammurabi of Babylon, 88, 145; period of, 109
hand-shaped: pin-head, 13; catch of fibula, 208–9, 261
Hathor curls, 119, 139–40
Hawkes, C. F. C., 130
headdresses, periods: Early Dynastic, 3, 9–10, 14, 80; Sargonid, 21–4; Late Assyrian, 251–4
headdresses (*see also* diadems), principal types: bead and chain (*brīm*), 9, 14, 21; crowns, 254; fillets, 69, 100, 251–2, 254; frontlet, 21–2; headbands, 44, 108, 119–23, (twisted guilloche) 197; jewelled Assyrian, 251–4; *polos* of Assyrian kings, 251–3; Queen Pu-abi type, 3–4, 21
Hencken, H., 217
Henschel-Simon, E., 113
Hepat, goddess, 149
Herrmann, G., lxiv
Herzfeld, E., 77, 91, 160
Higgins, R. A., 120, 129, 131, 263
Hittite: weapons, 57, 97; jewellery, 99–100; booty from Hurrian cities, 110–11; sun symbol and religion of, 146, 149
Hoffman, H., 234–5
horned gods and goddesses, 119
Hubushkia, 182
Hungary, 208
Hurrian: penetration of Mesopotamia, 40; axe head, 73; gold work, 90, 109–12, 135; deities, 110, 140, 143–4, 146–7, 149; pottery, 111, 127, 187; influences on Cypriote designs, 127–8; words, 133; influences on Kassite jewellery, 165
Hyksos, the, 107, 113

Ianzi, 182
Ibi-Sin, king of Mesopotamia, 77, 82
idols, double violin-shaped female, 46; stylized, as pendants, 49, 52, 60
Inanna (Inanna-Ishtar), goddess, 142, 151–7; temples of, 94, 164, 168
inlay (*see also* cloisons), 1, 65, 75, 95–6, 102, 118, 120, 133, 167–8
In-Shushinak, god, 160, 168–9
Iran, gold and silver of, lxiv, lxvi, 1, 18; Mesopotamian influence on, 20, 28; Talish region of, 20–1, 162; trade connection with Afghanistan, 21; spiraliform jewellery in, 35; trade route over, 36, 73, 77; at period of Third Dynasty of Ur, 77–81; end of third and beginning of second millennium B.C. in, 91–3; first half of second millennium B.C. in, 94–6; mid second millennium B.C. in, 158–62, 177, 179; terracotta figurines of, 162; at end of second millennium B.C., 185–97; in first millennium B.C., 206–23, 228, 232–3, 264–9
Iraq, 28, 177
Iron Age, 205, 224, 228
Ishtar, goddess, 85, 132–3, 135, 137, 140, 143–4, 219; symbol of, 141–2, 145, 147–8, 151–3; jewellery of, 153–7, 166
Isin-Larsa period, *see* Larsa period
ivory and ivories, 80, 127; Assyrian, 216, 241

Jamdat Nasr period, 1, 27, 35, 134, 140
jasper, 171
Jerusalem, 224

Kaletas, mines at, lxiv
Kandil Dağ mountains, 181
Kantor, Helene, 213
Karageorghis, V., 82
kārum, Assyrian, at Kültepe-Kanesh, 97–101
Kassite: period, 68, 89–90, 148, 163–79, 212–13, 265; gold work, 89–90, 164–5, 186; seals, 89–90, 155, 164, 166–7; symbols, 148, 153; origins, 163; gods, 164
Keban, mines at, lxv
Kenyon, K. M., 104–5, 108
Khorsabad, 183, 209
Khram river, 37, 74
Kirruri, land of, 181
Kramer, S. M., 153–4
Kuftin, B. A., 74–5
Kupper, J. R., 109
Kura river, 73–4
Kurdistan, 28, 158, 181
Kurigalzu II (III) of Babylon, 164, 166–7, 179

Labat, R., 168
Lagash, Second Dynasty of, 39
Lama, goddess, 85, 89–91, 155
Lamaštu, demon, 211, 261
lapis lazuli, 1, 3, 33, 66, 69, 127, 133, 138, 170–2, 176, 178–9; mines, lxiv, 77; trade in, 1, 6, 20–1, 36, 64, 77, 79
Laroche, E., 149
Larsa period, 41, 58–61, 59, 64, 70, 83–9, 142, 176
Layard, Sir Henry, 246
lead, 80; vessels, 77
leaf decorations, 3–4, 80, 191
Leemans, W. F., 133
Lehmann-Haupt, 235
Lemnos, 19, 49, 57, 60
lightning symbol, 89–90, 147
lion-headed demon, 211–12
lions, 203, 208–9, 222–3; heads, 196–7, 203, 210–12, 246, 248, 251; with two bodies, 210; with griffins, 221

Little Zab river, 182
Lloyd, Seton, 163, 204
lock rings (*see also* hair-rings), 45, 51
lotus, 212, 243–5, 262
lunula, *see* crescent
Lycia, 19, 63
Lydia, lxiv, 239, 263, 268–9

mace head, bronze, 191
Madhloom, Tariq, 235
malachite, 168, 170
Mallowan, Sir Max, lxiv, 15, 17, 27–8, 30–2, 34, 40, 77, 178–9, 211, 217, 220, 233–4, 246, 254
Maltese cross symbol, 148, 212
man-headed bulls, 201, 216, 220, 265
Mannai, 222
Mannean metal work, 207, 216
Marduk, god, lxi, 184, 202, 260
masks, frit, 178–9
Mazda, A., 192
medallions, 102, 203–4
Media and Medes, lxvi, 268–9; tribute to Assyria from, 183, 241; conquests of, 202, 232; conjectural metal work of, 206–7, 210–11, 216–17, 223, 250; jewellery of, 267
Mellaart, J., 39, 41
Mellink, Machteld, 63
Meluḫḫa, lxiv
mercury, 230
Meskalamdug, helmet of, lxv; grave of, 16
Mesopotamia, Third Dynasty of Ur in, lxi–lxiii, lxv, 2, 26–9, 31, 33–5, 37, 44, 49, 58–9, 61, 64–74, 140, 157; sources of ores for, lxiii–lxvi, 17–19, 94; Early Dynastic period in, lxv, lxvi, 1–16, 28, 31, 36, 78–9, 152, 193; Jamdat Nasr period in, 1, 27, 35, 134, 140, 151, 157; Sargonid period in, 2–6, 17–37, 47, 49, 61, 105, 141, 152; influence on Anatolian metal work, 18–20, 28, 35, 38, 40, 58; Guti-Gudea period in, 27, 41, 64–82; Akkadian period in, 31, 33; influences on Palestine, 32, 102, 105, 140; spiraliform jewellery in, 35; Gutian invasion of, 39–40; relations between Trialeti and, 73–4; influence on Tepe Hissar, 77; Larsa period and First Dynasty of Babylon in, 83–91; Hurrian principalities in, 110; influence on Syria, 140; deities of, 142–7; rosette symbol in, 151–2, 156
Minns, E. H., 74
Minorski, 182
Mitanni, lxiv, 111, 133, 143, 146, 165
Montet jar, 57, 102, 104
moon: god, lxiii, 141, 144–5, 147–8; goddess, 111, 150; symbols, 142, 149–51
Moorey, R., 251
Moortgat, A., 167–8
mosaic work, 164, 167, 179, 191
moufflon heads, 209–10, 213, 223, 246
moulds, for jewellery, 29, 61, 101, 108, 134, 136, 138, 229; for axe heads, 73, 101; for figurines, 136–7; for pottery plaques, 140; for sun disc amulets, 145
'mouth-pieces', 130, 189, 228
Murat river, 204
Murray, A. S., 81
Musasir, 183–4
Myres, J. N. L., 81

Nabu, god, 90
Nannar, Nanna, moon god, lxiii, 152
Naram-Sin of Akkad, 19, 39–40, 141, 215; palace of, Brak, 28–9, 40
Nebuchadnezzar of Babylon, 224, 268
necklace, of Pu-abi, 5–10; of Abbabashti, 27, 65, 74, 102; Dilbat, 88–91, 100, 117–18, 125–6, 145, 148, 160; *tudittu* and, 155–6, 174
necklaces, periods: Early Dynastic, 5–7, 10–12; Early Bronze, Anatolia, 43–4; Third Dynasty of Ur, 58, 65, 67–70; Larsa, 84–6, 88; Sargonid, 12, 22–3, 26, 29; Talish Moyen, 20; Simash Dynasty, 95; mid and late second millennium B.C., Iran, 159–62, 189, 192–4; Late Cypriote, 82; Mid-Assyrian, 168–71, 178; first millennium B.C., Iran, 197, 207–8; Urartian, 199–202
necklaces, principal types: bead, 5–10, 20, 22, 26–7, 30, 43–4, 58, 65, 67–70, 80, 85, 88, 95, 126, 137, 159, 161–2, 169, 178, 189, 192–4, 199–202, 207, 227; 'choker', 85, 155, 197; 'dog collar', 6–7; of plaques, gold and lapis lazuli, 169, 176–7; of spacer beads, 207; with counterweight, 85, 95, 155, (tassel) 156, 201–2; with pendants, 29, 88–9, 119, 156, 161, 169–71, 199, 207, 211, 254
Negahban, E. O., 189–90, 197
Neo-Babylonian: seal, 220; earring, 239, 268
Nikkal, goddess, 150
Ningal, moon goddess, 111, 150; jewellery of, lxi, 111, 132–3
Ningirsu-Ninurta, god, 118
Ninhursag, goddess, 35, 166
Ninmah, goddess, 84
Ninurta, god, 147
Nippur, 40
Nissen, H. J., 2, 9, 21
'nose rings', 109

Oates, David, 178–9, 191
onyx, 33, 65, 168, 170–1
Oppenheim, Max von, 260

Orontes river, 133, 229
Oxus treasure, 268
Özgüc, Nimet, lxii, 17, 41, 46–8, 100
Özgüc, Tahsin, 41, 48, 200

Pactolus river, lxiv
Palestine, Anatolian contacts, 14–15; Mesopotamian influences, 32, 102, 105, 126; Caucasian contacts, 47; Middle Bronze I in, 99, 108, 113; Amorites in, 104–6; Middle Bronze II in, 106–27; Hurrian penetration of, 110, 112; Late Bronze period in, 112, 122, 127, 138, 150; relations with Cyprus, 127–31, 136; mid second millennium B.C. in, 132–57; late second and early first millenium B.C. in, 224–30; Assyrian influence on, 226–9; cremation graves in, 230
Papkhi, booty from, 180–1
Parrot, A., 14–15, 215
Pazuzu, demon, 211
pectorals, 162, 168, 173–4, 215–22; *tudittu* and, 157
pendants, periods: Early Dynastic, 3, 10–12, 15; Sargonid, 19, 29–30, 33, 35; Troy IIg, 48–9; Late Bronze II, Anatolia, 63; Hissar III, 79; Larsa, 84, 87; Kassite, 89, 166; Middle Bronze II, Palestine, 108; mid second millennium B.C., Iran, 159–62; Mid-Assyrian, 168, 170–1; Iron Age, Palestine, 231
pendants, principal types: animal, 33, 130–1, 138, 170, 177; bird, 138, 195; button, 265; cage, 190, 198; chariot yoke, 227; circular, 44, 85, 100, 161, 202, 229, 234, (rosette) 89, 91, 152, 156, (with central boss) 87, 100, 162, 190–1, (with central suspension) 30, (with crescent) 88, (with granulation) 117, (with star) 140–1, 144, 147, 149, (with suspender strips), 29; coiled wire, 11, 29, 160, 200; crescent-shaped, 79–80, 87–91, 100, 141, 149–51, 159, 172, 188, 226, 229; disc, 161, 170–1, 190, (with rays) 89, 91, 140–9; double circle, 15, 189, (pyramid) 195, 198, (spiral) 11, 23, 78–9, 166, 172, 267; drop-shaped, 171; earring, 238, 240–1, 243–4, 266; forehead, 166, 172; fruit, 12; horn-shaped, 149–51, 226; idol, 49, 60, 89–90, 100; impressed cruciform, 231; inlaid, with winged disc and animal head, 108, 118–20; 'Ishtar', 135, 137, 160, 187–8, 234; lanceolate, 30; lantern-shaped, 207; leaf, 3, 10–11, 63; lentoid with cylinder, 171; lotus, 238; lozenge-shaped, 135; Maltese cross, 148, 168, 212; melon-shaped, 171; moon, 87–90, 141, 150–1; multiple cylinder, 171; nude goddess, 138–41, 234; oval, of chalcedony, 233; pomegranate, 11, 170, 192, 194–6, 199, 202, 243, (bud) 229; ring-shaped, 11, 14; seal, 234; square, 234; star-shaped, 140–4, 159, 178; sun disc, 141, 144–9, 162; triangular, 119, 170, 189; vase-shaped, 170–1; wheel-shaped, 198; winged, 108; with 'cup spiral' pattern, 168, 170–1; with lightning symbol, 89–90, 147–8
Persia, *see* Iran
Persian Gulf: trade, 35, 64; lands beyond, 40, 186
Petrie, Sir Flinders, 47, 117, 119, 224, 226, 228
Philistines, pottery of, 224–5, 227
Phoenicia, Bronze Age in, 102–27; goldsmiths of coastal cities, 136; Iron Age in, 203, 208, 269; pottery of, 226; tribute to Assyria from, 241
Phrygian: embroidery, 256–7; fibula 260, 262
pins, periods: Early Dynastic, 12–13; Talish Moyen, 20; Sargonid, 20, 22, 25–6, 31–2; Early Bronze, Anatolian, 42–3, 63; Troy IIg, 55–7; Troy II–V, 57; Third Dynasty of Ur, 66, 70, 72; Guti-Gudea, 69; Simash Dynasty, 94; *kārum* levels II and Ib, 98–9; Early and Middle Bronze, Syria, 105; Iron Age, Palestine, 228; first millennium B.C., Iran, 266
pins, principal types: ball-headed, 42, 68, (granulated) 74–5, (with studs) 42; bird-headed, 99; club-headed, 105; conical headed, 32, 70, 98; copper, 32, 62; curved, 13; double club-headed, 57, (spiral headed) 42, 57, 60; flat-headed (nail-headed), 62–3, 113, 203; fluted, with wings, 42; gold-plated, 96, 98–9; hammer-headed, 42, 46; hand-headed, 13; iron and silver, 266; knob-headed, 113; lion-headed, 193; mushroom-headed, 15, 98–9, 105, 191; pierced shank, 12–13, 25, 32, 96, 225; pot-headed, with spirals, 55–7, 60; shell and bitumen, 96; spatulate (racquet), 3, 13, 20, 32; toggle, 12, 32, 66, 72, 96, 98–100, 105, 112–13, 116, 121, 124, 130–1, 188, 191, (with threaded ring) 99; with bar-twisted shaft, 56; with cloisonné rosette head, 56; with curled or rolled head, 32, 105; with date-shaped head, 42; with decorated shaft, 98–9; with oval fluted head, 98; with rings or beads on shank, 96, 113
pin-through-sockets fastening, 108–9, 122–3, 250
Piotrovski, B. B., 202, 208
pithos burials, 63
plaques, principal types: 'Astarte', 107, 119, 138–9, 219; circular, 14–15, 100, 230; exorcism, 211; headdress, 254; ivory, 119;

necklace of, 169, 176; nude goddess, 138–40; shell, from Mari, 12, 25; terracotta, 85, 140; triangular, 266; used as armour, 216; winged bull, 201
Pontic region, 38, 42, 46
Porada, Edith, 102, 164, 166–7, 196
protective spirits or goddesses, 220
Pu-abi, Queen, jewels of, 3–4, 11–13, 36
punched dot technique, *see* repoussé
Purushkhanda, 18, 40

Qalparunda, 241

Reade, J. M., 243
Regolini-Galassi tomb, Etruria, 217, 220
repoussé work, 88, 135, 137, 161, 179, 187, 190, 221
Reshef, god, 119, 129, 150
rhyton, 210
ribbons, gold, 3, 22, 69; silver, 266
rings, periods: Early Dynastic, 13–14; Third Dynasty of Ur, 69; Late Cypriote II, 120; Middle Elamite, 187; second millennium B.C., Iran, 192, 196; Urartian, 199–201; early first millenium B.C., Iran, 262, 266
rings, principal types: cloisonné, 14, 199–200; coiled wire, 69; enamelled, 120; filigree decorated, 13, 187; gold 'glove' with, 213; granulated 187, 200–1; incised gold, 196; lotus-shaped, 262; serpentine, 192
Rizayeh, Lake (Lake Urmia), lxvi, 93, 182
rock crystal, 171, 241
rock reliefs, 79–80, 110, 143, 146, 215, 220, 250–1, 255, 260
rosettes: appliqué for garments, 151, 212–13, 219, 251, 255, 259–60; as symbol, 142, 151–2; on bracelet, 152, 246–8; on diadem, 214, 218, 251; on earring, 174, 176, 208; on pectoral, 221; pendant, 89, 91, 152, 156
rosettes, periods: Jamdat Nasr, 1; Early Dynastic, 3, 14; Early Bronze, Anatolia, 46–7; Troy IIg, 48–9, 55–7; Middle Bronze II, Palestine, 109, 121; Mid-Assyrian, 174, 176, 179
roundels, of Ziweye, 210–12; of Ghafantlu, 222
Riis, P., 219
Russia, Talish region (*see also* Caucasus), 11, 20–1; Pontic sites, 46–7

Salvini, Mirjo, 181
Samaria, 224
Sapia, gold from, 182
Sargon of Agade, lxiii, lxv, 17, 19, 39–40
Sargon II of Assyria, 145, 183–4, 199, 202, 222, 224, 241–2, 250, 253, 257
Sargonid Period (2370–2200 B.C.), 2, 6, 17–37, 47, 49, 61, 105, 141, 152; (721–705 B.C.), 242, 246, 248, 257, 259, 265
Sataran, god, 164
scarab, 113, 138, 226, 231; holder, 234
Schaeffer, C. F. A., 20, 137, 141, 205
Schliemann, H., 19, 48–9, 55–8
Scythians, 202, 208, 216, 232
'Sea Peoples', 136, 230
Seleucia, 230
Sefid Rud river and valley, 158, 189
Sennacherib of Assyria, 147, 184, 229, 232, 259; reliefs of period of, 242–3, 250
shaft graves at Ur, 68
Shalmaneser III of Assyria, 181–2, 240–1
Shamash, sun god, 141–2, 144–5, 147–8
Shamshi-Adad V of Assyria, 148, 182, 240; stele of, 147, 252
Shapash, sun goddess, 141, 219
Shaushga, goddess, 140, 143–4, 149, 219
silver, source of, lxiii, lxv, 19; increased use of, 59, 77–9
Simash Dynasty of Elam, 94
Sin, moon god, 141, 144–5, 147–8
siren figures with pectorals, 217–19
Solomonic period, 224–7
spacers, *see under* beads
Speiser, E. A., 110
sphinx with pectoral, 217, 219, 221
spindle-shaped flask, 128
spiraliform jewellery (*see also* bead, quadruple spiral; pendant, double spiral), 19, 35, 127, 166
Spycket, Agnes, 154
star symbol, 140–9, 152, 178, 187, 191, 213; to sew on garment, 212–13, 259–60
statue, statuette, jewellery on, from Susa, 94–6
Stewart, J. R., 112, 123
Stronach, David, 78, 260, 267, 269; his classification of fibulae, 260–4
studs, 1, 53, 203; ear, 63
Sumer (*see also* Mesopotamia), goldsmiths and jewellers of, lxi, lxv, lxvi, 77, 92; Early Dynastic period of, lxv, lxvi, 1–16, 19–24, 26, 28–9, 31–3, 35–6, 49, 78–9, 152, 193; Early Dynastic I of, 1, 14, 79; Early Dynastic II of, 1; Early Dynastic III of, 1–2, 7, 9, 15, 17, 19, 21, 33, 38, 51, 79, 155; Sargonid period in, 17–37, 77; trade routes from, 61, 73–4; Guti invasions of, 73; contacts with Iran, 77, 79, 92, 94; Larsa period in, 83; fenestrated axe of, 101, 104; rosette symbol in, 151, deities of, 151–3, 155, 157
sun disc, 141, 149, 219; winged, 118–19, 145, 148–9, 220; with stylized animal head, 118–19; with rays, 144–9; with Maltese cross, 148

Syria, Sargonid period in, 19, 35; influence of Mesopotamia on, 28, 32; Naram-Sin's campaigns in, 39–40; connections with Kültepe, 42, 47, 99; trade route through, 61; connections with Hissar, 77; connections with Cyprus, 81, 127–9; contacts with Anatolia, 100, 134; Early and Middle Bronze Age in, 103–5; fenestrated axe of, 104; Hurrian kingdoms of, 110; pottery from north, 111, 127–8; connections with Palestine, 127–9; Late Bronze Age in, 132–57, 177; deities of, 147; terracotta figurines from, 162; Egyptian influences transmitted through, 165, 167; cremation graves in, 230; fibulae from north, 260; Median dominion over, 268

Takht-i-Sulaiman mountain, 182
Termizer, Raci, 198
Terrace, E. B., 160
Teshub, storm god, 147, 149
throat ornament, 173
Thureau-Dangin, F., 243
Tiglath-Pileser I of Assyria, 180–1
Tiglath-Pileser III of Assyria, lxiv, 148, 182–3, 216, 235, 240, 242, 248, 252, 260; period of, 251, 254–5, 265
tin, 18–19
torques, 52, 114, 137, 197, 203, 215–16, 266–7
trade routes, 17–20, 28, 47, 61, 134
Transcaucasia, source of gold, lxiv, 18, 37; Mesopotamian jewellery in, 18, 20, 32, 36; barrow graves of, 27, 37; granulation in, 37, 43; contacts with Anatolia, 37, 38, 77; relations with Mesopotamia in Guti-Gudea and Third Dynasty periods, 73–4; Kassites and, 163–4; Scythians in, 216
Troad, the, 19, 58, 60–1
Troy IIg period, 19, 40, 48–60
Troy III period, 55
Tudhalia IV, king, 149
tudittu, tudinatu, 132, 135, 153–7, 174
Tufnell, Olga, 102, 112–13, 117
turquoise, 1, 80
Tushratta, king of Mitanni, 133, 143, 155
Tutankhamun, pharoah, 167–8

Ur, First Dynasty of, 15; Third Dynasty of, lxi–lxiii, lxv, 2, 26–9, 31, 33–5, 37, 44, 49, 58–9, 61–2, 64–74, 82, 83, 90, 102, 140, 155, 160–1, 167, 207, 215
Urmia, Lake, *see* Rizayeh, Lake
Uruk, First Dynasty of, 1
Utu, sun god, 152

Vanden Berghe, L., 264

Wainright, G. R., 147
Warpalawas, king, 220, 251, 255, 260
wheel, fast, 59, 108
whetstone with lion's head, 168–9, 187
Wilkinson, C., 206, 220–1
Wilson, Kinnier, 182
Wiseman, D. J., 89, 134
Woolley, Sir Leonard, 2, 4, 6–7, 9–10, 13–14, 21, 25, 51, 68–9, 134, 136, 194, 229, 244

Yadin, Y., 104
Yarim-Lim period, 137
Young, Rodney, 219, 260
Young, T. Cuyler, 91, 93, 188

Zab valley, 181–2
Zagros mountains, 19, 94, 163, 186
Zarineh river, 181–2

1

1, 2, 3, *see pp. 3, 10*

3

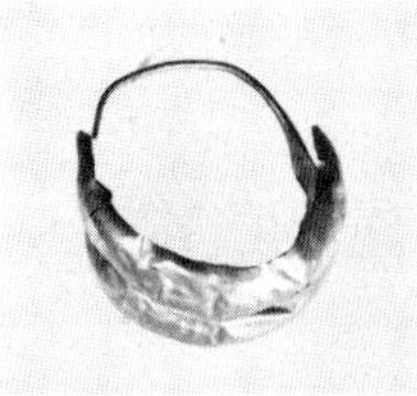

4, *see p. 4*

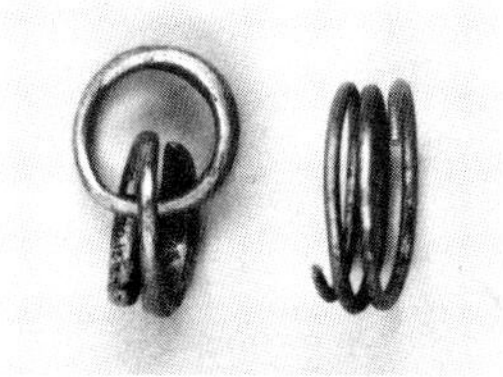

5, *see p. 5*

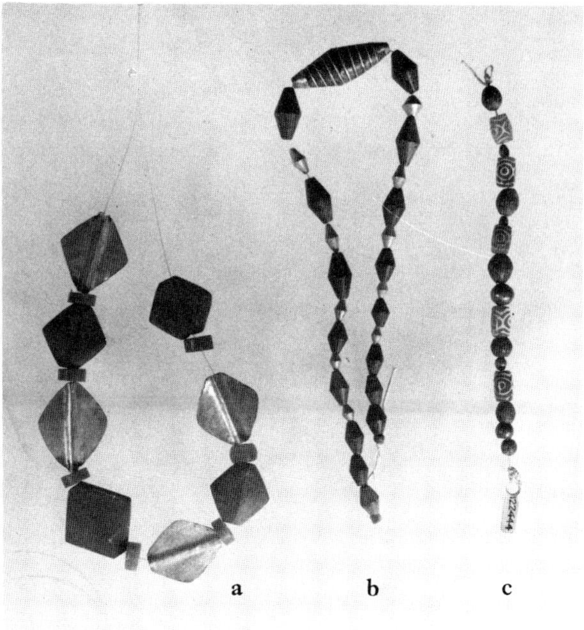

6

6 d

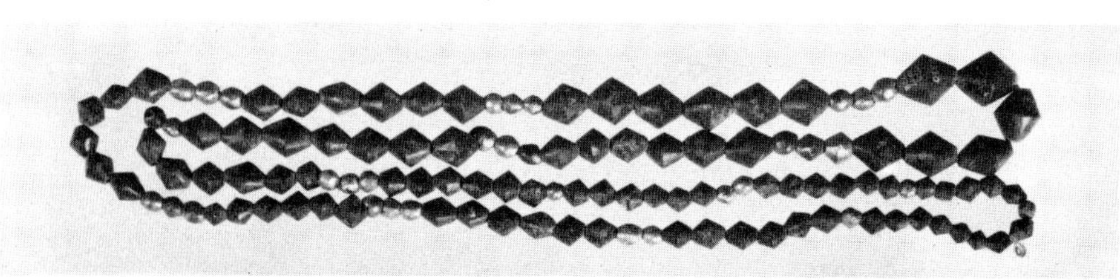

7

6, 7, *see pp. 5, 7, 9, 10*

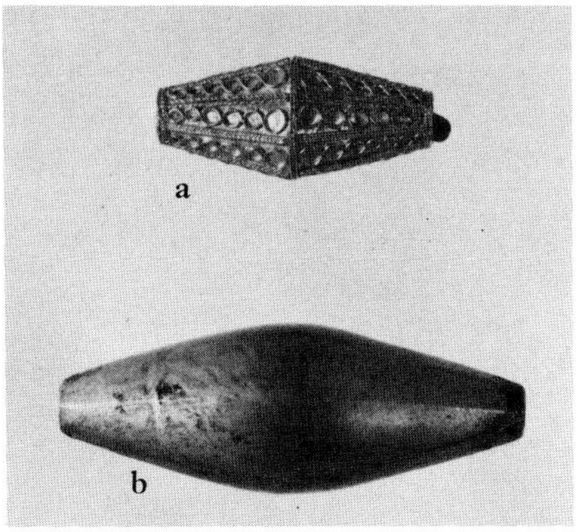

8, *see pp. 6, 9*

9, *see pp. 9, 11*

10, *see p. 11*

11 a b c 11, *see p. 13*

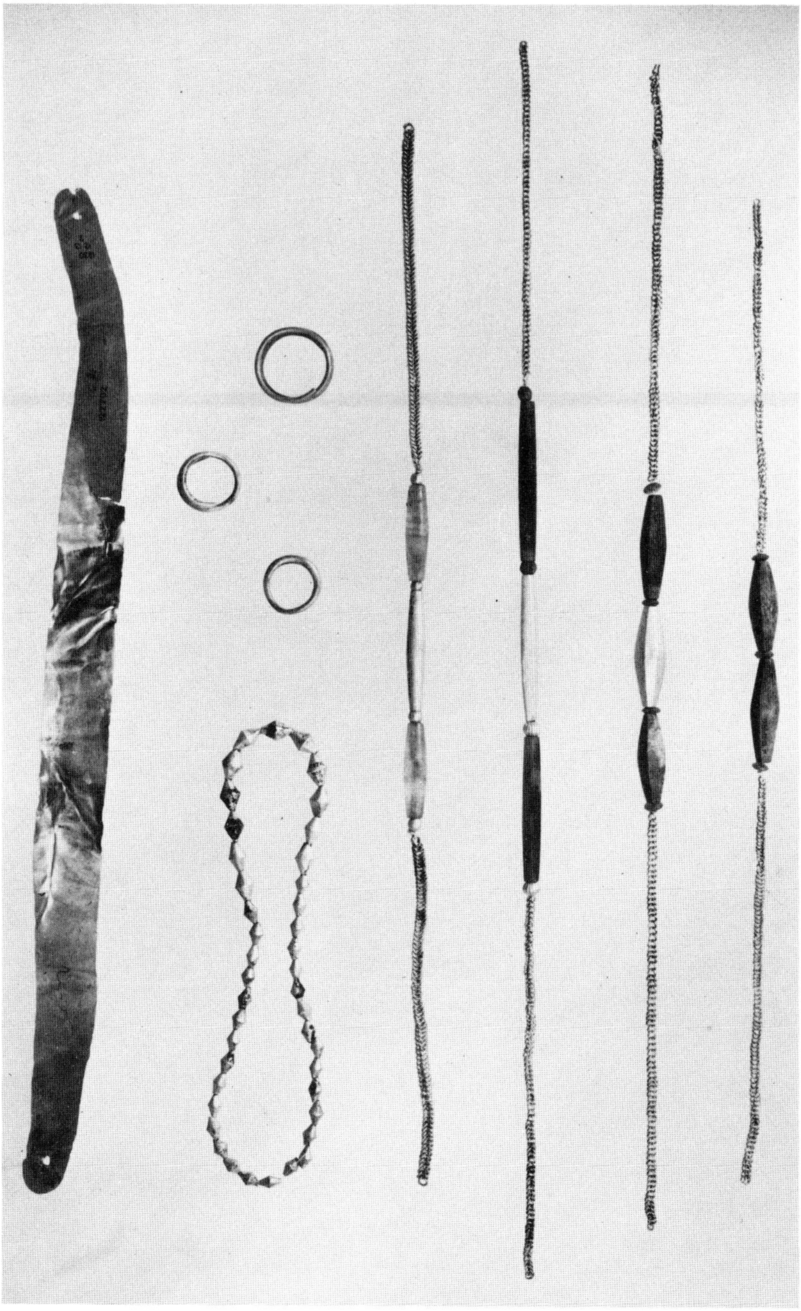

12, *see pp. 9, 14*

13, *see p. 6*

14, *see p. 15*

15 (a, b), *see p. 20*; (c), *see p. 205*

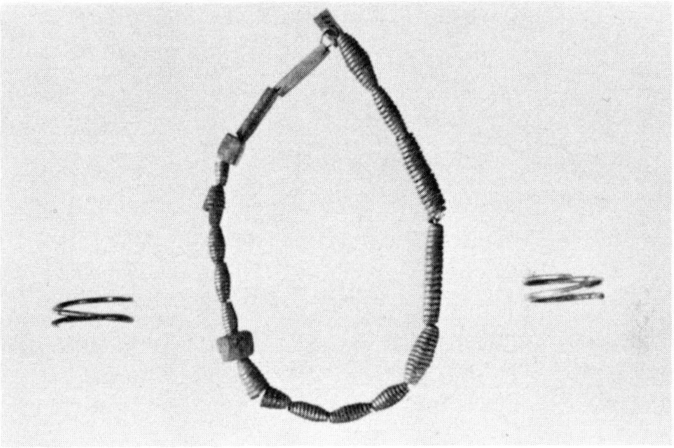

15 a

15 b

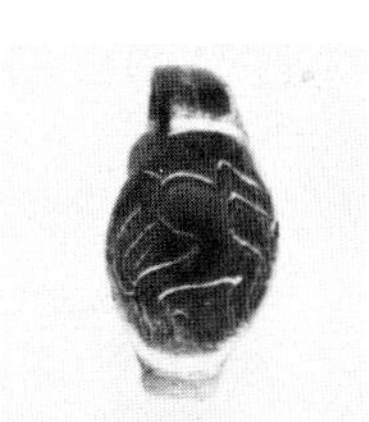

15 c

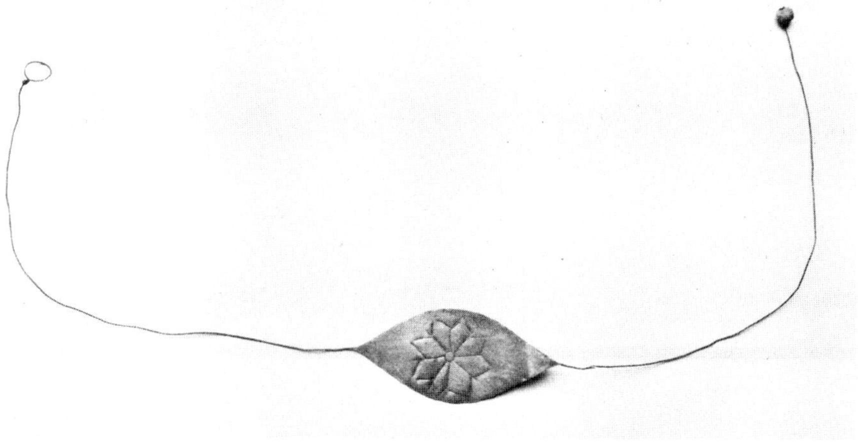

16, *see p. 22*

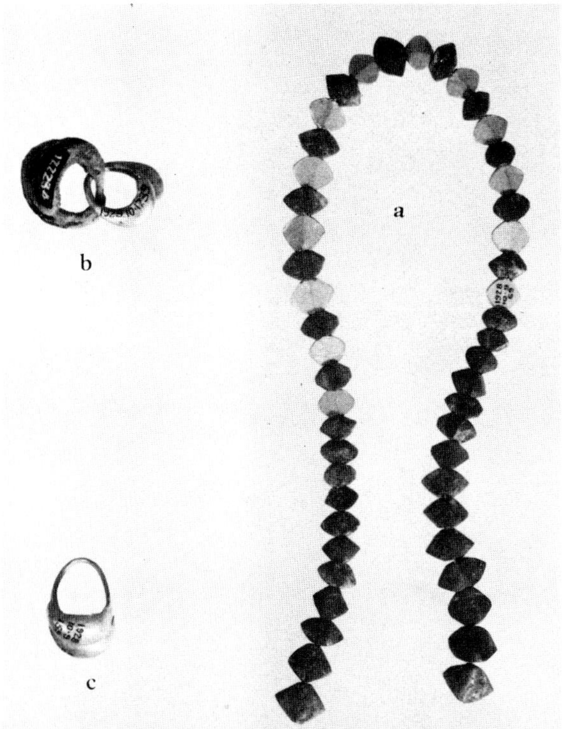

17 (a), *see pp. 10, 26;* (b), *see p. 23;*
(c), *see fig. 15a*

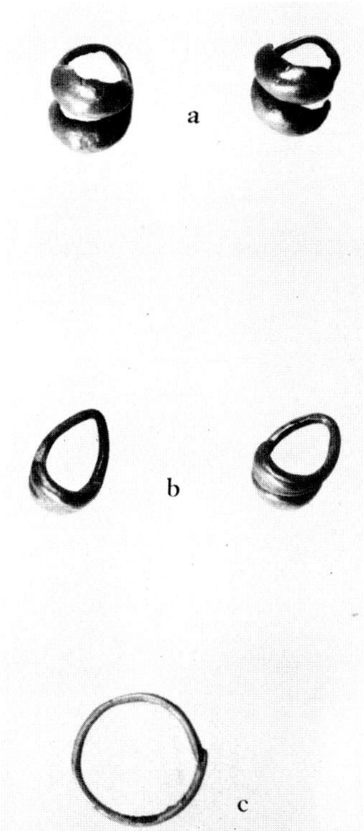

18 (a), *see p. 23;* (b), *see p. 24*

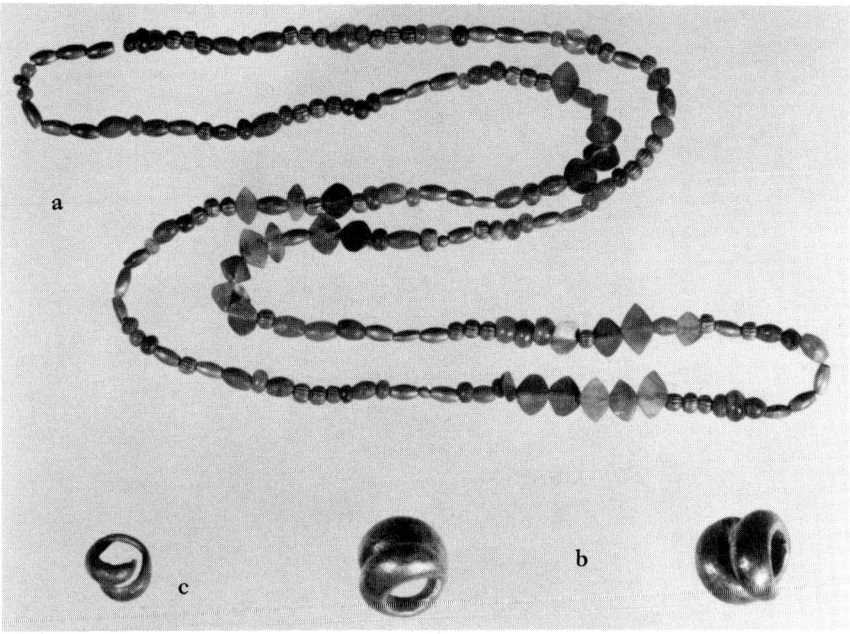

19 (a), *see p. 26*; (b, c), *see p. 24*

20 (a), *see p. 26*

20 (b), *see p. 26*

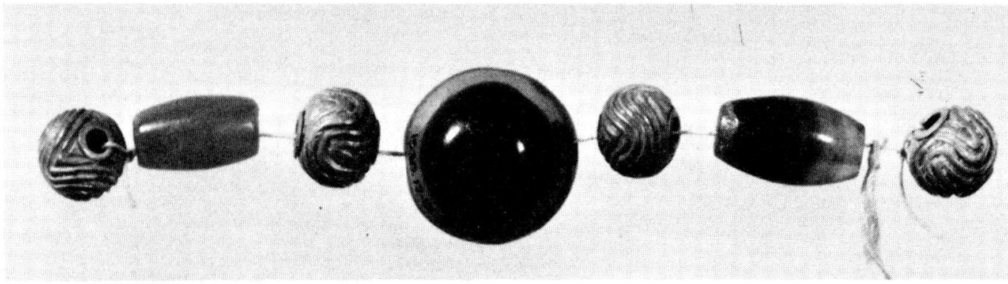

21, *see p. 26*

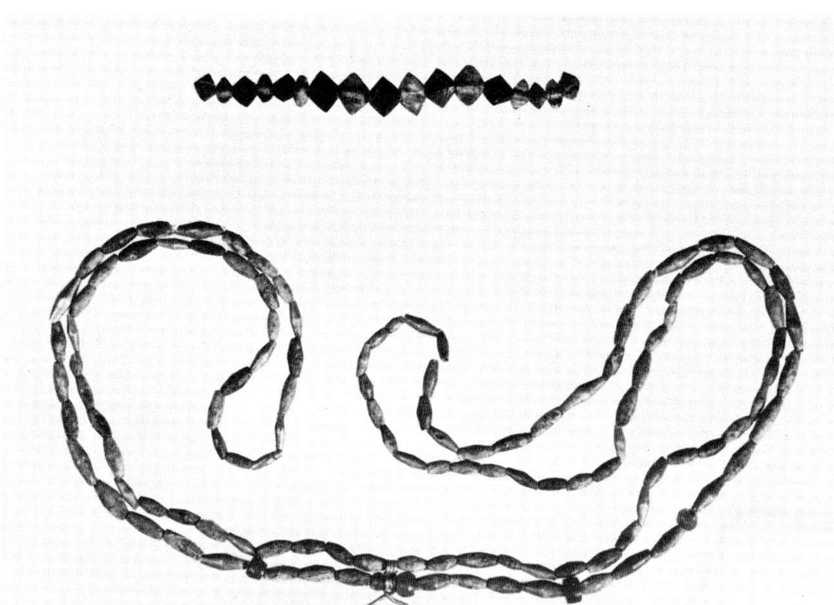

22, *see p. 23*

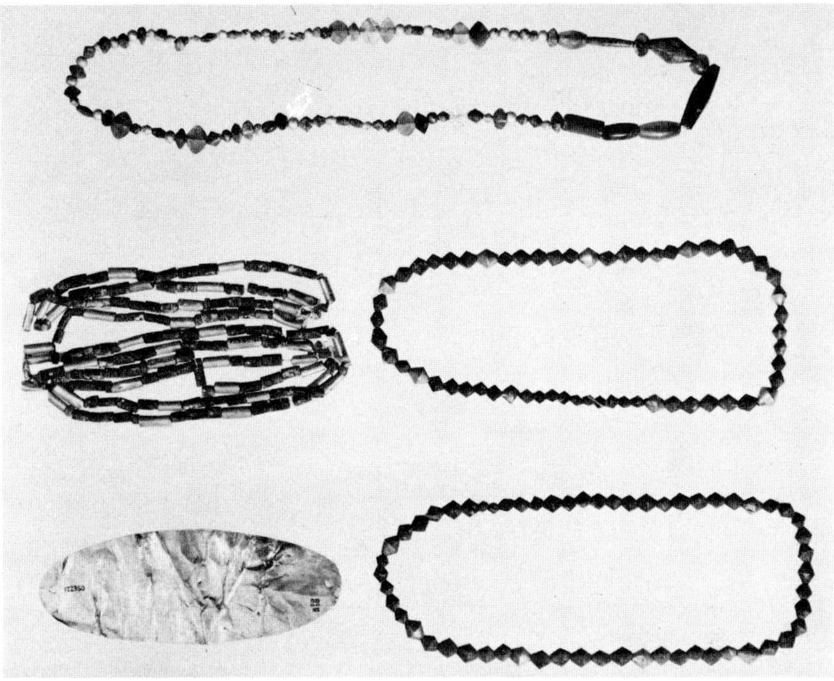

23, *see p. 22*

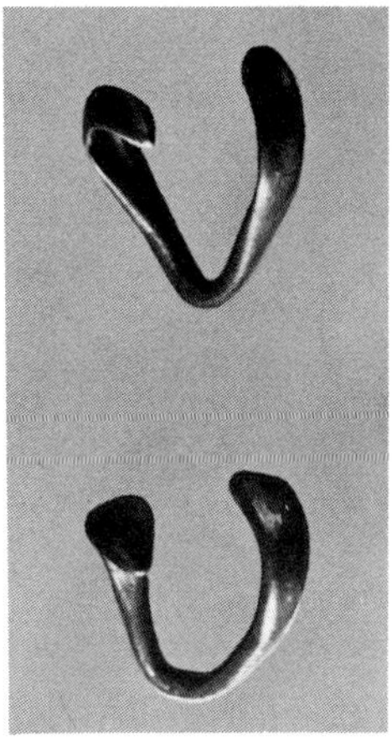

24 a

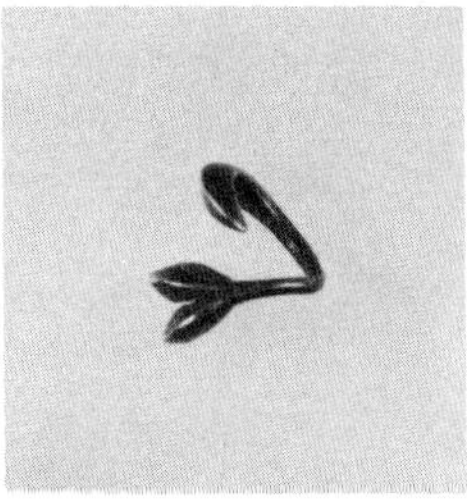

24 c

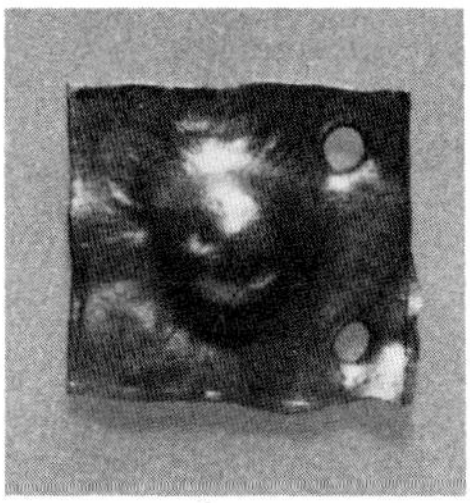

25 a

24 d

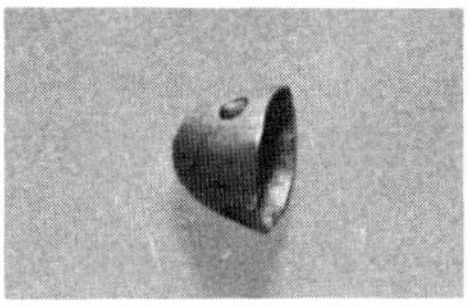

25 b

24 b

24, *see p. 28*

26, *see p. 29*

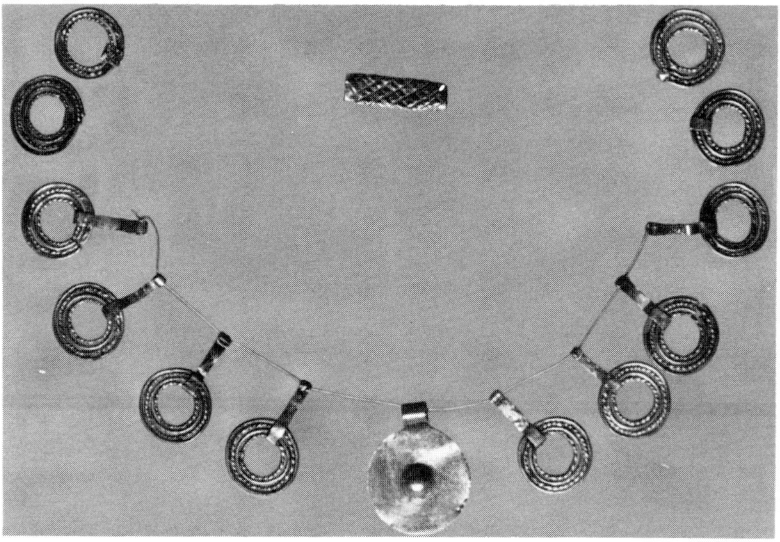

27

28

29

27–29, *see p. 29*

30, *see p. 30*

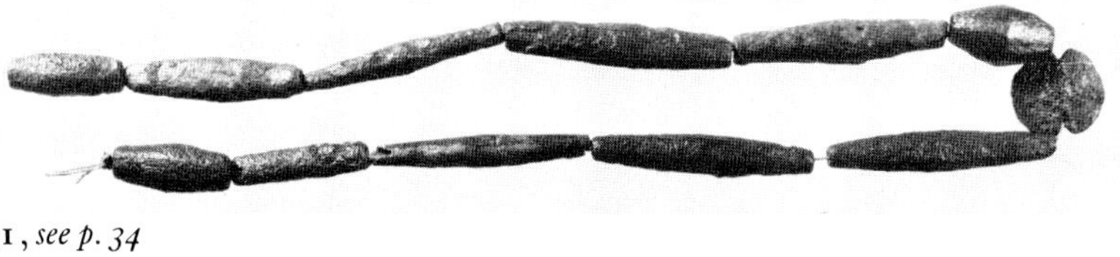

31, *see p. 34*

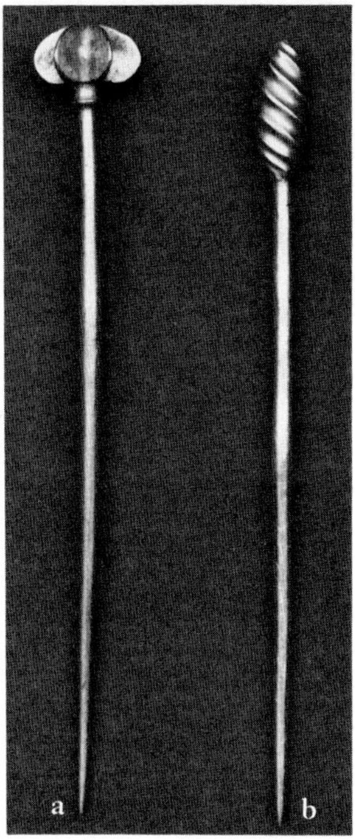

32, *see p. 42*

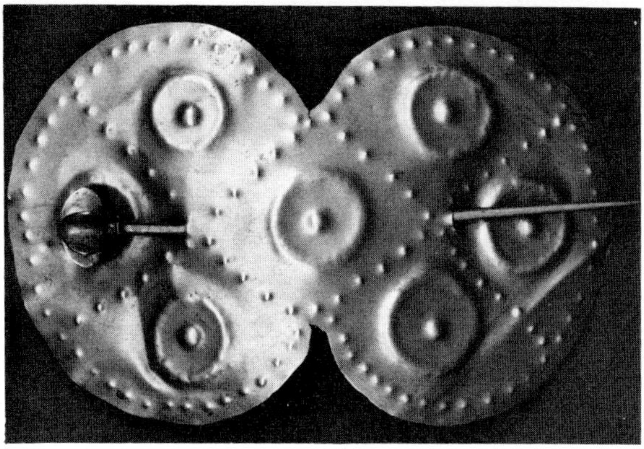

33, *see p. 43*

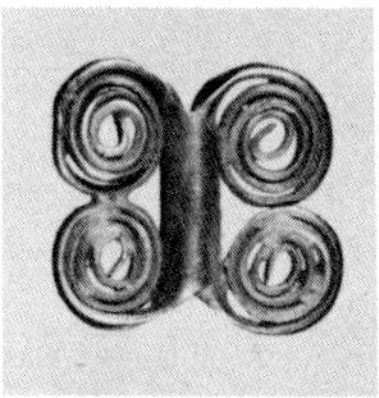

34, *see p. 34*

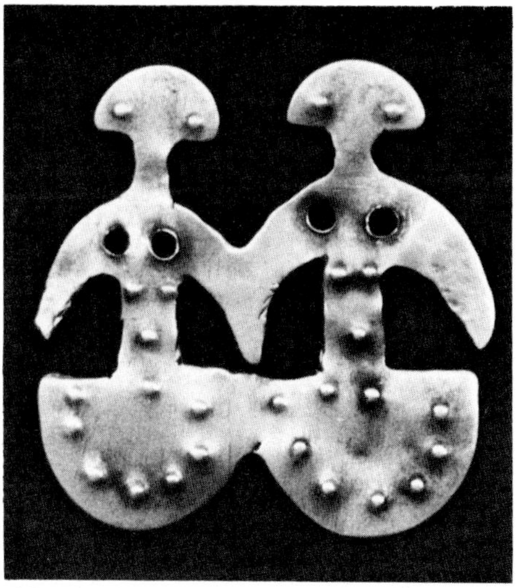

36, *see p. 46*

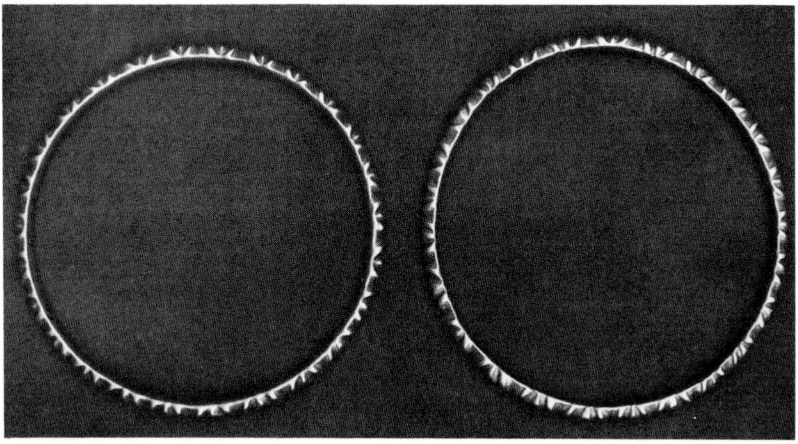

35, *see p. 45*

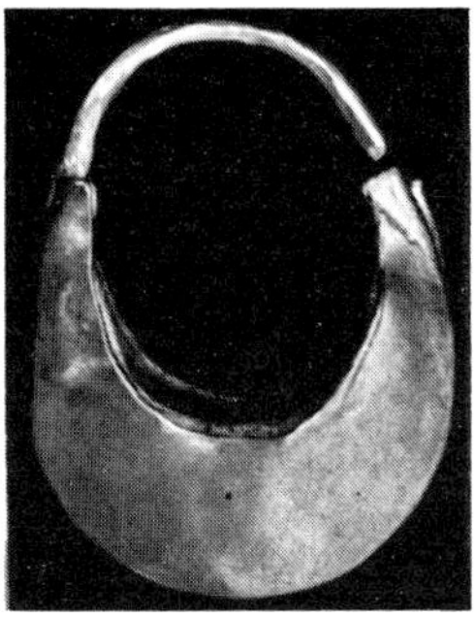
37 a

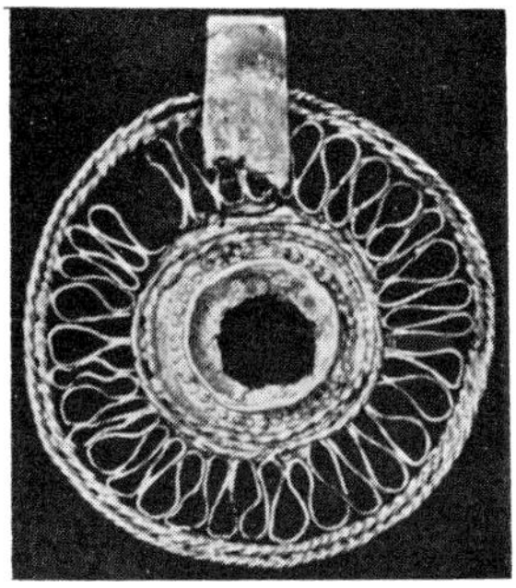
37 b

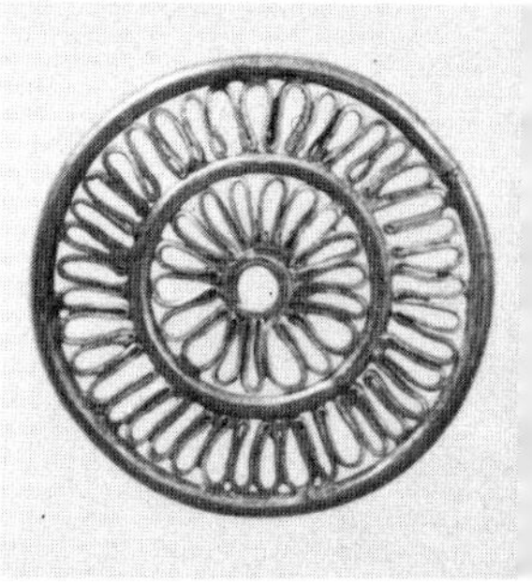
38

37, 38, *see p. 47*

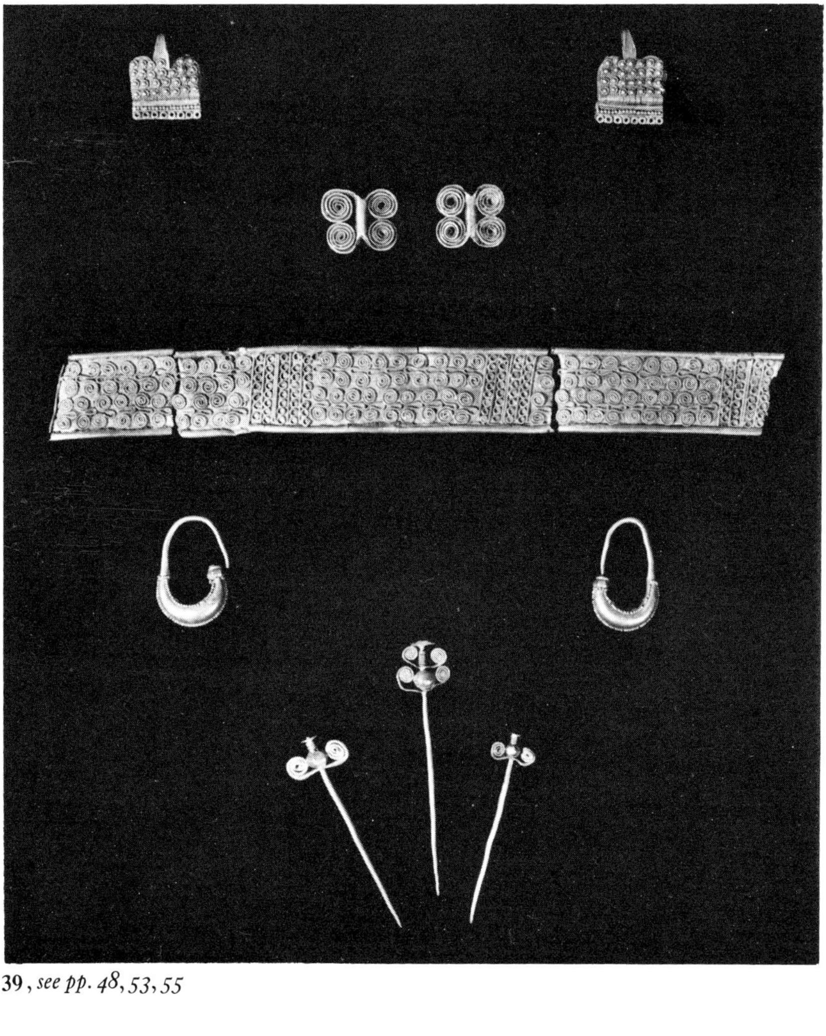
39, *see pp. 48, 53, 55*

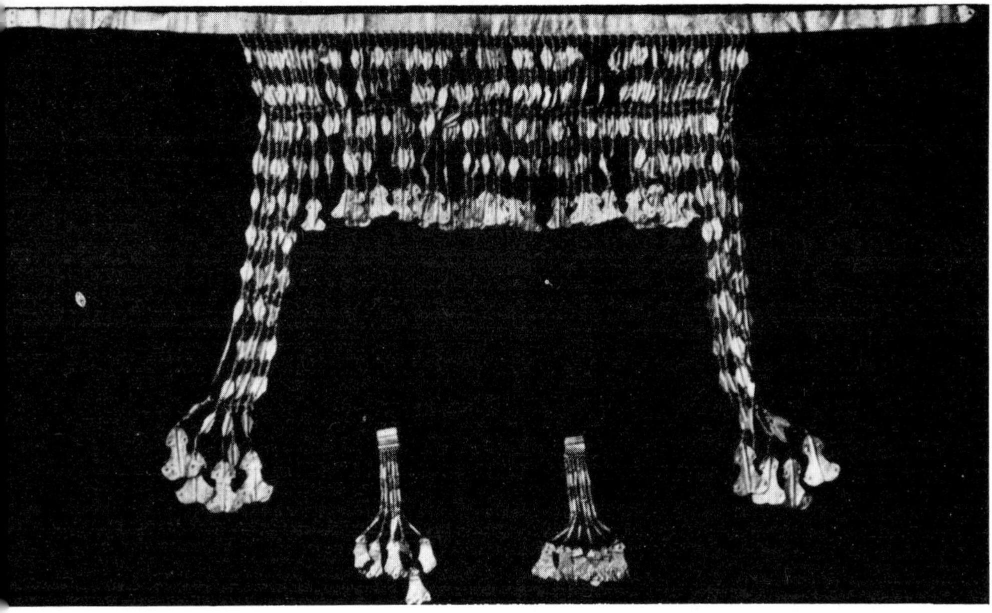

, *see p. 52*

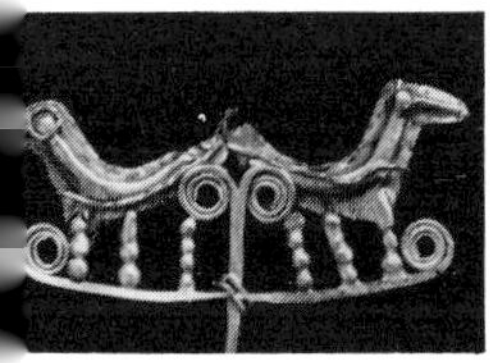

44

45, *see pp. 65, 102*

42, *see p. 60*
44, *see pp. 62, 63*

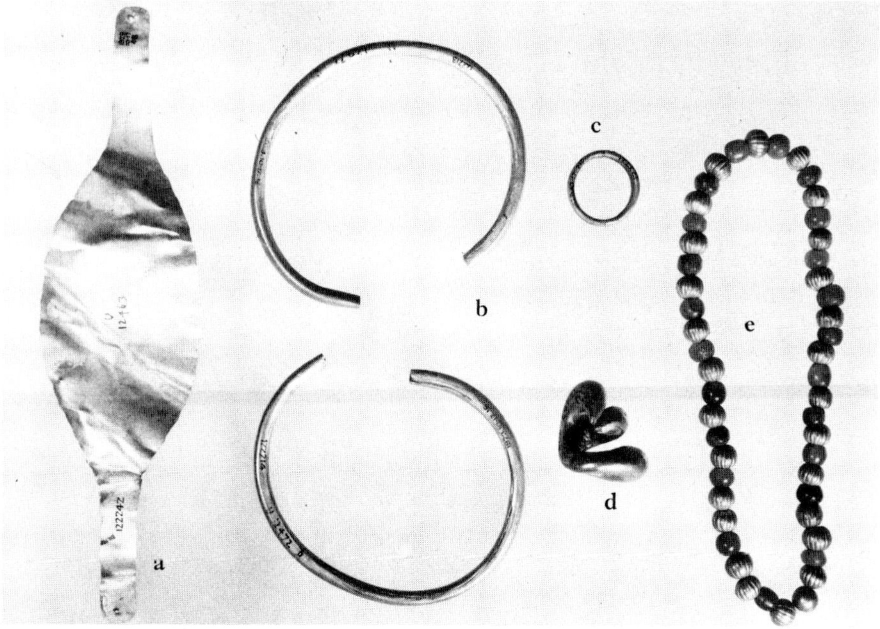

46

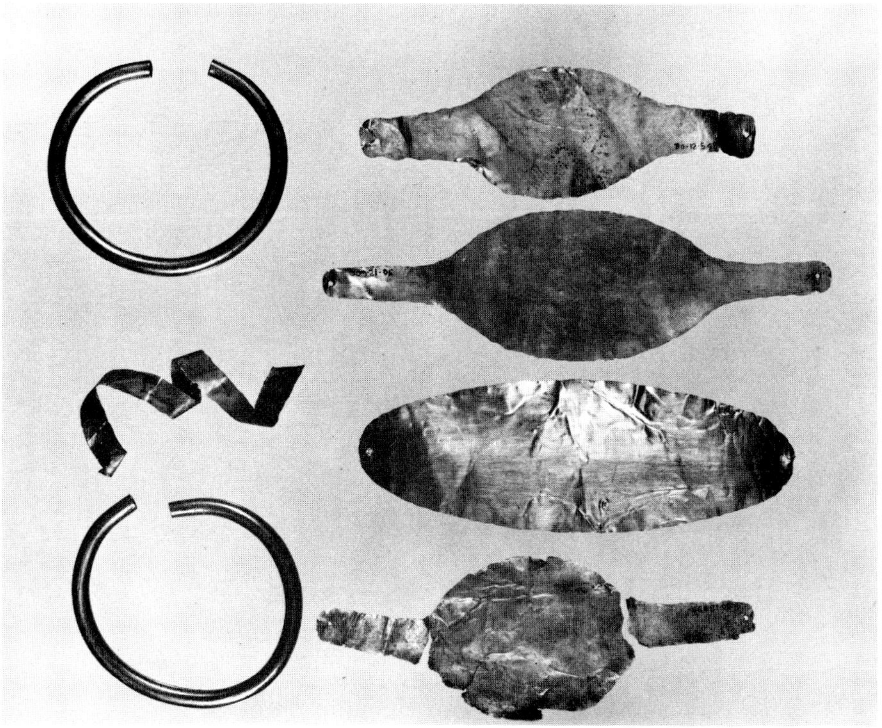

47

46, 47, *see pp.* 65, 67

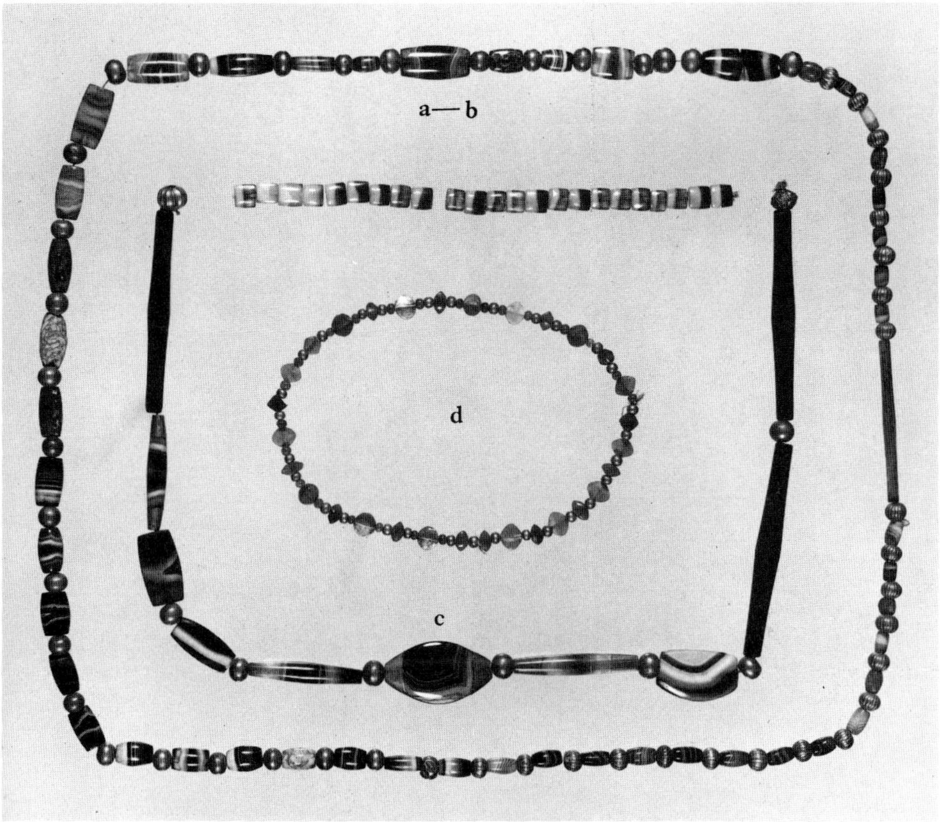

48, *see p. 67*

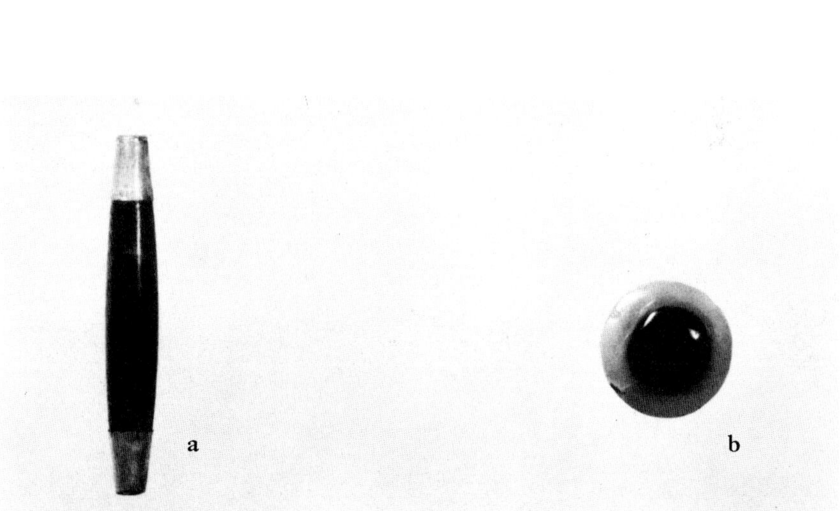

49, *see p. 68*

50, *see p. 69*

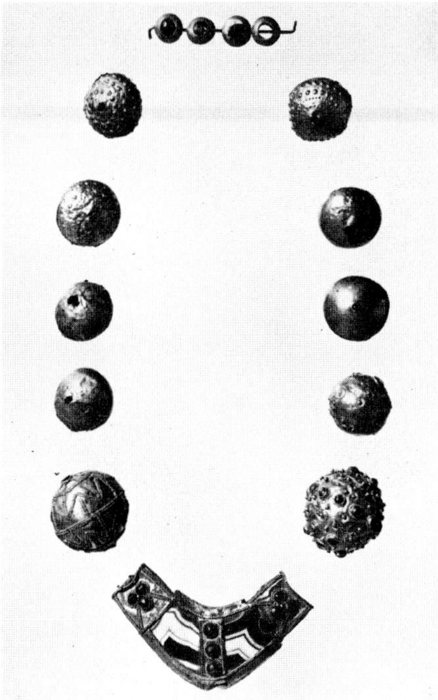

51

51–54, *see p. 75*

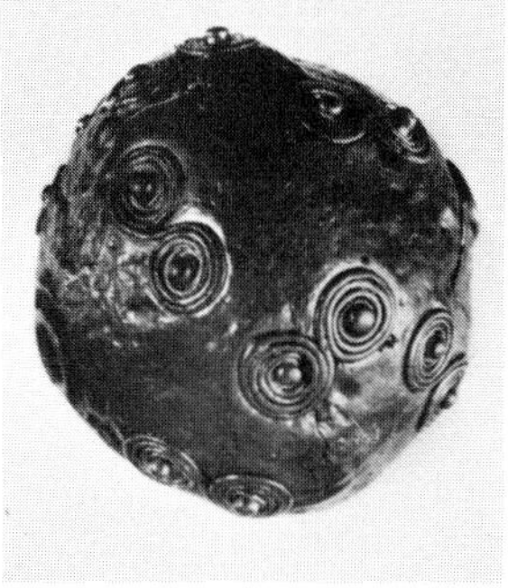

52

53

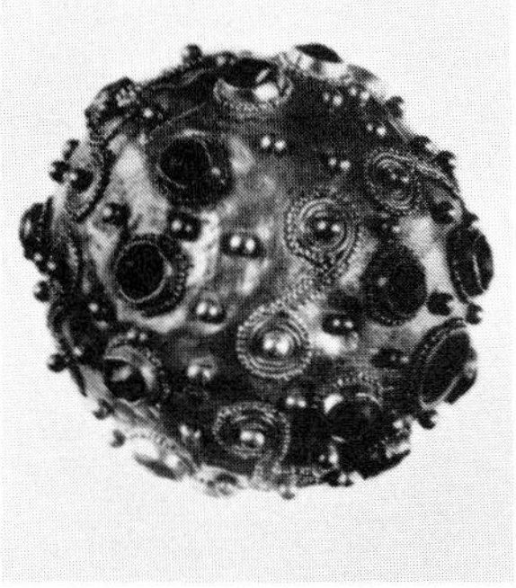

54

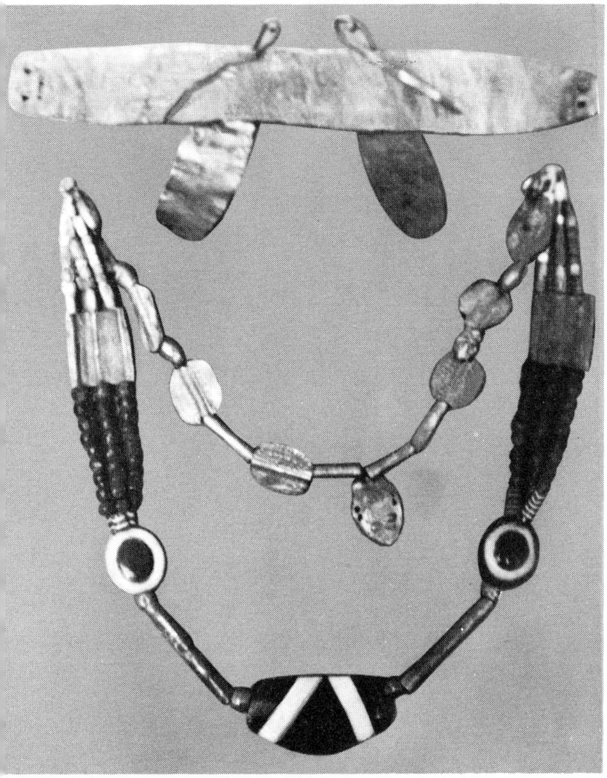

55 , *see p. 79*

56 *see p. 80*

57, *see p. 83*

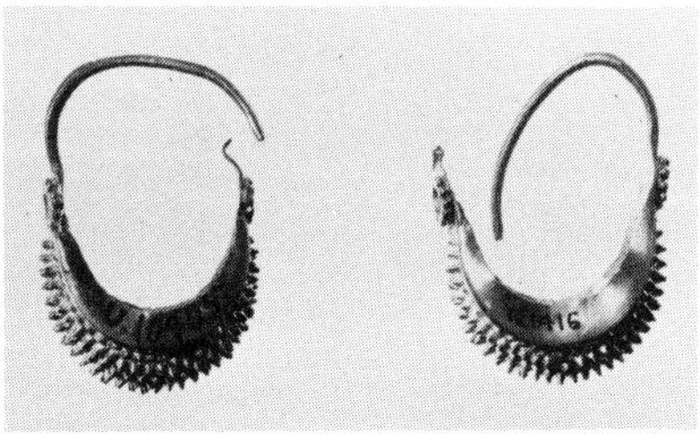

57 a

57 b

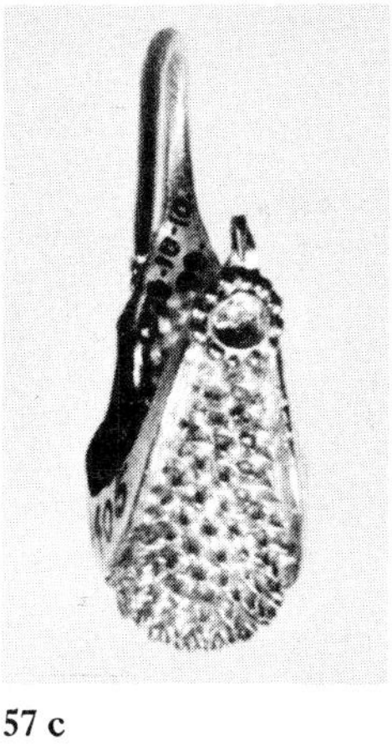

57 c

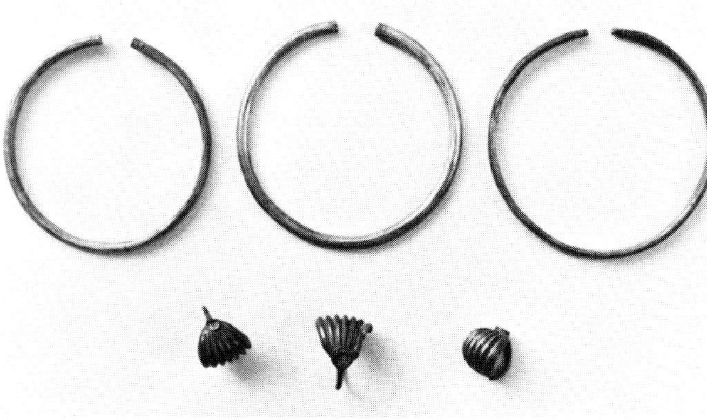

58 a

58 b

58 (a), *see pp. 84, 91*
(b), *see p. 84*

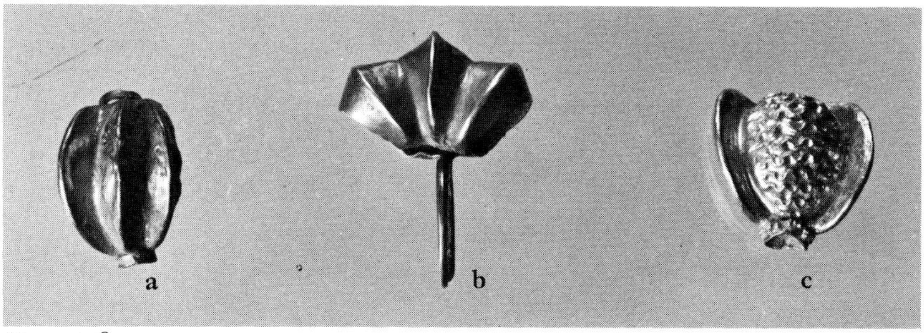

59, *see p. 84*

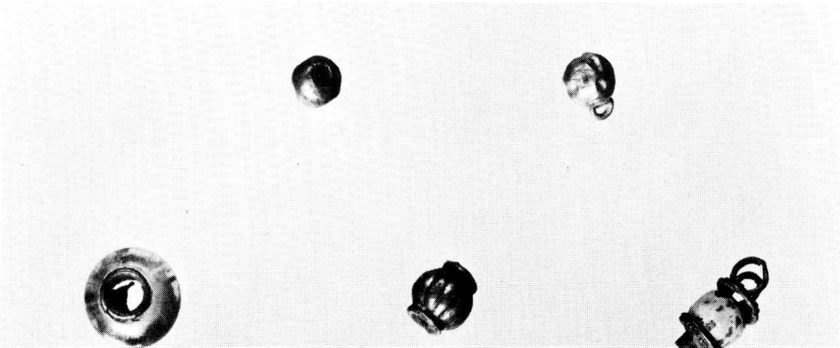

60, *see p. 88*

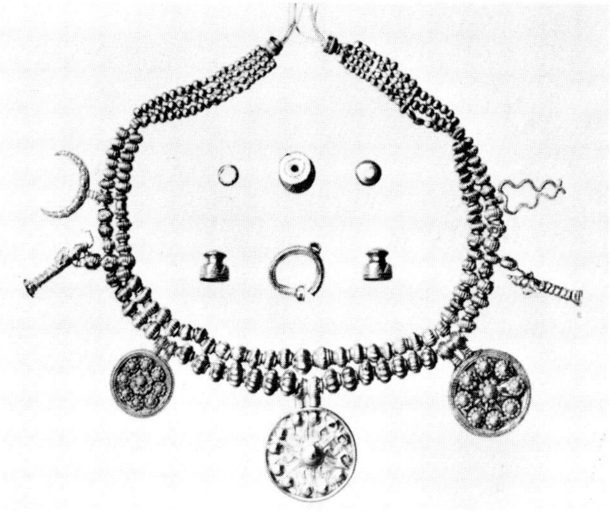

61, *see pp. 88, 145*

62 a

62 b

62 c

62–64, *see p. 89*

63 a

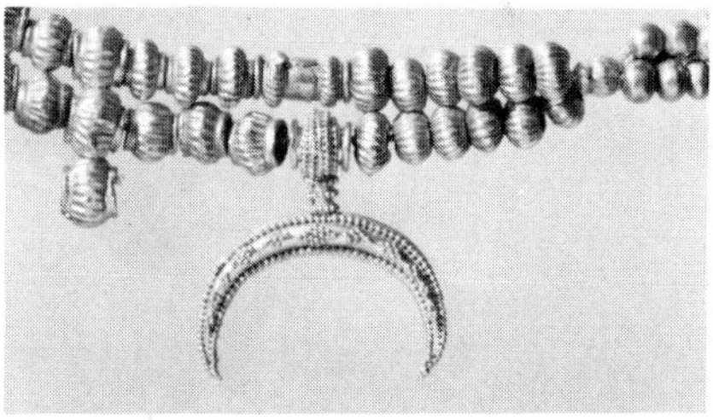

63 b

64 a

64 b

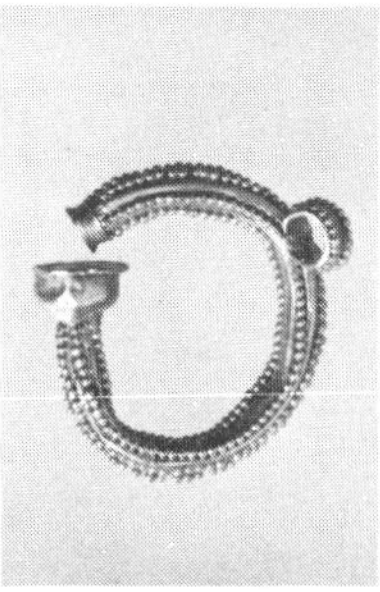

65, (a), *see p. 89* 65 b 65 c

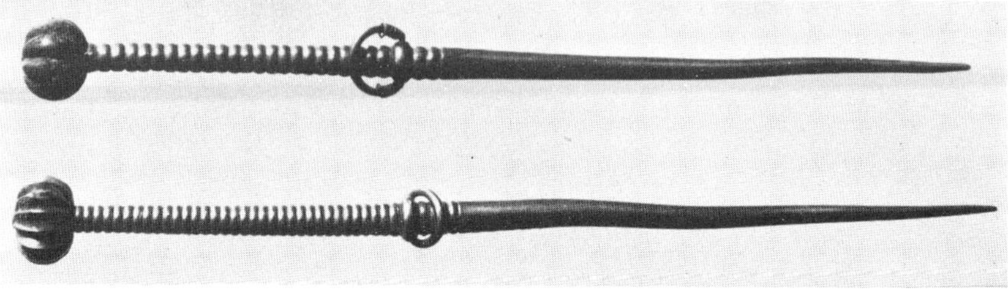

66

67 66, 67, *see p. 99*

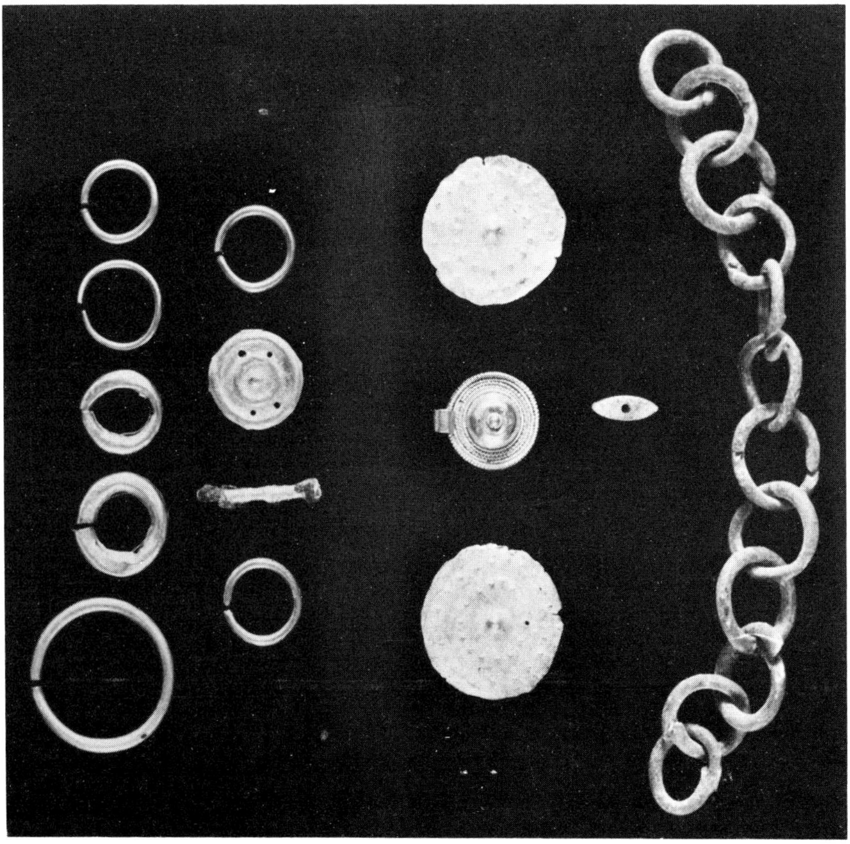

68, *see pp. 29, 134*

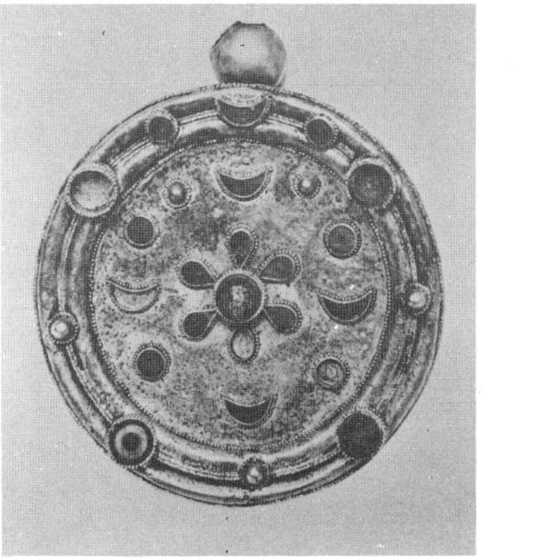

69, *see pp. 102, 104, 76*

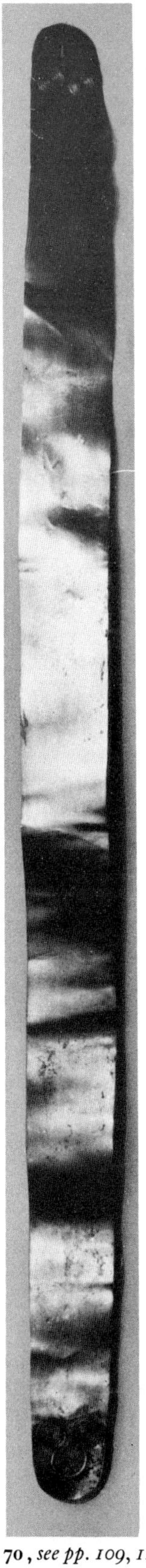

70, *see pp. 109, 122*

71, *see p. 108*

72, *see p. 109*

73

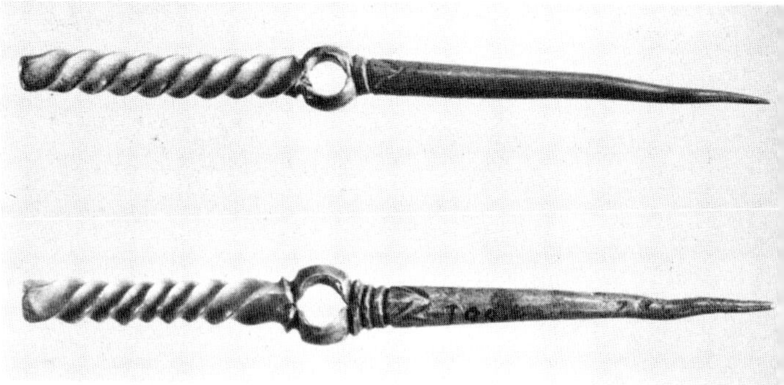

74

73, 74, *see p. 113*

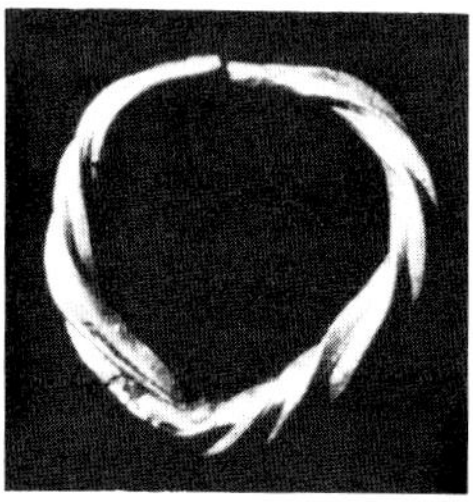

75 (a), *see p. 115*

75 (b), *see p. 114*

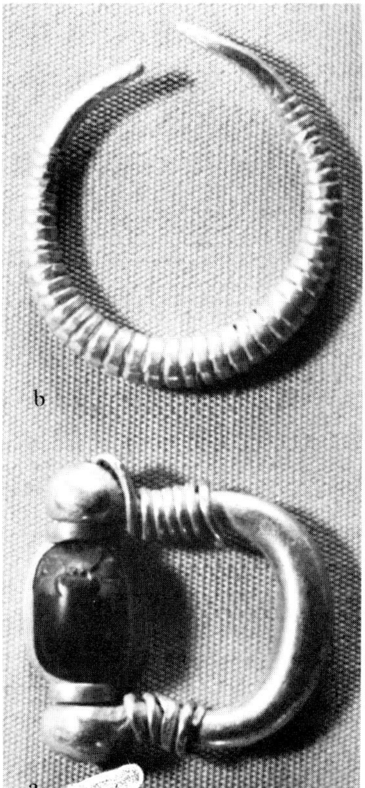

76, *see p. 114*

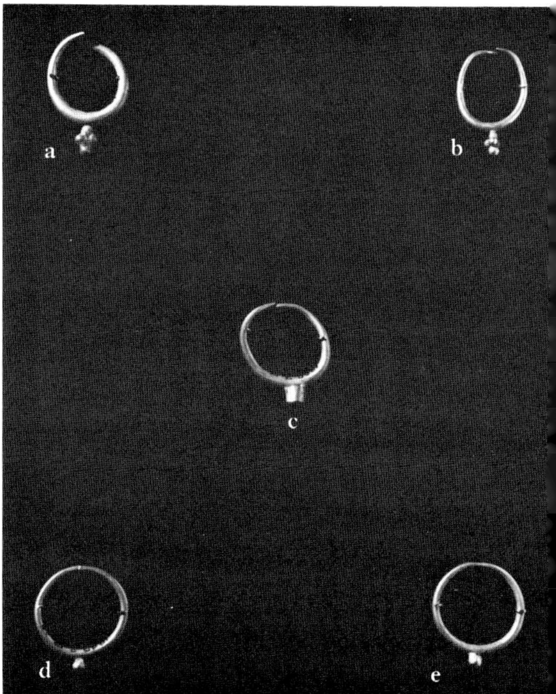

77 , *see p. 116*

78, *see p. 116*

79, *see pp. 116, 109*

80, *see p. 116*

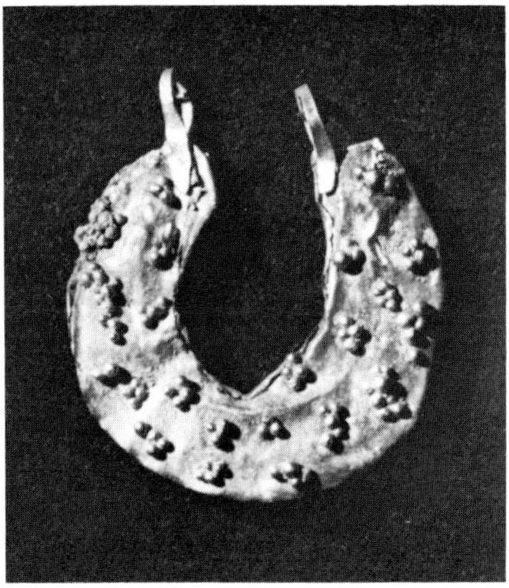
81, *see p. 117*

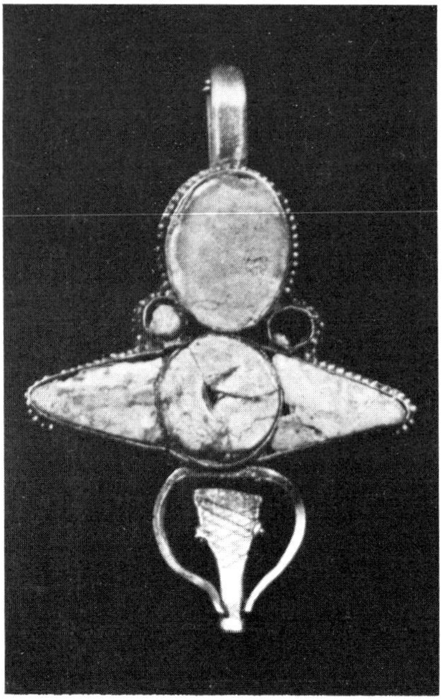

82

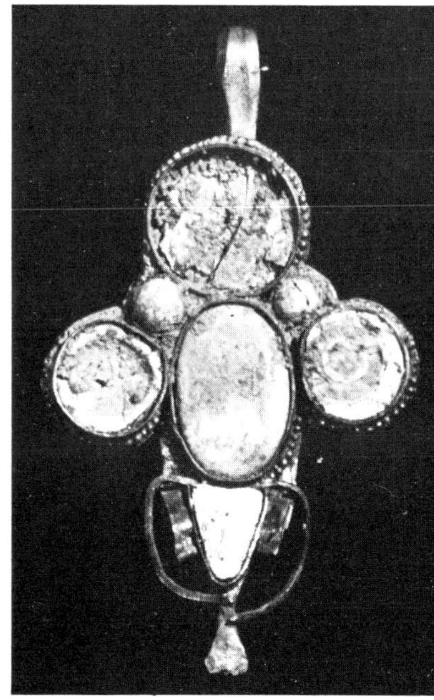

83

82, 83, *see pp. 118, 131*

84

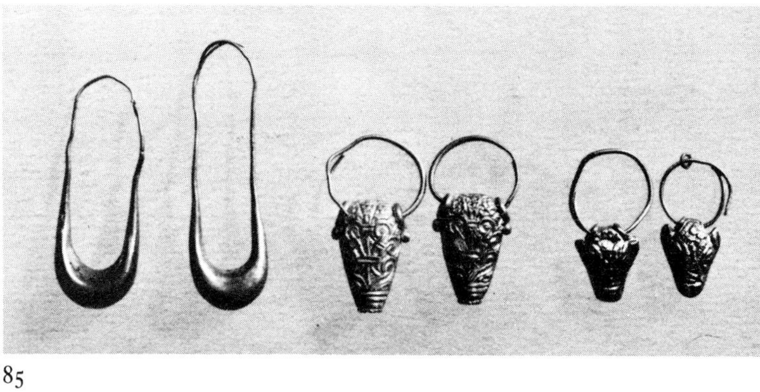

85

84, 85, *see p. 120*

86

86, 87, *see p. 121*

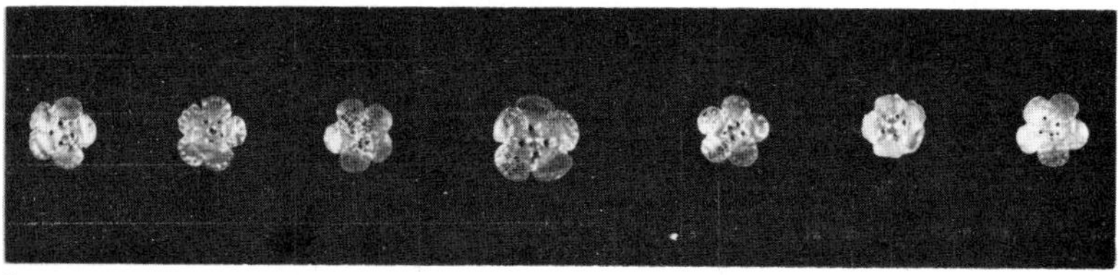

87

88, *see p. 122*

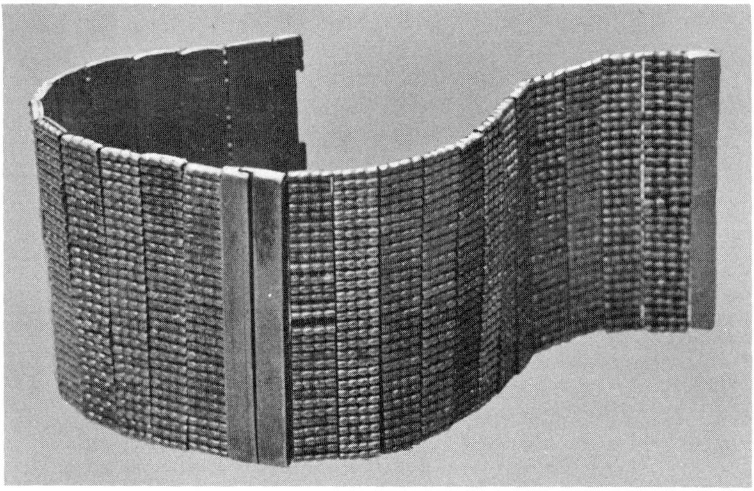

89

90

89, 90, *see p. 123*

91

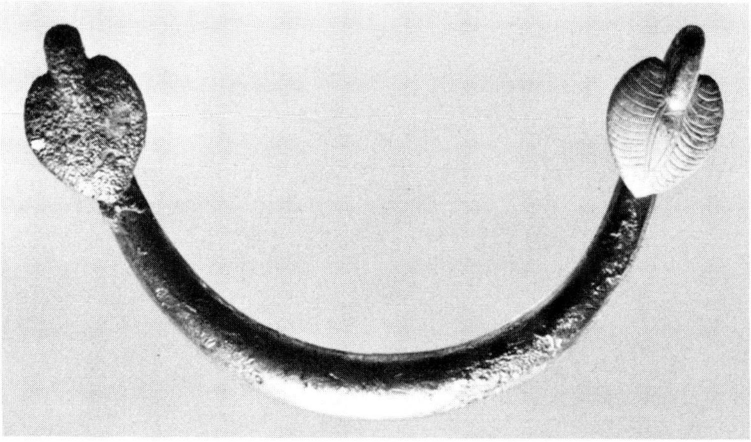

92

91, 92, *see p. 124*

94 a

94 b

94 c

93

93, 94, *see p. 126*

95, *see p. 127*

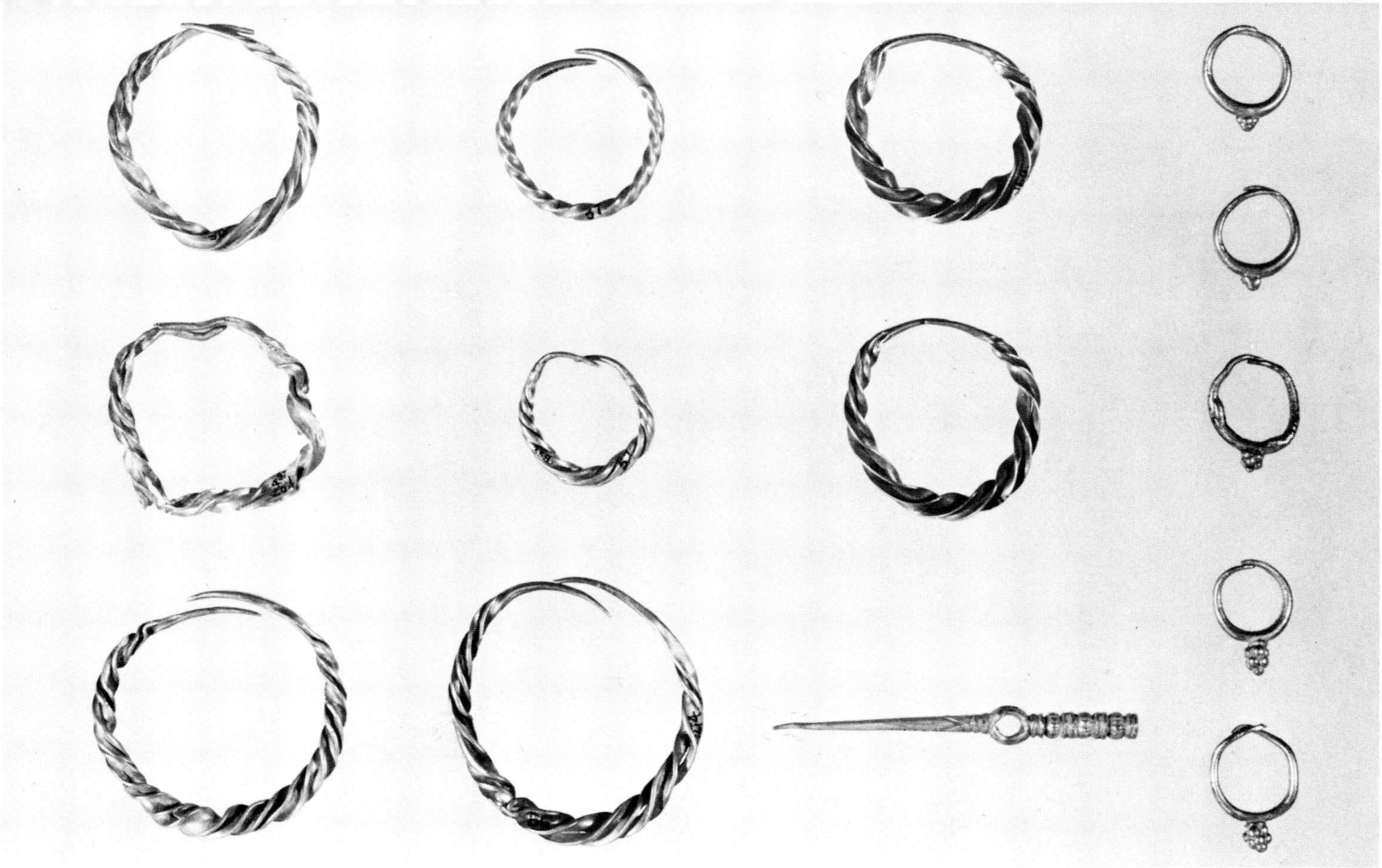

96, *see p. 130*

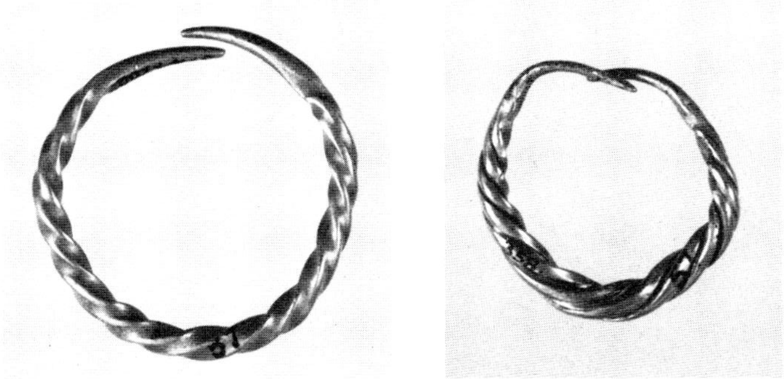

97

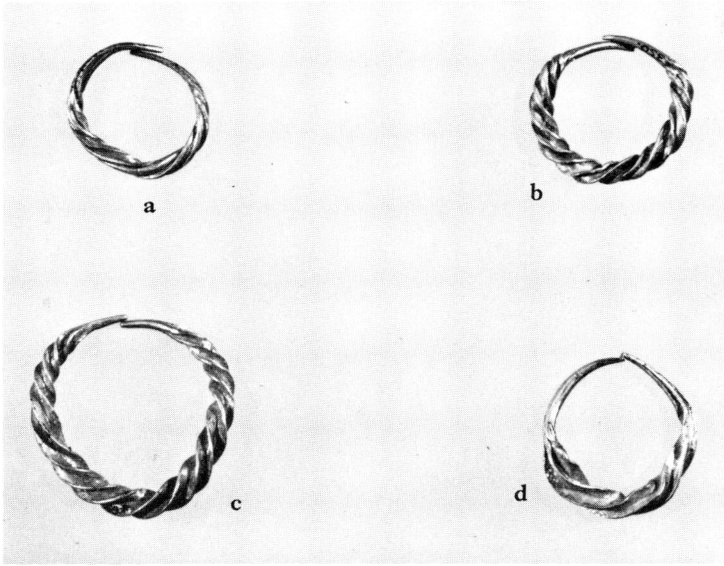

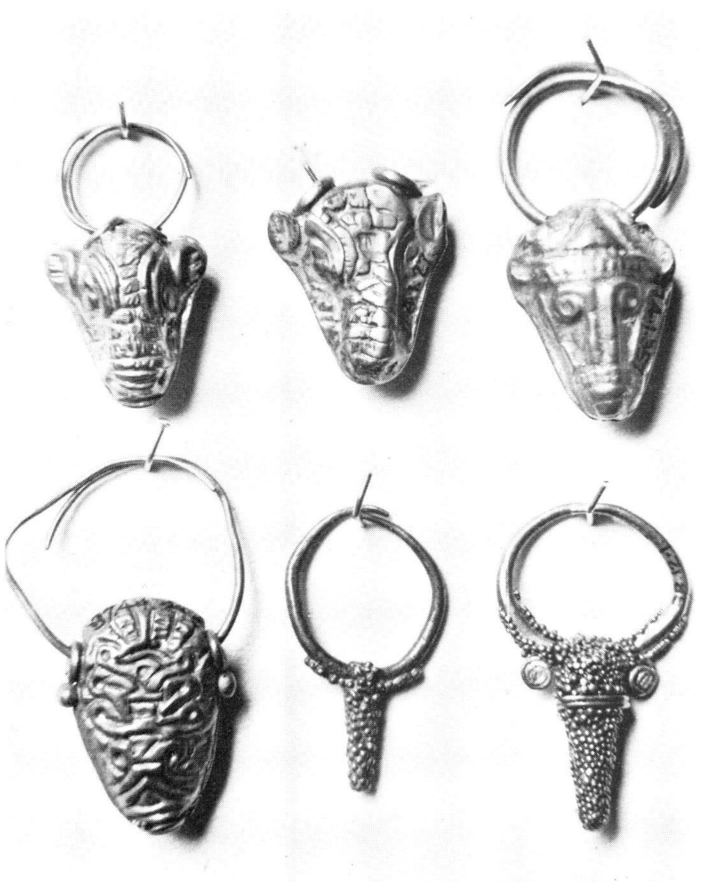

100, *see p. 135*

101, *see p. 138*

102

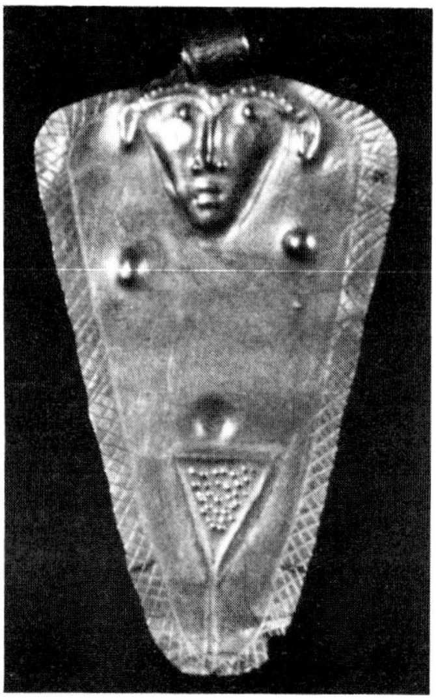
103

104

102–106, *see p. 139*

105

106

107, *see p. 139*

108, *see p. 141*

109, *see p. 141*

110, *see p. 150*

111, *see p. 141*

112, *see p. 142*

113, *see p. 149*

114, *see p. 144*

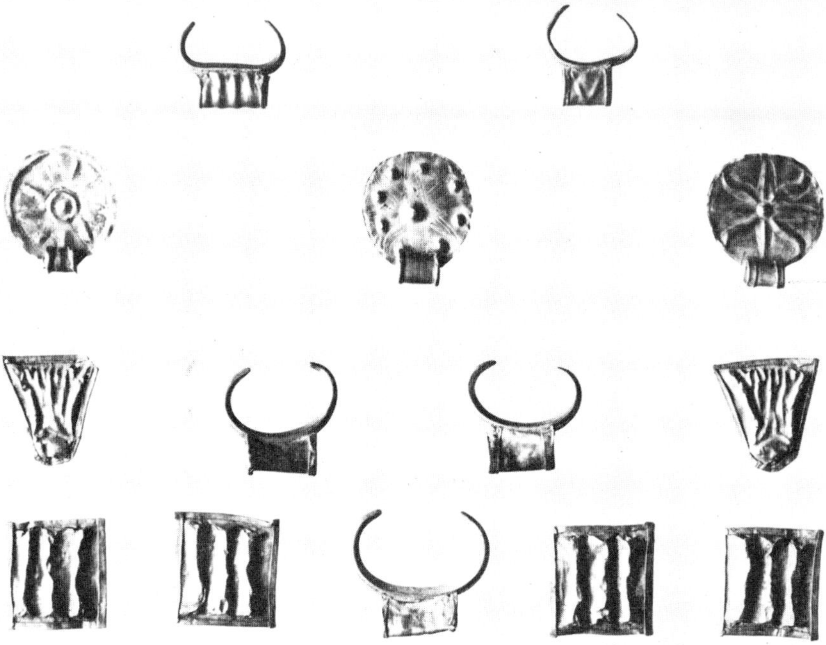

115, *see pp. 144, 150*

116, *see p. 147*

117, *see p. 148*

118, *see p. 148*

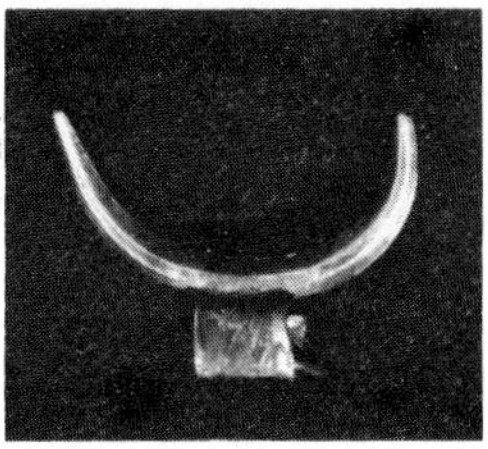

119, *see p. 150*

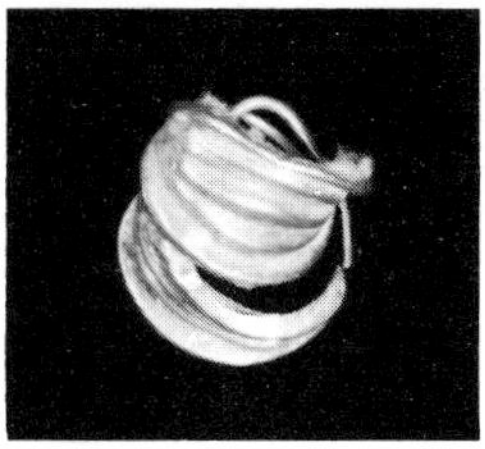

120, *see p. 158*

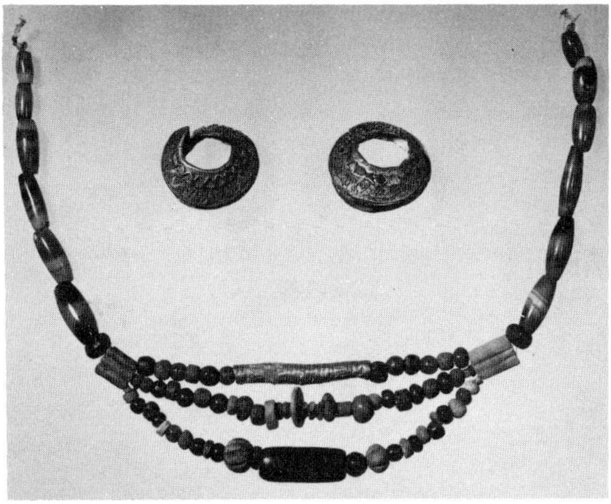

121

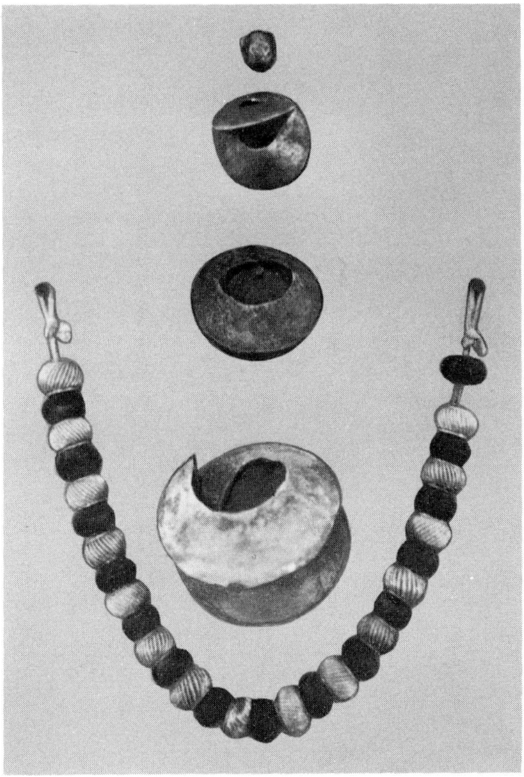

122

121, 122, *see p. 159*

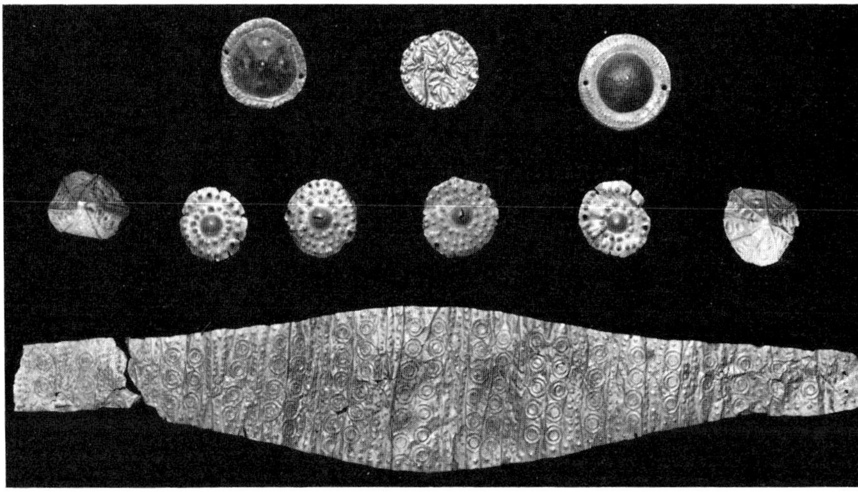

123, *see p. 160*

124, *see p. 161*

125, *see p. 162*

126, *see p. 162*

127, *see p. 164*

8, *see p. 187*

129

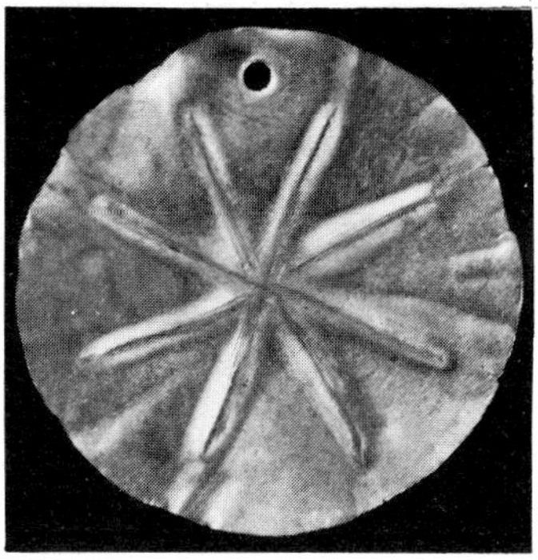

130

129, 130, *see p. 178*

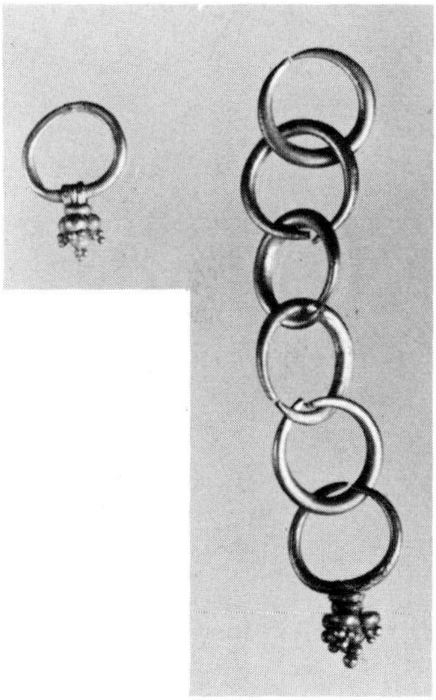

131, *see p. 178*

2, *see p. 187*

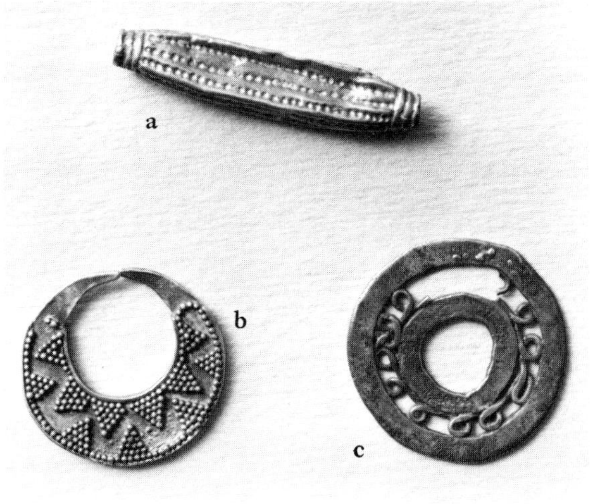

133, *see p. 187*

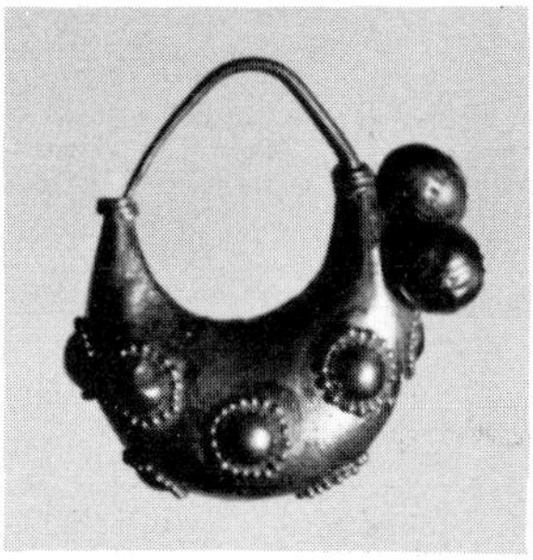

134, *see pp. 159, 188*

135

135, 136, *see p. 189*

136

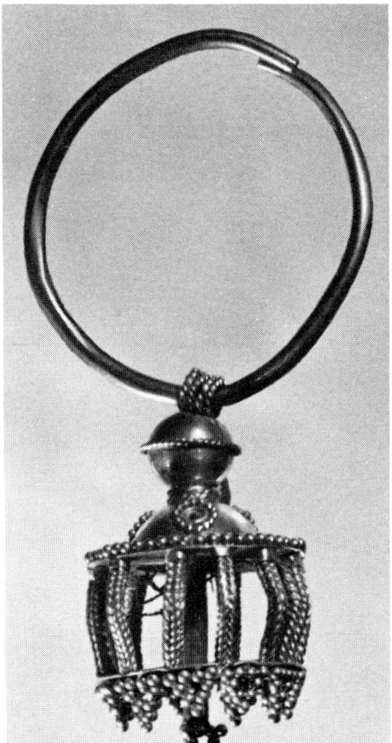
137, *see p. 190*

138

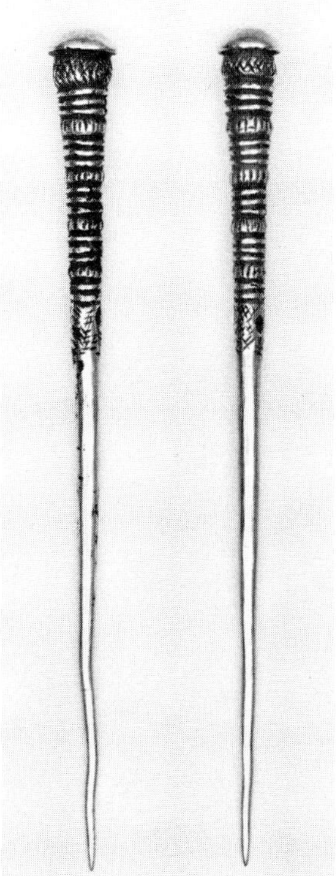
139

138, 139, *see p. 191*

140, *see p. 191*

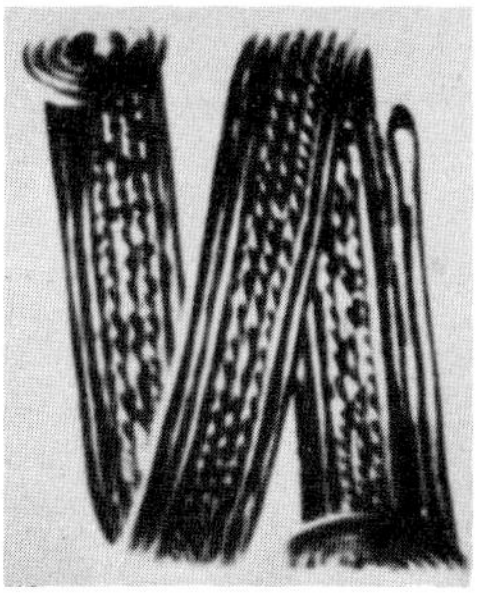

141

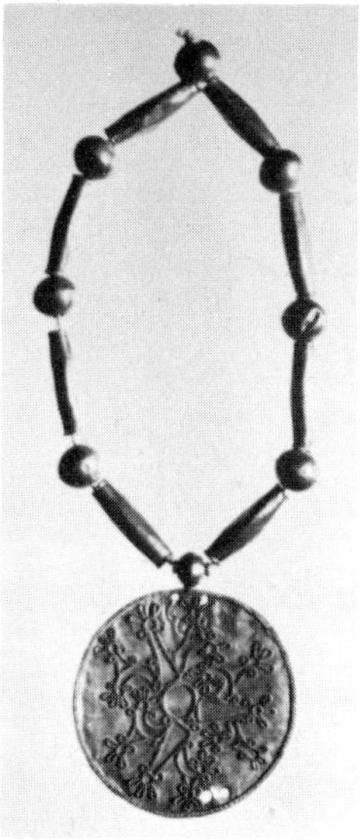

142

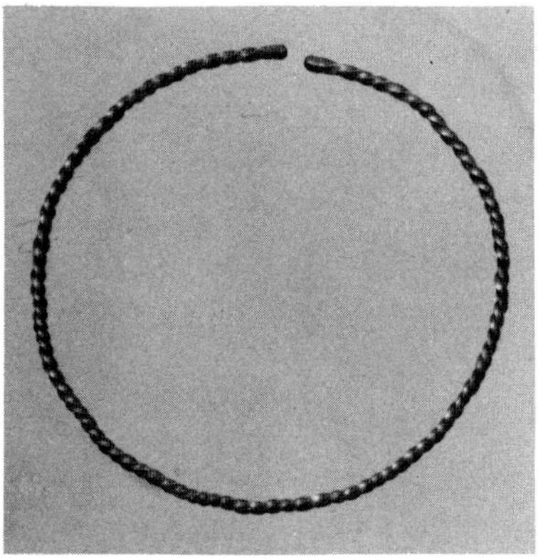

143

141–145, *see p. 192*

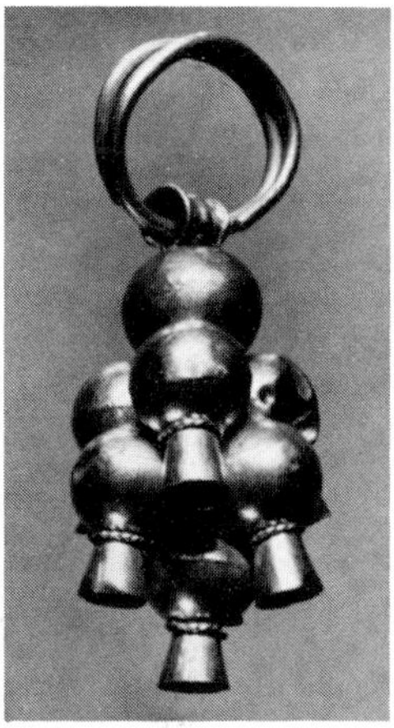

144

145

146, *see p. 193*

147

147, 148, *see p. 195*

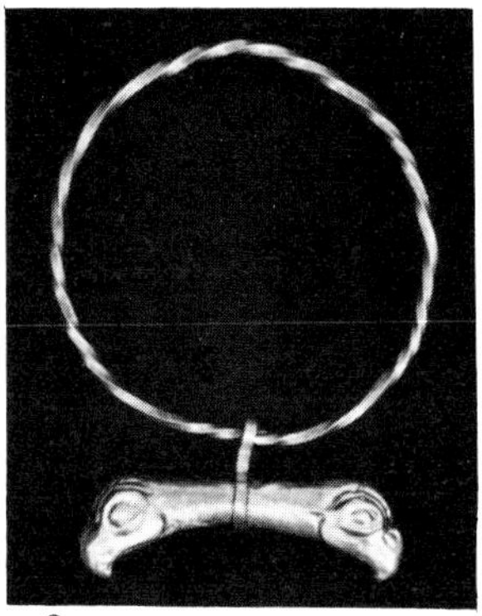

148

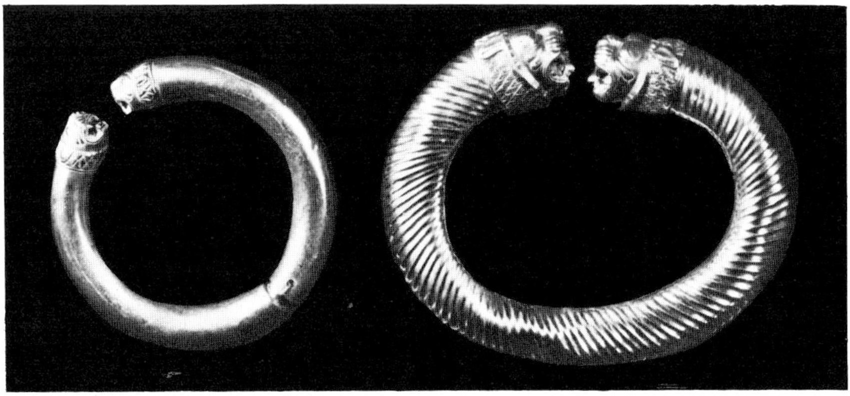

149

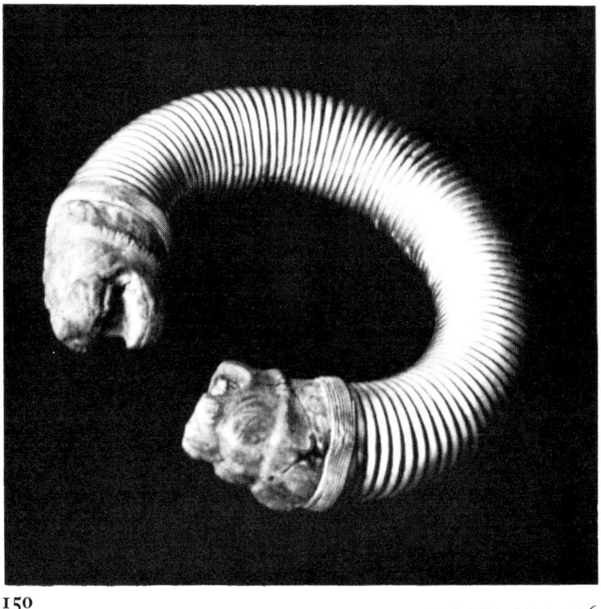

150

149, 150, *see p. 196*

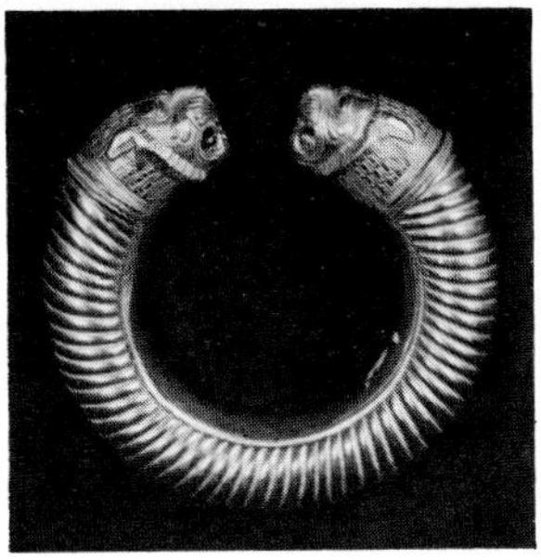

151

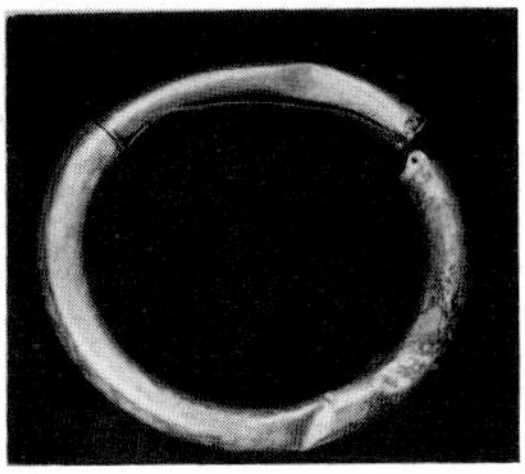

152

151, 152, *see p. 197*

153, *see p. 198*

154 a

154 b

154, *see pp. 200, 194*

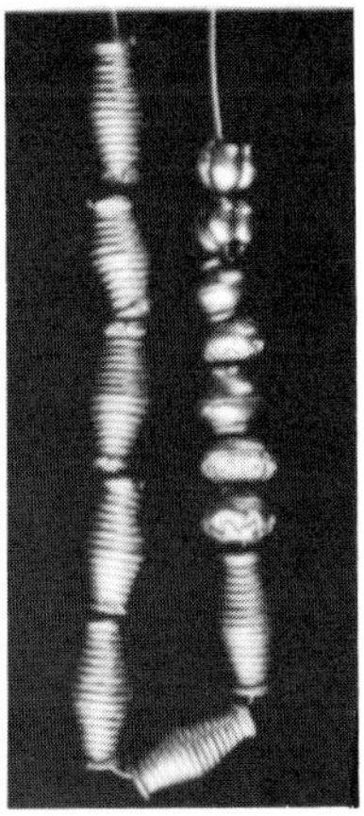

155, *see p. 200*

156, *see p. 201*

157, *see p. 202*

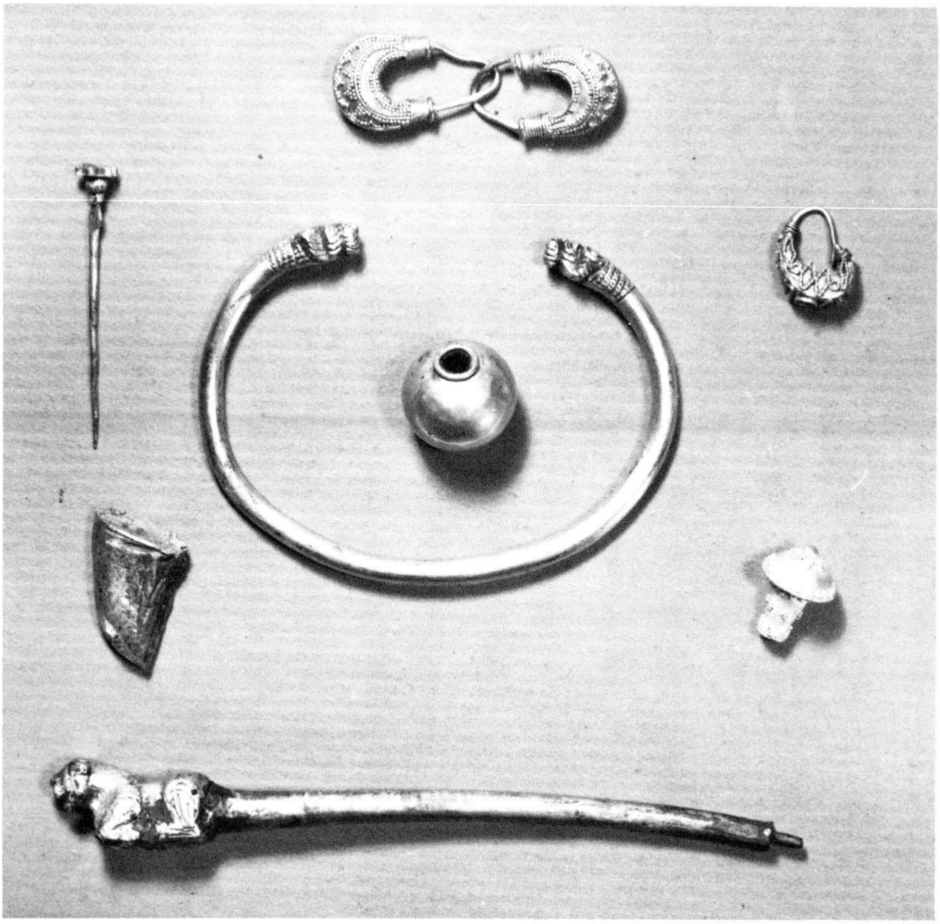

158, *see p. 203*

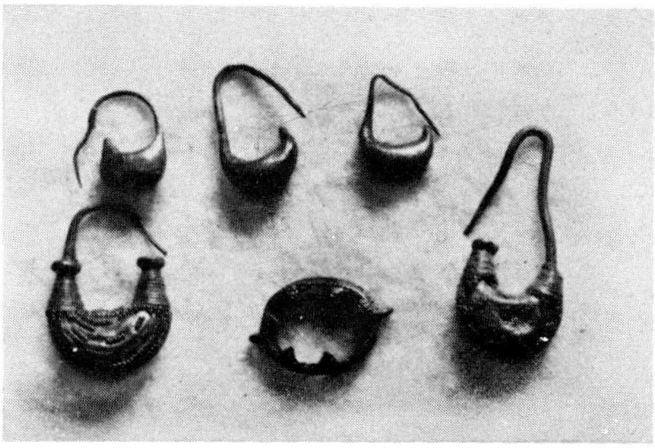

159, *see p. 208*

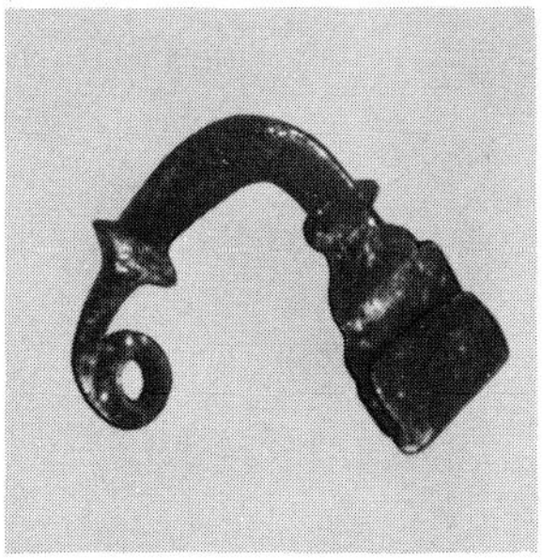

160, *see pp. 204, 263*

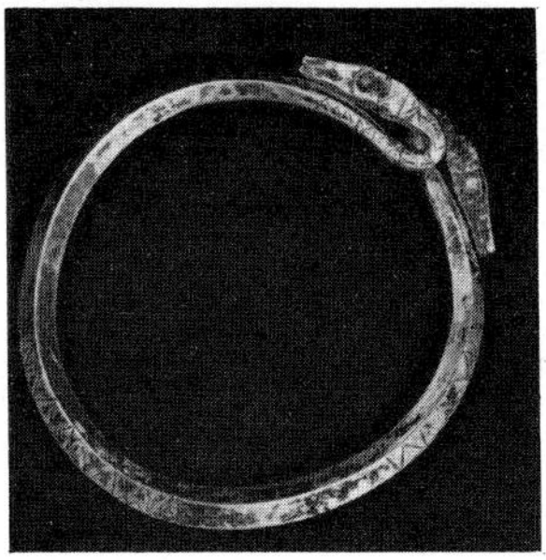

161

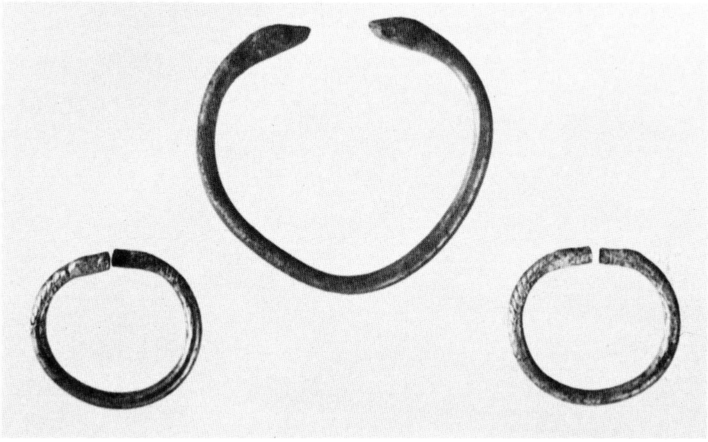

162

161, 162, *see p. 205*

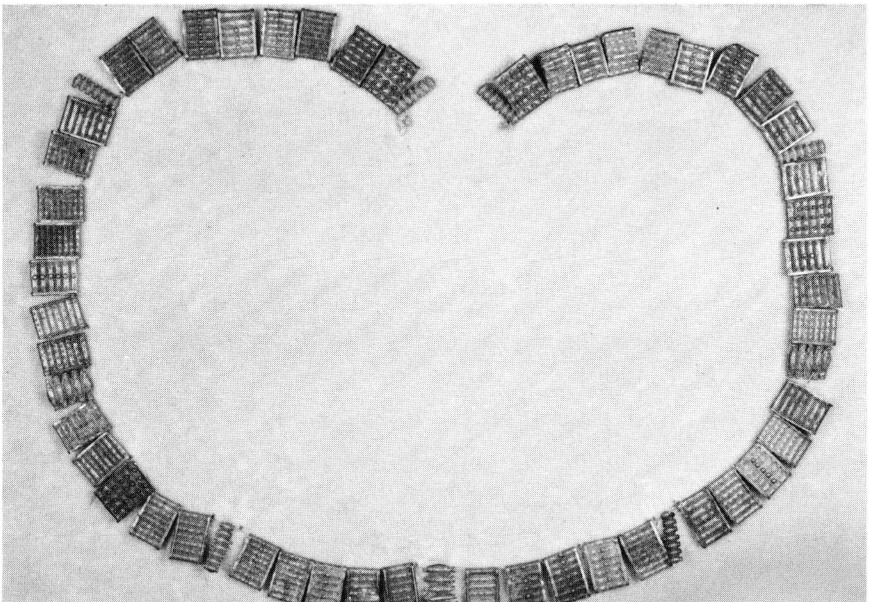

163, *see pp. 207, 195*

164

164, 165, *see p. 207*

165

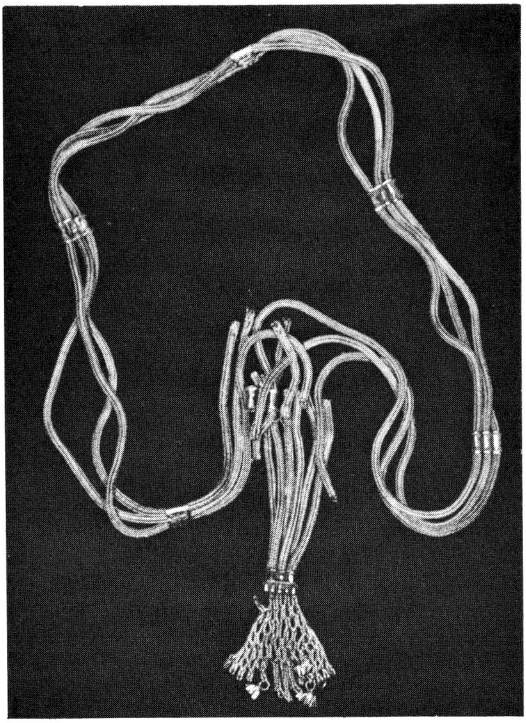

166 , *see p. 208*

167

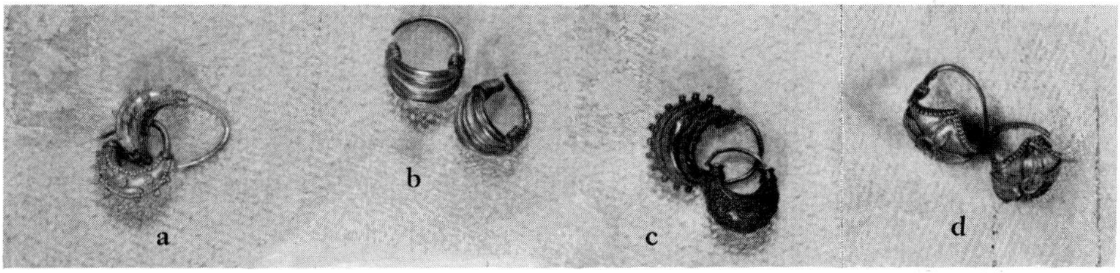

168

167, 168, *see p. 208*

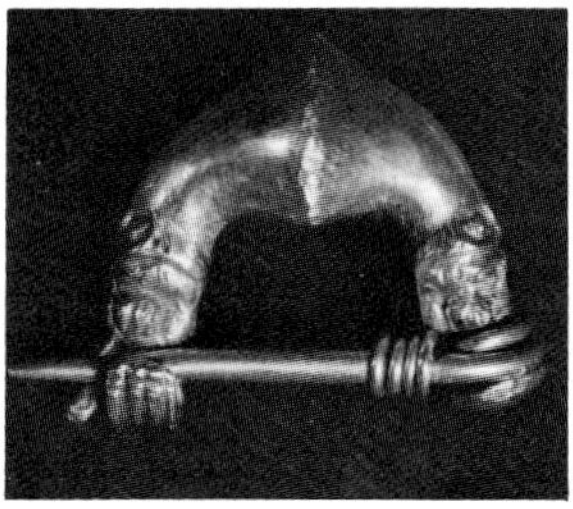

169, *see p. 208*

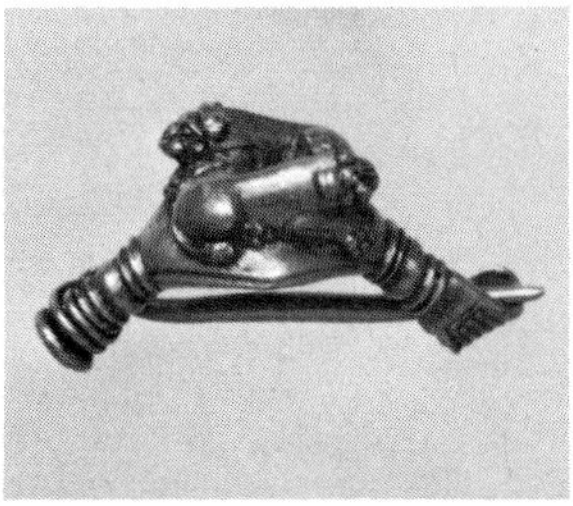

170 a

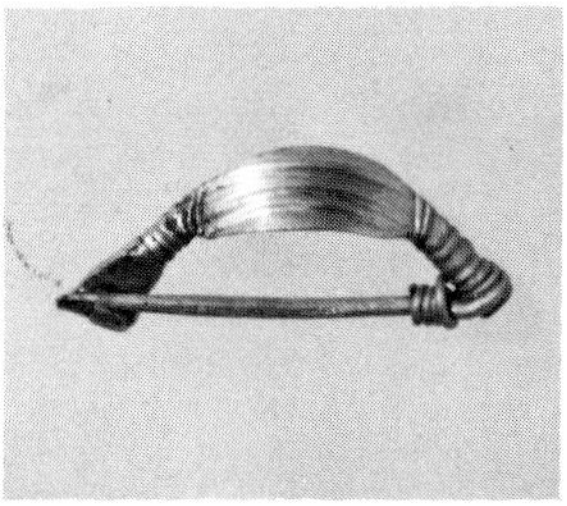

170 b

170, *see p. 209*

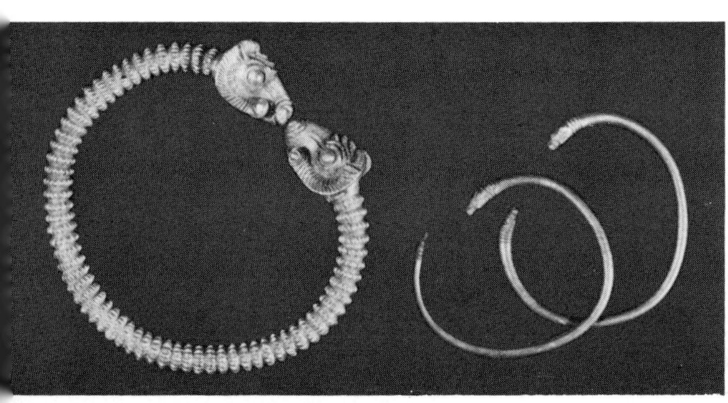

71, *see p. 209*

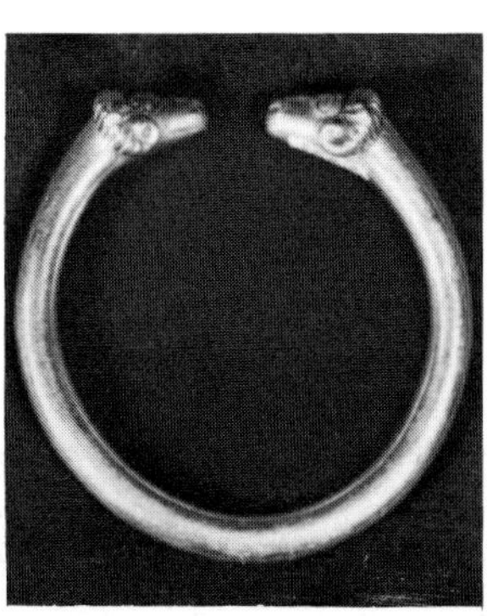

172 , *see p. 210*

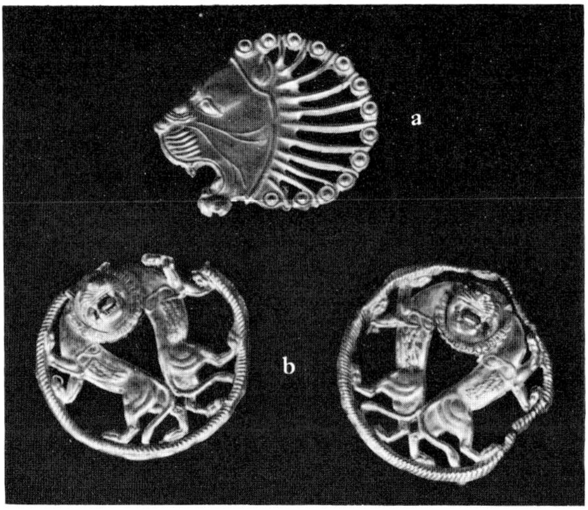

173 (a), *see p. 211*; (b), *see p. 210*

174

175

174, 175, *see p. 211*

176

pp. 211, 261

177

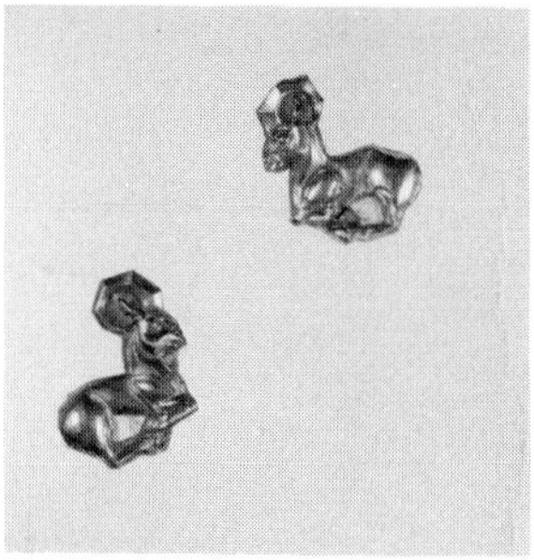
178

177–179, see p. 212

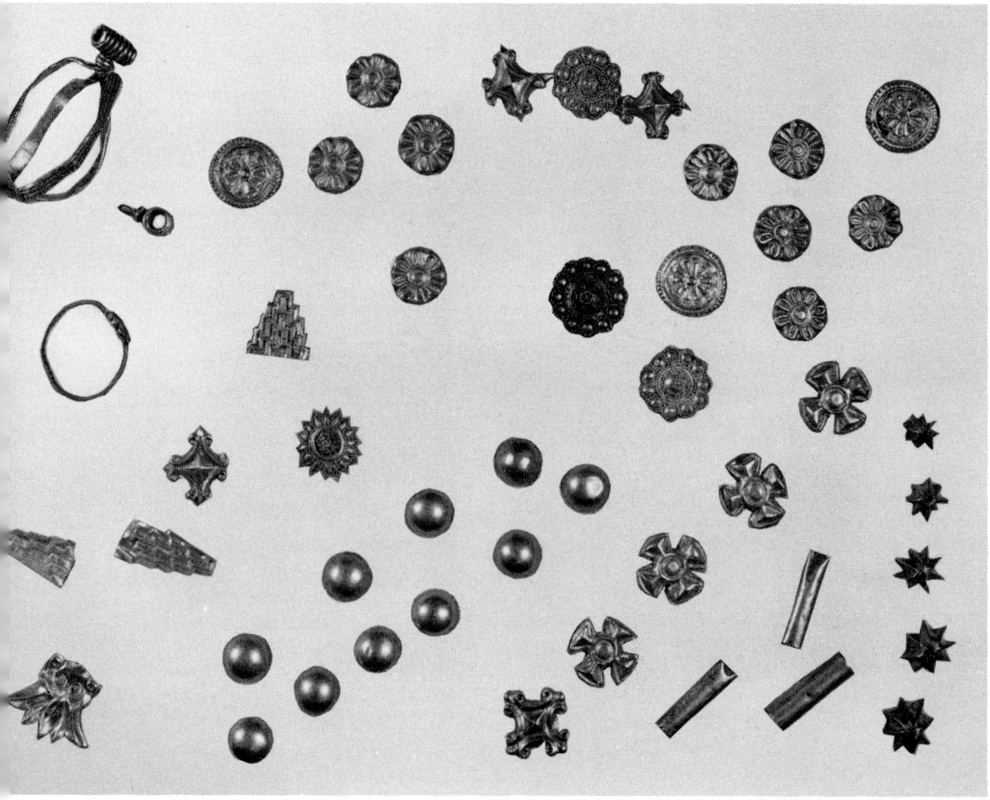

180 a

180 b

180, *see p. 212*

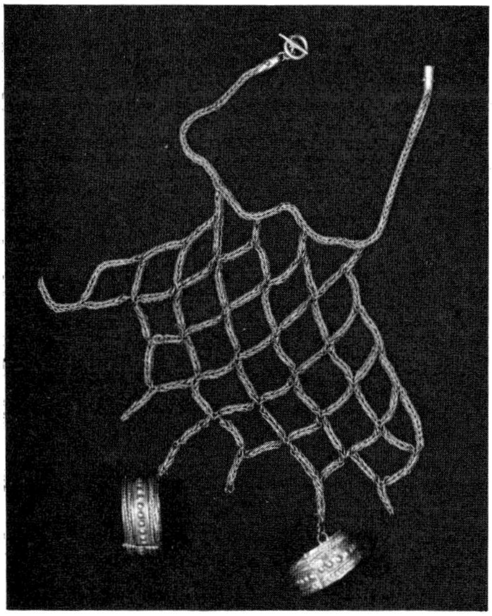
181

182

181–183, *see p. 213*

184–187, *see p. 214*

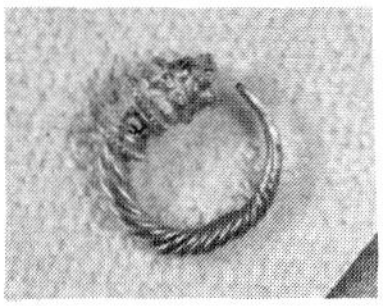
183

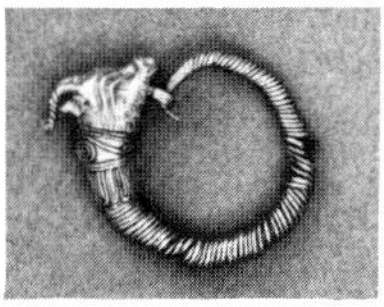
184

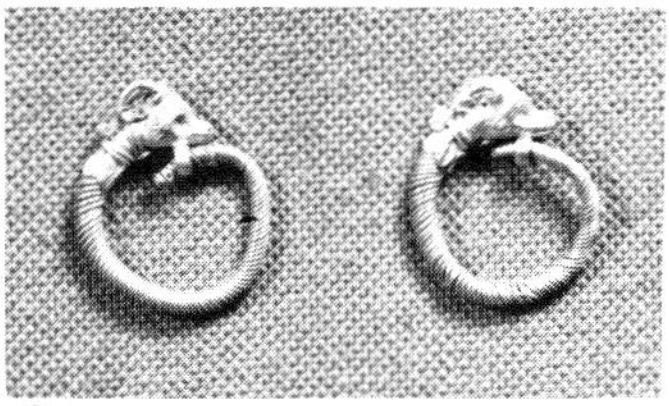
185

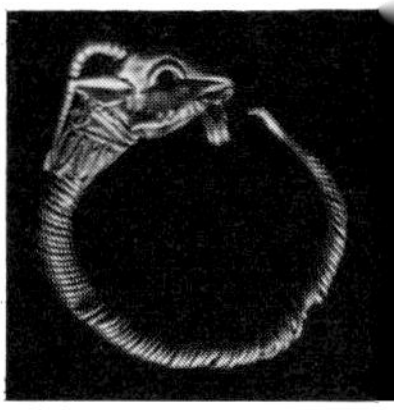
186

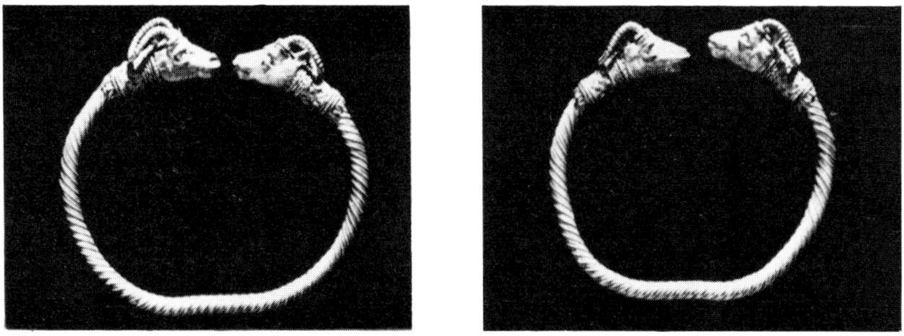
187

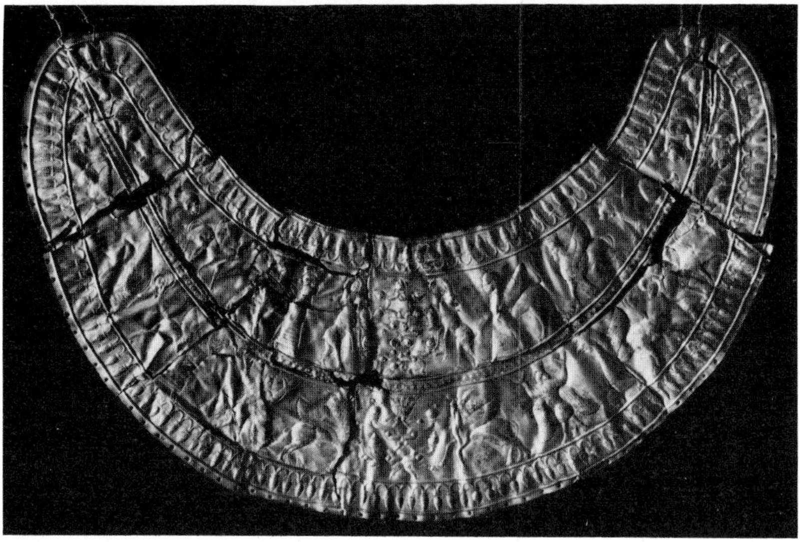

188, *see p. 216*

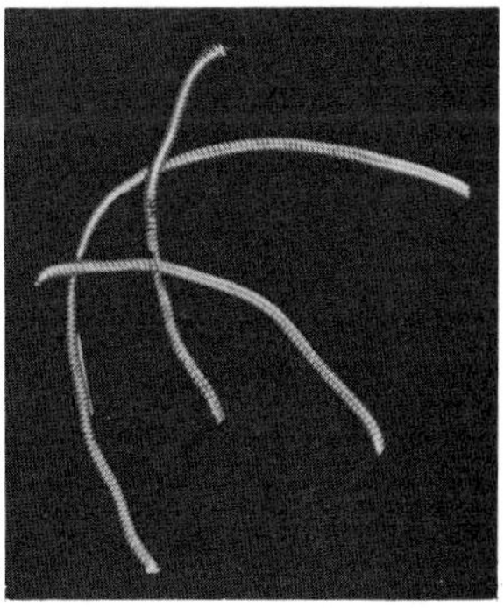

189, *see p. 215*

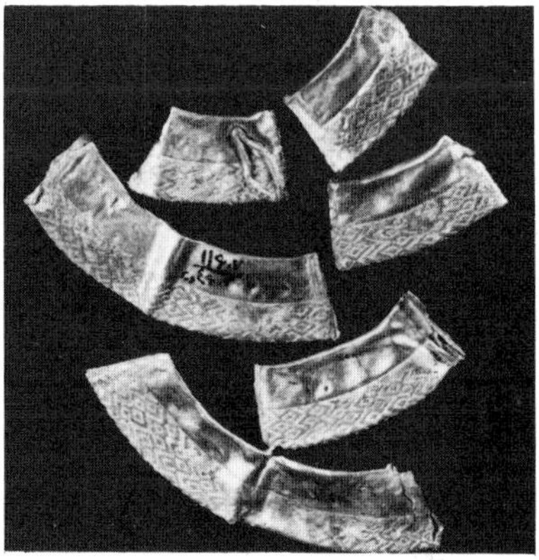

190, *see p. 217*

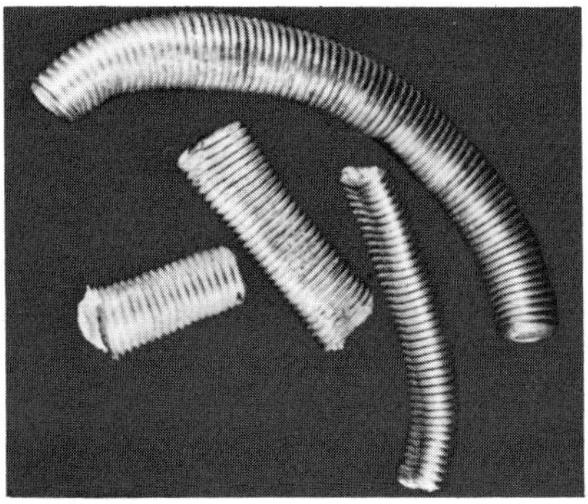

191, *see p. 215*

192

193

192, 193, *see p. 217*

194, *see p. 219*

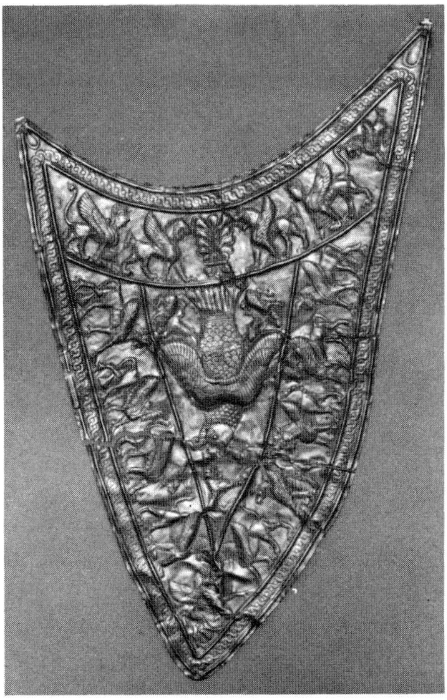

195, *see p. 221*

196, *see p. 222*

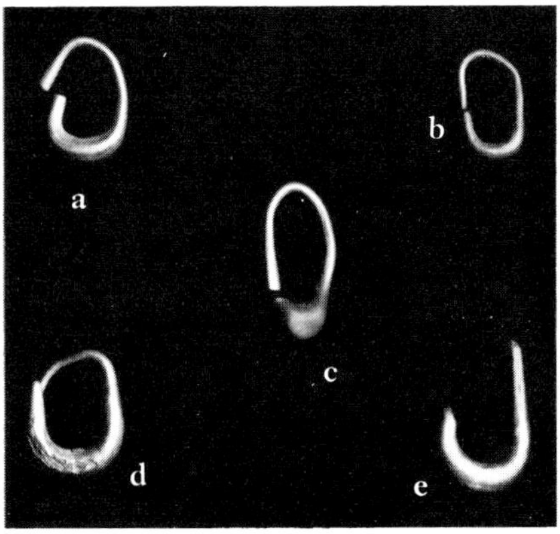

197, *see p. 225*

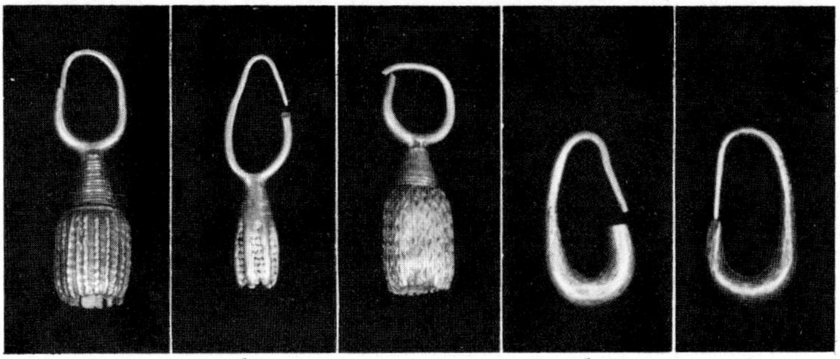

198 a b c d e

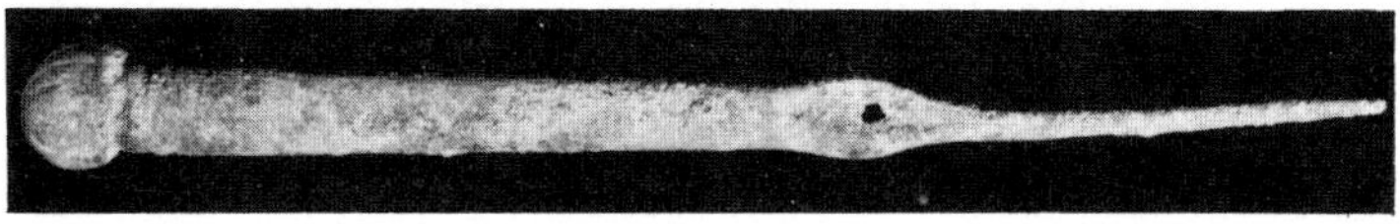

199

198–200, *see p. 225*

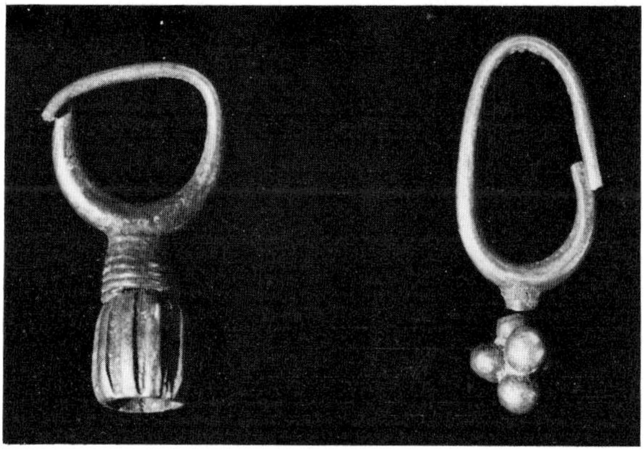

200

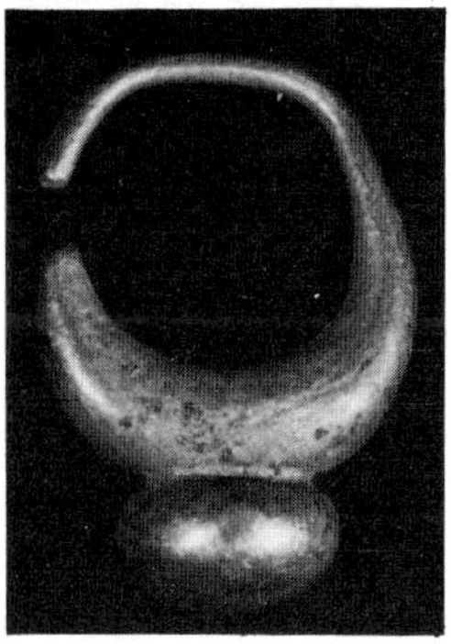

201

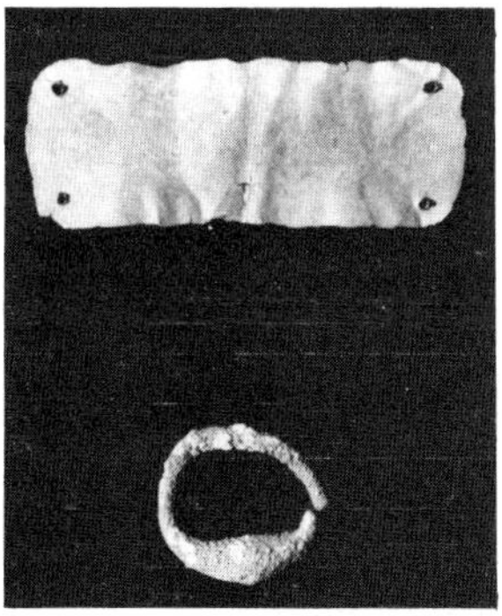

202

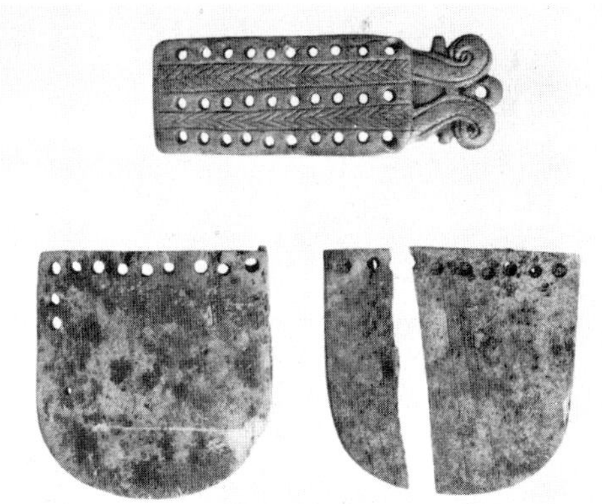

204

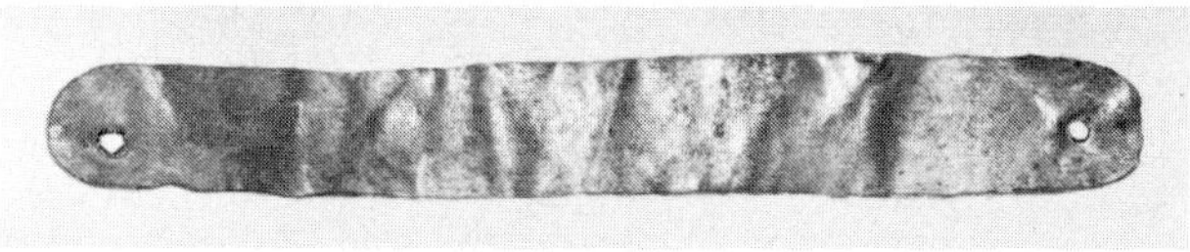

203

201–204, *see p. 226*

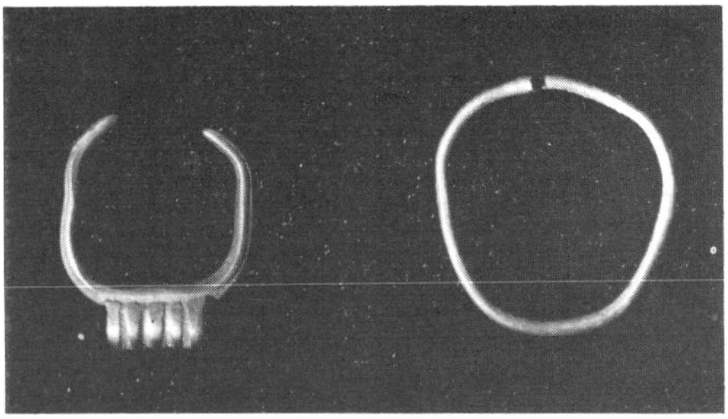

205, *see p. 226*

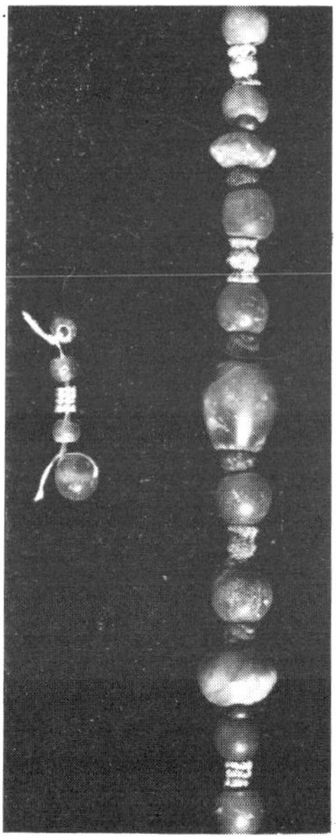

206

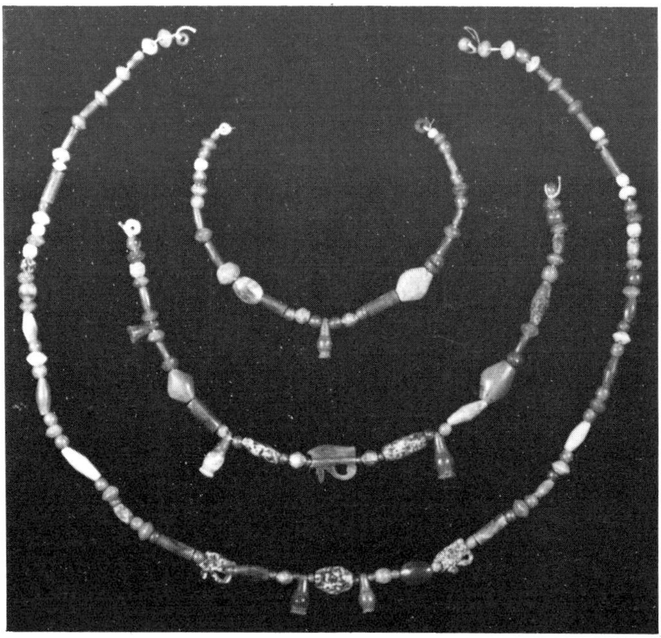

207

206–208, *see p. 227*

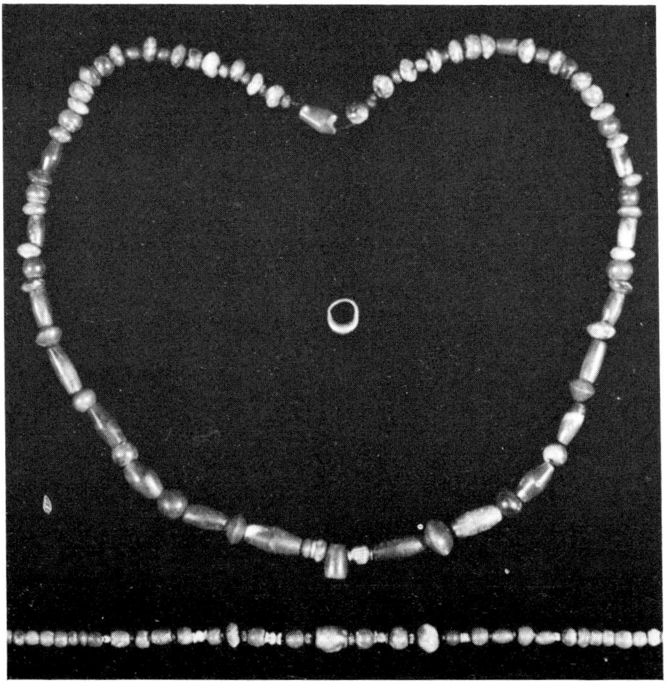

208

209

209, 210, *see p. 227*

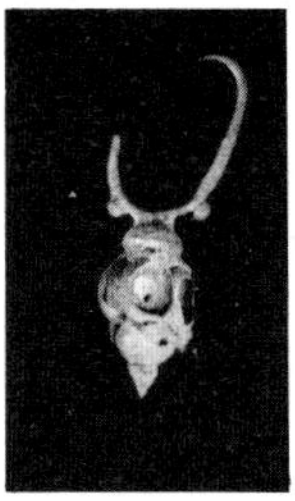

210

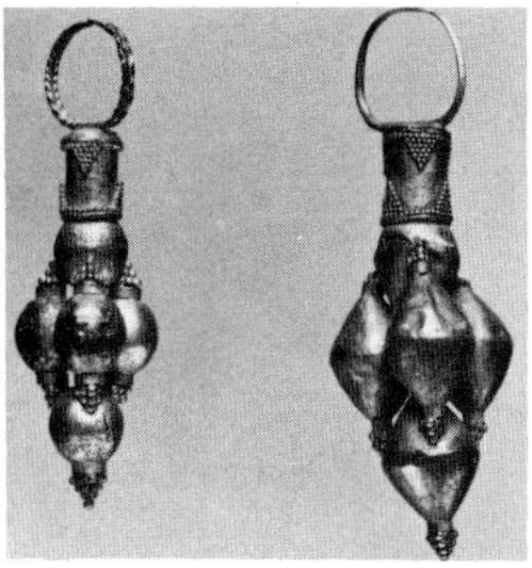

211

212

211, 212, *see p. 228*

213, *see p. 229*

213 a

213 b

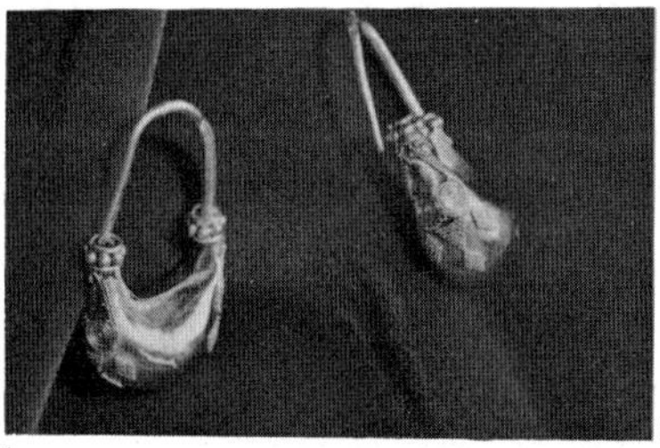

214

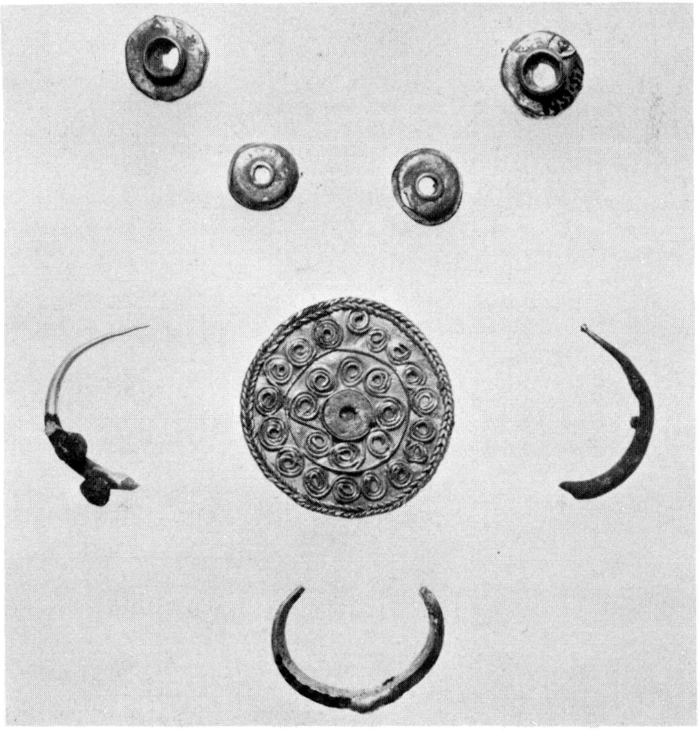

215

214, 215, *see p. 230*

216 a

216 b

216, *see p. 223*

217, *see pp. 239, 268*

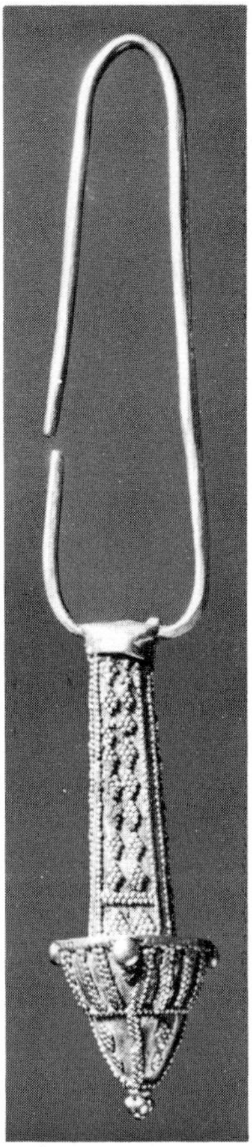

218 a

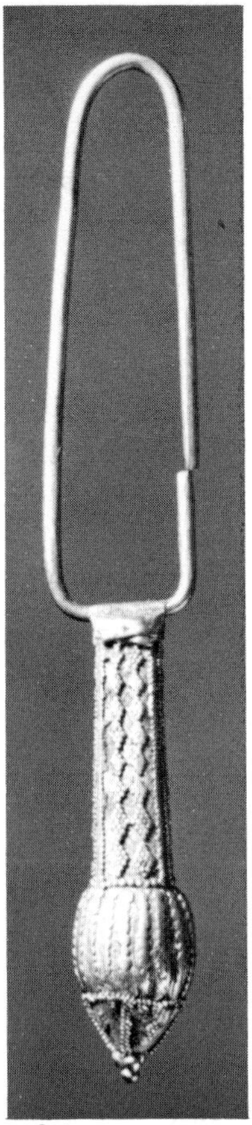

218 b

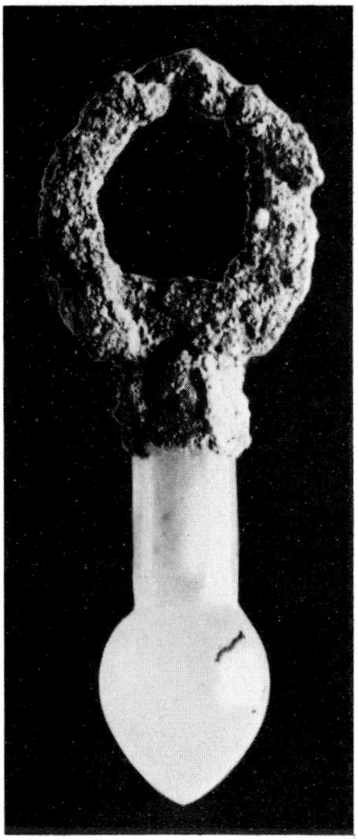

219

218–220 *see p. 241*

220

221, *see p. 242*

222, *see pp. 243, 350*

223, *see pp. 208, 244*

224, *see p. 244*

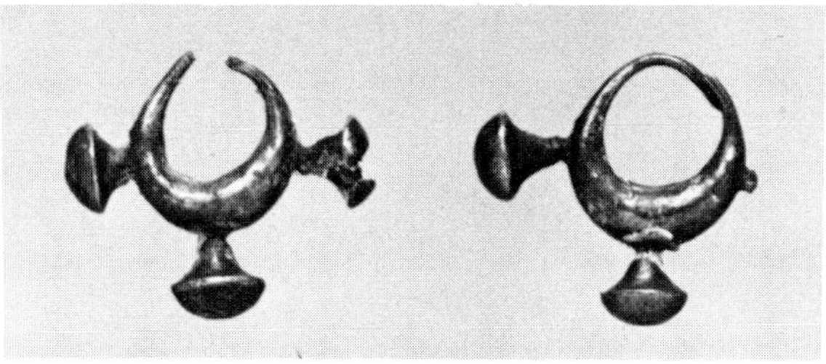

225, *see pp. 234, 241*

226, *see p. 244*

227, *see pp. 246, 250*

228, *see p. 246*

229, *see p. 246*

230, *see p. 251*

231, *see p. 254*

232

232, 233, *see p. 254*

233

234 a

234 (a), (b), *see p. 254*

234 b

235

235, 236, *see p. 254*

236

237

237, 238, *see p. 254*

238

239

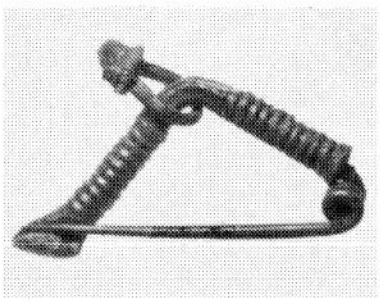

240

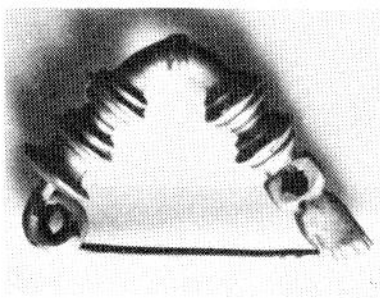

241

242

239–242, *see p. 261*

243 a

243 b

243, *see p. 261*

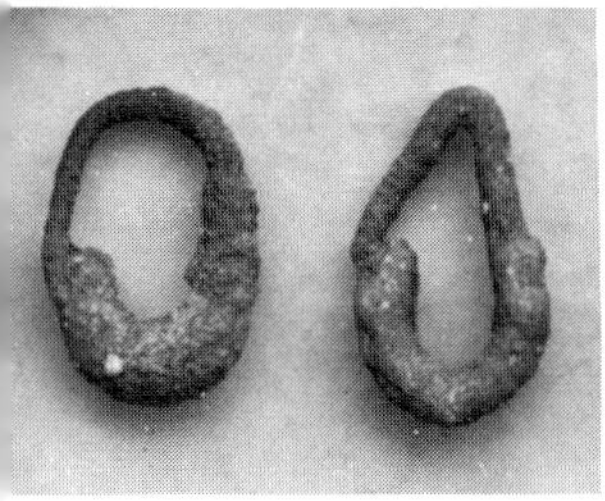

244

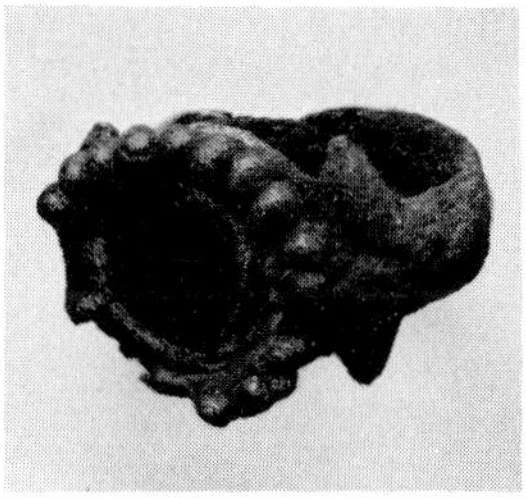

245

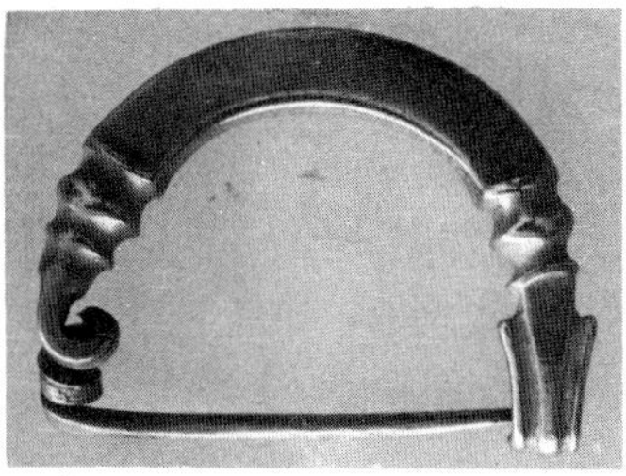

246

244–246, *see p. 262*

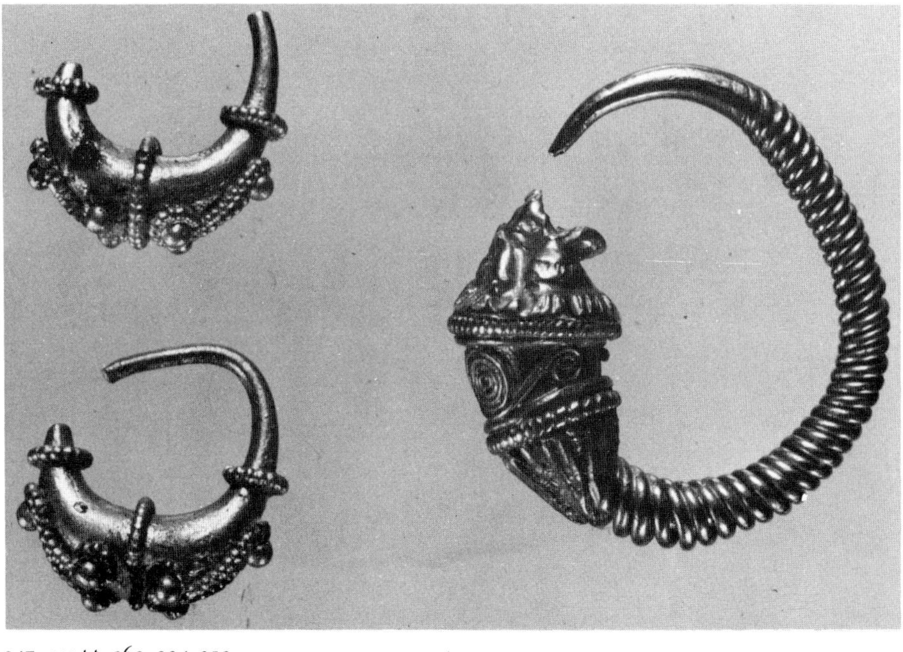

247, *see pp. 263, 234, 213*

248

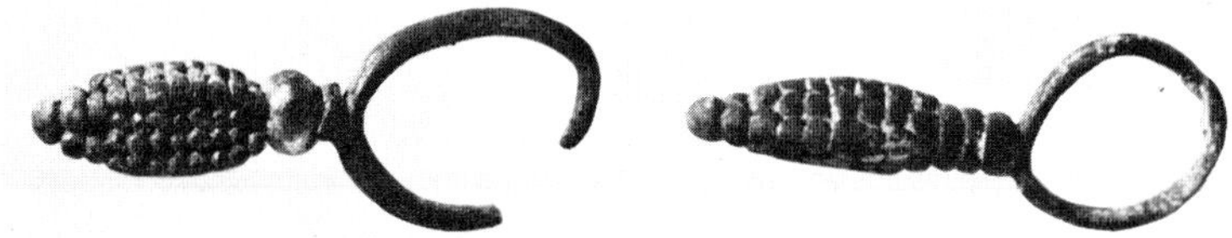

249

248, 249, *see p. 264*

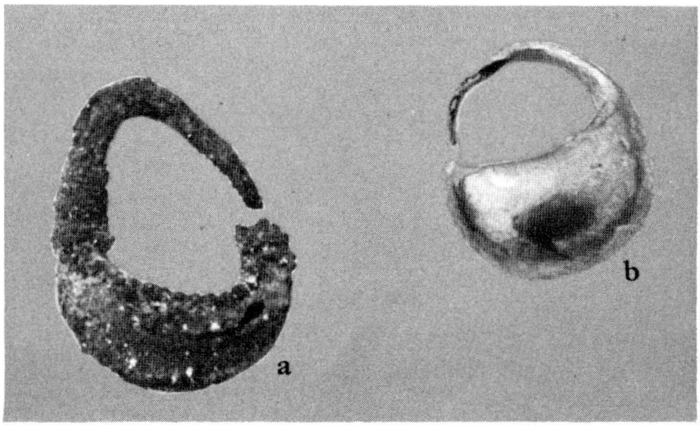

250 (a), *see p. 264;* (b), *see pp. 264, 240*

251, *see p. 265*

252

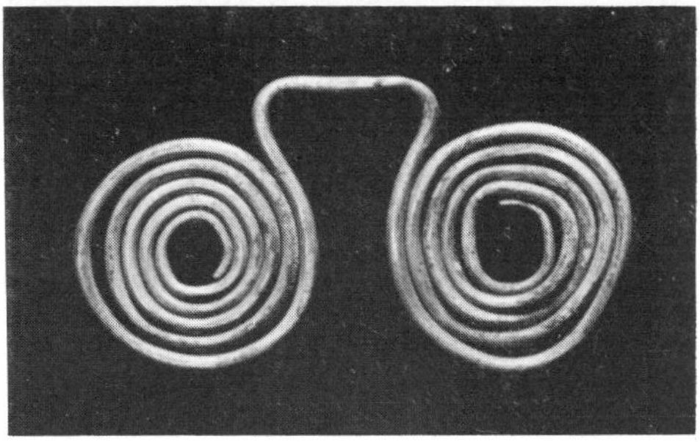

253

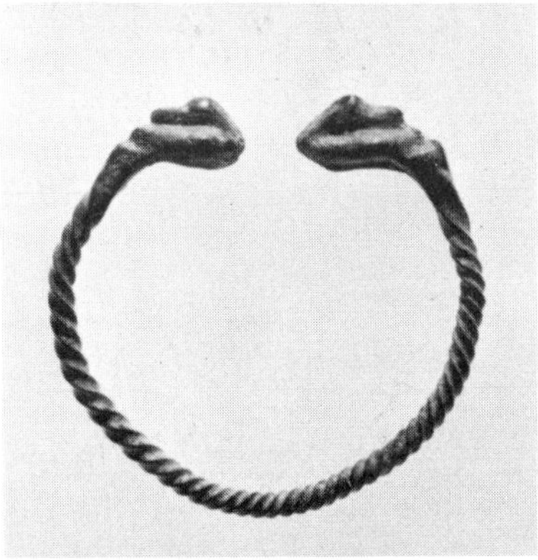

254

252–255, *see p. 267*

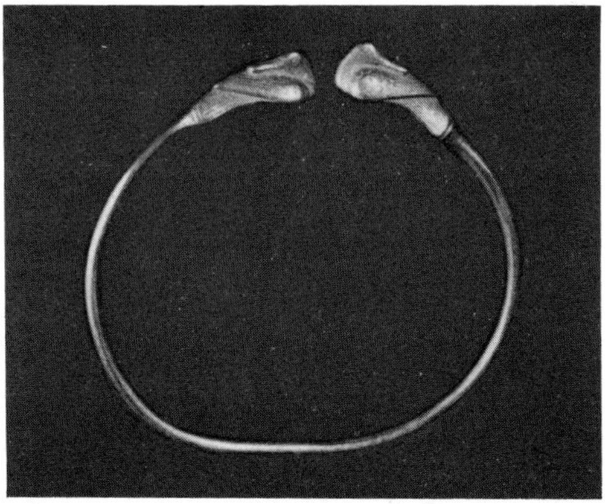

255

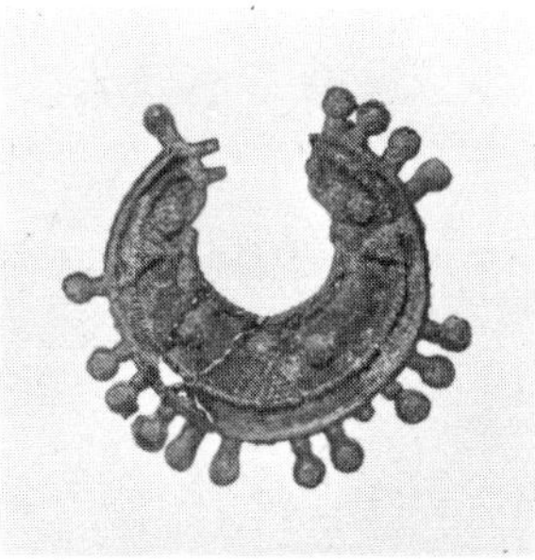

256, *see p. 268*

257

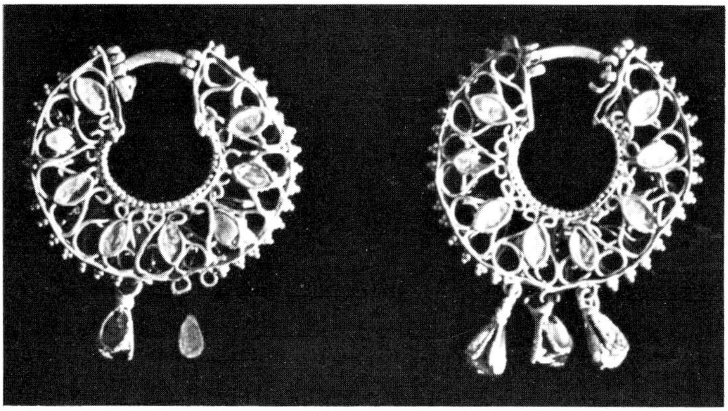

258

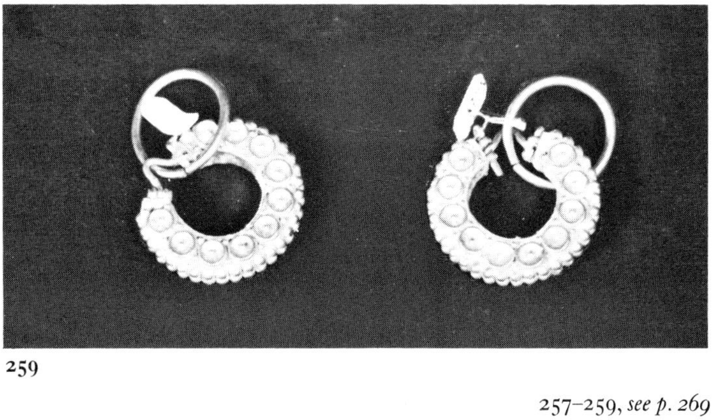

259

257–259, *see p. 269*